W9-DJE-767

DISCARD

54904

BR Labriolle, Pierre Champagne de, 1874–1940.
67   History and literature on Christianity from Tertullian
.L32 to Boethius. Translated from the French by Herbert Wil-
1968 son. With introductory foreword by Cardinal Gasquet.
        New York, Barnes & Noble ₁1968₎
            xxiii, 555 p. 25 cm. (History of civilization)
            Reprint of the 1924 ed.
            Translation of Histoire de la littérature latine chrétienne.
            Includes bibliographical references.
            1. Christian literature, Early—Latin authors. 2. Latin literature—
        History and criticism. 3. Fathers of the church, Latin.   I. Title.
        BR67.L32   1968   870.9′001   78–3495

History of Civilization

The History and Literature of Christianity
from Tertullian to Boethius

History and Literature of Christianity

from

Tertullian to Boethius

By

PIERRE DE LABRIOLLE

Translated from the French by
HERBERT WILSON

With Introductory Foreword by
His Eminence CARDINAL GASQUET

NEW YORK
BARNES & NOBLE, INC.

Published in the United States of America 1968
by Barnes & Noble, Inc., New York, N.Y.

No part of this book may be reproduced
in any form without permission from
the publisher, except for the quotation
of brief passages in criticism

First published in Great Britain in 1924
by Kegan Paul, Trench, Trübner & Co Ltd.

BR
67
.L32
1968

Printed in Great Britain

FOREWORD

I HAVE been asked to write a brief *Foreword* to this excellent translation of this important and scholarly work, the *Histoire de la Littérature Latine Chrétienne.* I gladly accepted the task, if only to testify my personal appreciation of the volume and to record my thanks to the author, M. Pierre de Labriolle, for having given us a work that has long been wanted by scholars and students of Latin literature.

M. de Labriolle is well-known from his numerous essays upon special points and persons connected with this subject. Here in England, it is to be feared, the study of the influence of Early Christian literature upon European thought and culture has been much neglected, and it would hardly be an exaggeration to suggest that many who have been educated upon the works of the Pagan classical authors would hardly know the names, and still less the works, of the great Christian writers of the early centuries. In France and in Germany the importance of this side of general literature is being more and more recognized, and its influence is clearly seen in the literary output of the last century. In France, for instance, Chateaubriand was deeply read in the Early Christian Latin literature. This is evidenced in his *Les Martyrs* and others of his

v

54904

works. So, too, to name only one other case: M. Gaston Boissier has given us many charming studies of Christian Latin authors in his always suggestive *Fin du Paganisme*.

At the present time in England there is, I believe, a distinct tendency to recognize the importance of the study of the Latin writers of the Early Christian ages. The late Dr Mayor of Cambridge lectured on Tertullian, and made a profound study of the text of the *Apologeticum*, and his notes were published with an introduction and translation by Professor Souter at the Cambridge University Press in 1917. In this the eminent scholar Dr Souter fully recognizes the importance of Early Christian literature. It is well to note here that in the very useful Tables printed at the end of M. de Labriolle's volume full justice is not done to the many excellent studies and translations of the Christian classics which have been made by English scholars. To judge from these tables only, a reader would suppose that very little indeed had been done by English scholars in this field of work. There are very many such studies and translations in existence. For example, to name but a few: We have the *Ante-Nicene Christian Library* (published by T. & T. Clark), the *Library of the Fathers of the Holy Church* (Newman and other scholars), *A Select Library of Nicene and Post-Nicene Fathers* (Wace and Schaff), various translations among the S.P.C.K.'s publications, etc. This is not said by way of criticism or to detract in any way from the great value of this work of our author, but to assist any student who may desire to profit by this volume and, taking up the study of the

Christian classics, would wish to know what English editions to consult.

M. de Labriolle's volume begins with a long Introduction of some thirty pages, in which, having pointed out the relatively recent interest taken by scholars in the study of Early Christian Latin writers, he examines the attitude of Christianity, both theoretically and practically, towards the old Pagan models, and the influence of these upon the formation of the literature of the Christian ages. The Introduction should be read in its entirety; it will repay a careful study. It concludes by introducing the reader to the chief collections of Latin texts contained in the *Patrologia Latina* of Migne and the Vienna *Corpus* still in progress.

The volume itself, after this Introduction, is divided into five books, which contain notices of the chief Christian writers from the beginning till what is known as the "Middle Ages," that is, from the great Tertullian at the end of the first century of the Christian era to St Isidore of Seville at the close of the sixth. The books are divided into Chapters, prefaced by bibliographical notices and enriched by notes of anything which could serve to inform the reader on the subject-matter treated of. The lives of the various writers are brief, but are complete, and contain the important historical settings which gave occasion to the writing of the various pieces. Only an examination of the volume itself can give an adequate idea of the rich material which the author has gathered together and here offers to the student of Christian literature.

No better idea can be given of the scope and purpose of this work than a quotation from the passage

with which M. de Labriolle concludes the volume.
He writes:

"After Boethius, Cassiodorus, and Isidore of Seville,
the frame-work of the intellectual life of the Middle
Ages was established for a long time. A natural line
of demarcation at this point closes the history of Latin
Christian literature.

"I believe I have not over-estimated its merits. I
have not concealed the fact that really finished literary
authors are rare. . . . But let us guard ourselves against
a certain rather rigid type of 'humanism,' which would
only judge the Christian writings from the point of
view of the classic ideal. . . . Whatever be its defects,
this vivid Latin Christian literature deserves to be
more carefully studied than appears to be generally the
case, and whoever is interested in the history of ideals
will not regret having made the effort. There are
numerous historical and literary problems which can
only be grasped fully after we have seen their factors
coming to light during the period we have just
traversed [in this volume]. And, again, how many
strong personalities are revealed, how many magnificent
minds and pathetic souls anxious for the destiny of
mankind, each one preserving, in spite of the community of their faith and the identity of its theoretic
solutions, their original action upon this eternal enigma!
On the day when our Higher Course of Studies shall
have taken a more generous interest in some of their
masterpieces, scholarly research will again turn in the
direction of patristic study."

With these words of M. de Labriolle we may
well leave the volume to speak for itself, in the con-

fidence that in this English version it will find many
readers, who will be grateful to the author and his very
competent translator for having given them so valuable
a help to the study of the Christian classics.

AIDAN CARD. GASQUET.

July 21st, 1924.

AUTHOR'S PREFACE

THIS History of Latin Christian Literature is the
outcome of over twelve years spent as Professor at the
University of Fribourg-en-Suisse. Thanks to the entire
liberty allowed to me in the arrangement of the course
of studies I was able to combine with my lectures
on classic Latin literature a profound study of the
Christian authors and thereby to follow the destinies
of the Old Learning through their vicissitudes up to
the threshold of the Middle Ages.

We do not possess in France any similar work.
*L'Histoire Générale de la Littérature du Moyen Age
en Occident* (Paris; E. Leroux), the French translation
from Ad. Ebert, was made as long ago as 1883, and
is only of value for its sufficiently conscientious analyses.
Bardenhewer's *Patrology*, translated in 1905 (Paris;
Bloud, 2nd ed.) is little more than a bibliographical
repertory. The recent contribution by M. Tixeront
(Paris; Gabalda) is an elementary *précis* in which Latin
literature only obtains its bare share. It seemed to me
that I might be performing a useful service in providing
for the first time an ample survey wherein I might
endeavour to bring again to life the leading figures in
Western Christianity, and to define the present stage
of matters still in dispute.

I trust I have not been too prodigal of information
that might be easily obtained. Those desirous only of

a general view can pass over the technical remarks and the notes. The latter, together with the Tables which I have grouped at the end of the volume, will assist the serious reader to find his way rapidly over the expanse of this vast Christian literature, still inadequately explored, wherein so many problems solicit his studious inquiry. I have pointed out numerous questions still to be studied; any manual giving the impression that our knowledge is complete would be wanting in scientific value.

P. de L.

BIOGRAPHICAL NOTE BY THE TRANSLATOR

PROFESSOR PIERRE DE LABRIOLLE, the distinguished Author of this painstaking, eloquent and authoritative work, has made the study of classic literature and of patristic Christian literature the solid foundation for the high esteem in which he is held among French *savants*. As he states in his preface, it is the fruit of nearly thirteen years spent as Professor of Classic Latin Literature at the University of Fribourg - en - Suisse, during which period he was able to make a profound study of the early Latin Christian authors.

Born at Asnières, near Paris, on the 18th June 1874, he became *Agrégé de Lettres* in 1895, and was chosen to be Professor of the *Faculté des Arts* in the University of Montreal, where he remained from 1898 to 1901. He was afterwards Head Professor at the Collège Stanislas (1901-3), and at the Lycée at Rennes (1903-4). From 1904 to 1918 he was Professor of Latin Literature of the *Faculté de Philosophie* at the University of Fribourg-en-Suisse, and at present fills the chair of Latin Literature and Roman Institutions at the *Faculté des Lettres* at the University of Poitiers. He attained the distinction of *Docteur es-Lettres* in January 1914, and in February 1923 was awarded very honourable mention as *Associé Correspondant de la Société des Antiquaires de France.*

During the War he was mobilised at Belfort on the 2nd August 1914, and in 1917 at the request of the French Ambassador at Berne was chosen to direct the course of studies for the students interned at Fribourg.

Professor Pierre de Labriolle is at present engaged on a French Translation of the Confessions of St Augustine, with critical text, for the *Collection des Universités de France* under the auspices of the *Société des Belles Lettres*, who are performing a most scholarly and admirable service by their series of critical editions and translations into French of the leading examples of classic Greek and Latin Literature.   From the wide learning and sympathetic appreciation of the life and writings of St Augustine, shown in the following pages, further understanding and enlightenment on the mind of that great Doctor of the Church may be confidently expected.

Amongst his other works may be mentioned *Vincent of Lérins;* the *De Paenitentia,* the *De Pudicitia* and the *De Praescriptione Hereticorum* of Tertullian; *La Vie de Paul de Thèbes et la Vie d'Hilarion, par Saint Ambroise; Saint Ambroise; La Correspondance d'Ausone et de Paulin de Nole; La Crise Montaniste,* which was crowned by the *Académie des Inscriptions et Belles Lettres; Les Sources de l'Histoire du Montanisme,* crowned by the French Academy, and the *Satires of Juvenal,* in collaboration with M. Villeneuve.

HERBERT   WILSON.

May 1924.

TABLE OF CONTENTS

PAGE

FOREWORD BY HIS EMINENCE CARDINAL GASQUET . . v

AUTHOR'S PREFACE xi

BIOGRAPHICAL NOTE xiii

EXPLANATION OF THE SIGNS xxi

INTRODUCTION.

LATIN CHRISTIAN LITERATURE AND THE OLD LEARNING.

I. Latin Christian Literature and Modern Criticism.—II. The Æsthetic
interest which this literature offers.—III. The intellectual formation of the Christian writers.—IV. The added Dignity received
from them by Roman literature.—V. The Old Learning and
Christianity : the Nature of the Problem stated. The dream of
St Jerome.—VI. Christian hostility to this learning—VII. The
compromises necessitated.—VIII. The middle course which
finally ensued.—IX. The handing on of the old literary culture
by Christianity.—X. To what extent profane learning has penetrated Christian thought.—XI. Bibliographical notes. Migne's
Patrology. The *Corpus Scriptorum Ecclesiasticorum Latinorum* . 1

BOOK I.

THE SOURCES OF ORIGIN.

CHAPTER I. THE FIRST LATIN VERSIONS OF THE BIBLE.

BIBLIOGRAPHY. I. The tardy coming into bearing of Latin Christian
Literature. Greek the dialect of the Mediterranean.—II. The
first Latin translations of the Bible. Their literary and grammatical character. Their influence on the Latin tongue . 39

PAGE

CHAPTER II. THE FIRST CHRISTIAN WRITERS IN THE
LATIN TONGUE: TERTULLIAN.

BIBLIOGRAPHY. I. Pope Victor. Apollonius, the "Senator." The
Fragment of Muratori.—II. The Origins of the Church in
Africa. Tertullian.—III. The Christian view of Tertullian.
The intellectual equipment of Tertullian.—IV. His life. His
transition to Montanism. Tertullian, Head of a Sect.—V. His
Apologetic Works.—VI. Tertullian in his relations to the
Pagans.—VII. Tertullian and Gnosticism.—VIII. Tertullian
and Montanism.—IX. Tertullian as Writer.—X. The *Martyrdom*
of Saints Perpetua and Felicitas. Was Tertullian the author
of the account ? 50

BOOK II.

THE IIIRD CENTURY DOWN TO THE PEACE OF
THE CHURCH, A.D. 313

CHAPTER I. THE *OCTAVIUS* OF MINUCIUS FELIX.

BIBLIOGRAPHY. I.—Minucius Felix.—II. The *Octavius* analysed.—
III. The religious bearing of the *Octavius*.—IV. Literary art
in the *Octavius*.—V. The priority of the *Apologeticum* over the
Octavius 109

CHAPTER II. ST CYPRIAN AND HIS TIMES.

BIBLIOGRAPHY. I. Tertullian and St Cyprian. — II. The life of
St Cyprian.—III. The ideas which dominated him. Influences
which determined them. — IV. How he realised them in
practice. The matter of the *lapsi*. — V. The writings of
St Cyprian.—VI. The prestige of St Cyprian. The Apocryphal
writings assigned to his name 131

CHAPTER III. NOVATIAN—COMMODIAN.

BIBLIOGRAPHY. I. The rôle of Novatian.—II. The *De Trinitate*.—
III. The *De Cibis Judaicis*.—IV. The works of Commodian.—
V. The *Instructiones* and the *Carmen Apologeticum*.—VI. His
language and metre. — VII. The riddle enveloping his
personality 169

CHAPTER IV. THE EVE OF THE PEACE OF THE CHURCH:
ARNOBIUS AND LACTANTIUS.

BIBLIOGRAPHY. I. The question of Arnobius. — II. The *Adversus
Nationes*. Arnobius and the Bible. His Metaphysical Con-

ceptions.—III. The Christianity of Arnobius.—IV. His Polemics
against Paganism.—V. The Rhetoric of Arnobius.—VI. The
Opinion of Christians regarding him.—VII. Lactantius. His
Life. — VIII. The *De Opificio Dei.* — IX. The *Institutiones
Divinae.* Lactantius's Method of Apologetics. Plan of his
Works.—X. The Blunders of Lactantius. The Salient Portions
of his Work. Stratification of the Views of Lactantius.—XI.
The *De Ira Dei.*—XII. The *De Mortibus Persecutorum.* Chris-
tian History. — XIII. Conclusions on Lactantius. — XIV.
Victorinus of Pettau, first Latin Exegetist.—XV. The *Adversus
Omnes Haereses* 188

Book III.

THE GOLDEN AGE OF LATIN CHRISTIAN LITERATURE.

CHAPTER I. The Morrow of the Victory.

BIBLIOGRAPHY. I. General view of the period opening with the Edict
of Milan.—II. The first transports over the victory : Firmicus
Maternus.—III. Reticius of Autun, an exegetist.—IV. Struggles
over doctrine. Arianism. St Hilary of Poitiers. His life of
warfare. His works. The *Fragmenta Historica.*—V. Lucifer of
Calaris. The *Libellus Precum.* — VI. Arian and anti-Arian
literature.—VII. Gregory of Elvira.—VIII. Marius Victorinus 227

CHAPTER II. St Ambrose, Bishop and Diplomat.

BIBLIOGRAPHY. I. A Bishop in the IVth century. The rôle of St
Ambrose.—II. His life until becoming a Bishop.—III. His
intellectual formation.—IV. His political action. The Altar
to Victory. The affair of Callinicum. The Penance of
Theodosius.—V. His literary work. The *De Officiis.*—VI.
Treatises on the ascetic life.—VII. Exegetic Treatises.—VIII.
Dogmatic Treatises and the Ambrosian Hymns.—IX. The
Prestige of St Ambrose 263

CHAPTER III. The Theologians of the Second Order.

BIBLIOGRAPHY. I. Ambrosiaster.—II. Donatism. Optatus of Milevis.
Tyconius.—III. Pacian of Barcelona.—IV. Filaster of Brescia.
Gaudentius.—V. Zeno of Verona. — VI. Hilarianus. — VII.
Niceta of Remesiana.—VIII. The affair of Priscillian . . 287

CONTENTS

PAGE

CHAPTER IV. CHRISTIAN POETRY IN THE IVTH CENTURY.

BIBLIOGRAPHY. I. General view of the Latin Christian Poetry.—
II. Paraphrases of the Bible. Juvencus. Cyprian's *Heptateuchos.*
—III. Didactic Poems.—IV. The *Centos.*—V. Paulinus of Nola.
The Conversion of Paulinus. Paulinus and Ausonius.—VI.
The Letters of Paulinus.—VII. His Poems . . . 311

CHAPTER V. ST JEROME AND HIS TIMES.

BIBLIOGRAPHY. I. St Jerome's Destiny.—II. His early years.—III.
The Biographies of the Monks.—IV. The *Chronica.*—V. The
translations of Origen.—VI. St Jerome in Rome. The Council
of Patrician Women. The Satirist.—VII. The *Discussion between
a Luciferian and an Orthodox.* The *Adv. Helvidium.*—VIII.
St Jerome the Translator of the Sacred Books. The First
Phase.—IX. His Departure for the East. The Second Phase.
—X. St Jerome and the *Hebraica Veritas.* St Augustine's
Reservations.—XI. The Commentaries on the Bible.—XII. The
de Viris Illustribus. The *Adv. Jovinianum.* The *Contra
Vigilantium.* The *Dialogues* against the Pelagians.—XIII. The
Origenist Dispute. Rufinus of Aquileia.—XIV. The Personality
of St Jerome.—XV. The Pilgrimages to the Holy Land. The
Peregrinatio Aetheriae.—XVI. Sulpicius Severus . . . 333

BOOK IV.

THE BREAK UP OF THE EMPIRE.

CHAPTER I. ST AUGUSTINE AND AUGUSTINIANISM.

BIBLIOGRAPHY. I. The taking of Rome by Alaric.—II. The Soul of
Augustine.—III. His Life. The Stages of his Conversion.—
IV. Augustine after his Conversion. — V. Polemics : Mani-
chaeans ; Donatists ; Pelagians ; Arians. Exegetic Treatises.—
VI. *The City of God.*—VII. The *de Catechizandis Rudibus.*—
VIII. The *de Doctrina Christiana.*—IX. Correspondence.—X.
Sermons. — XI. Conclusions on St Augustine. — XII. The
Disputes for and against Augustinianism. Cassian. St Vincent
of Lerins. Faustus of Riez. Arnobius the Younger. Marius
Mercator. St Prosper of Aquitaine.—XIII. Evagrius . . 389

CHAPTER II. THE CHURCH AND THE BARBARIANS—OROSIUS
—SALVIANUS—LEO THE GREAT—VICTOR OF VITA.

BIBLIOGRAPHY. I. Orosius and Augustine.—II. The Seven Books
against the Pagans.—III. The *de Gubernatione Dei*, by Salvianus.

CONTENTS

PAGE

—IV. Pope Leo the Great.—V. *The History of the Persecution by the Vandals,* by Victor of Vita.—VI. Vigilius of Thapsus . 433

CHAPTER III. CHRISTIAN LATIN POETRY IN THE
VTH CENTURY.

BIBLIOGRAPHY. I. Prudentius. His Life.—II. The *Cathemerinon.*—III. The *Peristephanon.*—IV. Didactic Poems. The Patriotism of Prudentius. The *Psychomachia.* The *Dittochaeon.* — V. The Poetry of Prudentius.—VI. The Poem of Orientius. The *Alethia.*—VII. Paulinus of Pella.—VIII. Claudianus Mamertus. —IX. Dracontius.—X. Sedulius.—XI. Sidonius Apollinaris . 446

BOOK V.

ON THE THRESHOLD OF THE MIDDLE AGES

CHAPTER I. WORKS IN VERSE.

BIBLIOGRAPHY. I. The Decline of Latin Learning.—II. Avitus.—III. Ennodius.—IV. Venantius Fortunatus . . . 485

CHAPTER II. WORKS IN PROSE: THE HANDING ON OF THE
LEGACY OF ANTIQUITY.

BIBLIOGRAPHY. I. Fulgentius of Ruspa.—II. St Caesarius of Arles. —III. Boethius, "The First of the Scholastics."—IV. Cassiodorus.—V. St Gregory of Tours. His Hagiographic Works. The *History of the Franks.* Gregory's Learning.—VI. St Isidore of Seville.—VII. Conclusion 495

INDEX 547

EXPLANATION OF THE SIGNS [1]

A.B. = *Analecta Bollandiana*, Brussels, 1882 et s.

** A.C.L. = A. HARNACK : *Geschichte der altchristlichen Literatur*, I. *Die Ueberlieferung und der Bestand*, Leipzig, 1893.

** A.K.L. = O. BARDENHEWER, *Geschichte der altkirchlichen Literatur*, Freiburg i. B., Vol. I (1913) ; Vol. II (1912) ; Vol. III (1914).

A.L. = *Anthologia latina*, sive poesis latinæ supplementum ediderunt Fr. BUECHELER et ALEX. RIESE, 2 parts 4 fasc. Leipzig, 1894-1906— *Anthologia latinæ supplementa*. Vol. I (1895), IHM's Edition.

A.L.L. = *Archiv für lateinische Lexicographie und Grammatik*, Leipzig, 1884 et s.

A.M. = *Anecdota Maredsolana*, Maredsous (Belgium).

A.S.C. = *Analecta sacra et classica*, ed. by dom PITRA, Paris, 1888.

B.A.L.A.C. = *Bulletin d'ancienne Littérature et d'Archéologie chrétiennes*, edited by P. DE LABRIOLLE, Paris, 1911 et s.

B.A.P. = *Briefe, Abhandlungen und Predigten aus den zwei letzten Iahrhunderten des kirchlichen Altertums und dem Anfang des Mittelalters*, hsg. von C. P. CASPARI, Christiania, 1890.

** *Bibliotheca scriptorum classicorum et græcorum et latinorum*, hsg. von Rudolf Klussmann. Zweiter Band, *Scriptores latini*. Erster Theil, Leipzig, 1912 ; zweiter Theil, 1913. (Supplementband au *Jahresbericht über die Forschritte der Klass. Altertumswissenschaft*)

B.K. = *Bibliothek der Kirchenväter*, eine Auswahl patristicher Werke in deutscher Uebersetzung hsg. von O. BARDENHEWER, TH. SCHERMANN und K. WEYMAN, Kempten et München, 1912 et s.

B.L.E. = *Bulletin de littérature ecclésiastique*, Toulouse.

B.ph.W. = *Berliner philologische Wochenschrift*, Leipzig, 1881 et s.

B.P.M. = *Beiträge zur Geschichte der Philosophie des Mittelalters*, Münster, 1891 et s.

* B.T. = *Bibliotheca Teubneriana*, Leipzig.

* C.B. = *Corpus* de Berlin : *die Griechischen christlichen Schriftsteller der ersten drei Jahrhunderte*, hsg. von den Kirchenväter - Kommission der Kön. preussischen Ak. der Wiss., Leipzig, 1897 et s.

** Chron. = A. HARNACK, *Geschichte der altchristlichen Literatur, die Chronologie*, Vol. I (1897), Vol. II (1904).

[1] The most important collections and works are marked with one asterisk. Two asterisks give the best informed Bibliographies.

C.I.L. = *Corpus inscriptionum latinarum.*

* C.P.T. = *Cambridge Patristic Texts*, Cambridge, 1899 et s.

* C.V. = *Corpus Scriptorum ecclesiasticorum latinorum*, editum consilio et impensis Academiae Litterarum Cæsareæ Vindobonensis, Vienna, 1866 et s.

C.V.S. = MAI, *Scriptorum veterum nova Collectio*, Rome, 1825-1838, 10 vol.

* D.C.B. = *A Dictionary of Christian Biography*, ed. by W. SMITH and H. WACE, London, Vol. I (1877), Vol. II (1880), Vol. III (1882), Vol. IV (1887).

DUCHESNE = *Histoire ancienne de l'Église*, LOUIS DUCHESNE, Paris, 1906-1910, 3 vol.

* F.P. = *Florilegium patristicum*, digessit, vertit, adnotavit, G. RAUSCHEN, Bonn, 1904 et s.

G.L. = *Grammatici latini*, H. KEIL'S Ed. Leipzig, 1857-1879.

* H.L. = *Textes et documents pour l'étude historique du Christianisme*, published under the direction of H. HEMMER and PAUL LEJAY, Paris, 1904 et s.

HURTER = *SS. Patrum opuscula selecta*, Hurter's Ed. Œnip., 1868-1885, 48 vol.

JORDAN ⇒ HERM. JORDAN, *Geschichte der altchristlichen Literatur*, Leipzig, 1911.

J.T.S. = *Journal of Theological Studies*, Oxford.

K.A. = CARL PAUL CASPARI, *Kirchenhistorische Anecdota*, Christiania, 1883.

K.T. = *Kleine Texte für theologische Vorlesungen und Uebungen*, hsg. H. LIETZMANN, Bonn, 1902 et s.

* MANITIUS = *Gesch. der lateinschen Literatur des Mittelalters*, by MAX MANITIUS, Münich, 1911, in I. VON MÜLLER'S *Handbuch.*

MANSI = *Sanctorum conciliorum amplissima collectio*, re-edited by WELTER, Paris, 1901 et s.

* M.G.H. = *Monumenta Germaniae historica. Auctores antiquissimi*, Berlin, 1877-1898, 13 vol.

* MONCEAUX = PAUL MONCEAUX. *Histoire littéraire de l'Afrique chrétienne depuis les origines jusqu'à l'invasion arabe.* Paris, 4 vol. 1901 et s.

N.P.B. = A. MAI, *Nova Patrum Bibliotheca*, 2 vol. Rome, 1852-1854.

**p = BARDENHEWER (O), *Patrologie*, 3rd ed., Freiburg i. B., 1910.

P.C. = Collection *la Pensée chrétienne*, Paris, Bloud et Cie.

* P.G. = *Patrologie grecque*, by J. P. MIGNE.

* P.L. = *Patrologie latine*, by J. P. MIGNE.

P.L.M. = *Poetae latini minores* recensuit et emendavit ÆMILIUS BAEHRENS. Leipzig, 1879-1886 (Bibl. Teubner), 6 vol.—Vol. VI is entitled *Fragmenta poetarum romanorum.*—The collection is continued under the same title by FR. VOLLMER, 1910 et s.

** P.W. = PAULY-WISSOWA, *Real-Encyclopädie der class. Altertumswissenschaft*, neue Bearb., Stuttgart, 1893 et s.

R. Bén. = *Revue Bénédictine*, Maredsous (Belgium), 1884 et s.

R.C. = *Revue Critique*, Paris, 1866 et s.

** R.E. = *Realencyclopedie für protestantische Theologie und Kirche*, 3rd ed., Leipzig, 1896 et s.

R.E.A. = *Revue des Etudes Anciennes* (formerly *Annales de la Faculté des Lettres de Bordeaux*).

Rh.M. = *Rheinisches Museum*, Frankfort, 1827 et s.

R.H.L.R. = *Revue d'histoire et de littérature religieuses*, Paris, 1896 et s.

R.L.M. = HALM, *Rhetores latini minores*, Leipzig, 1863.

R.Q.H. = *Revue des Questions historiques*, Paris, 1866 et s.

R.S. = M. J. ROUTH, *Reliquiae Sacrae*, 2nd ed. Oxford, 1846-1848, 5 vol.

R.S.R. = *Recherches de Science religieuse*, Paris, 1909 et s.

S.B.B. = *Sitzungsberichte der Kgl. preuss. Akad. der Wiss. zu Berlin.*

S.B.M. = *Sitzungsberichte der Kön Bayerischen Akademie der Wissenschaften zu München.* Philos.-phil.-histor. Klasse.

S.B.W. = *Sitzungsberichte der Kais. Akademie der Wissenschaften*, Wien. Philos.-histor. Klasse.

** SCHANZ = SCHANZ (M.), *Geschichte der römischen Litteratur*, in I. VON MÜLLER'S *Handbuch*, Vol. III (1905); Vol. IV (1914).

S.Q. = *Sammlung ausgewählter Kirchen-und dogmengeschichtlicher Quellenschriften*, hsg. by KRÜGER, Freiburg i. B., 1891-1896. Second series, 1901 et s.

S.S. = *Spicilegium Solesmense*, ed. by DOM J. B. PITRA, Paris, 1852-1856, 4 vol.

** TEUFFEL = *Geschichte der röm Litteratur*, 6th ed., revised by KROLL et SKUTSCH, Vol. III (1913), Leipzig.

* TILLEMONT = L. S. LE NAIN DE TILLEMONT, *Mémoires pour servir à l'histoire ecclésiastique des six premiers siècles*, Paris, 1693-1712, 16 vol.

T.L.Z. = *Theologische Literaturzeitung*, Leipzig, 1876 et s.

T.Q. = *Theologische Quartalschrift*, Tübingen, 1819 et s.

* T.S. = *Texts and Studies*, Contributions to Biblical and Patristic Literature, ed. by J. ARMITAGE ROBINSON, Cambridge, 1891 et s.

* T.U. = *Texte und Untersuchungen zur Geschichte der altchristlichen Literatur*, hsg. by O. v. GEBHARDT and A. HARNACK, Leipzig, 1882-1897, 15 vol. New series, 1897-1906, 15 vol. Third series, hsg. by A. HARNACK and C. SCHMIDT, 1907 et s.

V.M. = *Veröffentlichungen aus dem Kirchenhistor. Seminar München*, 1899 et s. (three series).

Z.K.T. = *Zeitschrift für Katholische Theologie*, Innsbrück.

Z.N.W. = *Zeitschrift für die neutestamentliche Wissenschaft*, Giessen, 1900 et s.

ABBREVIATIONS OF NAMES OF PLACES

B. = Berlin
Br. = Brussels
C. = Cambridge
L. = Leipsig
Lo. = London
O. = Oxford
P. = Paris

INTRODUCTION

LATIN CHRISTIAN LITERATURE AND THE OLD LEARNING

SUMMARY

I. Latin Christian Literature and Modern Criticism.—II. The Æsthetic interest which this literature offers.—III. The intellectual formation of the Christian writers.—IV. The added Dignity received from them by Roman literature.—V. The Old Learning and Christianity : the Nature of the Problem stated. The dream of St Jerome.—VI. Christian hostility to this learning—VII. The compromises necessitated.— VIII. The middle course which finally ensued.—IX. The handing on of the old literary culture by Christianity.—X. To what extent profane learning has penetrated Christian thought.—XI. Bibliographical notes. Migne's *Patrology*. The *Corpus Scriptorum Ecclesiasticorum Latinorum*.

I

IF we compare the histories and manuals concerned with Latin literature which have appeared during these last years with those which formerly were most in favour, we notice the increasingly important place occupied by Latin Christian Literature.

In the classic works of Pierron (1852), of Paul Albert (1871), and of Talbot (1883), this literature is not touched upon (with the exception of one short page devoted to the Christian hymns by Talbot). Out of 544 pages, Nageotte (1885) gives 32 to the Christian authors, but his appreciations are weak and inconspicuous. With the appearance of the short *Histoire de la Littérature latine* by Jeanroy and Puech (1891) some little progress can be seen, thanks to the personal ability of M. Puech, whose labours on Prudentius (1887) had made him familiar with a category of writers who had been systematically held in oblivion. It reached a decisive point in the hands of M. René Pichon, who out of 935 pages devoted 155 to strictly Christian literature—nearly a sixth of the total work—in the

first edition of his manual which is to-day so widely known :
" It is as living, as interesting, as profane literature," affirms
M. Pichon : " It is also almost Roman and much more
modern."

In Germany, since 1837, Baehr has added an appendix on
Latin Christian Literature to his *Histoire de la Littérature
latine*. However, Munk (*Geschichte der röm. Lit. für Gymnasien*,
Berlin, 1858–1861 ; review by Seyffert, 1875–1877) has only
a few words to say on the Christian authors. The same may
be said of Rudolf Nicolai (*Gesch. der röm. Lit.*, Magdebourg,
1881–1882). And it was only grudgingly and from time to
time that the *Jahresbericht* of Bursian and Muller condescended
to grant a short notice to detailed works relating to the period
following after the Antonines. Nevertheless, Teuffel had given
it a place in his system (1st ed. 1870). But so long-lived was
the prejudice that when Martin Schanz, who had been com-
missioned to write the History of Roman literature in Ivan
von Muller's *Handbuch*, thought it necessary to analyse at
some length the contents of the ecclesiastical works of the
first century, he drew down on himself lively criticism for
having encroached upon a domain reserved, as they said,
to other distinguishing features.[1]

From a historical point of view, this incurious spirit explains
itself fairly reasonably. From the time of the Renaissance,
a large number of humanists, altogether taken up with Cicero,
Horace and Virgil, made open profession of extending to the
early Christian writings and to the Latin Bible itself their
contempt for " scholastic " and " monastic " Latin.[2] With
the divine charm of the classic masterpieces they contrasted
its rustic and unadorned style. It was an easy matter for
them to take advantage of certain declared views, more or less
sincere, on the part of the Christian authors. Although
initiated, and for the most part on close terms with profane
learning, these Christian authors affected to hold them cheaply
and to contrast with their childish prodigality the noble
simplicity of the Scriptures. All that they were concerned
with was to take off the edge of the criticisms with which the
pagans loaded the language of the Holy Books from the

---

[1] Cf. Aly, in Bursian's *Jahresbericht*, ṭ. XCVIII (1898), pp. 8–9.
[2] The humanist, Pietro Bembo, disdainfully applied the term *epistolaccie* to the
Epistles of St Paul.

literary point of view ; and they thought they could do no better than to disqualify any principle pertaining to the art of style, try how they might to conform to it. They were taken at their word. And thus the text in which they wrote appeared to possess no more importance than so many documents on dogma, the liturgy, ecclesiastical history, etc. The philologists abandoned them to the theologians with a disdain in which prudence also found a place : for to touch upon them conduced to perilous disputes in which it was better worth their while not to get out of their depth. The transformation of the Latin tongue, brought about under the influence of Christianity, was considered in the light of a lamentable decadence. And right up to our times we have seen critics speaking with despair and disgust at the decline of Latin in Christian lands !

We are getting the better of an ostracism so wanting in intelligence, which explains but does not at all excuse the remarkable ignorance of the period condemned wholesale by these fastidious individuals. During the last fifty years philology has begun to turn its attention towards the Christian epoch. Undertakings such as the *Corpus Scriptorum Ecclesiasticorum Latinorum*, the programme of which was drawn up in 1864,[1] have greatly contributed to bring the philologists and theologians closer together ; and little by little the philologists have recognised the impossibility of forming a correct idea of the development of Latin literature if the Christian writings are excluded therefrom *a priori*.[2]

Upon this increasing attention which so many sound minds are giving to Latin Christian Literature, it will not be without purpose to bestow a brief justification, not for the pleasure of branching out into ambitious generalities, but in order to make some fundamental observations, which, once established, will serve in some sort as a substructure to our special studies.

---

[1] Cf. S.B.W., 1864, p. 385, et s.

[2] Max Bonnet, *La Philologie Classique*, Paris, 1892, pp. 172–174 ; Paul Lejay, R.H.L.R., 1900, p. 174 (" La science de l'antiquité n'est complète qu'à condition d'y faire entrer les monuments du Christianisme ") ; Heinze, *Die gegenwärtigen Aufgaben der röm. Literaturgeschichte*, in the Neue Jahrb. f.d. kl. Alt., 1907, p. 162. For Greek Christian literature, see A. Puech's interesting observations in *Atti del Congresso internazionale delle scienze storiche*, vol. II : *Atti della Sezione I, Storia Antica e filologica classica*, 1905, pp. 205–212, " *L'ancienne littérature chrétienne et la philologie classique*."

II

AT the outset, I will remark that for those who love to find in the works they are studying the qualities of composition and art which are characteristic of the classic writers, the reading of the Christian authors—especially the Latin authors—has some happy surprises in store. I repeat, especially the Latin authors. As a matter of fact, if it were our task to describe the development of Christian Greek literature, we should first of all have to extend our examination over a series of works, which are extremely interesting from the moral and religious point of view, but very feeble from a proper æsthetic standpoint. Letters, "revelations," simple and bare paraphrases from the Sacred Books—these are the channels through which this literature took its rise. Read the Διδαχή, the *Pastor* of Hermas, the *Epistles* ascribed to Barnabas or Clement of Rome; these are writings in quite popular language, for the purpose of calling to the minds of people of manifestly very humble conditions and culture, whether in a direct or allegorical form, the principles of fraternity (ἀγαπή) and the subduing of evil instincts (ἐγκρατέια), which they were too much given to forget. No literary care, no anxiety for the arrangement of ideas and phrases, is there betrayed.

It was only with prudence and circumspection that the Church, little by little, assumed the forms of profane literature in order to adapt them to her own ends. When the Canon of the New Testament had been closed up and placed outside all dispute, she recognised her right to draw upon them more largely. In the case of the first Greek apologists, Tatian, Athenagoras, Justin, etc., who addressed themselves to the Emperors or to the great pagan public, in order to refute the deadly accusations brought against them and to turn them against their accusers, the tone becomes more personal, more intense, the turn of phrase more polished, the arguments more closely rendered and philosophic. Notwithstanding, the diction is still incomplete, the composition flows haphazard : " What they borrow from Greek tradition is the Greek mode of thought," M. Maurice Croiset remarks,[1] " but they are as

---

[1] *Hist. de la Litt. grecque*, V, 326.

emancipated as may well be from a desire to satisfy the taste, or to charm or strike the imagination, without which there can be no literary creation properly so called." It was only gradually that the Greek Christian writers came to understand that to write well was not simple frivolity, and that the expression of ideas required that beauty of form which had for so long appeared to be an inconvenient and pretentious pursuit.

The Latin writers had been spared this long labour of accommodation, and that is explained at first by a chronological reason. The first Latin Christian works of which we shall have to speak are not of a date anterior to the end of the IInd century. Up to then, Greek was the language probably in use among the Christians of the West, especially in Rome. The only Christian writings in Latin were very literal, but very illiterate translations from the Greek Bible for the use of those of the faithful who had little acquaintance with Greek. Now towards the end of the IInd century, when Latin Christian Literature came to birth in Africa under the powerful impulse of Tertullian, a portion of the educated *élite* had been conquered. Some polished intellects, who had graduated under the best mental discipline, had given their adhesion to the new faith. These were destined to bring to it the powerful prestige of good diction in which they were past-masters and in which they would continue to excel, even while pluming themselves (doubtless in imitation of their Greek forerunners) in esteeming it as of slight value, and possibly experiencing some secret remorse at taking any further pleasure in it. Their skill in giving evidence of this facility will soon reveal itself to us in the *Apologeticum* of Tertullian and the *Octavius* of Minucius Felix. There is no dialogue of Cicero which surpasses in elegant grace the *Octavius*. Right from the dawn of its beginnings, Latin Christian Literature presents to us the same appearance as it will continue to present throughout its course, eager not only to spread abroad its ideas, but also to suggest them in polished language, and, after the simile of Lucretius, to spread honey on the brim of the cup in order to correct the sometimes bitter draught of truth :

Pocula circum
Contingunt mellis dulci flavoque liquore (IV, 13).

III

THERE has thus not been that divorce between Latin profane, and Christian, literature which for long separated Christian and pagan Hellenism. I will even go so far as to say that it is not possible for anyone to understand Tertullian, Cyprian, or Arnobius if he has not some little acquaintance with the purely secular literature of their time. They had been formed under the same system of education as all educated Romans under the Empire, and there is no need to suppose that when they embraced Christianity they had very profoundly altered their intellectual methods.

And what kind of education was this ? It is well to have a correct idea in order to understand the writers with whom the scholar's robe remained always so well marked a feature.

It was a hierarchy in two degrees : first in grammar, then in rhetoric. The grammarian took the child in hand when still very young, and his task consisted in teaching him to speak and write correctly either in Latin or Greek ; from this arose the study of grammar whether for the morphology or for the syntax. Then he read and commented upon the poets, Homer, Menander, Terence, Horace and Virgil, and it was only in connection with these explanations that he gave his pupils ideas in versification, philosophy, history, music, astronomy, etc. Education in general subjects was thus acquired by the accident of this literary exegesis, whether or not the texts paraphrased presented opportunity for it. Later on, the youth was entrusted to the rhetorician, whose principal ambition went no further than to make him able to speak correctly. He first of all rendered his faculties supple by written exercises, discourses, refutations, panegyrics and the development of matters of common knowledge. He then employed him on declamation proper, the pupil delivering a reasoning on some given subject, such as a case of conscience or a fictitious suit, etc.

This method was in conformity with the plan of studies which Quintilian had traced in his *Institutiones Oratoriae* which the Roman tutor continued faithfully to observe. For my part, I should not like to be too severe on it. If the prime virtue in a system of education is to interest the pupil, to shake him from his sluggishness, to force his imagination into a certain activity, it was not altogether bad. It obliged the young man to pay in his own person, to draw from his mind, barren or fruitful as it might be, all that he could, under pain of remaining awkward and mute under the eyes of his comrades. This presented a field for his emotions which he was not likely to forget, and success was as intoxicating as the humiliation was poignant. St Jerome relates, when he was about sixty, that it happened to him to see himself in a dream once more before the rhetorician in the act of declaiming his *controversy*, and that he experienced a profound relief, on awaking, at feeling himself delivered of his anguish.[1]

But on the other hand, from a practical point of view, how empty, how puerile ! One cannot imagine a course of instruction less *positive* than that given by the rhetors. Philosophy, history, law, all the sciences known at that time, had no further value in their eyes than in how far they enabled them to embellish fair phrases, impressive examples, arguments more or less juridical, and their eternal developments. Phrases, always phrases ! And if only they had drawn them from their own vat ! But the great thing was to ingeniously embody in them echoes of the classics, some hemistich from Virgil, some mocking satire from Horace, some sonorous grandeur from Cicero. All this kind of thing lacked virility and seriousness.

Thus, if we encounter in the writings of certain ecclesiastical scribes some rather puerile reasoning, such as that in which Tertullian, under the pretext of proving that the regeneration of man by water is a matter neither ridiculous nor impossible, delivers a panegyric on water and its virtues ; [2] or again an excessive propensity to take up and develop as of common interrelation the ideas and arguments already used by their predecessors ; if our taste is sometimes shocked by a profusion of shrill tones, by figures of style twenty times repeated, and by a certain lack of proportion, tact, and discretion, it is to the rhetoric class that we must go for the cause. And if we remember that this influence is always present with them it will enable us to avoid some occasional misconstruction. For instance, Villemain waxes very indignant over a passage in the famous letter of St Jerome to Heliodorus :

[1] *Contra Rufinum*, I, xxx.   [2] *De Baptismo*, III.

" If (in opposition to thy vocation) thy father were to lie
on the threshold of thy door to hold thee back, pass over the
body of thy father " (*Per calcatum perge patrem*). " What
religious ferocity ! " cries Villemain.[1] Pure rhetoric, will be
our reply. We have only to go back to the *Controversiae* of
Seneca the rhetorician, to establish the fact that St Jerome
had in mind a trait of character much admired in this school of
thought. A father was supposed to be desirous of keeping
back at all costs his son from going out to fight, and the
rhetorician Latro, puts into his mouth this final objurgation :
" If thou art determined to go, trample thy father's body
under thy feet." [2] *Ut ad hostem pervenias, patrem calca*
(I. viii. 15). Jerome had not forgotten this *sententia*—at an
unseasonable moment, we must believe, since he has given
scandal to posterity.

They preserved from their early training (which in the case
of many—St Cyprian, Arnobius, Lactantius, and even St
Augustine—had sunk into them long before from their profession as rhetoricians), a too self-satisfied virtuosity which
somewhat wearies the modern reader. They also owed to it
their greater consideration for elegance of form and the
literary charm of their writings.

IV

BUT the real interest which they offer us does not reside
solely, nor even principally, in their technical ingenuity.
Before all else it rests on this, that by the very fact of their
being Christians, their works were nurtured on a more virile
and sterner substance and one which speaks rather to our souls.

In order to estimate what gain in depth and sincerity
Christianity brought to them, consider the most noteworthy
of their contemporaries on the pagan side.[3] Frontonius, the
tutor of Marcus Aurelius, who passed his life in the pursuit of
elegant reasonings on futile subjects and in gathering the

---

[1] *Tableau de l'éloquence chrétienne au IV siècle*, p. 329.

[2] One will note that to contravene a father's wishes when they were in opposition
to a real vocation, is also one of the precepts of Epictetus. Cf. Colardeau, *Étude sur
Epictète*, Paris, 1903, p. 93.

[3] Put on one side once for all the great jurisconsults.

flowers of rhetoric; the foremost man of his time to extract from a paradox all the jests, and burlesque sequences gravely drawn out, which it was capable of producing; who wrote a panegyric on smoke, on dust, on carelessness, and sends to his pupil rules of gender, and has the simplicity to feel disappointed when he perceived that Marcus Aurelius would have none of these impassioned exercises and, withdrawing from him more and more, was turning his mind to philosophy. Apuleius, a man of doubtless finer intelligence who penetrates us in quite another way, but in whose case (even in his most beautiful passages, even in the eleventh book of the *Metamorphoses*, wherein he has come in touch with mystic accents almost Christian in their bearing) we experience so much *dilettantism* and touching complaisance for his own special talent. Again, examine such learned writers as Aulus Gellius, and further on the inept compilers of the history of Augustus, the correct and ceremonious Symmachus, and the poet Claudian—in all these it is not art which is wanting, but depth. When they are no longer borne up by the facts which they are relating, they have nothing, or next to nothing, to say.

In face of this verbose sterility, we are able to better estimate the merit belonging to the Christian authors. They alone have some certain intention; they alone have passion, an ideal. In the case of one of them, Tertullian, his great aim is to bring about the triumph, at all costs, of his conception of the faith and of life—a conception which is caustic, intemperate, violently hostile to nature, and drawing from his own paradoxes an indescribable, savage joy which incites him to go still further along a path deliberately narrow whither the Church is destined to refuse to follow him. In the case of St Cyprian, the organiser and administrator of genius, his efforts are directed to establishing so firmly the idea and *prestige* of the Church and of Episcopal authority that all the efforts of heretics should not be able to make a breach in the unbreakable solidarity of the faithful in union with their pastors. Lactantius is otherwise concerned; his purpose was to win over the men of letters, stubbornly unconvinced as yet, whose intellectual contempt caused him so much suffering; he inaugurated a method of apologetics which was more objective and more scientific, and, in full view of the doctrines

B

of the philosophers, he arrayed a real *summa* of Christian doctrine. A few years later, St Jerome was to realise the type of *savant*, and of philologist, at once studious and impassioned. And we know further from what experiences, from what a mediocre and blemished life St Augustine drew forth his profound conception of human nature, of his own inner corruption, of that indispensable aid which must come to him from above.

What characterises the Christian writers, however vexatious their ready compliance with the tastes of their time, and however fatiguing we sometimes find the too unrelieved oratorical trend of their style, or the subtilties of their exegesis, is that literature was not for them solely a play of the mind, an agreeable diversion, or a means of doing the honours to their talent. · They believed in what they said ; it was their soul which spoke ; all their moral being was engaged in their writings. I can hardly see in profane literature any single writer, who showed in his work any particle of this lively sense of conviction, save only Lucretius. But Lucretius is an altogether exceptional case. With the Romans, the art of writing always remained a little like what it had always been from quite the beginning—a simple relaxation from serious duties. They lent themselves to it for their pleasure without giving themselves up to it entirely.

With the Christian writers, on the contrary, it was a means of action, a lever to bring to bear on souls, to turn them away from error and to impel them to the truth. Their faith touched them in the bottom of their soul, and in their turn they were willing to acquiesce in the tastes of their readers just so far as that secret sanctuary where resolutions are born and acts take their rise.

We see what increase of dignity and interest Roman literature has received from their hands. From the end of the Ist century, it began to decline visibly : Greek was threatening to drive out Latin in the estimation and practice of lettered men. In order to bring it back to life, the proselytism of the new faith was required—the emotions, the mourning, the victories, which this faith aroused ; and thereby an influx of fresh ideas circulated anew under forms which were passing into decline, which by this means were rejuvenated and renewed once more.

V

THIS question of the literary quality of the Latin Christian works brings us to another which can be discussed here, once for all, with the amplitude which it deserves. It concerns the relations existing between the classic learning and Christianity, looked at from the historical point of view.

St Jerome relates in one of his letters a curious episode of his youth.[1] Having decided to embrace the ascetic life, he was bending his steps towards Jerusalem with the view of burying himself in the desert of Chalcis to the south-east of Antioch. With his passion for study, he had brought with him his books, procured in Rome " at the cost of much trouble and labour," which under no pretext whatever could he do without.[2] Here we must listen to him evolving in his own words the strange account which he related afterwards to one of the Roman patrician ladies to whom he had become the spiritual director :

> " Miserable man that I am ! I was fasting and then I began to read Cicero ; after many nights spent in watching, after many tears, which the remembrance of my faults of not so long ago drew forth from the depths of my heart, I took Plautus in my hands. If by chance, on recollecting myself, I started reading the Prophets, their unadorned style awoke in me feelings of repulsion. My eyes, blinded, saw no longer the light, and it was not on my eyes that I laid the blame, it was on heaven.
>
> " While the old serpent thus misused me, a violent fever penetrated the marrow of my worn-out body towards the middle of Lent, and, without any respite, in an incredible manner, it so consumed my poor members that I had scarcely any flesh left on my bones. Already people were thinking of my funeral. My body felt quite frozen ; a remnant of vital heat no longer palpitated save in the lukewarmness of my poor breast.
>
> " Suddenly, I felt myself ravished away in ecstasy and transported before the tribunal of the Judge. Such a

---

[1] *Ep.* xxii, 30, to Eustochium (Hilberg, in C.V., lib. 189).
[2] . . . bibliotheca . . . carere non poteram.

dazzling light emanated from those present that, crouched on the ground, I dared not lift up my eyes. On being asked my profession, I replied, ' I am a Christian.' Whereupon, he who presided said, ' Thou dost lie ; thou art a Ciceronian and no Christian ; where thy treasure is, there is thy heart also.'

" I forthwith held my peace, and under the stripes (for he had commanded that they should beat me), I felt myself tortured still more by the burning of my conscience. . . . At last, those present, casting themselves on their knees before the President, implored him to pardon my youth and to grant to my fault the time for repentance and freedom to carry out at a future date the penalty if ever I again read profane literature. And I, who in a moment so critical was ready to promise even more, made this oath : ' Lord, if ever it happens to me to possess or to read profane books, I shall have denied Thee ! ' On this undertaking, I was dismissed and came up to the earth again. To the great astonishment of all, I opened my eyes suffused with tears, and my grief convinced the most incredulous.

" This was not a case of deep sleep, one of those unreal dreams of which we are often the dupes. I call to witness the tribunal before which I lay prostrate ; I call to witness the awful sentence, the occasion of my terror ! May I never again be submitted to such an examination ! My shoulders were bruised ; on awaking, I still felt the blows. From that moment, I betook myself to the reading of the divine books with as much passion as I had given to reading the books of men."

That there is in this famous " dream " of St Jerome, a large portion of fiction I have not much difficulty in admitting ; and by pressing home certain details,[1] as also certain half-admissions subsequently made by St Jerome,[2] one feels inclined to think so.[3]

[1] Cf. the observations of E. Ch. Babut, *St Martin de Tours*, Paris, Champion, s.d., p. 99, et. s. Nevertheless, I do not get the impression that St Jerome wished to make people believe in a real death followed by a resurrection, as Babut suspected.

[2] *Apol. c. Rufinum*, I, xxx (P.L., xxiii, 441).

[3] A critical study of the *Dream of St Jerome* by P. de Labriolle, will appear in the *Mélanges* which will shortly be published in Rome for the centenary of St Jerome.

But what is open to no doubt is that the scruple which he thus vividly portrayed was for him as for so many other lettered Christians of the first centuries, the cause of very real and very grievous anguish.   In how far had a Christian, who was desirous of preserving in his intellectual and moral life an entirely logical attitude, the right to take pleasure in the reading of pagan books and in making of them his favourite mental diet ?   Here is a problem the interest of which seems to us rather remote.   However, it has excited, even in the modern world, burning controversies, at the time of the Renaissance,[1] in the XVIIth century,[2] above all in the XIXth century.[3]   In its initial form, it implied consequences of great historical importance : for instance, the future of Greco-Latin learning, firstly in the bosom of Christianity itself, and then in European civilisation.   At the given moment, the Church became practically the united mistress of this precious legacy. If she had rejected it decidedly, it would have been lost to us without hope of recall, and modern thought could not have rejuvenated and renewed itself from the sources of antiquity to the large extent which it has done.

VI

LET us try to begin by an effort of historical understanding to grasp the state of mind of the generations of Christians who lived in full and direct contact with the pagan world.

One must acknowledge that, in their case, there were not

---

[1] Cf. for instance, the Lucula Noctis by Fra Giovanni Dominici, published in 1908 by Remi Coulon, Paris, Picard, from two MSS., one in the Laurentian Library at Florence, the other in the Royal Library, Berlin.   The *Lucula* supplies most interesting information on the history of humanism in Florence at the beginning of the IVth century.   For the middle ages, consult G. Robert in his *Les Écoles et l'enseignement de la théologie pendant la première moitié du XII siècle*, Paris, Gabalda, 1909, pp. 76–92.

[2] We should remember the debate between Mabillon and Le Bouthillier de Rancé.   Cf. E. de Broglie, *Mabillon et la Soc. de l'Abbaye de Saint-Germain-des-Prés*, Paris, 1888, vol. II, pp. 97–196.

[3] Cf. L'Abbé J. Gaume's truculent work, *Le ver rongeur des sociétés modernes ou le paganisme dans l'éducation*, Paris, 1851 ; and again Daniels, S.J., *Les études classiques de la société chrétienne*, Paris, 1853 ; Krabinger, *Die klass. Studien und ihre Gegner*, Munich, 1855.   The Holy See has on several occasions uttered her opinion on the question (Encyl. of Pius IX, 21st March, 1853, to the Bishops of France ; Brief to Mgr. Gaume, 22nd April, 1874 ; Brief to Mgr. D'Avanzo, of the same date ; Letter of Leo XIII to Cardinal Parocchi, 20th May, 1885 ; to Mgr. Heylen, Bishop of Namur, 20th May, 1901).

wanting objects of scandal. At the circus, at the theatre, in the public exhibitions, in the institutions, in the daily scenes of their life, how many features recalled to them idolatry or breathed forth sensuality! And these detested vices they found in nearly all the works in which were expressed the soul of antiquity. What crude coarseness in the tales of mythology, what obscenities in its symbols! One could have no knowledge of even the prurient extracts from Greco-Latin literature over which the young men of the future toiled or slumbered, to deny that the sexual life, with its fires, its effeminacies, its enervating delicacies, sometimes even its most cynical perversities, held therein a considerable place. More than one amongst the educated Christians had learnt to beware of this profane fire from having in former days felt its scorch. Does not St Augustine go so far as to reproach himself in his *Confessions* [1] that he wept when still a child over the relatively extremely innocent pages wherein Virgil has recounted the sad love story of Dido! We might say that in this emotional tenderness of his boyhood he proved thus early the even then somewhat morbid initial stages of that sensibility whereof in later life his whole ardent desire was summed up in these two words *amare et amari.*[2]

Yes, Christian asceticism, or in other terms the distrust felt by Christians in regard to pleasure, could not fail to be bruised in the most painful manner by the licence of the pictures or allusions with which a large number of Greek and Roman writers, devout admirers of nature only and impervious to even the notion of sin, amused themselves.[3]

---

[1] I, xiii.

[2] Cf. II, 11 : " Et quid erat, quod me delectabat, nisi amare et amari." Here are some modern evidences which corroborate in an interesting manner that of St Augustine. Chateaubriand relates in his *Mémoires d'Outre-Tombe* (vol. I, p. 92, ed. Biré) that as a child he owed to an unexpurgated Horace, to the IX Book of the Aeneid, to Tibullus and to Lucretius, his first revelations of the world of the senses, and of his own voluptuous and melancholy nature : " One day I translated from the open book *Æneadum genitrix, hominum divumque voluptas* from Lucretius with so much vivacity," he states, " that M. Egault (his Latin master at the College of Dol) took the poem away from me and thrust me among the Greek roots." And again, Jules Lemaitre, in his *Les Comtemporains*, vol. VI (1896), p. 38 : ". . . If I consult my own experience, I know very well what the classics of antiquity have insinuated and left in me, and that is in short, the taste for a kind of voluptuous naturalism, the principles of an epicureanism and of a stoicism, alike full of pride, and possibly the germs of some virtues, but virtues totally wanting in humility." Cf. Ad. Boschot, *Une vie romantique, Hector Berlioz*, Paris, 1919, p. 5.

[3] For the misunderstandings which sometimes arise in connection with the *pecces* of Horace, *Satires*, I, II, 63, cf. P. Lejay, *Œuvres d'Horace, Satires*, Paris, Hachette, 1911, p. 32.

The old philosophy aroused prejudices of another kind. It contained within itself a principle of intellectual independence, of unrestrained and ironic criticism, which spared neither the traditional pagan religion—in this regard the Christians had passed condemnation—nor even (and that conveyed something quite different) the idea of God, the idea of a Providence, the belief in posthumous rewards.[1]   How could they maintain, in the face of such an audacious standard, the sovereign completeness of the *regula fidei ?*   The danger was no imaginary one.   Events had demonstrated its reality.   One of the most formidable intellectual movements amongst Christians which the Church at its birth had to combat, was Gnosticism, of which we see the traces at the end of the first century and which in the course of the second century developed an incredible growth.   Now there was an opinion current,[2] which was justified in part, that these speculative conceits passing all limits were closely related on more than one point to certain systems of profane philosophy—a compromising joint-interest which scarcely encouraged the faithful to sympathise with it.

Finally, it was not because of literary art in itself or because of its technique of style, which had been perfected to an astonishing degree in the course of centuries, that the awakening in them of a distaste very like to aversion was due.   We must recollect to what a degree of virtuosity, to what specious inventions, to what dialectical boastfulness had eloquence of speech and written literature arrived in the first centuries of the Empire.   By reason of the pleasure taken in frivolous mental acrobatics, in the inexhaustible niceties of their oratorical developments, Greco-Roman literature had lost in great part a sense of reality and the taste for truth.   It was the day of triumph of rhetoric and of Neo-Sophism, the strange seduction

---

[1] References in *La critique des traditions religieuses chez les Grecs,* Paris, A. Picard, 1904, by Paul Decharme.   See the index in this work at the words Athéisme, Impiété, Religion, Providence, Enfer.

[2] Tertullian associates Marcion with Epicurus (adv. Marc., V, xix; Kroymann, in C.V., vol. XLVII, p. 645, line 11).   In connection with this he notes that " omnes (haereses) ex subtiloquentiae viribus et philosophiae regulis constant."   Cf. *de Anima,* xxiii (Reifferscheid-Wissowa, in C.V., vol. XX, p. 336, line 16) : " Doleo bona fide Platonem omnium haereticorum condimentarium factum."   Hippolytus of Rome in his *Philosoph.,* associates Valentine, the Gnostic, sometimes with the Pythagoreans (VI, xxix), sometimes with the Academicians or the Peripatetics (VI, xxii), Marcus with the Pythagorean (VI, lii), Marcion with Empedocles (VI, xxix). E. de Faye admits certain affiliation of ideas between Greek philosophy and Gnosticism (*Gnostiques et Gnosticisme,* Paris, Leroux, 1913, pp. 28, 30, 41, 51, 97, 193, 419).

of which penetrated all the domains of thought, and assigned to intelligent minds as their supreme end skilfully deduced paradoxes, scholarly themes richly developed, and conceits of style. In a society intoxicated with literature, and become unaccustomed to truth, Christianity appeared to be entirely turned towards the interior life, and to be passionately convinced of the seriousness of human existence and of the tragedy of destiny, and to be *so far* removed from considering ideas as just simple incentives for dialectics ! How could the intellectual exercises in which this society placed its rapturous delight and pride fail to be accounted absurd and even pernicious !

It felt itself all the more drawn to this view by reason of the fact that the literary form of the Bible was a subject for astonishment in the eyes of lettered pagans, and became the pretext for scornful jestings without end. The Greek Bible, with its Hebraisms, its simplicity so closely related to the everyday language spoken, turned these people away in disgust, in whose eyes all was barbarian which was outside their own habits.[1] Matters became much worse when the Greek Bible had been translated into Latin by hands who, though well intentioned, had but moderate skill. These transpositions, very literal since the principal object was to render the Word of God in its exact tenor, very popular too in their language in as much as they were to be understood by the most ignorant, afforded some of the most scurrilous banter to the enemies of Christianity.[2] And, by an inevitable

[1] Celsus, ap. Origen, *Contra Celsum*, I, lxii (Koetschau, in C.V., *Origenes*, I, 113); Clement of Alex., *Protrepticus*, viii, 77. Origèn, *Hom.*, viii, i : " Deprecamur vos, o auditores sacrorum voluminum, non cum taedio vel fastidio ea, quae leguntur, audire, pro eo quod minus delectabilis eorum videtur esse narratio " ; Saint John Chrysost., *Hom. in Ioannem*, II, 2 (P.G., lix, 31); Saint Basil, Ep. cccxxxix ad Libanios (P.G., xxxii, 1085); *Hexam.*, 3 Homily (P.G., xxix, 120 D), in connection with the word φαῦσις in Genesis XVI : " Let not the singularity of the word cause you to laugh ; do not mock at us if we conform not to your choice of words, and if we seek not to arrange them in harmonious fashion, etc."

[2] Lactance, *Hist. div.*, V, i (Brandt, in C.V., vol. XIX, p. 400 ; P.L., vi, 500) : " Haec imprimis causa est, cur apud sapientes et doctos et principes huius saeculi Scriptura sancta fide careat, quod prophetae *communi ac simplici sermone, ut ad populum*, sunt locuti. Contemnuntur itaque ab iis qui nihil audire vel legere nisi expolitum ac disertum volunt, nec quicquam inhaerere animis eorum potest, nisi quod aures blandiori sono permulcet." See also *ibid.*, vi, 21 (Brandt, p. 562).— Arnob., *Adv. Nationes*, I, xlv (Reifferscheid, in C.V., vol. IV, p. 29, l. 20) ; I, lviii (ibid., p. 39, l. 8) ; I, lix, he cites a pagan objection ; " *Barbarismis, soloecismis* obsitae sunt res vestrae et vitiorum deformitate pollutae." Saint Jerome, Ep. liii, 10 (Hilberg, in C.V., vol. LIV, p. 463) : " Nolo offendaris in scripturis sanctis *simplicitate et quasi vilitate verborum,* quae vel vitio interpretum vel de industria sic prolatae sunt, ut rusticam contionem facilius instruerent et in una eademque sententia aliter doctus, aliter audiret indoctus." Cf. Ep. xxii, 30, 2.

reaction, the Christians were drawn to conceive an animosity against even the principle of art in style as being a deformity from the truth, and the leaven of vanity.

Greco-Roman civilisation, therefore, harboured for the supporters of the new faith more than one germ of bitterness and enmity. What still further poisoned this instinctive antipathy was the fact of the State becoming their persecutor, and employing against the Christians its gaols, its executioners, its tortures, and all the gamut of the atrocious Roman penalties.

It is necessary to give a complete representation of these data in order to obtain the full and impartial comprehension of a state of mind which I am now going to describe.

It has been proved that during the first centuries of our era,—in the East as well as in the West, contrary to what has been sometimes stated—there was a large number of Christians who were enemies of the old learning and who, contenting themselves with -their faith alone, and with one book, the Bible, had of their own free will, without distinction or examination, rejected the intellectual heritage of the old world. Clement of Alexandria, a man of distinguished intellect and a profoundly convinced Christian, but whose enlightened eclecticism would fain have allowed him to breathe freely the air of Greek thought which he admired, reveals to us that these *intransigeants* formed the majority around him towards the end of the IIIrd century ; [1] and this in a city in which the highest forms of scholarship were traditional, the city of erudition, of the museum, of libraries ! " The common herd," he declares not without melancholy, " fear the Greek philosophy, just as children fear goblins." [2] They went so far as to contest with Clement the lawfulness of his writing at all, or at least, to be much concerned that he should use his time on a task such as that. Clement was obliged to defend himself against these strange susceptibilities which readily were turned into matter of suspicion. [3] Even still later, in the IVth and Vth centuries, in Rome, in Cappadocia, in Cyrenäica up to Constantinople, the same misgivings were evident, not alone on the part of a few isolated protesting voices, but

[1] *Stromates*, VI, xi, 89 ; *ibid.*, VII, i.
[2] *Strom.*, VI, lxxx, 5.
[3] * * *Strom.*, I, 11–14. Cf. E. de Faye, *Clément of Alexandria*, 2nd ed., p. 139 et s.

throughout the Christian body.[1] Men like St Jerome,[2] St Gregory of Nazianzen,[3] Synesius of Cyrene,[4] and Socrates the historian,[5] were driven to give battle to the malevolence of which ἠέξωθεν πάιδευσις that is, profane education, was the object.

They introduced sometimes a little spite and bad temper ; but more often they displayed a longanimity which is astonishing ; there are justifications, adjustments of points of view, and even concessions, whereof the tone on certain pages nearly resembles that of the *intransigeants* which they were hoping to appease.

There emerges, therefore, the fact that we can state that during the first centuries of the Empire there is hardly a Christian writer in whose case there does not intrude, or show itself more or less sincerely, more or less diplomatically, a hostility in regard to the different forms of profane learning.

With some of them it was a mania and, we might almost say, a moral certainty. For example, Tertullian—in other respects the incomparable champion, the most original writer in Latin under the Empire—scarcely ever passes over an opportunity to dig still deeper the ditch separating the world from the Church. He proclaims that all the *doctrina saecularis litteraturae* is foolishness in the eyes of God, and that the Christian must reject it.[6] He treats the philosophers as " huxters of wisdom and eloquence," [7] as " animals of self-glorification," [8] and sees in the art of dialectic, invented by that " pitiable Aristotle," the mother of heresy. " What is there in common," he cries,[9] " between Athens and Jerusalem, between the Academe and the Church ? . . . So much the worse for those who have displayed a Christianity of the Stoic, of the Platonist, of the Dialectician ! For us, we have no need for curiosity,

---

[1] Οἱ πολλοὶ χριστιανῶν, said Gregory of Nazianzen (*Funeral Oration of St Basil*, xi, i ; P.G., xxxvi, 508).

[2] Ep. lxx (Hilberg, in C.V., vol. LIV, p. 700). A certain Magnus whom Jerome treats in the capacity of *Orator Urbis*, had asked him at the end of a letter " why he strewed here and there in his writings examples taken from profane literature, thus soiling the whiteness of the Church with pagan horrors." An insidious question wherein Jerome could suspect some snare contrived by the untiring hostility of his enemies in Rome. Cf. § 6 ; Hilberg, p. 708, l. 8 et s.

[3] *Op. cit.*

[4] *Ep.* cliii (P.G., xlvi, 1553).

[5] *Hist. eccl.*, III, xvi (P.G., lxvii, 420).

[6] *De Spectac.*, xviii.

[7] *De Anima*, III (Reifferscheid-Wissowa, p. 302, l. 32).

[8] *Ibid.*, I (p. 299, l. 10). Cf. Adv. Marc., I. xiii.

[9] *De Praescr.*, vii.

after Jesus Christ, nor for investigation, after the Gospel ! "
" The writings of philosophers, historians and poets, appear
to be worthy of credence because of their ornaments of style,"
declared Theophilus, the Bishop of Antioch, in the second half
of the IInd century, " but at bottom they are void and insen-
sate." [1] In the case of certain polemical writers,[2] these attacks
take the form of a systematic disparagement whose heavy
irony borders close upon the most overwhelming ineptitude.
Even the moderate minded, a Justin, an Athenagoras, a
Clement of Alexandria, an Origen, or a Lactantius, who in
their hearts could not bring themselves to admit that pagan
thought was altogether in error throughout, did not dare any
more than others to extend their feelings of goodwill and
equity to the length of depriving themselves of discharging
many criticisms.[3] Further, with a view to redeem their sympathies and their secret respect in this regard, they took refuge
on occasion in an unlikely hypothesis which had been invented
by the Alexandrine Jews previous to Christianity, according
to which the wisdom of the Greeks could have been no other
than a by-product of Hebrew wisdom, the philosophers having
taken toll of Moses and the Bible.[4]

In endeavouring to counteract the ironical strictures of the
pagans on the simplicity of the language of Holy Scripture,
they went so far as to dispute absolutely the importance of
style and of grammar, and to reduce those laws of language,
to which literary tradition attached so high a price, to mere
conventions or to simple prejudices. This paradox found
sometimes unexpected upholders. Of such a kind was the old
rhetorician, Arnobius, whose wordy eloquence, lacking discretion and fine distinctions, lingers over developing the idea
that the faith had no need of vain *technique*, and that, in

---

[1] *Ad. Autol.*, II, xii (P.G., vi, 1069) ; cf. III, II.

[2] E. G. Tatian, *Hermias.*

[3] Very numerous references : see K. Werner, *Gesch. der apol. u. polem. Liter.*,
Schaffhausen, 1861, etc., vol. I, pp. 316–335. For Clement of Alex., cf. W. Wagner,
in the Z. fur wiss. Theol., XLV (1902), p. 220, etc. For Origen, cf. J. Denis, *La
philosophie* d'Origène, Paris, 1884, p. 17, etc. Christian opinion in regard to divers
philosophies is well reviewed in the *Dict. of Christian Biography*, by Smith and
Wace, vol. I (1877), p. 143, etc.

[4] References equally numerous. See Harnack, *Gesch. d. altchr. Liter.*, erster
Teil, p. 877, etc. This theory of which St Augustine finally conceived some doubts
(Civitas Dei, VIII, xi), was transmitted to the middle ages by Cassiodorus (cf.
Inst. Div., I, xvii). We find some traces of this in the *Discours sur l'Histoire Univ.*,
by Bossuet (part II, chap. xv at the end). Bossuet's allusion is otherwise very
prudent.

accordance with every other form of speech, there was no such thing, *per se*, as a correct or a vicious form.[1]

In this way, the sentiment of intellectual Christians, whether sincere or not, joined hands over more than one article held by the exclusive *simpliciores :* such care for uniformity of thought is very much at the heart of Catholicism.   Under this train of reasoning more or less unfavourable to the Greco-Latin learning, there lay an element of rough but formidable logic.   What good to make any endeavour at conciliation, or pretence of coquetting with a civilisation wherein the true faith found so few points of contact, and so many occasions for becoming impaired or broken up ?   To live uprightly, to expiate one's faults, to keep oneself on the road to the eternal fatherland without too many deviations—was not this the essential duty of a Christian ?   Why aggravate a task already so difficult by mingling with it the study of writers brought up on polytheism, with no care for any moral law, who welcomed all undisciplined curiosities of the spirit, all carnal weaknesses, and whose contradictory speculations disclosed uncertainties deadly to the stability of the established faith ? By reading the Scriptures, were there not revealed therein more than one counsel susceptible of justifying the energetic prejudices already suggested by experience and even by good sense ?   The question then was no other than resolutely to take no account of that " wisdom of the world," which the Apostle Paul had called " foolishness," [2] in order to attach oneself to that which was the whole duty of man during his terrestrial pilgrimage.

VII

THIS psychological reconstitution which I have just sketched is not a fantastic one, nor one put together on any *a priori* principle.   It rests on an immense number of texts, in which there breathes the same asceticism, incurious of all that in life appeared to be but a superfluous decking and a useless gratification of the mind.   Nay more, in old compilations of ecclesiastical law, and in decisions of Councils, there are to be found

---

[1] *Adv. Nationes,* I. lix (Reifferscheid in C.V., vol. IV, p. 40).   " . . . Si verum spectes, nullus sermo natura est integer, vitiosus similiter nullus, etc."

[2] I *Cor.,* i, 20 ; cf. *Rom.,* i, 22 ; II *Cor.,* x, 5 ; *Coloss.,* ii, 8.

formal prohibitions against reading pagan books extended to the faithful and even to the Bishops.[1] These injunctions never possessed any but a local value, and, it would appear, only an uncertain efficaciousness. We see, however, the danger : the survival of the ancient patrimony of science and literature was directly menaced.

But for such a result the absolute principles of the *intransigeants* would have had to be pressed to their utmost limits and applied in all their rigour. Now life has its necessary requirements and reactions, wherein our preconceived notions, however ardently held they may have been, are brought up against their own limitations, with which they are constrained to make some attempt at composition. To have entirely rejected Greco-Latin learning might have been a bold and imposing attitude to have taken, but can we truly imagine that it could have brought about and realised its work of making a complete breach and destroying it ?

Let us consider what this Hellenic patrimony represented in power of research and creation, still further enriched as it was by Roman genius after the latter had appropriated it, and which in its decadence, already clearly visible, remained yet almost intact.

In the first place, it was the fruit of a long series of admirable strivings to explain the world to man, and man to himself. The Greek philosophers and critics had revealed, by their essays at a rational interpretation of the sum of human affairs, by their psychological intuitions, by their acute analyses of the human mind and its creations, the might of reason when applied by rule and method to its object. Then this field of humanity in which they had exercised their profound thought had become a delight to the imagination in other hands, those of their poets and artists, by virtue of their gift of sympathy, their instinct for the beautiful and graceful, sometimes sad, sometimes full of lightness, which were the marks of the Greek spirit. In all the domains of expression, especially of literary expression, the researches of the theorists aided by the grand creations of art, had revealed how all the delicate shades of sensibility and all the wealth of the intelligence

---

[1] *Const. apost.*, I, vi (Funk, 1 (1905), p. 13). (Text very curious.) Cf. IVth Council of Carthage (398), c. xvi, in Gratian, c. i. dict. xxxvii : " . . . ut episcopus gentilium libros non legat, haereticorum autem pro necessitate et tempore ".

might translate itself ; how the taste, at first instinctive, takes knowledge of itself and creates its own methods, how words acquire a power at once significant and suggestive, while the written phrase comes together duly ordered, balances itself, amplifies itself, and passes into rhythm, harmony and beauty.

Was Christianity, therefore, to sacrifice these lessons in lofty reasoning, this positive knowledge, this compelling art at once touching and refined, and these wise systems of *technique ?* Such a clean cut would have affected not only the virtuosities of art to which the serious-minded Christian had the right to remain a stranger. It would have suppressed, or paralysed for long, astronomy, music, rhetoric, dialectic, grammar and all the mental disciplines which at that time went to the make-up of a man of culture.[1] At one stroke Christianity would have condemned itself to intellectual indigence ; it closed up for itself the great avenues of thought, and with insurmountable difficulties complicated its mission of conquest and propaganda.

Had the Christian phalanxes been recruited indefinitely among the " wool-carders, cobblers and fullers," according to the sarcastic insinuation of the pagan philosopher, Celsus,[2] it would have been easy to make cheap of the intellectual treasures accumulated through the antecedent centuries. No one would have felt the loss due to such a holocaust. But quite early lettered men, and minds broken in to the traditional methods of teaching, had allowed themselves to be drawn to the new faith, and once they had become included amongst the faithful, they wished, in the proselytising of their new found certainty, to constitute themselves its apologists. How then, from that moment, could they have failed to introduce the necessary methods proper to their feelings as men of culture and self-respect ? For in their case it was a lively source of moral suffering, a real *cross*, to feel the overwhelming contempt which the learned among the pagans laid heavily on " this miscellaneous collection of ignorant people and credulous women gathered in from the offscourings of the populace," as

---

[1] " Orbis ille doctrinae quam Graeci ἐγκύκλιον παιδέιαν vocant " (Quintilian, *Inst.* Or., I, x, i).
[2] Ap. Orig. C. *Celsum*, III, lv.

one of them said in speaking of the sect,[1] and of the Book wherein they read the divine word.   They accused them of lowering their intelligence, and of sacrificing the exigencies of criticism and of intellectual refinement to an irrational faith.[2]   They formed the passionate desire to oblige these disdainful spirits to hold their peace, by proving to their adversaries the beauty and truth of the Christian doctrine by means of arguments which they could not challenge *a priori*, and by becoming their equals through the perfecting of their literary art and by their concern for correct language.[3]

It was the desire to raise themselves from the intellectual point of view which probably gave check to the rather fanatical tendency of which, however, some vestiges remained here and there even among those most open to reason.   They reflected that St Paul had no fear in quoting profane authors in his Epistles, such as Epimenides, Euripides and Aratus.   Here was ready to hand a precedent worthy of respect.   Tertullian

---

[1] Caecilius, in the *Octavius* of Minucius Felix, viii, 4.   This intellectual embarrassment was all the more grievous to them in that certain amongst their number recalled that they had been hindered in their own conversion by the form of the Biblical Latin.   Cf. St Augustine, *Conf.* III, v, 9 :   " Visa est mihi indigna (scriptura) quam Tullianae dignitati compararem."   See also St Jerome, *Ep.*, xxii, 30.

[2] Caecilius, *ibid.*, v, 4 : Celsus, *ap.* Origen, I, ix ; xxvii ; III, xviii ; III, xliv (" Here are some of their maxims : far from us be any man who possesses any knowledge, any learning, or any light.   But if it is a question of the unwise, of the ignorant and unlettered, let them come to us with confidence. . . .") ; Porphyry, the Neo-Platonist philosopher, comments in these words on the passage in St Matthew, xi, 25 (" I confess to thee, O Father, Lord of heaven and earth, because thou hast hid these things from the wise and prudent, and hast revealed them to little ones.") : " On this count he should have rendered clearer and less enigmatic what he was writing for children and for those still deprived of the light of reason.   If it is from the wise that the mysteries are hidden, and to children of tender years and still at the breast that, contrary to all good sense, they are allowed to be seen, all the more reason then is there to seek after unreason and ignorance with ardour.   The great work of Christ on this earth was to have concealed the rays of knowledge from the wise in order to unveil them to those who were bereft of sense and to sucklings " (*Ap.* Macarius Magnetes, Apocr., IV, ix).

The Emperor Julian used to say to the Christians : " *Believe in Him only* is the sum-total of your wisdom.   Your portion is ignorance and boorishness " (quoted by Gregory of Nazianzen, Or. c. *Julianum*, IV, cii (P.G., xxxv, 637)).   See also Lucian, *Peregrinus*, XIII.   The epithet *stutti* was commonly awarded to them (Lactant., *Inst. div.*, V, I ; Ps.—Augustine, *Quaest. in Vet. et Nov. Test.*, cxiv) ; Augustine, *Enarr*, in Ps., XXXIV, viii (P.L., xxxvi, 338) : " Ubicumque invenerunt christianum, solent insultare, exagitare, irridere, vocare insulsum, hebetem, nullius cordis, nullius peritiae."

[3] *Octavius*, xxxix ;   Origen, fragm. quoted in the *Philocalia*, V ;   Lactant. Inst. div., V, i–ii, and also I, i, 10 ;   II, xix, i ;   III, i, i ;   St Jerome, Preface to the *De Vir, illustr.*   The apocryphal collection of letters exchanged between Seneca and St Paul had been forged in order to combat by indirect means in the minds of the lettered pagans their repugnance to the form of the *Epistles ;* the forger represents the admiration of Seneca for the basic matter of these *Epistles*, in order to entice the scrupulous to pierce beneath the outer covering which displeased them.

himself, although by temperament inexorable, recognised that to forbid Christians to become acquainted with profane learning was to reduce them to an intellectual and practical helplessness well nigh complete.[1]   There were some who went so far as to admit that very nearly all of the truth was scattered throughout the pagan philosophical systems, but that no thoughtful mind had embraced it in its integrity, because none of them knew of the master idea which dominates life and which gives it its sense and end.   It was only necessary then to reconstitute again by the light of revelation these scattered morsels of truth and to bring them back to unity.[2] Clement of Alexandria notes that a knowledge of historical methods, of geometry, of astronomy, and above all of dialectics is capable of rendering great service in the interpretation of the truths of the faith and in the defence of these truths against those who misunderstood them.[3] St Gregory of Nazianzen considered that whoever developed in himself either piety or learning, and the one to the exclusion of the other, resembled a one-eyed man, but that the combination is truly complete when a man disposes of both these forces.[4]

We here have declarations which possess their value.   We must not exaggerate their importance, nor believe that this apparent liberalism was not frequently contradicted, even amongst those who lent themselves to it, by observations inspired by a totally different spirit.   I have already underlined these fluctuations and have given their origin.   We have no right to impose on facts and on written texts a uniform tendency which is by no means reflected therein, and which might be only an opinion or an assumption of our own mind. It is best to accept them as the evidence history offers, with their incoherencies and their contributions.

---

[1] " . . . cum instrumentum sit ad omnem vitam litteratura " (de Idolol., x; they were objecting to this, but he welcomes this objection); cf. de Cor., viii (Œhler, I, 436): " (Litteras) necessarias confitebor et commerciis rerum et nostris erga Deum studiis."

[2] This is the theory of Lactantius who in this respect is in line with Justin, Athenagoras, Clement of Alexandria and Minucius Felix.

[3] Detailed references in Wagner, Zeitsch. f. wiss. Theol., xlv (1902), p. 245, etc.

[4] Panegyric of Basil, xii (P.G., xxxvi, 509 C).

VIII

TOWARDS the end of the IVth century, after all, a *via media* between these confused disputations emerged, and, thanks to the illustrious names of those who were in favour of it, it acquired for later ages not indeed the force of a law, but a real power of influence and suggestion.

There is a celebrated tract, erroneously classed amongst the sermons of St Basil,[1] wherein the Bishop of Caesarea explains to some young people, his nephews, " the right way of drawing profit from the profane authors " ; this is really the title of the treatise which has often been reprinted since the Renaissance, and which has always been dear to lovers of the literature of antiquity. Truth to tell, we do not see the subject developed with the fulness and precision which we might have hoped from it. Basil brings to his discussion less of method than of agreeable *bonhomie* and abounding humanism. Nevertheless, some important principles disengage themselves. Basil considers that all was not tainted from the moral point of view in even this profane literature so much decried at the time ; that the poets, orators and historians knew how to give praise to what is good and that they provide an abundance of precepts and examples capable of bringing an ennobling influence into the soul of a young man. Only he insists on a proper selection in order that the suspect portions may be eliminated. Under reserve of this preliminary expurgation, Basil is of opinion that there is great advantage in young people having dealings with profane letters ; they will supply them with the beginnings of a formation of character which they will later on complete by the study of the Holy Books ; they will accustom their eyes, when still young, the better to support the dazzling splendour of the teachings of Scripture. They are, in short, for the young Christian of the IVth century, what had been in former days the learning of the Egyptians to Moses, and to Daniel, that of the Chaldeans. Their value consists in being a preparation and setting out on a still higher task which is, in its special bearing, the understanding of the Old and New Testament.

[1] P.G., xxxi, 563–590.

The point of view of St Basil is thus a special one and hardly escapes the reproach of narrowness. But when one calls to mind with what distrustful susceptibilities on such a subject he had to deal one feels more inclined to render homage to the generosity of his intentions.

Some years later, towards 400, St Jerome in his turn had occasion to define his ideas on the same problem. One of his correspondents in Rome had expressed to him his astonishment at seeing him intermingling his works with quotations borrowed from profane authors.[1] Jerome replied to him, and his justification amounts to no less than a vindication of his absolute right to make use of the Greco-Latin literature in the interests and honour of the faith. He reminds him that a long tradition going back beyond St Paul right to Moses himself, authorises this kind of quotation ; that polemical requirements obliged the defenders of Christianity to have recourse to them, and that anyone amongst them would have missed his mark had he felt bound to abstain from them. He sums up his own view in a comparison : just as in the Book of Deuteronomy (xxi, 12) God ordains that before marriage with a captive her head and eyebrows must be shaved and her nails cut in order to render her worthy of the bed of her husband, so likewise the Christian who has been seduced by the beauty of the *sapientia saecularis* must make a beginning by cleansing it of all that it holds of death, idolatry, voluptuousness, error, and passion, and, when thus purified and suitably prepared, it will become worthy for the service of God.

If we are perplexed to know how St Jerome reconciled in his mind this doctrine with the somewhat formal obligations whereof his dream of Cicero has furnished the testimony, St Jerome himself removes this difficulty when he retorts that after all a dream is only a dream and engages us to nothing, in answer to a similar charge made by his old friend, Rufinus who had become the most perfidious of his adversaries.[2] However this may be, let us bear in mind the compromise which he defends.

The opinion arrived at by St Augustine in his *De Doctrina Christiana*,[3] begun in 397 and finished only in 427, is somewhat analogous.

[1] See above p. 18, n. 2.
[2] *Apol. c. Rufinum*, I, xxx (P.L., xxiii, 441).
[3] P.L., xxxiv, 15–121.

St Augustine had a perfect knowledge of profane Latin literature. He had taught it at Thagaste, his native city, afterwards at Carthage, in Rome and at Milan. He could never forget—his *Confessions* bear witness to it—that to the *Hortensius* of Cicero, a noble and eloquent exhortation to the study of philosophy, he owed his first intellectual stirrings and that *there* was kindled his passion for wisdom and truth.[1] On the other hand, the further he advanced in life the more rigorous, the more exclusive, became his Christianity : to such a degree that in his *Retractations*, written when he had reached his seventy-second year, he felt it an obligation on him to disavow—among other imperfections—all that might savour in his former writings, whether in the matter of form or expression, of any complaisance he may have felt for the *liberales disciplinae*.[2]

This twofold trend, that of the man of letters and of the Christian rigorist, betrays itself in his *De Doctrina Christiana*, but the second preponderates, as might be expected, in a tract which is nothing but a treatise on sacred rhetoric, or a manual for the interpretation of the Scriptures for the use of clerics. According to St Augustine, in profane learning there are elements so evidently sullied by superstition that no upright man should think of making experiments in it : astrology, for example. There are others, such as history, natural history, astronomy, dialectics, rhetoric, etc. . . . which, provided that they guarded against the depravities and abuses to which they give rise, are worthy of study and should render the greatest service in connection with exegesis and oral commentary on the Scriptures. Augustine, like Jerome, breaks into an allegorical simile wherein he sums up his views. In imitation of the Jewish people in their flight from Egypt, Christianity must carry away the gold and silver vessels of her enemies and employ them for her own uses.[3]

Under cover of such authorities and of such reasonings the old learning was enabled to be preserved. We experience some surprise in realising that its defenders had never conceived for it any more convincing apology than to represent it as a kind of preliminary preparation to the profound study of the Bible.

[1] *Conf.*, III, iv.
[2] See the special points noted by Harnack, *Sitz.-Ber.* of the Berlin Acad., 1905, ii, p. 1106.
[3] *De Doctr.* chr., II, xl (P.L., xxxiv, 63).

Such is however the fact. Every age has its special reasons for loving the past, for attaching itself to it and for giving to it some breath of life, without which it would be nothing but dust and ashes. It is well then to commend the courage and good sense of those who, resisting the pressure of the zealots of pious ignorance, finally maintained the duty, or at least the lawfulness, of learning the art of thinking and writing in that school wherein this art had been pre-eminently brought to perfection.

IX

Now come the invasions of the barbarians—those great disasters of the Vth century. When Latin civilisation came to be broken down on all sides, the public schools to be closed, the whole framework of her intellectual life to be swept away, the Church of the West, in the complete overthrow of all regular institutions, was to appear as the one sole power able to preserve the old order now on its path to destruction. Will she make it binding on the conscience to safeguard the works of antiquity ? Will she exercise a *rôle* of official guardianship and prudent protection over this treasure already half fallen into ruin ? In order to sustain this thesis, we should have to resort to some special pleading in regard to the texts, or to exercise an arbitrary choice in their selection. In reality, according to time and place, they reveal such marked differences of attitude in regard to profane learning, that the idea of any systematic plan in their preservation must be scouted.

But what is not open to doubt is, that in the bosom of the Church, various initiatives were manifested which saved from disaster a large portion of what remained at that time to be preserved. In this connection, a decisive impulse was given by Cassiodorus. A former Consul, sometime *magister officiorum* at the court of King Theodoric, the Goth, Cassiodorus, renouncing the world, founded about the year 540, his convent of Vivarium not far from Squillace on the South-east coast of Italy, and resolved to establish there some means to the intellectual life which, according to his intention, might provide some stimulus to the religious calling. He explained to his monks the usefulness of the " liberal arts " for the *lectio*

divina, and how secular literature, vain indeed if they were to
seek their proper end in itself, might, on the other hand, receive
its full reward in the case of those who regarded it not as an
end, but as a means.[1] It must not then be desired for its own
sake, but only as a path whereby to approach to true wisdom.
There is always the same traditional idea, whose progressive
formation I have noted with a growing tendency to increasing
harshness. I ought rather to say the traditional illusion ; for
the method of conceiving of a study which, based on works
of the intellect, should neglect the real foundation in order
to attach itself only to the form, would be to reject the
thoughts conveyed and to pretend to retain only the positive
facts acquired and the mechanism of their expression. To
realise this prudent, but rather chimerical distinction, would
have necessitated the clerics under Cassiodorus to have killed
in themselves all imagination, all curiosity, all secret pleasure
in regard to the genius of Roman civilisation, whose *chefs-
d'œuvres* their abbot was placing at their disposal. Cassiodorus had got together in reality a fairly considerable library
at his monastery of Vivarium.[2] Certain recent researches might
lead us to think that this library was collected at a later date,
at least partially, at the famous monastery of Bobbio, founded
in 612 by St Colomban.[3] I think we may conclude that
Cassiodorus, in spite of his precautionary restrictions, rendered
eminent services to the old learning far superior to those to
which some ill-informed minds give the honour in the Rule of
his contemporary, St Benedict.[4]

There followed the Irish and British monks who gathered
together and maintained the light of learning. At what
period did the Church in Ireland and Great Britain receive
the first seeds of classic culture ? The question is disputed.
What is sure is that in the scattered regions of *Romania*, such
as Britain, or in those which had never formed a part of it,
such as Ireland (the Greco-Roman paganism, representing as
it did nothing concrete, and consequently nothing very
formidable), the study of classic literature was accepted as part
of their instruction with rather more sereneness than else-

---

[1] *Inst. div.*, I, *Praef.* (P.L., lxx, 1108) ; I, xxvii–xxviii (P.L., lxx, 1140).
[2] *Inst. div.*, I, viii.
[3] Cf. Paul Lejay, in the B.A.L.A.C., 1913, pp. 265–269.
[4] The *Regula* is in Migne, P.L., lxvi, 215–932. The best edition is that of G.
Butler, Fr. i. B. 1912, a French translation from Dom Guéranger, 1868.

where.[1] In the monasteries scattered in swarms throughout the West by the monk Colomban, or by his disciples,—Bobbio, in the province of Pavia, Luxeuil, near Belfort in 590, St Gall in 614—more than one *chef-d'œuvre* of antiquity found a protecting resting place which saved it from disappearing. And when the Anglo-Saxons had felt the influence of the Irish, other asylums, such as Fulda in Prussia, Gorze near Metz, etc., opened also their portals to the relics of the past.

In this way, while these centuries of the sword and of barbarity were unfolding their course, the handing down of the old learning was effected in the West up to the time of the bursting into flower of the Carlovingian period.[2] During the forty-five years of his reign, Charlemagne in company with Alcuin, gave strong support to the culture of the classics. The greater part of the manuscripts which we now possess date from the IXth and Xth centuries, or trace their descent to the originals transcribed during this period.[3]

X

I WILL not further extend this general view of the relationship that existed between the old learning and Christianity. Whatever precaution one should take before hazarding any general statements concerning so vast a domain, I feel that there is one factor that must be insisted upon at this stage. Received with distrust and even with a certain amount of aversion by the Christian, this culture was only in the last resort safeguarded

---

[1] See on this point M. Roger's fine work, *L'enseignement des lettres classiques d'Ausone à Alcuin*, Paris, Picard, 1905.

[2] As regards the East, the question is more obscure. According to one tradition, the Greek clergy are stated to have burnt a large quantity of works in verse, of a more or less erotic character, more particularly those of Menander, Diphilis, Philemon, Sappho, Mimnermus, etc. Krumbacher (*Byzant. Literaturgesch.*, p. 505) agrees with Bernhardy in thinking this fact very unlikely and not proven. He states that at Constantinople in the IXth century, Greek profane literature was hardly any more abundant than it is now, save in the matter of the later historians and in works of the specialists. He attributes the disappearance of a large portion of this literature to the intellectual decadence which marked the Byzantine Empire during the period enclosed between the years 650 and 850. The fires lighted on the occasion of the taking of Constantinople by the Crusaders in 1204 caused fresh disasters. Then the *débâcle* of the Empire in the XVth century brought to the West learned Byzantines whose manuscripts played a certain *rôle* (the value of which has been somewhat over-estimated) in the expansion of the Italian Renaissance. See Ph. Monnier, *Le Quattrocento*, Paris, 1901, vol. II, p. 21.

[3] Cf. Louis Havet, *Manuel de critique verbale*, Paris, 1911, p. 3 et s.

as the servant of theology, and as an auxiliary to the interpretation of the Bible.

Here we see the somewhat humiliating *rôle* to which it must have been reduced, if we had only the declarations which the best accredited spokesmen of Christianity have uttered in this connection to go upon. " *Non discere debemus ista, sed didicisse.*" This saying of Seneca might serve as the leading characteristic of the divers Christian tracts wherein the problem of the right to use the Greco-Roman patrimony was theoretically considered. Mere exercises for giving suppleness to the mind, practised just so long as was necessary for the resulting benefit to be acquired—herein, they maintained, consisted the sole office which all the labour of mankind anterior to the new faith had any right to serve.

That was the thesis, that the official principle ; that also, we may suspect, was the expedient of people driven this way and that between the urgent insistence of their own good sense and that of the iconoclasts of the old world of thought and of art.

But, taking the facts as they are, this art, this thought penetrated Christianity much more profoundly and intimately than one would have any reason to doubt if we took as current coin the opportunist professions of a Basil, a Jerome, or a Cassiodorus. I here am broaching a question the magnitude of which should at once deter me. We must however take note of certain features which will make us understand its bearing.

When in the second half of the IVth century, the great Bishop of Milan, St Ambrose, the counsellor of the Emperors Gratian, Valentinian, and Theodosius, undertook to furnish a synthesis of Christian morality worthy to take its place in opposition to the great pagan syntheses, did he endeavour to base it on the Gospel alone ? No ; but it was from the *De Officiis* of Cicero that he borrowed the general framework and even the title of his treatise. He likewise took a whole host of ideas from the Stoic morality of which Cicero had been the eloquent interpreter, such as the distinction between reason and the passions, the consideration of the " sovereign good," the classification of the virtues (wisdom, justice, courage, temperance), the division of duties into perfect duties and duties less binding, the value to be given to the judgment of the conscience, etc.   It is true that he fathoms these ideas in a far different spirit, that he justifies them by reasons which Cicero could not have thought of, and that he gives them finally a sense, a bearing and effectiveness entirely new.   However, with Ambrose, while the Christian morality affirms its originality, at the same time it resolutely assimilates all that is excellent which pagan morality could offer.

The resulting action was analogous in all domains— theological speculation, scriptural exegesis, Christian art, the liturgy, the different classes of literature and forms of style : The influence of profane ideas and customs made itself felt throughout.   This phenomenon of infiltration or co-pene- tration is one of those questions in which for several years religious critical ingenuity has played a special part.   It has sometimes happened that it has lost its way amid comparisons which are open to doubt.   Ascertained facts show that nowhere has there been any *hiatus*, breach or complete rupture, but throughout a correspondence and continuity.   In spite of the anathemas more than once pronounced against it, the genius of the ancient civilisation survived in the civilisation born of the Christian idea and largely contributed to form it. Thus through force of circumstances, the two great spiritual powers, which seemed to be wholly antagonistic, came together.   Christianity had sufficient vitality to escape any deformations in essentials by the fact of this accession of ideas. And it is due to this fusion that even men who are strangers to the Christian faith, are nevertheless willing to accept the fundamental notions of morality which she proposes, since therein is also included the legacy of the past.   " If we are Christians," M. Camille Jullian once declared, " if we must hold to this designation as to a formula of salvation, it is because it represents, together with all the visions which the Man of Galilee gave to the consciousness of mankind, all the lessons which the philosophers of antiquity had left there ; it is because, far from being in opposition to the past, Christianity has completed and crowned it."[1]

[1] *Revue historique,* vol. LX (1896), p. 342.

XI

NEARLY all the texts which will form the subject of our study will be found in the *Patrologie Latine* by Abbé Migne (Paris, 1844–1855, 221 vol., des Origines à 1216). Among these texts a fairly large number have been reproduced already in the *Corpus Scriptorum ecclesiasticorum latinorum,* now in course of publication. Some information on these two collections will not be)ut of place.

" Among the French clergy of the XIXth century," wrote Dom Cabrol,[1] "there were few of a more original type than that of the young priest arriving in Paris without money or special recommendation, of very moderate education, but active, enterprising, very well versed in wordly matters, fruitful in resources, and by no means averse to the desirability of self-advertisement, but placing it at the service of good causes : his imagination always busily at work over gigantic undertakings, possessing in a high degree the art of discovering hidden talent, and of cleverly extracting therefrom some portion, and of making it auxiliary to his own end ; endowed with a patience which no opposition could fatigue and with a strength of will which made all bend before it, creating work after work with no other capital than his confidence in himself and his energy, and realising the final achievement of one of the most distinguished undertakings of our century."

The Greek and Latin *Patrologies* were only one amongst many others published by Migne ; but it is in this that he showed the extent of his talent as an organiser.[2]

To bring to life again on a still vaster plan the great collections of ecclesiastical writers inherited from the XVIth, XVIIth and XVIIIth centuries ; to incorporate therein the recent discoveries ; to open to all access to the monuments of Catholic thought—this was the aim he pursued.

We may ask ourselves what might have been the fate of this inordinate task if Migne had allowed himself to be guided only by his own lights. He had the happy thought to write to Dom Guéranger, who gave him the name of Dom J. B. Pitra, at

---

[1] *Histoire de Cardinal Pitra*, Paris, 1893, p. 108.
[2] For further details, cf. P. de Labriolle, in B.A.L.A.C., vol. III (1910), p. 203 et s.

GARDNER HARVEY LIBRARY
Miami University-Middletown
Middletown, Ohio

that time Prior in Paris. P.tra who, though still very young (at this time he was 30 years old), was already profoundly versed in patristic literature, understood that there could be no question of getting together a new edition for each author after collating the manuscripts, but that they must choose among already existing editions those which were most worthy to form a part of the projected library. He suggested to Migne that they should have recourse to Benedictine works to supply the greater part of their material.

" The Benedictines had a less rigorous method than that demanded to-day," M. Paul Lejay states ; [1] " they were guided by their predilections and their acquaintance with the authors, and by the antiquity of the manuscripts. That was the method in vogue at that time, and it gave some good results. It is clear that no very minute comparisons in detail could be founded on texts established in this manner. But the principal fault does not consist in the nature of the text ; it is rather in the lack of certainty and in the insufficiency of the information on the contents of the manuscripts. The modern expert demands less a text than the materials wherewith to compile one. . . . Nevertheless," M. Lejay adds, " no one can reproach Migne with not having made a better attempt than the Benedictines. He was no philologist, and we must not forget that in France in 1844, and elsewhere, it would have been hard to discover men who were familiar with the method which was only to bear fruit some years later : if Lachmann had already published the greater part of his editions, his *Lucretius* nevertheless did not appear before 1850 ; Ritschl began the publication of his *Plautus* in 1848. We must not ask more of Migne than he could, or desired to, accomplish."

The *Patrologie Latine* began to appear in 1844. The printing press at Petit-Montrouge issued about 20 volumes yearly, an enormous output and superior to all expectations : in 1855, the 217 promised volumes were ready for the subscribers. From 1862 to 1864, Migne published four further volumes of *Indices*. The 162 volumes of the *Patrologie Grecque* were printed during the period between 1857 and 1866 at the rate of 18 volumes yearly. We can get some idea of the immensity of the undertaking, if we realise that the Latin

[1] R.H.L.R., I (1896), p. 98.

series represented 297,567 pages, and the Greek 235,724 pages, or a total of 533,291 pages, which were all stereotyped, that is reproduced on tin plates which permitted of successive re-impressions with no fresh corrections.

From the first moment, criticism was busy on this work and, beginning, as was natural, by taking exception to the most patent defects, went on to take note of the numerous typographical mistakes which marred certain volumes of the *Patrologie Latine*. Next, judges possessing the requisite authority, pointed out the confusion, the blunders and the unsatisfactory selection shown in some of the editions ; but at the same time, they rendered homage to the prodigious skill of the editor and signalised the immense debt which ecclesiastical studies henceforward owed to him.

In fact, Migne had grudged neither his time, his labour, nor his money. He had secured for his work the scientific aid of those most qualified to give it. He had also conceived the very happy idea of incorporating in his compilation the dissertations of the commentators of old. From a scientific point of view, was it not a real advantage to group together, as he did, the scattered works of the Ballerini, Basnage, Baronius, Dodwell, Constant, Garnier, Mabillon, Muratori, Ruinart, etc. ? If the *Patrologie* still remains indispensable to-day, even in the case of the volumes which have their *replica* in the *Corpus Scriptorum ecclesiasticorum latinorum*, it is due to the notes and learned studies which are helpfully embodied therein.

The Imperial Academy of Sciences of Vienna has been responsible for the appearance of the *Corpus*, volume after volume since 1866. The scheme of the collection embraces the accurate establishment of the text after an examination as complete as possible on the authenticity of the manuscript ; no exegetical notes (on principle), except to indicate the sources of the author ; and detailed *Indices*. Its scope was to include all the Latin ecclesiastical writers up to the VIIth century inclusively. Broadly speaking, these editions are of important value. Some portions have succeeded less well.[1] From the bibliographical point of view, we have to regret the incon-

---

[1] e.g. Hartel's *St Cyprian ;* certain portions of St Augustine's writings edited by Knoll and Zycha (cf. T.L.Z., 1892, p. 130 et s. ; 412 et s. ; 1895, p. 364 et s. ; 1898, p. 136 et s. ; R.C., 1894, 2, 277 ; 1896, 2, 104 ; 1898, 1, 227).

venient and illogical system of numbering the volumes in the collection.

Some Christian authors have also been published, in part or in their entirety, in other collections of which a list will be found further on. But the two which we have been discussing are of fundamental weight.

BOOK I
THE SOURCES OF ORIGIN

CHAPTER I

THE FIRST LATIN VERSIONS OF THE BIBLE

BIBLIOGRAPHY

FOR a reconstruction of the Latin versions of the Bible anterior to the Vulgate of St Jerome, we have the following sources at our disposition:— 1. An important store of manuscripts scattered among the European libraries; 2. Quotations from ecclesiastical writers; 3. A few rather rare quotations in the inscriptions on tombs; 4. Portions of the Vulgate wherein St Jerome has been contented to reproduce pre-existing texts (see lib. III, chap. v). Sabatier, the Benedictine, has collected the manuscripts known in his time in an important work called *Bibliorum sacrorum latinae versiones antiquae*, etc. . . . Paris, 1749-1751. Since Sabatier, many discoveries have been made in the libraries: see Schanz, III, 486; art. *Latin Versions* in the *Dict. of the Bible*; art *Bibelübersetzungen*, in R.E., vol. III, 28; art. *Itala* in the Index of *Thesaurus linguae lat.* Whence arose the idea of a "new Sabatier". This idea, adumbrated by Wölfflin, A.L.L., VIII (1893), p. 311, and defined by C. Weyman, *Hist. pol. Blätter* 144 (1909), pp. 897-905, was in process of being realised before the war by Joseph Denk (*der neue Sabatier*, L. 1914) who announced in 1915 three ample volumes of 1000 pages each, then a volume of *Prolegomena* and *Indices* (at a subscription of 400 marks). Denk's plan has had objections made to it elsewhere: cf. Jülicher, T.L.Z. 1917, n. 2.

For the language of these versions, see H. Rönsch, *Itala und Vulgata*, Marburg and Leipsic, 2 edit. 1875; ID. *Collectanea philol.*, Bremen, 1891; Goelzer, *Etude lexicog. et gramm. de la latinité de saint Jérôme*, thèse, Paris, 1884; G. Koffmane, *Gesch. des Kirchenlateins*, Breslau, I, 1879; II, 1881 (unfinished and otherwise mediocre); Burkitt, *The old Latin and the Itala*, in T.S., iv, 3 (1896): cf. C. Weyman, in B. ph. W., 1897, pp. 11-16, Heer; *die Versio Latina des Barnabasbriefes und ihr Verh. zur altlat. Bibel*, Frib. i. B., 1908; L. Wohleb, *die latein. Uebers. der Didache*, Paderborn, 1913 (in the *St. zur Gesch. u. Kultur des Alt.* hsg. von. Drerup, Grimme and Kirsch. VII, 1); numerous indications scattered throughout the *Archiv. f. lat. Lexic.*, of Wölfflin (2 tables, one for volumes I-X (1898), the other for volumes XI-XV (1909)).

SUMMARY

I. The tardy coming into bearing of Latin Christian Literature. Greek the dialect of the Mediterranean.—II. The first Latin translations of the Bible. Their literary and grammatical character. Their influence on the Latin tongue.

I

LATIN Christian Literature offers no landmark of any importance before the end of the second century. At that time,

Greek Christian literature had already produced a number of conspicuous works, in particular all that brilliant crop of apologies destined to plead the cause of Christianity before the authorities of the State and public opinion itself.

Such a tardy appearance is at first a matter of astonishment. Very simple reasons can explain this. Greece had made such a thorough conquest of the Roman world that there was hardly any town of importance in the West in which the Greek tongue was not in everyday use. During the period of the Emperors, the West was linked with the East by extensive commercial intercourse. From Greece, from the Euxine Sea, from Syria, and from Egypt, merchandise of every kind, directed in the first case to Brindisi, to Ostia or Pozzuoli, was then sent by road to Rome, the centre of the world's traffic, who then re-distributed a large part over Gaul, Spain and Africa. The *pax Romana* rendered easy these transactions : " Sed et mundus pacem habet per eos (sc. Romanos) "—wrote St Irenaeus about 180—" et nos sine timore in viis ambulamus et navigamus quocumque voluerimus." At the same time, the Levantine merchants, together with their importations brought with them their ideas, their beliefs, their religions— and their tongue. In his discourse *Pro Archia* (X, 23) Cicero had said before : " *Graeca leguntur in omnibus fere gentibus ; latina suis finibus, exiguis sane, continentur.*" In an increasing degree since his time Greek had become, during the first centuries of the Empire, a Mediterranean dialect.

Even in Rome, popular epigrams, satirical catchwords and puns at the expense of the Emperors, were current in Greek, and Suetonius has preserved for us a fairly rich collection.[1] These sayings were evidently understood by a very large public. One could readily find equally significant facts in Northern Africa. It would seem exaggerated to speak of a kind of elimination with which the Latin tongue was being threatened, as Mommsen suggests, if Rome had not made it the official language.[2] But in the towns along the coast, Adrumyttium, Carthage, Oea, Leptis Major, etc., Greek was very much in use as is evidenced by the inscriptions on the tombs.[3]

---

[1] They will be found collected in A. Macé's *Essai sur Suétone*, Paris, 1900, p. 274 et s.

[2] *Rom. Gesch.*, V, 643 : French translation, XI, 284.

[3] Toutain, *Les Cités rom. de la Tunisie*, Paris, 1896, p. 200 ; Audollent, *Carthage romaine*, Paris, 1904, p. 701 ; and especially Thieling, *der Hellenismus in Kleinafrica,*

The men of letters liked to make use of it. The work on the eternity of matter, which the painter, Hermogenes, had written at Carthage and which Tertullian was to refute, appears to have been composed in Greek.[1] Tertullian himself oscillated for some time between the two languages : he had given a first rendering in Greek to his *Virginibus Velandis*, to his *De Spectaculis* and to his *De Baptismo*. Similarly with the *De Ecstasi*, which was never subsequently rendered in Latin.[2] The same conditions are noticeable if we pass on to Gaul. The use of Greek had been prevalent for a long time in the South.[3] Varro had already noted the fact.[4] The infusion of Greek elements was continually replenishing this linguistic foundation. " The traces left by the Phocaeans," as E. Renan remarks,[5] " had not been entirely effaced. People from Asia and from Syria, much given to emigrating towards the West, were in the habit of ascending the Rhône and the Saône, carrying with them a portable bazaar of varied merchandise, or rather of remaining on the banks of these large rivers in places which offered to them some hope of subsistence."

Furthermore, the fashion in literature from which no one can completely escape, exercised its influence. Claudius,[6] Nero, and then Hadrian,[7] had a taste, a passion and a mania for Hellenism, and had encouraged its general use. Favorinus the Gaul, who was born at Arles between the years 70 and 80 of our era, gave conferences in Rome in Greek just as a little later did Apuleius at Carthage,[8] and his numerous works in Greek won for him the highest honours. From Suetonius we learn

Leipsic and Berlin, 1911, p. 30 et s. (inscriptions) ; p. 43 et s. (*tabulae defixionis*) ; p. 48 et s. (*amulets*). Out of 90 African *tabulae defixionis* of the second and third centuries after Christ, Thieling enumerates (following the collection made by Audollent) a total of 20 Greek, 29 Greco-Latin, and 41 Latin, with here and there some Greek letters.

[1] Zahn, Gesch. d. neut. Kanons, I, i, 49.

[2] Note also the number of Greek expressions in the *Passion of Perpetua and Felicitas*, xii : Audivimus vocem unitam dicentem : Agios, agios, agios. § x : in oromate ; § iv : machera ; § v–vi : catasta ; § vii : diastema ; § viii : fiala ; § x : afa ; § xv : cataracterius, etc.

[3] Ch. Lecrivain, *Les Grecs dans le Sud de la Gaule, Bull. de la Soc. archéol. du Midi de la France,* 1907, pp. 30–34.

[4] " Quod et Graece loquantur et Latine et Gallice," quoted by St Jerome, *Comm. in Ep. ad Gal.,* ii, pref.

[5] *L'Eglise Chrétienne,* p. 468.

[6] Suetonius, *Claudius,* xlii.

[7] Cf. Renan, *Origines de Chr.,* vi, 34 et s. We possess some Greek poetry by Hadrian : *Anth. Pal.,* vi, 332 ; vii, 674 ; ix, 17 ; ix, 137 ; ix, 387 ; Kaibel, *Epigr. gr.* n. 811 ; 888 ; 1089.

[8] *Florides,* IV, xviii. Some indications of the use of Greek in Africa among cultivated circles, *Apologia,* X ; LXXXVII ; XCVIII.

C

the titles of a dozen Greek *opuscula* on divers historical subjects, on archæology and literature. We see Elienus who was
born at Preneste quite close to Rome and had never left
Italy, rendering his books in Greek; in speaking the Attic
tongue he even passed as a native-born Athenian.[1]   The
Stoic philosopher, Cornutus, a native of Leptis in Africa, who,
even in Rome numbered amongst his pupils Persius and
Lucanius, composed his writings on grammar in Latin, but
made use of Greek exclusively for his philosophic essays.
And many others could be quoted. It was only during the
second half of the IIIrd century that the set-back from Greek
became noticeable in the West. This set-back was accentuated in the IVth century and it is at this latter date that men
like Rufinus and St Jerome were to undertake the useful
mission of translating the most notable productions of Greek
Christian thought for the use of the Western world.

But Christian propaganda, having found its *points d'appui*
and obtained its first recruits principally among the Jewish or
pagan element speaking the Greek tongue, had quite naturally
made use of Greek as its vehicle. Even in Rome, at the heart
of the Empire, Greek had for long been familiar to the communities of Christians.[2] It was in this language that the
author of the Epistle to the Romans exhorted them. Rossi
is of opinion that Divine Service was celebrated in Greek up
to the end of the IIIrd century. The principal Christian
opuscula written in Rome during the IInd century, such as the
letter sent by St Clement to the Church in Corinth in the name
of the Roman community, the *Pastor* of Hermas, and the
Dialogue of Caius with Proclus, the Montanist, were written in
Greek. St Justin, who, though born in the East, had made
several sojourns in Rome, where he had founded a school
and was destined later to undergo his martyrdom, does not
appear to have experienced any temptation to use any other
dialect than Greek for his *Apologia*. When, in about the
year 177, " the servants of Christ dwelling in Vienne and
Lyons " wrote " to their brethren of Asia and Phrygia having
the same faith and the same hope of redemption "—(it is in
these terms that they began their famous letter containing the

[1] Philostratus, *Vita Sophist.*, II, xxxi, i (p. 123, 3 Kayser). We may compare
the testimony of Aurelius Victor, *Epist.* x, on Septimus Severus (born at Leptis).
[2] The principal facts are gathered together by Caspari, *Quellen zur Gesch. des
Taufsymbols*, Christiania, 1875, vol. III, p. 267–466.

detailed account of the martyrdom and heroic sufferings of Sanctus, Blandinus and their companions), the writer (possibly St Irenæus who was to be elected Bishop in place of St Pothinus who died beneath the blows received when he was arrested) made use of the Greek tongue in inditing his message of victory and of peace.[1] At the beginning of the IIIrd century, St Hippolytus, a Roman priest, wrote his mediocre works in the same language. We do not come to any inscriptions which were not worded in Greek until those engraved on the tombs of Popes Fabianus († 250), Lucius († 254), and Eutychianus († 283).[2]

These facts are significant; they make us understand why Christian literature in the Latin tongue did not take its birth until a century and a half after the preaching of Christ.

II

As with Latin profane literature, Latin Christian literature had its beginning in translations.

" The manner in which the Hebrew Bible penetrated the Western world through the vehicle of the Latin tongue is an event which, with good reason, invites the curiosity of the learned and the reflection of the philosopher," says Gaston Paris.[3] " It is not through the agency of the Jews that it was introduced there : the translation of the Hebrew books into Greek at Alexandria, a truly memorable act, which had been one of the most remarkable consequences of the Hellenisation of the East, had no counterpart in Latin. The Jews, so numerous in Rome from the time of Augustus, were Hellenised Jews : if they read the law and the prophets, it was in Greek, and the converts which they made belonged to this Greek or semi-Greek world, which was as numerous perhaps in Rome as the purely Latin population. It was in a world of this kind that Christianity issuing from the Hellenistic synagogues, also made its first conquests. . . . Soon, however, it recruited in Rome and in the provinces proselytes who did not understand Greek or understood it very badly. For their use the New

---

[1] One of the martyrs, Sanctus, is shown nevertheless as replying in Latin to the Governor (Eusebius, H.E., V, i, 20 ; note also *ibid.*, V, i, 44).

[2] De Rossi, *Rom. Sot.*, II (1867), p. 236.

[3] *Mélanges linguist.*, I, 60.

Testament was without doubt the first to be translated, and then, when the doctrine had become established that the Old Testament was the introduction and the symbol of it, the Jewish books followed."

It was to little purpose that Greek was the cosmopolitan and international language *par excellence*, for, according to the just observation of Gaston Paris, there were certain elements in the Christian Churches of the West, who, varying in importance according to time and place, had only a slight acquaintance with Greek, or none at all.   How could they have allowed the written text of the Bible, which played so important a *rôle* in the life of the Christians and which was read privately and in public,[1] to remain a dead letter to a more or less considerable portion of the faithful ?   The same necessity, which was at different times to occasion the appearance of Syriac, Coptic, Armenian, and Arabian, etc., translations of the Bible, in good time made imperative the translation of versions in Latin.[2] The origins of the Latin Bible are in most respects very obscure.   St Augustine himself was not at all sure of the exact date of their first appearance.   " We can count those who have translated the Scriptures from the Hebrew into Greek " : he wrote in his *De Doctrina Christiana* (II, xi) : " in the case of the Latin translators that is quite impossible. In fact, in the earliest days of the faith, the first comer, if there happened to fall into his hands a manuscript, and he thought himself to have some knowledge of the two languages, considered himself at liberty to translate it."   " Qui scripturas ex Hebraea lingua in Graecam verterunt numerari possunt, Latini autem interpretes nullo modo. Ut enim cuique *primis fidei temporibus* in manus venit codex Graecus et aliquantulum facultatis sibi utriusque linguae habere videbatur, ausus est interpretari."   This *primis fidei temporibus*

---

[1] L. Duchesne, *Orig. du culte chrétien*, Paris, 1898, p. 106 ; Harnack, *Ueber den privaten Gebrauch der hl Schriften in der alten Kirche* (*Beitr. z. Einl. in d. Neue Test.*, VIII [1912]).

[2] Sundry *opuscula* outside the Old and the New Testament, but specially dear to the piety of the faithful, were quite early transposed into Latin : for example, the *Didache* (ed. J. Shlecht, F.R. i. B., 1900 and 1901), the first *Letter* of Clement of Rome *to the Corinthians* (Dom Morin, in A.M. II [1394]), the *Pastor* of Hermas (*versio vulgata*, Hilgenfeld, L. 1873 ; the version called *Palatina* is at the end of the IVth century [ed. Gebhardt and Harnack, *Patr. apostol. op.*, fasc. 3, L. 1877]), the *Epistle of Barnabas* (Heer, Fr. i. B., 1908), certain apocryphal writings such as the *Acta Pauli* (T.U. xxii, 2 [1902]), etc. . . . a compact review of what remains of the literature of the early days of Christianity in translation would be welcome. See the list drawn up by Harnack, A.C.L., 883–884.

is rather vague as a chronological indication. Many critics still hesitate to admit, or even expressly deny, that Tertullian had at his disposal at the end of the IInd century one or more Latin versions of the Bible either in part or complete. In reality we find in Tertullian passages which are sufficiently explicit to enable us to have the right to uphold a contrary opinion.[1] These passages show (1) that Tertullian himself habitually translated his quotations from the original Greek ; (2) that he had before his eyes Latin versions ; not that they were indispensable to him but for the satisfaction of his curiosity which was always on the alert.

The first translations must have been made in the course of the IInd century. Under what conditions, in what country, and by whose hands ? These are so many questions which cannot be solved at the present time.[2] The hypothesis of an African origin is that which would most commend itself. However this may be, these Latin versions were to multiply themselves throughout the West up to the time of the great revision by St Jerome, who has preserved them in part in his own translation of the Holy Books. More ancient than the most ancient Greek manuscripts of the Bible which have been preserved to us, they offer great interest to theologians.[3] From the literary point of view likewise their importance is considerable. They have largely contributed to shape the imagination, language, and style of the Christian writers. They have been the starting point of a mighty work in the creation and adaptation of words which has had its repercussion throughout Christian literature. We can even trace its influence much further. " The pre-Hieronymic versions," to again quote G. Paris, " have left their traces down to much later centuries : the Middle Ages without exception quoted with complaisance so-called Messianic prophecies which are found neither in the Hebrew text nor in the Vulgate, and which owe their existence only to misinterpretations of the Septuagint diffused by their old Latin translators ; and even in our days the infant Jesus is pictured between an ox and an ass

[1] I have quoted and discussed them, B.A.L.A.C., IV (1914), pp. 210–213.

[2] It will not be possible to classify and give the genealogy of these versions until after the completion of a series of studies of which Heer (Rom. Quartalsch. XXIII (1909), p. 218) has very happily outlined the salient features.

[3] " Even the most literal version," remarks Burkitt, " is also in a certain sense a commentary. Many of our current theological conceptions have come to us through this Latin channel." The old Latin and the Itala, p. 4.

because of a passage from Habacuc (III, 2) which, when translated by the Septuagint (between two animals), signifies in
reality quite another thing."

And how many words, how many biblical expressions preserved by St Jerome in his translation has our language
accepted, whether through imitation by our own writers or the
intermediary of translations from the Middle Ages ! [1]   The
Latin Bible has been " one of the elements of the alloy out of
which was made the solid metal of our French tongue " [2] and
one of the principal factors of our Western civilisation.

The philological character of these Latin versions was in
strict correspondence with the principles which the faith of
their translators could not fail to impose on them.   The
respect felt by the primitive Church for the Greek of the
Septuagint equalled that which the Greek of the Gospels
inspired in her.   To be valued as authentic in all controversy
connected with morals or doctrine, the texts from Scripture
required that the Greek of the Old and New Testament
should be transposed with the utmost exactitude and literalness.[3]   On the other hand, there could be no question of
delaying over the scruples of the fastidious, or the exclusive
and condescending rules of the purists in their choice of words
and expressions.   The determining reason for these undertakings was to render the sacred texts accessible to those who
could not understand them under their Greek form : it would
have been scarcely reasonable to frighten them away by a too
aristocratic style of Latin (always admitting that the translators had it at their disposal), or by a quantity of fine distinctions which would have escaped their notice.

Here we come upon quite a new conception of the qualities
requisite in a translation.   As a means of comparison, let us
take the example of Cicero.   He was fond of this exercise.
Beginning in his early youth, he translated the *Phenomena* of
Aratos into Latin hexameters ; after that came Xenophon's
Economics, Plato's *Protagoras* and *Timaeus*, without counting

---

[1] First French *Psalters* about 1100 ; Bible of the University of Paris, between
1225 and 1250.

[2] Trénel, *L'Ancien Testament et la langue française du moyen-âge*, Paris, 1904,
p. 58.

[3] *Adv. Marc.*, II, ix, Tertullian points out the mistake of certain translators
who, simply by the maladroit substitution of the word *spiritus* for the word *afflatus*
in Genesis ii, 7, afforded a pretext to heretics for attributing the sins of mankind
to the " Spirit " of God.

the numerous passages from Greek authors (Homer, the Tragedies, etc.) which he translated here and there in order to embellish his own reasonings. In his treatises on philosophy and rhetoric he had to cope with the technical formulae employed by his models. When one studies his method, we realise that, if he sometimes attempts to render the Greek word for word (*infinitio* for ἀπειρία ; *anticipatio* for πρόληψις ; *mulierositas* for φιλογύνεια, etc. . . .), he more often re-duplicates his Latin equivalent (*intelligentia et ratio* for νόησις ; *genitorem et effectorem* for δημιουργόν ; *fluens et tractus* for εἰρομένη [λέξις], etc.), or rather he has recourse to some ample periphrase conveying the equivalent with irreproachable exactness (*qui animo cernuntur et ratione intelliguntur animantes* for τὰ νοητὰ ζῷα ; *quod est ad cultum deorum aptissimum* for τὸ Θεοσεβέστατον ; *genus quod in laudandis aut vituperandis hominibus ponitur* for ἐπιδεικτικόν γένος, etc.).[1] Such redundancies were in conformity with his customary play of style, and perhaps he thereby saw a means of demonstrating his favourite and perhaps rather paradoxical theory on the richness of the Latin *verborum copia*.

These literary prepossessions remained a sealed book to the translators of the Latin versions of the Bible. Their purpose was to make a faithful copy as accurately as possible of the inspired Greek, while remaining intelligible : this is the ideal which they approached more or less closely.[2] From this have resulted consequences of grave bearing from the point of view of the history of the Latin language. Already very receptive of Hellenisms on the part of the profane authors of the Empire,[3] this tongue thus incorporated a quantity of new words formed on the Greek,[4] and her syntax itself underwent

[1] There are numerous examples of these different processes in Causeret, *Etude sur la langue de la rhét, et de la crit. litt. dans Cicéron*, treatise, Paris, 1886, p. 13 et s. ; V. Clavel, *de M. Tullio Cic. Graecorum interprete*, treatise, Paris, 1868, p. 292 ; Atzert, *de Cic. interprete Graecorum*, Diss, Göttingen, 1908, p. 6 et s. ; 19 et s. ; Leo, in *Hermes*, 1914, p. 192.

[2] In this connection, St Augustine points out differences between the Latin versions with which he was acquainted (*De Doctr. christ.*, II, xv). St Jerome remarks that only a very literal translation is admissible where Scripture is concerned, " *ubi et verborum ordo mysterium est* " (Ep. LVII, 5). A similar scruple obtained in the bosom of Judaism : from the point of view of literalness, the versions of Aquila and Symmachus went beyond the Septuagint. See also Gaston Paris, *Mél. ling.*, I, 75.

[3] Cf. Goelzer, *op. cit.*, p. 221 et s. ; *id., Revue intern. de l'Enseignement* 1908, p. 105.

[4] Acedia, agonia, aporiari, apostata, apostolus, baptisma, blasphemia, catholicus, diabolus, diaconus, ecstasis, eremus, episcopus, eleemosyna, homilia, laicus, martyr, monachus, parabolari, scisma, etc.

the same process as the Greek Bible.[1] Certain terms or
Hebraic idiosyncrasies (much more restricted in number than
has been sometimes stated) filtered into the Latin across the
Septuagint and the Gospels.[2] Vulgarisms, such as the
devotees of *elegantia* would have proscribed, crept in likewise.[3]
A quantity of old words authentically Latin were called upon

[1] For example, a case of the genitive absolute, "et cogitantium omnium
(διαλογιζομένων πάντων, Luke III, 15) "; "omnium autem mirantium (πάντων
δὲ θαυμαζόντων, Luke IX, 43) ". (It is quite likely that this turn of phrase was
already current in the popular language, for we come across it in the de Bello
Hisp., xiv, i, and xxiii, 6); the comparative genitive: "major ejus est (μείζων
αὐτοῦ ἐστίν) " (there are some examples in profane Latin which are frequently
met with after Apuleius); *adjuvare* used with the dative ; also *adorare, decet ;
benedicere, nocere* with the accusative ; expressions such as "cum esset in loco
quodam orantem " (. . . ἐν τῷ εἶναι αὐτὸν ἐν τόπῳ τινὶ προσευχόμενον, Luke
xi, i), etc.—We notice also that the faithful imitation of the Greek caused the
translators to multiply the forms of the participle. The abundance of participles
is one of the *traits* of "Church Latin." As Latin was very poorly provided with
forms of this kind, ecclesiastical writers were led to a more or less abusive extension
of the sense of existing forms, giving to the present participle, for instance, the
value of an aorist, The prose of the classics already offered a few rare examples
of this extension.
[2] Cherubim, Rabbi, Hosanna, alleluia, gehenna, Pascha, Sabaoth, etc. . . .
The influence on the Greek of the Bible, previously attributed to the Hebrew,
diminishes in importance in proportion as the knowledge of popular Greek became
more pronounced. And more than one turn of phrase supposed to be of Hebraic
origin attaches to even Latin of good style. The expression *vanitas vanitatum*
usually considered as a Hebraism, is foreign neither to classic Greek nor even to
Latin : Sophocles, *Œd. Col.* 1238, κακὰ κακῶν, *Œd. R.* 465, ἄρρητ' ἀρρήτων ; *Anth.
Pal.*, vii, 45, Ἑλλάδος Ἑλλάς 'Αθῆναι ; cf. Varro, L. I., vii, 27, divum deus ; Plautus,
Trin. 309 : victor victorum ; *Capt.* 825 : rex regum (also Horace, *Ep.* I, i, 107) ;
Petronius, *Trimalch.*, nummos nummorum. According to Pfister, this practice
would seem to have gone back as far as Gorgias and Prodicos (B. ph. W., 1914,
1449). The qualifying genitive (judex iniquitatis, filius caritatis, abominatio
desolationis) unaccompanied by an adjective appeared in profane prose since the
time of Apuleius. For the genitive of apposition (of the type *aevitas temporis,
cupiditates libidinum* [numerous examples in Sittl, *Die lok. Verschied., d. lat. sprache*,
Erl. 1882, p. 92 et s.]), compare such Greek classical expressions as πῆμα κακοῖο,
εὐνῆς λέχος. In his work on the *Mathesis*, Firmicus Maternus wrote when he was
not yet a Christian : *temporis aetas, erroris confusio, artis disciplina, malitiae impro-
bitas.* Cf. Kroll, Rh. M. vol. LII (1897), 584 and Wölfflin, A.L.L., X (1898), 538.—
Against the theory that the ablative of comparison accompanied by a (major ab illo)
was of Semitic origin, the *Thesaurus ling. lat.* is of opinion that this is not true
(I, 39). It quotes examples from Pliny the Elder, A.N., xviii, 126 : "alius usus
praestantior *ab* iis non est " ; xxxv, 198 : "saxum utilius a sulphure." Sittl
(*die lokalen Verschiedenh.*) and Wölfflin (A.L.L., vii [1892], p. 471) thought they
saw in this use an imitation of the Hebrew preposition *min.* Benedixisti bene-
dictionem has also analogies in archaic Latin : *cenam cenare*, Plautus (*Rud.* 507) ;
messem metere (*Epid.* 701) ; *noxam nocere*, Titus Livius (quoting an ancient expression [IX, x, 9]). For the use *morte moriemini*, we may compare *luce lucebit,*
Plautus (*Cure.*, I, iii, 26) ; *curriculo currere* (Most. 349) ; Cicero, *occidione occidere*
(*Phil.*, XIV, xxxvi) ; *morte mori*, Sallust (*Hist.*, III, xxv) : we have already in
Homer, *Odyss.*, xi, 410 : ὣς θάνον οἰκτίστῳ θανάτῳ·
[3] Some critics, such as Ronsch, have grossly exaggerated the importance of
this. Cf. Corssen in Bursian's *Jahresb.*, vol. CI (1899), p. 82. Nevertheless, the
repeated declarations of ecclesiastical writers do not permit us to unduly minimise
it.

to render new meanings [1]—moral ideas which up till then had not been developed, and liturgical ceremonies. Others were coined in a manner sufficiently conformable to the rules governing their Latin derivation. Has not Cicero himself claimed the right to impose new names on new ideas, *imponenda nova novis rebus nomina?* [2] How could the translators have refused new formations and the adaptations of which they felt the necessity? The Roman vocabulary the poverty of which has been deplored by Lucretius ("*propter egestatem linguae . . .*"), and which Seneca himself found to be wanting, [3] enriched itself by superabundant additions whose composite variety completely disconcerted those lettered men who had been formed on the prudent eclecticism of the traditional discipline.

[1] Devotio, aedificatio, transgressio, praevaricatio, remissio, vocatio, conversio, praedicatio, paenitentia, virtutes (miracles), tentator (the devil); tingere (baptize), absolvere (absolve), etc. The development of the Judaisms of certain of these words has lent itself to some interesting studies. Much still remains to be done in this connection.

[2] *De Finibus*, III, i. St Jerome was to learn later how to avail himself of this and similar passages to justify his own verbal creations which be it said were very discreet. *Comm. in Gal.*, I, 12 (P.L., xxvi, 323): " Si itaque hi qui disertos saeculi legere consueverunt, coeperint nobis de novitate et vilitate sermonis illudere, mittamus eos ad Ciceronis libros qui de quaestionibus philosophiae praenotantur, et videant quanta ibi necessitate compulsus sit, tanta verborum portenta proferre quae nunquam latini hominis auris audivit, etc. . . ." " And," adds Jerome, " nevertheless, although I have been translating not from the Greek but from the Hebrew, I have ventured upon fewer novelties in my ample transpositions than did Cicero in works of far lesser dimensions."

[3] *Ep.* LVIII: " . . . quanta verborum novis paupertas, immo egestas sit."

CHAPTER II

THE FIRST CHRISTIAN WRITERS IN THE LATIN TONGUE: TERTULLIAN

BIBLIOGRAPHY

I. TERTULLIAN : The question of the manuscripts of Tertullian demands a careful examination. These manuscripts fall into two families :—

A. The *Agobardinus*, so called from the name of its owner, Agobard, Bishop of Lyons, who died in 840. He had it transcribed, and bequeathed it to the Church of St Etienne at Lyons. This manuscript is to be found in the Bibliothèque Nationale in Paris (*Parisinus*, No. 1622, saec. IX). At the present time it contains no more than thirteen treatises, namely : the *Ad Nationes*, the *de Praescriptione*, the *Scorpiace*, the *de Testimonio Animae*, the *de Corona*, the *de Spectaculis*, the *de Idolotria*, the *de Censu animae* (*de Anima*), the *de Oratione*, the *de Cultu feminarum*, the *Ad Uxorem*, the *de Exhort. Castitatis*, and the half of the *de Carne Christi* (up to § x, to the words *sed animae nostrae*). In its original make-up it contained many others as is proved by a very precious index which can be read on page 2. This index enumerates twenty-one works as belonging to Tertullian. The second part of the manuscript having been torn out, eight of them have disappeared —a mutilation all the more to be regretted as out of these eight treatises, five have never been found reproduced in any other manuscript and are totally lost, namely, the *de Spe Fidelium*, the *de Paradiso*, the *de Carne et Anima*, the *de Animae Submissione*, and the *de Superstitione saeculi.*

B. The second family falls into two groups of manuscripts, the one older and the other of more recent date.

(*a*) The *oldest group* is represented by the *Montepessulanus* (biblioth. municipale de Montpellier), XIth century, which includes seven treatises, and by the *Paterniacensis* (MS. *de Payerne*), now at Schlettstadt, of near kinship with the *Montepessulanus*, and which traces its descent from the same archetype. The *Paterniacensis* comprises nine treatises.

Two other manuscripts, the *Hirsaugiensis* (from the monastery of Hirschau in Wurtemberg) and the *Gorziensis* (from the monastery of Gorze near Metz), belonged to the same group. Both of them have been lost and we only know of them through the works of Beatus Rhenanus (Bâle, 1521 ; 1528 ; 1539).

(*b*) The more recent group is made up of manuscripts of the XVth century, Italian for the most part ; Kroymann traces them to two archetypes now at Florence. Several treatises, such as the *ad Martyras*, the *de Pallio* and the *de Fuga*, are only found in the manuscripts of this group. Of these two archetypes, one traces to the *Montepessulanus*, either directly or rather through an intervening one ; the other to the *Hirsaugiensis* through an intervening one which has been likewise lost.

Kroymann is of opinion that the archetype of the *Montepessulanus*, the *Paterniacensis* and the *Hirsaugiensis* ought to be found at the Abbey of Cluny. An old catalogue (XIIth century) of the library of Cluny has led him to this hypothesis.   He supposes that a *Corpus* of the works of Tertullian must have been put together independently of that which we find in the *Agobardinus*.   And it is from this *Corpus*, in two volumes, preserved at Cluny, that our manuscripts should come.

Such is the state of the text of the manuscripts of the second family that there are no grounds to hope for a completely accurate edition of the treatises which have not come to us through the *Agobardinus*.   That is the essential point to bear in mind.   We shall also note that three treatises, the *de Baptismo*, the *de Jejuniis* and the *de Pudicitia* are only known to us in Cagny and Mesnart's edition, Paris, 1545 (Gangneius).   They are not extant in any manuscript.

The *Apologeticum*, by reason of its great historical importance, has enjoyed an exceptional handing down in manuscript.   It figures by itself in nineteen MSS.   Montfaucon quotes three more in addition in his *Bibliothèque des Bibliothèques*.   By successive eliminations, the critics have established that the only one which ought really to count is the *Parisinus lat.* 1623, of the Xth century (P).

Its rival is a certain *Fuldensis* (F).   This manuscript, formerly preserved in the library of Fulda, has been lost.   The first editors of Tertullian were ignorant of it.   A learned Belgian, François de Maulde, a Canon of Bruges (the Latinised form of his name is "Modius"), had noted in 1585 the different readings from his copy of the edition, which had appeared shortly before in 1580 through the instrumentality of De la Barre.   These very numerous readings (more than 900), were communicated to Fr. Dujon (Junius), who published them as an appendix in his edition of 1597.   It is through Junius that we come to know of them.   A copy collated by Modius as far as chap. xv, 8, was discovered by Hoppe in the library of the town of Bremen.   In some respects it is more carefully done than the transcription by Junius.   M. Waltzing published it in the *Musée Belge* in 1912.

The attention of critics was not drawn to the *Fuldensis* in any decisive manner until after it had been aroused by C. Callewaert in an article in the *Revue d'Hist. et de Litt. religieuses*, vol. VII (1902), pp. 322-353.   Confining his examination to the seven first chapters of the *Apologeticum*, Callewaert came to the conclusion that the *Fuldensis* derives from a source independent of the other manuscripts of this treatise, and represents in itself a tradition which has disappeared, the traces of which can be followed in the Greek translation of the *Apologeticum* up to the IIIrd century.   He signalised the excellence of several of the variants provided by the *Fuldensis*.   Since then, he has brought fresh proofs to support his theory, in the *Mélanges Ch. Moeller*, in 1914.

Lively discussions have been aroused during all these latter years on the value of P. and of F.   I have dealt with these in the B.A.L.A.C. 1914, 4 fasc. (published in 1917), pp. 315-316.   Since then, an *Etude sur le Codex Fuldensis* by M. Waltzing has appeared (*Bibl. de la Fac. de Philos, et Lettres de l'Univ. de Liége*, fasc. 21, 1917).   M. Waltzing concludes that an authorised edition of the *Apologeticum* should be based on the *Fuldensis*, but that caution must be used with even the *Fuldensis*.   See also Rauschen, *Emendationes et adnotationes ad Tertulliani Apologeticum*, F.P., XII (1920).

BIBLIOGRAPHY of Tertullian in *La Crise Montaniste*, 1913, pp. vii-xx, by P. de Labriolle.

LIST OF WORKS : See Table No. 2.

II. The Fragment of Muratori.—Text in P.L., III, 173-194 ; Preuschen, S.Q., Heft. 8 (1893), p. 129 ; Rauschen, in F.P., III (1905) ; Jacquier, *le Nouveau Testament dans l'Eglise Chrétienne*, vol. I (1911), p. 189 et s. (with commentary and bibliogr.).

III. The Martyrdom of Perpetua and Felicitas. — Text in P.L., III, 13-58; Robinson, T.S. 1, 2 (1891); Franchi de Cavalieri, in *Röm. Quartal-schrift*, Suppl. Heft. 5 (Rome, 1896).—French translation by Dom Leclercq, *The Martyrs*, I, pp. 120-139; translation of the Prologue and the Conclusion in the *Sources de l'Hist. du Montanisme*, by P. de Labriolle, p. 9 et s.—For a general view of the Martyrdom, cf. the excellent analysis by P. Monceaux, I, p. 70 et s.   H. Delehaye, *les Origines du Culte des Martyrs*, Brussels, 1912, p. 430, gives proofs of the long popularity of Perpetua and her companions in Africa.

SUMMARY

I. Pope Victor.   Apollonius, the " Senator ".   The Fragment of Muratori.— II. The Origins of the Church in Africa.   Tertullian. — III. The Christian view of Tertullian.   The intellectual equipment of Tertullian. —IV. His life.   His transition to Montanism.   Tertullian, Head of a Sect.   V. His Apologetic Works.—VI. Tertullian in his relations to the Pagans. —VII. Tertullian and Gnosticism.—VIII. Tertullian and Montanism.—IX. Tertullian as Writer.—X. The *Martyrdom* of Saints Perpetua and Felicitas.   Was Tertullian the author of the account?

I

IF we take away the translators of the Bible, were there any Christian writers before Tertullian who wrote in Latin? Certain hints given by St Jerome in his *de Viris Illustribus* permit us to believe that there were.   In § liii he wrote: *Tertullianus presbyter nunc demum primus post Victorem et Apollonium ponitur*.   In another place, in Epistle LXX, 5, while giving a list of the principal Christian authors, he places Tertullian first.   He does not mention Victor and does not breathe a word of Apollonius, whom he quoted some lines previously, it is true (§ 4), but amongst the Greek authors.

As regards Victor, the indication given in the *De Viris Illustribus*, LIII, may be completed by another offered in a very short paragraph, § xxxiv: "Victor, thirteenth Bishop of Rome, wrote on the subject of Easter, and certain other *opuscula*. . . ."   In the *Chronicle*,[1] Saint Jerome qualifies these *opuscula* (called *volumina* in this work) as *mediocria*.   It appears probable that he was simply dealing with the letters of Pope Victor at the time of the lively disputes with the Bishops of Asia over the controversy about Easter; [2] Jerome was also in a position to know of other writings analogous to those of Victor, as for example concerning the Montanist affair.[3]

[1] *Ad ann.*, 193 (Helm, p. 210).
[2] Cf. Eusèbe, H.E., V, xxiii et s.   The letters given by Migne, P.L., V, 1483, are not authentic.
[3] P. de Labriolle, *La Crise Montaniste*, p. 271 et s.

Some of these *quasi* official documents were perhaps rendered in Latin, or in Latin and Greek. St Jerome, who was very zealous in swelling as far as possible his catalogue of the writers of the Church, did not forget to make much of it however meagre was its literary importance.

As regards Apollonius, Jerome mentions in his *de Viris Illustribus*, § xlii, an *insigne volumen* which, in the reign of Commodus, he had read before the Senate " in order to give an account of his faith " which was imputed to him as a crime. He attributes to him the rank of *Romanae urbis senator*. This mention was taken from Eusebius with certain fanciful additions with which Jerome supplements it. Eusebius relates in his *History of the Church*, V, xxi, that Apollonius when denounced for being a Christian was invited by the judge, Perennius, who knew him to be a very cultivated man, to justify himself before the Senate (Eusebius does not say that Apollonius was himself a Senator) ; that in front of all he made " a very eloquent apology of the faith for which he was bearing witness," and that after that his head was cut off. The words of Apollonius had been inserted by Eusebius in his *Relatio* of the early martyrs, which has unhappily been lost. The *acta* of Apollonius as we now possess them in Greek and in Armenian, do not give any *apologia* properly so called, but only the replies of Apollonius to the judge. The matter rests very obscure. Jerome himself, who knew no more than Eusebius, could not have been sure that this alleged apology had been written in Latin and it is from this uncertainty that his hesitating attitude without doubt proceeds.

All this is therefore of little account and doubtful, and we must pass on to more solid ground.

We will only mention, lest we forget it, the explanatory list of the New Testament, known under the name of the *Fragment of Muratori*. This index in eighty-five lines, mutilated at the beginning and possibly at the end also, was discovered by Lodovico Antonio Muratori, the learned librarian of Milan, in a manuscript of the VIIIth century in the Ambrosian Library, and published by him in 1740.[1] This manuscript, which is the only one to contain the text, came from the Monastery of Bobbio in Lombardy. The Fragment is of interest, especially to philologists, on account of its faulty Latin

---

[1] *Antiquitates Ital. medii aevi*, III, 851.

from which several critics (Hilgenfeld, Zahn, Chapman) suspect a translation from a Greek original, and to the historians of the Canon of Scripture who find therein much information of great value.   The anonymous author begins by laying down what he knows of the origin of the Gospels of Luke and John, and then lays stress on the fundamental agreement of the Gospels ; he passes on to the Acts of the Apostles, to the Epistles of St Paul, of St Jude and St John (to which he joins in a quite unexpected manner the Book of Wisdom), to the Apocalypses of John and of Peter, to the *Pastor* of Hermas of which he recommends the reading in private and discountenances its public or liturgical reading.   Then at the end come some very obscure lines [1] from which we may gather the opinion that we must explicitly exclude from the Canon certain heterodox books which aspired fraudulently to creep in to it, and which amongst certain sects passed for divinely inspired works.   We cannot be far out in placing the writing of this fragment about the year 200.   Th. Zahn [2] thinks that it must have been compiled in Rome or in some neighbouring community.   But his own method of proving this somewhat impairs the conclusion at which he arrives.   In fact, he notes himself that the expression *urbi* (lines 38 and 74–76) were used throughout the Empire—not only in the capital—to mean Rome ;   that *sedente cathedra urbis Romae ecclesiae Pio episcopo* (I, 15–76) is a well recognised phrase on the lips of a Roman speaking to Romans ;   finally, that the author shows no special *pietas* for the Church in Rome nor claims for her any exceptional privilege in the matter of deciding what was the authentic Canon.   We may here add an observation which has been developed by Dom Chapman.[3]   The author of the *Muratorianum* declares (I, 71) : " We also accept, and these only, the Apocalypses of John and of Peter."   Now there exists no proof that the Roman Church in the IInd century admitted the Apocalpyse of Peter, which, on the other hand is quoted just like a canonical book by Clement of Alexandria.[4]

---

[1] Cf. P. de Labriolle, *La Crise Montaniste*, p. 288.
[2] *Gesch. d. neut. Kanons*, II, 14.
[3] R. Bén. XXI (1904), p. 240 et s.
[4] *Eclogae ex scriptis proph.*, § 41, 48, 49.

II

It was Northern Africa which gave to Christian literature the greater part of the writers who shed their lustre on it for the space of nearly three centuries. Up to the IVth century, Africa was the home of Western Christian thought. We know that during the same period her contribution to profane literature was by no means insignificant. Here is the right place to give an account of the " genius " of Africa, her tendencies and her special characteristics. We must guard against any complete synthesis of these attributes, however brilliant the partial glimpses we may obtain : as a matter of fact, it is as embarrassing to note down the specific *nuances* of the African temperament as to define with exactitude the " Africanisms " in the vocabulary and syntax around which the school of Ed. Wölfflin made so great a stir some while back.[1]

We know nothing of the beginnings of the Church in Africa. Towards the end of the IVth century, there were noteworthy Christians in that country who were hardly better informed than ourselves. One would gladly consider her as an offshoot of the Church in Rome. This is a plausible hypothesis but one which goes further than the texts we have to prove it.[2] She emerged on a sudden from the twilight in 180. On the 17th July, 180, twelve Christians[3] of the town of Scillium (possibly in the Pro-Consulate of Numidia, but the exact spot has not been located), seven men and five women appeared before the Pro-Consul Vigellius Saturninus. They remained steadfast in their wish to continue Christians ; they even refused the reprieve of thirty days which the Pro-Consul offered them for the purpose of thinking over the matter again, and heard their sentence to perish by the sword. We possess both in Latin and in Greek several specimens of the *Acta* of their martyrdom. These *Acta* were originally composed in Latin. The passage, which is very short, bears the sobriety of language of a lawyer's statement wherein no rhetoric mars the stern truth of their words and attitude.

---

[1] Cf. Wölfflin in the *Sitz.-Ber.* of the Academy of Bavaria, 1880, p. 333, and in several articles in A.L.L. ; Sittl, die lokalen Verchiedenheiten der Latein. *Sprache*, etc., Erlangen, 1882.

[2] Paul Lejay, *les Origines de l'Eglise d'Afrique et l'Eglise romaine*, in the *Mélanges Godefroid Kurth*, Liége, 1908.

[3] It appears to be probable that out of the twelve names, six were added after the event and do not belong to the group of martyrs of the 17th July. Cf. Saltet, in B.L.E., 1914, p. 108-125.

Some days previously, the same Pro-Consul had struck down four other martyrs at Madaurus. A period of calm seems to have followed this short persecution [1] and during this respite the Christian communities swelled rapidly in Africa, especially at Carthage. " If we are willing to offer to die," Tertullian was to say to the Pro-Consul Scapula [2] about the year 212, " what would you do with so many thousand people, with these men and women, these living beings of every sex and age, and of every condition, who would come forward to hand themselves over to you ? How many butchers, how many swords would you need ? What would happen to Carthage thus decimated by you when everyone would recognise there his near relations, his neighbours, perhaps men and women of your own rank, the leading citizens and the parents, or the friends of your friends ? " In short, towards the end of the IInd century, the Church in Carthage was provided with all the organisation which assured its vitality : it counted a considerable number of the faithful, and the disputations on moral and doctrine excited there an interest which betrayed the ardour of her faith. Such was the *milieu* wherein was born the father of Latin Christian Literature, Quintus Septimius Florens Tertullianus.[3]

III

TERTULLIAN became for the early ages of Christianity a famous example of the lamentable falling away to which men of rare intelligence are exposed. If a man like him fell into the snares offered by the wild speculations of Montanism, who could dare to feel sure of himself ? They gave expression to words of grave pity in his regard not altogether lacking in bitterness. And they took advantage of his unsound reputation to copy from his writings abundantly—without giving his name !

[1] Tertullian, *ad Scap.*, IV.
[2] *Ad. Scap.*, V (Œhler, I, 550). Cf. *ibid.*, II : " cum tanta hominum multitudo, *pars paene major civitatis cujusque*, in silentio et modestia agimus."
[3] These names are vouched for by testimony of differing value. Tertullian called himself *Tertullianus* (*de Bapt.*, XX ; *de Exhort. cast.*, XIII : this last passage besides being very much spoiled is not found in the better manuscript, the *Agobardinus*) and *Septimius Tertullianus* (*de Virg. vel.*, XVII). Lactantius calls him likewise *Septimius Tertullianus* (Inst. Div., V, 1, 23). *Quintus* and *Florens* are only provided by a subsequent tradition, gathered in the XVth century by the humanist J. Trithemius (John of Trittenheim) and Politianus (Angelo Poliziano).

However, admiration found its way through censures and scandalised looks. And it was for Tertullian's knowledge that it was especially felt. His style is sometimes accounted obscure and not sufficiently polished. But what prodigious erudition! St Jerome, whose competence no one will deny, exclaims in one of his letters : " *Quid Tertulliano eruditius, quid acutius ; Apologeticus ejus et contra Gentes libri cunctam saeculi continent disciplinam.*" [1] Vincent of Lerins went still further than these flattering terms in his famous *Commonitorium.*[2] In his view, Tertullian was to the Latins what Origen was to the Greeks : " Who was more learned than this man ? who as competent as he in things divine and human ? So much so, that all philosophy, all the different sects of the philosophers, their founders, their adherents, and the systems defended by the latter, history and science under their multiple forms—all these, the wonderful extent of his intellect embraced. . . ." His praise of him goes on increasing in ample measure, to end, it is true, in regret that a man so eminent made so bad an ending and could become " a great temptation " in the Church.

Tertullian's scholarship is really remarkable. It will appear still more so if we compare it to that of the most learned pagans of his time. Nowadays we have become more scrupulous and harder to please, and are sometimes tempted to find it superficial, unreliable and second-hand. But we should be wrong in minimising its solid parts and especially its amplitude. Tertullian wrote with equal facility in Latin and Greek : many of his treatises were composed in both these languages. He was familiar with the greater part of the great systems of Greco-Roman philosophy, and, however incapable he was of following with impartiality and sympathy the ideas of others, he knew how to extract from them their leading characteristics for the purpose of refuting them, or compelling them to coincide with his contention. He borrowed much from profane philosophy especially from Stoicism. He was no stranger even to physiology : in an age when all development of an argument was evolved in the abstract by a simple chain of interlinked reasonings, or by texts placed together one after the other, Tertullian had the merit of enlarging the habitual field of the logicians and psychologues, his pre-

[1] *Ep.* LXX, 5.   [2] § xxiv.

decessors or his contemporaries ; he interested himself in the results arrived at from natural sciences ; he foresaw what the thinker might draw from them in the pursuit of his own speculations ; and of all the Greek and Latin writers for whom he gave evidence of the greatest consideration and even of respect, men of science held the first place.[1] To this we must add his vast knowledge of law, which in a large measure gives to his work its general tone and individual colouring. It is easy to see that in this respect he is a past-master. When he touches on law, he is not like some amateur who ventures on ground which is not his own, but, if not quite like a consulting lawyer, at least like a *causidicus* who knows all its secrets, all its machinery, all its tricks, I was going to say, and who makes them cleverly serve his own purpose.[2] If subtilty, strength of logic, the art of following without losing the thread of a fundamental axiom in its application to a multitude of different cases are the essential marks of the legal mind, Tertullian possessed them all in a high degree. We must also consider the great number of texts from Scripture which he has quoted, interpreted, and paraphrased with so much aptness and stubborn desire to convince. It is quite easy to see that he had at his service every *instrumentum fidei*, and his wonderfully accurate memory, whatever else one may say of it, provided him on each occasion with the deciding points of which he had need.[3]

Neither the primitive Christian literature, nor that of the IInd century even though heterodox, were strangers to him. He had read the *Pastor* of Hermas, which for long he treated with respect, then with fury and hatred when he saw the party view which his anti-Montanist adversaries drew from it ; the

[1] This is what I have tried to demonstrate in an article in the *Archives générales de Médecine*, 1906, pp. 1317-1328.

[2] Cf. P. de Labriolle. *Tertullien jurisconsulte*, in the *Nouv. Revue histor. de Droit français et étanger*, Jan.-Feb. 1906 ; and Schlossmann, *Tertullian in Lichte der Jurisprudenz*, in Z. *fur Kirchengesch.*, XXVII (1906), 251-275, 407-430. Schlossmann emphasises the exaggerations which tend to identify Tertullian with the lawyer of the same name whose five fragments are quoted in the *Digeste* (I, iii, 27: Mommsen, Berlin, 1908, p. 34 ; XLI, ii, 28 : p. 701 ; XXIX, i, 23 and 33 : p. 437, and XLIX, xvii, 4 : p. 890).

[3] He possessed the Old Testament in the text of the Alexandrine Canon, and of the twenty-seven books of which the New Testament is composed, he omits in his quotations only the IInd Epistle of Peter, the IInd and IIIrd Epistles of John, and the Epistle of James (a passage in the *Scorpiace*, XII, proves that he was not acquainted with the latter) He attributed to Barnabas the Epistle to the Hebrews. His blunders in quotations from the Bible are rare ; thus, in the *de Fuga*, II, he confuses the heretics of I Tim., i, 20, with those of II Tim., i, 15.

Acta Pauli on the origin of which he gives in the *de Baptismo*, XVII, much careful information; perhaps also the *Acta Pilati* (cf. *Apol.* XXI).

Among the Montanist *opuscula*, a collection of oracles of the Phrygian soothsayers came into his hands. In the *de Anima*, he quotes the *Acta* of Perpetua and Felicitas, certain portions of which are penetrated with the Montanist spirit. Further he examined the work of the anti-Montanist Apollonius, which appeared in about the year 212, next he was to add almost at once a seventh book directed against this polemist to the six books of his *de Ecstasi*. With regard to the Greek apologists, he did not perhaps testify all the gratitude which was their due. He only mentions Justin, and even then only on the score of his being an opponent of Gnosticism, not in his capacity of apologist. He is content to sum up *en bloc* and in a somewhat scornful manner at the beginning of his *de Testimonio Animae* the methods of his forerunners, their unfruitful efforts at conciliation between the wisdom of the pagans, and the truths of Christianity. Two of them, nevertheless, he has laid under large contribution, namely, St Justin, whose *Apologies* and his *Dialogue* with Tryphon he exploited, and Tatian, who provided him with some important notions on the theory of the Logos and on Christology. He also stripped bare, in pursuing his polemics against individuals, the writings of the Gnostics and anti-Gnostics. The longest of his treatises, the *Adversus Marcionem*, rests on an analysis of different documents emanating from Marcion himself, in particular the New Testament retouched by the heresiarch, and his *Antitheses*, in which he placed in strong relief the contradictions between the Gospel and the Law. While taking toll of the refutations previous to his own, Tertullian had read with his own eyes the *Phaneroseis* of Apelles, the work by Hermogenes on the eternity of matter, and several other *opuscula* which were circulating amongst the Gnostics, for example, a treatise on the lawfulness of flight in face of martyrdom. He made extracts from a large portion of the orthodox disputations, such as those of Irenæus and Theophilus of Antioch, but in more than one case he went in quest of first-hand documents and thoroughly explored the prolific output of the Gnostics. He was equally familiar with the work of Melitos of Sardis whose mental equipment was not without analogy to his own. As regards Clement of Alexandria, his contemporary, it seems that he did not know him and that Clement also was equally unaware of Tertullian.

This is but a very rapid inventory. It will suffice however to reveal the amplitude of the breadth of his intellect. And what gives a correct estimate of its trend from this point of view, is to recognise that the cast of his mind was not purely speculative. There was nothing about him of the learned recluse, nor of the mystic absorbed in his dreams. He was admirably cognizant of the pagan and Christian world in the midst of which he was living. We find in his writings, interspersed in the midst of discussions and polemics, a host of features which make Carthage his native city, with its exterior and picturesque aspects, live again before our eyes, as well as its moral and religious life.[1] And all this precise information extended far beyond the horizon of Africa, as far as the most distant regions of scattered Christianity.

Endowed with a mind fundamentally positive and practical, with a talent tempered to a superior fineness, which knew how to bind together in vigorous systems, theology, moral, and discipline, without mentioning the Latin tongue itself which he constrained with so much learning to new uses, this original and powerful personality inaugurated Latin Christian Literature in the West in a manner which was most resplendent.

IV

A SHORT notice in St Jerome's *de Viris Illustribus*, § liii, and a few rare confidences of Tertullian about himself, offer us almost the only data at our disposal for relating his life.

He was born probably between the years 150 and 160 : in any case, he had reached the full maturity of his talent by 197 when he wrote the *Apologeticum*. He was a native of Carthage. According to St Jerome, his father fulfilled the duties of " proconsular centurion," which may mean either a centurion of the town cohort stationed at Carthage, or an official

---

[1] I would especially mention the *ad Scap.*, III–V ; *de Res. carnis*, XLII ; *Apol.*, XVI ; *ad Nat.*, I, xiv ; *Scorp.*, VI ; *de Idol.*, XV ; *de Pallio*, I ; *adv. Val.*, VIII, etc. Tertullian is an authority of the first order on the times of the Emperors.

personage bearing the title of centurion, not officially but one in use by common parlance.[1] His family was pagan. He himself deplores his errors of former days, and his sarcastic observations in regard to Christian beliefs : " *Haec et nos risimus aliquando : de vestris sumus. Fiunt, non nascuntur Christiani.*" [2] He confesses that he was a sinner, that he frequented the public shows,[3] that he committed adultery.[4] He may possibly have had himself initiated into the mysteries of Mithra.[5] He gives no very clear explanation of the reasons which influenced his turning to Christianity. The spectacle of the heroism of the Christians must have produced in his mind a lively impression : " Everyone, in the face of such prodigious endurance feels himself as it were struck by some doubt, and ardently desires to find out what there is at the bottom of this matter : from the moment that he understands the truth, he forthwith embraces it himself." [6] He also energetically extols the evidence that existed of the power of exorcism possessed by the Christians : " What proof can be more certain ? Here we see the truth displayed in its simplicity under the eyes of all, and strong in its own virtue. It is impossible to suspect any trickery." [7] Reading the Scriptures does the rest.[8] Tertullian therefore was a convert who exchanged a very free manner of living for the rigours of Christian discipline. His horror of paganism, even where it was least open to blame, might have proceeded from his hatred of a past whereof he felt in himself the re-awakenings.

He was married. In his *Ad Uxorem*, he addresses himself to his wife and asks of her not to contract a second marriage. Was this jealousy for himself after he should be dead ? Certainly not, since Christ predicted the altogether spiritual conditions of the Resurrection. But a salutary counsel of which every Christian will know how to draw profit.

He was a priest. St Jerome gives us formal testimony on

---

[1] M. René Cagnat courteously communicates the following : This information of Jerome is confirmed by a passage in the *Apolog.*, IX, 2, if we can admit the reading *patris nostri* which the *Fuldensis* alone gives. On this text, see Dessau in *Hermes*, XV (1880), 473, n. 2 ; Tissot, *Fastes* . . . , p. 8 ; Pallu de Lessert, *Fastes des Prov. Afr.*, 1 (1896), p. 296 ; Audollent, *Carthage Rom.*, pp. 399 and 720.

[2] *Apol.*, XVIII, 4. Cf. *de Paen*, 1.

[3] *De Spect.*, XIX.

[4] *De Res. Carnis*, LIX.

[5] A rather enigmatic allusion in the *de Praescr.*, XL, 4.

[6] *Ad Scap.*, V ; cf. *Apol.*, L, 15.

[7] *Apol.*, XXIII, 7.

[8] Cf. *Apol.*, XVIII, 1.

this point. This testimony is in opposition to the false interpretation of critics by which they have sought to invalidate it. How can one believe, after all, that Tertullian, a layman, could constitute himself without opposition the apologist, the polemist, the Doctor, which he was, and that he could have dared to give rules to a whole community in the intimate relations of their life with so much authoritative minuteness ? Such a case would have been too exceptional in the early days of Christianity for no one to have stigmatised it as unusual. After the deceptions inflicted on the Church by Tertullian, there would not have been wanting people to diminish their importance or to give some explanations of their cause by reminding themselves that he had assumed the responsibilities of a teacher to which no official charge had appointed him, and that such a usurpation had intoxicated him with pride and finally ruined him. Now these considerations—so natural from the pen of writers in the Church—are nowhere apparent, and this silence completes our conviction that the information given by St Jerome can be and should be accepted as authentic.[1]

The great event in his life as a Christian was his going over to Montanism. How could such a man, with a mind so positive, so staunch a promotor of organised regulations, in full possession of his intellectual maturity and his *prestige* amongst his brethren, have allowed himself to become mixed up with an Oriental sect whose more or less frenzied external aspects were so little calculated to attract him ? This is a somewhat confusing problem the solution of which, however, as we shall see, is not beyond attainment.

This sect had its birth in Phrygia, probably about the year 172, under the impulse of Montanus, a " Prophet," in which apostolate, two women, Maximilla and Priscilla, were associated. Far from separating themselves from the " rule of faith," the Phrygian prophets formulated no proposition which was of a nature to stand in its way, and allowed themselves no rash speculations. It was not in this field that they directed their special efforts. Penetrated with the feeling that the world was shortly coming to an end (we know that this belief was common among the first generations of Christians, but these appeared to have sensed it with a quite special

[1] Cf. P. de Labriolle, B.A.L.A.C., 1913, 161–177.

intensity of apprehension), they desired above all to awaken souls from the moral lethargy under which they seemed to them to lie numbed, to arouse them by the fear of judgment to come, and to prepare them for this dread event through the agency of ascetic rules of a very precise nature. With a view to this, Montanus prescribed fastings, the carefully regulated programme of which left nothing to individual caprice ; he advocated the joyful acceptation of martyrdom ; he refused on principle all pardon to sinners convicted of grave delinquencies, in order not to encourage their weakness by any too accommodating amnesties.

This rigorousness, however formidable, did not go however to the excessive lengths to which asceticism is sometimes tempted to carry itself. Montanus possessed a certain sense of the practical, the impress of which he had shown in the clever organisation of his propaganda. Thus, he counselled that people should suffer martyrdom patiently, but not that they should go to meet it without necessity. Similarly, though distinctly hostile to re-marriage—and on this matter he had on his side a large part of the prevalent Christian opinion—he avoided any condemnation of the conjugal union in itself. He intuitively realised what human nature was capable of, but he had no hesitation in claiming from nature the most painful detachment in view of the imminent catastrophy.

Montanism might seem at first sight to have no other aim than to draw to itself, in order to carry them to the highest degree of exaltation and enthusiasm, the several strains of belief issuing from the purest vigour of Christianity. Notwithstanding, even in his native country, he soon awakened mistrust, and the Bishops of Asia were not lenient with him. The reason was that Montanus and his wives by no means gave themselves out as ordinary preachers of asceticism and virtue, as single-minded zealots seeking to communicate to others the flame by which they were animated. They considered themselves as the habitation of the Holy Spirit, or rather that they were identical with the Holy Spirit, the state of ecstasy being considered to have annihilated in them all that appertained to their own personality. Further still, the adherents of Montanus regarded him, and he regarded himself, as the living incarnation of this Consoler, this Intercessor, this

Paraclete, the coming of whom Christ had announced to his disciples according to the IVth Gospel (xvi), and who, in accordance with the promise of Jesus, was to lead them to the truth in its entirety. Thenceforward the oracles of Montanus became, as it were, a new Testament which in no way rendered void the Gospels, but completed them by filling up the gaps which Christ had left therein of His own will.

Montanism was not merely a movement, a simple guidance in the moral order, an aspiration towards a more rigid and purer life : it was belief in the mission of the Paraclete incarnate in the person of Montanus and in a lesser degree in that of his prophetesses, and in the absolute character of his precepts.

Such were the fundamental conceptions of the sect to which Tertullian gave his intellectual adhesion and the support of his rugged talent. He was not long in separating himself from the community at Carthage, and also in practically cutting off himself and his partisans from those whose lukewarmness he judged to be an offence. A passage from the *de Anima*, IX, proves that he celebrated the ritual ceremonies apart.[1]

However, the Montanist group at Carthage could never have been very numerous. People are not in the habit of giving themselves airs for loving the truth backed up by an *élite*, nor of mocking at the " vainglorious *crowd* of Psychics " ;[2] nor do they haughtily quote the *multi vocati*, *pauci electi* (Matth., xxii, 14), when they have the consolation of numbering around them close ranks of adherents.

The little we know of the later history of this group in Africa comes from St Augustine who informs us in chapter lxxxvi of his *de Haeresibus*. He tells us : (1) that Tertullian did not hesitate to embroil himself with the Montanist sect, and from that moment established " his own conventicles " ; (2) that the " Tertullianists "—by this name people distinguished his followers—lasted at Carthage up to the time of Augustine ; that they there possessed a basilica ; (3) that Augustine held a conference with the last adherents of the party, with the

---

[1] See P. de Labriolle, *La Crise Montaniste*, p. 461 et s.
[2] Gross, carnal beings. It was by this expression, borrowed from the vocabulary of St Paul, that the Montanists described those of the Catholics who had no desire to know anything about their apocalypses. See P. de Labriolle, *La Crise Mont.*, p. 139 et s.

result that they reconciled themselves to the Church and handed back their basilica to the Catholics.

Why should we question such precise and authoritative testimony ? A man of intractable character, always prone to find fault with others, embittered further by disputes in which no mercy was shown, by the loss of his former authority, by the dull remorse due to his own inconsistencies, it is not to be wondered at that Tertullian did not succeed in keeping under his rod all his adepts in their first fervour, and that he withdrew himself from them with a handful of irreconcilables. Besides, Augustine, having come into contact with the " Tertullianists " of his time, was able and must have questioned them on their origin. We must also note that he speaks of their reconciliation with orthodoxy as a matter of common notoriety (*basilicam, quae nunc etiam notissima est . . . ; quod etiam te* (he is writing to Quodvultdeus), *meminisse arbitror*). Neither any psychological likelihood nor any reasons of history invalidate the deliberate testimony which he gives.

When did Tertullian die ? We do not know. A. Réville [1] supposed that he entered again " within the pale of the common Mother." " It is evident," he declares, " that a man of such ecclesiastical character, so episcopal as Cyprian, would not have made the writings of a Doctor, who had formed a separate sect, his favourite reading " (cf. St Jerome, *de Vir. Ill.*, LIII). Réville's mistake is clear, and springs from the following considerations : (1) St Cyprian did, in fact, study Tertullian much. He closely imitated him in several of his treatises. But he never named him one single time, not even in the controversy around the baptism of heretics in which, however, he might well have availed himself of his opinion. (2) In addition, the tone in which ecclesiastical writers have spoken of Tertullian excludes the hypothesis of a tardy repentance. What cries of victory would have been heard had he finally recognised his error ! Now, from no quarter whatever did these hosannas resound.

Many of the details, which it would have been interesting to know, elude us in the life of this tempestuous genius. It seems probable that he made one or several sojourns in Rome.[2]

---

[1] *Nouv. Revue de Théol.*, 1858, I, p. 100.
[2] P. de Labriolle, *op. cit.*, p. 355.

The supposition of a journey to Greece rests on a false interpretation of *de Jejunio*, XIII.[1]   However, the general line of
his biography may be approximately sketched, and the
examination of his works will render more precise its various
stages.

V

It is necessary to consider the books *ad Nationes* and the
Apologeticum together.   These two treatises were written in
the year 197 at a few months' interval:[2] precise allusions to the
revolt of Albinus against Septimus Severus and to the reprisals which followed the defeat sustained by Albinus near
Lyons on the 19th February, 197, enable us to give the priority
to the *ad Nationes*.   Besides, the *ad Nationes*, in more than
one place, indicates the developments in the *Apologeticum* ;
and in places where the same arguments are arrayed in both,
it is in the *Apologeticum* that they are clothed in a more
finished form.   The difference between the two *opuscula* is
shown in the aim which the author pursues in them : the
principal objective of the *ad Nationes* is to attack the pagan
morals and beliefs ; that of the *Apologeticum* is to defend the
morals and beliefs of the Christians.   Again, the *ad Nationes*
is addressed to the " nations," that is to say, to the pagans,
to the unbelievers without ; the *Apologeticum* was destined
not for the Roman Senate, as the historian Eusebius of
Caesarea has wrongly supposed, but for the *praesides provin-
ciarum*, the Governors of the Provinces—that is to say, for the
Pro-Consul of Africa, and beyond Africa, for the entire body of
those high magistrates on whom depended practically the
fate of the Christians.   Tertullian wrote his *Apologeticum* in
the form of a speech by counsel.   As a matter of fact, no
defence whatever was allowed to a Christian accused before
the tribunal.   It is just this lack of legal fairness that Tertullian takes for his text in developing his plea in writing,
which endeavours to anticipate the judgment of the *praesides*
whom he pretends to harangue.

---

[1] By the words *quibus tunc praesens patrocinatus est sermo*, the word *sermo*
does not mean the speech of Tertullian taking part personally in the Council
meetings which he mentions as taking place in Greece, but the word of God.

[2] *Ad Nat.*, I, xvii ; *Apol.*, xxxv, 9.

What were the occasions offered to Tertullian for lifting up his voice in protest ?   For some fifteen years past, the Pro-Consuls of Africa had shown a certain tolerance in regard to the Christians.   But unequivocal indications revealed the viru-lence of the popular hatred, to which a few years later in 202, the edict of Septimus Severus was to give free licence.   " Day by day the people beset us," Tertullian affirms ; [1] " day by day they betray us, and very often they come to do us violence while at our meetings and assemblies."   And again,[2] " how often, without consulting you (the *praesides*), on their own initiative do not the people who hate us, attack us, with stones and torches in their hands ?   In their Bacchanalian fury they spare not even Christians who are dead ; from their repose in the grave, from the resting place of death, they snatch their bodies rotting in corruption, they tear them in pieces and scatter their poor remains."   To violence, they added derisive mockery.   An apostate Jew had devised a representation of the God of the Christians under the form of a two-footed ass and had circulated this caricature in Carthage.

" Here," relates Tertullian,[3] " is a new blasphemy against our God which the people pass from mouth to mouth.   Not long ago, in this very town, an unmitigated scoundrel—a renegade from his own religion and who is only a Jew through the hurt which his own skin has undergone (we note the allusion to circumcision), exhibited a cartoon against us with this inscription : Onochoetes.   It represented a personage with the ears of an ass, a cloak, a book, a cloven foot.   And the crowd of people who believe this rascally Jew ! . . .   There is only talk of Onochoetes throughout the town."

It was necessary at all costs to create a reaction against popular prejudices partaking of a more educated state of mind.   Tertullian on the whole did no more than yield to the pressure of the same circumstances which had brought forth the Greek Apologists.   These apologetic works he exploited : but he placed his characteristic mark, so vigorous and easily recognisable to all, on what he borrowed from them.   It is by

---

[1] *Apol.*, vii, 4.
[2] *Ibid.*, xxxvii, 2.
[3] *Ad Nat.*, I, xiv.   Cf. *Apol.*, xvi.   The meaning of *onochoetes* has not yet been fixed (*asinarius sacerdos :* Œhler, Rauschen ; " He who lies amongst the asses " : Audollent : " engendré par accouplement avec un âne " : Dom Leclercq, etc.).

comparing Justin with Tertullian that we are able to form a better estimate of the masterful literary talent and of the strength of mind of the inexorable dialectician. Whether it was from scorn of vain *technique* or from an incapability of setting forth his ideas in order, Justin did not bind himself down to any settled plan of reasoning. When he wished to present a picture of the life of the Christians, he scattered their principal features in chapters xii, xiv, xv, xxix, lxii, of his first *Apology* and in chapter x of the second. He strikes some happy developments, but does not carry them to a point or extract the pith. The *Apologeticum*, on the other hand, is a compactly written and powerful composition. This has been sometimes contested : it could only have been otherwise without a very attentive consideration of the landmarks which Tertullian himself took pains to establish throughout the plan of his work.[1] First there is an introduction (i–vi) in which he lays down, in the first place, the *iniquitas odii erga nomen christianorum* (I, 4), and secondly, the uncertain character of those human laws which were put in force against the Christians as though they were irrevocable. In § iv the general line of his argument is indicated : " I am going to demonstrate positively the innocence of the Christians. And I shall not only refute the accusations brought against us, but I shall return them against their authors (such is, as a matter of fact, his method throughout this work) . . . ; I shall reply to each category of complaints which refers to the clandestine crimes which they bring against us (this point will be studied from § vi, 11 to § ix, 19), and to those which we perpetrate (as they say) within the knowledge of all (such as the *crimen laesae divinitatis*, examined from § ix, 20, to § xxviii, 2 ; and the *crimen* — or *titulus* — *laesae maiestatis* which is the subject of § xxviii, 3, to xlv), — crimes on account of which we are held to be abominable, mad, worthy of punishment and meet subjects for derision, *in quibus scelesti, in quibus vani, in quibus damnandi, in quibus inridendi deputamur*." [2] A summing up in five chapters (xlvi to l)

---

[1] These points to note are marked in the following passages : i, 4 ; iv, 1–2, 3 ; vi, 11 ; ix, 1, 20 ; x, 1 ; xv, 8 ; xvii, 1 ; xxviii, 3 ; xxxix, 1 ; xl, 1 ; xlii ; xlvi, 1, 2 ; L.

[2] These last qualifications are too vague to my mind to allow one to connect them, as Callewaert would have it, with the separated parts of the development of his thesis from § vii to § xlix.

opposes the Christian doctrine to the doctrines of the philosophers and appeals to the justice of God against the ridiculous justice of man.

All this possesses a connected order as rigorously followed
as the texture of the *Apologies* of St Justin is indecisive and
wavering. It is especially in the passages dealing with law
that the superiority of Tertullian declares itself. Thus, in
chapter iv of his Ist *Apology*, Justin briefly criticised the
illegality of the procedure practised against the Christians.
Tertullian again takes up this point, but with a force, a
sequence, and technical precision, which only a long practice
in Roman law could have permitted him. The arguments
which fill the first chapters of the *Apologeticum* are irresistible
in logic and eloquence. They concentrate themselves into
well hammered formulae, they narrow themselves down into
irreducible dilemmas in which are shown the stupidity, and
the entire lack of logic of a procedure which was opposed to
all traditional forms of administering justice. In face of a
contest conducted in this manner, the Romans were to learn
that the issue was not with any haphazard attorney with more
zeal than knowledge, but rather with a man of law, broken in
to all the *finesse* of the bar, familiar with history and with law,
and whose wrongs were worthy to move (if not to convince)
their chief magistrates.[1]

The general tone of the work has an imperious and ironical
ruggedness very different from the conciliatory amenities of
Justin. Even when pleading for the sacred cause, Tertullian
is not the man to have recourse to concerted accommodation
or to diplomatic prudence. His keen wit takes his fill of
mythology, and revives those discussions inherited from
Greek apologists which likewise had received their full
measure of Jewish apologetics and Hellenic philosophy.
More respectful towards public authority, as the precepts
of St Paul enjoin as a duty, he claims however for his brethren
the right to shun the orgies for which the name-days of the
Emperors provided occasion, and to avoid all deification
of the Caesars. Where philosophers are concerned, there
must be no concession, no coquetting with them : where he

---

[1] M. Monceaux has, however, conceived with much subtilty what the Roman
magistrates could have opposed to the arguments of Tertullian, and to the reflections which his juridical thesis might have suggested to them. *Hist. litt. de l'Afrique
chr.*, i, p. 249 et s.

desires to place in relief the humility, the purity and dignity of the Christians, it is to the pride of Plato and of Diogenes, to the depravity of Socrates and Speusippus, to the base flatteries of Aristotle that he marshals them in opposition. He only slightly unbends when describing the altogether simple and correct life of the believers : yet he mingles with this more moving picture some mordant shafts which he knows not how to forgo.

He is almost completely himself in this work, with his powerful logic, the virtuosity of which is sometimes near neighbour to sophistry, with his incisive and haughty ruggedness which, one may say, seeks to humiliate his adversaries rather than to convince them, and with his nervous vigour of style.

It sometimes happens to writers to put their best selves into their first works. Tertullian has thrown into his *Apologeticum* a quantity of reflections which he is to resume later on in order to develop and make a profound study of them, and they were to form the substance of several of his treatises. Nearly all the thesis *de Testimonio Animae* is to be found in chapter xvii. He only had to accentuate in his *ad Scapulam* his proud declarations on liberty of conscience taken from chapter xxvii. In chapter xxxviii, he makes a preliminary flourish with vigorous invective against the theatre, which he is to thunder forth in the *de Spectaculis*. The leading motive of the *de Praescriptione* is already sketched out in chapter xlvii, 9 et s. And chapter xxi traces the outlines of the theory of the Word, which is to re-appear completed in the *Adversus Praxean*. All these questions, touched on *en passant* which he had neither the leisure nor the wish to study exhaustively at the time, he had in mind to take up again, when the right moment came, in order to clearly elucidate them and to extract therefrom their full measure.

The *Apologeticum* is one of those works which survive the circumstances which gave them birth and which enter into the common treasury of civilised nations. Nowhere shall we listen to more fervid demands for justice, tolerance, or the rights of an accused man ; to more vivid protestations against the tyranny of unjust laws assumed to be irrevocable ; lastly, to a more eloquent defence of Christianity, of its moral nobility, of the heroism of its martyrs. If there be in this admirable special pleading forms which are worn out, arguments which have perished with time, the contrary would have been the more wonderful. Taken as a whole, his work holds good, it still lives. " Tertullian," said Chateaubriand, " speaks like a modern ; the *motives of his eloquence have their roots in the circle of the eternal verities.* One part of his plea in favour of religion might still serve the same cause to-day " (*Génie du Christian.*, III, iv, 2).

The educated Christians immediately felt this startling superiority. The *Apologeticum* was translated into Greek a few years after its appearance, it seems. Tertullian himself did not trouble to do this, for some fragments preserved by Eusebius betray slight errors of interpretation.[1] At a time when translations of Latin works into Greek were so rare,[2] it was to the advantage of the faith to encourage these exchanges between West and East, in disregard of the national susceptibilities of Hellenism.

Compared with this masterpiece of passion and eloquence, the *De Testimonio Animae* appears a little weak. In it we see Tertullian endeavouring to establish an original method for gaining access to the heart of non-Christians. He states that the tactics of the Apologists, his predecessors, had not succeeded. They had attempted to prove through the instrumentality of a quantity of extracts drawn from the profane philosophers and poets that there were agreements more pronounced than disagreements between the new doctrine and the old pagan wisdom. These attempts at conciliation had resulted in no good : the enemies of the faith had contented themselves with rejecting their most admired masters in places where they seemed to offer support to the truth of Christianity. It was useless to have recourse to this vain pursuit of learning ; useless too, to eulogise the Holy Books, since in order to believe in them one must first be a Christian (*ad quas [litteras] nemo venit, nisi iam Christianus*). For the faith, the real point of contact must be sought for

[1] For example, compare Eusebius, *Hist. Eccl.*, II, ii, 4, with *Apol.*, v, 1–2 ; E. II, xxv, 4, with *Ap.* v, 3 ; E. III, xx, 7, with *Ap.* v, 4 ; E. III, xxxiii, 3, with *Ap.* ii, 6–7 ; E. V, v, 5, with *Ap.* v, 6–7. For inexactitudes in translation, see especially Eusebius, II, xxv, 4.

[2] Cf. E. Egger, *Mémoires d'Hist. anc. et de Philologie*, Paris, 1865, p. 266 et s. One might quote the *Georgics* translated by a certain Arrienus (who must be distinguished from the disciple of Epictetus) under Hadrian : The *Historiae* of Sallust, translated by Zenobius the sophist, likewise at the time of Hadrian.

in the human soul before it had undergone deformation through any learning : *te simplicem et rudem et impolitam et idioticam compello*. If we listen to the testimony of this yet whole-hearted soul, we shall realise the Christianity latent therein (*testimonium animae naturaliter christianae*). In the spontaneity of his language, of his entreaties, and of his exclamations even, his soul proclaims the unity and goodness of God, the existence of demons, a future survival and a reality of rewards beyond the grave. These are the truths which nature herself, nature pure and simple, had confided to him. And we must beware of seeing in these self-revealing phrases mere stereotypes, void of all thoughtful reflection, of the vicious forms and formalities to the use of which his familiarity with letters must have contributed. From what had literature herself borrowed these *eruptiones animae*, if not from the very soul itself ? Let the sincere-minded pagan offer an attentive ear to this truth which he carries enshrined in himself, whose accents he knows not how to comprehend !

There is nothing more curious than the divergences of criticism over this *opusculum*. Moehler and Neander admired it. Viala, a Protestant theologian, wrote : [1] " Of all the works of Tertullian this one seems to me to be the deepest, most universal, and possibly also the only one which will last out." Others, on the other hand, consider it as " one of the most feeble " by this author, and remark " that it is made up entirely of studies in Sophism and of conventional phrases in the current language of the day." [2]

Perhaps in the *De Testimonio Animae* there may be something to justify in a certain measure this enthusiasm and these slighting references. Tertullian promises more than he gives ; he traces out the main lines of a method further than he has succeeded in applying it : he sketches the theory of an agreement between the supernatural and the human soul, without establishing it by adequately defined facts. He possessed an intuition which is full of interest and he seems to have owed this to the Stoic philosophy,[3] but not sufficient psycho-

---

[1] *Tertullien considéré comme Apologiste*, Strasbourg, 1868, p. 29.

[2] Guignebert, *Tertullian* . . . , p. 252.

[3] The idea of " universal consent " is a stoic idea. See Diog. Laert., VII, LIV. We even find in stoicism whispers of a similar kind in the vulgar tongue, as revealing certain truths : Chrysippus, *Fragm. Stoic. Veterum*, fragm. 892 (Arnim, II, 243) ; Seneca, *De Benef.*, V, vii, 2 ; *Marc. Aurelius*, v, 8 ; x, 21.

logical penetration to enable anything vital it might contain to emerge, and his prescience has only approximately arrived at results.

The *Ad Scapulam* is a short " caution " in five chapters addressed to Scapula, the Pro-Consul of Africa, who, breaking away from the relative longanimity of some of his predecessors, in the year 212–13 began to persecute the Christians with hate, and did not hesitate to extend to them the penalty of burning which the worst criminals were generally able to avoid. The soldiery profited by this official rigour to despoil suspects likewise menaced by their own private enemies who denounced them freely. Right from the outset of this work, Tertullian lays down with perfect dignity the position which he intends to take up and maintain ; it was not pity he demanded for the Christians,—in becoming Christian they made the sacrifice of their life ; but it was to the self-interest of their enemies that he determines to appeal. He takes himself to task : " What am I saying ? Of their enemies ? rather of their friends, for ' to love those who love us ' is a sentiment natural to all ; it belongs only to the Christians to love their enemies (*amicos enim diligere omnium est, inimicos autem solorum Christianorum*)." He recalls certain fundamental principles : firstly, liberty of conscience (this he affirms in such formal terms that Pamelius, one of the editors of his works in the XVIIth century, cannot conceal his anxiety and observes that in the beginning of the *Scorpiace* there are precepts of quite a contrary kind) : [1] " Every man receives by natural law liberty to worship what seems good to him. . . . It is no part of religion to exercise restraint upon religion which should be embraced of one's own free will and not by force (*nec religionis est cogere religionem quae sponte suscipi debet, non vi*)." From this ensues the perfect loyalty of the Christians : " The Christian is no man's enemy, least of all the Emperor's. Inasmuch as he knows that he (the Emperor) is established by his God, he necessarily must cherish him, must respect and honour him and must desire his welfare, as well as that of the whole Roman Empire so long as the world shall last, for the Empire will last so long as the world. We therefore honour the Emperor as we are permitted to honour him, as it is fitting for him to be honoured, that is to say, as

---

[1] *Ap.* Migne, P.L., I, 777, note 2.

a man who is second after God. . . ." What subjects are
more pacific than the Christians ?—yet nevertheless if we had
a mind. . . . A muffled threat here rumbles. Already a
hint of this might have been discerned in chapter xxxvii, 3,
of the *Apologeticum*. In other respects, the *Apologeticum*
supplied the greater part of the reasonings which are developed
in the *Ad Scapulam*. There is one however which is new and
which gives to this work its particular intention. Tertullian
enumerates a certain number of recent facts wherein Scapula
should read the portending signs of divine anger : devastating
rains, balls of fire suspended over the walls of Carthage, and
an eclipse of the sun.[1] We here recognise a development
to which Roman historians were partial. We must note that
Tertullian hits back in a very spirited manner against the
pagans, and lays to their charge the common complaint,
which imputed all public calamities to the Christians as
despisers of the national gods. Then joining issue directly
with Scapula he draws up for his consideration the warning
spectacle of the punishments by which certain persecuting
magistrates had been overtaken : one, Vigellius Saturninus,
had lost his eyesight ; another, Claudius Herminianus, was
attacked by gruesome sores festering with maggots : he
recognised his mistake and died almost a Christian. Was not
Scapula himself, even at this moment, bowed down by illness ?
Now when had this illness begun ? Just after he had
delivered up to the wild beasts the martyr, Mauilus of
Adrumyttium.

The idea that Providence manifests in the world below the
effects of its rigour by the chastisement whereby it strikes the
impious in their bodies and in their life had for long brought to
the Christians (as to the Jews of old) its avenging consolations.
Josephus[2] had shown Herod falling into putrefaction, consumed while living by worms, maddened with suffering, and
putting an end to his unspeakable woes by suicide. Herod
Agrippa, the persecutor of the Apostles had expired, he too
devoured by worms.[3] Pilate was reputed to have fallen
under the yoke of such misfortunes that he was " compelled

---

[1] This eclipse took place, according to the calculations of modern astronomers,
on the 14th June, 212. This allusion enables us to give a more or less authentic
date to this treatise.
[2] Quoted in Eusebius, H.E., I, viii, 3–14.
[3] *Acts*, xii, 23 ; cf. Eusebius, I, x.

to become his own murderer and his own hangman."[1]
Lactantius was to trumpet forth an ample score to the same
strain in his *De Mortibus Persecutorum*. Tertullian already
draws from these events their powerful effect in his *Ad
Scapulam ;* but he has sufficient moral and literary tact not to
swell them to excess. The work possesses a noble and
vigorous energy whose pathos becomes still more insistent
towards the end where Tertullian supplicates the Pro-Consul
one last time " not to fight against God " ($\mu\grave{\eta}\ \theta\epsilon o\mu\alpha\chi\hat{\epsilon}\iota\nu$; the
expression, borrowed from the Acts of the Apostles, xxiii, 9,
is quoted in its Greek form).

It was not only against the hostility of the public powers
and the ill-usage of the crowd that the Christians had to defend
themselves ; it was also against the Jews. Born of Judaism,
long confounded with it by common opinion, Christianity did
not have long to wait before undergoing the effects of the
hostility of Israel for whom it cherished itself a profound
antipathy. " *Nam et nunc adventum eius (Christi) expectant
(Judaei), nec alia magis inter nos et illos compulsatio est,
quam quod jam venisse non credunt* " : " The Jews are still
expecting the coming of Christ and between them and us no
subject of disagreement is stronger than their refusal to
believe that He has already come." [2] This in reality was the
cardinal point of dispute between Jews and Christians. But
many other secondary subjects of strife had arisen to add to
this fundamental grievance.[3]

Very numerous in Africa,[4] the Jews did their best to stir up
the hatred of the pagans. *Synagogas Judaeorum, fontes
persecutionum* is another phrase of Tertullian's.[5] A recent
disputation in public which had resulted in failure on account
of the bad behaviour of some of the audience, was to suggest to
Tertullian the idea of putting in writing the arguments which
it had not been possible to deliver orally. From this incident

---

[1] H.E., II, vii.
[2] *Apol.*, xxi, 15.
[3] Regarding this question, which deserves to be treated to its fullest extent,
see the documents collected by Jean Juster, *les Juifs dans l'Empire Romain*, Paris,
1914, vol. I, pp. 35–76. A good general aspect is given in *Disc. et Conf.*, by Renan,
p. 311 et s. ; Harnack, *Mission u. Ausb. des Christentums*, I, pp. 39, 50, 399 ; II,
p. 77.
[4] Monceaux, *les Colonies juives de l'Afrique romaine* (*Rev. des Etudes juives*,
XLV [1902], pp. 1–28) ; *Dict. d'Archéol. chr. et de Lit.*, I, 745 ; Audollent, *Carthage
romaine*, p. 705.
[5] *Scorpiace,* X.

arose the *Adversus Judaeos*. The general purpose of this treatise is quite clear. Tertullian sets out to show the Jews that the general idea of revelation does not allow us to attribute to the Law of Moses any but a temporary value and that they were wrong in clinging to it, since the New Law had almost entirely taken the place of the ancient rites which had been abolished. An examination of the Prophecies proved that the expected Messiah had brought to mankind his message of salvation. From the time of Adam up to Christ, the divine ordinances had been evolved continuously, but from henceforth their end had been attained : " *Non potes futurum contendere, quod vides fieri.*" In matters of detail the discussion suffers from some confusion. The last chapters (ix–xiv) are borrowed for the greater part from the IIIrd book of the *Adversus Marcionem* ; [1] and this, together with instances of clumsiness, make us doubt whether it was Tertullian himself who made this unskilful transcription.[2]

VI

THE apologetic writings of Tertullian form the most generous, the most vibrating portion of his works, but not perhaps the most curious to whosoever would seek to penetrate within this soul of wrath and passion. From this point of view, far more significant are the treatises wherein he undertakes to define the attitude of the Christians in Africa as regards pagan society, and the various forms of the civilisation of his day. Here we shall learn to know him through and through with all the fierce ardour and rage of his temperament.

" Christianity and the Empire," Ernest Renan [3] stated, " regarded each other like two animals who would like to devour each other. . . . When a society of men . . . be-

---

[1] We may compare *Adv. Jud.*, ix with *Adv. Marc.*, III, xii, xiii, xiv, xvi, xvii ; *Adv. Jud.*, x with *Adv. Marc.*, III, xviii–xix ; *Adv. Jud.*, xi–xii with *Adv. Marc.*, III, xx ; *Adv. Jud.*, xiii with *Adv. Marc.*, III, xxiii ; *Adv. Jud.*, xiv with *Adv. Marc.*, III, xx–xxi.

[2] This problem in criticism can be studied anew in Monceaux, *Hist. litt. de l'Afr. chr.*, I, 295 et s., and Harnack, *Chron.*, II, 290, who both hold to its authenticity. Likewise Akerman, *Ueber die Echtheit der letzteren Haelfte von T adv. Judaeos*, Lund, 1918, but Einsiedler, *De Tert. adv. Judaeos libro*, Diss., Augsbourg, 1897, and Kruger, *Gott. Gel. Anz.*, 1905, p. 31 et s., raise very strong objections.

[3] *Marc. Aurèle*, p. 428. A very similar argument occurs in E. Schuerer's *die aeltesten Christengemeinden in roemischen Reiche*, Kiel, 1894, p. 9.

comes a republic apart in the State, it is a scourge even though it be composed of angels. It was not without reason that they hated these men so gentle and benevolent to outward appearance. In very truth they were rending asunder the Roman Empire. They sapped her power. It was no good saying that a man is a good citizen because he pays his taxes, because he is an alms-giver and orderly, when in reality he is a citizen of heaven and only accounts his native land on earth as a prison in which he lives enchained side by side with the outcast." There are many who represent the first generations of Christians in the same light as did E. Renan ; they imagined them as voluntary exiles from social life, and as stubbornly opposed to the temptations which it presented to them. We must not take too literally the somewhat emphatic declarations of certain apologists and the chiding unreasonableness of certain moralists. The reality appears to be very different. It is enough to read attentively the *opuscula* wherein Tertullian regulates matters dealing with questions of their interior economy to see how various were the leanings of the faithful in Carthage and Africa. There were the simple-minded, incapable and careless of speculative theories, who contented themselves with the quiet possession of their faith, but by reason of their simplicity were exposed to enervating sophisms ; [1] there were the intellectuals, who prided themselves on broaching the most abstruse questions in religious metaphysics ; [2] there were the weak, " the Christians fickle as air," [3] who, far from savouring of martyrdom,[4] persecution,[5] and repentance,[6] before all else showed themselves desirous of their own tranquillity,[7] and pretended to contrive here below as comfortable a life as possible ; even though at the

---

[1] " Qui simpliciter credidisse contenti non exploratis rationibus traditionum intentam probabilem fidem per imperitiam portant " (*De Bapt.*, I) ; " rudes animas " (*Adv. Marc.*, I, ix) ; " Nam et multi rudes et plerique sua fide dubii, et simplices plures quos instrui, dirigi, muniri oportebit " (*De Res. C.*, 11) ; " Simplices enim quique, ne dixerim imprudentes et idiotae, quae major semper credentium pars est " (*Adv. Pr.*, ii ; cf. *ibid.*, i).

[2] Cf. *De Praesc.*, ix ; *Adv. Marc.*, I, ii.

[3] ". . . Plerosque in ventum et si placuerit Christianos . . ." (*Scorp.*, i).

[4] Cf. *ibid.*, i : " sauciatam fidem vel in haeresin vel in saeculum exspirat (infirmitas)." See Harnack, *Mission*, I, 404, note 2.

[5] Arguments advanced by the partisans of flight in times of persecution are given in the *De Fuga* in § v, vi, vii, viii, x ; note in § vi (Œ., i, 471) the words : " Sic enim voluit quidam, sed et ipse fugitivus, *argumentari*. . . ."

[6] *De Paen.*, v, 10–12.

[7] " Mussitant denique tam bonam et longam sibi pacem periclitari " (*De Cor.*, i).

price of the most grievous compromises ;[1] there were the
" liberals ", who dreamed of reconciling Christianity with the
world, or at least set themselves against all useless provoca-
tion ;[2] lastly, there were the rigorists, like-minded with
himself. Tertullian assumed the task of herding this
fluctuating and diversified human flotsam and jetsam willy
nilly into the narrow paths which formed for him the only way
permitted to a Christian.[3]

What in reality did Christianity mean for him ? A faith
with no doubts, a *regula fidei*, in other words, a conglomerate
compounded of precepts laid as of obligation upon the intelligence, whose authenticity was guaranteed by the unanimous
voice of the Churches ; but before all else, a discipline, that
is a rule of life, and a check upon the will. His legal mind
approved of the idea of a doctrine which throws upon human
life in all its different activities, in the infinite multiplicity
of its acts, a closely circumscribed network of regulations,
with the promise of eternal recompense for those who shall
accept its enchaining hold, and the threat of eternal punishment against whomsoever shall set himself in opposition
with a view to escape from it. The God whom he cherishes
is the inflexible and jealous Judge who has established *timor*
as the solid base of man's salvation, who scatters temptations
in this world in order to prove His faithful ones, and who holds
His vengeance ever ready. From this arose the strictures of
Tertullian against the heretic, Marcion, who was given to
making much of the anthropomorphic attributes of the God
of the Old Testament.

"Hearken, ye sinners," cries Tertullian, " and you
who are not yet sinners, in order that you may learn
how you may become so. People have invented a God
who doth not take offence, who neither groweth angry

---

[1] A goodly number of Christians were not at all disposed to deprive themselves
of the theatre. Tertullian enumerates their excuses in the *De Spectac.*, i, ii, iii,
xx, xxix. We may compare the distress of the author of the *De Spect.* (generally
attributed to Novatian) in regard to certain analogous sophisms (Hartel, *Opera
Cypriani*, III, p. 3). Mixed marriages had likewise their partisans (*Ad Ux.*, II).
We shall notice, without wishing in any way to confuse these very distinct categories, that Tertullian admits that Christians could render themselves guilty of
offences in common law (*Apol.*, xliv, 3, and xlvi, 17) and of crimes against nature
(*De Pud.*, iv, 5).

[2] See especially the *De Idololatria*. It is easy to mark off the position taken up
by his adversaries by following each refutation on Tertullian's side.

[3] *De Fuga*, xiv (Œ., i, 491).

nor taketh vengeance; a God in a hell wherein no flames bubble forth, and which hath no outer darkness, no terrors to make you tremble, no gnashings of teeth. He is all good, I tell you, He forbiddeth sin surely, but only on paper. He holdeth you in regard, if you are kind enough to grant Him your obedience, for making some show of honouring Him. As for Fear, He will have none of it." [1]

A conception such as this enabled Tertullian to logically deduce for himself the necessity of a mortified life, entirely co-ordinated and hanging upon the thought of his own individual salvation. But he was not the kind of man to confine his efforts to the pursuit of a perfection purely egoistical. In addition to his duty as priest obliging him to exterior action, he was too combative, too passionate, too bent on winning over souls, and infusing into them his ideas, affections and hates, not to strive to impress on others his own ideal in so far as a perfect resemblance was possible.

To come to facts : see him busied in defining certain rules of conduct for the use of his brethren in cases of doubt or controversy. For example : in what measure was it lawful for a Christian to take part in the life of the pagans (*De Idololatria*), for a Christian woman to adorn herself (*De Cultu Feminarum*) ? Must young girls wear the veil (*De Virginibus Velandis*) ? When and how was it becoming to pray (*De Oratione*) ? He is never content with stating general principles. He enters into particular facts, in every little detail which makes up the thread of day to day. The *De Idololatria* is a kind of treatise in moral theology wherein, after having laid down the gravity of the crime of idolatry, Tertullian passes in review the different phases of life in the world, its callings, ceremonies, even its language, and sets himself to define in each case how far the Christian, who should be the enemy of indolence, might take part therein. And with what minuteness does he determine the conditions of prayer, the tone, the gestures and the attitude to observe (*De Oratione*) ! With what scrupulosity does he measure the length of the veil suitable for virgins, showing how it should be disposed before and behind, and just how long it should fall, and the exact age at which they should

---

[1] *Adv. Marc.*, I, xxvii.

begin to wear it ! He is not one of those moralists who suppose that the spirit alone is sufficient to vivify everything. He likes to foresee, so as to give rules for everything, because he is aware of the feebleness, the perversity of man, and fears that he may escape by some side issue wherein he had omitted to trace the road he should follow or to erect warning notices. Rigidly defined explanations must therefore adapt the injunctions of the law to everyday realities.

This is the spirit, at once authoritative and punctilious, in which he treats of the problems sustaining the development of Catholic life in a heterogeneous *milieu*. Not that he was incapable of a kind of grave gentleness, even of a certain unction. Let us run hastily through the *De Paenitentia :* it is not a didactic treatise on penance as an ecclesiastical institution, but far more a kind of sermon wherein Tertullian addresses himself especially to the catechumens still only slightly familiar with the demands of Christian life, or too ready to elude them. One is struck by a certain soothing solicitude and benevolence in the tone which he adopts. Harshness, in very truth, is not wanting. He is prompt to anger against the " hearer of the word " who, while confessing to the purifying virtue of baptism, has thoroughly made up his mind, at the moment of receiving the rite, not to give up the sins which he loves (cf. § vi) ; against the sinner who grows weak with alarm at the thought that he will have to live " without taking the baths, sordidly deprived of all joy, in the coarse garb of sackcloth, under the unsightliness of ashes, with countenance disfigured by fasting " (XI). But in several places we are able to notice a gentle and compassionate mysticism, and accents of pious and tender charity : for instance, when in order to re-assure the sinner against every temptation to despair, he insists on the fatherhood of God (VIII).

The *De Patientia* and the *De Oratione* breathe the same relative serenity. In like manner, a virile emotion, with nothing insipid about it, permeates the entire *Ad Martyres* with a vein of consolation, the sustaining influence of which Tertullian brings to the *benedicti martyres designati*, who were awaiting the ordeal of torture and death in prison at Carthage. Here again, however, under an outward show of humility (*nec tantus sum, ut vos alloquar . . .*), together with respectful entreaties to accept their glorious destiny, the rigour of his asceticism pierces through, which would quickly make itself pitilessly felt before even the shadow of any weakness.[1]

This asceticism is the foundation and leading principle of Tertullian's nature. Even before he had given his full and entire adhesion to Montanism, he never ceased combating faint-heartedness, falling away, and weakness, whose deadly languor in his view weighed down the atmosphere. Formal refusal to allow the Christians to take part in the public shows under whatever form (the circus, theatre, athletic contests, gladiatorial encounters)—for all these reminded them of idolatry or exhaled pleasure (*De Spectaculis*) ; formal injunctions against exercising any calling which, from near or far, might give any colour to the worship of false gods ; against the teaching of profane literature ; express reservations in connection with engaging in commerce which thrives by cupidity and fraud and is often near neighbour to idolatry ; the forbidding of any participation in any feast-day, in any ceremony, in any custom inspired by the worship of false gods ; a formal interdict against accepting any public office ; the incompatibility existing between military service and one's duty as a Christian ; a proscription of every kind of verbal expression savouring of paganism (*De Idololatria*) ; the forbidding of the re-marriage of widows ; of Christians to contract mixed marriages (*Ad Uxorum*). These are some of the stern limitations which he exalts, and with what merciless harshness, with what resolute, brutal acceptance of all the consequences involved in the principles which he sets forth !

There are pages, on the other hand, admirable for their dialectic, their subtil vigour and their ardent desire to convince. The curious thing is that in this fiery inquisitor there smoulders one lingering weakness : he has preserved some kindly feeling for rhetoric, its refinements and its tricks of style. Amid so much rugged exhortation, certain passages of a refined and delicate turn give a singular effect. This is how at the end of the *De Culta Feminarum*, he enumerates the virtues with which alone it becomes Christian women to embellish themselves :—

" Show yourselves adorned with the cosmetics and ornaments imitated from the prophets and the apostles.

[1] Cf. § ii and iv.

Derive your white vesture from simplicity, from modesty
your red, paint your eyes with reserve, your lips with
silence, hang on your ears the words of God, bind on your
neck the yoke of Christ . . . , array yourselves in
the silk of probity, the fine linen of sanctity, and the
purple of chastity, and, decked out in this manner, you
will have God for your lover ! ''

He once gave free rein to this hidden disposition.   It is in
the prodigious *De Pallio* which, of a surety, is the most difficult
from its Latinity, and in regard to which Claude de Saumaise,
that incomparable exegetist of the XVIIth century expended
large stores of ingenuity without succeeding in unravelling
all its hard sayings.   Under colour of justifying himself for
having exchanged the toga for the rough cloak, Tertullian
lets himself go (on a subject otherwise well-defined in Christian
tradition) [1] in the most astounding developments, as if he were
desirous of proving to the lettered men of his age what an
unrivalled rhetorician he might have been if it had pleased
him to have made a profession of *belles-lettres*.   Such purposely
trifling virtuosity in the author of the *De Idololatria* and the
Apologeticum scandalised the good Tillemont :   " We find
in the *De Pallio*," he says,[2] " great erudition, but I do not
think that we find in it all the wisdom and gravity which we
might expect from a man with Tertullian's reputation."
Malebranche,[3] for his part, in whose opinion Tertullian is
a type of those " strong imaginations " whom he dislikes
because " they throw passion over everything," declares
that there is no excuse for " this foolish idea of making himself
obscure and incomprehensible."   And we must confess that
it is strange that a man so penetrated with the seriousness of
human life and so quivering with expectation of the eternal
fatherland, should have indulged in these distilled literary
conceits.   A contradiction like this reveals how far Tertullian
remained a man of his time, and how profoundly its profane

---

[1] Cf. Varro in his satire entitled *Modius*, fr. 314 ; Apollonius de Tyana, *Philostr*,
p. 307, 19 Kayser ; Dion Chrys, *Or.*, lxxii ; Apuleius, *Apol.*, xxii.   Geffcken,
Kynika und Verwandtes, Heidelberg, 1909, has well studied the question of its
sources.   He refers the *De Pallio* to the " Diatribe " class and suspects Tertullian
to have made extended use of Varro.   The Christian note is discernible especially
in § ii, iv, v and towards the end of the *opusculum*.
[2] *Mémoires pour servir a l'Hist. Eccl.*, Paris, vol. II (1701), p. 227.
[3] *De la Recherche de la Vérité*, Book II, part 3, chap. iii.

learning, which in all other respects he affects to hold in distrust, had set its mark on him.

VII

It is not only in the practical order, but also in the intellectual, that Tertullian practised his magisterial scolding. The Gnostics had no more formidable enemy.

The unbridled imagery of these pseudo-Christian intellectuals, deeply infected with individualism, and eager to promulgate new doctrines, who turned topsy-turvy the theory of creation, distinguished between the true God, and God the Creator and Legislator of the Old Testament, and placed between this supreme God and the visible universe their married Aeons, their *syzygies*, their *pleromata*, their *ogdoads* and their *archons;* who made light of the reality of the events recorded in the Gospels and whittled down the historic Christ into a phantom Jesus who had neither suffered nor risen again, who enclosed in straitly circumscribed categories the benefits of a redemption reduced to absurdity, from which the greater part of mankind was excluded ; who distorted the idea of the Church which they personified in one of the Aeons of their grotesque cosmogonies ; of whom some ended by proclaiming that " it is quite lawful for gold to drag itself in the mud without soiling itself,"[1] that the destinies of the soul are in no wise solidly compact with the weaknesses of the flesh— acts not being able to change the spiritual nature of the human being—and that no one is obliged to suffer for an unreal Christ whose Passion was entirely fictitious :   this unrestrained criticism, this pride which refused to bow before the beliefs common among the faithful inspired in Tertullian the most furious opposition.   All the more so that the Gnostics excelled in awakening doubt in the hearts of those who had the weakness or presumption to hold discourse with them,[2] and that many souls felt themselves discouraged by certain desertions which had just afflicted the Church.

In the *De Praescriptione Haereticorum*, Tertullian applied himself energetically to counter this formidable contagion of

---

[1] *St Irenæus*, I, vi, 2 (P.G., VII, 508).
[2] Cf. *de Praescr.*, VIII, i.

scandal. After an out-and-out indictment of profane philosophy, of Aristotelian dialectics,—that past mistress of subtilty, contradiction, and of vain curiosities of the mind,— he raises the juridical argument of " prescription " as a supreme counter-stroke against this heresy. The true bearing of this can only be appreciated through the practice of Roman Law, and some explanations are here necessary.

The Law of the Twelve Tables established that whosoever shall have enjoyed for the space of two years the use of any property in land, and for the space of one year any other form of property, shall become the legitimate owner thereof (with the exception of certain cases reserved).[1] This form of acquiring property was called *usucapio*. But it was reserved only to those possessing citizenship.[2] A different procedure was needed for property in the provinces which did not carry with it legal (Quiritian) ownership, and for aliens who, lacking the title of citizens, were not qualified to obtain the *dominium*.[3] " It was permitted to anyone who had obtained possession of any property in the provinces in a regular manner, and had been in possession thereof for at least ten years, to rebut all claim on the part of the former possessor by means of a plea in demurrer, *longae possessionis praescriptio*." [4] Supposing a claimant came forward to claim any such property as belonging to him. The Praetor then handed to him a written form in which were defined the points on which the judge designate would have to pronounce. But at the head of this written statement he drew up, on the prayer of the defendant, a conditional restraint setting forth that, if the defendant had in reality possessed the property for the legal space of time, the plaint brought against him would be non-suited *a priori*. The *praescriptio*, therefore, was an exception enabling the possessor to render void the action which was being brought against him for the recovery of the property.[5]

Such was the method of procedure which Tertullian introduced into the domain of theology. The heretics arrogated to

[1] Cf. Cuq, *Les Institutions Juridiques des Romains,* vol. I, 2 ed. (1904), p. 85 ; May, *Eléments de Droit Romain,* 3 ed. (1894), p. 168 et s.

[2] May, *op. cit.,* p. 143.

[3] For further details, see Cuq, II, p. 249 et s.

[4] Cuq, II, p. 249. The author adds, " This exception of which Gaius is unaware and which is mentioned for the first time in a rescript of 29th Dec. 199, was very likely embodied in certain provincial edicts before being made of general application by the emperors."

[5] May, *op. cit.,* p. 170.

themselves the right to make dissertations on the Scriptures ; they interpreted them arbitrarily ; sometimes even they corrected and mutilated them. Now the whole question resolved itself into this : had they the right to touch them ? To whom did the Scriptures belong ? This point, once decided, would render unnecessary any plea on the question of principle.

It was historically indubitable, affirmed Tertullian, that they are the property of the Catholic Church who is heir to them through the channel of legitimate transmission. It was a fact that Christ charged the Apostles to preach His doctrine and made them its depositaries ; this fact they had transmitted in their turn to the Churches called Apostolic ; and, by the intermediary of these Churches, they had passed to other centres of Christianity in proportion as they became enlightened throughout the world. And what proved this uninterrupted succession still more was the identity of the traditions which perpetuated themselves among the different groups of Catholics.

This is the leading idea of this treatise, which is one of the most vigorous and most strongly put together of the writings of Tertullian and the one which modern theologians have most admired.[1] Strict logic would have demanded that, after it had been thus firmly supported upon law and upon history, any further disputation with the heterodox should have been refused. But it was too much to ask of this game fighter to obey the dictates of logic. It was above all for the use of the Catholic masses that he had hammered out his system. Once the bulk of his following had been placed in safety in the stronghold handed down to them, he did not hesitate to make on his own account the most brilliant *sorties* against the enemy as much to give additional assurance to his own people as to throw into confusion the opposite camp. The *De Baptismo*, which gives a complete theory of Christian baptism, is directed against a " viper " of the Cainite heresy. In the *Contra Hermogenem*, he joins issue with the painter of that name, " that heretic and mischief-maker who confounds eloquence with loquacity and impudence with stability." Hermogenes maintained that matter is eternal,

---

[1] I have made a study of the protracted fortunes of the argument from " prescription ", R.H.L.R., xi (1908), 408–428 ; 497–514.

and that God made everything from it. Against him Tertullian opposes a certain number of difficulties, in addition to copious abuse. In giving to matter eternity—an attribute belonging to God—Hermogenes, in his opinion, made matter the equal of God. Further, he raised it above God by reducing God to the necessity of having need of it in order to accomplish His work of creation. God, therefore, did not certainly make use of it *ut dominus*. He could only make use of it *precario*, for if He had used it *ex dominio*, it would be necessary to make Him responsible for the existence of evil in the world, since He would not have permitted matter, an attribute of Himself, to spread abroad the evil which it holds within itself. Not having possessed it *ex dominio*, He could not on that account have made use of it except as of a property outside Himself,—*aut precario* because He had need of it, *aut ex injuria*, because He was the more powerful. Let Hermogenes choose ! Thus, in each detail of the discussion, the argument from law crops up every moment. The *Adversus Valentinianos* is little more than a compilation of passages drawn from the great work of St Irenæus, *Irenæus omnium doctrinarum curiosissimus explorator*, as Tertullian calls him (§ v). He makes a point of bringing in some jesting and a rather amusing satire on the mystery in which the sect of Valentinus, the Gnostic, was presuming to involve itself. The five books of the *Adversus Marcionem* represent an original effort in quite another way.[1] I will only mention here the essence of the Marcionist thesis. Marcion had been keenly struck by the differences existing between the idea of God as revealed in the Old Testament, and that which appears in the Gospels. On the one hand, a severe and even cruel God, in whom some of the passions belonging to man live and boil over, who loves, hates, takes vengeance, and is subject to indecision and repentance ; on the other hand, a God of clemency and goodness, the celestial Father of all creatures. Marcion started from this opposition in order to accommodate to his liking the ideas contained in Revelation. In his view, the true God, the supreme God, had been in very truth and for the first time manifested in Christ ; as for the God of the Old Testament, in his eyes He was a simple Demiurge, a

[1] The beginning of the *Adversus Marcionem* is very curious in the history of the book in days of antiquity. The author explains there how this work had three editions the third of which he intended should cancel the two others.

secondary God, responsible for the creation of the ὕλη, of matter evil in itself. Of course the Catholics could not accept these views. By denying Judaism, Marcion committed not only a " colossal historical error " ; [1] he robbed Christianity of the majesty which the long vista of the centuries, previously preparing for the event, had added to the new religion. So Tertullian waged against this heresiarch a particularly implacable warfare. Each one of the five books of his treatise taken separately is longer than his other works. And what a mine of information (still indifferently well explored) for theology, history, exegesis, and the forms of Christian polemics !

However grateful the Catholics might be for such a champion, it is evident that with his mania for domineering over his fellow-Christians, Tertullian could not fail to excite around him the most lively opposition. People did not suffer themselves to be kept under as docilely as he could have wished. A coalition was set up against him, consisting not only of the " laxists," but also of the moderate minded who, pained at seeing the evangelic yoke weighted to excess, took occasion to entrench themselves behind the Scriptures and to oppose any exaction which did not find sure support in them. It is probable that the Bishops, whose actions Tertullian did not hesitate on occasion to criticise, were in favour of this reaction. How could the Bishops have supported this *intransigeant* to whom *quieta non movere* would have appeared the worst form of abdication, and who were constantly required to resolve questions on principle instead of leaving them to be cleared up by the exigencies of life itself ?

Tertullian was well aware of this spirit of opposition ; and he was the more exasperated thereby because the Scriptures, even when appealed to by the most accomplished of advocates and twisted by the most dexterous of tormentors into making the most convincing texts speak on his behalf, left him sometimes defenceless in the face of particular cases which the Holy Spirit (as they would have said) had not foreseen.[2]

In order to fill these terrible gaps, he essayed a fresh expedient. He made appeal to his studies as a man of law. He reminded himself that custom (*mos, mores majorum,*

---

[1] E. Renan, *L'Eglise chrét.*, p. 359.
[2] For instance, as regards the question of the public shows : *De Spect.*, III. From the point of view of the prohibition of flight in times of persecution, the text from *Matth.*, x, 23 caused him a great deal of worry.

consuetudo), was one of the sources whence flowed *jus civile*.
Custom was considered by the Roman jurists as expressing
the tacit consent of the people, the source of all law. Having
been proved by long use, " it was equally binding on the judge
as was the law," [1] and although its original influence was
becoming progressively feebler, none the less in principle
it remained one of the modes whereby law was fashioned. In
certain instances therefore in which the Scriptures were
either mute or ambiguous, and a certain tradition seemed to
favour his views, Tertullian bade people note that custom,
by the very fact that it is a custom, enshrines its justification
in itself.[2] *Consuetudo* evidently proceeds from *traditio*. But
in order to render valid this *traditio*, was a written origin
necessary as the " liberal " party pretended ? Not the least
in the world. Tradition, even without this *point d'appui*
of origin, was perfectly admissible. Did not a thousand
examples drawn from Christian practice prove this super-
abundantly ? Had Christ anywhere ordained the pro-
nouncing at the moment of baptism the words : " I renounce
Satan, his pomps and his angels " ? Where is it written
that we must sign ourselves with the sign of the Cross on so
many occasions ? etc. . . . All these practices have no other
authority than that of custom : *traditio auctrix, consuetudo
confirmatrix, fides observatrix*. And, as a final deduction,
it is reason which brings her support to tradition itself :
*Rationem traditioni et consuetudini et fidei patrocinaturam aut
ipse perspicies aut ab aliquo qui perspexerit disces*. From this
follows, concludes Tertullian, that in default of a definite law
it is custom which provides the law—just as in civil law—and
this law has sufficient justification in the authority of reason.

Has he made an end of it ? By no means. He hastens to
exclude a portion of this last consideration in order to guard
himself against " customs " which are too beneficent to prevent any objections which might by chance be brought against
him. If reason is a legitimate authority, why should she not
pass judgment on a tradition whenever the latter should be
found not to have explicit connection with a precept of our

---

[1] E. Cuq, *les Instit. Jurid. des Romains*, vol. I, p. 20–21 ; 168 et s. ; vol. II,
p. 17, and the article *Mores* by the same author in the *Dict. des Antiq.* (III, 2,
2001) ; Ihering, *Esprit du Droit Romain*, trans. Meulenaere, Ghent and Paris
2 ed. 1880, vol. II, p. 28 et s.

[2] *De Cor.*, ii et s.

Lord or of the Apostles ? Better still, why not reduce to law all that reason prescribes ? Why should it not be lawful to each believer (*omni fideli*) to do this, provided that the rule established be in conformity with the designs of God and that it be profitable in the matter of discipline and contribute to salvation ? Has not God said : " Judge not of yourselves that which is just " ? And did St Paul do anything else when he gave counsels in his own name under the patronage of divine reason ?

Here we can well discern the real character of Tertullian : a passionate attachment to his own private judgment which, instead of frankly avowing it, seeks to justify his craving for making rules by a complete, complicated, and abstruse system. Tertullian would have liked to rigidly define every single thing by authority. But his Catholic sense of tradition, of things to be respected on account of their long continuity, or of the source whence they derived, restrained this individualistic craving. And it was a question with him how to reconcile more nearly these contradictory tendencies through the instrumentality of stratagems and sophisms.

Moreover, this kind of artifice, though useful in masking the weak spots in a line of argument carried to its last extremity, could not satisfy his own sense of logic nor long deceive those whom he had for a moment dazzled. He was in the position of a judge firmly convinced of the necessity of repressing certain evils for whom the " arsenal " of the law provided no suitable weapon. A living and divinely inspired message alone would have been capable of supplementing the insufficiencies of the *Sancti Commentarii*, or the silences and lack of rigour of tradition. But where could this voice be found to make itself heard in warning the *frivola et frigida fides* of the mass of Christians and in supplying a remedy against their weakness of character ?

Such was the moral condition of the inexorable *intransigeant* when he came into touch with Montanism, or at any rate when he decided to make a profound study of it.

VIII

How did he come to know about it ? We cannot tell. It is certain that he had in his hands a collection of Montanist oracles, thanks to which he was put into direct contact with the thought and manner of life of the Phrygian prophets. Many things therein must have shocked him : for instance, the *rôle* that devolved upon women in the sect, and the leaven of anarchy that was contained in this doctrine wherein the " Holy Spirit " was everything. But side by side with these displeasing features, what seductive ideas he there met with ! It will suffice to record his confessions thereon.

What struck him first was the respect in which doctrine was held by Montanus, and his disdain for purely theoretical questions.

Montanism accepted the Christian revelation as an accomplished fact, as a venerable tradition, and as a heritage on which no man might lay hands. Far from endeavouring (as was the case with Gnosticism) to dissolve by analysis its elements in order to put them together again with the aid of speculation, he reverently sought from them the means of justifying his own task and advertised no other ambition than to realise an expressed promise of Christ. There was nothing among those who propagated his doctrine to render them open to the charge of spiritual pride.

In addition, this doctrine appeared to have no other object in view than how to live. The ideal which it proposed to itself was altogether moral, and its object was not at all *knowledge* so much as *practice*. With its face set entirely on the future of mankind, whose destiny it assumed henceforward to be tottering to its fall, it took care not to go in search of any justifications which might favour dereliction from ordinary duties, which might serve as a cloak to laxities of the senses, or to secret infamies of the flesh. What could be more appetising to the soul of Tertullian ? What more reassuring to the rigour of his puritanism ?

Then, what a delightful surprise to see blossoming again in the bosom of Montanism all those religious phenomena whose signification the Scriptures, and especially the Epistles of St Paul, had revealed to him—predictions about the future, the reading of hearts, improvised psalms, visions, spiritual utterances spoken in ecstasy ! As more and more fully he gave credence to the Phrygian seers, a twofold feeling came over him : first he felt better, purer, and had the impression of a moral renovation in which his *ego* was lifted up ;[1] then, thanks to their clear teaching on the Paraclete, a host of problems on which hitherto his explanations had had an uncertain note through lack of explicit and unequivocal texts, received the most luminous solution, and one too which was least tolerant of the lack of firmness shown by so many Catholics.[2]

Tertullian was in search of a Code, and here he had found one which at once supplied him with a moral rule conformable to his secret desires, and an authority able to impose it by referring it to a divine source. How could he refuse to make it his own ? It was the mind of the ardent lawyer that was first conquered and fixed his choice when it came to having to decide between Montanism and the Church.

It was not sufficient for him to be personally convinced that he had made this choice with discernment and wisdom : he felt bound in addition to impose it upon others and to discover arguments which would be likely to make them become its adherents. His whole personality was formed upon opposition, and had grown great thereby. From the first awakening of his curiosity in Montanism up to his complete submission, a long and burning series of meditations took place in him, stirred up by the attacks or the replies of his enemies. It is probable that influences came from without to spur him on and to precipitate the rupture. St Jerome mentions one of them definitely : " *Invidia posthac et contumeliis clericorum romanae ecclesiae ad Montani dogma delapsus. . . .*"[3] It was therefore jealousy and the insults of the Roman clergy that drove Tertullian to the point. We do not know the details of this quarrel. But to make up for this we can clearly distinguish the fundamental questions around which the dispute turned whether at Carthage, or perhaps at Rome. These were : (A) Ecstasy ; (B) Flight during Persecution ; (C) Re-marriage ; (D) The Fasts ; (E) Penance.

A.—ECSTASY

In default of the *De Ecstasi*, which has been unhappily lost, several passages scattered through the works of Tertullian

---

[1] *De Pudic.* I, ii.
[2] *De Resurr. Carnis*, lxiii ; *De Fuga*, i ; *Adv. Pr.*, xiii.
[3] *De Vir. Ill.*, liii.

allow us to piece together approximately the thesis he there
defends so far as it touches upon the lawfulness of ecstatic
revelations.

Were they bound not to accept these "*charismata*" as
authentic? This was certainly not the only question for
him, but it was the point round which centred the disagreement between the Catholics and Montanists. He has too
often stated this to allow of any doubt in the matter. It
was important therefore to justify the form in which these
"*charismata*" manifested themselves in the Montanists, since
their adversaries drew therefrom a pretext for declaring them
diabolic.[1] In the eyes of Tertullian *ecstasis* was a state
produced in a normal manner during sleep. The soul lost
in that state its sense of its surroundings; its faculties of
sense were suspended; the power of conscious reflection
became stupefied; images, which it ceased to direct of its free
will, assailed it. However, it preserved the memory of what
it had thought it had seen and heard. God permitted this
mode of special activity sometimes to take on a religious
character and signification. Whether in sleep *or even apart
from sleep*, the state of ecstasy, *amentia*, was the modification
through which of necessity the human reason passes at the
moment when it enters into direct relation with God. Visions
and prophecies therefore postulated it of necessity.

This is the essence of Tertullian's doctrine, under reserve of
supplementary proofs on which he had to support it.

We note how wise, serious, how little revolutionary it is.
Of the " frenzy " with which in the course of their vaticina-
tions the heralds of the new prophetic spirit were animated,
not a word. He eliminates this element from his definition,
although it was of capital import as an historical reality,
and had excited so much distrust. Avoiding in this manner
all confusion with the pagan *mantique*, he retains only the
theory of the occasional loss of personality by the seer in
order to give it strenuous support.

---

[1] See especially the *De Anima*, xliii et s., and P. de Labriolle, *La Crise Montaniste*, p. 365 et s. This treatise *De Anima* is extremely rich in the matter of
psychological and even physiological observations; it is one of those which best
shows the variety of Tertullian's learning.

B.—FLIGHT DURING PERSECUTION

To be prepared for martyrdom was, in those uncertain times, one of the objects with which every fervent Christian was concerned. But the Church did not impose upon the faithful the absolute duty of steadfastly waiting for arrest, torture, and perhaps death. Polycarp, the Bishop of Smyrna, yielding to the entreaties of his friends, had taken refuge in a small house in the country in the outskirts of the town. A similar attitude had been, or might have been, that of Clement of Alexandria, Origen, St Cyprian and of many other personages of incontestable courage. In Africa, not only the laics, but also the pastors themselves did not hesitate, when the occasion arose, to place themselves beyond the reach of their persecutors. Not long before, Tertullian had taken no scandal at this : " Etiam in persecutionibus," he had written in his *Ad Uxorem* (I, iii), " *melius est ex permissu fugere* quam comprehensum et distortum negare." And again, in the *De Patientia* (xiii) : " *Si fuga urgeat,* incommoda fugae caro militat."

The teaching of the Paraclete forced him to withdraw this concession. " Nearly all the utterances " of the Paraclete were an exhortation to martyrdom ; two of the *oracles* quoted by Tertullian expressly requested this of the faithful Christian. As for those who ran away, the Paraclete did not hesitate to " brand " them ; to make up for this, he promised his assistance to whosoever should not shrink from its terrors and torments.

There is nothing to equal the easy assurance with which Tertullian executed the necessary *volte-face*. Without troubling to excuse his inconsistency, he and his new associates set themselves to denounce as unlawful every attempt to elude persecution.

In his *De Fuga*, he laid down a principle destined to make clear all that followed. Did persecution come from God or from the devil ? Of a surety it comes from God since it exalts the faith and makes the servants of God " better." The devil is only its instrument ; it is God who is its author, and who unchains it when it pleases Him in order to prove or to chastise the just. Therefore, however evil it may appear to man's fallible judgment, persecution was a good thing in itself : *nullo modo fugiendum erit quod a Deo evenit* (§ iv). It was likewise unworthy to buy oneself off at the price of money, to treat with informers, soldiers or the judges. These negotiations were a disguised form of apostasy, a crafty method of " flight " : *Pedibus stetisti, cucurristi nummis. . . . Negatio est etiam martyrii recusatio. . . . Non quaeritur qui latam viam sequi paratus sit, sed qui angustam.*

C.—RE-MARRIAGE

Was it, aye or no, lawful from the religious point of view to re-marry ? To-day the problem appears to be without much interest ; it is curious to have to state that during several centuries eminent minds were preoccupied—and doubtless as many souls were tortured—with moral difficulties which are nothing more than a matter of individual delicacy.

But if discussions on re-marriage have lost almost all value at the present time, at least they retain an historical importance : they clearly show the strength of the principle of asceticism held towards the beginning of the IIIrd century ; on this question also Tertullian betrays some of his most secret *arrière-pensées*, and, in the opinion of St Augustine,[1] it was the unbending attitude which he took up on this question which made him a " heretic," by the very fact that he assumed a position contrary to that maintained by the Apostle St Paul.

St Paul[2] had nowhere concealed his very clear preference for the celibate ; but, preserved by superior good sense from all excessive severity, he had contended on principle that the change from celibacy to marriage was in no wise sinful, and he had even gone so far to admit the lawfulness of re-marriage.

Such approximately are the *nuances* of the Pauline view. It was to interpret these *nuances*, to press them to an undue point, or even to force them against their real tenor, that

---

[1] *Haer.*, lxxxvi ; *Ep. ad Julianam Viduam*, iv, 6 (P.L., XL, 433).
[2] Cf. Ist Ep. to the Corinthians, vii.

Tertullian applied the infinite resources of his sophistic reasoning in three treatises.

The order of succession of the *Ad Uxorem*, of the *De Exhortatione Castitatis* and of the *De Monogamia*, is easy to determine. We do not notice in the *Ad Uxorem* any declaration relating to Montanism. Further, Tertullian expressly recognises in it that a Christian may take flight from persecution, which he was to deny in the *De Fuga*. In the *De Exhortatione Castitatis*, the ditch had been leapt over, for Tertullian there quotes an oracle of the " holy prophetess Prisca " ; but, besides this being the only mention of her, the fact that he abstains from all savage allusions to the Catholics, gives colour to the idea that, though he had already been conquered by Montanism, he had nevertheless not yet entirely effected his breach with the Church. On the other hand, no doubt is possible in regard to the *De Monogamia*. It is an aggressive and violent work in which he no longer extends any compromise.

In one work after another, therefore, further advances are made manifest, and we can follow the development of Tertullian's opinions on re-marriage from entire orthodoxy to declared Montanism.

It becomes evident that Montanism had scarcely modified his ideas radically. The *Ad Uxorem* contains, at least in germ, the greater part of the arguments developed in the two subsequent treatises. From the time when he wrote it, the antipathies in his mind gained in strength. Nevertheless, he represented perseverance in widowhood as being eminently profitable to the moral life rather than as a positive obligation : " *Nam etsi non delinquas renubendo. . . .* " [1] Once he had become attached to the Phrygian doctrine, he changed a counsel into a precept, and such a formal precept that all derogation therefrom was likened by him to *stuprum*. The tone of his discussion changes also. In the *De Monogamia*, he affects to consider his adversaries as beings wholly in servitude to their senses, and whose reasonings had nothing intellectual about them. He takes them to task even in their persons, their secret vices, and the shamelessness of their party. He makes no hesitation in alluding to an ignominious scandal in which, it appears, he had included the Bishop of

[1] *Ad Ux.*, I, vii.

Uthina, one of the Roman colonies in Africa. He fights for his cause with all his heart and soul by crushing these sensual-minded people who disguise their passions under principles.

His attitude towards marriage in itself is fairly ambiguous. On several occasions he repeats that he has no wish to proscribe it, but only to apply thereto the rule of temperance. But looking at it closely, however, what contradictions, what malevolent insinuations, what morose lectures ! If he does not go quite to extremes, if he is content to cast over marriage a sour discredit, instead of simply disapproving of it, the reason is that at first Montanus himself had not gone to that length, and secondly because he feared to be mixed up on this account with the ranks of his detested enemies, the Marcionists, who themselves condemned without restriction the union of the sexes. He had eloquently fought Marcion on this point ; he did not dare, however much he might have wished, to appear to justify subsequently the heresiarch and his deep-rooted asceticism.

D.—FASTING

With regard to fasting, his principal effort seems to have aimed at setting up in Carthage the practices enjoined by Montanus, which consisted either in complete obligatory fasting, or in prolonging, of obligation, certain fasts far beyond the usual limits of the " xerophagies." [1]

We can imagine how these rigorous and precise Montanist rules must have pleased Tertullian : all the postulates of his reason and all the instincts of his authoritative temperament there encountered their absolute satisfaction and blossomed forth in combative activity.

What seemed to be outrageous to the non-Montanist Catholics was this arrogant attempt to render nugatory, in the name of the *prophetia nova*, all individual initiative, and the substitution of a series of heavy mortifications *ex imperio* for mortifications which were *ex arbitrio*. Herein lay an encroachment whose lack of moderation threatened

[1] For the nature of the xerophagic *régime*, see *De Jej.*, I. Cf. P. de Labriolle, *op. cit*, p. 399–400, for a picture of the Montanist fasts as compared with the Catholic.

the daily independence of everyone much more than his prohibition relating to re-marriage. Hence arose a general revolt against the pseudo-Paraclete, author of these dangerous concepts, whom the Catholics identified with the " devil " and " Anti-Christ," and against the band of " false prophets." The safest refuge offered for their defence seemed to the Catholics to lie in the Scriptures and in tradition, that is to say, the customs hitherto in force. All non-scriptural and non-traditional rules were proclaimed as a foolish novelty and a suspicious imitation of Judaic devotions, or the rites of Apis, Cybele and Isis.[1]

Tertullian could not fail to defend the authority of the Paraclete thus diminished.

His discussion is one of most rare insolence. The word *gula* occurs a dozen times in the *De Jejunio*. Guzzlers, greedy to fill their bellies, who covered their disgusting appetites under respectable terms—these are some of the features under which he depicts his adversaries. Further, gluttons were voluptuous : gluttony with them resolved itself into lasciviousness, *per edacitatem salacitas transit*. And Tertullian develops the picture and defines its leading characteristics with entire lack of modesty. The whole of chapter I is full of obscenities. There is nothing in his language more unchaste than this raving preacher of chastity.

E.—PENANCE

There remains the question of penance. Of all those we have found space to study in regard to Tertullian, this question is the most important. Not that Tertullian had approached it with any new dispositions : he shows himself in the *De Pudicitia*, which is especially devoted to this subject, such as we have seen him in the *De Monogamia* and the *De Jejunio*,—just as violent, just as sternly decided to *oblige* men to become better, and to transform the Church so far as it depended upon him, into a community of saints. But this time the dispute between Catholics and Montanists was not concerned solely with discipline : *a problem of a dogmatic order, the problem of the " Power of the Keys," was*

[1] *De Jej.*, xi ; xiv ; xvi.

involved in it. Tertullian was bound to take up a position ; and thus he was forced to modify, not only his old treatises on penance, but also some portions of his conceptions of the Church and of the prerogatives attaching to the clerical hierarchy.

To begin with the *De Paenitentia.* I have mentioned the comparatively temperate and benignant character of this work. In it Tertullian admitted that the sinner who had fallen after baptism into one or more grave sins, had still the right to be pardoned *once.* How different appears the spirit animating the *De Pudicitia,* even from the most superficial study !

From the very first pages, Tertullian allows his wrath to break forth. The adversary to whom he takes exception is a Bishop, a Roman Bishop without doubt. The identification of this Bishop is a problem to which very different solutions have been given. It is commonly enough admitted to-day (but without decisive proofs), that it was Callistus who was aimed at.[1] Now at that time, Callistus, by a public act, by a ruling read in the assemblies of the faithful, had just made known that he authorised fornicators and adulterers to re-enter the Church after due penance. With what abusive irony does Tertullian turn into ridicule the proud language of the Pontiff and (to him) the cunning hypocrisy of his allocution ! And it is not only by this sectarian mood that his Montanism declares itself, but also by a notable change in his ideas as regards penance and to all purposes by an appreciable evolution in doctrine. " The marks of shame borne by the flesh which has been soiled subsequently to baptism cannot be washed away by penance " (XII, I), is the new principle with which he is inspired. There are some sins which a Christian must no longer commit : the Church, the spotless virgin, cannot countenance a stain. For sins like these there is no pity ; and the guilty one need look no further to her ! He disavows without hesitation the restrained conception which he had developed in the *De Paenitentia.* In chapter xxi, he even goes so far as to take away her power of pardoning from the Church of the " psychics " (in these words he describes the Catholic Church constituted

---

[1] For recent discussions however, cf. K. Adam, *das sogen. Bussedikt des Papstes Kallistus,* Munich, 1917 (*Veroff. aus dem Kirchenhist. Seminar Munchen,* iv, 5).

with her Hierarchy) in order to transfer it into the hands of the truly " spiritual " Church, the Montanist Church which at any rate will not make use of it except in altogether exceptional cases.   And he is by no means sure that in this he has not exceeded the hardihood of Montanus himself in order to satisfy the demand of his own personal views and of his controversial attitude.

Taken as a whole, a careful examination of the Montanist treatises of Tertullian proves that we should be wrong in rigorously identifying the original Montanism with that bearing the mark of Tertullian's works.   At the time when he fell under the influence of the doctrine of the Phrygian prophets, he was in the full maturity of his thought and in full exercise of his talents.   From that moment it was inevitable that in giving in his adherence he should put his impress on it and should adapt it in some degree to his own conception.   In his theory of ecstasy, as we have seen, he guards against lègitimatising the physical excesses whereof the protagonists of the sect had given a rather scandalous exhibition in the East ;   with knowing hand he shaded off all that savoured of irregularity, incoherency, and morbidity in the Phrygian cult of prophesying.   He also endeavoured (it is one of the *leit-motifs* of his discussions) to link it up with the past, and to persuade his readers that these so-called innovations of the " Paraclete " had nothing revolutionary in them, and that they might be found outlined or in germ if one only read the Scriptures carefully.   On the somewhat frail theological web of primitive Montanism, he wove his fantastic theory of successive revelations explaining the necessary outcome of the plan inaugurated by God from the beginning of Creation by the operation of the Paraclete— a gradual development in discipline, in the sense of an ever-increasing rigour, and not as an evolution of the rule of faith which, according to him, was not susceptible of any further progress in matter of doctrine.

In his heart of hearts, he would have passionately liked to have the Montanist cult of prophecy " recognised " and authorised.   Feeling at last that the Church—an organism founded on a Hierarchy and containing the great majority of the faithful—would be irreducible, he took the step of separating himself from her.   In other respects, he preserved intact his symbol of faith, his respect for the Scriptures, and his theory of prescription and the apostolic character of the Churches. Against dissentients, he continued to write vigorous treatises wherein, on more than one occasion, he has given to certain dogmatic formulae their almost definitive expression, as in the *Adversus Praxean*, the *De Resurrectione Carnis*, the *Scorpiace*, the *De Carne Christi*, etc.

Hampered by a past which he was not willing totally to disavow, he arrived at strange compromises and disastrous combinations, whereof no one better than he could appreciate the weak points. From the psychological and religious point of view, his case is one of extreme interest, in which there mingles some pity in regard to this strong mind struggling on incoherently and without succeeding, in spite of so much sophistry, in getting away from himself.

IX

FROM the literary point of view, Tertullian may perhaps be compared with the most striking representatives of Latin literature in the time of the emperors. This is a truth which is sometimes overlooked but of which anyone who shall have held any close commune with his works will be irresistibly convinced. It is distressing to see with what ill-natured incompetence his language and style have been sometimes appreciated : we have David Ruhnken, the German philologist of the XVIIIth century,[1] pedantically declaring : " Tertullianum latinitatis certe pessimum auctorem esse aio et confirmo " ; and Auguste Matthiae [2] branding him on account of his " barbarous " language ; Courdaveaux [3] deplores " that such a man, as great from the qualities of his heart as from the courage of his views, should only have as a vehicle for his ideas *a poor provincial patois* even more unsuited than the real Latin tongue for abstract discussions, and which he wrote in so obscure a style that his thought is even more difficult to disentangle than that of St Paul."

---

[1] Ruhnken passed a portion of his life at Leyden, but he was a native of Pomerania. Ruhnken's opinion is quoted at length by E. F. Leopold in the *Zeitsch. f. hist. Theol.* VIII (1838), p. 33.

[2] *Grundriss der Gesch. d. griech. und rom. Litt.*, 3rd ed., Iena, 1834, p. 221.

[3] *Revue de l'Hist. des Relig.*, XIII (1891), p. 1.

The truth is that Tertullian adhered strictly to the literary tradition of his age. He knew the methods of "artistic prose" as they had been formed among the Greeks under the influence of Gorgias, Isocrates, Theophrastus of Eresos and of the rhetoricians of Asia, which Cicero had permitted himself to appropriate, adapting them to the genius of the Latin tongue. Anaphora, alliterations, and symmetrical divisions by κῶλα, etc.—all this *technique* of rhetoric was familiar to him ; and his works present numerous examples. It was not a question of the metrical rules governing the cadence of a sentence, which he generally observed in his terminations.[1] This was the common ground of the Roman tradition which the schools had preserved and transmitted from one generation to another. In addition, Tertullian was contemporary with Apuleius whose works he had certainly read.[2] A taste for variety in his vocabulary, a love of " uncommon "' forms of expression, certain affectations in style, and certain obscurities of thought may have come to him from that source. We shall never know all the richness of his vocabulary until a complete inventory, which does not exist at present, shall have been drawn up of it. He has been called " the real creator of the Latin of the Church." [3] This opinion is perhaps not absolutely exact, for we must reckon the part which belongs to the anonymous translators of the Bible. But it is clear that he largely contributed to that collective work by which the appearance of the Latin tongue was renovated. His creations of new words are innumerable : the specialists hold that they appear to be conformable after a general fashion to the rules governing their Latin derivation.[4] Likewise his syntax, with the exception of slight peculiarities, remains in line with that used by his contemporaries.[5] But he coined words and phrases such as no writer since Tacitus had had the ability to do, because his genius animated, vivified and inflamed all he wrote.

[1] Out of 852 terminations to chapters, one can count only 43, or 5 per cent. in which the closing words are not certainly of a rhythmic cadence.
[2] Cf. Kellner, *Ueber die. sprachl. Eigentumlichkeiten Tert.*, in *Theol. Quart.*, lviii (1876), p. 229 ; C. Weyman, *St zu Apuleius u. seinen Nachahmern*, in the *Sitz.-Ber. d. Bayer. Ak.* 1893, II, p. 340–343 and 352 : Van Der Vliet, *Studia eccles.*, Leyden, 1891, I, p. 9 et s. ; E. Norden, *die Antike Kunstprosa*, p. 614–615.
[3] Harnack, A.C.L., I, 667 ; cf. Norden, *op. cit.*, p. 607.
[4] Hoppe, *Synt. u. Stit. des* T., L. 1903, p. 115.
[5] *Ibid.*, p. 114.

Formed on the discipline of juridical learning, he illuminated his theological discussions with clear-cut forms which the West was to appropriate (*una substantia, tres personae ; duae substantiae, una persona ;* and, for the distinction between the Divine persons, *distinctio, non divisio, discreti, non separati ;* for the distinction between the two natures in Christ, *conjunctio, non confusio,* etc.). Then, although marked by a hereditary culture, his dominating and original personality exercised a sovereign mastery of the forms he used. Unlike Minucius Felix or Lactantius and so many other Christian writers, we hardly ever surprise him practising the art of stealing his turns of phrase and similies from the classics. He disdained these lawful pilferings. It is in very truth his own vigour which circulates through so many sturdy and subtile pages. Far from impairing his literary gifts, Montanism gave them their full scope. Here and there there may be found a certain fastidious oppressiveness in his treatises at the beginning, in the *De Baptismo* and the *De Paenitentia,* for example. Montanism put his temperament at ease, long held in check by the fear of saying too much, and by certain scruples which were henceforth to vanish. And this wrathful and passionate soul breathed itself forth still more freely in that he believed that he was representing the true religious ideal in face of the lapses which dishonoured it in bringing it down to their level. His last treatises are brimful of sophistry, yet, notwithstanding, Tertullian was never so keen, so vibrating, so urgent and at the same time so pathetic.

When one has tasted the pleasure produced by his combative prose, one experiences some difficulty in not finding a certain insipidity in the purer and more sugary style recommended by classic "good taste." It has some strange condensations which in places render it formidable ; but it is a triumph of mind to have succeeded in piercing through some of its obscurities.

X

A CONSIDERATION of the *Passion* of Saints Perpetua and Felicitas should be taken in connection with Tertullian. We shall see a little further on the reason for this. On reading this celebrated little account, instinct with such ardent and pure exaltation and with such touching and graceful simplicity, hardly spoilt here and there by a suspicion of rhetoric, we can easily understand it.   Chapter I forms a prologue which we owe to the compiler who has pieced together the different portions of the account.   In Chapter II, this compiler relates in a few words the simultaneous arrest of Vibia Perpetua, a young woman of twenty-two, educated and of good family, of two young people, Saturninus and Secundulus, and of two slaves, Revocatus and Felicitas—all catechumens. (Shortly after, a certain Saturus, who had instructed them, was to give himself up of his own free will : § iv.)   He then states that he will leave Perpetua to continue the narrative, who drew up in her own hand the account of their sufferings. We then have the narrative of Perpetua herself beginning at § iii : she brought it to a close at the end of § x remarking that she stopped on the eve of the combat, and that it must be left to another to relate, if he will, what was to take place in the amphitheatre.   At the beginning of § xi, the compiler takes up his pen again, but only for an instant : he merely adds the description given by Saturus himself of the visions which were vouchsafed to the martyr in his prison.   All the last part of the *Acta* from § xiv is by the compiler who, in carrying out his own wish or rather as he says, the *fideicommissum* of Perpetua, traces a picture of the wonderful struggle of the martyrs and their bloody death, and in a peroration whose spirit is altogether analogous to that which is breathed in the prologue, accentuates the lesson which comes forth from these examples.

We must therefore represent to ourselves the incidents very much as follows : Perpetua and Saturus found leisure in their dungeon to draw up a short account of the sufferings they were enduring, and especially of the " graces " which God sent to them.[1]   These notes fell into the hands of a witness of their torment who takes information therefrom complementary to what he had not been able to see with his own eyes,[2] completes the narrative given by the martyrs and, out of these diverse elements, forms a complete story which he encloses in a moral and religious exhortation.   There are

[1] § ii : " sicut conscriptum manu sua et suo sensu reliquit " ; § xi : " visionem, quam ipse conscripsit ".   Cf. § xiv.
[2] E.G. § xv.

thus two portions to distinguish in these *Acta :* the portion of the compiler and that of the martyrs themselves.

Some traces of Montanism have sometimes been thought to emerge from the passages explicitly attributed to Perpetua and Saturus. Thus, a point has been made of the four *visions* of Perpetua and that related also by Saturus. But how were these visions a Montanist phenomenon in a special degree ? There were very few in ancient times (I will say pagan as well as Christian) who had any doubts as to the religious signification of such warnings.

The case of the compiler is very different. I think we may boldly identify him with Tertullian, and for reasons of an entirely philological order. It is *his* style, *his* language, *his* phraseology.[1] His Montanism, which had not yet been declared but was already in full religious effervescence, is likewise betrayed (the text must have been written shortly after the years 202–3, the date of the martyrdom).

What was his aim in the twofold dedication with which the *Passion* begins and closes ? He desired to show that the activity of the Holy Spirit has in no way diminished ; that its " virtue " remains permanent ; that God continues to fulfil his promises in " invisible proofs for infidels, favours for believers." Only a weak faith, a faith at its last gasp (*imbecillitas aut desperatio fidei*) could imagine that the Divine grace only dwelt within " the men of old time " and that the present age was excluded from it. It was thus a pious duty and a sure means to edification to put on record in writing (*digerere*) the graces recently given, just as it had been at the birth of Christianity in the case of the " old examples of faith." No preoccupation could be more correct.

But there is something else in this prologue. In the opinion of the author, the flood of grace had never been so abundant : there was an *exuperatio gratiae* and that was because the end of the world was quite near, and because God, by the mouth of his prophet Joel, had promised an " outpouring " of His Spirit " on all flesh " during the last days.

What is still more startling is that the compiler (let us say, Tertullian) takes upon himself to include in the *instrumentum Ecclesiae* the recent visions and also the " new prophecies." *Instrumentum* in legal language meant every

[1] Cf. P. de Labriolle, *la Crise Montaniste*, pp. 345–351.

document claiming credence, and all written proof. It is evidently in this sense that he here uses this word. But if we are to believe that by *instrumentum* Tertullian means merely the *Corpus* of Scripture, we must note an ambiguity, under cover of which some vexatious confusion might arise.

The *Passion*, which is very attractive of itself, becomes still more so in so far as it reveals to us the state of mind of Tertullian in the first phase of his adhesion to Montanism.

E

BOOK II

THE IIIʀᴅ CENTURY

DOWN TO THE PEACE OF THE CHURCH (313)

CHAPTER I

THE *OCTAVIUS* OF MINUCIUS FELIX

BIBLIOGRAPHY

THE manuscript numbered 1661, IXth century, in the Bibliothèque Nationale in Paris, which contains the seven books of Arnobius, *Adversus Nationes*, holds also an eighth book which is no other than the *Octavius*. The difference in tone and style between the *Adversus Nationes* and the *Octavius* is striking. However, the title *Octavius*, without doubt, read incorrectly as *Octavus* (the eighth), conduced in the Middle Ages to a confusion which the first editors of Arnobius did not perceive. It was only in 1560 that the oversight was rectified by François Beaudoin (Balduinus) in his Heidelberg edition.

The text of the *Parisinus*, transcribed by a copyist who was clearly very ignorant, swarms with mistakes. There is in Brussels a manuscript of the XIth-XIIth century, which is only a copy of the *Parisinus*.

Editions: P.L., III, 239-376; C.V., II (1867), by Halm; H. Boenig, in B.T. (1903); J. P. Waltzing, Louvain, 1903; Bruges, 1909, B.T. (1912): there is important documentation in these three editions; G. Rauschen, F.P. fasc. VIII (1913).

French translations: J. P. Waltzing, Louvain, 1902; Bruges, 1909; Louvain, 1914.

Consult: J. P. Waltzing, *Lexicon Minucianum*, Liége and Paris, 1909; Monceaux, I, 462-508; B. ph. W. 1914, 1452 (*coup d'œil* of collective bibliography relating to the *Octavius*); C. Synnerberg, *Die neuesten Beitraege zur Minutius-Literatur*, Helsingfors, 1914; *Hermes*, 1915, 456-463 and 609-623; *Bursian*, vol. 170/173 (1916), p. 57.

SUMMARY

I. Minucius Felix.—II. The *Octavius* analysed.—III. The religious bearing of the *Octavius*.—IV. Literary art in the *Octavius*.—V. The priority of the *Apologeticum* over the *Octavius*.

I

" THE pearl of apologetic literature " is what Ernest Renan called the *Octavius*.[1] To this judgment it is difficult not to subscribe after reading this well-ordered dialogue, so happily written, in which is revealed such agreeable goodwill to convince without offending anyone.

Lactantius wrote of the author in his *Inst. Div.*, V, 1, 21 :

---

[1] *Marc. Aurèle*, p. 389.

" Among the defenders of our cause known to me, Minucius
Felix occupied a very distinguished rank at the bar.　His
book entitled *Octavius* shows what an excellent champion
of the truth he could have been had he devoted himself
entirely to this kind of study."　St Jerome mentions him in
various places, notably in the *De Viris Illustribus*, LVIII :
" *Minucius Felix, Romae insignis causidicus, scripsit dialogum
christiani et ethnici disputantis, qui Octavius inscribitur.*"
He tells us that Minucius had also composed a *De Fato*.

The information given by Lactantius and Jerome is
corroborated by the work itself from which doubtless Lactantius and Jerome obtained it.　As a matter of fact, it
comes out in § ii, 3, and xxviii, 3, that Minucius was
practising the calling of an advocate.　He calls himself
Marcus Minucius Felix (cf. III, 1 ; V, 1).　From his own
testimony (I, 4 ; V, 1), he had been a pagan for a long time,
and then he was converted.

Jerome tells us that he exercised his profession in Rome,
and this is confirmed by § ii.　It is thought that he must
have been of African origin.　The name of a Minucius Felix
has been discovered on a column at Tebessa [1] and on a dedication found at Carthage.[2]　Certain very strong expressions
on the Roman sway (xxv, 4–5), surprising from the lips
of a Roman of the old stock, are more comprehensible in the
case of a provincial.　In another respect points of style reveal
the familiarity of the author with African writers such as
Frontonius, Flaurus, Apuleius and Tertullian.

The other characters taking part in the dialogue are not
necessarily imaginary, which does not imply nevertheless
that the conversation which Minucius is supposed to be
describing really took place.　It was the ordinary practice of
Cicero, the model favoured by the author, to represent
characters he had known or whose name was familiar to
the Roman public in discussion, in order to convey his views
in a more or less fictitious setting.

About Octavius Januarius (cf. XV, 2), who gives the name
to the work, we know nothing more than what is contained
in it.　A married man and father of a family (II, 1), he was
converted at the same time as Minucius or even a little before

---

[1] C.I.L., viii, 1964.
[2] *Ibid.*, Suppl. 12, 499.

him (I, 4). The name of one Octavius Januarius figures in an inscription found at Bougie (C.I.L., viii, 1962).

As regards the third interlocutor, Caecilius Natalis, some lively discussions have been provoked by certain epigraphic discoveries made between the years 1853 and 1859. In two places in the course of the dialogue, allusion is made to Frontonius who was born at Cirta. In § ix, 6, Caecilius says : " *id etiam Cirtensis nostri testatur oratio* " ; and Octavius goes on to refute the alleged calumny by employing these words : *Fronto tuus* (xxxi, 2). From merely reading the dialogue there is then some temptation to suppose that Caecilius was a native of Cirta. Now five inscriptions have been recovered at Cirta of the years 212–217, which come from a triumphal arch erected by M. Caecilius Natalus as a mark of appreciation for his election to the dignity of quin-quennial triumvir.[1] This coincidence is interesting. However there are some difficulties which render the identification uncertain and we have no reason to insist too much on it.

II

THE dialogue opens with the author confiding to us his ardent affection for Octavius now no longer living. The memory of this dear friend and the perfect community of their senti-ments had recently returned to him with singular force. From being both pagans had they not together passed " to the light of wisdom and of truth " ? And his thoughts thus wandering over those happy years dwell on the conversations in which Octavius succeeded in bringing in Caecilius to the true religion.

Minucius Felix details in a leisurely manner the circum-stances which surrounded the incident which he is going to relate (II–IV).

Taking advantage of the Courts being in vacation, Octavius, Minucius Felix, and Caecilius his intimate friend, have betaken themselves to Ostia, a country resort favoured by the Romans. One morning they direct their footsteps towards the sea, with the breeze blowing in their faces, when Caecilius, per-ceiving a statue of Serapis, brings his hand to his mouth

[1] C.I.L., viii, 1, 7094–7098 ; cf. 6996.

after the pagan rite, and imprints on it a kiss. His friends notice the action, and in a few ironical words Octavius reproaches Minucius Felix for allowing his dear Caecilius to fall into such childish practices. These stinging words are not noticed at first. The three friends continue their walk and amuse themselves with looking at the different objects which meet their eye. But the taciturn and wounded expression of Caecilius at last strikes his companions. On being questioned, Caecilius confesses that the shaft levelled by Octavius just now has wounded him keenly and that he wishes to have a thorough explanation with him. The three friends take up a position on a dyke going out some distance into the sea ; Minucius Felix is to preside over the debate. All is ready : Caecilius opens the discussion and begins to plead his cause.

This prelude written in a soothing cadence and refined elegance, discloses a skilful art and one fully master of its own resources.

The speech of Caecilius (V–XIII) is appreciably shorter than the reply which Octavius is going to give. However, in making the " Devil's advocate " speak, the author has not thought it necessary to put in his mouth futile arguments which might be refuted with ease. No intentioned arrangement weakens the expression of the pagan's complaint.

Caecilius begins with a formal declaration of agnosticism. Mystery envelops us. For us the universe is a riddle which passes our understanding, and it is at once wiser and more religious to leave it in peace. The Christians pretend to solve it—they, unlettered people ! How ridiculous ! It was a fact that nowhere have we been able to discern in action any Divine intervention, a Providence, an intelligent will anxious to counteract chance and to regulate the course of events for the betterment of good people.

After such an avowal, we may ask how Caecilius is going to defend the pagan religion. Will he content himself with insinuating that, in the universal ignorance, the Christians at least should acknowledge that they have not been wise much longer than the rest ? By no means. He concludes that, since everything evades man's grasp, he ought to cling with all the more tenacious energy to those fixed points which are open to him. Now the religion of Rome is seen as a body of venerable traditions with which her greatness has always been bound up. Here the tone of Caecilius becomes warm and he is moved in recalling the beneficent action of those gods to whose solicitude the great festivals in the history of Rome bear witness. He who but now was relegating Divine intervention to the ranks of unverified hypotheses, now gets near to the approaches of a real faith; and his Roman nationality comes to his aid in getting over this difficult step.

After having thus exalted " this religion of such antiquity, so practical and so salutary ", Caecilius hits back angrily against those who would like to destroy it. The speech for the prosecution, to give it its true name, now begins. He first loads with contempt the Christian sect which is recruited among the dregs of the people and " forms a coalition of impiousness out of this rabble." The chief points of his accusation define themselves : their disdain for things that are holy, their iniquitous mysteries which, with these wretched people, bind them together in infamous intercourse at their nocturnal meetings. He then attacks the conception of the God of the Christians, whose inquisitorial ubiquity appears to him to be a marvel of presumptuousness and madness, and the Christian eschatology, especially the doctrine of the Resurrection, for which he reserves his most mordant irony. The speech ends with an appeal to humility and to that prudent doubt which the new Academe had enjoined, and which is the safest attitude of mind to adopt.

From a historical and moral point of view, these few pages are of exceptional richness. Caecilius is an admirable representative of those lettered pagans who were very sceptical as regards the foundation of things, but who, from civic *pietas* and from respect for the *mos majorum*, thought it to be their duty to energetically defend the religion of tradition—an essential element in the prosperity and greatness of Rome. The author must have possessed a rare openness of mind to lend so eloquent and so persuasive an accent to the cause which he detested.

After a short respite (XIV–XV), Octavius takes his turn to speak (XV–XXXVIII). His method is as follows : to pursue his adversary step by step in order to refute all his complaints without omitting one, then to turn them the moment he can against the pagans ; to select his examples

and his *points d'appui* from among the pagan thinkers in
order not to lead Caecilius astray and to prove to him that
these *semi-nudi*, whom he despises, are not so far removed
from him as he appears to think.

As against the transcendental scepticism of Caecilius,
Octavius first defines the notion of Providence.   In a broad
and full development in which his talent and his Ciceronian
recollections have full play, he describes the splendour of the
heavens, the ordered course of the seasons, etc.   All reveals
the highest intelligence which has an eye to details as well
as to the whole.   Must we believe from these manifestations
that there is one God or many ?   It is enough to behold what
passes on the earth, which is the image of the heavens :   every
kingdom which is divided perishes.   God is therefore one.
Reason attests it, and the mind of the philosopher so near to
Christian thought recognises it equally.

After having established these fundamental truths, Providence and the oneness of God, Octavius makes a point against
the pagan religion.   On this question the arguments of
Christian apologetics were already fixed—namely, the entirely
human origin of the gods, the scandal of mythology and of
the rites consecrated by law.   Octavius does not parti-
cularise them except by the allusions he makes to the
very words which Caecilius had employed.   He points out in
particular the danger of an education, which corrupts by all
these untruths the minds of children, and renders them
impermeable to the truth.   He seeks to loosen the bonds of
solidarity which Caecilius wished to establish between the
glories of Rome and the pagan religion.   He does not dare
to deny outright the prodigies vaunted by the pagans, but he
attributes them to demons, wandering and impure spirits
who have fallen from heaven, and who console themselves
for their misfortunes by deceiving and destroying souls.

He next approaches the charges brought by Caecilius
against the Christians.   Here his line of argument becomes
more solid :   reasons of heart and also reasons of Reason.
He declares to his friend that he pardons him his mistake for
he remembers that he himself had likewise shared the same.
But let him give up believing in these miserable fables !
Only those give credence to such shameful things who are
capable of perpetrating them themselves.   Then step by

step Octavius justifies the different conceptions of Christianity over which Caecilius had been scandalised—the watchfulness exercised by God over his creatures, the catastrophe of the end of the world, the resurrection and punishments beyond the grave.

In these latter pages and in those which follow, there are all the constituents of a picture of Christian life : virtue under suffering piously accepted, the heroism of the martyrs, the purity of heart which refuses consent to everything that might soil it. And these things are said with a fire of enthusiasm which throws its final brightness over the warm and vibrating peroration.

The three friends remain for a moment silent (**XXXIX**). It was then Minucius' part to give judgment. But Caecilius anticipates him, declaring himself to be convinced on the principal points discussed. A few further interchanges of views will do the rest.

" We then separated," the author concludes, " happy and enraptured, Caecilius at having found belief and Octavius at having won the day, and myself at the faith of the one and the victory of the other."

III

A PERFECT naturalness in the setting of the work or, if you will, in the setting of the scene ; a remarkable attempt at impartiality in exposing the charges brought by pagans ; much warmth and conviction in the reply of the Christian, Octavius ; an extremely supple style of many lights and shades, wherein the elegance of the Ciceronian age is heightened by a freshness of quick and picturesque expressions—such are the merits which all agree to recognise in this work by Minucius Felix. Nevertheless even those who most gladly render homage to the literary beauty and seduction of this dialogue, are astonished at only finding such fugitive examples of Christian doctrine in it. Octavius claims to convert the pagan Caecilius and appears to have succeeded in doing so : but is it not true that Caecilius at the close of the discussion is almost as ignorant of the faith to which he gives his willing adherence as at the beginning ? Octavius gives proof of a very strange discretion and, what is more serious, certain of his words only give very imperfect expression to Christian doctrine which he appears to shrink from explaining completely.

This complaint may be readily brought against the *Octavius*. Let us examine more precisely what failings from an intrinsically Christian point of view can be justly brought against it :

(*a*) In the first place, the conception which Octavius, the mouthpiece of the author, makes to himself of God is, in the opinion of certain critics, of Gaston Boissier [1] among others, " far more abstract and philosophic than intrinsically Christian." " We must not," says Octavius, " seek out a name for God : His name is—God. We only require names when we have to distinguish by some special appellation each individual among a multitude : to God, who is alone of His kind, the name of ' God ' belongs in every respect. If I call Him ' Father,' people might believe He is of flesh ; if ' King,' people might suppose that He is of earth ; if ' Master,' people might certainly understand that He is mortal. Put aside all these accessory names and you will perceive it in all its clearness." [2] Certainly we have not here quite the God of the Christians. True, but the intrinsically Christian idea comes out elsewhere. G. Boissier himself perceived this for he brings back his reader to chapter xxxv, 4, in which God is called *parentem omnium et omnium dominum*. He could have chosen a far more significant passage (xxxi, 8). " What is troubling you," says Octavius to his interlocutor, " is that we love each other with mutual affection because we know not hate ; again (and that makes you envious) we call each other ' brethren ' as being the sons of one God our Father (*ut unius Dei parentis homines*), as being participators in the same faith, as being heirs to the same hope."

There is thus no reason to insist on this point.

(*b*) A second charge of more weight is the roundabout, ambiguous, almost equivocal manner in which Octavius makes allusion to Christ : " You attribute," he says, " to our religion the worship of a malefactor and his cross ; but you err very far from the truth in supposing that a malefactor has deserved to pass for a God, or that a being of earth could have passed for such. Assuredly that would be

[1] *Fin du paganisme*, I, 284.   [2] *Otavius*, xviii, 10.

worthy of pity if all our hope should rest on a man subject to death : for all our support in him would cease in the death of this man, etc." [1] Baehrens,[2] one of the editors of the *Octavius*, has thought to see in this passage a manifest negation of the Divinity of Christ. The idea which seems to me to emerge from it, on the contrary, is this : you may make quite certain that we are not the people to adore a man and especially a malefactor ; our hope rests on something else than what is ephemeral and perishable. In transposing the expression in a positive sense, we can almost draw from it an affirmation of the virtue and of the Divine immortality of Christ. But we must readily agree with M. Boissier that we might expect something else " than a brief and obscure phrase " [3] on such a subject : " What is he doing," M. Boissier exclaims, " that in an apology of Christianity he has been unwilling to pronounce the name of Christ ? " In fact, this *is* surprising : we should however remember— a fact which is too often ignored—that amongst the apologists of the IInd century, Aristides, St Justin and Tertullian are the only ones who have uttered the name of Jesus Christ.

(c) We likewise find that in several places in the *Octavius*, the doctrine of grace seems either to be ignored or contradicted. Hear again what G. Boissier says : [4] " In order to give an answer to the jeers of his opponent, who makes fun of these ignorant people, of these worthless nobodies who dare to discuss God and the world, Octavius says to him : Know that all men, without distinction of age, sex or position, are capable of reason and of good sense, and that of themselves they can arrive at wisdom." If nature alone leads them thither, if they have no need of God's aid in obtaining it, what becomes of the necessity of grace ? He adds a little further on that in order to know God, instead of listening to the errors of those by whom we are surrounded, it is enough to interrogate ourselves and to believe in ourselves, *sibi credere*. This is just how Seneca expresses himself (*Ep.* 31, 3) ; but Athenagoras the apologist, a contemporary of Minucius, speaks very differently. He attacks those wise men of the world who pretend that reason unaided can lead them to the truth and who flatter themselves that they

---

[1] xxix, 2 ; cf. ix, 4.
[3] *Fin du Paganisme*, I, 280.

[2] Ed. Teubner, 1886, p. xi.
[4] *Op. cit.*, p. 280–281.

can know God by their own lights. " Unlike them," he says, " in our search for what we should believe, we place our trust in the testimony of the prophets who, being inspired of God, speak to us of Him in His name." Here we have language which is truly Christian and which appears to be a direct reply to the words of Minucius.

And G. Boissier adds in a note : " See also the following passage in which the necessity of grace, in order to arrive at the truth, appears to be not admitted : *Cum sit veritas obvia, sed requirentibus*, 23, 2." [1]

I do not know if these criticisms ought to be accepted in their entirety. G. Boissier first tells us : " The doctrine of grace is nowhere mentioned." As a matter of fact, it is nowhere expounded didactically ; but more or less enveloped allusions to it are made. See XXVII, 7, in regard to the power of exorcizing demons possessed by the Christians : " In spite of themselves," Octavius says, " the wretches (he is speaking of impure spirits) tremble with fright in the body and take flight at once, or rather disappear little by little according to the aid which the faith of the sufferer is able to provide, or according to the succour which the grace proceeding from the deliverer lends to him (*prout fides patientis adjuvat aut gratia curantis adspirat*)." Compare again XXXVII, 5–6, concerning the martyrs : " Our children, our weak women laugh at crosses and tortures, at ferocious beasts and all the terrors of their sufferings, with a patience which comes to them from on high (*et omnes suppliciorum terriculas inspirata patientia doloris inludunt*). And do you not understand, unhappy man that you are, that there is no one . . . who could support these tortures *without help from God ?* " Finally, can we not see an allusion to grace, fully or slightly comprehended, in this reproach of the pagan Caecilius : " *You attribute to God all our actions*, just as others attribute them to fate : thus, it is not from a spontaneous act that people adhere to your sect but because they are chosen by God." [2] Boissier's assertion appears therefore to be a little rash. As for the arguments which he brings forward in order to show that Octavius speaks as a Stoic rather than as a Christian, possibly they too have not all the weight which he deduces from them. If Octavius affirms that all men,

---

[1] The correct reference is xxiii, 8.   [2] xi, 6.

without distinction of age and social position, are capable of arriving by nature at wisdom, *natura insitos esse sapientiam,* it is because he desires to offer a protest against the aristocratic disdain of Caecilius who, in his estimate of these bare-footed Christians appeared to believe that, in order to be a thinker, a man must be well clothed.   Octavius aims at making him understand that reason is the most freely distributed thing in the world, and that it is of little importance what rank a disputant holds if he argues well.   It would have been altogether without purpose to confuse the question by making the doctrine of grace intervene, and we ought to be thankful to the author for not having done so.   The same may be said for the other passages to which Boissier takes exception. Let us put back into its context the *sibi credere* in which he perceives an echo of Seneca.   Octavius has just been speaking at length on the deplorable credulity of their ancestors and of the mass of errors with which tradition, reinforced by education, encumbered the spirit, and adds : " You fear them (these contemptible gods) . . . : this is because you foolishly strive to follow your parents, and because you prefer to fall into the mistakes of others *rather than to place confidence in yourselves."* [1]   One can easily catch the sense of these words. The following lines from Renan might serve as a commentary to them : " Se convertir au christianisme n'était pas un acte de crédulité ; c'était presque un acte de bon sens relatif. Même au point de vue du rationalisme, le christianisme pouvait être envisagé comme un progrès ; *ce fut l'homme religieusement éclairé qui l'adopta."* [2]   As for the last passage brought forward : " Truth offers herself of her own accord but on condition that men seek for her," the idea that truth is before all else a conquest of the soul is such an elementary factor in psychology [3] that we ought not to wonder that Minucius Felix advanced it as a fact without further widening the debate.

(*d*) Another criticism : Minucius Felix has allowed imprudent expressions to escape which he never would have ventured to make if he had been a sincere Christian.   For example the following, on pagan prodigies : " *Quae si essent*

---

[1] xxiv, 2.
[2] Marc. Aurèle, p. 582.
[3] Especially for a mind brought up on the writings of Plato.

facta, fierent ; quia fieri non possunt, ideo non sunt." [1] Baehrens cannot believe that Minucius Felix did not perceive how
easily the argument could be turned against the Christian
miracles. G. Boissier himself makes a *piquant* [2] analogy
between the above reflection and the following one of Renan :
" Nous repoussons le surnaturel par la même raison qui
nous fait repousser l'existence des centaures et des hippo-
griffes : c'est qu'on n'en a jamais vu."

In reality, Minucius Felix would only have thought of
applying to his own faith the reasoning by which he claimed
to destroy belief in the pagan miracles if he had himself been
a hesitating Christian, which is just the point debated.
Let us rest assured that he believed in the reality of supernatural " graces " whose favours the Christian communities
received with so much happiness and pride. If the argument
which he used has been retorted against Christianity, what
does this prove ? Any phrase isolated from the context
may cut both ways. At that rate we ought to suspect
Arnobius, for he has cast ridicule on mythology by methods
very analogous to those which Voltaire was to employ
against the Bible ; and it would be prudent to be mistrustful
of Lactantius, who has one quite " Protestant " passage
on the right of everyone to make his own religion.[3] If we
are to see in the incriminated words some sceptical insinuation,
we must be in the state of mind of Baehrens who, without
blinking, calls Minucius Felix " a forerunner of Strauss and
Renan " !

(*e*) G. Boissier is also amazed at the antipathy displayed
by Minucius Felix against the externals of worship, against
temples, statues and every representation or, if I may dare
to say so, any definition of what is divine. In the mind of
Octavius there was only one good way of praying to God,
and that was the offering to Him of a pure heart : " Here
we have doubtless a fine profession of faith," G. Boissier
remarks ; " but Seneca could have subscribed to that as well

---

[1] xx, 4.

[2] *Fin du Paganisme*, I, 277.

[3] *Instit. Div.*, II, viii. " Everyone should trust to himself in what is the most
important affair in his life, and should use his own judgment and his own sense in
seeking after and weighing up the truth ; our predecessors in time have not necessarily been before us in the paths of wisdom, etc." A Jesuit of the XVIIIth century, Father de Laubrussel, remarks, not without a tinge of spite, that " critics
have always made use of this maxim of Lactantius which is little understood."
Traité des Abus de la Critique en Matière de Religion, 1711, p. 70, note.

as Minucius.   If that is all the doctrine held by the Christians, they were nothing more than a sect of philosophers just like others." [1]   G. Boissier's surprise is quite legitimate ; but it is not only in the case of the *Octavius* that he has a right to show it.   Among the apologists of the first centuries and up to the time of Lactantius, there was a marked disdain for all ceremonial in matters of religion.   They feared even the shadow of idolatry and shrank from it ; and besides there were texts from Scripture like those from Isaias, i, 11 ; lxvi, 1 ; from the Acts, xvii, 24 ; vii, 48–50, which urged them to oppose to all the exterior forms of religion the far more preferable holocaust of piety and virtue.   The question only arose little by little under pressure of the requirements of public worship.   It is not then surprising that Minucius Felix seems to be here and there very intemperate, and he a Catholic, in his hostility against certain outward manifestations of religious sentiment.

(*f*) We come lastly to the principal charge which we should specially notice.   The most disconcerting thing in the *Octavius* is not its contradiction of Christian doctrine— it is nowhere proved that this exists in reality—it is the silence on Christian doctrines preserved by the author.

Octavius deliberately kèeps himself to the domain of the most general philosophic truths—the need for a Providence who organises and rules the universe, the oneness of God, the discussion and reprobation of the scandalous fables put to the account of the gods, and of the rites by which the pagans pretended to honour them, and an apology of the life of the Christians.   These are the principal points which the champion of Christianity successively touches upon.   It is impossible not to be struck by so many gaps.   In his pleading there are some things which remind one of the Scriptures ; [2] but nowhere does he explain what are the sacred sources of the faith.   He completely neglects the proof from the accom-

---

[1] *Fin du Paganisme*, I, 281.   Similar declarations by Seneca are, as a matter of fact, pointed out by Fr. X. Burger, *Minucius Felix und Seneca*, Munich, 1904, p. 28.

[2] A few in number : compare *Octavius*, XXXIII, 3, and *Josue*, X, 11 ; *Oct.*, XXIX, 3, and *Jeremias*, XVII, 5.   Some expressions are taken from St Paul : *spei coheredes* (xxxi, 8), cf. *Ep. to Titus*, III, 7 ; *Ep. to the Romans*, viii, 17 ; *unum bonum sapimus* (xxxi, 6) and *Ep. to the Romans*, xv, 5 et s.   In many places we may ask whether he has drawn from St Paul or from Seneca ; very probably from Seneca to judge from the analogy of certain of his expressions. (See *Oct.*, xxxvi, 8, and Seneca, *De Prov.*, ii, 2.)

plishment of the prophecies, which had appeared so decisive
to St Justin.[1]   We have here a very paltry, a very incomplete
account which gives an entirely inadequate idea of the
economy of the Christian revelation.

On this point the fact is indubitable and it would be idle
to try and elude it.   We must therefore give some explanation.   Let us see what has been put forward.

At first people had recourse to an interpretation which
was formerly in favour, but which has since lost much of its
credit.   Minucius Felix was bound to silence by that " discipline of the secret," which it is alleged obliged the faithful
" never to speak openly of the faith and of their worship
before catechumens and unbelievers."   But why should
he have been more mysterious than St Justin who, in his
first apology, unfolds all the mystery of the Eucharist,[2]
or than the author of the *Cohortatio ad Graecos*, who, however
little explicit he is on dogma, nevertheless is able to explain
in a few words the doctrine of the Word ?[3]   What is this
obligation which must have weighed on him (Minucius Felix),
from which St Irenæus and Tertullian escaped ?   As a matter
of fact, it has been shown that the " discipline of the secret "
was enclosed in far more rigorous bounds than people for a
long time believed.[4]

Roeren, who suggested the above hypothesis in 1859,
relied principally on this phrase in the *Octavius :* " We never
speak of God in public unless it be that anyone interrogates
us." [5]   This is a too brief indication in which we can hardly
seriously see any hint of the *disciplina arcani*.

Another critic, Keim,[6] thought that Minucius Felix was
a catechumen still little versed in matters of faith and who
could only say what his zeal as a neophyte had already taught
him.   But does he reflect that Minucius Felix wrote long
after his conversion when his friend, Octavius, was already
dead ?[7]   Unless we are to suppose that all is fictitious in
the dialogue and that the confidences of the author, as well

---

1 See the *Apol.*, xlv–lv et s.
2 1 *Ap.*, lxvi et s.
3 Ch. xxxviii.
4 Cf. Batiffol, *Etudes d'Histoire et de Théol. Positive*, Paris, 1902.
5 xix, 15.
6 *Rom. und das Christenthum*, Berlin, 1881, p. 472.
7 Cf. Chap. i.

as the characters that he puts in it, are imaginary, Keim's hypothesis falls to the ground of itself.

It has been upheld, on a better foundation, that if Minucius Felix showed himself so reserved, it was simply because he did not wish to go further than his own particular conviction. In that case, he must have been an altogether soft-spoken and prudent heretic. The most moderate expression of this interpretation is found in Kuehn.[1] According to Kuehn, Minucius Felix, an eclectic philosopher, must have *chosen* among the Christian doctrines those which best suited his cast of mind and thus he must have advanced his " personal doctrine," buoyed up on beliefs which could not have been accepted. Baehrens[2] took up the same idea but pushed it to extremes. In his eyes, the reticences of Minucius Felix, as well as his unskilful arguments, are explained by the excellent reason that he was not a believer. It was the case of a philosopher and man of letters who had seen an excellent rule of discipline in Christianity nearly approaching the wisdom of the Greeks, but one better adapted to the daily wear and tear of life. He connected himself therefore with it thinking to show his brethren a highly refined interpretation of it ; and to the untrained crowd he abandoned chimeras which were repugnant to reason.

This is an evident paradox the falseness of which cries aloud. If Lactantius and St Jerome recognised him as one of themselves, without doubt this was because they did not find in him any trace of " rationalism."

Ernest Renan too advanced his own explanation which is much more elaborate. He thought to see in the gaps of the *Octavius* the concerted dissimulation of a " skilful lawyer " passing over the points in his belief that he found difficult in order the more easily to win the adhesion of his uninformed hearers. Once more yielding to his mania for comparisons he likens Minucius Felix to the preacher at Notre Dame[3] " addressing people of the world who are easy to satisfy, making himself all things to all men, studying the weaknesses and passions of the persons he desires to convince, affecting under his heavy cope the gestures of the man of open mind

---

[1] *Der Octavius des M.F.*, Leipsic, 1882.
[2] See the Preface to his edition.
[3] *Marc. Aurèle*, p. 403.

and falsifying his office in order to render it acceptable. Become a Christian on the faith of this pious sophist—nothing can be better ; but remember that all this is a bait. . . ."

Here indeed is a lively thrust : should we accept these severe words in all their rigour ? Would not Minucius be an unctuous Tartuffe and a juggling devotee in that case ? In order to establish the exact shade of the truth (at least this is how it seems to me), I think we must put before our eyes the end which Minucius Felix is pursuing in his work. It is the indispensable condition to thoroughly appreciate the method which he used in order to attain to it.

Minucius Felix clearly did not write the *Octavius* for the popular eye : he wrote it for men of the world, for educated men. His characters have a high distinction and an evidently very refined culture if we consider the number of allusions and quotations which they grasp without the least effort. Minucius Felix was not a Christian after the manner of Tertullian ; he was living amongst his people, he numbered excellent friends in pagan circles and he was well aware of the anti-Christian prejudices with which his caste was especially imbued.

It was just because he was well aware of them and possible because some work, some discourse of Frontonius, the rhetorician, had shown him once more all their virulence, that he wished to endeavour to dissipate them.

In order to prove to his pagan hearers that he was by no means unmindful of the force of their reasons, he gave logical sequence to the leading speech of Caecilius and employed the most closely-reasoned eloquence ; his refutation must consequently assume all the greater authority.

What was the spirit in which he drew up this refutation ? A very characteristic passage in which Minucius, the arbiter in the debate, reviews his impression of the discourse of Octavius, will show us : [1] " As for me, my admiration was so great that I was quite beside myself ; I marvelled that he should have proved all those things which it is easier to feel than to speak, by arguments, by examples and by authorities derived from what he had read ; that he should have vanquished the perverse with these same weapons from philosophy which he employed, finally, that he should have demonstrated

[1] XXXIX, 1.

the truth to be not only easy to understand, but congenial "
(to reason). According to this confession, which is without
any doubt the view of the author, it was for him first of all
to give a form to his belief, to make it emerge from the limbo
of sentiment, and to explain it in the light of day to minds
accustomed by long practice to the art of disputation—
assuredly a task needing tact. Next, to support his apology
by arguments which the pagans could not refuse *a priori*.
From that arose the necessity of so many reflections from
good authors and his satisfaction in backing up his argument
by profane philosophy. Finally, it was desirable to give his
doctrine a happy turn, to render it pleasing and to incline
their hearts to make it their own.

But it remained an understood thing that the general
orientation of his detailed apology must not deviate from the
line which the opening speech of Caecilius had previously
traced out for him. Octavius says so in so many words at
the beginning of his reply. He wishes " to blot out the
defilement proceeding from these bitter insults in the living
water of the words of truth." That is why he takes the
allegations of his adversary one by one, in order to endeavour
to demonstrate their nothingness. Apart from the oneness
of God, and Providence, he only lays down two dogmas,
the dogma of the resurrection and that of future punishments :
these are just those which Caecilius had attacked. He
attempts to purge the mind of his friend of his false ideas
and erroneous judgments. Caecilius little by little is won
over by the warm conviction of this antagonist, who, besides,
is so dear to him. His prejudices fall to the ground, he confesses himself beaten ; but it is not quite the *Je vois, je sais,
je crois, je suis désabusée* of Pauline in *Polyeucte*. He gives his
adhesion to the points laid down, which have been the subject
of the discussion, and to those alone.[1] Difficulties remain to
him, but the solution is put off to the morrow.

Octavius avoided adding any debatable matter pro-
visionally beside the mark, which, by turning him from his
object, might have caused him to overlook the refutation of
any charge already definitely brought : and he followed this
line not only on the question of religion but also on the ques-

---

[1] " *Itaque quod pertinet ad summam quaestionis, et de providentia fateor et de
Deo cedo et de sectae jam nostrae sinceritate confido.*" (xl, 2.)

tion of purely natural order. That is why he only makes a hasty allusion to the special methods in vogue against the Christians.[1] Similarly, he makes no defence of the loyalty of the Christians or of their respect for the heads of the State : Caecilius had made no charge against them in these respects. He sets before himself the establishment of a common ground of agreement, a perfect symmetry between attack and defence, and eliminates every question which does not enter into his plan.

But after all, he was the designer of this plan. Why did he not enlarge it sufficiently to admit the principal doctrines of his faith ?

Without doubt, the reason is that he wished to reach by his work, a veritable propagandist pamphlet, a definite class of readers, men like Caecilius, rather sceptical as to the real foundation of things, and rather inquisitive on metaphysical questions, but whose agnosticism was compatible with a very sensitive and a very ardent Roman piety ; men who for these reasons despised the Christians for their dogmatic intrepidity which seemed all the more outrageous coming from inferior people ; men who feared them owing to the evil reports current about them and vowed to destruction these despisers of Rome and of the gods.

In order to find points of contact with minds thus fashioned, would it have been suitable to lay down at the outset, from a kind of somewhat fanatical bravado, incomprehensible positive statements on the Word, the prophecies, and the relationship existing between the Father and the Son, etc. ? Clearly not. It was necessary to discuss their charges dispassionately, to compel them to recognise their lack of foundation, to bring them to more right-minded views, and, since to remain on the defensive is always a rather awkward attitude, to drive home a few vigorous points.

This is just what Minucius Felix has done. Of the three elements of which the first apologies are composed, namely, the justification of the Christians, the criticism of the pagan beliefs, and the dogmatic explanation of Christianity, he developed the two former and passed over or adjourned the third. These are the tactics of an advocate, if you will (Minucius Felix quite clearly was versed in the artifices of the

[1] xxviii, 3.

bar and we can find evidences of it here and there), but
legitimate tactics on the whole if we consider that there is a
proper way of giving instruction in belief and that this proper
way presupposes gradual exercises and a progressive advance-
ment towards an initiation by definition.[1]

Certainly the work is not perfect and we agree that from
motives of prudence and policy, Minucius Felix has *minimised*
doctrine to an excessive degree.[2]   But in conclusion, many
omissions in which some people wish to see ignorance,
dissimulation, and equivocal *ruses*, explain and almost justify
themselves if we consider that the *Octavius* is not a *summa*,
but simply a kind of introduction to Christian doctrine
written for the use of cultivated men of the world.

IV

JUST as Minucius Felix brings forward no fresh view of the
pagan religion, and no original synthesis of the truths of his
own faith, so his inspiration needs to be constantly urged on
and supported by the help of others.   He does not possess
that power of reflection which permeates a style, giving a
personality and a life-like form.   It is enough to consult
one or other of the recent editions giving his sources to
realise that the *Octavius* is, according to the expression of
M. Paul Monceaux, " a mosaic of ideas, scenes and details
taken from all quarters." [3]   He borrowed from Cicero the
general plan of the dialogue,[4] and that tone of perfect urbanity
which the interlocutors maintain face to face with each other
in the most burning parts of the discussion.   The choice of
an arbiter to settle the debate came to him perhaps from
Tacitus.[5]   Cicero also furnished him with the refined and
delicate opening, and the greater part of the " motifs " of
the eloquent leading speech of Caecilius.   To Seneca he is

---

[1] See Lactantius, *De Ira Dei*, 2.   " *Nam cum sint gradus multi, per quos ad
domicilium veritatis ascenditur, non est facile cuilibet evehi ad summum . . .*" and
the whole passage.   Cf. Orig., c. *Cels.*, III, liii.

[2] His successors appear to have felt what was wanting in him.   See Lactantius,
Div. Inst., i, ix, 22.

[3] *Hist. Litt.*, I, 490.

[4] Previous examples of the use of dialogue in apologetics are to be found in
Ariston of Pella, Justin Martyr, and Caius of Rome.   Lucian of Samosata, on the
pagan side, had given to this class of writing a veritable second spring.

[5] *Dial. Or.*, IV.   Cf. Plato, *Protag.*, 337 E ; *Symp.*, 175 E.

indebted for a quantity of pointed expressions and nearly all the developments in chapters xxxvi and xxxvii where Octavius, replying to the disdainful charges of Caecilius, exalts the poverty of the Christians and opposes to the dangers of wealth and honours the sovereign good of a pure heart. Seneca had said of the " wise " Stoic : [1] " Ecce spectaculum dignum ad quod respiciat intentus operi suo Deus, ecce par Deo dignum, vir fortis cum fortuna male compositus, etc." And Octavius repeats concerning the Christian martyr : " Quam pulchrum spectaculum Deo, cum Christianus cum dolore congreditur, cum adversum minas et supplicia et tormenta componitur. . . ." Philosophers, historians, poets—from all of them Minucius Felix takes his toll. His work is a fabric of recollections, but so cleverly interlaced and so finely adjusted that the joints do not appear. In this treatise, made up of different bits and pieces, all presents one single whole, all is ordered with the same enthusiasm. This ingenious art of adaptation (with at least some degree of originality) is that of a Ronsard, a Chénier. Minucius Felix was of the same family as these humanist experts. He was the most learned and the most delicately tempered of lettered men.

V

THE characteristics of his talent themselves furnish us with a valuable indication for taking up a position in the so much controverted question of the priority of Tertullian's *Apologeticum* as regards the *Octavius*. It is not open to doubt that between these two works there are analogies of foundation and of form. " There are long or short developments, but of a cast which is characteristic, quotations, reflections, special features, and bursts of eloquence, of bitter or ironical ridicule and of mere raillery." [2] This fact is not disputed by anyone ; but the reasons given are so contradictory as to form one of the most remarkable collections of cacophony that modern criticism offers. Up to 1868, with the exception of a few rare dissidents, it was believed that the *Apologeticum*

[1] *De Provid.*, II, ix.
[2] Massebieau, *Rev. de l'Hist. des Relig.*, vol. XV (1887), p. 325. For a detailed account of these resemblances, see the editions of Boenig and Waltzing.

had the priority. The *Octavius* had been printed half a century after the *Apologeticum* (1484 ; 1543) and Tertullian's *chef-d'œuvre*, already held in universal admiration, continued to be regarded as anterior to all Latin writings of a similar kind. Ad. Ebert shook the prevailing opinion in a memoir which appeared in 1868.[1] Since then, a host of articles, dissertations, and treatises have appeared on this much debated problem. Three theories emerge from all this printed matter. One, upheld principally by Hartel, advances a source common to Tertullian and to Minucius Felix. According to this, they both made use of a Latin apologist who must have drawn upon Varro, Cicero and Seneca. But who was the apologist ? Here the difficulty commences. And then, which of the two was the first to exploit him ? The question debated would still remain even if this mysterious source could be marked down. The second theory, that of Ebert, which places the *Octavius* before the *Apologeticum*, has recruited a number of " authorities " (Schanz, Boenig, Ehrhard, Geffcken, etc.). Lastly, the third, which is the traditional idea, was taken up in 1887 by a French scholar, M. Massebieau, in a remarkable article in the *Revue de l'Histoire des Religions*, which more than any later discussion strikes at the real root of the question debated. Massebieau states the numerous resemblances in detail between the *Apologeticum* and the *Octavius*, and asks this question : if Tertullian really borrowed from Minucius Felix, would he have utilised him by taking his words and his expressions but without ever mentioning him by name ? Such a proceeding is unlike his methods. Tertullian likes to quote his authors by name. In addition, he takes from them their ideas and the facts which they cite, but he preserves his own style and marks with his own impress all that has come to him from other sources. Minucius Felix on the contrary has no scruples in making his own the turns of phrase which he meets with in other authors. Does it not seem fairly reasonable from this that he would have made use of Tertullian for the Christian part of his treatise just as he used Cicero and Seneca for that portion which was essentially philosophic ? In other words, that he largely drew upon the *Apologeticum*

---

[1] *Tert. Verh. zu Minucius Felix* reprinted in the *Abh. d. saechs Ges. d. Wiss.*, XII (*Phil. Hist. Kl.*, V), 1870, pp. 319–386.

(and also upon other treatises of Tertullian, such as the *De Paenitentia*, the *De Resurrectione Carnis*, the *De Testimonio Animae*, the *De Corona*) to extract from them what he found suitable to his purpose ?

Another observation which has its value is the following :[1] supposing that the *Octavius* had in reality begun the series of works by Latin apologetics, would not this treatise have enjoyed among Christian antiquity (however confused the literary tradition of the first two centuries soon became) a renown superior to what he seems to have attained ? Minucius Felix would have justly been held as a pioneer of great merit.   Now we do not find that this homage was anywhere meted out to him, and it is a new reason of quite a general order to give the first place to a meagre comparison of texts in which criticism has vainly exhausted itself during the last fifty years.

[1] Harnack, *Chron.*, II, 329. The not uniformly conclusive arguments of Harnack have been keenly criticised by G. Kruger in the *Gott. Gel. Anz.*, January 1905, p. 36 et s.   These will be found analysed by A. d'Alès, in his *Etudes des PP. Jésuites*, vol. CIV (1905), pp. 289–317.

CHAPTER II

SAINT CYPRIAN AND HIS TIMES

BIBLIOGRAPHY

WE are able to check the manner in which the collected works of Cyprian have been got together. With his methodical habits, St Cyprian kept by him a copy of his letters. To these *dossiers* he added the letters which he himself had received on such and such religious question ; and he was glad to be able to communicate them on occasion in order to justify his conduct or to give authority to his opinion. Around these documents, thus grouped together, other letters must have come to be annexed after his death. Side by side with a division into subjects, we find in the manuscripts traces of a division into persons to whom they were sent. It does not appear that there was any general collection of the letters of Cyprian before modern times. This explains how a certain number of documents, attested by the explicit witness of the Bishop, have gone astray [1] in the course of this more or less capricious juxtaposition. As for the writings themselves, a list drawn up by the deacon Pontius in § vii of his *Vita Cypriani*, or rather a series of transparent allusions of an oratorical kind, permit us to affirm that even in the lifetime of Cyprian a first collection of eleven treatises had been established. Mommsen [2] discovered in a manuscript of the Xth century belonging to the library of Philip de Cheltenham a stichometric catalogue drawn up in 359, about a hundred years after the death of Cyprian, which nearly coincides with the list of Pontius, but some writings and some letters are added. Dom Morin [3] lastly has noted another *index* in an unpublished sermon of St Augustine : the *Quod Idola Dii non sint* only figures in this last document. It is through the aid of these three lists, checked by the text of the quotations from the Bible, that we can circumscribe those writings of St Cyprian which are certainly authentic.[4]

The authority enjoyed by the Bishop was such that certain sects made a selection of his works for their own particular use. Reitzenstein [5] has made a study of one of this series included in two manuscripts, one at Wurzbourg and the other at Munich, whose Donatist origin is not disputed.

[1] Harnack (in T.U., xxiii, 2 [1902]) enumerates eleven properly belonging to Cyprian.

[2] Cf. *Hermes*, XXI (1886), p. 142, *Gesamm. Schriften*, VII (1909), p. 282.

[3] B.A.L.A.C., IV (1914), p. 16 et s.

[4] K. Mengis has recently drawn attention to the index which is found on f. 43 of the manuscript of Wurzbourg Theol. 145 (W. in Hartel). He considers it to be an important document which should represent a tradition anterior to that of the manuscript of Cheltenham, and near to the time of Cyprian. Cf. B. ph. W., 1918, pp. 326-336.

[5] *Sitz.-Ber. d. Heid. Akad. d. Wiss.*, 1913, n° 14, p. 34 et s. ; *Nachr. von der Kon. Ges. d. Wiss. zu Gottingen, Phil.-Hist. Kl.* 1914, Heft I. These two manuscripts are the *Cod. Wirceburgensis theol.*, fol. 33, and the *Cod. Monacensis*, 37-39, both dating from the beginning of the IXth century. Cf. Mengis, *Ein donatistiches Corpus Cyprianischer Briefe*, Diss. Freib.-i.-B., 1916.

The most complete modern edition is that of G. von Hartel, in vol. III of the *Corpus Script. Eccl. Latinorum.*

Hartel established his text after comparing fifty manuscripts. Taken as a whole, the classification given by him is correct, although he has not valued at its true importance such a manuscript as the *Veronensis;* his edition marks a real improvement on those of Pamelus (Antwerp, 1568), of Rigaut (Paris, 1648), and of Baluze-Maran (Paris, 1718). Since Hartel, the inventory of the manuscripts of St Cyprian has been pursued. Hans Frhr von Soden in his *die Cyprianische Briefsammlung* (T.U., xxv, 3 [1904]), has counted 157 which make up a *Corpus Cyprianicum;* in addition, 274 which furnish writings or isolated pieces. Among these manuscripts, some go back to a very early date, back to the VIth and VIIth centuries. This abundant material is an almost unique occurrence in Latin Christian litera-ture. The labours of von Soden have shown the necessity for a fresh edition of the works of Cyprian. Particularly scrupulous attention will have to be given to the quotations from Scripture, which are so important in the history of the Latin Bible. Moreover, another publication by H. von Soden, *das latein. Neue Testament in Afrika zur Zeit. Cyprians* (T.U., xxxiii [1909]), has appreciably cleared the way.

Works. See TABLE III.

The fundamental work on Cyprian is that by Paul Monceaux, *Saint Cyprien et son Temps (Hist. litt. de l'Afr. chr.,* vol. II, 1902). Other recent works will be pointed out in the notes.

SUMMARY

I. Tertullian and St Cyprian.—II. The life of St Cyprian.—III. The ideas which dominated him. Influences which determined them.— IV. How he realised them in practice. The matter of the *lapsi.*— V. The writings of St Cyprian.—VI. The prestige of St Cyprian The Apocryphal writings assigned to his name.

I

ST CYPRIAN called Tertullian his master. He used to like to say " *Da magistrum* " when he wished to have in his hand some work of his vigorous predecessor for his daily reading.[1] He was profoundly under the impress of that dominating genius. What a difference however between the intemperate ascetic, the crafty sophist Tertullian, and this essentially loyal and true, though very experienced soul ! Cyprian had those qualities of heart which attract, which draw sympathy ; I mean charity, prudence, and love of order, of harmony and of peace. Quite from the beginning these gifts clearly belonged to his cast of mind : he was made like that. But they proceeded also from the exercise of his function. At a very early age he had the charge of souls, having been appointed scarcely two or three years after his conversion to direct the group of Christians at Carthage.

---

[1] St Jerome, *de Vir. Ill.,* liii.

There is nothing to equal a responsibility of this kind in making a man wise, in helping him to discern those limits where what is possible ends and what is chimerical begins. When a man knows that the opinion which he is defending, that the measure which he is putting in force will affect a whole body of people who trust in him and who consider him as the mouthpiece of the Holy Spirit, he is readily inclined to keep himself from all exaggeration and to remain carefully within the bounds of what is reasonable. Tertullian succeeded in pressing his ideas to their extreme limits, and in treating as timid and perverse those who did not range themselves on his side : this intemperance only compromised himself. Perhaps if he had assumed the hard task undertaken by Cyprian we should have seen him softening down his fine *intransigeance*, like certain politicians, who are terrible busy-bodies so long as they are in opposition, but become relatively prudent, conservative, and pacific when they are in power.

However this may be, what attracts us in Cyprian is the quality of just balance, the lack of which did most harm to Tertullian. He was face to face with grave trials, the persecution under Decius which was the most formidable that had yet laid its heavy hand on the Christians ; the schisms and bickerings of insubordinate priests ; disagreements with the Roman Episcopate, etc. . . . When we make a study of his conduct in each separate case, we realise that he always maintained a certain rigidity, that he was keenly alive to his own prerogatives and that he entertained the conviction that God Himself, in more than one case, had dictated his conduct by direct command.[1] But this somewhat exalted faith in his mission and this rigidity of principles did not exclude a very skilful diplomacy in their application because he had the advantage of that considered wisdom which gives a profound knowledge of men and matter.

From the strictly literary point of view, Cyprian is far inferior to Tertullian. Apart from the Bible, the principal

---

[1] The *visions* or revelations to which he appeals in justifying such and such an act or in bringing support to such and such a decision, are numerous : *Ep.*, xi, 3, 4, 5, 6 (Hartel, II, p. 497 et s.) ; *Ep.*, xl, 1 (H., 585) ; lxvi, 10 (H., 734) ; *Ep.*, lxiii, 1 (H., 701) ; *Ep.*, lxxiii, 21 (H., 799). Other allusions to phenomena of the same kind, which had not been vouchsafed to him personally, *Ep.*, xvi, 4 (H., 520) : ecstasy in children ; *Ep.*, lvii, 5 (H., 655) ; *de Mortal.*, xix (H., 138), etc. . . There had only been the Montanists who believed in the permanent outpouring of the Holy Spirit in the Church, but here it is the Catholic Church, the Bishop who proclaims its privilege, and no longer those " spiritually " without the pale.

food of his mind and of his faith, and apart from Tertullian his constant model, the suspicion attaching to whose name he moreover killed, he does not appear to have been acquainted with any writings of the old Christian literature. His reading is strictly limited and his philosophy is very brief. He was a man to rule rather than a man of doctrine. The tradition of cultivated intellectual curiosity of which Tertullian had given such a brilliant example, was to be renewed only in the second half of the IVth century by St Hilary, Marius Victorinus, St Ambrose, St Jerome, St Augustine and Rufinus. Once more Greek Christian erudition, richer still than Tertullian had the opportunity of becoming acquainted with, was to be incorporated by these masters of Latin thought. The horizon of St Cyprian was much more limited.

He had received a classic education and faithfully applied the methods of style which he had been taught—the balancing of the parts of a sentence, *homoioteleuton*, cadenced terminations [1] (more strictly followed than by Cicero himself), etc. . . . But it is enough to read through some of his letters and one or two of his treatises to realise that he had none of the biting satire, intellect, or eloquence of his predecessor. Neither too has he the same variety in the subjects treated, nor in the manner in which he treats them. When we read Tertullian, we are ceaselessly spurred on by the pointed characteristics and the passion which he betrays and by his keenness to convince. The works of Cyprian are unrolled in a more uniform and more tranquil movement of speech.[2] Interest in him arises from the root matter of the subjects and practical problems which he discusses and solves. This is due to the fact that all that Cyprian wrote was in strict relation to his office as a Bishop, and to the actual circumstances in which he was engaged. It was not enough for him to enlighten his flock by word of mouth : he desired also to reach those who could not hear him. Then on several occasions he found himself obliged to leave his flock. This is why he writes without literary vanity, although never losing

---

[1] See de Jonghe, *Rec. des Travaux de l'Univ. de Louvain*, 14 fasc. (1905).

[2] " Erat ingenio *facili, copioso, suavi* . . .", Lactantius says (*Inst. Div.*, V, 1, 25). And St Jerome (*Ep.*, lviii, 10) : " Beatus Cyprianus *instar fontis purissimi dulcis* incedit et placidus." And Cassiodorus (*Inst.*, I, xix) : " . . . *velut oleum decurrens in omnem suavitatem* ". All three had a just impression of this mellow prodigality spreading out over a wide surface. On the language of Cyprian, see the conscientious work of L. Bayard, *Le Latin de Saint Cyprien*, thèse, Paris, 1903.

proper regard for and even the niceties of form in order to convince, exhort, and lead back the unruly, and confirm the faithful. We can reproach him with a certain contempt for speculation, with a lack of interest in purely theoretical questions : he hardly had the time to delay over such things. Moreover, he amply makes up for these omissions by a very penetrating intuition of soul, by an ardent mysticism which in no wise impairs his energy, lastly by all those qualities of a man of action, who, in making himself a man of letters, still continues to be a man of action. " A whole people lived on his word ; each one of his sermons, each one of his discourses was a real act, right up to that last hour in which, for reply to the Pro-Consul, he discovered a still more eloquent silence, and placed in a resolute ' No ! ' his soul which up to that moment he had laid bare by his spoken words." [1]

II

THE sources from which we can trace the life of St Cyprian are fairly abundant. (1) A few months after the martyrdom of St Cyprian a clerk in his *entourage*, named Pontius, took in hand to preserve in writing a portrait of the great Bishop. Persuaded in his inmost heart that no such remarkable figure had appeared in the Church since the days of the Apostles, he desired to make posterity share his admiration by relating the *opera ac merita* of Cyprian from the time of his conversion to his martyrdom. This *Vita Cypriani* [2] of which 23 manuscripts are known to exist at the present time, is the first Christian biography, the first specimen of a class which was to enjoy such a remarkable *prestige*. (We know that the *Life of Antony*, by St Athanasius, and the *Life of St Martin*, by Sulpicius Severus [to only mention two] obtained perhaps the most remarkable circulation in Christian antiquity.) It is far from being a *chef-d'œuvre*, and it does not appear a matter of doubt that Harnack has overrated

---

[1] Ernest Havet in the *Revue des deux Mondes*, 15 Sept. 1885, p. 311.

[2] The name of Pontius does not figure in it, but it is furnished by St Jerome in his *De Vir. Ill.*, § lxviii. His name is found on an inscription at Corubis of the IIIrd century (C.I.L., VIII, 980), a little town on the North-west coast of the Roman province of Africa, where St Cyprian found shelter during his exile. Cf. Dessau, *Hermes*, LI (1916), p. 70 et s.

its merits.[1] In the first place, it suffers from the defect common to the greater part of the early Christian *Lives ;* the author having no other concern than to exhibit the exceptional action of the Holy Spirit on his hero, the psychological and really human interest is too much relegated to the second place. Then its rhetorical grandiloquence hardly conceals the scarcity of positive information. The recital of facts offers disconcerting bare patches (which it is true the contemporary reader could supplement). Pontius does not even mention by name the two Pro-Consuls before whom the Bishop appeared. He is aware that everyone was acquainted with the life of Cyprian (§ i), that the *Acta* of his martyr will provide many details which he omits (§ xi), and almost his entire interest is given up to edifying.—(2) The *Acta Proconsularia Cypriani*, which have been excellently analysed by Paul Monceaux,[2] are made up of three parts : (*a*) The report of the examination of Cyprian before the Pro-Consul Aspasius Paternus, and his exile to Curubis, on the 30th of August 257 ; (*b*) The report of his second examination before the Pro-Consul Galerius Maximus and his condemnation to death on September 258 ; (*c*) The account of his execution on the 18th of the Kalends of October 258 at Villa Sexti near Carthage. The document is remarkably precise. It must have been the work of a contemporary who had seen everything with his own eyes, had heard everything with his own ears and who at once consigned to writing what he had seen and heard.—(3) St Jerome only devotes to Cyprian a short notice in his *De Viris Illustribus*, § lxvii. Not that he holds the saint in mediocre literary esteem, but on the contrary, because his works were, as he states, " *luce clariora.*" We owe to him a few details which we do not find elsewhere.— (4) Lastly, Cyprian's letters provide a precious source of information for the period of his episcopate. Taken as a whole, this correspondence has a *quasi*-official character. Whether he writes under his own name, or whether he is

---

[1] *Das Leben Cyprians von Pontius, die erste christliche Biographie, unters,* von Adolf Harnack, Leipsic, 1913 (T.U., xxxix, 3). Compare with this Reitzenstein's appreciations in the *Sitz.-Ber. der Heidelb. Ak., phil. Hist. Kl.* 1913, Abh, n° 14, p. 46 et s. ; those of Corssen, in Z.N.W., xv (1914), 221 et s. ; 285 et s. ; xvi (1915), 54 et s. ; and that of C. Weyman, in B. ph. W., 1915, p. 1271 et s.

[2] II, 179–190. Adverse criticisms of Reitzenstein, ill-founded, are to be found in the *Sitz.-Ber. der Heidelb. Ak. d. Wiss.*, quoted above. See also Corssen, Z.N.W., 1916–1917.

acting as interpreter to the Synods over which he is presiding, it is always in his character as a Bishop that Cyprian shows himself. He had occasion to deliver an apology for his action in answer to certain false imputations, as we find in letter lxvi. But as a rule, he leaves himself out, and effaces himself behind the problem with which he is dealing, and does not speak of what concerns himself personally except when he is forced to. The correspondence of St Jerome was to be of quite another order. This is because Jerome was somewhat of a *franc-tireur* in the great army of the Church. St Cyprian, not requiring to express himself freely and frankly, as was to be the case with Jerome, was ruled entirely by the interests of which he was the guardian.

Cyprian was born in Africa. The date and place of his birth are not known. His family was pagan. Like all the young men of a certain position he passed through the usual course of studies and learned rhetoric, which later on, according to the testimony of St Jerome, he was to teach before his conversion. On his own confession, his youth was by no means chaste.[1] A priest, Caecilius,[2] or Caecilianus[3] by name, made him decide to change his mode of life. Cyprian adds the name of his spiritual instructor to that of his own : from that date, as it seems, he called himself C. Caecilius Cyprianus, *qui et Thascius* (the meaning of this sobriquet, *qui et Thascius*,[4] is unknown). He made a gift to the poor of part of his fortune, was baptised, became a priest, and shortly afterwards his talents caused him to be elected Bishop of Carthage at the end of the year 248 or at the beginning of 249, notwithstanding the opposition of certain members of the clergy.[5] A few months later, the persecution under Decius broke out. Cyprian did not feel it to be his duty to wait for martyrdom : he hid himself during the first month of the year 250 till April or May 251 : " He judged, and with reason, that with a Church it is the same as with an army, in which the death of a leader, however heroic this may be thought, may become the signal of defeat." [6] His flight however provoked hostile comments in Carthage and even in Rome. Cyprian felt the

[1] Cf. *Ad Donatum*, iii–iv.   [2] *De Vir. Ill.*, *l. c.*   [3] *Vita*, § lv.
[4] Monceaux, *op. cit.*, II, 202. For this form *qui et* cf. *Glotta*, IV (1912), n° 1–2.
[5] *Ep.*, lix, 6.
[6] Freppel, *Saint Cyprien*, Paris, 1890, p. 164.

F

need to justify himself.[1] But he gives the best apology for
his conduct in the admirable solicitude which he extended
from a distance over the interests of his Church. When he
came back to Carthage a series of difficult cases offered themselves for his decision. It was necessary to regulate the
question of the *lapsi*, that is to say, of Christians who had
" fallen away " during the recent persecution, and who were
seeking to re-enter the Church or even to slink back into it by
very equivocal methods. He had to combat a body of
rebellious priests who, with Novatus and Felicissimus at their
head, were setting themselves up against the authority of the
Bishop. While the Pontifical See of Rome was vacant
(from the 21st of January 250 to the beginning of March 251),
he energetically supported Cornelius after he had been
elected a candidate together with Novatian. His influence
among the Christians in Africa continued to grow, and the
Churches from all parts solicited his directions. The edict of
Gallus and Volusianus in the year 252 did not bring about the
general persecution which at first had been feared. But
other trials came upon the Christians in Africa, and Cyprian
extended to them the full measure of his devotion ; these
were raids on the Christians of Numidia for whose ransom
it was necessary to open a public subscription, and a devastating plague which was accompanied by a real weakening in
public morality and brought down on the Christians, who
were made responsible for this scourge, fresh ill-usage. His
last years were preoccupied by the question of the validity of
baptism conferred by heretics. Cyprian entered into conflict on this subject with Pope Stephen (254–257), and the
dispute soon became bitter on both sides, even to serious
danger. But soon the edict of Valerian, promulgated in
August 257, caused the first summons of Cyprian before the
tribunal of the Pro-Consul, who banished him to Curubis.
A year later, an order came to bring him back ; this time it
was for his martyrdom, to which he submitted on the 14th
September 258.

---

[1] *Ep.*, vii ; xiv, 1 ; xx, 1. Cf. *Ep.*, viii, written from Rome by the clergy in
Rome to the clergy in Carthage.

III

LET us begin with taking a glance at the ideas which really dominated the views and conduct of St Cyprian. By this means we shall lay hold of the thread which will help us to find our position when we follow him through one or other of the crises in which he took part.

We find a conception of the Church, a conception of the *rôle*, the prerogatives, and the duties of a Bishop diffused throughout the entire writings of Cyprian, which clearly explains his permanent attitude. I will endeavour to set it out in relief principally with the aid of the celebrated treatise *De Catholicae Ecclesiae Unitate* and his letters.

A firmly convinced apology of oneness,—considered as the leaven, the unifying link and the mark of the true Church —forms the foundation of the *De Catholicae Ecclesiae Unitate* and of all the pages in which Cyprian dealt with the same question. The worst enemy which the Christians had to fear was not that which let loose persecution ; for against persecution it was sufficient to arm oneself with courage.[1] It was that which cunningly, by intrigues hatched under cover, *per pacis imaginem* [2] prepared the way for schism and heresy. There was no greater crime than to sow hatred among the faithful, than to separate them from their shepherds. At most the apostate only destroyed himself ; but the instigator of dissension applied himself to efface the fundamental and pacific character of the Church—namely, oneness. Words which come unceasingly from the pen of Cyprian are these : *unanimitas, concors, consensio.*[3] He multiplies mystical symbols borrowed from Scripture prefiguring this " unanimity " of will, this unbreakable cohesion of the faithful with their pastors : it was the seamless garment of Christ, the dove of the Canticle of Canticles (the faithful bird bringing peace, *par excellence*), the bread and wine of the Holy Sacrifice formed, the one of a handful of grains of wheat, the other of many clusters of grapes, etc. Certain of Cyprian's adversaries

[1] Cf. *de Unitate,* 1 et s.
[2] *Ibid.* (Hartel, I, 209, line 13).
[3] See Hartel's *Index,* or better still, the list drawn up by Chapman in the *R. Bén.,* 1902, pp. 365–367.

exploited the words of Christ : " Wheresoever two or three shall be gathered in My name there will I be in the midst of them," and drew from them a reason for justifying their desire for schism. Cyprian turns against them the text which they make a false use of, and proves to them that this maxim, far from justifying, condemns them. In uttering these words, the intention of Christ had been to testify His love of concord and union, since He allows it to be understood that He will be *more willingly* present with two or three persons animated by the same sentiment than with a great number of men whose hearts are beating out of unison.[1]

From such premises, Cyprian could only draw conclusions of total exclusion against those who seceded from, or remained outside, a society so closely bound up in the spirit of obedience and charity. He did not at all recoil from the consequences, or rather insisted on them with determination. The most laudable actions, in his view, lose their merit outside the Church : martyrdom was fruitless, graces were without value, and salvation became impossible.[2]

His attitude in the matter of the baptism of heretics [3] is logically explained by the view which he held. Was it necessary to rebaptise converts who, abandoning the different sects which flourished on the outskirts of the Church, asked to be admitted within her pale ? Was the imposition of hands and anointing with oil according to the Roman practice, or *consignatio*, sufficient ? When the question was put to Cyprian by certain bishops of Mauretania, he seems to have nowhere experienced the scruples over which these latter were hesitating. Moreover, he had already expressed his opinion in the *De Catholicae Ecclesiae Unitate* (§ 11). The definitions by which he affirms it anew are of a preciseness which lends itself to no equivocation. " Baptism is one, just as the Holy Spirit is one, just as the Church is one." [4] " There can be no baptism outside the Church." [5] " We do not re-baptise ; we baptise those who come to us from among the heretics : they could not have received anything from the heretics, since these latter are of no account." [6] He added another reason which was not that of a psychologist of

---

[1] *De Unit.*, § 12. [2] § 14-15.
[3] The most important items in the *dossier* are letters lxix to lxxv and the Acts of the Councils held on this matter.
[4] *Ep.*, lxx, 3. [5] *Ep.*, lxxi, 1. [6] *Ibid.*

mediocre intuition : [1] " Do not think that the heretics, scandalised at our opposition to their baptism, in which they see a second baptism, will be the less disposed to come back to the Church. Very much the contrary ; this public declaration of our faith will convince them the more profoundly of the necessity in which they are placed of embracing the truth. If they see that our decisions make their baptism valid and legitimate, they will believe that they are in legal possession of the Church and of its privileges. Hence they will have no further motive to come back to us. Make plain to them on the contrary that outside the Church baptism is without virtue . . . you will see them very quickly imploring the favours and gifts of the Mother Church." We know with what inflexibility Cyprian opposed this absolute theory to that of Pope Stephen. The dispute grew keener almost to the point of a rupture. The letter of Firmilian of Caesarea to Cyprian (*Ep.*, lxxv) [2] reveals to what a pitch the dispute had reached. The death of Stephen, which took place on the 2nd of August 257, somewhat calmed down the nervous tension of the controversy. On the whole, it was through his passion for the unity and integrity of the Church that Cyprian had been drawn, in agreement with his colleagues in Africa [3], to maintain so vehemently a doctrine which the future was to decide in a contrary sense.

We can see without difficulty the *rôle* which the Bishop played in the organisation of the Church. He was the essential part of that collectivity of which the Church is composed, and it was on him as the successor of the Apostles that in a special degree was laid the charge of maintaining its entire unity. [4] Without doubt, it was the suffrage of the people which elected him (nowhere does Cyprian protest against this altogether democratic method of election) ; [5] but it was God who conferred on him his sacred character.

---

[1] *Ep.*, lxxiii, 24.

[2] P.L., iii, 1154 ; Hartel, II, 810–827.

[3] On the Councils relating to this matter, cf. Monceaux, ii, chap. ii. See also H. von Soden, *Sententiae* lxxxvii *Episcoporum. Das Protokoll der Synode von Karthago am 1 Sept.* 256 *textkritisch. dargestellt und uberliefe-rungsgeschichtlich unters.*, in the *Nachrichten* of Gottingen, 1909, 3, pp. 247–307 ; Id., *die Prosopographie des afrikanischen Episkopats zur Zeit Cyprians*, extract from *Quellen und Forsch. aus ital. Archiven u. Bibliotheken*, 1909.

[4] Cf. *Ep.*, xlv, 3 (Hartel, II, 602).

[5] He seems even to have had full confidence in the wisdom of popular choice. Cf. *Ep.*, lxvii, 4–5 (Hartel, II, 738).

And, once provided with this twofold human and divine investiture, the Bishop enjoyed the widest prerogatives. He was the director, and the administrator of his flock, and God will punish those who revolt against his authority.[1] The price paid for this pre-eminence was the devotion, moral integrity, and constant zeal of which he ought to give proof. The rights of Bishops corresponded to their duties which were much more formidable than those which weighed on the faithful : it was by these that they were justified.[2] In other respects, even and above all for a Bishop, union with the body of the faithful, with the Church, was the mark of orthodoxy. If he compromised this unity, however regular his promotion may have been, he loses his title.[3]

Such, shortly reviewed, is Cyprian's theory of the Church and of the Episcopate. There is still a point nevertheless on which it is necessary to touch. Did Cyprian admit that there was somewhere a head of this great body of the Church ? Did he accept a centralisation in this ecclesiastical unity of which he was so ardent a defender ? In other words, did he bow before the Roman Primacy, before the magistracy of the successor of Peter ? Here is a problem which has been very often discussed [4] and to which even at this day divergent solutions are brought. Hugo Koch, an old pupil of F. X. Funk, the celebrated professor of the Faculty of Catholic Theology of Tubingen, devoted to it in 1910 quite a collection of *Texte und Untersuchungen* (xxxv, 1), as a first token of the evolution in doctrine which he had just accomplished outside the ranks of Catholicism. " Cyprian did not recognise popery either as of doctrine or as of right " (p. iv). His fundamental contention may be summed up as follows. In order to demonstrate it, Koch could have endeavoured to follow the evolution of the views of Cyprian in the course of his works,— the chronological order of his treatises and his letters being sufficiently established in spite of a few doubtful points. He preferred another plan in which his method of dialectics suited him better. He goes straight to the *De Catholicae*

---

[1] *Ep.*, iii, 1 (Hartel, II, 470, I, 1) ; *Ep.*, lxix, 4 (Hartel, II, 670, I, 16).

[2] He did not hesitate to counsel the people of Léon and Asturias to no longer " be in community with " two unworthy Bishops (*Ep.*, lxvii).

[3] *Ep.*, lv, 24 (Hartel, II, p. 643, I, 4) ; *Ep.*, lxv, 4 (Hartel, II, p. 724, I, 18).

[4] In J. Turmel's *Histoire de la Théologie Positive*, vol. II (Paris, 1902), p. 216 et s., 269 et s., we can see in what warm controversy Catholic and Protestant polemists have engaged around the disputed texts of Cyprian.

Ecclesiae Unitate and chooses two short chapters for his treatise —the ivth and the vth. From a very minute analysis, he deduces the following conclusion : If Christ first established the Church on Peter alone (cf. Mt. xvi, 18 et s.), this was solely, in the opinion of Cyprian, in order to render tangible and as it were visible by means of that unity among its members, the moral unity which was to reign in His Church. But such a priority in point of time did not at all confer on Peter any pre-eminence in authority or honour : it had a purely symbolical bearing, and the other Apostles continued to be the equals of Peter, *pari consortio praediti et honoris et potestatis.* St Cyprian too considered the Episcopate as the heir of the Apostolic College, as forming one whole, in which each Bishop, jointly and severally, held a portion of the whole (*cuius a singulis in solidum pars tenetur*), in full equality with his colleagues.

It is in the light of these fundamental principles thus deduced from the *De Cath. Eccles. Unitate,* that Koch proceeds to examine each of the declarations scattered through the writings of Cyprian, in which people have sometimes read a confession of the exceptional preponderance of the *Cathedra Petri.* He finds nothing in them which goes beyond or which contradicts them, but only the reiterated affirmation of the independence of each Bishop in his diocese. Cyprian's attitude in face of Pope Stephen over the question of the baptism of heretics, the rather curt style which he makes use of in regard to the Roman Pontiff, his manner of acting in certain ecclesiastical matters in which Rome was interested, for example, the deposition of Basilides and of Martial (*Ep.,* lxvii), the excommunication of Marcian, Bishop of Arles (*Ep.,* lxviii),—all confirm Koch in the justness of his interpretation.

His reasoning has such stern force and his putting together evinces so much logic, that on reading it for the first time we may ask how we can draw any other conclusion than he has, basing ourselves on the same texts. However, we have not to draw attention solely to his religious prejudices. Koch himself, in his introduction, partitions off the critics, his predecessors, into three groups : those who think that Cyprian explicitly admitted the primacy of jurisdiction of the Bishop of Rome ; those who make him the representative of an " episcopalism " with special characteristics, excluding any kind of primacy ; lastly, those who, taking up an intermediate position, believe that Cyprian recognised in the Roman Church, if not a primacy of jurisdiction, at least the authority belonging to a real centre of unity for the universal Church. Now Otto Ritschl is in company with Dom Chapman in the first category ; Ehrhard and Tixeront rub shoulders with Loofs and Benson in the second ; and we are surprised to see associated, in the third, Harnack, Funk and Batiffol.

The real fact of the matter is that a certain number of points are obscure, and remain so even after Koch's penetrating study. That the interpretation given by Koch to § iv of the *De Cath. Eccl. Unit.* is the only likely, the only legitimate one, and that every other does violence to the words of Cyprian or introduces into them arbitrary shades of thought, we must not hesitate to recognise. The investiture specially conferred on St Peter is very rarely taken into consideration by Cyprian in this chapter under the aspect of a symbolic prefiguration. But before adhering fully to the consequences which Koch deduces from it, one would like to rest secure on one or two preliminary certitudes whereof the correctness is in doubt. In this treatise, in which Cyprian had in fact no other object than by an energetic appeal for union and " unity " to baffle the intrigues incessantly being hatched against him by the group of restless Christian spirits, has he given us a formal and full instruction on his theory of the organisation and the hierarchy of the Church, or rather was he not at pains to demonstrate the heterogeneous nature of the spirit of schism as contrasted with the spirit of Christianity, by a series of illustrations which are not at all equivalent to considered and complete theological formulæ ? Then does Cyprian himself count for nothing in the famous " interpolation " (which is appreciably more favourable to the *primatus Petri*) of § iv in that other reading of the text in which Dom Chapman,[1] who has the support of Harnack,[2]

---

[1] Louis Saltet (B.L.E., 1920, 170–206), as against Dom Chapman, recognises a real contradiction in doctrine between the two recensions of the famous passage in the *De Unit. Eccl. Cath.*, iv. He does not think that St Cyprian retracted it, and admits unreservedly the hypothesis of an interpolation.

[2] T.L.Z., 1903, col. 262. Cf. *R. Bén.*, 1902–1903. Ernest Havet wrote in 1885 (*Rev. des Deux Mondes*, 1st Sept., p. 67) : " I do not see in it anything which formally contradicts Cyprian's ideas, and instead of supposing that additions were made to the text in the interests of the Church at Rome, we can equally well suppose on the contrary that people who were in opposition to the pretensions of that Church may have suppressed certain portions ; or further, perhaps Cyprian himself as a consequence of his quarrel with Stephen ".

recognises his style and handiwork, while Laurand even
perceives in it indications of his favourite way of ending his
sentences ? [1] Even if this twofold difficulty be definitely
decided in the sense favoured by Koch, we should still have
to ask ourselves if he does not, by despoiling them of their
essence and fulness, press to an extreme limit certain of the
expressions which Cyprian uses to indicate the Church in
Rome (v.g. " navigare audent et ad Petri cathedram atque ad
ecclesiam principalem unde unitas sacerdotalis exorta est " in
Ep. LIX, 14 : Pope Cornelius, to whom the letter is addressed,
must at any rate have understood it in a rather less narrow
sense than Koch makes of it) ; or if, on the other hand, he
does not too much exaggerate the importance of the *rôle*
played by Cyprian, however ample this *rôle* may have been,
when he represents the Bishop of Carthage as being the
" conscience " of the whole Western Church. A man who
held such personal ideas on the Episcopate and on baptism
might well have formed (keenly jealous as he was of his own
authority) a particular conception of the precedence of Rome.

It still remains none the less clear that the inner core of
his theological system was the imperious need for co-ordination
and discipline. This principle, so firmly established in his
mind, served him as a criterion in all doubtful cases which it
was his duty to decide.

It is worth our while to examine the influences which fixed
in him this zeal for close solidarity.[2] There is no doubt that
the scenes of political life which he had witnessed in his youth
partly contributed to this result. We know to what prolonged anarchy the Roman Empire had been a prey during
the period following the death of Marcus Aurelius. In the
space of forty-three years (192–235), the Praetorians and the
Legionaries brought about no less than six military *coups
d'état.* The world saw itself governed by madmen or
profligates, such as Commodus and Heliogabalus. The rivalry
between candidates for power drenched many provinces
in blood. How was the Empire able to withstand such
shocks ? It was due to Roman administration, to their

---

[1] B. ph. W., 1909, col. 1016.
[2] On this point, see some interesting ideas which have had their influence on me
in an article in the *Revue de théologie et de philosophie*, 1893, p. 105 et s., *Saint
Cyprien et les Influences qui l'ont formé*, by Eug. de Faye.

system of municipal government and to the army. Thanks to their well-geared machinery, these great organisations upheld the framework of the national life and prevented it from breaking up in disorder and chaos. A mind so keenly observant as that of Cyprian could not fail to have been struck by the conservating force of the principle of order and hierarchy whose effects he could see all around him. Had he remained a pagan he would have made an excellent Pro-Consul : as a Christian, he was an admirable Bishop.

I will add that the incidents which marked his Episcopate without doubt accentuated in him this passion for moral union and some sort of material cohesion. In the very bosom of the Christian body, to his perpetual vexation, he had to deal with restless spirits who did not cease to hatch intrigues and to work against him in an underhand manner. Dom Chapman has very ably demonstrated that the *De Catholicae Ecclesiae Unitate*, in which the views of Cyprian are summed up, was composed at the time of his differences with Felicissimus.[1] This Felicissimus had been made a deacon, without the consent of the Bishop, by Novatus, one of the five priests who were implacable adversaries of Cyprian, and after the departure of Novatus he had become the head of the small hostile *clique*. Harassed as he was by schism within at a time when all Christians should have faced the enemy hand in hand, how could Cyprian have failed to feel keenly the value of a unity which his enemies were struggling hard to relax, in proportion as he himself was strengthening their bonds ?

Lastly, we may add that Cyprian's theory of the Church and of the *rôle* of the Episcopate was in some ways the outcome of a long series of facts which had prepared it beforehand. Throughout the crises which one after the other had failed to weaken the Church—the intellectual crisis connected with Gnosticism, and the moral crisis arising from Montanism, the Episcopate had become more and more strengthened as the guardian of the rule of faith, and as the authorised interpreter of the Spirit. It was thus natural that Cyprian, improving on St Irenæus and Tertullian (I am speaking of the Tertullian of the *De Praescriptione*), should accentuate this idea of the preponderating authority of the

[1] *R. Bén.*, 1903, p. 26 et s.

Bishops, who were the sole organs of doctrine and the representatives of living tradition in the Church.

Such views, held by a man of such high intelligence and of such an upright heart, could not but reinforce his zeal for doing well and his ambition to be equal to his task however heavy it might be. We will now see how he put them into practical application.

IV

ONE of the first difficulties to present themselves to Cyprian when he became a Bishop was the famous question of the *lapsi*,[1] which followed on the edict of the Emperor Decius which was put in force at the end of the year 249 or at the beginning of 250. The complete text of this edict has not come down to us ; but we know fairly well the manner in which it was applied. The procedure had been perfectly set out with administrative precision. On a fixed day throughout the Roman Empire in the towns and villages, the inhabitants were obliged to present themselves before a local commission composed of magistrates and notabilities.[2] On his name being called out, each one came forward and found himself under the necessity of proving by an act, or some sort of idolatrous gesture, that he had never been a Christian, or if he had been that he renounced it. The commissioners gave him in exchange a certificate, *libellus*, duly signed and dated.[3]

These well-devised dispositions threw the Christians into panic. At Carthage, where the ceremony took place at the Capitol, there was a rush to apostatise : " There were those," Cyprian tells us,[4] " who did not wait to be apprehended before mounting to the Capitol, nor to be questioned in order to apostatise. Defeated before the battle, laid low before

---

[1] These are the principal relevant documents in the *dossier :* the treatise *De Lapsis ;* letters xv, xvi, xvii, xviii, xix, xxv, xxvii, xxx, xxxiii, xxxv, xxxvi, xxxix, lv, lvi.

[2] As regards Carthage, cf. *Ep.* xliii, 3 (Hartel, 592) : " . . . quinque primores illi qui edicto nuper magistratibus fuerant copulati, ut fidem nostram subruerent."

[3] See P. Foucart, *Les certificats de sacrifice pendant la persécution de Decius,* in the *Journal des Savants,* 1908, p. 177 et s. ; Dom Leclercq, *Les certificats de sacrifice paien sous Déce en* 250, in B.A.L.A.C., vol. IV (1914), p. 52 et s. ; 188 et s. (Dom Leclercq gives the text and the translation of 25 *libelli* coming from different localities in Egypt) ; Faulhaber, in Z.K.T., 1919, p. 439 et s., 617 et s.

[4] *De Lapsis,* viii.

being assaulted, many did not even stay to make the excuse of appearing to sacrifice to idols by constraint. These people ran to the Forum and freely hastened to (spiritual) death, as if they had for long desired to do so, as if they took advantage of an opportunity long cherished in the depths of their heart. How many of them did not the magistrates, in view of the late hour, put off till the following day! How many of them begged that their death might not be deferred![1] . . . And to fill up the measure of these crimes, there were seen children being brought forward and led by the hand of their parents, to lose still so young the divine mark which they had received at the very threshold of their lives."

A certain number of the faithful, shrinking from a heroism the refusal of which would have been the inevitable punishment of incarceration or death, and from a formal apostasy, bethought themselves of an ingenious expedient. Thanks to the interested good-nature of minor functionaries, they secured, for a sum of money, the *libellus* which it was enough to show in order to remain henceforth unmolested.

Hence arose two categories of *lapsi :* the *sacrificati* and the *libellatici*, culpable in an unequal degree without doubt, but both reprobated by the consciences of those who had not given way.

What had been the former attitude of the Churches relative to failures of this kind ? The procedure of doing penance was not probably the same in all communities.[2] But it would appear that thirty years before Cyprian, apostasy counted as one of those crimes to which most of the Churches accorded no forgiveness.[3] Without doubt the sinner was bound to do penance ; but pardon was reserved to God, whose decision the Bishop did not recognise in himself any right to anticipate.

Such sternness seemed discouraging to those who had fallen away. Before even the rigours of the Government had ceased, several were trying how to be reinstated in the Church, from which their desertion had excluded them. Some zealots presented themselves anew before the tribunal recanting their recent weakness.[4] Others subjected themselves

---

[1] This relates, of course, to the death of *the soul*, as above.
[2] We may conclude this from St Cyprian, *Ep.* lv, 20–21.
[3] Cf. P. de Labriolle, *La Crise Montaniste*, p. 425 et s.
[4] *Ep.* xxiv.

to expiations which they might expect would last as long as their lives. But for the great majority such a method appeared extremely severe and they looked about for some less stony path whereby to re-enter the fold.

From the time of Tertullian, and doubtless even before that, it was admitted that those who had suffered for the faith disposed of a certain right of intercession on behalf of sinners. Pope Callixtus had even, as it seems, officially sanctioned this right, without our being able to know exactly in what way he had fixed its limitations. The greater part of the *lapsi* very soon conceived the idea of utilising for their benefit the merits accumulated by the heroism of the confessors.[1] In this they were encouraged by the group of priests who detested Cyprian and who were not at all indisposed to favour in his absence—for the Bishop, as we have said, had left Carthage when the storm broke out—any moves of a nature to diminish his authority.[2]

However praiseworthy had been the firmness shown by them in the face of the Roman power, the confessors were not all of them of irreproachable moral eminence. Some of them were of the kind to feel flattered at playing the *rôle* of liberator in regard to their less staunch brethren. By an act of generosity which cost little, and without requiring any guarantee of repentance or of doing penance,[3] they granted permits of reconciliation to those who solicited them. People succeeded in obtaining these under fictitious names for the benefit of their friends. A traffic arose in them.[4] Certain permits were issued in these terms : *Communicet ille cum suis,* an elastic formula which under the pretext of kinship more or less authentic allowed a host of people to obtain pardon *en bloc.*[5]

We may imagine the feelings of Cyprian when he became aware of such regrettable abuses. These unauthorised and unrestrained proceedings, this total forgetfulness of the just prerogatives of the Bishop and of the methods in use up till then for the pardon of faults committed, and all this lack of order must have shocked in the highest degree his instincts

---

[1] Several of them had perished under torture or in prison, cf. *Ep.* xxii, 2 (Hartel, 534). But the trial which the majority had to undergo was prolonged incarceration under very painful conditions.

[2] Cf. *Ep.* xv, 2 (Hartel, 513).

[3] *Ibid.*   [4] xv, 3.   [5] xv, 4.

as a conscientious administrator. His *rôle*, however, was a most delicate one. To restore in its entirety the old discipline was (and this he knew well) to range against him quite a large portion of public opinion which found these cheap pardons to their advantage. Had there not been in certain towns open sedition against their Bishop in order to compel him to authorise these premature reconciliations ? [1] And in face of these outbreaks many had yielded.

However, Cyprian did not hesitate. Any weakness would have meant the abdication of the rights with which he considered himself to be invested. He entered into the struggle without resorting to fruitless strong measures, or to impulsive violence, but consistently imbued with certain very clear-cut principles : (1) By personally inaugurating the measures necessary, but taking care to inform his colleagues of the other Episcopal Sees, his clergy, and the clergy in Rome (at that time without a Bishop), so as to clearly assure himself at each step that he had been approved and followed by all those whose moral collaboration he desired ; (2) By straining longanimity as far as possible, but without permitting any encroachment on his authority as a Bishop. In the case of open and persistent rebellion, by acting with energy and cutting into the quick.

Moreover, he understood perfectly well the complexity of the problem offered to him, and did not flatter himself to be able to resolve it by himself. He realised that it would be inhuman to impose a life expiation on the " fallen," who had undergone the pressure of such difficult circumstances and of the example given by a movement that was well-nigh general. But, on the other hand, was it lawful that they should be exonerated from all penalty when, for far less grave offences, other sinners must go through the series of trials by " exhomologesis " ? [2] The difficulty did not only arise at Carthage, but in all the Churches over which the storm had passed : *Non paucorum, nec ecclesiae unius, nec unius provinciae, sed totius orbis haec causa est.*[3] Only a general Council would have the authority to adjudicate definitely on the question once tranquillity had returned.[4] But pending this

---

[1] *Ep.* xxvii, 3. [2] Cf. *Ep.* xv, 2. [3] *Ep.* xix, 2. Cf. xxx, 5.
[4] *Ep.* lv, 4, etc. Such was likewise the opinion of the Roman clergy : cf. *Ep.* xxx, 5.

authoritative decision which would without doubt assure uniformity of procedure, Cyprian felt it to be his right and his duty to pronounce on facts which seemed to him to admit of no hesitation. And this, shortly reviewed, was his line of theological reasoning :

With regard to those *lapsi*, who insolently demanded their reconciliation as a right and appeared to be determined to carry it by assault, he showed himself unbending and without pity. He told them that if they were in such a hurry they had at their disposal a very simple means of curtailing the delays : the field was still open to them ; why did they not hasten to suffer martyrdom ? With one blow the taint of apostasy would be wiped out.[1] He likewise blamed without hesitation those priests who, obligingly facilitating demands which were inadmissible, had communicated with *lapsi* before they had received any official absolution.[2] As regards the confessors his position was more embarrassing, for he could not diminish the claim to consideration which their courage had won for them. He was anxious when the question arose to give evidence of the real value which he attached to their intervention. Thus he decided that when one who had fallen away had received a permit of reconciliation from a martyr and found himself in danger of death, it should be lawful to him to obtain peace by the ministry of a priest or, in case of urgency, of a simple deacon without waiting for the decision of the Bishop.[3] But this concession was to be exceptional. He formally invited confessors to refrain from giving out plenary and summary immunities. Let them be content to designate by name in their *libelli* those sinners whom they thought worthy to be absolved and fitting recipients of the benefits pertaining to the right of intercession which they desired to exercise. As soon as security should return, the Bishop would submit these requests to the assembled Church, and with their advice, would give his decision with full knowledge of what he was doing.[4]

Their prerogative thus remained subordinated to due examination by the *Ecclesia* and to the decision of the Bishop. This was the principle firmly established in the mind of Cyprian : hence his indignation on receiving some such kind

---

[1] *Ep.* xviii, 2.
[2] *Ep.* xv, 2.
[3] *Ep.* xviii, 1.   Cf. *Ep.* xviii, 2
[4] *Ep.* xvii, 1.

of permit [1] in which martyrs notified to him in a peremptory tone the pardon which they were granting to all those whose conduct posterior to their apostasy should be judged to have been irreproachable.

Further, when he perceived sincere repentance and a wish to expiate the failure of the past, he leaned at once towards indulgence. Thus, in *Epistle* LVI,[2] he examines the case of three Christians who, after having victoriously emerged from a first trial, had ended by giving way before their atrocious tortures. Since then,—three years had already intervened,—they had not ceased doing penance. While reserving the decision for an approaching Council, Cyprian clearly expresses his own personal view : the circumstances of their " fall " and their present goodwill gave them the most legitimate claim to a pardon.

In the first days of April, 251, a Council was convened at Carthage to regulate these distressing questions.[3] Without doubt it was to this assembly that Cyprian read his admirable treatise *De Lapsis* in which he made as it were an examination of conscience of the Church in Africa on the morrow of the formidable crisis through which it had just passed. The work begins with an utterance of joy at peace having at last come back to the Church, and with a pious testimony of admiration in regard to those confessors who had proved stronger than their tortures. Then he enters upon the painful problem offered by the numerous desertions which the Church in Africa had witnessed. He shows that if God had been thus pleased to test His followers, it was because the weakness of their faith called for a chastisement which should reinvigorate them.[4] It was the previous attachment of nearly all to the goods of this world which by enervating their souls had led to the basest abdication. The last part of the treatise is a long exhortation to penance conceived in the most pathetic terms, but which evolves a very precise definition as to the rights of confessors, rights too often widened to excessive limits by pardons giving scandal.

This work is of surprising unction, profundity of sentiment,

---

[1] Cf. *Ep.* xxiii and *Ep.* xxvii, 2.
[2] Hartel, 648.
[3] It is not impossible that there may have been two Councils in 251. Cf. Monceaux, II, 43.
[4] *De Lapsis*, vi.

and tact. All that he had to say is said, but with dispositions full of a most attentive regard for charity.

Finally, the Council came to the following decisions (these are known to us, not by the acts of the Council, which we no longer have, but by Cyprian's letters, *Epistle* LV, in particular) : (1) All hope of making peace with the Church was not taken from the guilty, but a long penance was imposed upon them with the obligation to solicit the indulgence of the Bishop who would have to pronounce on particular cases ; [1] (2) Different treatment was given to the *libellatici* and the *lapsi*. The former, as being less blameworthy, would be authorised to re-enter into communion after due enquiry. The *lapsi* could only obtain their pardon *in articulo mortis*.[2] On this last point, therefore, the Council showed itself more rigorous than Cyprian himself was disposed to be ; (3) Those *lapsi* who should refuse the *exhomologesis* could not be reconciled even *in articulo mortis*.[3]

In the spring of the following year, a fresh Council consisting of 42 Bishops accorded a general amnesty to those *lapsi* who should submit to the requisite penance, but all hope of recovering their priesthood was denied to Bishops, priests and deacons who had yielded during the struggle.[4]

The question of the *lapsi* was not definitely closed. It had too profoundly shaken the conscience of the Christians not to entail lengthy consequences. In Rome, the rigorist party who were grouped around the priest Novatian protested against the lenient treatment which the Councils thought to be legitimate and necessary. However, the lenient party under Cyprian won the day. It was he who had thought out in advance the most equitable solution, and the most practical at that time. These words sum up his consistent moderation and firmness : " *Conscientiae nostrae convenit*," he wrote to Pope Cornelius, " *dare operam ne quis culpa nostra de Ecclesia pereat*." He had suffered deeply from the thought that too much severity would plunge so many souls into despair ; but equally, his goodness of heart had been restrained by reasonable anxiety for the prerogatives of a Bishop and for the " sacrament " of union.[5]

---

[1] *Ep.* lv, 6.   [2] *Ep.* lv, 2, 6, 17 ; lviii, 1 ; lix, 13.
[3] *Ep.* lv, 23.   [4] *Ep.* lvii, 1 and 5.
[5] The expression *sacramentum unitatis* occurs frequently in his works (Hartel): pp. 213, 11 ; 215, 11 ; 600, 4 ; 668, 8 ; 754, 15 ; 786, 13 ; 808, 3 ; 809, 9 ; 820, 1.

V

WE now have a grasp of the principles governing St Cyprian
and the methods he followed in adjusting them to realities.
A brief appreciation of his treatises and his *libelli* will be
sufficient : this latter expression he frequently employs to
designate them.

The *Ad Donatum* must be placed very shortly after the
passing of Cyprian to Christianity. It is the outburst of
a new convert who recalls his moral blindness before baptism,
and the weight of the chains which his passions had riveted
on him, and who feels himself delivered and flooded with
light. He makes his friend Donatus, also a Christian but a
little less ardent as it seems, his confidant in the marvellous
work which the revivifying faith has operated in him.

Some have desired to transform this enthusiastic mono-
logue into a dialogue : [1] to do this, it is enough to place at the
beginning certain very commonplace lines which have been
relegated by Hartel [2] to the category of apocryphal documents,
in which Donatus clumsily asserts the community of thought
which has always linked him with Cyprian, and appears to
remind him of a promise : the *Ad Donatum* begins merely
with these words : " Bene admones, Donate carissime ;
nam et *promisisse me memini*, etc. . . ." But this conjecture hardly appears to be a happy one. Why should
this tag have been eliminated from most of the manuscripts ?
Does it not destroy the parallelisms at the beginning and
the end of the work between the two descriptions with which
he opens and closes it ? The epithet " *sanctissime* Cypriane "
is also very strange at this date. Then, there is no allusion
in the rest of the work permitting us to think that the author
really made use of the form of a dialogue.

Cyprian represents Donatus as climbing with him a high
mountain from which they see the wide perspective of human
life : on all sides reign corruption and unrest, at the games,
at the theatre, in the homes, in the law courts and public life,
and even in the palace of the Emperor. In contradistinction,
the Holy Spirit brings equilibrium and peace to whosoever
shall take God for his sole support.

A tone of strong sincerity animates the *Ad Donatum*

---

[1] Goetz in T.U., xix, 1 (1899).   [2] Hartel, III. 272.

and yet its form is wordy and verbose, and void of all simplicity. St Augustine tactfully noted [1] the service which
serious and " sane " Christian doctrine had rendered to
Cyprian's style by gradually diverting it from these conceits :
" . . . ut sciretur a posteris, quam linguam doctrinae
christianae sanitas ab ista redundantia revocaverit et ad
eloquentiam graviorem modestioremque restrinxerit. . . ."
When Cyprian wrote the *Ad Donatum* the rhetorician still
survived in him. He was never quite to renounce the
niceties and affectations of his former school, but he was to
become far more sparing of them than such a beginning
would have allowed us to suppose.

The *Ad Demetrianum* is an eloquent denunciation of a
certain Demetrianus, without doubt a magistrate,[2] or possibly merely a rhetorician, in any case an implacable enemy
of the Christians, who had spread abroad the rumour that
certain recent calamities—war, pestilence, famine and drought
—must be put to the account of their impiousness. We are
acquainted with this complaint which was for a long time yet
to be revived : Tertullian had already drawn attention to
it ; [3] it is mentioned at the beginning of the *Adversus Nationes*
by Arnobius ; Lactantius makes allusion to it in his *Institutiones Divinae ;* [4] St Augustine examines it fully in his *Civitas
Dei.* It was St Cyprian who pinned down the fundamental
points of the Christian refutation. He did not concern
himself to question the acts of Providence, but to demonstrate
the anger of Heaven called down against the vices of the
pagans, who were alone responsible, which furnished to the
Christians themselves the opportunity of trials which they
accepted with resignation and confidence, whereas the pagans
had nothing to oppose to the sufferings which fall upon them.
In § viii, we note a curious passage on slavery : here the
Christian is assuming the accents of Stoicism : [5]

" From thy slave thou dost exact absolute submission.
Thou art man and dost oblige a man to obey thee. You

---

[1] *De doct. Christ.*, iv, 14.

[2] Cf. § viii (Hartel, p. 356), x, xii, xiii. Some have objected to the tone of this
work as lacking respect. Was Tertullian much more deferent in regard to the
Pro-Consul Scapula ?

[3] *Apol.*, lx ; *ad Nat.*, I, ix ; *ad Scap.*, iii.

[4] V, iv, 3.

[5] Cf. Seneca, *Ep.* xlvii, 6 : " Vis tu cogitare istum, quem servum tuum vocas,
ex iisdem seminibus ortum, eodem frui caelo, aeque spirare, aeque vivere, aeque
mori ? "

are both called to birth by the same chance, subjected
to death by the same condition, formed of the same
matter, endowed with the same soul ; by the same law
by which you enter into this world, you go out from it.
In spite of this, if he serve thee not according to thy
wish, if he bend not to thy least desire, imperiously
and without pity thou dost make him pay the penalty
of his servitude : stripes, hunger, nakedness, even the
sword or the dungeon are the punishments which thy
cruelty exercises against him."

The tone is harsher and more biting in places than even
that of the *Ad Scapulam.* Cyprian had to deal with a dangerous fanatic whom he made it his business to unmask.
In the first pages he still lingers over a fastidious rhetorical
development on the growing decrepitude of the universe.
The rest of the pamphlet is of a fine, passionate vigour.

The authenticity of the *Quod Idola Dii non Sint* is not
absolutely certain. St Jerome,[1] however, and St Augustine [2]
attributed it to Cyprian, and such testimony should not
lightly be set aside. This mediocre *opusculum*, borrowed
almost entirely, not only in its ideas, but even sometimes in
its expressions, from Tertullian and Minucius Felix, is divided
into three parts : a criticism of mythology from the Evhemerist
point of view (§ i–vii) ; the attributes of God, among which
unity is placed first (§ viii–ix) ; an outline of a Christology
(§ x–xv). Without doubt, this is a work which came soon
after the conversion of Cyprian, who in his zeal as a neophyte
thought he could not do better than review the ideas which
he had come across in the most well-known apologies of that
period.

The three books of the *Testimonia ad Quirinum* are no
longer in dispute as being by Cyprian. At most, we can
admit that certain interpolations have crept into the third
book. When Cyprian put together this compilation—this
is the most suitable description—he must already have been
a priest, perhaps a Bishop : he calls Quirinus " *Fili carissime.*"

" The plan of this treatise," he explains to Quirinus,
" conforms to your desire : it is a *compendium*, an

---

[1] *Ep.* lxx, 5, *ad Magnum.*
[2] *De Bapt.*, VI, xliv, 87 ; *de Unico Bapt. c. Petie.*, iv, 6.

epitome. I did not wish to present any developments, but to group and bind together extracts so far as my poor memory can supply them. See in this, not a formal treatise, but material for the use of those who might wish to write one. This brevity has great advantages for the reader. Without confusing his mind over too long an explanation, it supplies useful summaries to his memory which it can faithfully preserve."

Each chapter opens by setting forth a thesis : thus, in the first book, the failure of the Jews and the call of the Gentiles is demonstrated in twenty-four theses ; in the second book, the divinity and the mission of Christ are developed in thirty theses ; in the third book (added afterwards, for the introduction only announced two books), the duties of a Christian in the moral and disciplinary order are given in detail in 120 theses. Under each of these theses, a certain number of quotations capable of illustrating them are given. Thanks to the *Testimonia*, we have a very good knowledge of the Latin text of the Bible as it was read in Carthage towards the middle of the IIIrd century. From this time there was something like an " official " Bible in Africa. Cyprian does not give to his quotations the variety of readings which Tertullian used. He makes his references from an almost uniform text. Thus, out of 886 verses from the New Testament quoted in the *Testimonia* and in his other works, there are 382 which are found repeated twice or several times with only insignificant variations.

For the polemists of the IIIrd and IVth centuries, the *Testimonia* became an arsenal to which they came to equip themselves. This collection of relevant and classified passages placed at their disposal appropriate weapons, and the value of such convenient resources was keenly appreciated.

The *Ad Fortunatum de Exhortatione Martyrii* has much analogy to the *Testimonia*. It is a collection of exhortations borrowed from Scripture with the view of preparing the *milites Christi* for the struggles which they might have to face. Cyprian explains his plan in a preface addressed to Fortunatus (possibly the Bishop of Thuccabori) : [1] " military " metaphors abound in accordance with the practice of Chris-

[1] This Fortunatus of Thuccabori is mentioned in the *Sententiae episcoporum* (Hartel, I, 444).

tians in the first centuries. Certain fundamental principles, such as the vanity of idols, the warning of Heaven against those who offer sacrifice to them, Jesus Christ to be preferred in everything, and the hatred of the world to Christianity, serve as a peg for quotations from the Bible with which Cyprian mingles his own observations. A fine peroration on the signal honour of martyrdom brings to an end this manual of heroism through which blows the breath of combats.

It has been remarked that all this *apologia* draws its arguments not from juridical demonstrations, nor from philosophic principles nor from " adverse " witnesses, but only from the lights derived from the Christian revelation. Such exclusiveness was to draw upon Cyprian the criticisms of some of his successors, the partisans of a more eclectic method.[1] It is difficult to decide whether Cyprian's method was better adapted than the other to his aim of defence and conquest. In any case, it is just what we should expect from a profoundly Christian mind like his, which paid little attention to methods from outside, and felt that he could do no better than offer to others the reasons which had appeared to him to be of decisive importance in the work of his own conversion.[2]

Another group of St Cyprian's writings bears a more strictly " homiletic " character. As is almost always the case with men of action, eloquence constituted one of the forces of Cyprian. " Such was his passion for speaking," Pontius[3] tells us, " that he wished, when the hoped-for day of his martyrdom should come, to meet his end while he should be speaking of God." He often preached both at Carthage and outside his Episcopal city.[4] The admirable vigour of his exhortations during the pestilence re-established order and the exercise of charity among the demoralised Christian community. Some of the treatises enable us, though imperfectly, to obtain an idea of what a " sermon " meant to Cyprian.

The *De Habitu Virginum* must belong to the beginning of his episcopate. This eulogium of virginity, specially

---

[1] Lactantius, *Inst. Div.*, V, vi, 4. " . . . Non enim Scripturae testimoniis, quam ille (Demetrianus) utique vanam, fictam, commenticiam putabat *sed argumentis et ratione* fuerat refellendus." St Jerome, *Ep.* lxx, 3, *ad Magnum*.

[2] *Vita Cypriani*, § xiv (Hartel, III, 3, p. cvi).

[3] Cf. *Ep.* lviii, 1 ; lxxvi, 1.

[4] *Vita Cypriani*, ix–x.

written for those young girls who had offered themselves to
Christ, is for the greater part based on ideas borrowed from
Tertullian's *De Pudicitia, De Virginibus Velandis* and *De
Cultu Feminarum.* He forbids them to adorn themselves,
to dye their hair, to take part in marriage banquets which
were so often immodest, to frequent public baths common to
both sexes, and, in a word, to court sensual temptations or
expose others to them. More clearly than Tertullian,
nevertheless, he points out that continence is not an absolute
duty or a necessity imposed by God, but that it remains
a matter of choice as free as it is meritorious.[1]

In his *De Dominica Oratione,* Cyprian likewise had before
his eyes Tertullian's *De Oratione.*[2] But he followed it with
a certain amount of independence. His plan is very different
from that adopted by Tertullian. The work is important
for its Christian conception of prayer, especially as regards
its *social* character, which does not exclude but broadens our
individual concerns : [3]

> " We do not say : *My* father, who art in heaven . . . ,
> give *me* this day *my* daily bread . . . ; forgive *me my*
> trespasses. . . .   No, prayer is general, collective (*pub-
> lica est nobis et communis oratio*).   When we pray, it is
> not for one person alone but for all the people, because
> all the people form but one single body. . . ."

The *De Mortalitate* is an admirable " instruction " on
suffering and death considered from the Christian point of
view. Cyprian makes more than one maxim of the Stoics
his own ; but the resignation which he recommends is not
only the stiffening of a proud soul against destiny ; the
promises of immortality are also opened wide to it. The
disasters entailed by a scourge almost without precedent—
that terrible pestilence which towards the middle of the
IIIrd century ravaged the Roman Empire—had brought in
its train an incredible falling away of souls. Many Christians
revolted against the injustice of seeing their brethren struck
down without distinction together with the pagans themselves, and, what was more, baulked of the hope of a glorious

---

[1] § xxiii (Hartel, I, 203, I. 26 et s.).
[2] See E. Frhr. von der Goltz, *das Gebet in d. aeltesten Christenheit*, L., 1902,
pp. 279–287.
[3] § viii (Hartel, I, 271).

martyrdom. Cyprian endeavours to inspire these dis-
heartened people with his vivifying energy. What was life,
and what was death ? The first was a battle to which the
second puts an end, bringing to us, if we have triumphed,
the eternal reward. To grieve so much over the death of our
near relations was to betray the lack of vitality of our faith.
People were complaining that Christians had not been
spared. Was then faith a guarantee against misfortune ?
Why should the Christian expect to break through for his own
benefit that solidarity which united the whole human race ?
The sole privilege which he ought to claim was that of suffering. It was only idolatry that despaired ; the Christian
acquired new strength through trials. Martyrdom, it was
true, escaped us if we were struck down (by the pestilence).
Let them therefore replace this loss by entire resignation to
the Divine Will, which we daily pray " may be done."
Whosoever believed in a morrow that shall make amends,
should dry his tears. We may regret those whom we have
lost, but we must not weep for them. Let us rather look
forward to the celestial country where we shall find again our
dear ones, reassured henceforward of their destiny, but still
solicitous for our own, who hold out their arms and ardently
call to us to come and partake of their happiness.

In the *De Opere et Eleemosynis*, he develops the idea that
good works and the giving of alms are for the Christian a duty,
and also an advantage as a principle to sanctification and
a leaven of divine favour. He supports himself by examples
and declarations drawn from Holy Scripture, and brushes
aside the maxims current on the inconveniences of a too
great liberality. The ideal which he invites the faithful to
approach is the disinterested life of the first community of
Christians wherein (according to the account in the Acts
of the Apostles) each one made his brethren share in what he
possessed, or rather desired to possess nothing but what was
in common with them.

The *De Bono Patientiae* is inspired by Tertullian's *De
Patientia*,[1] but Cyprian adapts his counsels to the circumstances of which he is speaking and to his constant purpose
of entire " unity." Against the Stoic philosophy, he extols
patience,—that is to say, the ability to bear that which is

---

[1] See the comparison in Benson's *Cyprian*, 1897, p. 443 et s.

contrary to nature,—as a specially Christian virtue, of which God himself, Christ, and the Just, have defined the marks and furnished the model. It is that which preserved the Christian in temptations and trials. Lack of patience, on the contrary, had always brought with it a train of evils, from the original fall, to schisms and heresies. He ends by appealing to Christians not to call down vengeance from on high so *impatiently* on those who persecute them, and to reverently wait for the infallible day of divine punishment.

His constant preoccupation, continually kept alive by the ill will of certain people, can easily be seen too in the *De Zelo et Livore* (concerning envy and jealousy). It represents this twofold fault as a pitfall, most formidable from being hidden, into which the devil endeavoured to precipitate the Christian.

We might fairly state that these treatises are all the more attractive in that they are more closely connected with the actual questions which pressed upon the mind of Cyprian. When he merely develops ideas or general precepts with the aid of abundant quotations from the Bible, the interest languishes a little. It revives, on the other hand, the moment that Cyprian comes into contact with contemporary reality. Then his accents become more keen and more impassioned ; his mysticism stands out more alluring and persuasive in arriving at the relative value of the diverse attractions making their call on the soul. Cyprian's talent grows, we should say, in proportion as he uses it in collaboration with his work as a Bishop and his daily struggles.

VI

ST CYPRIAN'S prestige was great in Christian antiquity.[1] Those who had known him were penetrated with admiration, and the biography compiled by Pontius is a proof of this. His life so fruitful in results, his compelling eloquence, his absolute devotion to his flock, lastly his heroic death coming as the crown to such exceptional virtues, possessed material whereby to pass on to posterity a figure more glorious than

---

[1] Evidence of this is collected in A.C.L., I, 701–717. His guidance was asked for from Gaul, Cappadocia, and Rome. People learned his letters by heart (*Ep.* lxxv, 4).

any other. Especially in Africa was his memory exalted :
" Carthage raised three basilicas in his honour, one on the
spot where he met his martyrdom, signalised by the *mensa
Cypriani*, another over his tomb at Mappalia, and a third
not far from the port." [1] The anniversary of the saint, the
κυπριανὰ, was celebrated on the 14th September, not only
in his Episcopal city, but throughout entire Africa,[2] in Rome,[3]
in Constantinople [4] and in Spain.[5] His renown radiated over
the whole Christian world. He was read with ardour.[6] The
reservations of Lactantius on his methods in apologetics,[7]
and those of St Augustine on his theories regarding baptism,[8]
detract in no wise from the respect which both of them have
dedicated to the Doctor and martyr. Prudentius rises to
enthusiasm in his *Peristephanon :* [9]

> "Dum genus esse hominum Christus sinet et vigere mundum,
> Dum liber ullus erit, dum scrinia sacra litterarum,
> Te leget omnis amans Christum, tua, Cypriane, discet."

At the Council of Ephesus in 431, Cyprian was one of the
ten Fathers on whose testimony the Council based its condemnation of Nestorius.[10] He had become one of the
accredited representatives of the mind of the Church. When
St Augustine had to discuss any opinion of his, he found
himself obliged to remind his own adversaries that the works
of the great Bishop must nevertheless be distinguished from
writings that were properly canonical to which universal
respect had wellnigh raised them.[11]

From all this we need not be astonished that so many
opuscula to which he had not put his hand, have been placed

---

[1] H. Delehaye, *les Origines du Culte des Martyrs*, Brussels, 1912, p. 433. Cf.
Monceaux, II, 375 et s.

[2] Saint Augustine, *Sermo* cccx, 1.

[3] *Depos. martyrum*, xviii kal. Oct.

[4] St Gregory of Nazianzen, *Or.* xxiv.

[5] Prudentius, *Peristeph.*, xi, 237.

[6] " Quae enim regio in terris inveniri potest, ubi non ejus eloquium legitur,
doctrina laudatur, caritas amatur, vita praedicatur, mors veneratur, passionis
festivitas celebratur ? . . ." (*Tractatus* of St Augustine, edited by Dom Morin,
Munich, 1917, p. 103.)

[7] *Div. Inst.*, V, 1, 24.

[8] Cf. *De bapt. contra Donatistas.*

[9] *Perist.*, xiii, v, 6 et s.

[10] Hefele-Leclercq, *Conc.* II, i, p. 302.

[11] *Contra Cresconium*, II, xxxi, 39 ; *Ep.* xciii, 35. See also Batiffol, in R.B.
1917, 29 et s.—In connection with the confusion between Cyprian of Carthage and
Cyprian of Antioch, a converted magician, cf. R. Reitzenstein, *Nachr. Gottingen,
Ph.-Histor. kl.*, 1917, pp. 38–79 : I have made an analysis of this study in the *Revue
de Philol.* (*Rev. des Revues*), 1918.

to his account. The list of the *apocrypha*, attributed to him will be found elsewhere. Among the works which have been erroneously ascribed to him there are several reflecting the questions and disputes of his period and must have been written at about his time. For instance, the *Ad Novatianum,*[1] a kind of pastoral instruction in which Novatian is taken to task in a very sharp tone, and which brings forward the efficaciousness of penance and the salutary effect of the divine pity in opposition to the excessive rigours which he (Novatian), promulgated in regard to the *lapsi*. The *Liber de Rebaptismate*, the text of which, much spoilt, has been unfortunately preserved in only two late manuscripts which are not even independent, gives in a curiously paradoxical form the thesis maintained by certain of the adversaries of Cyprian on the question of the baptism of heretics.

The *Exhortatio de Paenitentia* is a collection of quotations from the Bible of the kind that Cyprian had drawn up in his *Testimonia*, and inspired by a similar spirit on the question of penance.

Other *apocrypha* give us several interesting ideas in connection with the history of customs. Thus we can gather in reading the *De Spectaculis* some of the excuses, which are at times *bizarre*, brought forward by Christians fond of the public shows, to give a theological justification for their taste :[2]

"Where has this been forbidden in the Scriptures ? " they asked (§ ii). "Moreover, was not Elias the ' charioteer (*auriga*) of Israel ' ? Did not David dance before the Ark ? We find mentioned therein harps, stringed instruments, brazen instruments, drums, flutes, zithers and choirs. In the conflicts which we have to sustain against evil spirits, the Apostle offers us the model of the contest with the *cestus*. In another place, borrowing his example from the *stadium*, he promises a crown as the reward. Why then should a faithful

[1] The attribution to Pope Sixtus IInd of this tract, suggested by Harnack in 1895 (T.U., xiii, 1) is taken up by D'Alès, R.S.R. 1919, 320 et s., who likewise assigns the *Adversus Judaeos* to Sixtus.

[2] The *De Spectaculis* is claimed for Cyprian by Hartel, A.L.L., 1892, 1–22. A certain number of critics assign it to Novatian, see D'Alès, *art. cit.*, p. 298 et s., who holds the same opinion. The similarities in style do not appear to me to be very significant.

Christian be forbidden to see what Holy Scripture does not fear to mention by name ? ''

A line of argument similar to that upon which Tertullian had already laid stress is developed against these complaisant advocates of vice (*vitiorum assertores blandi et indulgentes patroni*) ; and they find themselves invited to substitute the contemplation of the splendours of nature and the reading of the marvellous narrative of the Bible for an altogether idolatrous amusement. . . .

The author of the *Adversus Aleatores*, who is a Bishop, takes the gamblers to task, and declares to them that he considers it as one of the first duties of his charge to make known to them the perils of that passion to which they abandon themselves. Their '' sedentary and idle perversity '' (*sedentaria et pigra nequitia*, § vi) was the sure means taken by Satan to lead them on the road to mad passion, perfidy, ruin and debauchery ; for prostitutes prowl round the gambling table. Gambling was of the devil ; it was the unforgivable sin against the Holy Spirit, and a violation of the temple of God, which every Christian was.

These inexorable anathemas are expressed in language whose incorrectness almost rivals its vehemence. Solecisms and even barbarisms abound in it, especially in those manuscripts which have suffered the least amount of retouching.[1] Philologists find in the *Adversus Aleatores* (with which, from the point of view of form, we may compare certain letters coming either from the Roman clergy or from different correspondents of Cyprian),[2] precious lights on '' vulgar '' Latin. Harnack[3] thought he saw in it a work by Pope Victor. At the same stroke the *Adversus Aleatores* was promoted to the dignity of being the first work of Latin Christian Literature. But the hypothesis has not been able to withstand the investigations of which it has been the starting-point, and Harnack has had to abandon it.[4] All that remains to be said is that the author of the *Adversus Aleatores* makes a great point of his privileges as a Bishop,

---

[1] *Monacensis* 208, IXth century ; *Trecensis* 581, VIIIth – IXth century ; *Reginensis* 118, Xth century. There is also the *Parisinus* 13047, IXth century, to which Hartel and Harnack give the preference.

[2] *Ep.* viii, xxi, xxii, xxiii, xxiv, in the series of St Cyprian's letters.

[3] T.U. Bd. V.H. I (1888).

[4] A.C.L., II, 2, p. 379.

which, in his eyes, corresponded to imperative duties.[1] We may think of him either as an " African Bishop of Cyprian's school "[2] (who is frequently imitated in the treatise as regards language and the form of its Biblical quotations), or as some anti-Pope from the camp of Novatian.

The *De Singularitate Clericorum* reminds clerics in a long " instruction " in 46 chapters of the duty which is incumbent upon them of not living in the same house with women. For centuries the Church was to fulminate against this abuse without eradicating it. We already find traces of it in Hermas and St Irenæus in the IInd century. St Cyprian denounces it with great vigour. St Jerome uses harsh and outspoken terms to brand it. The author of this doctrinal letter is not known. He was certainly a Bishop,[3] and it appears a Bishop in charge of a schismatic community.[4] The manner in which he speaks of martyrdom and supposes the clerics whom he is reprimanding speak of it,[5] hardly enables us to place its appearance further back than just after peace had come to the Church.

The *De Singularitate Clericorum* provides a curious abstract of the more or less specious arguments with which the delinquents endeavoured to palliate their lively appreciation of a woman's presence, or simply their lusts. What mattered the opinion of men, they said (§ viii) ; we seek a meritorious opportunity of overcoming ourselves (ix) ; did not St Paul write : " Bear ye one another's burdens and thus ye shall fulfil the law of Christ " (x), and in another place : " Everyone of us shall render an account of himself unto God " (xiii) ? If scandal on both sides was to be feared to such an extent, how may the faithful dare to mingle the sexes when they meet together in Church (xiii) ? we are practising in our own way the duty of *caritas* (xxix), etc. The list of sophistries is further lengthened and these are refuted one by one with a perspicacity which does not allow any doubt as to their real meaning.

[1] 1 : " In nobis divina et paterna pietas apostolatus ducatum contulit et vicariam Domini sedem caelesti dignatione ordinavit et originem authentici apostolatus super quem Christus fundavit (et) Ecclesiam in superiore nostra portamus, accepta simul potestate solvendi et ligandi. . . ."

[2] Monceaux, II, 115.

[3] See Hartel's edition, p. 173, I, 5–10 ; 174, 4–12 ; 219, 6.

[4] *Ibid.*, § xxxiv (p. 210, 6) and § 1 (174, 7). For the attempts to attribute it to Novatian, cf. D'Alès, R.S.R., 1919, 312 et s.

[5] § xxxiv et s. (p. 210). § iv (p. 177, i, 27) is less convincing.

We must also mention the *De Bono Pudicitiae*, a kind of pastoral letter in imitation of Tertullian's *De Pudicitia* and of St Cyprian's *De Habitu Virginum*, on the virtue of modesty, which " locum primum in virginibus tenet, secundum in continentibus, tertium in matrimoniis " (§ iv). The critics who admit the assignment of the *De Spectaculis* to Novatian likewise attribute to him the *De Bono Pudicitiae*,[1] which is closely allied to it in language, style, and the models whom the authors follow in it. The *De Laude Martyrii* and the *Adversus Judaeos* hold a special position among the *apocrypha* attributed to St Cyprian. They figure in Cheltenham's list. The principal reason which prevents us from believing that the *De Laude Martyrii* was written by Cyprian is the preponderance of an ambitious rhetorical effect which displays itself from the first chapter and hardly squares with the gravity of the circumstances under which the work was written, when pestilence was raging and a persecution had quite recently broken out (§ viii). This reason did not appear decisive to Baronius, Bellarmine or Tillemont. However the study of this treatise gains in importance if one only compares with it the serious concern customary with the Bishop when he felt the sufferings of his flock. Harnack wishes to saddle it on Novatian, the convenient beneficiary of any works whose authorship is unknown. He advances the same solution for the *Adversus Judaeos*, one of the numerous homilies of the first centuries against the Jews. In any case, the work is not by Cyprian for the text of the Scriptural quotations differs from that which Cyprian followed. The *De Pascha Computus*, according to the author's own testimony was written in the fifth year of the reign of Gordian in the Consulate of Arrianus and Papus (§ xxii), and therefore before Easter in the year 243. The question of Easter had much exercised the Christian Churches since they had emancipated themselves from the Jewish reckoning. Already Hippolytus of Rome, about the year 222, had applied himself to deep calculations. The author of the *Pascha Computus* was inspired by Hippolytus or some source common to him. Animated with a lively enthusiasm for his dry subject (cf. § i ; xxiii), he first gives an explanation of his system, and

---

[1] Paul Lejay in the *Bull. des Humanistes franc.*, IV (1895), p. 54, has drawn attention to an interesting manuscript of the *De Bono Pud.*, Bibl. Nat. *lat.* 1658, which Hartel has wrongly made light of.

then draws up a Paschal table as Hippolytus himself had done, perhaps with the intention of correcting the latter on diverse points. The *De Montibus Sina et Sion* need not hold our attention except as a written document illustrating the history of allegorical exegesis and its fantasies. The author commits some strange mistakes of history : he places Sinai in Palestine (§ iii) ; he confuses the first temple with the second (§ iv) ; he relates things concerning the death of Christ which he could not have read either in the Synoptics or in the Gospel of St John (§ viii). The style is poor, without skill and full of gross solecisms.[1] The *De Duodecim Abusivis Saeculi* belongs to a period far removed from Cyprian, and was probably written in Ireland in the VIIth century. This enumeration of the " abuses " of the world consists in superficial commonplaces and transpositions in imitation of the style of certain rhetorical methods practised by antiquity. The *Caena Cypriani*, " more worthy of a Turk than of a Christian," declared Tillemont, who was scandalised by the ineptitudes and the incongruities of this *bizarre* production, is a kind of mnemonical *resumé* of the Bible in the form of a " banquet " at which appear the personages in the Bible with the marks and the particularities which characterise them. The second part of the work is taken up by a lawsuit which Joel, who presides over the said banquet, brings against the guests suspected of having committed larcenies to the prejudice of the royal furniture ! It is painful to think that this depressing buffoonery should have found a host of admirers if we are to judge by the manuscripts which have come down to us. As to the date of its composition, we can only form guesses (end of IVth century ?[2] or beginning of Vth ?).[3] The *Acta Pauli* are used therein as a *quasi* canonical book.

R. Reitzenstein published in 1914 in the *Zeitsch. fur die neutest. Wiss.*, p. 60 et s., following the *Codex Wirceburgensis theol.*, f. 33, s. ix, and the *Codex Monacensis* 3739, IXth century, a rather curious treatise, which may be mentioned here, on the " three kinds of wages that human life offers "

---

[1] See Corssen, Z.N.W., 1911, pp. 7–8.
[2] Brewer, in Z.K.T., 1904, p. 105 et s.
[3] Harnack (T.U., n.f. iv, 3b, p. 21 et s.), who attributes the *Caena* to Cyprian, a poet of Gaul. A. Lapôtre's attempt (R.S.R., 1912, p. 497 et s.) to transform the *Caena* into a satire by Julian the Apostate is purely fanciful.

(cf. St Matth. xiii, 8), that is to say, on the varying quality of the rewards which await the just, according to whether they had been martyrs, ascetics or ordinary Christians. This work is related in many details to the *De Habitu Virginum* of St Cyprian·; to admit that Cyprian had been influenced by it, as Reitzenstein supposes, we must have cogent reasons which this critic does not furnish ; it is the opposite which is without doubt true. The traces of Gnosticism, which he discovers in it, only appear to be very feebly marked.[1]

---

[1] See Harnack in T.L.Z., 1914, 220 et s. Observations on the syntax in B. ph. W., 1915, n 16, by Schmalz.

CHAPTER III

NOVATIAN—COMMODIAN

BIBLIOGRAPHY

I. Novatian—P.L., III, 861-970; *de Trinitate*, ed. by W. Yorke Fausset, Cambridge, 1909 (including a study); *de Cibis Judaicis*, ed. by Landgraf and C. Weyman, in A.L.L., XI. (1898), pp. 221-249.—Consult: A. d'Alès, *le Corpus de Novatien*, in R.S.R., 1919, 293-323.

II. Commodian—P.L., V., 201-282 (the *Instructiones* only); Ludwig, L., 1877 (B.T.); B. Dombart in C.V., vol. XV (1887).—Consult: Monceaux, III, 451-489. Recent Bibliog. on the question of the date of Commodian analysed by P. de Labriolle, in B.A.L.A.C., 1912, pp. 79-80; Monti, *Bibliographia di Commodiano*, extract from the *Athenaeum* III, 2 (1915): completed in B. ph. W., 1915, 1304; Lindsay, *The MSS. of Commodian*, in B. ph. W., 1914, 509; J. Martin, in S.B.W., 181, 6 (1917) (I have reviewed Martin's study in the *Rev. de Philologie* [*Rev. des Revues*], 1918). For the language and style of Commodian, see also Durel, *Commodien, Rech. sur la doctr., la langue et le vocab. du poète*, Paris, 1912 (mediocre); Sisto Cucco, *La grammatica di Commodiano*, in the *Didaskaleion*, 1913, p. 307, et s.; Vrow, *de Commodiani metris et syntaxi*, Utrecht, 1917.

French Translation of the *Instructiones* by J. Durel, Paris, 1912. The *Carmen Apologeticum* of Commodian is only known through a single manuscript, the *Cod. Cheltenhamensis*, n° 12261, VIIIth century.

For the *Instructiones*, the *Berolinensis*, 167, VIIIth/IXth century, formerly at Cheltenham, must be placed first. Lindsay suspects, from certain abbreviations of a special type, that the *Cheltenhamensis*, n° 12261 and the *Berolinensis* 167 formed originally one and the same manuscript coming from Verona.

The *Cod. Berolinensis* very probably represents the Angers manuscript (*Andecavensis*) which J. Sirmond had used, and which was given up as lost.

We may also mention for the *Instructiones*, the *Cod. Cheltenhamensis*, n° 1825, XIth century and the *Cod. Parisinus*, n° 8304, XVIIth century (B) (whence derives a Leidensis Vossianus 49 (A), of the same period). A and B furnish readings which are only conjectures by Sirmond and to which Dombart has attached too much importance. This is one of the faults of his edition. In addition, Dombart made the mistake of relying upon Sedlmayer and Knœll for the collating of the Cheltenham MSS., who did not bring to this task all the care that might have been desired. More than one erudite question must remain in suspense until a fresh edition has been established, which is more correct.

SUMMARY

I. The rôle of Novatian.—II. The *De Trinitate*.—III. The *De Cibis Judaicis.*—
IV. The works of Commodian.—V. The *Instructiones* and the *Carmen Apologeticum.*—VI. His language and metre.—VII. The riddle enveloping his personality.

G

I

AMONG the correspondence of St Cyprian, we come across
two letters, the XXXth and the XXXVIth, coming from the
clergy in Rome and addressed to the Bishop of Carthage
in connection with the question of the *lapsi*. In reply to
a communication from Cyprian, who was anxious to assure
himself whether he was in full agreement with the clergy
of that city, Letter XXX insists on the duty imposed upon
the Church of maintaining a rigorous discipline with regard
to the apostates under whom were included the *libellatici* ;
it thanks the Bishop in warm terms for the encouraging
words he had addressed to the confessors who were in prison,
and concludes by declaring that the Church of Rome did not
feel that it had the right to decide definitely the question of
the *lapsi* before the Bishop of Rome, who had recently died,
had been replaced ; that in the meantime, the *lapsi* could
only do penance without trying to extort a premature amnesty,
it being understood that in case of peril of death, he should
take into consideration the merits which they shall individu-
ally have acquired, with a view to their reconciliation with
the Church. Letter XXXVI relates to the same discussion.
It is in reply to Letter XXXV, in which Cyprian had drawn
the attention of the clergy in Rome to the reprehensible
obstinacy with which certain *lapsi* had refused to enter upon
the way of penance, under the pretext that they had already
received their pardon from the martyr Paulus. In it,
Cyprian's attitude is fully commended while the inconsistency
of certain martyrs, and the rebellion of certain sinners,
receives a strong reprimand.

These two letters had been written by the Roman priest,
Novatian. Cyprian indicates this as regards Letter XXX
(*Ep.* lv, 5) ; the general contents and style of Letter XXXVI
scarcely leave any doubt that it was from the same pen.

One happy result of modern criticism is to have brought
to light the vigorous personality of Novatian. We have
little knowledge of his origin. According to a rather doubtful
piece of evidence given by the historian Philostorgius, he
was a Phrygian (H.E., viii, xv). In one letter, part of which
Eusebius has translated,[1] Pope Cornelius depicts him in the

[1] H.E., VI, xliii.

blackest colours. He brands his mischievousness, his false-hoods, his perjuries, his unsociable temperament and cunning hypocrisy, and is not disposed to see anything else in him than an " astute and evil monster," long possessed of the devil, and one who had received baptism under very equivocal conditions of validity. But certain expressions used by Cornelius to describe him, in spite of their sarcastic turn,[1] enable us to obtain a glimpse of the important place which Novatian held among the clergy in Rome, and of his intellectual worth which encouraged his ambitions. We may gather the same from the significant criticism whereby St Cyprian shows him as pluming himself on his eloquence, and deplores his regrettable familiarity with profane philosophy.[2]

Novatian had hoped to secure his own election as Bishop of Rome. Cornelius was chosen. His disappointment must have been poignant. A certain Novatus (with whom he has been on more than one occasion wrongly confused),[3] a priest of Carthage of a very mischief-making temperament, incited him to break with Cornelius. Novatian found the means to exact his own ordination as a Bishop from three Italian Bishops, who were very simple-minded people, and whose understanding, if we are to believe Cornelius, had been obscured with the fumes of wine. This was schism (251). In addition, his personal rivalry was complicated by divergent ideas. Novatian had set himself to protest against any reconciliation of the *lapsi*. He reserved their pardon to God, and denied to the Church the right to anticipate the Divine verdict.[4] The *clique* on which he leant for support was too limited to cause this rigour to prevail. He was excommunicated both in Rome and in Carthage. His party was numerous throughout the Roman world,[5] and it appears that his theories later on went to the length of refusing absolution for mortal sins whatever they were.[6] According

---

[1] ὁ δογματιστής, ὁ τῆς ἐκκλησιαστικῆς ἐπιστήμης ὑπερασπιστής. ὁ ενδικητής τοῦ εναγγελίου.

[2] *Ep.* xliv, 3 ; lv, 16 and 24 ; lx, 3.

[3] The error has been favoured by the defective form of the name by which, even in Rome, his partisans called themselves : *Novatiani* (instead of *Novatianani*). See note 28 in P.G., xxxix, 420. In the East, he is usually called Νοουάτος.

[4] Cf. Cyprian, Ep. lv, 27–28 ; lvii, 4.

[5] To the West as far as Spain, to the East as far as Syria. In the East, his disciples called themselves the " Pure " (καθαροί (Katharoi) : cf. Eusebius, H.E., VI, xliii, 1).

[6] St Ambrose, *De Paen.*, I, x (P.L., xvi, 489).

to information given by Socrates, which is suspect, Novatian died a martyr during the persecution of Valerian.

He wrote much. In his *De Viris Illustribus* (§ lxx), St Jerome cites the following works : *De Pascha, De Sabbato, De Circumcisione, De Sacerdote, De Oratione, De Cibis Judaicis, De Instantia* (concerning Perseverance), *De Attalo, De Trinitate ;* he adds " *et multa alia,*" which has encouraged his critics to impute to Novatian more than one work whose authorship is doubtful. We have seen that the *De Spectaculis* and the *De Bono Pudicitiae* should possibly be retained among the writings placed hypothetically to his account. For the *De Trinitate* and the *De Cibis Judaicis*, the literary tradition is much more solid. It will be noticed that Novatian is the first Roman writer who wrote exclusively in Latin. We have here an indication of the decline of Greek in the Christian community at Rome.

II

THE *De Trinitate* was published in 1545 by Gagny-Mesnart among the works of Tertullian. Jacques de Pamèle (*Pamelius*) restored it to Novatian in 1579. This confusion of the authors goes back to antiquity. Rufinus had already made that mistake and St Jerome had to rectify his error : " Nec Tertulliani liber est nec Cypriani dicitur (he declares) sed Novatiani, cujus et inscribitur titulo, et auctoris eloquium stili proprietas demonstrat." [1] Without doubt, the title was not due to Novatian himself, for the word *Trinitas* does not appear in the treatise. Still less is a complete theory of the Trinity developed therein ; it is rather an essay on the relationship of the Son to the Father. The plan is clear and comprises four parts : God the Father (i–viii) ; Jesus Christ distinct from the Father, true God and true Man (ix–xxviii) ; the Holy Spirit (xxix) : an appendix on the method of reconciling the Divinity of the Son with the Oneness of God (xxx–xxxi). The Christology of the author is based in essentials on that of Tertullian. Nevertheless, St Jerome has gone a little far in making the *De Trinitate* a simple *resumé* of Tertullian's " whole work " (he is doubtless thinking of the *Adversus Praxean*) : Novatian has his own

---

[1] *Contra Rufinum*, II, xix (P.L., xxiii, 444).

personal ideas, which he freely expresses in a form limited to the syllogism,[1] sometimes with an amplitude which one might have wished had been more discreet.[2]

III

UP to 1893, the *De Cibis Judaicis* as also the *De Trinitate* were only known in the old edition of Gagny-Mesnart, reproduced and more or less made correct by those of Ghelen, Pamèle, Jackson, Gallandi, etc. At that time, a manuscript containing in addition to the *De Cibis*, Latin versions of the Epistle of St James and of the Epistle of Barnabas, and the works of Filaster, the heresiologist, was discovered in the library of St Petersburg. This manuscript, of the IXth century, had originally belonged to the Monastery of St Pierre de Corbie. It was taken to Paris in 1638, and during the French Revolution it fell into the hands of P. Dubrowski, a secretary in the Russian Embassy. It served as the material for Landgraf's and Weyman's recension.

The *De Cibis Judaicis* is in the form of a letter which Novatian, who at the moment was separated from his flock, addresses " to the people steadfast in the gospel " (plebi in Evangelio perstanti). In two previous instructions, he had already pointed out to them how defective was the understanding of the Jews of their own Law. They were ignorant of what the real circumcision meant and the real Sabaoth, and understood no better the true meaning of the distinction between pure and impure animals as laid down in Leviticus.

Taken literally, as the Jews did, this distinction would mean nothing less than to favour the Gnostic heresy according to which part of the Divine creation would not be good. If God had divided animals into categories, which in the beginning had all been blessed by him equally, it was for our mental and moral instruction. In itself, every animal was " pure." But God wished to make the Jews, carnal beings, understand the obligation of fleeing those vices which the forbidden animals symbolised : " In animalibus mores depinguntur humani et actus et volontates ex quibus ipsi homines fiunt vel mundi vel immundi " (§ iii) : for example, the life of the

---

[1] Cf. xvi (Fausset, p. 56) ; xxx (id., p. 112).
[2] V.g. § ii (Fausset, p.9, I. 5–14).

pig passed in the muck, the thefts of the marten, the haughtiness of the swan, the hatred of the owl for the light, etc. . .
On the contrary, the pure animals represented the virtues loved by God : are not the ruminants representative of man who chews without ceasing the Divine precepts ? Do not the fishes with their rough scales bring to our minds the harsh, bristling, untutored, solid and grave manner of thought of virtuous men ? The forbidding of certain foods was a punishment to the Jews for having preferred the flesh-pots of Egypt to manna, and taught them temperance. But all that had passed away. The religion of Christ consisted of something very different to restrictions of this sort. " Deus ventre non colitur." Truly pure and holy nourishment was an unspotted conscience, an innocent life. Does it follow from this that all excess shall be henceforth lawful (§ vi) ? By no means. The religion of Christ was also a severe religion. And those who took pleasure in good cheer, and filled themselves with undiluted wine even on awaking from sleep,[1] or gave themselves up to debauchery should be mindful of this.

The interpretation given by Novatian to the regulations in Leviticus was not at all new. We already find it in the letter in which under the name of Aristeus, a hellenised Jew had endeavoured to explain to the Greeks who despised Judaism, not only the origin of the translation of the *Septuagint*, but also the motive of those precepts which scandalised them.[2] It likewise appears in the *Epistle of Barnabas*,[3] the work of a converted Jew who wrote without doubt in the first half of the IInd century of our era. Tertullian himself outlines it in his *Adversus Marcionem.*[4] But in the *De Cibis Judaicis*, it is developed with a clearness, a choice of examples and also an ease of style revealing a methodic mind familiar with the best profane writers. It has been remarked to what a high degree Novatian carries the spiritual meaning in regard to enactments about food. He is behind the Christianity of his time from this point of view. Another interest attaching to this work is the first opening out, as it were, of the symbolic

---

[1] This last feature is a reminiscence of Seneca, *Ep.* cxxi, 6.
[2] § 143 ; 144 ; 164 ; 306 (Wendland's ed.).
[3] x, 1-9.
[4] II, xviii.

ideas of the Middle Ages, which was to develop a liking for personifying some human vice or virtue in each animal.[1]

IV

CHRISTIAN antiquity is almost mute as regards Commodian. Gennadius of Marseilles, who seems to have written the first 82 notices in his *De Viris Illustribus* between the years 467 and 469, devotes to him the following paragraph (§ xv) :

> " It was through reading our Christian writings, together with profane writings, that he was touched by the faith. He therefore became a Christian, and desirous of offering as a gift to Christ, the author of his salvation, the fruit of his studies, he wrote against the pagans in a mediocre and *quasi* metrical style (*mediocri sermone quasi versu*). With the little familiarity that he possessed with our holy books he showed himself better able to destroy pagan errors than to fortify our own beliefs. This is why in treating of the Divine promises against them he conducted his discussion in a sufficiently gross and, as it were, heavy spirit (*vili satis et crasso ut ita dixerim sensu*) which threw them into astonishment and us into despair. Having studied in the school of Tertullian, Lactantius, and Papias, he inculcated upon his readers a doctrine which is perfectly moral, and above all, the love of voluntary poverty, which he had himself embraced."

One other mention of Commodian appears in the Decretal attributed to Pope Gelasius (P.L., lix, 163) : " The writings of Commodian are apocryphal (that is to say, non-canonical)."

No other ancient writer speaks of him. His works were only printed at a late date. Jacques Sirmond, the Jesuit, drew attention to the *Instructiones* and quoted two pieces from it in his edition of Ennodius (1611). Nicolas Rigault published them for the first time at Toul, in 1649. As regards the *Carmen Apologeticum*, it was only discovered in the middle of the XIXth century by J. B. Pitra in a manuscript of the VIIIth century belonging to the library of Thomas Philipps at Middlehill. Pitra inserted it in his

[1] See H. O. Taylor, *The Mediaeval Mind*, 1914, 11, p. 67–130.

Spicilegium Solesmense, vol. I (Paris, 1852), p. 21 et s. The poem is without a title and without the name of the author, but the identity of certain verses (for example, *Instr.* I, xxviii, 1, *Carm. Apol.* 229), the similarity of ideas, style and metre, enabled Pitra to attribute it with certainty to Commodian.

Of very moderate interest in themselves, Commodian's works have regained a present-day prominence whereof the personality of the author and the date of his works have been the subject of discussion in recent years. Before entering upon these discussions, we must give an indication of the contents and the spirit of the *Instructiones* and the *Carmen Apologeticum*.

V

THE *Instructiones per litteras versuum primas* comprises 80 pieces of 6 to 48 verses. These pieces are " acrostics," that is to say, that the first letters read vertically form one or several words. Two of them (I, xxxv ; II, xix) are alphabetical, the first letters corresponding to the series of the letters of the alphabet. The division running into two books (41 pieces + 39) is not very satisfactory. The division would be better if it were placed after II, iv in accordance with the nature of the subjects. The title of the collection is explained by verse I, i, 9 : " *Ob ea perdoctus ignaros instruo verum :* " " I who know, instruct in the truth those who are ignorant of it." The first book is addressed specially to outside unbelievers. The second book is more esoteric. In it Commodian sets forth his " eschatological " ideas, then distributes moral and disciplinary counsels to the various classes of Christians—catechumens, matrons, confessors, ecclesiastics, etc.

The *Carmen Apologeticum* comprises 1060 verses grouped two by two. It opens with a warning by the author to the pagans (1–88) ; then follows an exposition of a rather vague theology (principally from the point of view of the Trinity) on God, Christ and Revelation (89–578) ; a demonstration of the necessity of faith for salvation (579–790) ; lastly, a picture of the end of the world (791–1060). Speaking generally, the *Carmen Apologeticum* seems superior to the

Instructiones, doubtless because the author has not subjected himself to the limitations of the acrostic. But the spirit animating the two works is the same.

Commodian has none of the speculative spirit which sets forth ideas for the pleasure of seeing them grouped into a system and appealing to each other by natural affinities. In his eyes, as with Tertullian and Cyprian, Christianity was the great, the only matter. He concerns himself with discouraging his enemies and in confirming in their faith those who, although Christians, were tending to forget the duties to which their profession bound them.

He first takes to task the pagans among the unbelievers, and does not spare them his sarcasms. The word *stultus* is his favourite epithet. He directs against them many gibes of this sort : " Poor fool, dost thou think then that Jupiter thunders, he who was born upon the earth and was nourished on the milk of a goat ? And supposing Saturn had devoured him at that time, what wouldst thou have done now that he is dead ? "[1] " Do you dare to call gods statues made of brass ? Make of them therefore rather pots for your use."[2] He inveighs against the " ignorant brutes " whose sluggish hearts are indifferent to the truth, and who, like fatted swine, take pleasure in their bestial delights.[3] How are you to live, however, if life is not ruled by one law ?[4] As for the Jews, " ever froward, and stiff-necked without suppleness,"[5] he reproaches the obstinacy with which they shun the evidences of history. " You will not allow yourselves to be convinced, and therefore shall you be disinherited."[6] In the *Carmen Apologeticum*, he devotes a special piece to them (V. 617–744) in which he stigmatises their pride and their pretence of filling by rites the place of purity of heart which they lack : " Nos sumus electi ! dicentes."[7] Neither does Commodian forget the pagans of Judaistic tendencies who pass their lives " hesitating between two parties "[8] and run to the synagogue and then come back from there to their temples. This equivocal attitude will be their ruin : it will give them over to tortures beyond the grave.

With regard to the believers themselves, he displays little

---

[1] *Instr.*, I, vi, 7–10.   [2] *Ibid.*, I, xx, 6–7.
[3] *Carmen Apol.*, 16 et s.   [4] *Instr.*, I, xxiii, 4.
[5] *Ibid.*, I, xxxviii, 1.   [6] v, 2.
[7] *Carmen Apol*, 676.   [8] *Instr.*, I, xxiv, 1.

gentleness, to whatever rank they belong. He reproaches
the Christian women with their finery, their curls, their painted
eyelids and dyed hair, and all that vain show which they
should leave to courtesans.[1] " Triumph over the evil one, ye
modest women of Christ, and only display your wealth by
bestowing it." He stigmatises too the sumptuous funerals,[2]
the brutishness of drunkenness,[3] and frivolous gossiping in
Church.[4] Neither do his criticisms spare people connected
with the Church, the " Doctors," who in their hopes for the
present, accept the persons of men and authorise certain
relaxations,[5] and clerics who do not observe the Law which
they presume to teach.[6] Quite other is the Christian's ideal.
He should fulfil like a man a joyless task[7] in this life which is
but a long chain of woes and tribulations :

> " Esto ergo talis qualem vult esse te Christus :
> Mitis et in illo hilaris, nam saeculo tristis.
> Excurre, labora, suda, cum tristitia pugna." [8]

To accomplish this, he must avoid the public shows ; [9]
he must consider how little worth are profane studies at the
price of rectitude of the will ; [10] he must give alms largely and
accept with entire resignation the trials which God sends
him. . . . [11]

These chiding exhortations, addressed to the *rudes* (the
word signifies not the " ignorant " as G. Boissier believed,
but those who were not acquainted with Christianity or who
were not inspired with its real spirit), assume a still more
urgent intensity in the light of the eschatological views
which the poet discloses in certain pieces of the *Instructiones*,[12]
and especially in the *Carmen Apologeticum*. G. Monceaux [13]
remarked that the picture traced by Commodian of the end
of time is the most complete which has been bequeathed to
us by the fantasy of the Christian " millenarists." " Guided
by his faith and the Bible, Commodian vividly calls up
before his eyes these grandiose spectacles which he paints
with the enthusiasm of a devotee sure of going to paradise,
and with the precision of an ocular witness."

[1] *Instr.*, II, xviii ; xix.
[3] II, xxxvi.
[5] II, xvi, 1–2.
[7] I, xxvi, 10 et s.
[9] II, xvi, 4–6 ; 21–23 ; *Carmen Apol.*, 207 et s.
[11] *Inst.*, II, xxxii.
[12] III, 479.
[2] II, xxxiii.
[4] II, xxxv.
[6] II, xxxiv.
[8] II, xvii, 15–17.
[10] *Carmen Apol.*, 583–4.
[12] I, xli ; II, 1–4 ; xxxix.

The following are the special features of the *Carmen Apologeticum* :

At the end of six thousand years the immortality promised to man will come. Man will rise from the dead, will recognise the truth of the promises which have been made to him, and will feel to the fullest extent his moral and physical happiness (v. 791–805).[1] There will be signs foretelling this resurrection. King Apollyon[2] invades Rome with the Goths ; he treats the pagans harshly, makes the Senate pass under the yoke and contrariwise manifests his entire benevolence towards the Christians. This episode lasts for five months (v. 805–823).[3] Meanwhile, Cyrus arrives, whom Commodian identifies with Nero, who has been held in reserve in a mysterious place for the work he had to accomplish.[4] His coming had been prophesied by Elias during three and a half days.[5] The Jews and Romans fall to adoring Nero and under his leadership take steps to massacre the Christians. Elias makes reprisals with formidable scourges.[6] Notwithstanding, at the instigation of the Jews, Nero causes seven thousand Christians to perish,[7] whose bodies God takes up into heaven (v. 823–865).[8] The persecution redoubles. The Christian people are exiled from Rome.[9] Nero joins two Cæsars[10] to himself, and issues general edicts and orders all to do sacrifice.[11] For three and a half years blood is poured forth. But Nero is to be despoiled of the power which he has abused (v. 865–890). A king rises up in the East and advances towards Rome at the head of four nations (Persians, Medes, Chaldeans and Baby-

[1] For a picture of this happiness, cf. *Apocal.*, xxi, 4.
[2] Cf. *Apocal.*, ix, 11.
[3] *Ibid.*, ix, 10.
[4] Some people thought that Nero would come back under another name, in order that the Jews might accept him as a Christ (cf. Victorinus of Pettau, *in Apoc.*, xiii, 16 ; Lactantius, *Inst. Div.*, VII, xvi, 4). The choice of the name of Cyrus here given by Commodian is perhaps explained by Isaias, xliv, 28, and xlv, 1. On the legend concerning Nero, cf. Geffcken, *Nachrichten* of Gottingen, *Phil.-Hist. Kl.*, 1899, pp. 441–462. The incidents relating to Nero are scattered in the following passages in Commodian : *Carm Apol.*, 813–838 ; 851–858 ; 869–874 ; 885–897 ; 909–918 ; 927–935 ; *Instr.*, I, xli, 7–11.
[5] A combination probably of Malachias, iv, 5, with *Apocal.*, xi, 11.
[6] Cf. *Apocal.*, xi, 6.
[7] For the figures, cf. *Apocal.*, xi, 13 (it is there applied however to the enemies of God).
[8] Cf. *Apocal.*, xi, 9 and 12.
[9] *Orac. Sibyll.*, iv, 135.
[10] Cf. *Daniel*, vii, 24.
[11] For the cessation of the *oblatio* to Christ (v. 879), cf. *Daniel*, ix, 27.

Ionians).[1]   Nero marches against them with the two Cæsars.
They are all three massacred and their bodies become food
for the birds.[2]   Their armies pillage Rome, and the proud
city, which deemed itself to be eternal, is burnt and wiped out
(v. 891–926).[3]   The victorious king directs his steps to Judea
and endeavours to seduce the Jews by prodigies.[4]   " He is
anti-Christ for the Jews, as Nero was for us." [5]   Soon the
disappointed Jews are reduced to implore the succour of the
true God (v. 927–940).   God then causes the advance of a
people whom he had been keeping in the regions beyond
Persia.   This people consisted of nine and a half of the
tribes of the Jews out of the twelve traditional number.[6]
The innocence and happiness of this people are described.
They march towards Judea in the midst of universal rejoicings.
The tyrant flees to the North and raises an army.   But he is
taken prisoner and also the devil, and they are both plunged
into flames.[7]   The saints enter into the Holy City and
beseech God to raise up the dead as He had promised (v. 941–
992).   God begins by making a fire rain down upon the
impious.   Very few escape from it.   Then is let loose the
final catastrophe heralded by the strident sounds of the
trumpet.   During the night, there is a terrifying falling to
pieces of the universe accompanied by the hurling of thunderbolts, the falling of the stars, earthquakes, and the roaring
of the hurricane.   A fall of dew protects a few privileged
ones who have been marked out beforehand by Christ.   For
the space of seven months, the fire purifies the earth.   The

---

[1] These four nations recall perhaps the four angels of the *Apocalypse*.   This
was to be the interpretation of St Epiphanius, *Panarion*, LI, xxxiii.

[2] Cf. *Apocal.*, xix, 17 ; 21.

[3] Cf. *Apoc.*, xviii, 7.   The idea of a punishment hanging over Rome quoted
as the sinner and the persecutor, is frequent in the *Sibylline Oracles* (III, 356–364 ;
V, 162–178 ; 386–397 ; VIII, 37–49 ; 80–106 ; 165).   The Latin apologists only
allude to them with the greatest discretion ; Tertullian, *Apol.*, xxxii, 1 ; St Cyprian,
ad Demetr., xxi (Hartel, p. 336, 8) ; Lactantius, VII, xv, 18.

[4] Cf. *Apocal.*, xiii, 13.

[5] Commodian thus distinguishes *two* Anti-Christs.   This duplication is also
met with in Victorinus of Pettau, *in Apoc.*, xiii, 16 (P.L., v, 338 C) ; in Lactantius,
de Mort. Pers. II, who alludes to the popular belief founded on the declarations of
the Sibyl (*quidam deliri credunt . . . Sibylla dicente*) according to which Nero
would appear at the end of time as the precursor of Anti-Christ.   See also Sulpicius Severus, *Dial.* II, xiv ; *Chron.* II, xxix, 5 ; St Jerome, *in Dan.*, ix, 29 (P.L.
xxv, 568).   Neither the *Apocalypse* nor Hippolytus of Rome mention two Anti-
Christs.

[6] Cf. Esdras, IV, xiii, 40 et s. ;   *Apoc.* of Baruch, lxxviii–lxxxvi (Schurer,
esch. d. Jud. Volkes, III, 305).

[7] Cf. *Apocal.*, xix, 20.

humble come down from heaven surrounded by angels. The bodies of the Just rise from the tomb and are borne on the clouds to Christ. The executioners of Jesus rise also from the tomb in order to gaze at this spectacle ; then they are plunged back again into the abyss (v. 993–1060).

The *Instructiones* furnish in a supplement some curious notions which Commodian indicated in the *Carmen Apologeticum*. Thus, according to the succession of events given in the *Instructiones* (II, i ; iii ; iv), the descent of the Heavenly Jerusalem is placed, between the first conflagration of the world (*Carmen*, v. 993–998) and the second (v. 999–1041), when the just receive the recompense which they have merited by their heroic resistance to anti-Christ. " They reproduce in wedlock for a thousand years. There, all the attributes which life on earth distributes in abundance by a perpetual renewing are brought together. No more rain, no more cold, in this golden city . . . ; the light given by lamps is no longer necessary there ; it gleams with the brightness of Him who created it, and night never reigns there " (II, iii, 9 et s.).

VI

APOCALYPTIC reveries inspired from Jewish and Judaeo-Christian sources ; injunctions of unaccommodating severity aimed at Christians who were too much inclined to escape from the rigour of the law of Christ, as much as at outside unbelievers—of such is made up the work of Commodian.

When compared with the rules of classic literature, his language swarms with inaccuracies. He jumbles up declensions and conjugations ; he confuses the query *ubi* and the query *quo ;* he is indifferent to the syntax of agreement and to the rule governing the right relation of tenses. His verses " contain the finest collection of barbarisms which the worst Latinist could have dreamt of." [1] Nevertheless, his style is not that of an *indoctus*. Apart from Holy Scripture, the principal food of his mind, and Christian authors (Tertullian and St Cyprian), Commodian had at least some slight acquaintance with certain profane writers, such as Terence, Lucretius, Virgil, Horace, perhaps also Sallust, Cicero, Tibullus and

[1] Monceaux, III, 483.

Ovid.[1] He makes awkward attempts at different methods—
alliterations, parallelisms between his verses, antitheses, and
piling up of synonyms. He sometimes attains to very forcible
compendious phrases in his turn of expression. But any
appreciation of art was wanting to him ; with the exception
of a few happy points, the whole is prosaic, heavy and maladroit.

As regards his hexameters, they have been compared to
those of a modern schoolboy who knows fairly well the general
rules pertaining to Latin verse in connection with the *caesura*
and the form of the last two feet, but is very ignorant of
quantity. Commodian did manage to write some good
hexameters (there are 37 in the *Instructiones*, and 26 in the
Carmen Apologeticum) ; but for the most part, his versification is wrong because the poet had not an idea of prosody.
Of the usual classical pauses he has hardly retained any but
the *penthémimère* which he almost always uses.[2] He reproduces in the two last feet the classical distribution of words
and accents, but here, as elsewhere, he pours into the traditional mould elements which do not at all belong to it.

Should this clumsy imitation of the classic hexameter
be considered as a fact by itself marking " the beginning of
a new art " ? [3] I think not. M. Monceaux has shown [4]
how in two-thirds of the metrical inscriptions, whether Christian or pagan, which have been discovered in the Roman
provinces, especially in Africa, quantity is confused. On
the other hand, the pause is given to the fifth foot ; a habitual
rhythm in the last two feet is observed ; and, as is the case
with Commodian, the acrostic, assonance, and sometimes
even the rhyme, are preserved. Commodian therefore made
no new innovations. Neither did he prepare the way for
any future innovation, for his verses present nothing in
common with the " rhyming " verses of the centuries that
succeeded.[5]

We may remark, moreover, that the perplexities experi-

---

[1] Notice is given of these resemblances in Dombart's edition, and in Manitius
(R.L.M., xlv [1890], p. 317, and xlvi [1891], p. 151), Ciceri (*Didascaleion*, II [1913],
363) ; J. Martin (S.B.W., vol. 181, 6, p. 108).

[2] There are also some examples of the *hepthémimère*, and four cases at least of
the *caesura* κατὰ τρίτον τροχᾶιον (*Instr.*, I, 10, 8 ; II, 7, 15 ; 11, 10 ; 31, 6).

[3] G. Boissier, *Fin du Paganisme*, II, 37.

[4] III, 430 et s.

[5] On his metre cf. Vernier, in the *Rev. de Philol.*, v. XV (1891) ; Havet, *Métrique*,
§ 496 ; Vrow, *op. cit.* ; and especially Monceaux, III, 481 et s.

enced by specialists relating to the system of versification followed by Commodian [1] will not be removed until we have an edition more faithful to the manuscripts than that of the *Corpus* of Vienna.   In more than one place, Dombart has retouched the text in order to accommodate it to the metre which he attributes to his author.

It has been sometimes supposed that Commodian deliberately wished to adapt his methods of expression to an unlettered public which he had specially in view.[2]   In itself, this hypothesis does not seem to be unlikely.   St Augustine followed the same practice when he wrote his *Alphabetical Psalm* against the Donatists,[3] as he explains in his *Retractiones*. But the case of Commodian appears to be very different. Nowhere does he limit the circle of his readers to the illiterate : In this connection I have pointed out the mistake which people commit about the word *rudes*.   If he wrote badly, as did many of his contemporaries, it was in spite of himself and not of set purpose.   Passionately convinced in his views and his faith as he was, he would surely have defended them with other weapons if he had not been at bottom rather ignorant notwithstanding certain passing breaths of classic literature.

VII

THE personality of Commodian is still an enigma, and all efforts of the critics have not succeeded in unravelling it or in determining with certitude the period at which he lived. Difference of opinion is considerable in relation to the date of the *Inscriptiones* and of the *Carmen Apologeticum*, since it bears on a period of time extending over more than two hundred years.   For long this question had been in dispute

[1] These difficulties are extremely perplexing and not a little disconcerting. Boissier and Scheifer declare that Commodian does not take quantity into account at all.   Haussen affirms that the system of the grammatical accent has been in no way substituted by the poet for the system of quantity both before the *caesura* and at the end of the line, and that the quantity is observed to a certain extent. Vernier maintains that Commodian never replaced a short syllable by a long accented one : this critic admits moreover that there are words where the accent is wrongly placed.   Meyer seeks an explanation in Semitic poetry which only takes into account the number of the syllables, and whose principles Commodian blended with those of the *cursus* of prose writers, etc. . . .

[2] Boissier, II, 40 ; and before him Gaston Paris, *Lettre à Léon Gautier sur la versification latine rythmique*, Paris, 1866 (Extract from the *Bibl. de l'Ec. des Chartes*, sixth series, v. II), p. 28.

[3] P.L., xliii, 23–32.   Cf. *Retr.*, I, xix.

when in 1906 Brewer was believed by some to have settled it in an important study on Commodian. According to Brewer,[1] Commodian must have been writing neither in the middle of the IIIrd century (Ebert, Boissier), nor at the beginning of the IVth (F. X. Kraus), nor between the years 260 and 350 (Harnack), nor in the second half of the IVth century (Maas), but between the years 458 and 466, in the south of Gaul. This is the conclusion to which Brewer came from considerations of a linguistic order and from an examination of historical allusions which he thought he saw in the *Instructiones* and especially in the *Carmen Apologeticum*. Shortly after the appearance of this learned work, J. Draseke wrote : " There is no longer any question concerning Commodian ; Brewer has offered a definite solution." [2] This was going rather too fast. Draseke's conviction did not impose itself on all minds with the same clearness. A very lively attack was brought to bear upon Brewer's comparisons by M. Paul Lejay,[3] which was soon followed up by Carl Weyman,[4] F. Zeller,[5] d'Alès,[6] Revay [7] and J. Martin.[8] We may say that to-day Brewer's thesis is held to be more than doubtful. This thesis relied in the first place on a passage in the *Carmen Apologeticum* (v. 805–822) in which Brewer thought he recognised more than one incident taken from the capture of Rome by Alaric in the year 410. The following is a literal translation of this passage : Commodian is here indicating some of the signs announcing the end of the world :

" ' But,' some may say, ' when are we to believe that all this is going to take place ? ' Here, in a few words, are the events following which those I am announcing will be realised. There will be many signs which will mark the end of this mighty disaster. But the beginning will be the seventh persecution directed against us. Already he is knocking at our gates and is girding himself with his sword who shall soon cross over the river while

---

[1] *Forschungen*, A. Ehrhard and J. P. Kirsch, VI, 1-2, Paderborn, 1906 ; *ibid.*, X, 5 (1910).
[2] T.L.Z., 1907, p. 80 ; *ibid.*, 1911, p. 364.
[3] R.C., v. LXIV (1907), pp. 199–209 ; LXVIII (1909), p. 125.
[4] *Theolog. Revue*, v. VII (1908), p. 523 et s. ; vol. VIII (1909), p. 485 et s.
[5] T.Q., vol. XCI (1909), p. 161–211 ; 252–406.
[6] *Rech. de Sc. rel.*, vol. II (1911), p. 479 et s. ; 599 et s.
[7] *Didaskaleion*, vol. I (1912), pp. 455–480.
[8] T.U., xxxix, 4 (1913).

the Goths are making their on-rush. King Apollyon, the name to be feared, will be with them. He will put an end, with sword in hand, to the persecution of the saints. He will march upon Rome with many thousands (of warriors) of his own race, and, by God's decree, ·he will make some of the vanquished his captives. At that time many senators, made captive, will lament ; and, conquered by a barbarian, they will blaspheme the God of heaven. Nevertheless, these pagans everywhere keep alive the Christians. Filled with joy, they seek for them more as if they were their brothers. As for those living in luxury and worshippers of vain idols, they hunt them down and make the senate pass under their yoke. These are the evils which those who have persecuted the loved ones (of God) will undergo : for the space of five months they will be slaughtered by this enemy."

An analysis of the details of this description is sufficient for us to see that in no particular do they fit in with the information bequeathed to us by historians contemporary with the taking of Rome in the year 410. The invaders are represented as pagans : now the Goths had become Arians from the time of Valens (364–378). Commodian insists on the benevolence with which they favour the Christians exclusively : now, according to Orosius [1] and St Augustine,[2] Alaric displayed equal clemency to the pagans themselves. Lastly, the senate is shown as a pagan *collegium*, and as the stronghold of paganism, and on this account suffers humiliating treatment. How can we apply to the Vth century such a picture of the senate when, by the testimony of St Ambrose, the Christian senators formed the large majority from the end of the IVth century ? [3] In reality, Commodian imagines much more than he can remember ; and, mingling historical touches with recollections of the Apocalypse, he gives an eschatological rôle to the Goths in the middle of the IIIrd century, whose menace the empire had already felt so heavily.

[1] VII, xxxix, 10 (Zangemeister, p. 546, 14).

[2] *De Civit. Dei*, I, 1 (Hoffmann, p. 4, 1, 21) ; III, xxix (H., p. 156, 26 ; 157, 3).

[3] *Ep.* xvii, 9 : " Cum majore jam curia christianorum numero sit referta " ; xvii, 10 : " pauci gentiles," " innumeri christiani senatores." Commodian lays stress in more than one place on the " paganism " of the Senate (*Carmen Ap.*, v. 815–820 ; 824 ; 831–849 ; 851 ; 855 ; 910).

Brewer likewise endeavoured to establish a connection between a passage in the *Instructiones*, II, x (the poet was exhorting certain children who had been carried away by the enemy and reduced to some form of slavery, to re-enter the bosom of the Church when grown up), and a decision of Pope Leo I in the year 458, relating to the question whether it was necessary to re-baptise children who had been carried away by the Vandals, when they returned to the Catholic faith. But certain characteristics are little favourable to the comparison : if these children were captives, how could the poet counsel them to flee " a terrible and ever bloodstained, impious and rebellious race, living the life of brute beasts " (v. 8–9), if that depended upon them ? We are under the impression that this " enemy " is rather the persecuting State which had usurped possession of their young consciences.

The fact is that nothing in the *Instructiones*, any more than in the *Carmen Apologeticum*, reveals that Commodian wrote after the reconciliation of the Church with the Roman authorities. The life of a Christian, as he depicts it, was a life under constant menace,[1] a life of struggle, in which peace itself when it should arrive, would be a " traitor's " peace.[2] One or two passages even offer some curious analogies with certain episodes at the time of St Cyprian, such as the schism of Felicissimus.[3] Nevertheless, it would not be unlikely if Commodian, insufficiently equipped with information on his own account, had applied even expressions of Cyprian to a case different from that which the saint had in view. Taking all in all, I think that we can with some certainty place the works of Commodian between the year 250 and the Edict of Milan (313). St Jerome does not speak of him in his *De Viris Illustribus* published in the year 392 : this was because the illiterate character of Commodian's work would not have contributed to the aims which he professes in his preface. As regards Gennadius, the place given by him to Commodian (between Prudentius and Audentius on the one hand, and between Faustinus and Rufinus on the other) is of little value, for it looks very much as if he knew nothing of him except what he had learnt from the *Instructiones*.

---

[1] Cf. *Instr.*, II, ix, xiii, xxi, xxv, xxix.

[2] *De Pace subdola* (xxv)

[3] xxv and xxix. Cf. Zeller, in T.Q., 1909, p. 359 et s., for these verbal analogies which are striking.

Commodian was born a pagan.[1] He often deplores his past errors and confesses that he had been given up to every kind of superstition.[2] The *explicit* of the *Carmen Apologeticum* gives him the rank of Bishop : there is nothing in his writings to confirm this information, which perhaps is due to the imagination of a scribe. He calls himself *mendicus Christi*,[3] which may perhaps mean an " ascetic," [4] or " one who solicits alms for Christ." [5] At the head of the last portion of the *Instructiones*, in the place where he gives his own name in an acrostic, these two words *Nomen Gasaei* figure, which so far have had little explanation although hypotheses are not wanting. Do they mean " the man of Gaza " ? [6] Or the name of the " treasurer " ? [7] We cannot tell exactly. If Commodian is believed to have been a native of Africa, or an African by adoption, this is due to his name, his language, his numerous references to St Cyprian, and the use which he makes of the *Testimonia ad Quirinum*. It is possible that a more profound knowledge of " Christian " Latin, and of the history of Christian ideas, will one day permit of absolute conclusions which would be premature at the present time.

[1] The words *parentibus insciis ipsis* (*Instr.*, I, l. 5) have been wrongly interpreted by G. Boissier (*Fin du Paganisme*, II, 39) : they mean " (I used to frequent the temples), my parents being themselves ignorant people " and not ". . . without the knowledge of my parents ".

[2] *Instr.*, I, 1, 4 ; I, vii, 21 ; I, xxvi, 25 ; I, xxxiii, 2 ; *Carm. Apol.*, 3 ; 11 ; 83.

[3] *Instr.*, II, xxxix : *Commodianus mendicus Christi*, is the group of words obtained by reading the first letter of each verse of this piece from the bottom to the top.

[4] Cf. C. Weyman, *Miscell. zu lat. Dichtern*, printed by the IVth International Congress of Catholics at Freibourg (1898), p. 9 et s. Weyman appeals to Cassiodorus, 10th Collatio, in which the expression is used of one " qui de aliena largitate cotidianum poscit auxilium." For the ascetic spirit of Commodian, cf. *Instr.*, I, xxvi–xxviii, and *Carmen Apol.*, v, 579–616.

[5] Monceaux (III, 463 ; cf. 83) remarks upon the insistence with which Commodian solicits the alms of the faithful and scolds them for not giving enough. He regards Commodian as one of those *seniores laici* who (this practice is given as at the beginning of the IVth century, but it goes back to an earlier date without doubt) helped the Bishop in his work of administration.

[6] Gaza, in Syria : the ordinary ethnological term is *Gazensis ;* we find however *Gazeus*, at a rather later date.

[7] *Gazaeus*, derived from *gaza* or *gazum*, treasure, is not established elsewhere.

CHAPTER IV

THE EVE OF THE PEACE OF THE CHURCH

ARNOBIUS AND LACTANTIUS

BIBLIOGRAPHY

I. ARNOBIUS.—P.L., V, 718-1288; Reifferscheid, in C.V., vol. IV (1875). For the sole manuscript of Arnobius see Minucius Felix on a former page. The text of Arnobius has drawn the special attention of philologists: Meiser, in S.B.M., 1908; Lofstedt, *Arnobiana*, Lund, 1917 (cf. B. ph. W., 1917, 1291); Brakman, *Arnobiana*, Leyden, 1917; K. Kistner, *Arnobiana*, Progymn. St-Ingbert, Pfatz, etc. . . . A fresh edition of the *Adv. Nationes* is much to be desired.—Consult: Monceaux, III, 241-286.

II. LACTANTIUS.—P.L., VI and VII; Brandt, in C.V., xix (1890) and xxvii (fasc. 1, 1893; fasc. ii, 1897). — Consult: René Pichon, *Lactance*, Paris, 1901; Monceaux, III, 287-359; Th. Stangl, *Lactantiana*, in Rh.M., LXX, 224-252. Brandt (*Wochensch. f. kl. Phil.*, 29 [1912], 1383) declares that a revision of his own edition is indispensable.—
The question as to the authenticity of the *De Mortibus Persecutorum* has lost much of its importance since an almost unanimous agreement has been reached on this long-debated problem between the most authoritative critics. The work was one out of a collection of manuscripts bought by Colbert at the Convent of Moissac (Tarn-et-Garonne), on the advice of Baluze. The latter, when he published the work for the first time (1679), following a much spoilt manuscript of the IXth century (Bibl. Nat. 2627, *Colbert*, 1297), had no hesitation in identifying it with the *De Persecutione* attributed to Lactantius by St Jerome (*de Vir. Ill.*, lxxx). This assignment was almost at once contested by Columbus, in 1684, then by Dom le Nourry in 1710. Brandt, the editor of Lactantius in the *Corpus Script. Eccl. Lat.* has appraised the *rationes dubitandi* (S.B.W., vol. 120 [1890] and 125 [1891]). His reasons were very skilfully refuted by René Pichon (*Lactance*, p. 338 et s.), who won over the assent of Brandt himself (B. ph. W., 1903, 1257). With the exception of a few dissentients (v.g., Silomon, in *Hermes*, 1912, pp. 250-257), the authenticity is commonly accepted to-day. The same does not quite hold good for the two dedications to Constantine included in book I, 1, 13-16, and in book VII, xxvii, 2, of the *Instit. Div.* Brandt and Monceaux consider them to have been interpolated, for the triumphant tone of the author does not at all agree with the work as a whole, in which the suffering anger of an oppressed man is plainly visible. Pichon thinks that the opposition between these pieces and the rest of the *Institutiones* is exaggerated. It is possible, too, that Lactantius himself re-edited his *Inst. Div.* (see Batiffol, *La Paix constant. et le Cathol.*, Paris, 1914, p. 224 et s.). In fact, these dedications are wanting from certain excellent manuscripts. These same manuscripts likewise do not include three theological dissertations in which opinions of a very pronounced dualism are expressed. Monceaux (III, 302) regards them as subsequent additions. According to Pichon, these pieces are conformable

to the train of ideas habitual with Lactantius who was rather uncertain as a theologian. Brandt ended by accepting Pichon's point of view (B. ph. W.).

III. VICTORINUS of PETTAU.—P. L., V, 281-344 (reproducing Routh, R.S., III, 451-453, in the *De Fabrica Mundi*); Haussleiter, in C.V., vol. XLIX (1916). See later observations on the manuscripts.

SUMMARY

I. The question of Arnobius.—II. The *Adversus Nationes*. Arnobius and the Bible. His Metaphysical Conceptions.—III. The Christianity of Arnobius.—IV. His Polemics against Paganism.—V. The Rhetoric of Arnobius.—VI. The Opinion of Christians regarding him.—VII. Lactantius. His Life.—VIII. The *De Opificio Dei*.—IX. The *Institutiones Divinae*. Lactantius's Method of Apologetics. Plan of his Works.—X. The Blunders of Lactantius. The Salient Portions of his Work. Stratification of the Views of Lactantius.—XI. The *De Ira Dei*.—XII. The *De Mortibus Persecutorum*. Christian History.—XIII. Conclusions on Lactantius.—XIV. Victorinus of Pettau, first Latin Exegetist.—XV. The *Adversus Omnes Haereses*.

I

THE position which Arnobius occupies in Christian antiquity is exceptional and very curious. After having taught rhetoric all his life at Sicca-Veneria, in proconsular Africa, Arnobius was converted late in about his sixtieth year. His Bishop, a little distrustful of this labourer who had engaged at the eleventh hour, whom he had always known as being very violent against the Christians, demanded from him a pledge of his sincerity.[1] Arnobius thought he could do no better than to transfer to the service of the cause which he had just embraced his sustained eloquence, his concise erudition and his heavy irony. He wrote a work, the *Adversus Nationes*, which appeared about the year 300.[2] It is amusing to observe what this old man and improvised apologist understood of Christianity, and how he mingled adventitious ideas without troubling himself over their incongruities and without considering that his Christian readers might be offended.

II

THE *Adversus Nationes* comprises seven books. Arnobius begins by a refutation of a grievance the import of which Tertullian and St Cyprian have already made us understand.

[1] This story is related to us by St Jerome in *Ep.* LXX, 5.
[2] Probably between the years 304 and 310.

On all sides people were saying that since the Christians had appeared the human race had been afflicted with a thousand ills proving that the offended gods had abandoned the earth. Arnobius draws attention to the puerility of any argument fixing a date for the beginning of these scourges, whose very name goes back to most remote antiquity, so as to make them coincide with the coming of Christianity. How could any-one doubt that these ills proceeded from the general laws of the universe which are in no way subject to our convenience ? In any case, there was nothing in the Christian doctrine to justify the wrath of heaven. From this doctrine Arnobius sketches the leading points, after his own fashion, in books I and II. Then he turns round on the pagans : you say that it is because of us the gods load humanity with misfortune. Not at all ! If they exist, it is with you that they are angry on account of the gross conception which you have of them, and the incoherent rites by which you pretend to honour them. Books III to VII form the polemic of an ironical and vehement despiser of the Greco-Roman religion. And continually the same sarcastic question crops up : " Is it then on account of such mad conceptions that you persecute us ? . . ."

What first of all strikes us in the *Adversus Nationes* is the almost total absence of quotations from Scripture. Arnobius unfolds his line of argument in the abstract ; nowhere does he place his support upon the Sacred Books. We barely find three or four passages giving a more or less clear echo of them.[1] Is this discretion, so rarely found in Christian writings of the first centuries, the considered policy of Arnobius ? In addressing himself to the pagans, did he avoid on principle laying weight on documents which the pagans could have challenged ? This would be to give him a too subtle intention. In several places Arnobius confuses points, or labours them excessively, thereby purely and simply betraying his lack of knowledge. Thus he affirms that Christ was heard by the different nations whom He addressed as though He had spoken in the proper language of each one of them [2]—a manifest transposition of the facts reported on the Day of Pentecost in the Acts of the Apostles. A

---

[1] Compare Arnobius, C.V., vol. IV (1875), 1, 6 (p. 6, line 7), with *Matthew*, v, 49 ; ii, 6 (p. 108, l. 26), and *Romans*, xii, 7 ; ii, 65 (p. 101, l. 11), with *John*, x 7-9 ; xiv, 6, etc.
[2] 1, 46.

little further on, he greatly exaggerates the prodigies that
followed the death of Christ : " Novitate rerum exterrita
universa mundi sunt elementa turbata, tellus mota con-
tremuit, *mare funditus refusum est*, aer globis involitus est
tenebrarum *igneus orbis solis tepefacto ardore deriguit.*" [1]   He
had read the gospels very carelessly ! More singular still
is his total lack of curiosity as regards the Old Testament.
We might say that he had no idea of the filiation between
Judaism and Christianity, nor of the link which united the
New with the Old Testament.   To the pagans who returned
against him his accusation of anthropomorphism by bringing
forward the anthropomorphisms of the Old Testament, he
retorts in these words : " And let them not bring against us
the fables of the Jews as if we also attributed different forms
to God. . . .   In reality, these fables do not concern us and
have absolutely nothing in common with us ; or if, as people
think, they have a community with us, you must look for
more learned doctors who will teach you how to clear up the
obscurity and the mysterious words of these writings." [2]
Here we have a very rash repudiation and one which does
not seem to have caused him any embarrassment.   Again,
if he had ever opened the New Testament, would he have
insisted so much on declaring as incompatible the idea of
anger and the idea of Divinity itself ? [3]   The God of Arnobius
is a God who is indifferent and peaceable, who is neither
moved, nor given to vengeance.   The Divine impassibility
as he imagines it, has an altogether pagan and Epicurean
quality.   Remarkable minds like Tertullian and Clement
of Alexandria had energetically combated this view, and,
even at the time when Arnobius was writing, Lactantius
devoted a whole work, the *De Ira Dei*, to refuting it.   Arnobius
has the appearance of considering as null and void all this
long labour of Christian thought.

We find the same singularity in his metaphysical conceptions, for example, in what concerns the soul, its origin,
its nature and its destinies. [4]   In the eyes of Arnobius, it
was veritable blasphemy to attribute to God the fatherhood
of the soul—a presumptuous filiation invented by human
pride.   If the soul proceeded directly from God, would God

---

[1] 1, 59.   [2] iii, 12.
[3] i, 17 ; vi, 2 ; vii, 5 ; 36, etc.   [4] See book II.

have permitted that it should fall into so many moral and
religious errors ?   Would He not have foreseen the consequences of His act as Creator ?   From the perfect, only
the perfect could come forth :   Plato saw this well, and
Arnobius does not hesitate to place himself under his
patronage.   That the soul has for its author some demiurge,
" inferior to God, although belonging to His court," [1] appears
to him to be the most likely hypothesis.   Fashioned in this
manner, the soul was certainly corporeal.   There was such
a close solidarity between the life of the body and the life
of the soul that these reciprocal influences implied an identity
of material.   Was it at least immortal ? in itself, it was not :
it may become so when the case arises by virtue of its merits,
and thanks to a special favour of God.   If it has sinned,
it will. be plunged into the flames, and these flames will have
the effect of rarefying it, and of destroying it little by little
in cruel tortures.   The immortality of the soul was quite
conditional and subordinated to the efforts made in this
life to know God and to follow His law.[2]

The principal points of this doctrine come from Plato
for whom Arnobius does not spare flattering epithets and
whose authority he willingly invokes.   If he takes away
from God the responsibility of having created souls, if he
imagines them as being materially linked with the body
up to the last *dijugatio*, it is because he is making use of the
conceptions of Plato.   He only formally separates himself
from the philosopher to deny the pre-existence of souls.   But
it is not Plato only upon whom he draws.   In Arnobius
there is a whole series of intellectual influences which intersect
each other and do battle in his thoughts.   What he says of
the demiurge, the artificer of the soul, singularly resembles
certain Gnostic dreamings.   His views on the corporeal
nature of the soul are reminiscent of those of Tertullian in
his *De Anima*.   If we examine his theory of knowledge,
we see that it is related to the empiric point of view of the
Stoic school :   for him, the soul is a *tabula rasa* on which
impressions from without come to be inscribed, and only
experimental knowledge can bring certitude.   In flagrant
contradiction, Arnobius only makes an exception of the idea

[1] ii, 36 (C.V., p. 77, 15).
[2] II, 32 and 61 (C.V., p. 74, 13 and 97, 16).

of God, which he declares to be innate. Certain vestiges of Neo-Platonism have been noticed in him. In fact, he is an example of the most surprising eclecticism, and he borrows his explanations in turn from the different systems of lay philosophy.

III

BUT what place then does Christianity occupy in such a complex whole ? Does it form only a secondary part of the edifice ? Does it play only a subordinate and purely accessory rôle ? To state this would be to come to a too rapid conclusion.

To begin with, Arnobius was veritably changed and con-verted by grace : " What blindness ! " he cries. " Up to now I still worshipped images that had come forth from the foundry, gods fashioned by blows of the hammer on the anvil, from the bones of elephants, from pictures, and garlands suspended from ancient trees ; when I saw a polished stone all glistening with oil, I adored it as though some power were present in it ; I paid my addresses to it, I asked favours from a senseless stone. . . . But now, led by so great a master (Christ) into the paths of truth, I know the value of all that, I pay my respect to Him who is worthy of respect, I no longer insult the name of God, and I render unto each one his due." [1] He thus whole-heartedly renounces his former self. I will add that there are certain truths in Christianity which Arnobius appears to have felt with force and sincerity : for example, the majesty of God, whose existence and all-power man recognises as it were spontaneously ; the goodness of Christ, and His divinity. Even here doubtless a scrupulous theologian might find much to reprehend. Arnobius had so much fear of lowering the notion of Divinity by making it have any points of contact with Humanity, that he estab-lishes only a very feeble link between the Divinity and the Humanity of Christ.[2] And, from the purely literary point of view, how much want of taste ! Does he not go so far as to laud Christ in several passages with the same turn of words which had already served Lucretius in his praise of Epicurus ? [3] But if we except these relatively theological and unfortunate

---

[1] i, 39.   [2] Cf. Tixeront, *Hist. des Dogmes,* Paris, 1908, I, 443.
[3] Compare i, 32, and Lucretius, *de Nat. Rerum,* v, 1 et s. ; v, 471 et s. ; 281 et s.; 592 et s., etc. . . .

resemblances Arnobius speaks in a worthy manner of the
Saviour and of the immense benefit brought by Him to
humanity.

He likewise makes observations on the conditions regulating the acceptance of the Christian belief.   Thus he sketches
in book II some sort of theory of the necessity of " faith "
for life.   Every enterprise, he observes, postulates some
preliminary faith; such is the absolute law of all our initiatives.
Who makes a journey or a voyage, or enters into business
transactions without firmly counting upon coming back to
his home with his affairs brought to a satisfactory conclusion,
etc. ?   In the same way, every philosophic doctrine to which
we adhere implies that we refer it in a more or less degree
to the authority of a master.   Therefore, why jeer at the
Christians for attaching themselves to Christ ?   They were
doing nothing more than conforming to the normal methods
of human action.

This theory of faith, in itself a legitimate concession to the
intelligence, had already been put forward by Origen in his
great work against Celsus,[1] and we can find other traces of it
in Christian writers of an anterior date.[2]   More than a century
after Arnobius St Augustine was to give it a far higher
meaning and to make of it a real " principle of reason."
With Arnobius, it is only an occasional consideration from
which he does not dream of deducing all the consequences.
Also we must not expect to see him establishing his defence
of Christianity on any very profound psychology.

He insists more on the powerlessness of human reason to
discover the truth by its natural forces.   Arnobius was the
first in date of these hardy, and very probably rash apologists
who based religious doctrine on philosophic Pyrrhonism.
Confessions of incertitude from the great philosophers ;
specious arguments on which the most contradictory metaphysical reasonings base their authority ;   man's ignorance
of the true explanation of the phenomena surrounding him ;
the uselessness of his presence in the universe ;   the basic
equality of man and the animal in spite of the superiority
which, in his pride, the former attributes to himself, and in
a certain sense even the greater innocence of the animal,

[1] I, ii (Koetschau, in C.B., vol. I, pp. 63–64).
[2] V.g. Theophilus, *ad Autol.*, 1, 8.

as an ox, in whose mouth Arnobius places a veritable speech for the prosecution against his master,[1] eloquently affirms,— such are the reasons upon which our author prides himself in order to counsel man to despise himself entirely. He is also as far removed as possible from the optimism of his pupil Lactantius who was so ready to marvel at the beauty and admirable arrangement of the human being. To Arnobius man was a creature without grace and without distinction, miserable and vile.[2] And his conclusion is that we must abandon vain speculations which exhaust our frail reason, in order to give ourselves entirely to God, *ad Dominum rerum tota mente atque anima proficisci*.[3]

IV

In order to understand the real character of the work, we must remember that it is a speech for the prosecution which Arnobius develops far more than a piece of special pleading ; or rather, it is a furious assault with a prodigality of wounding phrases.[4] He takes no trouble to win over rebellious minds. His aim is only to confound and humiliate. Mythology is his butt ; it bears all the burden of his demonstration.

We must not suppose that the Christians were the first to be shocked at the " scandal " of mythology. The truth is that, if we put aside the *Iliad* and the *Odyssey*, wherein faith in the reality of the events belonging to mythology appears to be entire, lengthy protest had not ceased to make itself heard from the first awakening of critical reflection. There were very few thoughtful minds in Greece who refrained, from motives of respect, from giving expression to their reservations and from offering some more acceptable interpretation. The legends of the past shocked at once their moral and religious

---

[1] vii, 9 (C.V., p. 243, 13).

[2] " Nam quid in homine pulchrum est ? " (iii, 16). " In humanis vero corporibus quidnam, quaeso, inerat pulchritudinis ? " (iv, 23). Man was an " animal himself well saw the moral danger of this systematic lowering of man's dignity : *Inst. div.*, II, 1, 2 et s.

[3] ii, 60 (C.V., p. 96, 24).

[4] " O parvuli (Reiff., 28, 24) ; O mentes incredulae, difficiles, durae (34, 27) ; miserum et supervacuum " (ii, 38) ; " animal vile " (vii, 4), etc., etc. Lactantius O nescii (36, 7 ; 50, 13) ; O impii (159, 13) ; O sancti atque impolluti antistites religionum (118, 2) ; O theologi (181, 1) ", etc.

sense of what was fitting, and their reason. And it was on the score sometimes of morality and religion, and sometimes of reason, that they took up their attitude against it.[1]

Did the advocates of Christianity bring to bear any very new methods of exegesis ? B. Aubé, whose learned works on the first centuries of our era are well known, wrote in one of his books that Christian polemics had made no fundamental additions to pagan criticism of mythology.[2] Speaking frankly, we cannot contradict him over that. The object the Christian writers had in view was not to interpret mythology, but to demonstrate it as infamous and ridiculous. Among the hypotheses bequeathed to them by Greek philosophy they were content to choose those which best suited their particular purpose. For the most part they confined themselves to seizing upon the evhemerist hypothesis [3] which had in their eyes the advantage of controverting all the pseudo-divine element in paganism on the most ordinary historical grounds. But on the other hand, not daring altogether to deny the prodigies proceeding from the oracles and magic of the pagans, they attributed them to demons. Other methods of explanation which had been tried before did not offer them any attraction. Or rather, they saw the danger of people drawing from them reasons for saving polytheism by lending a more or less philosophic appearance to the most impossible legends. This is why they refused all credence and even violently denounced them,—especially the Stoic method of exegesis, that last refuge of the defenders of Hellenism.

Their wellnigh constant method was irony. To obtain a correct idea of this we must read Arnobius especially. The *Adversus Nationes* is the most complete repertory of Christian criticism of mythology. Archæologists will there find a mass of information on pagan legends, and on the details of their rites and sacred ceremonies. We can clearly see that his erudition is not first-hand. Arnobius draws upon Clement

[1] See Paul Decharme's fine work, *la Critique des traditions religieuses chez les Grecs*, Paris, 1904.—Bodo von Borries, *Quid veteres philosophi de idololatria senserint*, Gottingen, 1918.

[2] *St Justin, Philosophe et Martyr*, 1875, p. 326.

[3] The fundamental conception which Evhemerus had put forth in his famous romance *The Ἱερὰ Ἀναγράφη* may be summed up as follows : " The gods were originally powerful kings whom their subjects, from gratitude or from flattery, deified after their death."

of Alexandria, Tertullian, and other more obscure authors,[1] without counting Cicero, whose *De Natura Deorum* furnished Christian writers with so many valuable resources. But he developed the traditional themes with such ample fecundity that it is interesting to examine them in his book. Arnobius was possessed of a realistic imagination of exceptional vigour. His triumph is to seize upon some metaphysical hypothesis, or popular belief, and deduce from it accurately and with the most precise details all the ridiculous consequences which he perceives in it. The way in which he relates the adventures of Jupiter should be read. Without any compunction at the most licentious pictures, this pitiless satirist describes the ridiculous positions to which the libidinous god had to stoop ; he imagines all the circumstances of his seductions with a copious *verve* with which the reader ends by being amused in spite of the puerile tinsel of his phraseology.

V

ON the whole, Arnobius may be considered as a kind of Voltaire, far less polished, but possessed of an irony almost as impetuous as that of Voltaire himself. He derives the legends of mythology by a procedure very like that which the Voltaire of the *Taureau Blanc* or of the *Lettres d'Amabed* was to employ against the Bible. I will add that he was in addition what Voltaire never became in the slightest degree—the most verbose of rhetoricians. In reading him we seem to be hearing his sonorous and indefatigable voice ; we feel him delighting himself with the amplitude of his periods and the fecundity of his vocabulary. No theme comes his way without its supplying him with all that it is capable of producing, and even more.[2] The art of amplification, understood in the most superficial sense, could not be illustrated by

---

[1] For example, a certain Cornelius Labeo, whom he does not mention by name. He was a philosopher, probably a Neo-Platonist of the Ist or IInd century A.D., who was much interested in the national religion of Rome. In comparing the *Adv. Nationes* with texts of St Augustine and Macrobius, wherein Labeo is explicitly mentioned, we can see that Arnobius often took him as his point of departure, in order to refute him. Cf. Kroll, Rh. M., 1916, 309–357 ; Boehm, *De Corn. Labeonis aetate*, Konisberg, 1913 ; Bousset, in *Archiv. f. Religions wiss.*, XVIII, 137.

[2] Thus I, xxxviii (Reiff., p. 24, l. 29 et s.), when enumerating the benefits conferred by Christ, he allows himself to be drawn on to attribute to Him some which do no less than make Jesus to be an initiator into the secrets of universal matter.

better examples than those which may be drawn from the *Adversus Nationes*. Interrogations repeated up to the fifteenth and twentieth time, apostrophes, exclamations, antitheses, alliterations, anaphora—the whole arsenal of the schools can be found. The verbal dexterity of Arnobius is extraordinary. We suspect that he must have been a great consulter of glossaries.[1] He delivers his words with the prodigality of a man sure of not drying up his sources. He has always two, three, four, or five words for the same idea, and instead of choosing one of them he piles them all up.[2] In addition, his tenacious memory furnishes him with a large quantity of recollections borrowed from classic writers, and even from the most ancient Latin authors.[3] In his rounded periods he observes the metrical rules of the *clausula*.[4] All this goes to make up a style of singular *verve* in which, as I have said, we end by finding a species of entertainment which is not of a very high order.

VI

WE shall not be surprised after all this that Arnobius enjoyed in Christian antiquity only a very mediocre *prestige*. When St Jerome speaks freely of him, that is to say in his letters (not in his *De Viris Illustribus*, in which the exigencies of apologetics are the ruling note), he shows what he makes of him (*Ep.* lviii, 10). He is moreover almost the sole writer to make any mention of him. The famous decretal attributed to Pope Gelasius quotes the writings of Arnobius as " apocryphal," that is to say, not as being unauthentic, but as being very suspect from the doctrinal point of view. The same suspicions are to be found in modern times. The *Mémoires* of Trévoux, the organ of the Jesuits, only consents to exonerate Arnobius from Bayle's insidious criticisms after observing " that he does not hold a sufficiently distinguished

---

[1] Cf. Tschiersch, *De Arnobii Studiis Latinis*, Jena, 1905, p. 39 et s.

[2] Ex.: Reifferscheid, p. 16, 30; 164, 16; 24, 22 (. . . quid fecerint, egerint, pertulerint, actitarint); p. 58, 1: "qui estis unius mentis et per easdem vias placitorum inceditis unitate "; p. 175, 3: " victos somnos atque altissimi soporis oblivione demersos, etc. . . ."

[3] Tschiersch, *op. cit.* (Lucretius, p. 8 et s.; Plautus, p. 11 et s.; Cato, p. 16 et s.; Varro, p. 18 et s.).

[4] Spindler, *de Arnobii genere dicendi*, Strasbourg, 1901, p. 30–32; Th. Lorenz, *de clausulis Arnobianis*, Breslau, 1910.

rank among the Fathers to urge us keenly to take up his defence." Further, just as with Lactantius, the *Mémorial* refuses him the title of Father. " We should not call them Fathers of the Church while attributing error to them, but rather only give this title to those to whom the common and recognised belief of the faithful accords it."

A Christian who knew nothing of Scripture, or made very little use of it ; who misunderstood some of the leading ideas of Christianity and, I will add, formally proscribed all exterior forms of worship,[1] was in fact a very strange Christian ! It is matter for astonishment that Arnobius was never invited by his Bishop to revise his work. How are we to believe that the latter could have declared himself satisfied with this token furnished by his white-haired catechumen ? However this may be, the interest attaching to the case of Arnobius lies in the contradictions offered by a line of thought which had for long been fashioned on the reading of profane works, and had then been remodelled by a late *crise religieuse* which, powerless to bring into unity these contradictory influences, serenely placed the most anomalous assertions side by side in the same work.

VII

LACTANTIUS too is not an intelligence of the first order. Gaston Boissier often quotes him in his *Fin du Paganisme*, but he did not judge him to be sufficiently " representative " to devote to him a special study. M. René Pichon who wrote a lengthy volume on him instinct with very scrupulous literary sentiment, acknowledges with a good grace that his author is mediocre, " in the Latin sense of the word,—and a little also in the French sense." [2] The very fact that he has been called the Cicero of the Christians,[3] and that he was wellnigh the equal of the classic masters whom he admired in the purity of his style, is proof to us that he kept himself to well-worn grooves : a more vigorous and fresher mode of

---

[1] vi, 2 ; vii, 1 et s.

[2] *Op. cit.,* p. viii.

[3] It was Pic de la Mirandole who gave him that title (*Opera Omnia*, 1573, p. 21). But quite early his name had been associated with that of his model of predilection : cf. St Jerome. *Ep.* lviii, 10 : " quos (libros) si legere volueris, dialogorum Ciceronis ἐπιτομήν (abridgment) reperies."

thought would have upset this fine classic harmony. Even when we exert ourselves to say something good of him it would be puerile to endeavour to cover up the weaknesses in the train of thought of this conscientious professor, whose traditionalism was more pronounced than his critical sense was acute. Nevertheless we carry away with us after reading his works the impression that, notwithstanding his too exclusively literary culture, Lactantius counts in the long series of the first apologists ; that the attempt which he made possesses its own originality, and reveals certain interesting modifications in the state of mind of the lettered Christians.

He styled himself L. Caecilius Firmianus qui et Lactantius.[1] People have sometimes tried to make him out an Italian, from Firmum in Picenum. But the ethnological derivative from Firmum would be Firmanus, not Firmianus. From St Jerome's notice of him (*De Vir. Ill.*, lxxx), we may conclude that he was an African. The chronology of his life is little known. However, we possess certain distinguishing marks. He was born a pagan in about the year 250. He studied under Arnobius at Sicca. Nowhere does he mention him by name as his instructor, even in the passage of the *Institutiones Divinae* in which he gives the names of his predecessors. We know that Arnobius wrote his apology very late in life. He appears, besides, to have exercised no influence on the mind of Lactantius. The latter in his turn took up the teaching of rhetoric.[2] He acknowledges that his ability in the art of eloquence was of limited extent, and that he never appeared in the Forum.[3] All the same, he must have acquired a certain reputation for he was nominated for the post of professor in that subject at Nicomedia in Bithynia. Since the winter of the year 285 the town had become the place of residence of Diocletian and had acquired all the importance of an imperial city. In this entirely Greek town he had only a few pupils and was obliged to take to writing : " *Penuria discipulorum ob graecam videlicet civitatem ad scribendum se contulit*," said St Jerome.[4] Possibly this " *penuria* " was not felt until the active measures taken against the Christians deprived

---

[1] The MSS. vary between Caecilius and Caelius. An inscription found at Cirta (C.I.L., viii, 7241) mentions an L. Caecilius Firmianus who must have belonged to the same family. The " qui et Lactantius " is the *signum* or familiar name.

[2] *Inst. div.*, I, 1, 8.

[3] *Ibid.*, 10.

[4] *De Vir. Ill.*, lxxx.

him of his official title of rhetorician. Meanwhile, he had been converted.[1] The terrible persecution of 303 came. Lactantius did not suffer personally any punishment, and remained in Bithynia until 305 or even 306.[2] But when, after the abdication of Diocletian (May 305), Galerius made war upon the schools, Lactantius decided to leave Nicomedia.[3] We do not know where he took refuge during this time of trouble. Possibly he came back to Nicomedia between 311 and 313, when Galerius issued his Edict of toleration (10th April, 311).[4] He had experienced some very hard times, lacking even the necessaries of life, if we are to believe St Jerome's account.[5] His last years were more peaceful than he could have hoped. Constantine appointed him to teach Latin literature to his son Crispus born in 307. Lactantius was then " in extrema senectute." [6] He died doubtless at Trèves but we do not know at what exact date.

VIII

THE first work of Lactantius preserved to us is entitled *De Opificio Dei.*[7] Up till then, he had confined himself to poetry and to the somewhat dry walks of the old learning.[8] Now that he had become a Christian he set himself to do some good work for the use of those whom he called " the philosophers of our sect." The work is not based on the circum-

---

[1] *Inst. Div.*, I, 1, 8 ; *Epit.*, xliii, 3 ; *de Ira Dei*, 11, 2 ; cf. St Augustine, *de Doctr. Christ.*, II, lxi.

[2] *Inst. Div.*, V, xi, 15.

[3] *Ibid.*, V, ii, 2.

[4] We conclude this from certain indications in the *de Mort. Persec.*, xxxv, 1 and 4 ; xlviii, 1. See, however, Pichon, *op. cit.*, p. 360.

[5] *Chronical* (II, p. 191 Schoene).

[6] *Ibid.*

[7] Composed in 303–4 (Harnack) or at the end of 305 (Monceaux).

[8] St Jerome (*De Vir. Ill.*, lxxx) attributes to him : 1. A *Symposium*. The " tabulated form " arose in Greece and had enjoyed much favour in the philosophic schools (Plato, Xenophon, Aristotle, Aristoxenes of Tarentum, Hieronymus of Rhodes, Prytanis, Epicurus, Persaeus, Lucian of Samosata, Plutarch, etc.). Cf. *Cena Trimalchionis*, in the *Satiricon* of Petronius ; 2. A 'Οδοιπορικόν, an itinerary from Africa to Nicomedia in hexameters ; 3. A work entitled *Grammaticus*, doubtless dealing with questions of grammar ; 4. Four books of letters to Probus, two books addressed to Severus and two books to Demetrianus (these are quoted by St Jerome, *Ep.* lxxxiv, 7, and *Com. in Gal.* II, 4 (P.L., xxvi, 373)). Pope Damasus pronounced these letters very wearisome on account of their length and for the scant interest of the subjects treated therein (the rules of versification, geography, philosophy) : cf. St Jerome, *Ep.* xxxv, 2. The date of these different collections is uncertain ; 5. Two books to Asclepiades, who had himself dedicated a book on Providence to Lactantius (cf. *Inst. Div.*, VII, iv, 17).

H

stances of current events although the author makes allusion in it to the clouds held in the sky over the Christians.[1] He addresses himself to one Demetrianus, a former pupil of his own, a Christian, and, without giving to his explanations any supporting aid from Scripture, endeavours to vindicate Providence from the attacks of certain philosophic schools, who denounced any Divine work in connection with man, his soul and his body. Cicero had already undertaken this task;[2] but, according to Lactantius, he had not understood how to draw all that might have been possible from such rich material. To counter the pessimism affected by the Epicureans in order to discredit the very notion of Providence, Lactantius demonstrates that man is not at all degraded to the point to which those paradoxical minds had debased him, since he had to his credit language and reason, which made up for what he lacked,[3] and that even those very people who placed the animal superior to him would not go to the extreme limit of exchanging their alleged meanness as men against the stupidity of the brutes.[4] Then analysing in detail the physical constitution of man, he shows the perfect adaptation of his organs to their end. Next he passes on to the nature of the soul, whose creation he deliberately attributes to God, in contradistinction to his former tutor Arnobius. Here and there some rather *naïve* remarks make us laugh[5] (similar works by Fénelon and Bernardin of Saint-Pierre have some difficulty in guarding against these trifling ironies); taking him as a whole, this spiritual apology, thoroughly imbued with Aristotle, Cicero, and Varro, is of value from its clearness and the æsthetic feeling which dominates it, as well as its eye to usefulness which is thoroughly in accordance with Roman tradition.

IX

As soon as he had written the *De Opificio Dei*, Lactantius occupied his mind with a work of quite another bearing,

---

[1] I, 1; I, 7; xx, 1.
[2] *De Rep.*, IV, l. 1; *de Nat. Deorum*, II, xlvii; *de Finibus*, III, xviii.
[3] " Quae desunt ratio rependit " (iii, 5).
[4] iii, 12.
[5] V.g. xiii· " Conglobata in nates caro quam sedendi officio apta ! "

and began preparing the materials.[1] In writing his *Institutiones Divinae*, Lactantius had a very clear view of the object which he wished to attain, and of the proper method of approaching it. Formed by his education and also by his profession to hold in esteem things intellectual, he had often suffered from the cultured contempt lavished by educated pagans on Christianity. He himself quite appreciated the fact that those amongst the Christians who constituted themselves the interpreters of divine truths were not always up to the level of their task.

This feeling of inferiority, so painful for his *amour propre* as a proselyte, appears to have been emphasised in Lactantius by the writings of two opponents of Christianity whom he had known when he was teaching rhetoric in Bithynia.[2] The scholarly art and the cruelly skilful arguments made use of by one of them had inflamed him with an ardent desire to refute them, and with them, all those who either in Greek or Latin had accomplished the same detestable task.

It was thus to educated minds that he wished to address himself by preference. Not by any means in any spirit of lofty superiority as was the case with the Gnostic. In nowise did he despise the humble. He knew better than anyone that religion found access more easily to simple and pure hearts because they had fewer secret antipathies to it.[3] But he marks out in his mind the audience which he wished more particularly to convince.

This end dictates the principal features of his methods. Lactantius claims to be making a literary apology adorned with every attraction of style, and capable of charming the most disdainfully punctilious minds. He is not ashamed to confess it ; and the desire to write well is co-ordinated in him with a more lofty design, which is to obtain access to minds still obstinate whom he must convince at all costs.

---

[1] *De Opif. Dei*, xv, 6 ; xx, 2. The *Institutiones* appeared between 304 and 313.
[2] *Inst. Div.*, V, ii. He mentions neither of them by name. One of them was a philosopher by profession : Porphyry has been suggested, but Porphyry had written a work in fifteen books against the Christians. Now Lactantius speaks of a work in three volumes. It is, besides, doubtful if Porphyry was living at the time of Lactantius. The second was a judge. He was referring probably to Hierocles, the Neo-Platonist, the author of a Λόγος φιλαλήθης προς τοὺς χριστιανοὺς. For the intellectual condition of pagan society at the beginning of the IVth century read some penetrating pages in Father Batiffol's *La Paix Constantinienne et le Catholicisme*, 1914, p. 142 et s.
[3] *Inst. Div.*, VII, 1, 12.

In addition, he understood that the days of pure and simple refutation had passed, and that in face of the imposing systems of pagan philosophy, he must erect an edifice more firmly held together and of a cohesion which should be of a far superior kind. As was to be the case with Bossuet at a later date, he thought that for the defence of Christian doctrine the better part was to " la proposer simplement." The title, *Institutiones*, borrowed from the language of the law, is also significant. Lactantius is the first Latin apologist to offer to the men and women of his time a complete doctrine, elementary without doubt, but connected throughout by the singleness of his inner principle and capable of giving satisfaction to minds keenly appreciative of logic and harmony. Here we have no vague spiritual metaphysics : a whole history of religion is unfolded, a complete moral system is stated, and an entire philosophy is offered for acceptance, dominated by the doctrine of a Providence, the Christian doctrine *par excellence*. We are dealing with a thorough and fully conscious Christian who in his desire to communicate his belief to others does not disguise any portion of it nor extenuate any requirement of faith. As M. Thamin has happily expressed it, the *Institutiones* are " la véritable *Somme* des premières années du IV. siècle."

Newer still is the method of discussion which Lactantius imposed upon himself and which he faithfully followed. Addressing unbelievers, he did not wish to propose arguments which predicated faith in order that their validity might be appreciated. Thus he deliberately puts on one side the testimony of Scripture. It was useless to make use of Scripture to convince minds 'who judged it to be *vanam, fictam, commentitiam*. In his treatise *Ad Demetrianum* he blames St Cyprian for having so constantly had recourse to it. Proofs taken from the Holy Books were assuredly excellent in themselves, but only for Christians. Others must be convinced by arguments from comparison, " *argumentis et ratione*." When he decided to bring forward some sacred text, he always took care to corroborate it by extracts from other sources in the same sense, which the pagans could not reject. Thus he makes appeal to the authority of philosophers, historians and poets, and to the *carmina sacra*, and oracles, for those whom profane writers would otherwise have left cold. His literary tastes made this excellent method easy and agreeable to him. Sometimes we even see literary recollections intruding into his views at moments when we might have hoped for a less literary fervour : a reminiscence of the *In Verrem* comes rather coldly in connection with the crucifixion of Jesus Christ (IV, xviii). As a rule, however, he restrains them and adroitly makes them serve his purpose.

The two first books (*De Falsa Religione* and *De Origine Erroris*) are given up to a criticism of polytheism : no other point of view of the author is developed in it.

Book III, *De Falsa Sapientia*, has for its object to prove the falsity of pagan philosophy, its contradictions, and its uselessness in practice. Lactantius has little love for the philosophers although his strictures are unequally distributed between the different schools. He treats them very harshly : the arbitrary nature of their constructions, sometimes too the lie direct which their bad morals give to principles which they proclaim so loudly, irritate him and he delivers against them a strong attack. He goes so far as to say that their virtues, if by any chance they *are* virtuous, are as if they did not exist. This is because the echoes of the persecution still rumble in the *Institutiones*, and because certain philosophers had not shown themselves to be the least implacable enemies of the Christian. Moreover the tactics imposed by Lactantius upon himself, as well as his own loyalty, restrained him as a rule on the brink of the abusive exaggeration into which Tertullian had fallen. To defame without measure the leaders of pagan thought would have been to discredit points of agreement which he selected between *their* ideas and Christianity. He savoured too much of a Cicero or a Seneca to believe that even though lacking the faith human reason could not catch any gleam of light ; and it was upon points common to both, and undisputed, found in almost all moral writings (VI, ii, 16–18), that he claims to base the sound foundations of his own in order to make them as broad as possible.

From Book IV (*De Vera Sapientia et Religione*) onwards, Lactantius, without entirely renouncing polemics, sets himself to build up rather than to criticise. He demonstrates the indissoluble union between " wisdom " and religion. He develops the cardinal articles of his faith : God, Christ,

miracles, the Incarnation, the Church and heresies. In Book
V (*De Justitia*), he makes a study of the idea of " justice,"
which had been notoriously confused in pagan philosophy.
Book VI (*De Vero Cultu*), establishes the fundamental principles of Christian morality, so far as it proceeded from God,
its true origin. Lastly in Book VII (*De Vita Beata*), he
approaches the highest problems : the wherefore of creation,
of the immortality of the soul, and the problem of our latter
end ; and he closes his work with an exhortation to fight the
good fight for God.

The *Epitome*, by the testimony of Lactantius himself
written some time after the *Institutiones* at the request of one
Pentadius, reproduces its essential points in a much briefer
form, with corrections of details which prove that Lactantius
had reconsidered his plan in order the better to adapt it to
the daily life of the Christians. It is like an amended second
edition of the *Institutiones* after the elimination of useless
developments, repetitions and quotations from profane
authors.

X

VOLTAIRE showed himself greatly amused over the errors of
" that man Lactantius whom the students at the Alexandrian
school of his time would have derided if they had deigned to
cast their eyes over his rhapsodies." [1] As a matter of fact,
it would be easy to draw attention to his insufficiencies from
the critical point of view.

With the same credulity as his predecessors (with the
exception of St Irenæus and Origen), he makes use of the
Sibylline oracles, and of the compilations which had come
wholesale from Jewish or Christian hands in which he thought
he found so many clinching confessions wrenched from the
pagan Sibyls by the force of truth. He had an excellent
opportunity of proving any analogies existing between these
predictions and his own ideas. He does not suspect either
that the books attributed to Hermes Trismegistus might
have been written after the advent of Christianity by pagans
desirous of making them compete with Christianity itself
and of defending the national religion. Impressed by the
wonderful knowledge of Trismegistus, and with his marvellous

---

[1] *Dict. philos.*, article *Ciel matériel.*

similarity to Christian thought, he is happy to bring his example before the pagans in order to prove to them that they were wrong in rejecting his teaching which was so very well adapted to the highest views of their religious philosophy.

Thus a portion of his argument rests simply on wrong interpretations. As a theologian, he does not count. He is a far from trustworthy exponent, and some of his interpretations are wholly lacking in taste.[1] He recklessly plunges into dreams of the Millennium at a moment when, at least in the East, they were tending to disappear under the influence of wiser explanations ; and he is even pleased to give lengthy descriptions of the phases of the strange apocalypse which he announces.[2] His fantastic eschatology is all the more surprising in that the entire work of Lactantius is decidedly that of a man offering a doctrine applicable to a long continuity of mankind. Now he declares that these appalling prodigies would happen before two hundred years.[3] He passively accepts a tradition which should have been repugnant to him, and classes himself among those disciples of the letter, *solius litterae discipuli*, whose superficial exegesis the great Origen when treating of this question of the Millennium, had already denounced more than fifty years before.[4]

We must understand then that Lactantius was possessed of an intelligence of no very great compass. " Utinam tam nostra adfirmare potuisset quam facile aliena destruxit ! "[5] St Jerome mournfully said. Whence is it that each time that he touches upon moral questions, he interests and almost moves us ? It is no longer the aggressive and rough dialectic of Tertullian, or the rather despondent language of St Cyprian : we meet with fine intuitions, and all the *clairvoyances* of a delicate soul which really feels the truth of Christianity and which knows how to make it appeal to the heart. In truth, what is perhaps the most novel trait in Lactantius is the really profound sense which he possesses

[1] E.g., *Inst. Div.*, IV, viii, 7.
[2] *Inst. Div.*, VII, xiv–xxvi.
[3] *Ibid.*, VII, xxv, 5.—We may note the following expressions : " The cause of this desolation and of this carnage will be that the name of Rome, which now rules the universe (it costs me much to say this, but I say it because it must happen), the Roman name will be effaced from the earth. The Empire will go back to the East ; once more the East will reign, and the West will be under its heel."
[4] *Periarch.*, II, ii, 2 (P.G., xi, 241–2).
[5] *Ep.* lviii, 10.

of the moral efficaciousness and of the renovation which it
has brought to the soul of mankind.

No one before Lactantius had better grasped the difference
between the two religions, Christian and pagan, the one consisting principally in the reform of the will by adhesion to
certain doctrines bound together and entirely dependent on
a God conceived as Father and as Master ; [1] the other resting
wellnigh solely on rites in which the " fingers " alone had a
part,[2] and which exacted neither purity of heart, assent of the
intelligence, nor a right intention. In the love of God lay
the norm of every true Christian. Therefore, in order to
bring unity to his interior life, the Christian must not suffer
the wholly pagan divorce of religion from intelligence. He
must not form his philosophy in one way, and his religious
life in another, but must identify his religion with his philosophy, the one interpenetrating the other, the one being the
other in its foundation. *In sapientia religio et in religione
sapientia est.*[3]

In another place, on meeting with a definition of virtue
included in some verses of the satirical poet Lucilius, he shows
how virtue in the mind of the pagans consisted in *knowing*
where good and evil are to be found. This definition is far
too intellectual to his taste. What use is there in knowing
where good and evil are to be found, if the will is not sufficiently
strong to turn us towards the one and away from the other ?
Knowledge is a thing extrinsic to the soul, our will lies in our
inmost heart and must be the moving spirit. Moreover,
to do good implied that we know already what it is, in such
a way that the principle advanced by Lucilius, which was
false because incomplete, entered into a juster and more
comprehensive principle (VI, v).

Again elsewhere he discusses with penetration a statement
of the philosopher Carneades. Carneades maintained that
the man who would be wholly just cannot escape from falling
sometimes into evident follies, since he will speak or act
against his most certain interests. An honest man who owns
an insanitary house, and who at the moment of selling it feels
himself bound in conscience to make known to the purchaser

---

[1] *Inst.*, IV, iii.
[2] Ritus ejus in manu et digitis est (IV, iii, 9), ritum ad solos digitos pertinentem
(V, xix, 29).
[3] IV, iii.

its state ; or a man who, in a shipwreck, seeing one weaker than he supporting himself on a plank, shrinks from seizing upon it, and prefers to die rather than to commit an injustice— such a man cannot fail to be taken for a fool. From the purely human point of view, replies Lactantius, this argument cannot be gainsaid. It had caused much embarrassment to Cicero. It was clear that if we limited everything to things of earth, even egoism became right reason, and sacrifice was folly or pure illusion. But if, on the other hand, we hold the doing of our duty by obeying God to be our foremost concern, the sense of the words was changed as it were. Wisdom, as conceived by Carneades, was but a snare and delusion ; folly, on the contrary, was what he exalted under the name of wisdom, in responding to one's immediate interest even though it be to the hurt of another. To the man holding the true principle, everything was clear ; to the man who was ignorant of it, everything remained obscure and disconcerting.

Many other passages could likewise prove to us that in places Lactantius reached the real foundation of the Christian spirit. And what gives a real interest to the study of the *Institutiones* is that we find very different tendencies inter-mingled and confused in them, some the legacy of the past, and others indications of a new spirit. His writings contain more traces than we might think of the *intransigeant* attitude hostile to every concession which had animated certain writers of the first centuries. Lactantius had some liking for logic carried to extreme lengths, the weapon dear to Ter-tullian which, if carried out to the letter, would have extin-guished the possibility of any social life for the Christian and would have cut him off from the civil. Neither trade nor war concerned the Christian : [1] it is true that Lactantius immediately admits that necessity may constrain him, but, only for a moment, and he adhered to the old mistrust which had so long dwelt in the minds of Christians of strict observance against *cupiditas acquirendi* and against the shedding of blood. Lactantius is so unbending over the *Non occides* that in his view a Christian has not even the right to require the penalty of death against an accused man, for " it was equally criminal to kill people by word as by the sword." [2] More severe than Tertullian,[3] who only condemned

---

[1] V, xvi, 2, and I, xviii.   [2] VI, xx.   [3] See the *De Idolol.*, xiv.

art in so far as it ministered to pagan worship, Lactantius
discountenances it without any extenuation. More ruthless
than Clement of Alexandria, he denounced perfumes and
flowers : if God created them, it was in order that man might
exercise his virtue by not making use of them. As regards
music, he only authorised it on condition that it be consecrated to the praise of God.[1]

These traits of absolutism are so much the more surprising
because, taken as a whole, his work is of a moderate and
tranquil tone. Did so much rigorousness enter into the
heart of this " University Christian " ? Was he then an
implacable adversary of the world in which he lived ? Not
at all. He was possessed of a very lively sentiment of the
majesty of Rome : he did not believe in the eternity of Rome
since he was convinced that the world was shortly coming
to an end, but in predicting her fall, he could not help himself
from trembling at an announcement which was almost
a blasphemy : *Horret animus dicere.*[2] Let me further add
that Lactantius had nothing about him as a rule of the intemperate ascetic who derives a sour pleasure from hurling
defiance at all the instincts of human nature. He experienced
no misgivings on the lawfulness of marriage, on flight in times
of persecution, or on a liberal amnesty in matters of penance.

How can we reconcile such irreproachable uprightness
and so just a sense of what may be demanded from human
frailty, with the violent extremes of thought to which we have
just drawn attention ? These incongruities must be explained by the diverging influences which weighed upon his
mind. Lactantius was at once a man of tradition and a man
of his own time. On one side of him he was very respectful
of all that he inherited from past generations of Christians.
He even accepted, as we have seen, beliefs already almost
superannuated, such as the Millennium, and introduced them
somewhat artificially into the material of his work. A horror
of war, disdain for commerce, a distrust of all that renders
life on earth smoother and more attractive were forms of
sentiment which were survivals of a former state of mind,
that of the first Christian communities, or at least of certain
elements contained in those communities.

On another side, however, Lactantius did not isolate
himself from the surroundings in which he was living. We

---

[1] VI, xx, 16.   [2] VII, xvi, 2 ; cf. xxv, 7.

know with what decision he inaugurated a novel method in apologetics, more scientific and more accessible to those whom he wished to win. He must have understood the moral problems which changing times presented. He belonged to a period when the masses were streaming into the Church, when the Church herself was shortly to seal a pact of alliance with the Empire, thanks to which all material obstacles paralysing her free scope were to be removed. Would it be possible henceforth to uphold the Kingdom of God at so high a level above so many hesitating and lukewarm souls ? Must not a system of morality which was strained and seeking after extremes be made more supple, and while preserving virtue and doctrine, give the preference to more moderate solutions ? His good sense said " yes," but the numbing influence of the old rigorism suggested " no " ; and something of these contradictory tendencies which disputed a place in his thoughts and gained the upper hand each in turn, remained in his theological reasonings.

XI

THE *De Ira Dei* is plainly announced in the *Institutiones Divinae :* " Some people think that anger is absolutely foreign to God, in as much as God is not subject to passions, which are violent upheavals of the soul, and that every living thing is doomed to perish which experiences the action of their shock. This ⸢thesis shatters the very foundation of true religion. But let us leave for the moment this question of the anger of God : the material is too abundant and I will defer it for more ample development in a special work." [1]

The following are the terms of reference presented by this problem from the philosophic point of view.

The God of the Old Testament was a severe God, sometimes even cruel ; who loves, hates, is irritated, and takes vengeance : " And I will execute great vengeance upon them, rebuking them in fury : and they shall know that I am the Lord, when I shall lay my vengeance upon them " (Exek. xxv, 17). Now the idea of God which had been developed in the Greek philosophic schools implied on the contrary ἀπάθεια impassibility, amongst the Divine attributes. On this point,

[1] *Inst. Div.*, II, xvii, 4.

they were almost all in agreement. " Num iratum timemus Jovem ? " Cicero asks in his *De Officiis*, III, 102, where he gives an explanation, as we know, of Greek thought. And he replies : " At hoc quidem commune est omnium philosophorum . . . nunquam nec irasci Deum nec nocere."

The Jewish and Hellenic conceptions were therefore in absolute opposition to each other. Hence arose a great difficulty for minds formed in the Greek school, whose faith forbade them to sacrifice any portion of the Old Testament.

It is curious to see how this conflict of views for some possessed extreme importance, while for others it remained null and void, or of little account. Thus the apologists of the IInd century, Justin, Aristides, etc., in their restrained commerce with profane philosophy accepted the notion of ἀπάθεια—a complaisance which in no wise hindered them from making allusions to the ὀργή Θεόυ. How these matters could be reconciled they have not troubled to tell us. Similarly, among the Latins at the beginning of the IVth century, Arnobius, as we have seen, insisted with such warmth upon the absolute necessity of the Divine impassibility, that we are justified in asking ourselves how he accommodated his views with the Bible, or even if he had ever read it. There were also others (such as Cyprian and Commodian) who, entirely leaning to the practical, and desirous only for the interests of discipline, brandished over the sinner the threat of the Divine anger without thinking of regarding it from the philosophic point of view.

But for a goodly number of ecclesiastical writers this was a real problem which they felt bound to discuss and to solve. The influence exercised by Greek philosophy on the thought of those whom we might imagine to be most unbending, is striking. Thus Tertullian, in his polemics against Marcion who had taken upon himself to point out the " anthropopathisms " of the Old Testament in order to draw from them a conclusion as to the inferior quality of the God of the Jews. The features to which Marcion took offence —the picture of a God provoked to anger and prompt to vengeance—were just those of which Tertullian was most enamoured. Nevertheless, the objections of the heresiarch moved him more than he cared to acknowledge. This was because he felt that they were inspired by Greek thought, which alarmed him, whatever he might have said about it. Also, after having brought divers arguments against it,— texts from Scripture proving that Jesus Himself had been a " jealous God " ; [1] teachings of St Paul on God the avenger and lover of justice ; [2] the folly of taking literally that illusion of language by which we imagine the Divine nature to be entirely similar to human nature and susceptible of the same shortcomings,[3]—we see him making the most unexpected concession : he admits that it is the Son, the Son alone, who, destined from all eternity to assume contact with humanity, invested Himself in some manner from the beginning with the sentiments and passions of mankind ; that it is He who rages, repents, pardons, and shows Himself to the Patriarchs in the Old Testament : and during that time, the Father remained invisible in His transcendent majesty.[4]

Origen traced out the solution which the Greek Church should favour. Taking inspiration from Philo, he admitted that God has acted in regard to man as man himself acts in regard to the child : God feigns to make experiment of human affection (anger, repentance, etc. . . .) in order the better to lead him into the paths of salvation ; but it would be puerile to take literally the expressions used in the Old Testament, which are adapted to the feeble mentality of the generality of mortals,—for the Divine Essence is excluded from all " passion."

Lactantius leaves these discussions outside his programme. They appear to have only a very small interest for him. More of a jurist than a philosopher, he takes up a very different point of view. " Sine ira Deum esse credentes dissolvunt omnem religionem " : [5] " Omne imperium metu constat, metus autem per iram. . . . Deus autem habet imperium, ergo et iram, qua constat imperium, habeat necesse est." [6] To dispute this Divine aptitude was to do no less than to destroy the doctrine of a Providence. If God is not angered against the impious, neither does He cherish the just. The very idea of Providence comprehends that of a God who knows how to punish just as He knows also

---

[1] *Adv. Marc.*, IV, xxvii.   [2] *Ibid.*, V, xiii.   [3] *Ibid.*, II, xvi.

[4] Cf. *Adv. Prax.*, xvi ; *Adv. Marc.*, II, xxvii : " Igitur quaecunque exigitis Deo digna, habebuntur in Patre invisibili incongressibilique *et placido*, et, ut ita dixerim, *philosophorum deo*, quaecunque autem ut indigna reprehenditis, deputabuntur in Filio. . . ."

[5] *De Ira Dei*, xxii, 2.   [6] *Ibid.*, xxiii, 4.

how to reward. Moreover—and this was the error made by Epicurean and Stoic philosophies—this Divine anger was pure at its source, possessing no other attribute than holy indignation against evil. It had nothing of the sudden and irrepressible violence which characterised our own. It was patient and long-suffering and it allowed sinners time for repentance. And, faithful to his customary method, Lactantius does not omit to quote certain passages from the Sibylline books where the threat of Divine anger breaks forth, in order to show that the pagan religion itself had a belief in this primordial truth, that God cannot be impassible. In fact, putting aside speculations for which he cares nothing, he draws a picture of a God at once just and good, quite like the father of a family or the head of a State, upon whom their responsibilities imposed the duty of exacting the necessary punishment. And the interpretation which he puts forth is not very different from that which St Augustine was to lay down : " Ira Dei, non perturbatio animi, sed judicium quo irrogatur poena peccato." [1]

XII

THE *De Mortibus Persecutorum* is no longer, as was the case with the *De Ira Dei*, a quiet dissertation on the lawfulness of the Divine anger. It is the setting forth of the formidable effects of this anger, partly based on the most recent events.

When the author wrote it,[2] peace had at last been given to the Church. Addressing himself to a certain Donatus, he intones a Hosanna in honour of Providence who had at last brought moral and material repose to the Christians, and who had laid low their enemies at the same time. He sets himself to relate their successive downfalls. He first passes in review in a very summary manner the first persecutors of Christianity, Nero, Domitian, Decius, Valerian, and Aurelian, upon whom a cruel or premature death had avenged their attacks (§ i–vi). Beginning with Diocletian, he comes to contemporary events, and to these he devotes no less than forty-five chapters (§ vii–lii). He starts with the Government

---

[1] *De Civit Dei*, XV, xxv.
[2] 313–4 (Harnack) ; 318–320 (Monceaux).

of the Tetrarchy, Diocletian and Maximian, "Augusti";
Galerius and Constantius Chlorus, "Cæsars"; the hateful
exactions of the first three; the cruelties exercised against
the Christians by Diocletian, whose hatred, inflamed by
Galerius, commanded the general persecution of 303. Then
follow the illness of Diocletian, and the intrigues whereby
Galerius succeeded in compelling his abdication, and in causing
Maximin Daïa and Severus to be associated in the Imperial
rule; the abominable cruelties of Galerius when he became
supreme; and Constantine, after his escape from his mur-
derous designs, elected Emperor by the soldiers on the death
of Constantius Chlorus. The very confusion of these succeeding events (there were no less than six "Augusti" in 307),
renders difficult a succinct analysis of the last part of the work.
While following closely the tangled web of these circumstances,
the author does not forget the particular preoccupation
which caused him to undertake the work. What he seeks to
demonstrate is the manner in which the hand of God had lain
heavy on those Princes who had done evil to the Christians,
while it spared and favoured those who had seen fit to recognise the goodness of their cause.[1] One of these persecutors,
Severus, was compelled to open his veins (§ xxvi); another,
Maximian, had hanged himself (§ xxx); Galerius, a truly
ferocious wild beast who deserved the most exquisite form of
punishment, died corrupted and devoured by worms (§ xxxv);
Diocletian had expired in sorry and destitute circumstances
(§ xliii); Maximin Daïa had poisoned himself and his agony
had been terrible (§ lxix). Even the families of these cruel
men had not been spared (§ l). And the *De Mortibus Persecutorum* finishes, as it had begun, with a hymn of gratitude
to the Lord: "The Lord who hath purged the earth of those
proud names. Let us then celebrate the triumph of God
with joy; day and night let us offer Him our prayer and
praise, that He may establish for all time this peace which
has been given to us after ten years of war." The leading
characteristics of this treatise emerge from this brief glance:
the terrible end suffered by the greater part of these wicked
rulers had been meted out by the Divine dispositions, not
with reference to any particular crime, but especially to the
persecuting measures taken against the faithful. "In spite

[1] ix, ii.

of the punishment which his crimes had deserved, Diocletian had reigned perfectly happily so long as he did not soil his hands in the blood of the just." Only those had escaped the rigour of heaven who had proved themselves friendly to the Christians, Constantine for example, whose death had been calm and peaceful; "In lecto suo requiem vitae, sicut optabat, accepit." [1] Lactantius had been for a long while penetrated with the conception of Divine vengeance exercising itself upon those who had braved it when the hour came. This he had clearly indicated in the *Institutiones*, and also in the *Epitome*. [2] Is there any need to say that this was by no means a new idea, and that in it Lactantius revealed himself, as Bossuet would have said, as " un homme de l'ancienne marque " ? There is no doubt that the Christian idea of Providence admitted these " special exercises " (of the Divine will) on which, according to some, Lactantius too much insisted. Let us bear in mind, however, something of this complaint. Lactantius is indiscreet in the zeal which he displays in endeavouring to unravel God's designs with the intrepid certitude which he reveals in all their details, as if these had been confided to him from above. All the more that, following the example of Tertullian, he avoids any useful explanation of the fact that " good " emperors had treated the Christians without any clemency. The intoxicating and unlooked-for victory, coming after such severe experiences, had so far confirmed him in his views on the avenging initiatives of Providence, that the least suspension of judgment would have seemed to him culpable and almost sacrilegious scepticism.

What gives a particular value to this work is that Lactantius was compelled by his thesis to give an historic substructure to the demonstration which he was proving. From the point of view of an historical document, what value should be placed on the *De Mortibus Persecutorum* ? For some years, critics have appreciably reconsidered the contemptuous views of Lactantius as an historian held by Duruy, Burckhardt and Schiller. M. Maurice has demonstrated his trustworthiness by irrefutable numismatic and

---

[1] xxiv, 5.
[2] *Inst. Div.*, V, xxiii, 1–5. Cf. IV, xxvii, 5 ; V, xxii, 23 ; *Epit.*, xlviii, 4–5. The most important texts are translated in Monceaux, III, 343.

iconographic testimony.[1] M. Pichon, after a minute comparison of the information furnished by Lactantius with what we can gather from contemporary and subsequent historians, comes to this conclusion regarding the *De Mortibus :* " This is not a unique treasure-house of perfect truth ; neither is it a tissue of errors and misstatements : it is a historical source useful to consult and necessary to correct, a source mingled with the truth, with what is likely and with what may be romance, a historical source just like the others, no more and no less." [2] " The more one studies his account," M. Monceaux concludes,[3] " the more one is brought to recognise its rigorous and detailed exactitude. It cannot be denied that Lactantius was wonderfully well informed on the history of official events as also on the *chronique scandaleuse ou anecdotique* of his times." Where Lactantius lays himself open to more real criticism is the way in which he interprets the facts which he had truthfully set down. He is partial ; he hates with such a vigorous hatred the persecuting rulers that he can hardly bring himself to admit that any good could possibly proceed from souls so fundamentally corrupt. Thus, he censures measures which from the political point of view were quite defensible, such as the Tetrarchy, or the financial enactments of Galerius. He is profuse in unfriendly interpretations however fair he wished to be, although the latter trait comes out through much passionate invective.

At the very time when Lactantius was composing his *De Mortibus Persecutorum*, Eusebius, Bishop of Cæsarea in Palestine, himself also one of Constantine's great administrators, was endeavouring to give an account of Christianity from its beginnings in Greek, or more accurately, to make a careful choice and a suitable classification of the documents handed down by tradition. The attitude of mind in which he pursued his task was not essentially different from that of Lactantius. In the mind of Eusebius, ecclesiastical history was evangelical proof of a particular kind. It was an account

---

[1] See numerous mentions of Maurice in Monceaux. III, 347. Add *Comptes rendus de l'Acad. des Inscr. et B.-Lettres*, 1908, p. 146 et s. ; *Numismatique Constantinienne*, vol. I (1908) ; vol. II (1910) ; *Bull. de la Soc. des Antiq. de France*, 1913 (*Nouvelles observations à propos du Labarum*, and various articles) ; B.A.L.A.C. 1914, p. 37 et s.

[2] *Op. cit.*, p. 383.

[3] III, 347.

of the stages by which the Church, firmly established upon the tradition embodied in the Bishops, and illuminated by the Holy Spirit which spoke through her foremost men, had successively passed, before her Providential reconciliation with the Roman power. And in the attempts of dissident sects, Eusebius always perceived the hand of the devil greedy for the ruin of souls, who used every endeavour to arrive at his hateful end. Such had been the innermost tendency of Christian history when, emerging from purely chronological investigations to which it had hitherto confined itself, it conceived higher ambitions ; such it was to remain during the passage of time, setting forth the Divine will by recording the facts by which this will had been manifested. Lactantius had his share in impressing this character upon it. The *De Mortibus Persecutorum* marks a date.

At the present day this work still deserves to be read. Spurred on by passion, the former professor of rhetoric laid bare therein his somewhat tasteless conceits. By a rapid narration of a succession of events, by the dramatic unfolding of certain scenes, and the piquant character of certain features, he stimulates interest from one end to the other and renews it again and again.

XIII

THAT Lactantius was not a great mind is a conclusion emerging clearly enough from the review which we have just made, and there is no need to insist on this again. His train of thought has so little of what was new about it that it felt no need of expression in any other than the old mould of Ciceronian prose. It found itself at home there and did not seek to create from it any other form. The excellent pages of M. René Pichon [1] should be read in which, defining " classic " style, he shows with what happy scrupulousness Lactantius strove to observe its rules and to imitate its elegances ; and his assiduity in " formulating the most novel and special ideas in the traditional language, and in clothing in terms of irreproachable classic purity matters which belonged exclusively to Christianity." A stranger to the attractive originalities of a Tertullian or an Apuleius, he does not deviate

---

[1] *Op. cit.*, p. 307 et s.

from classic syntax except in a small number of points.[1]   He invents no new metaphors and does not resuscitate current expressions.   In revenge, what he possesses in a remarkable degree is the instinct and taste for oratorical style, with its copiousness, its symmetry, and its large, harmoniously-balanced developments.   Everything about him, in form and foundation, gives an impression of disciplined and seasoned balance, and only the revengeful ardour of the *De Mortibus Persecutorum* had a momentary effect of disturbing this balance.

Moreover, the writers who had any traffic with new channels were few.   It was something in those times of changing literary methods, to have preserved a language that was correct, clear and abundant.   Also, more intellectual resources than we might at first suppose that a quiet professor of rhetoric could possess must have been required to form such a personal idea of the needs of contemporary apologetics ;   to give so much sequence and careful application in the realisation of the design thus conceived ;   to cling with such tenacity to the Christian doctrine of Providence, and to follow up its demonstration with ever-increasing aptitude through a series of works from the altogether tranquil and philosophic deism of the *De Opificio Dei*, to the burning accents of the *De Mortibus Persecutorum.*

What influence had his effort on those cultivated pagans whom he had in view throughout ?   We have no indication which might enable us to gauge it.   He found far more admirers at the beginning of the Renaissance than in Christian antiquity.   Hardly any ecclesiastical writer has been so often published.   Since then, sympathy in his regard has grown colder, and I think, this disfavour is somewhat excessive.   However this may be, his name remains " inseparable from one of the most important facts in history, not only in that of Rome, but of all humanity, namely, the reconciliation of the Church with the Empire and the appearance of the first Christian Government." [2]

---

[1] For example, as regards the agreement of the tenses, and the use of *quod* and even (rarely) of *quia* after verbs of explanation.
[2] Pichon, p. 454.

XIV

IT is principally from St Jerome that we derive our knowledge of Victorinus of Pettau. Jerome was interested in Victorinus as the earliest specialist in exegesis among the Latins, and also from his being a compatriot from Illyria. Otherwise he held him in little esteem. While recognising in him a certain amount of learning,[1] or at least some desire of erudition,[2] he allows it to be understood that this attempt was paralysed by his literary unskilfulness[3] and by his incompetence in the Latin language.[4] In addition he reproaches him for having been addicted to the wild dreams of the millennium,[5] after Papias, Irenæus, Apollinaris, Tertullian and Lactantius. According to Jerome, Victorinus had been Bishop of Poetovio[6] (in Upper Pannonia, on the Drave on the borders of Noricum). He certainly died a martyr under Diocletian,[7] but we do not know in what year. His life therefore may be placed in the second half of the IIIrd century. Of the works attributed to him by St Jerome in the *De Viris Illustribus* one only remains, the Commentary on the Apocalypse.[8] There is quite a history attaching to the text of this Commentary. We have it (thanks to the labours of Haussleiter) in four different forms. A manuscript in the Vatican Library[9] mentioned by Angelo Mai gives the first version of Victorinus, which is very strongly imbued with millenarism.[10] A second

---

[1] *Prol. in Is.* (P.L., XXIV, 20): "etsi imperitus sermone, non tamen scientia."
[2] *Ep.* lxx, 5 (Hilberg, in C.V., liv, 707): "licet desit eruditio, tamen non deest eruditionis voluntas."
[3] *Ep.* lviii, 10 (*ibid.*, p. 539): "quod intellegit, eloqui non potest."
[4] *De Vir. Ill.*, lxxiv: "Non seque làtine ut graece noverat."
[5] *De Vir. Ill.*, xviii; in *Ez.* XI, xxxvi, 1 (P.L., XXV, 339).
[6] Petavionensis episcopus, *de Vir. Ill.*, lxxiv. It was often read as *Pictaviensis* before Launoy in a dissertation of the year 1653 (2 ed., 1664) restored the true reading and showed that Victorinus had been the Bishop of Pettau and not of Poitiers.
[7] We may conclude this from the manner in which Jerome signalises his name in the *De Vir. Ill.* and elsewhere (v.g. *Adv. Rufinum*, III, xiv). Adon. was the first to state this explicitly in his martyrology (P.L., CXXIII, 389).
[8] For traces of other writings mentioned by Jerome, see Haussleiter, in C.V., vol. XXXXIX, p. xiv et s.—The enumeration of St Jerome is not final: he adds *et multa alia*, a very vague expression of which he makes excessive use in the *De Vir. Ill.* Cassiodorus, *Inst. Div.*, vii (P.L., LXX, 1119) alludes to a comm. by Victorinus on St Matthew; likewise Jerome (P.L., XXVI, 20 and 223).
[9] *Codex Ottobonianus latinus* 3288 A., XVth Century. This manuscript is very difficult to read. There is a photographic reproduction of some leaves in C.V., vol. XXXXIX. There are two copies of this, of the XVth and XVIth Century.
[10] Especially beginning from chap. xix et s.

version is due to St Jerome. At the request of a certain Anatolius Jerome consented to revise the Commentary of Victorinus. He gives an explanation in a prologue wherein, in order to escape the criticisms of his detractors, he is careful not to exaggerate the importance of this revision, which he confined to certain additions, suppressions and corrections.[1] As a matter of fact, a comparison of his rendering with that of Victorinus brings out emendations of a certain importance. Jerome has improved the style of Victorinus ; in many passages he has substituted a new Latin rendering of Scripture to that used by Victorinus ; his emendations also bear upon the root of things, especially upon his " millenary " passages, nearly all of which he has cut out ;[2] to make up for this, he has improved and amplified the rendering of Victorinus by different supplementary paraphrases, some of which are borrowed from Tyconius.[3]

In a later recension, the authorship of which is unknown, the text of the *Apocalypse* carries a more liberal admixture of the editing of Jerome, undergoing some further rather incompetent revision.[4] Lastly, a final recension has united the three preceding ones, with the introduction of some additions and many transpositions[5] under pretext of better methodical arrangement.

Another very short work, the *De Fabrica Mundi*, of which there is no mention in antiquity, was claimed for Victorinus by G. Cave, in the XVIIth century, on account of the superscription on a manuscript in Lambeth Palace Library,[6] containing a series of fragments and extracts. This assignment is commonly admitted : the mediocre and obscure style, and the ideas coloured by millenarism,[7] clearly favour it. In it Victorinus draws moral and religious lessons from the Creation in Genesis ; he insists especially on the virtue of

---

[1] C.V., XXXXIX, p. 14.

[2] The arrangement of Haussleiter's edition enables us easily to take these into account : see C.V., XXXXIX, p. 138, 1 to 154, 18.

[3] Jerome's recension figures in four manuscripts. The two principal ones are the *Cod. Taurinensis lat.*, G.V. 3, XIth century, and *Cod.* 1079 in the Municipal Library of Arras, Xth century.

[4] Six manuscripts. The principal one is the *Codex Harleianus*, saec. ix–x, now in the British Museum.

[5] One manuscript only, *Cod. biblioth. Casinensis* CCXLVII, saec. xi–xii. This is the only text which figures in Migne's *Patrology*, in which Galland's edition is reproduced.

[6] *Cod. bibliothecae Lambethanae Londinensis* 414, saec. x–xi.

[7] See especially § vi (Haussleiter, p. 6, l. 10 et s.).

the number seven, and makes it fit in with his own conceptions of the economy of the universe.[1] The arrangement of this little treatise hardly enables us to think with G. Cave that it originally belonged to a commentary on Genesis or on the Apocalypse.

In a great number of manuscripts of Tertullian there figures an *Adversus Omnes Haereses*, resembling the *De Praescriptione*.[2] This catalogue gives a characteristic summary of thirty-two heresies : the first is that of Dositheus, the last that of Praxeas. There is general agreement in recognising that Tertullian could not have been the author. Taking up a hypothesis already suggested by Œhler (*Tertull. Opera*, II, 752), Harnack proposed to attribute it to Victorinus of Pettau.[3] The arguments adduced by him cannot but have their value.   (1) In his *De Viris Illustribus*, § lxxiv, St Jerome quotes an *Adversus Omnes Haereses* among the works of Victorinus. (2) Now Jerome must surely have known the work we are speaking of.   In his treatise against the Luciferians, § xxiii there is a passage which, with the exception of a few emendations of form, is a close imitation of the beginning of the *Adversus Omnes Haereses*.   Then Jerome only mentions by name one work bearing this title and makes use of just this one which we possess.   We have here a presumption favourable to its identification.   (3) On the other hand, in a letter addressed to Damasus (*Ep.* xxxvi, 16), Jerome connects the name of Victorinus with that of Hippolytus in relation to the interpretation of the history of Esau and Jacob : " . . . *Hippolyti* martyrii verba ponamus, a quo et *Victorinus* noster non plurimum discrepat, non quod omnia executus sit, sed quo possit occasionem praebere lectori ad intelligentiam latiorem. . . ." Victorinus had thus borrowed certain things in his exegetic treatises from Hippolytus where he followed him very closely.   This proceeding of borrowing material conforms with the idea of the relation-

---

[1] *Ibid.*

[2] We do not find it in the *Agobardinus*.   It is joined without any special reason to the *De Praescriptione* in the *Paterniacensis* 439, saec. xi.   In more recent manuscripts, especially those of the Italian tradition (*Florentinus Magliabechianus*, Conu. sopp. VI, 9, s. xv ; *Florentinus Magliabechianus*, Conu. sopp. VI, 10, s. xv, etc. . . .), the *Adversus Omnes Haereses* immediately precedes the *De Praescriptione*.   The first editors of Tertullian printed it after the *De Praescriptione*.   Since Rigault it has been separated from it : see Œhler, II, 751 ; Kroymann, 213.

[3] *Zeitsch. f. wiss. Theol.*, xix (1876), 116 et s. ; cf. *Chron.*, II, 430.

ship between the *Adversus Omnes Haereses* and the *Syntagma* of Hippolytus.[1]

The combination is ingenious, nevertheless Harnack himself in the course of time became far less favourable to it ; and, from reasons of matter and form, he confesses that the drawing up of this list is far more intelligible if we place it at Rome about the year 220 rather than at Poetovio at the end of the IIIrd century.[2]

Various other works [3] have been attributed to Victorinus of Pettau, without any of these conjectures appearing to be required. Taking him as a whole, his was a mind of mediocre originality, his temperament that of a follower formed on the school of writers of Greek culture, such as Papias, Irenæus, Hippolytus, and, above all, Origen,[4] and one who appeared, although writing in Latin, to have been ignorant of the Latin literary tradition.

---

[1] On this relationship, cf. P. de Labriolle, *Les Sources de l'Histoire du Montanisme*, pp. xxxvi–xlviii.

[2] For further details, *ibid.*, p. lxxxiv.

[3] The *Tractatus Origenis de libris ss. Scripturarum*, and a Homily *de Decem Virginibus*, etc.

[4] Jerome insists on different occasions on the subordination of Victorinus to the views of Origen ; cf. Haussleiter, in C.V., vol. XXXXIX, p. viii et s.

BOOK III

THE GOLDEN AGE

OF

LATIN CHRISTIAN LITERATURE

CHAPTER I

THE MORROW OF THE VICTORY

BIBLIOGRAPHY

I. Firmicus Maternus.—P.L., XII, 981-1050 ; Halm, in C.V., vol. II (1867) ; Ziegler, in B.T. (1907).—Consult : Cl. H. Moore, *Julius Firmicus Maternus, der Heide u. der Christ*, Munich, 1897 ; Boll, in P.W., VI, 2365-2379 ; Spiegelberg, *das Isis-Mysterium bei F.M.*, in *Archiv. f. Religionswiss*, XIX (1918), p. 194 ; F. Groehl, *de Syntaxi Firmiciana*, Breslau, 1918 (cf. B. ph. W., 1918, pp. 1231-1235). French Translation in Buchon's *Choix de Monuments primitifs de l'Egl. Chrét.*, 1840, pp. 747-771.

II. Reticius of Autun.—Consult : *Hist. litt. de la France*, I, 2 (1733), pp. 59-63 ; D.C.B., IV, 544 ; *Chron.*, p. 433.

III. Saint Hilary de Poitiers. See Table, No. IV.—Consult : Largent, *Saint Hilaire*, 1902 (Coll, les Saints, Gabalda) ; Feder, in *Stimmen aus Maria-Laach*, 1911, pp. 30-45 ; C. Weyman, in B. ph. W., 1917, p. 1165 ; Beck, in Z.K.T., 1906, pp. 108 and 305 ; Rauschen, *ibid.*, p. 295 ; H. Jeannotte, *Le Psautier de saint Hilaire de Poitiers*, 1917.

IV. Lucifer of Calaris.—P.L., XII, 765-1038 ; Hartel, in C.V., vol. XIV (1886).—Consult : Hartel, A.L.L., 1886, 1-58 ; Kruger, in R.E., XI, 666.

V. *Collectio Avellana.*—Gunther, in C.V., vol. XXXV (1895-8).

VI. *Libellus Precum.*—P.L., XIII, 82-107 ; C.V., vol. XXXV, pp. 5-40.

VII. Faustinus.—*Contra Arianos*, P.L., XIII, 37-80 ; *Fides Theodosio Oblata*, *ibid.*, 79-80.

VIII. Arian and anti-Arian Literature.—Potamius Olisopo : *Ep. ad. Athanasium* (written about 350, according to Dom Wilmart, *R. Bén.*, XXX [1913], 284) ; P.L., VIII, 1416-1418 : cf. *R. Bén.*, *ibid.* The other works are in P.L., VIII. According to Dom Wilmart, *op. cit.*, the *Epist.* called *Beati Hieronymi de Substantia Patris et Filii et Spiritus Sancti*, published by Guillermo Antolin, in the *Revista de Archivos, Bibl. y Museos*, XII (1908), p. 207, is by Potamius.

IX. Fragments from Bobbio.—P.L., XIII, 593-672.

X. *Sermo Arianorum sine nomine auctoris.*—P.L., XLII, 677-684.

XI. *Opus imperfectum in Matthaeum.*—P.G., LVI, 611-946.

XII. *Dissertatio Maximi contra Ambrosium*, in Fr. Kauffmann, *Aus der Schule des Wulfila*, Strasb., 1899, pp. 65-90.

XIII. Foebadius of Agen.—*Liber c. Arianos* (c. 357-8). P.L., XX, 13-20.

XIV. Hosius of Cordova.—*Ep. ad Constantium*, P.L., VIII, 1327-1331, and P.G., XXV, 744-748 (translated in Tillemont, VII, 313) ; *Hosii Sententiae* : P.L., VIII, 1317-1328 ; *Ep. ad Papam Julium*, Mansi, *Conc.*, VI, 1909-1910.

XV. Eusebius of Vercelli.—*Ep. ad Constantium* (355), P.L., XII, 947 ; *Ep. ad Presbyt. et Plebem Italiae*, XII, 947-954 ; *Ep. ad Gregorium*, X, 713-714 (cf. Feder, S.B.W., 162 [1909], p. 64) ; *Symbolum Quicumque* : P.G., XXVIII, 1581-1596 (cf. Turner, in J.T.S., XI [1910], 401-411).

XVI. *Altercatio Heracliana Laici cum Germinio Episc.* (January 366) ; Caspari, K. A., pp. 131-147.

XVII. *Tractatus contra Arianos.*—Sedlmayer, in S.B.W., 146 (1903), p. 11.

On Arian literature in general, cf. L. Duchesne, *Hist. Anc. de l'Eglise*, vol. II (1907) ; Jacques Zeiller, *Les Orig. Chrét. dans les Provinces Danubiennes de l'Empire Romain*, 1918 (a very full bibliography is given therein).

XVIII. GREGORY of ELVIRA.—The five sermons on the *Cant. of Cant.* have been published by Gotth. Heine, *Biblioth. Anecdotorum*, part I, L., 1848, p. 134.—See further on in detail the works which have been attributed to him.—Consult: P. Lejay, in *R. Bén.*, 1908, 435-457 ; Butler, in J.T.S., 1909, 450-459.

XIX. MARIUS VICTORINUS. — Non-Christian works : *Ars Grammatica*, G.L., VI, p. 3 ; *Explanatio* on the *de Invent.* of Cicero, R.L.M., pp. 155-304, and Stangl, *Tulliana et Mario-Victoriniana*, Progr. Munich, 1888, p. 49 ; *De Definitionibus*, P.L., LXIV, 891-910, and Stangl, *ibid.*, p. 17.—Christian works in P.L., VIII, 1019-1236.—Consult : Monceaux, III, 373 et s.

SUMMARY

I. General view of the period opening with the Edict of Milan.—II. The first transports over the victory : Firmicus Maternus.—III. Reticius of Autun, an exegetist. — IV. Struggles over doctrine. Arianism. St Hilary of Poitiers. His life of warfare. His works. The *Fragmenta Historica.*—V. Lucifer of Calaris. The *Libellus Precum.*— VI. Arian and anti-Arian literature. — VII. Gregory of Elvira. — VIII. Marius Victorinus.

I

WE now enter upon a new period, that of the first pact between Christianity and the Roman Empire. Promulgated in March 313 by Constantine and Licinius, the Edict of Milan inaugurated a system of liberty, but a liberty already privileged, and one which granted to the Christians something rather more than the just reparation to which they had a right. Constantine was not content with showing his favour to Christianity by the building and endowment of sumptuous basilicas at Constantinople, Nicomedia, Antioch, Jerusalem, Bethlehem (the only one still remaining), Naples, Capua, Ostia and Albano ; by immunities granted to the Catholic clergy ; and by the juridical powers assigned to the Bishops. These favours he intended to be reserved to the orthodox Church—the Church he only entered effectually on his deathbed—to the exclusion of heretics and schismatics. As regards the traditional religion of Rome, he did not hesitate to designate it in an official document by the word *superstitio* : [1] " Too circumspect to suppress the old forms of worship, he contented himself with leaving to them their own life which

[1] The Law of May 25, 323 (*Code Theod.*, XVI, ii, 5 : Mommsen, p. 836) ; inscription at Spello (between 333 and 337). Dessau, p. 705.

was almost at an end, while taking care that no one should be unaware that he was no longer faithful to them." [1]

His policy towards paganism was accentuated in the most rigorous sense by his sons Constans and Constantius. But strange contradictions retarded its effects. Though he forbade sacrifices and pagan worship, Constantius gave proof, on more than one occasion, of a want of logic of which the pagan Symmachus, in the face of arbitrary measures of quite another kind, was later on to take advantage. In his famous *Relatio* addressed in 384 to Valentinian II,[2] he recalled that " Constantius had taken away none of the privileges of the consecrated virgins ; he had filled the priestly offices with nobles ; he had not refused financial support to the Roman ceremonies ; he had followed the Senate with much complacency along the streets of the Eternal City ; he had viewed the temples without emotion ; he had read the names of the gods inscribed on their frontals ; he had enquired as to the origin of those sanctuaries, he had expressed admiration for the architects. . . ."

In these strong measures which were only partially efficacious, there was, however, matter to exasperate minds still faithful to the old religion on account of the fascination which its classic literary souvenirs exercised,—those glorious souvenirs in which it seemed bound up,—or who found in the " mysteries " sufficient outlet for their religious sense. Such minds were still numerous, especially among the upper classes. St Augustine has noted in his *Confessions* (VIII, ii, 3), possibly with some exaggeration, the pagan sympathies of " nearly all the Roman nobility " (*tota fere Romana nobilitas*) in the second half of the IVth century. To Prudentius the word *nobilitas*, taken by itself, meant the pagan aristocracy. Highly placed personages submitted to the unclean and bloody rites of the " taurobola." Amongst those whom we know practised this rite, Claudius Hermogenianus Cæsarius was Pro-Consul of Africa from 368 to 370, and Prefect of the City in 374 ; another, Sextilius Agesilaus Aldesius was director of the principal services of the Chancellery, and member of the Consistory of Public Worship ; yet another, Vettius Agorius

---

[1] P. Batiffol, *la Paix Constantinienne et le Catholicisme*, 1914, p. 399.

[2] § vi (ed. Seeck, M.G.H., VI, l, p. 280 et s.). This is translated in my *Saint Ambroise*, Paris, 1908, pp. 37–44. On the visit of Constantius to Rome in 356, see also Ammianus Marcellinus, XVI, x.

Praetextatus, " sacrorum omnium praesul," " princeps religiosorum," as Macrobius [1] calls him, was Prefect of the City in 367, and Praetorian Prefect in 384.[2] The momentary success of the short reaction inaugurated by Julian can be understood. However, twenty years later, St Ambrose could speak of his times as Christian, *christiana tempora*.[3] Ambrose was too clear-sighted to exaggerate the full meaning of this expression. He knew on what compromises so many minds lacking any real devotion depended for their adhesion to Christianity. But from the political point of view the victory of the Christian faith, so long harassed and hunted down, was now no longer in doubt.

> " See," cried the poet Prudentius in his *Contra Symmachum* (I, 544 et s.), when speaking of the Senate, " see the Assembly of old Catos donning the white robe of catechumens and laying aside the insignia of High Priest ! Barely a handful of them still remains on the Tarpeian rock ; the rest hasten to the pure sanctuaries of Christianity ; all the Curia of Evander is running to Apostolic sources. At their head are marching the Annii and the Probi. Rome, the illustrious, takes pride in having seen the noble Anicius the first to give lustre to the Assembly of the Chiefs of the City by his conversion. The heir of the Olybrii, after having inscribed his name on the Fasti and having donned the palm-bordered mantle, seeks to lower the fasces of Brutus before the gates of the martyrs, and to bow the axe of the Latins before Christ. The prompt faith of the Paulinii and the Bassi has not hesitated to give itself up to Christ, and to offer to the world to come the proud scions of their patrician race. Need I mention too the Gracchi, those friends of the people, those men invested with power and place at the head of the Senate, who have given orders to destroy the images of the gods, and with their Lictors have consecrated themselves to Christ, the All Compelling."

The pagan historian Ammianus Marcellinus notes on his

---

[1] *Saturn.*, I, xvii, 1 ; I, xi, 1.

[2] Other facts are quoted by Wissowa, *Rel. u. Kultus der Romer*, pp. 98–102. Cf. Geffcken, in *Neue Jahrb. f. d. Kl.*, 1918, p. 109.

[3] *Ep.* xvii, 10 (P.L., XVI, 964) ; cf. St Augustine, *Sermo* xliv, 2 ; Enarr. LIV, 12 ; cf. ii, 5.

side that if the candidates for the Roman Episcopate show so much ardour to compete for this office, it is because practical advantages are not wanting : gifts from Roman ladies, comfortable carriages, magnificent robes, and repasts whose luxury is not surpassed by kings.[1] However ill-natured, this remark reveals the prestige and state with which the Bishop of Rome was surrounded.

The reconciliation of the Christian Church with the Roman State held consequences of the first order for the future of Christianity : " In our days," observes M. Paul Lejay,[2] " people are too much inclined to limit its importance. Until the peace of the Church, the hostility of the public powers had weighed heavily on the life of the Christian communities. On the day when it had been definitely removed we see the Church coming forth, as it were, from a long winter, consolidating and developing her ranks, dis- cussing her hierarchical powers, defining the lines of her doctrines, drawing up the formulæ of her faith, regulating her worship, surrounding the holy places with public marks of veneration, providing holy retreats for souls desirous of per- fection, and giving to the Latin half of the Church a more faithful version of the Bible. All these fruits are the harvest of the IVth century." This expansion of the spiritual power of the Church and of her material prosperity made itself felt too in the domain of literature. Still we must exclude from our survey the rich output of Athanasius, Basil, Gregory of Nazianzen, Gregory of Nyssa, John Chrysostom, Synesius, or Ephrem, in order to confine ourselves to works written in Latin. In Biblical exegesis, speculative and moral theology, the hymns of the Church, didactic, epic, and lyric poetry, Christian effort was manifesting itself in every direction. Even art, from this time onward, became a " complete system of instruction, a theology in images, an *apologia* in sculptured design." [3] We can measure the importance of this revival if we consider that profane literature had no other representatives at that time than men like Libanios, Symmachus, Macrobius, or Claudian.

[1] *Res Gestae*, XXVII, iii.
[2] R.H.L.R., 1900, 187.
[3] L. Bréhier, L'Art Chrétien, 1918, p. 107.

II

UNDER the name of J. Firmicus Maternus we possess two works of quite dissimilar character : a manual of astrology, *Matheseos Libri* VIII, the most ample legacy from antiquity we have on this subject, and the *De Errore Profanarum Religionum*.[1]

Did the same Firmicus write both these works ? Cl. H. Moore's study scarcely allows us any doubt. The two works were written at a distance of some years apart, one between 335 and 337, the other (the *De Errore*) between 346 and 350. The author of the *Mathesis* informs us that he was born in Sicily ;[2] now the author of the *De Errore* was personally acquainted with that country.[3] Lastly, the resemblance in details of language and analogy of expression are striking :[4] taken together, identity of authorship seems to be imperative.

The *Mathesis* is dedicated to Lollianus Mavortius, Governor of Campania. Firmicus himself belonged to the order of Senators. He tells us that he had at first devoted himself to the Bar, and that disgusted, by the annoyances and enmities which the exercise of his profession had brought him, he had finally given it up. His eight books on Astrology according to his intention were to contain " omnem disciplinam divinae matheseos." There are, however, *lacunae* and mistakes :[5] the author agrees that he was not very cognisant of the matter of which he treats. He works upon Greek and Latin sources, the origin of which he rarely defines, being anxious above all things (as he confesses) to annex a new province for Roman literature.[6] We need not lay too much stress upon this technical treatise here. It will suffice to note the curious tendencies which appear in it. Firmicus counsels certain prudent restrictions in the use to be made of astrological conclusions. Care must be taken to make no deductions on

---

[1] Dom Morin (*Histor. Jahrb.*, 1916, pp. 229–266) attributes to Firmicus the *Consultationes Zacchaei et Apollonii* (P.L., XX, 1071–1166) ; likewise, with reservations, A. Reatz, in *der Katholik*, XXI (1919), p. 300 et s.

[2] I *Prooem.*, iv : " Siciliae situm, quam incolo et unde oriendus sum ". Cf. VI, xxx, 26.

[3] *De Err.*, vii (description of the neighbourhood of Henna).

[4] These resemblances are shown in Ziegler's edition, L., 1907. One of the most significant is in *De Err.*, xxvi, 3 ; cf. *Math.*, V, *Praef.* 3 (Skutsch, p. 280, line 17).

[5] See Boll, in P.W., VI, 2374.

[6] V *Prooem.*, iii.

matters of State nor upon the Emperor. Lord of the Universe, the Emperor, by reason of his very divinity, was immune from stellar influences.[1] What is most significant, from our point of view, is that Firmicus seems to be concerned with different moral problems connected with his favourite science. He seeks to reconcile, in an otherwise very superficial manner, regard for the moral order and respect for Astrology.[2] He wishes people to approach this science with a pure and sober heart, for he is compelled to have daily intercourse with the gods.[3] The prayers with which he opens books V and VII are written in accents that are almost Christian.

We could not reasonably venture to maintain that he had already embraced the faith when he wrote his *Mathesis* and was projecting other works of the same kind.[4] Astrology had been for long held suspect by Christianity [5] as being contrary to the very idea of a Providence whose free decisions could not be bound by anything. By pretending that destiny is immutably written in the stars, the astrologers seemed to render superfluous all recourse to the true God. What we can say is, that Firmicus betrays certain inner dispositions which render less surprising the fact of his conversion, which happened during the ten years separating the *Mathesis* from the *De Errore Profanarum Religionum*.

The beginning of the *De Errore* is wanting : the two first leaves have been torn from the only very much spoilt manuscript, a Vaticanus Palatinus (n°. 165, Xth century) from which Mathias Placius Illyricus made the first edition at Strasbourg in 1562, and which Bursian discovered at the Vatican in 1856. Firmicus arraigns firstly divination by the elements : water (the cult of Osiris and Isis), earth (cult of Cybele and Atys), air (cult of *Juno Caelestis*), and fire (Persian, the Magi, the cult of Mithra) ; and he points his more or less scandalous anecdotes with pathetic exhortations addressed to those who favoured those ridiculous figments. He then applies (§ vi,

---

[1] *Math.*, II, xxx, 4 et s.
[2] I, vi, 3.
[3] II, xxx, 1.
[4] V, i, 38 ; VIII, i, 10 ; VIII, iv, 14.
[5] See *Dict. of Christian Antiquities*, Lon., 1893, art. *Magic* and *Astrology ;* R.H.L.R., 1903, p. 431 et s., and 1906, p. 40 ; *Rev. Histor.*, vol. LXV (1897), p. 262 et s. The Christian attacks upon these practices have not yet been studied in any deep manner.

et s.) the critical method of Evhemerist exegesis to a series of other beliefs, especially to those coming from the East which were particularly dear to pagan religious sentiment (the *Liber* of Crete and that of Thebes ; the Ceres of Henna ; Adonis ; Jupiter Sabazios ; the Corybantes ; and the Cabires of Macedonia) : parricide, adultery, pederasty, theft, incest,—there was no crime which these gods did not authorize by their example, or by the legends relating to them.[1] Firmicus even gives an eloquent discourse on the sun, dealing with the identification which some people some-times wish to establish between Bacchus and the heavenly body of light, and protests against such extravagance and invites them to listen rather to the Divine Word (§ viii, 1–3). A few chapters are devoted to explaining the etymology of the names of certain gods : Serapis ($\Sigma \acute{a} \rho \rho a \varsigma$ $\pi a \hat{\iota} \varsigma$, the child of Sarah), was the Joseph of Scripture, worshipped by the Egyptians in a manner he would certainly never have wished ; the Penates (from *penus*, provisions) were originally only the daily meats by which man sustained his life, etc. These fancies are followed by (xviii, et s.) very precious information from an historical point of view on the signs, and symbols or passwords, used in the mysteries.[2] " I have eaten from the dulcimer, I have drunk from the cymbal and have learnt in their true meaning the religious mysteries " (cult of Atys and the Eleusinian Mysteries) ; " Hail, new spouse, hail, new spouse, hail, new light ! " (Mysteries of Iacchus) ; " Alas ! O thou who hast two horns and two shapes ! " (Mysteries of Bacchus) ; " Be of good courage, ye initiates of the god set free ; for ye shall be freed from your woes " (Mysteries of Isis, Atys or Adonis) ; " The bull is father to the serpent, and the serpent is father to the bull " (Mysteries of Dionysus).

The refutations of Firmicus and the resemblances indicated by him between these formulæ and passages from the Bible have not much interest. But what are significant in quite another way are the energetic appeals to the secular

---

[1] xii, 5.

[2] M. Paul Foucart writes in this connection (*Les Mystères d'Eleusis*, Paris, 1914, p. 377) : " Firmicus Maternus made a mistake, I think, about the value of these formulæ and their use. It was not a password used by the initiates to recognise each other, but a reply to the question put by the ministers of the temple ; each of the recipients declared that he had accomplished the acts enjoined by the ritual." Cf. *ibid.*, p. 383 ; and Graillot, *Le Culte de Cybèle* (Bibl. des Ec. franç. d'Ath. et de Rome, fasc. 107 [1912], pp. 132 and 543).

arm with which he points his demonstrations. He turns to
the Emperors Constantine and Constans (*sacratissimi imperatores, sacrosancti imperatores, sacrosancti principes, domini
imperatores*) and implores them to destroy, once for all, these
demoralizing and impious forms of worship :

> " Needs must, most holy Emperors, that you extirpate
> these abominations, destroy them, and apply to them
> the most severe enactments in your Edicts. Suffer
> not this fatal and senseless delusion longer to soil the
> Roman Universe. . . . There are some who refuse,
> hide away, and passionately crave after their own ruin.
> Nevertheless, assist these unhappy men, deliver them,
> they perish ! If God from on high has entrusted the
> Empire to you, it is that you may heal these wounds. We
> know what peril their crime makes them run, what pun-
> ishment is reserved to their error : better to free them
> from it in spite of themselves than to abandon them in
> their full contentment to their ruin." (They are like
> sick men who ask for food likely to do them harm, and
> it is necessary to make them take the most active
> remedies and to suffer the cautery of fire and sword.
> Once healed, they will realize the benefit of this con-
> straint). . . . " As for you, most holy Emperors,
> necessity commands you to overcome and to punish this
> evil. God orders you in His Law to pursue with your
> severity in every place the crime of idolatry. Hearken
> and merit in your sacred minds what God ordains for
> this crime " (then follows the text of Deuteronomy, xiii,
> 6–10, 12–18).

And again :

> " It wants but little, thanks to your laws, for the devil
> to be completely overthrown, for idolatry to be extin-
> guished, and for this fatal contagion to be stamped out.
> Already the poison has lost its virulence ; each day, the
> food for profane passion grows less. Rear the standard
> of faith : this is the rôle which Divinity has reserved
> to you. Thanks to His favour, you have overthrown
> in a wonderful manner all your enemies by whom the
> Roman Empire was becoming enfeebled. Give to it the

revered mark of law. Draw up sanctions, promulgate
the necessary edicts. . . . In His benevolence, Christ
has reserved to His people through the work of your
hands the destruction of idolatry and the overthrowing
of profane temples." . . . " Strip without misgiving
from the temples the ornaments which these gods,
out of your revenues, fashion in the fire of your foundries,
and in the furnaces of your mines. Confiscate for your
benefit all their offerings ; make them your own. From
the time of the overthrowing of the temples, the Divine
Power has not ceased to add increase to your own
might. . . ."

There is something a little painful in the spectacle of this
intolerance on the part of those who had formerly been
persecuted, and, scarcely delivered from their own nightmare,
were hastening to become persecutors in their turn. These
vengeful exhortations did not remain a dead letter. If the
work of Firmicus is of the year 346, it may have contributed
to the promulgation of the rigorous edict of that same year
which (these are the very words used in the edict), ordered
sacrifice to be discontinued and the closing of the temples
in order " to take away from those who had strayed the
occasion of sin." Some years later (353–356), the provisions of a similar law passed in 341 were renewed. As
regards the Christians, extenuating circumstances were
certainly not wanting, and Gaston Boissier has skilfully
pleaded them : [1] " Their feelings of anger and hate can be
understood," he observes ; " Paganism was the enemy, the
implacable enemy who, for three centuries, had prevented
them from living in peace, whom they had all been brought
up to fear and to abhor. . . . After all, paganism had given
the example of these rigours ; the first to strike with the
sword, it seemed just that they should perish by the sword."
Then too, they were in the first enthusiasm of a victory which
seemed like a miracle. The reaction traced by the Emperor
Julian was to counsel more prudence and discretion, while
at the same time it was to revive the hopes of the pagans
which had for some time disappeared. It remains to say that
such a sudden evolution cannot fail to be disheartening

[1] *Fin du Pag.*, I, 67, 69.

to those who remember the fine words which Lactantius at the beginning of the IVth century had written about the duty of exercising persuasiveness and of discountenancing all violence in religious controversies.[1]

The *De Errore Profanarum Religionum* deserves a careful commentary, the material of which would be easy to find in the learned works published during these last few years on the pagan mysteries. The work is not tedious : an ardent rhetorical style gives life to it. Moreover, when we appraise what Firmicus owed to his Christian predecessors [2] (Cyprian especially, for his quotations from the Bible, Minucius Felix and Arnobius), and the turns and expressions which he gathered from his profane models (Terence, Sallust, Ovid, Titus Livius, Virgil, Plotinus, Porphyry, etc.), his own original contribution appears modest. But he has the merit of putting together a very precise documentation of the contemporary forms of the cults which he wished to denounce as absurd and abominable.

In addition, his work shows us the extravagant transports caused to certain Christians of passionate temperament by the astonishing turn of fortune which seemed to place the forces of the Empire at the service of their faith. It appeared to them that so unlooked for a triumph, such a stroke of Providence, should at once display all its effects, and that it was necessary that the truth, henceforth sure of its future, should exercise its indefeasible right by doing away with obstacles capable of retarding its march.

III

RETICIUS, Bishop of Autun, was one of the great influences of the Church in Gaul in the first years of the IVth century.[3] He played an important part in the Synod of Rome held in 313, when Donatus was condemned,[4] and at the Synod of Arles in 314.[5] St Jerome attributes to him a voluminous work against Novatian, and a *Commentary on the Canticle of Canticles*. In the *De Viris Illustribus*, where his purpose is to

---

[1] *Div. Inst.*, V, xx, 9 (C.V., XIX, p. 468). Cf. *Epitome*, liii.
[2] Cf. Ziegler's edition, p. xlv.
[3] St Jerome, *De Vir. Ill.*, lxxxii ; St Augustine, *Contra Jul. Pelag.*, I, iii, 7.
[4] Augustine, *ibid.*
[5] St Optat, I, xxiii.

enhance the prestige of Christian literature, Jerome refrains
from letting us know what little merit he conceived for this
Commentary. More liberal in his letters,[1] he notices its
insufficiencies, not so much from the point of view of its form
as of its interpretation : Reticius must have forgotten the
first duty of the exegetist, which is to facilitate for the reader
the understanding of the text which he has undertaken to
paraphrase. The *Commentary* of Reticius was still existing
in the XIIth century : Béranger quotes a fragment of it in
his *Apologie d'Abélard*.[2] Since that date all traces of it have
been lost.[3]

IV

THAT the advantage of friendship with those in high places
has not always been an unmixed benefit for the Church, is
shown unmistakably by the life of St Hilary of Poitiers.

The IVth century was the period of the great controversies in doctrine,—Arians, Priscillianists, Origenists, Donatists, Manichæans, and Pelagians. Of these intestine dis-
sensions none was graver or more disintegrating for the
Christian faith than the controversy raised by Arius. The
fundamental economy of Revelation was threatened. In
addition, the Emperors when constituting themselves the
protectors of Christianity were fully determined to place
her in a state of tutelage and to take sides, in the name of their
omnipotence, in the factions which had been let loose. The
favour manifested by Constantius towards the partisans of
Arianism as against the holders of the faith of Nicaea might
have been a deciding factor in the development of events if the
admirable tenacity of a St Athanasius in the East, and
of a St Hilary in the West, had not offered a counterpoise.
The first " Doctor "[4] of the Latin Church, St Hilary appeared
in the light of history for the space of only ten years, but
during this short period lasting from 355 to 367 his action
was of sovereign efficacy.

---

[1] *Ep.*, xxxvii, 3.
[2] P.L., CLXXVIII, 1864.
[3] According to St Jerome, *De Vir. Ill.*, 97, Fortunatianus of Aquileia, another
exegetist, wrote in the time of Constantine.
[4] This title was officially conferred upon him in the XIXth century by the
Decree *Quod potissimum* of the Congregation of Rites (29 March 1851) and the
Apostolic Brief *Si ab ipsis* (13 May 1851).

Hilary was born at Poitiers in the first years of the IVth century. His family which occupied a high position was pagan.[1] In the Gaul of the IVth century, which was " an Italy much more than a Province," [2] Hilary received a very careful education. In the introduction to his work on the Trinity he gives the motives which determined his conversion. He had felt keenly that he would never be contented with material and bestial (*beluinae*) enjoyments, with idleness and riches. An upright life securely swathed in the prudent maxims of Epicureanism no longer satisfied him. He had a hunger after the Divine which the contradictions of philosophy ill satisfied. Contact with the Sacred Books brought light into his soul which up till then had been in darkness and uncertainty. We know nothing of the period between his baptism and his becoming a Bishop. He had been married, if we may believe the poet Venantius Fortunatus, who wrote his life in verse at the end of the VIth century. We have even a letter from Hilary " to his daughter Abra " ; but it is so affected that it is hard to believe it authentic.

Once Bishop of Poitiers, Hilary shortly after 350 made no delay in entering upon the struggles which were to fill his life. Up till then he had remained quite outside the Eastern disputes on the ὁμοούσιος and the ὁμοιούσιος,[3] and had rested in the quiet possession and preaching of the truths he had acquired.[4] His first work, the *Commentaries* on St Matthew, in which he treats of different questions connected with the text of the Gospel, although he does not give any continuous paraphrase of it, shows him to be faithful to the tradition of the Trinity held by Tertullian and Novatian : the formulæ of Nicaea had not yet exercised any influence on him. The Synods of Arles (353) and of Milan (355), the exile of Paulinus of Trèves, Eusebius of Vercelli, Lucifer of Calaris, and Denys of Milan, opened his eyes to the Arian menace : " *Horum furori respondere* animus exarsit," he remarks.[5] He resolutely opposed Saturninus, the Primate of

---

[1] In Ps. 146, 13 (C.V., vol. XXII, p. 853, 1, 9).

[2] The expression is from Pliny the Elder, *Hist. Nat.*, III, iv. It was still truer in the IVth century than in the Ist. For his education at Poitiers, cf. Ausonius, *Prof.*, xi, 46–48 ; *Epigr.* xlvii, 2, 208.

[3] He confesses this himself : *De Syn.*, xci : " . . . fidem Nicaenam nunquam nisi exsulaturus audivi."

[4] Cf. *De Trin.*, I, xiv.

[5] *Ibid.*, I, xvii.

Arles, who had gone over to the Arian idea. The ardour
of his proceedings marked him out to the Arian Bishops as
a dangerous adversary. At the Synod of Béziers (356) they
prevented him from offering a defence of Athanasius and the
faith of Nicea, denounced him to the Emperor as a factious
person, and obtained a sentence of exile against him.

Hilary was banished to Phrygia.[1] He profited largely
during this unhappy time to add to his intellectual per-
fectioning. He initiated himself into Greek Christian literature (it would be interesting to know on what theologians
he nourished his thought). It was a form of culture which
was already somewhat rare at this time, and conferred
upon him a superiority among the dialecticians of the West,
of which his *De Trinitate*, composed during his exile,[2] bears
the stamp. In these twelve books he was principally stirred
against the Arians, although his polemics were sometimes
aimed at the Sabellians, the Jews and the Gnostics. He was
well aware of the extent of the evil against which he desired
to forearm men's minds.[3] Here and there he traces with
clairvoyance the Arian psychology—that *haeretica subtilitas*
which played upon words in order to deceive the simple,
and adapted itself so complacently to *prudentia saeculi*.
The discussions of Hilary disclose on more than one page the
penetration of his mind, and enable us to understand the
details of the Arian contention. Evidence of this has been
preserved to us, thanks to him.[4] On such a question, the
difficulty of which dismays him,[5] St Hilary makes his readers
understand that the words which he is obliged to employ,
and the images and comparisons he uses, are hopelessly
inadequate to the ineffable truths which he has to render
intelligible, and that they should only see in them distant
approximations destined to lead them from the known to the
unknown.[6] The *De Trinitate* is one of the monuments of
lofty Christian speculation of the first centuries : never up
till then had the problems of Christology been examined
in the West in such minute detail. The *De Synodis*, which

---

[1] Cf. St Jerome, *De Vir. Ill.*, c ; Hilary, *De Syn.*, lxiii.

[2] Cf. *De Trin.*, X, iv (P.L., X, 346) : " Loquemur exsules per hos libros, et
sermo Dei, qui vinciri non potest, liber excurret."

[3] Cf. XI, 1 : " . . . multis jam per omnes ferme Romani imperii prouincias
ecclesiis morbo pestiferae hujus praedicationis infectis."

[4] Cf. the letter of Arius to Alexander, VI, v.

[5] II, v.   [6] I, xix.

is joined to the *De Trinitate* in nearly all the manuscripts, presents a speculative character in only certain portions (§ lxvi–xcii). The principal object of the work, which is addressed to the Bishops of Gaul, the two Germanies, and Britain, is to put the people of the West in touch with the struggles in the East against Arianism. Thus Hilary is led to quote and to appraise several formulæ of the faith of the East :—the second formula of Sirmium (357), clearly Arian in colour, the twelve anathemas of Ancyra (358), the formula of the Synod of Antioch *in encaeniis* (341), the " confession " of Philippopolis (343–344), and the first formula of Sirmium (351). It is a precious work from the historical point of view ; it prepared the way to appeasing men's minds by giving them a clearer view of the questions in dispute, and the position of the opposing parties.

The authority of Hilary made itself felt even in the East. Although a Latin Bishop, he was invited to take his place at the Synod of Seleucia in 359, and there he upheld the conclusions of Nicea against the semi-Arian majority and against the Anomoeans. He likewise took part in the deputation sent to Constantinople to inform the Emperor of what had taken place at Seleucia. Saturninus of Arles was at that moment at Constantinople. Hilary solicited an audience of Constantius. We possess his petition, the *Ad Constantium Augustum*. In it he went over in twelve chapters the circumstances of his unjust exile, and begged the Emperor, in the interest of peace between the East and the West, to hearken to the language of the authentic faith, which had been altogether confused by intrigues, subtilties, and vain disputes. Constantius did not heed the prayer of Hilary. Thereat the latter allowed his indignation to burst forth in a pamphlet which perhaps was not published until after the death of the Emperor (3rd Nov. 361). After enumerating the attempts made by the Arians and protected by Constantius, Hilary did not hesitate to compare him with the worst persecutors :

" I will therefore cry aloud to thee, Constantius, what I would have said to Nero, what Decius and Maximin would have heard from my lips. Thou art fighting against God, thou art laying waste the Church, thou persecutest the Saints, thou dost hold in detestation the proclaimers of Christ, thou dost overthrow religion, a tyrant not of human things, but of things Divine. Up to now I have said what crimes are common to thee and to those persecutors : learn now those which proceed from thyself alone. Thou dost falsely pretend to be a Christian, and art a fresh enemy to Christ ; precursor of anti-Christ, thou art accomplishing his works of darkness. . . . Thou dost distribute the Episcopal Sees among thy partisans and thou dost replace good Bishops by evil ones. Thou dost imprison priests, thou dost put thine armies in the field to terrorise the Church, thou dost assemble Councils, and thou dost constrain to impiety the Bishops of the West who are shut up at Rimini after having frightened them with thy menaces, and weakened them with hunger enfeebled as they are by winter, and led astray by thy false-hoods. . . ." [1]

Such intrepid activity was matter to be feared by the Arians of the East. They had Hilary sent back to Gaul under the pretext that he was " *discordiae seminarium et perturbator Orientis.*" [2] Received with great demonstrations of joy in his Episcopal city, Hilary had no mind to give himself the least rest. To drive out Arianism from Gaul was the task he pursued without intermission. After various Provincial Synods, the Council of Paris, held in 361, anathematised Auxentius, Ursacius, Valens and Saturninus, the leaders of the Arian movement. The Nicene doctrine triumphed in Gaul ; Hilary carried the war into Italy. A conference at Milan brought him into opposition with Auxentius, the Bishop. The latter extricated himself by making use of equivocal methods, and St Hilary, who protested, received orders to leave Milan.[3] He obeyed, but in his *Contra Auxentium* he denounced the underhand proceedings of his adversary, " that angel of Satan, that enemy of Christ, that cursed despoiler, that renegade from the faith which he confessed by a lie and which he outrages by blasphemy." [4]

His last years passed in his diocese were fruitful in exegetic and historical works. A disciple of Origen,[5] he applied the

---

[1] § vi–vii.
[3] *Contra Aux.*, § viii.
[5] Cf. St Jerome, *Ep.* xxxiv, 3.

[2] Sulp. Severus, *Chron.*, II, xlv, 4.
[4] § xii.

methods of allegorical interpretation to the study of the Psalms in his *Tractatus super Psalmos*, which has only come down to us in an incomplete form : [1] in it the Psalms are explained in their function of *evangelica praedicatio*. The *Tractatus Mysteriorum*, discovered in 1887 by Gamurrini in the famous manuscript of Arezzo, is conceived in the same spirit and, although much spoilt, clearly presents the purpose of Hilary :

> " Every work contained in the sacred volume," declares Hilary, " announces by word, explains by facts, and corroborates by examples the coming of our Lord Jesus Christ, sent by His Father, and born a man of a Virgin, through the operation of the Holy Spirit. From the beginning of the world, Christ, by authentic and absolute prefigurations (fulfilled) in the person of the Patriarchs, gives birth to the Church, washes it clean, sanctifies it, chooses it, places it apart and redeems it : by the sleep of Adam, by the deluge in the days of Noe, by the blessing of Melchisedech, by Abraham's justification, by the birth of Isaac, by the captivity of Jacob. . . . The purpose of this work is to show that in each personage, in every age, and in every act, the image of His coming, of His teaching, of His resurrection, and of our Church, is reflected as in a mirror." [2]

And further on :

> " These acts, signified by the different personages (in the Old Testament), but understood and fulfilled in Christ alone, it is fitting should be preserved to posterity in works written and drawn up. Thus future generations, instructed in the actions of former times, may con-

---

[1] There are remaining the paraphrases of *Ps.* 1, 2, 9, 13, 14, 51–69, 91, 118–150. Certain references mentioned by Hilary reveal evident lacunæ. The MSS. thus give us only a *selection*.—The commentaries on *Ps.* 15, 31, and 41 are not authentic. There are some additional fragments in R.B., vol. XXVII (1910), p. 19. The word *tractatus* carries two principal acceptations in ecclesiastical language. It means (1) a treatise, a commentary, explanations principally on the Bible (v.g. the African Confessors, in St Cyprian, *Ep.* lxxvii, 1 ; the " *Tractatus super Psalmos* " of St Hilary of Poitiers ; St Jerome, *de Vir. Ill.*, xxxvii, xlviii, xlix, etc.) ; (2) a discourse (cf. Ps. Cyprian, *de Op. et Eleem.*, xii [Hartel, III, l, p. 383] : St Augustine, *Ep.* ccxxiv, 2 [C.V., vol. LVII, p. 453, l. 5]) : " . . . tractatus populares, quos Graeci homilias vocant " ; Optat, *Contra Parmen*, vii, 6 : " . . . Omnis tractatus in ecclesia a nomine Dei incipitur et ejusdem Dei nomine terminatur ".

[2] § 1 (C.V., LXV, p. 3, l. 10 et s.).

template the present even in the past, and may venerate the past still more in the present. . . ." [1]

Such is his method : St Jerome, who under the influence of Origen, was in his turn to practise it, recognised its difficulties which Hilary hardly seemed to have foreseen.

Of his Commentaries on Job there only remain two fragments. Doubtless therein Hilary made no great effort as he did elsewhere to expound the mystical relationships of the *typica significantia*.

But he was not unmindful of the Arian question, or rather, his mind remained obsessed with it. The *Fragmenta Historica* do great honour to his zeal as an historian. They deserve special attention by reason of their importance as a fountain-head for ecclesiastical history and also on account of the problems in modern criticism which they arouse.

The dogmatic conflicts of the IVth century provoked, as we know, the formation of several very valuable documentary collections both in the East and in the West. It was necessary to find suitable material for their polemics and to provide the means of enlightening public opinions. We should bear in mind the pieces included by St Athanasius in his *Apologia* against the Arians, in his *History of the Arians* addressed to the Monks, and in his treatise on the *Decrees of the Council of Nicea ;* the letters collected by Arius and Alexander ; the Συναγωγή of Sabinus of Heraclea ; the *Gesta Purgationis Caecilii et Felicis*, etc. . . . More complete than any other, the collection known under the title *Fragmenta Historica* is drawn up on a very similar plan : there are letters from Popes, Bishops, and Emperors, Acts and Decrees of different Councils, and professions of faith, each contribution as a rule being connected to the preceding one by a more or less lengthy explanatory text.

These *Fragmenta Historica* were first published in Paris in 1598 by Nicholas le Fèvre according to the edition which Pierre Pithou, who died two years before, had already compiled and nearly finished. Pithou had worked on a manuscript of the XVIth century in which the fragments had been classed under two series, one anonymous and the

---

[1] *Ibid.*, ii, 14 (C.V., p. 37, l. 5).

other attributed to St Hilary by name. Le Fèvre took into account this division and attribution of authorship ; nevertheless, for chronological reasons he inverted the order of the series, placing the anonymous series second. A century later, Pierre Coustant, the Benedictine, admitted that *all* the documents included in Pithou's manuscript were fragments of a great historical work on the Councils of Rimini and Seleucia [1] written by St Hilary : this is why in his edition of the works of St Hilary which he published in 1693, and which has long been held as an authority, he called the whole collection *Fragmenta ex libro sancti Hilarii Pictaviensis Provinciae Aquitaniae,* etc., after arranging them under a more exact chronology, the name which, variously abbreviated, has since passed into ordinary usage.

Charged by the commission of the *Corpus Script. Eccles. Latinorum* to bring out a certain number of the works of Hilary—the *Fragmenta Historica* among others—Father Feder, a Jesuit, took in hand the study of the tradition of the manuscript and the historical contents and origin of this collection as a preliminary,[2] which he designated under the title *Collectanea Antiariana Parisina,* without prejudice.

Feder established in the first place that the Cod. Parisin. Armamentarii lat. 483, of the IXth century (A) preserved in the Arsenal Library, of which Fèvre and Coustant were ignorant, is the archetype of the two manuscripts utilised by them, namely the Cod. Pithoeanus (T) now lost, and the Cod. Paris. lat. 1700, of the XVIIth century (C), which latter moreover is only a copy of T. He also drew up a list of other manuscripts wherein appear many isolated pieces from the *Coll. Antiar. Par.,* and furnished complete references to the printed collections (especially those dealing with Councils) in which these several documents had been inserted.

He then took in hand to settle the origin of these *Fragmenta Historica.* The name of Hilary of Poitiers figures at the head of the second series of the Manuscripts—which the first resembles very closely as a matter of fact. Now this notion is confirmed by the intrinsic study of the fragments composing the above series. Thus the opening piece is by

[1] This work is attested by St Jerome in his notice on Hilary (*De Vir. Ill.,* § C) : " Est ejus . . . liber adversum Valentem et Ursacium, historiam Ariminensis et Seleuciensis synodi continens."

[2] S.B.W., CLXII, 4 (1910) ; CLXVI, 5 (1911) ; CLXIX, 5 (1912).

all evidence an introduction to a historico-polemic work by a Bishop who played an important part at the Council of Béziers, who made vain attempts to obtain an audience of the Emperor, and was determined to fight to the end for Athanasius and the Nicene confession of faith. How is it possible not to recognise Hilary under this description ?

Moreover this attributing of the authorship to him is hardly contested. But there is this fine point about it : are these extracts material for a work which Hilary had not been able to finish, or are they extracts from a finished work which we no longer possess ? It is to the second solution that Father Feder rallies. By a series of considerations in which the historical analysis of the texts in dispute and the evidence of contemporary events mutually help each other, he advances the following hypothesis. In 356, immediately after the Council of Béziers (and not during his exile at Constantinople from 359–360 as had been believed since the time of Coustant), Hilary wrote an historical and polemical work which was none other than the *Liber adversus Valentem et Ursacium* mentioned by St Jerome. Many fragments of this work are still in existence, namely two and probably three from the *Fragmenta Historica*,[1] to which must be added two other documents which have come down to us under the misleading and now obsolete title *Ad Constantium Liber Primus*—the letter from the Council of Sardica to the Emperor Constantius and the narrative text accompanying it.

Father Feder borrowed the essential portion of these views from a remarkable article by Dom A. Wilmart which appeared in the *Revue Bénédictine* in 1907,[2] but while he appropriated Dom Wilmart's ideas, Father Feder systematised them and carried them further than Dom Wilmart wished to do. He thinks that St Hilary wrote a sequel to his work against Valens and Ursacius about December 359, after the Councils of Seleucia and Rimini. What he was wishing to do on this occasion was to influence the Bishops who had " fallen " at Rimini to retract. The *Epistola legatorum Synodi Seleuciensis ad legatos Synodi Arimensis*,

---

[1] The *Praefatio ad opus historicum*, the *Varia ex actis synodi Sardicensis*, also doubtless the *Epistola synodi Sardicensis Orientalium*.

[2] " *L'Ad Constantium liber primus* de Saint Hilaire de Poitiers et Les Fragments historiques."

and probably also seven other of the *Fragmenta Historica* would belong to this second portion.

As regards those *Fragmenta* not susceptible of being classed in the two first portions of St Hilary's work against Valens and Ursacius, Feder supposes that they were incorporated in a third portion which appeared in 367, shortly before or after the death of Hilary.

The formation of the collection such as we now have it could be explained as follows. An anonymous writer, with the view of giving a fresh account of the Arian struggles, must have extracted for his own purposes from Hilary's work the numerous documents which the latter had included in it, and added thereto ample marginal notes. These useful *excerpta* were transcribed and circulated at an early date; certain indications enable us to state that the collection was made up in Italy at the beginning of the IVth century.

Clearly, conjecture occupies a large space in these combinations; it could not be otherwise on such a matter. At any rate, the leading ideas on the literary enigma offered to the curiosity of critics by the *Fragmenta Historica* are henceforth defined in a useful manner. And it is interesting to discover in the great Bishop the Roman taste for administrative conciseness and methodical order which furnished these oratorical contests with documents and facts.

St Hilary also made use of poetry in giving expression to his views. He was the first to write hymns for the Church in Latin. Isidore of Spain affirms this,[1] and before him St Jerome had noted the *Liber Hymnorum.*[2] His sojourn in the East had given him the opportunity of appreciating the effective propaganda of which the use of sung words is capable. Had not Arius composed songs for the use of sailors, millers, and travellers, set to profane airs?[3] This method of the Gnostics[4] had been revived and Hilary thought good to appropriate it. We know that he experienced difficulty in imposing the use of the chant of the Church upon his compatriots.[5] In 1887 a few hymns were known under his name,

[1] *De Eccl. Off.*, I, vi (P.L., LXXXIII, 743).
[2] *De Vir. Ill.*, c.
[3] Cf. Philostorgius, H.E., II, xxvii (P.G., LXVI, 464).
[4] Texts in P. de Labriolle's *La Crise Montaniste*, p. 62 et s.
[5] Jerome, *ad Gal.*, I. II : " Hilarius . . . Gallos in hymnorum carmine indociles vocat."

THE MORROW OF THE VICTORY

without sufficient guarantee of authenticity. The Arezzo manuscript has given three which might reasonably be attributed to him. The first piece, *Ante saecula qui manes* is written in the rhythm known as second asclepiad (one glyconic line followed by a minor asclepiad). The four last strophes are missing. There follows next—after a gap of six leaves in the manuscript—the piece *Fefellit saevam* in iambics of six feet; the first five strophes are missing. These two fragments are alphabetical. The third hymn, *Adae carnis gloriosa*, is in catalectic trochaic tetrameters; the end has been lost. These three pieces (to which some critics add a few others of a more or less resemblance) are dogmatic in character, which is specially pronounced in the *Ante saecula* treating of the relationship of the Son to the Father. In the second hymn the soul regenerated by baptism explains how Christ has triumphed over death and made the resurrection possible. The third celebrates Christ, the heavenly Adam, and His first victory over Satan. The versification shows many licences, especially a rather frequent hiatus.[1] These are clearly the kind of hymns, at once liturgical and popular, which it was necessary to oppose to the Arians in order to imprint on the memory the essential truths which the former were threatening.

St Hilary was thus a man of action and a fighter even in his verses. One thought only filled his life and made it one whole—the fight against Arianism. He was persuaded that the entire faith was at stake, that this rationalistic theology, this formalistic and literal exegesis, would kill the Catholicism that had been handed down. He had no hesitation in calling the Arian Bishops " anti-Christ " : *nominis antichristi proprietas est, Christo esse contrarium.*[2] Giving the appearance of preaching Jesus Christ, but in reality denying Him since they would only give Him attributes by means of which He could in nothing be distinguished from the creature, the angel or man ; carrying out this detestable work under the mask of a false piety ; seeking their support in the " world," and basing it on *ambitio saecularis*, and on *suffragia terrena*, whereas the Apostles themselves had known how to struggle

---

[1] For example, in the *Ante saecula*, lines 26, 32, 53, 72.
[2] *Contra Auxentium*, § ii.

against every power leagued against them—is how he upbraids them, and with these familiar grievances he mingles
pity for the Christian people thus deceived by bad shepherds :
" *Sanctiores aures plebis quam corda sunt sacerdotum.*" [1]

Hilary possessed the qualities of a leader of men, and this
he showed wherever he went, in the East as well as in the
West. His reputation was immense.[2] He enjoyed the
prestige of having suffered for his ideas. How can we deny
him the title of " disciple of truth,"[3] which was his ambition ?
Then too the eloquent vigour of his language completed the
effect of a very noble example.

In contradistinction to many other ecclesiastical writers
Hilary never concealed his desire to write well. At the
beginning of his great work on the Trinity he asks God to
grant him " verborum significationem, intellegentiae lumen,
dictorum honorem. . . ." [4] In another place, in his Commentary on the Psalms,[5] he declares that " he who treats of the
word of God should do honour to the Author of that word,
even in the beauty of his phrasing, just as those who compose
the wording of a king's rescript must proceed with diligence
and care in order to be worthy of the dignity due to a prince."
He always drew up the plan of his works with an eye to wise
composition,[6] and here and there excused himself for having
allowed himself in the ardour of discussion to be drawn further
than the limits he had set.[7]

In addition he had received a good formation as a scholar.
He did not know Hebrew,[8] but he had learnt Greek in the
East.[9] He had some knowledge of philosophy[10] and natural
sciences.[11] In a word, he had at his disposition all the resources giving a wide range of culture to a man who has not
been endowed with an original style and a form of expression

---

[1] *Ibid.*, iii–iv.
[2] We have the witness of St Jerome on this point, *Ep.* xxxiv, 3 : ". . . ubicumque romanum nomen est, praedicatur."
[3] *Contra Const.*, xii.
[4] I, xxxviii (P.L., X, 49).
[5] xiii, 1 (P.L., IX, 295).
[6] Cf. *De Trin.*, I, xx et s. : " Nihil enim incompositum indigestumque placuit
afferre."
[7] *Ibid.*, V, xii (X, 136).
[8] Cf. *In Psalm*, cxxxviii, 43 (P.L., IX, 775) ; cxlii, 1 (IX, 805) ; and St Jerome,
Ep. xxxiv, 3.
[9] St Jerome (*ibid.*) is too exact when he wrote : " Graecarum quoque litterarum
quandam aurulam ceperat."
[10] Cf. the introduction to the *De Trinitate.*
[11] *De Trin.*, XII, liii ; *In Ps.* cxxxiv, 11 ; lxviii, 29 ; cxx, 12, etc.

of his own. It is classic, and formed in the school of Quintilian, whom he imitates occasionally, but with more discretion than a phrase of St Jerome [1] would allow us to suppose. His periods are of an oratorical amplitude, with an abundance of similes which are too rigorously developed and driven home,[2] and endings adroitly balanced off.[3]

The strong vigour of eloquence does not permeate Hilary's writings. With Villemain we might say that it is on a lower level than the genius of the author, and that all this contentious and arid theology only half expresses him. But a burning sincerity breathes throughout which does not exclude charity. A fanatic like Lucifer of Calaris, himself passionately anti-Arian, was to attack Hilary for the concessions he made by his practical liberalism. He is a worthy figure in the list of those skilful and powerful organisers of Christianity, the Fathers of the Church, victorious, but harassed by intestine discords almost as grievously as it had been persecuted till lately from without.

Hilary died in 367, on the 1st of November, without doubt.[4]

V

PUTTING on one side all question of literary talent, Lucifer of Calaris (Cagliari, in Sardinia) makes one think of Tertullian whose *intransigeance* and restrictions he copied. Exiled with three other Bishops shortly after the Council of Milan (355)[5] for having refused to subscribe to the condemnation of St Athanasius, when the greater part of those who took part in it were weak enough to adhere to it, Lucifer lived in different countries from 356 to 361. We find him successively at Germanicia in Syria Commagene, Eleutheropolis in Palestine, then in the Thebaid. It was here he was found by the edict of the Emperor Julian who recalled to their Sees

[1] *Ep.* lxx, 5: "Hilarius . . . duodecim Quintiliani libros et stilo imitatus est et numero." Cf. Kling, *De Hilario Pict. artis rhetoricae . . . studioso.* Fr.-i.-B., 1910, p. 31.

[2] There is a characteristic example in the *De Trin.*, XII, 1. "Longis interdum periodis involvitur," Jerome caustically remarks, *Ep.* LVIII, 10. Hilary uses fifteen times running *cum* in a complementary sense : *In Ps.* li, 6.

[3] Kling, *op. cit.*, p. 33 et s.

[4] See the discussion on the date in Feder, S.B.W., vol. CLXII, fasc. 4, p. 126.

[5] Athanasius, *Hist. Arian.*, xxxiii et s. (P.G., XXV, 732; XLI, 741); Sulp.-Severus, *Chron.*, II, xxxix.

the Bishops who had been exiled or interned by the decision
of the Council, with the secret design of rekindling hostile
feelings within the bosom of Christianity.

Lucifer's writings were all written during his exile, and
were aimed uniformly at Constantius who is treated therein
without any attempt at conciliation. Their titles are
significant beforehand in their brevity : No truck with
heretics (*De non conveniendo cum haereticis*) ; Saint Athanasius
(*De Sancto Athanasio*) ; No pity for the enemies of God (*De
non parcendo in Deum delinquentibus*) ; Let us die for the Son
of God (*Moriendum esse pro Dei Filio*). These pamphlets,
largely reinforced by texts specially taken from the Old
Testament, which have come to us in one only manuscript
(*Vatic.*, 133, ix–x cent.), have as their object to stigmatise the
policy of Constantius, his complaisance towards the Arians,
those sons of darkness,[1] and his claim to justify them by
alleging his then prosperity to be a kind of dispensation from
God, while there were so many examples which showed the
long delay of the inevitable vengeance of heaven.[2] Lucifer
also protests against the procedure observed at the Council
of Milan when St Athanasius was condemned without having
been heard (*De Sancto Athanasio*). As against the Emperor
who had taxed him with arrogance he alleges his duty as
a Bishop to proclaim the truth without respect of persons
(*De non parcendo*). The *Moriendum Esse*, a mosaic made up
from Tertullian, Lactantius, the letters of St Cyprian,[3] and
the *De Laude Martyrii*, shows the energetic temper with which
Lucifer declares himself ready to leave everything in order to
defend the orthodox belief proclaimed at Nicea.

The imperial prerogative was not wanting in a certain
longanimity since it put up with such intemperate language
without wrath. " He allowed himself to be called the Ahab
of the Christians by the new Elias." [4] Possibly he thought
these anathemas too uninteresting to trouble about. Lucifer
had no claim as a man of letters ; he boasted of it and affected
to have been brought up on the Bible alone.[5] For skill in

---

[1] C.V., XIV, p. 20, l. 4.
[2] *Ibid.*, p. 35, l. 7.
[3] Especially letters vi, x, xxxvii, lv (perhaps also lviii). See Merk, in T.Q.,
1912, p. 1 et s.
[4] Duchesne, II, 340.
[5] C.V., XIV, p. 256, l. 6 ; p. 294, l. 23 ; p. 306, l. 19 and 23.

developing arguments he substituted a wealth of quotations from Scripture. Anchored upon certain unshakable principles, he deemed it to be superfluous to strengthen them by any demonstration from reason. Philologists (rather than men of letters or even theologians) find something to glean from his combative writing, whether in the text of the version of the Bible or in his language packed with anacoluthons, ellipses, and smacking of the popular orator.[1]

Towards the end of his life this passionate defender of orthodoxy outlined a movement very similar, as I have said, to what had already been effected by Tertullian. When Pope Liberius and Bishop Athanasius were inclined to exercise indulgence in regard to those Bishops who had allowed themselves to sign a formula favourable to the Arians at the Council of Rimini (359), Lucifer opposed their pacificatory desires with all his force. He rallied to his uncompromising views Hilary the Deacon, and Gregory the Bishop of Eliberis, about whom we shall have to speak on a future occasion. Hilary went so far as to maintain that the defaulters at Rimini, and those who followed them,[2] must be rebaptised. Such rigour was no longer in season and condemned Lucifer to remain by himself or nearly so. He spent the last years of his life in his diocese in Sardinia, and died there about the year 370–371.

Some of his partisans caused talk up to about the year 384. The *Collectio Avellana*[3] contains a *Libellus precum*,[4] a kind of petition addressed in 383–4 to the Emperors Valentinian II, Theodosius, and Arcadius, by the priests Faustinus and Marcellinus, as a form of protest against the annoyances to which they were exposed on the part of the Catholics, and against the odious name of " Luciferians " by which they were caricatured. An imperial rescript recog-

---

[1] Hartel's study in A.L.L., III (1886), p. 1, of Lucifer's Latin is well summed up in the *Rev. de Philol.* (*Revue des Revues*), 1888, p. 197–199.

[2] St Jerome, *Dial. adv. Lucifer*, xxi (P.L., XXIII, 175) and xxvii.

[3] A collection of more than two hundred pieces put together by an unknown scholar who lived in Rome in the time of Pope Vigilius (537–555). This collection comprises letters, edicts, etc., of emperors, magistrates, Popes, and Bishops and spreads over the years 367–553. The Ballerini brothers gave it this name in the XVIIIth century, because they thought (wrongly) that a manuscript in the Umbrian Convent of Santa Cruce in Fonte Avellana (now *Vaticanus* 4961) was the principal source from which the collection was drawn.

[4] This title is not attested by the written manuscript. It was invented by J. Sirmond, who published the work for the first time in 1650.

nised the reasonableness of their request.[1] We possess also
two other *opuscula* of Faustinus, composed as a guarantee
of the purity of their orthodoxy. In one, the *Fides Theodosio
Imp. Oblata,* he defends himself against any leaning to
Sabellianism ; in the other, the *De Trinitate sire de Fide
contra Arianos,* he enlightens Flaccilla the Empress on the
fundamental points of the Arian controversy.

The literary activity of the Luciferians may also have
assumed a more subtle and underhand form. They were
suspected, for sufficiently striking reasons, of having fashioned
weapons to be used for the glory of their cause which was
dear to them and too little understood—in particular, two
pretended letters of St Athanasius to Lucifer,[2] and the first
eight books of the *De Trinitate* by the pseudo-Athanasius.[3]

VI

WE must also glance at the Arian and anti-Arian literature
which reflects the burning polemics of the time, but offers
little real attraction except for theologians and students of
the history of doctrine. The confusion surrounding these
thorny controversies reveals but few agreeable surprises.

The writings on the Arian side are by no means numerous.
We know the fate of heterodox literature, and what dangers
it must have run in avoiding so many occasions for its
destruction.[4]

We may make passing mention of Potamius, Bishop of
Olisopo (Lisbon), a supporter of Arianism in the Episcopacy
of Spain. We have a letter from him to St Athanasius,
also two sermons, one on Lazarus, and the other on the
martyrdom of Isaias, which are characterised by a deliberate
seeking after the horrible. The writer complacently describes
in detail the different phases of the decomposition of the body
of Lazarus in the tomb, and notes its deliquescence and putrid
odour ; he lets us hear the *stridor* of the saw through the body
of Isaias and follows its hideous progress.

---

[1] P.L., XIII, 107–108.
[2] We have only the Latin text : P.G., XXVI, 1181 et s. ; C.V., XIII, 322 et s.
[3] P.L., LXII, 307–334. Books IX–XII form another work, and they have
been wrongly incorporated with the first eight in the *Patrol. lat.* See L. Saltet,
B.L.E., 1906, 300.
[4] Cf. P. de Labriolle, *Les Sources de l'Hist. du Montanism,* 1913, p. ix–xiii.

The Vatican Library and the Ambrosian Library at Milan share a palimpsest containing curious fragments of Arian origin. This palimpsest came from the Monastery of Bobbio. " The monks of the Abbey of Bobbio, founded by St Colomban in 613, to whom had been given the task of combating the influence of Arianism which had been perpetuated in Italy by the Gothic, and afterwards by the Lombard, domination, were obliged to collect ample Arian material in their library." [1] These twenty-one fragments all refer to Arianism, with the exception of the last two which are made up from extracts from an apocryphal work, the *Ascension of Isaias*. Angelo Mai first edited them in 1828. They belong to different works, of a homiletic, dogmatic, or polemical character. There is no positive difficulty in attributing them to the same author, whom certain indications invite us to look for among the Bishops of the region of the Danube. Maximin, Auxentius of Durostorum, and Palladius of Ratiara, have been suggested, but no deciding reason enables us to place any likelihood on its authorship. Another palimpsest from Bobbio, also deciphered and published by Mai, has given us fragments of a commentary on St Luke. In it there are mingled very characteristic statements of " homoian " Arianism with its edifying phraseology.[2]

The treatise by St Augustine, *Contra Sermonem Arianorum*, has preserved for us an anonymous Arian sermon (*Quidam sermo Arianorum sine nomine auctoris sui*) used as a preface to it. In the same way an Arian commentary on Job has slipped in among the works of Origen. These little treatises are of a tiresome mediocrity. This is not the case with the *Opus imperfectum in Matthaeum*, an " incomplete " collection of homilies on the Gospel of St Matthew, of which St John Chrysostom has long been regarded as the author, although Arian doctrine is there betrayed in statements lacking no ambiguity.[3] St Thomas Aquinas (who probably read the work in an amended edition) declared that if he had to choose between owning Paris or this book, he would choose the *Opus imperfectum*, if the choice were given him. In it the author speaks in the tone of a Bishop, with much force and

---

[1] J. Zeiller, *Les Orig. chrét. dans les Prov. Danubiennes*, etc., 1918, p. 491.
[2] *Ibid.*, p. 499, where the principal texts are quoted.
[3] *Ibid.*, p. 474.

authority, and extreme bitterness at having seen the erroneous doctrine of Nicea triumph over that of Arius. He also wrote— he alluded to it himself—Commentaries on St Mark and St Luke. Can he be identified with Maximin ? This hypothesis does not pass the bounds of mere probability. The same may be said of a learned attempt to show that the work had been written originally in Greek, which does not seem to have resulted in any sound conclusions.[1]

The *Dissertatio Maximini contra Ambrosium* (such is the title coined by Kauffmann, its first editor) is without literary value. But it is of real importance from the point of view of the Arian attitude towards St Ambrose and of the fortunes of Arianism in Illyria. This compilation is compressed in the margin of a manuscript at Paris (Bibl. Nat. lat. 8907) containing the two first books of St Ambrose's *De Fide* and the Acts of the Council of Aquileia. It comprises three distinct parts. First it is a commentary on a part of the Proceedings at Aquileia ; we know that the Council of Aquileia, which opened on the 3rd September 381, and of which Ambrose was the moving spirit, deposed summarily Palladius of Ratiara (Arcer), and another Illyrian Bishop, without doubt Secundianus of Singidunum (Belgrade), both convicted of Arianism. The Commentary, which is by the Goth Bishop, Maximin, follows the debates in the Council step by step. In a second portion, Maximin quotes various evidence in favour of the Arian doctrine, among others a letter in which Auxentius, the Bishop of Durostorum and a disciple of Ulfila, relates the life of his master. A profession of faith by Ulfila himself is inserted in this letter, which is a source of information of the first order on the life of the Arian apostle of the Goths.[2] After a space, which was no doubt left by the copyist in order to transcribe other texts which were finally neglected, comes the testimony of Palladius —a vehement diatribe against the *De Fide* of St Ambrose, and against his diplomatic methods. The collection closes with a brief appendix which relates the failure of the steps taken by Ulfila, Palladius, and Secundianus, and their partisans, before Theodosius. This last paragraph must

---

[1] Cf. Stiglmayr, Z.K.T., XXXIII (1909), p. 594–597, and XXXIV (1910), p. 1–38 ; p. 473–499. See also Dom Capelle in R. Bén., 1922, pp. 224-233.

[2] Cf. Jacques Zeiller, *op. cit.*, p. 440 et s. This profession of faith is quoted on p. 461.

have been added afterwards in the Vth century, and is not by Maximin.[1]

On the orthodox side we may mention the *Liber contra Arianos* by Foebadius of Agen, who, during St Hilary's exile, held a position of some prominence in Gaul. His mind was without originality, for whom Tertullian's *Adversus Praxean* seems to have been his favourite work, to judge from the clippings and abridgments which he took from it for his treatise addressed to the Bishops of Gaul. In it he aims especially at the second formula of Sirmium (357) which was strongly tinged with Arianism, and at Bishop Hosius of Cordova who had weakly subscribed to it.

Hosius was a hundred years old at the time; this fact explains his error, which his sturdy and long-held sympathy with Nicea made so unexpected, and which he was soon to disavow on his death-bed. When already a very old man he had taken an important position at the Council of Nicea, and had presided at the Council of Sardica, at which apparently the canons were drawn up under his immediate influence. Isidore attributes to him in his *De Vir. Ill.*, § v, two small works which have not come down to us. All that remains by him is a letter to St Athanasius, and another to Pope Julius.

Eusebius, born in Sardinia, and Bishop of Vercelli in 345, after having been for some time a Lector of the Church in Rome, became a courageous co-operator in the work of St Hilary, and suffered exile in 355–6, at the same time as Lucifer of Calaris. He lived at Skythopolis in Palestine, then in Cappadocia, and afterwards in Upper Egypt. Julian's edict set him at liberty; he died on the 1st August 370 or 371. The Church venerates him as a martyr. Among the treasures of the Cathedral of Vercelli is preserved a manuscript of the Gospels, written very probably in the IVth century, perhaps even by the hand of Eusebius, representing one of the most famous pre-Hieronymean texts.[2] According to the testimony of St Jerome,[3] Eusebius of Vercelli had translated the *Commentaries on the Psalms* by Eusebius of Cæsarea, leaving out passages of doubtful orthodoxy. We

---

[1] *Ibid.*, p. 484–488.

[2] Cf. P.L., XII, 9–948. The text has been re-edited by Cardinal Gasquet in the *Collectanea Biblica*, fasc. 111, Rome, 1914.

[3] *De Vir. Ill.*, xcvi. Cf. *Ep.*, lxi, 2.

have only a few letters of his. Some have wished to attribute to him the *Symbolum Athanasianum*, called the *Quicumque*.[1]

The most original of this group of anti-Arian writings is the *Altercatio Heracliani Laici cum Germinio Episcopo Sirmiensi de fide Synodi Nicaenae et Arimensis Arianorum.* It is dated the 6th of the Ides of January, 366. In it we must see, not an imaginary dialogue but an authentic tilt between Heraclianus, a layman, representing the orthodoxy of Nicea, and Germinius the Bishop of Sirmium [2] professing Arianism. Heraclianus who was thrown into prison with two other confessors, vigorously kept up the dispute, which bore upon the divinity of the Holy Spirit as much as on that of the Son. The arguments used are not those of dialectics : at a given moment at the Bishop's orders Heraclianus is boxed on the ears by a reader and a deacon. Nevertheless Germinius refused to hand him over to the imperial justice as urged by the shouts of the crowd. The whole setting of this colloquy has movement and life. It will be noticed that the profession of faith pronounced in the course of the debate by Heraclianus is taken word for word from a passage of Tertullian's *Apologeticum* (§ xxi).

Let me mention further among extant traces of anti-Arian literature a *Tractatus contra Arianos*, the fragments of which, included in a papyrus of the VIth century at Vienna (Cod. 2160, Theol. C 50a) following after St Hilary's *De Trinitate*, are not unworthy of our attention. This work seems to go back to the second half of the IVth century.

VII

To Gregory of Eliberis (Elvira, in Betica) St Jerome attributes quite justly some *tractatus* written "*mediocri sermone,*" and an "elegant book" *de Fide*.[3] Modern commentators have been far more generous, and his "heritage" has been swollen with a quantity of additions of which I should not dare to say all formed part of the original stock.

A great enemy of Arianism,[4] pitiless towards all com-

[1] Cf. C. H. Turner, in J.T.S., I (1900), p. 126.
[2] Cf. Feder in S.B.W., vol. CLXII, fasc. 4, pp. 100–104, on Germinius.
[3] *De Vir. Ill.,* cv.
[4] St Jerome, *Chron.*, ad ann. 2386, i.e. 370 A.D.

plaisance where the Arians were concerned, the fine rigidity of his orthodoxy deserved the praise meted out to it by the Luciferian compilers of the *Libellus Precum*.

A manuscript (XIth century) in the Church of St Vincent de Roda, in Aragon, imputes five sermons to him on the Canticle of Canticles, which were published by Gotthold Heine in 1848. Owing to the disturbance produced by the Revolution of 1848, Heine's publication had passed unnoticed. Dom Wilmart brought it back to the light in 1906,[1] and used it as a criterion to restore other works to Gregory,—in the first place the famous *Tractatus Origenis*, which were published in 1900 by Mgr. Batiffol and Dom Wilmart himself. These consist of twenty homilies, nineteen of which are on the Old Testament, and one on the mission of the Holy Spirit, written by a clever allegorist of moderate literary talent and saturated throughout with Minucius Felix, Tertullian, Novatian, Origen, Hippolytus and St Hilary. The first editors, accepting the tradition of the manuscript,[2] attributed them to Origen whose Greek rendering must have been translated, as they thought, by Victorinus of Pettau. Certain indications[3] compel us to recognise that this is no case of a translation but that we are confronted with a Latin original. It was necessary to go in search of some author who wrote in the Latin tongue, a difficult and often deceptive endeavour. Novatian appeared to be the one, but a deeper examination rendered the combination difficult to adhere to, and disclosed the likelihood of a post Nicene origin for the *Tractatus*. Dom Wilmart found a " close parallelism " between these *Tractatus* and Gregory's sermons on the Canticle of Canticles : " The same methods of style, the same system of quotations, the same turn of exegesis, the same theological trend ; or, if you prefer, the same characteristic traits reappear throughout, clearly and well defined—a ready suppleness of expression, original views on the Bible, freshness of allegory, and doctrinal *naïveté*, not excluding firmness." [4] What is very singular is that the *Tractatus* (sic) *Origenis*, which combat errors such as anthropomorphism or *patripassianism*, do not

[1] B.L.E., 1906, pp. 233–299.
[2] An Orleans manuscript, no. 22, Xth century ; one at St Omer, no. 150, XIIth century.
[3] V.g. p. 6, 1 ; " ex *humo homo* dicitur."
[4] B.L.E., 1906, p. 249.

breathe a word about the Arian question which outweighed all others in the life of Gregory. This objection has an answer to it ; we have said that St Hilary himself only interested himself very late in Arianism. The West showed some strange ignorances, but it did not fail to make its impression notwithstanding.

A sermon on Noah's Ark, a " type " of the cross, has since been " restored " to Gregory,[1] and the *Liber de Fide* which St Augustine erroneously imputed to St Gregory of Nazianzen,[2] and has come down to us in two editions, the second of which bears traces of retouching by the author.[3] The question of the ὁμοούσιος is frankly approached this time.[4]

VIII

St Augustine has related the attractive history of C. Marius Victorinus in his *Confessions* (VIII, ii). He obtained it from a priest, Simplicianus by name, who had been the intimate friend of Victorinus. Born in the African Pro-Consulate about the year 300, Victorinus followed the calling of rhetor in Rome. He was accounted one of the wisest and most eloquent men of his time. He had even allowed a statue to be erected in his honour in the Roman Forum (or perhaps in the Forum of Trajan). In spite of a certain urbanity natural to him which he preserved throughout his life, he does not spare the Christians some hard knocks of this kind : " In the opinion of the Christians the following argument is not conclusive :—' If she brought forth a child it was because she had connection with a man ' ; nor this either :—' If he was born, he will die.' For the Christians admit the existence of a Being who was born without the intervention of man, and who did not die." Augustine tells us that his heart was " the impregnable retreat of the devil " (*pectus, quod tam inexpugnabile receptaculum diabolus obtinuerat*, VIII iv, 9), and that his tongue, like a sharp arrow, had slain many souls.

In order the better to combat Christianity, he set himself to read assiduously " Holy Scripture and all the Christian

---

[1] *R. Bén.*, XXVI (1909), p. 1.
[2] *Ep.* cxlviii, 10. It occurs in various places in Migne (XX, 31 ; XVII, 549 ; LXII, 449, and P.G., XXXVI, 669).
[3] Dom Wilmart, in S.B.W., vol. CLIX (1908), fasc. I.
[4] V.g. P.L., XX, 35 ; 37–38 ; 39 ; 40 ; 41 ; 44 ; etc.

literature." Undertaken with a frankly hostile intention
this inquiry was to start him on the way to unexpected
conclusions. He felt a growing sympathy springing up within
him for the doctrine against which he was seeking weapons.
He went so far one day as to say privately to Simplicianus,
" Don't you know well that I am already a Christian." To
which Simplicianus replied, " I shall not believe you, and
I shall not count you as a Christian so long as I do not see
you in the Church of Christ." " Do walls then make men
Christians ? " Victorinus laughingly exclaimed. The fear
of causing sorrow to his friends and arousing lively hatred
for some time made his steps slow along the road he was
taking. One day, however, blushing over his delays, he
said suddenly to Simplicianus, " Come to the Church !
I mean to be a Christian." Without restraining his joy
(*non se capiens laetitia*), Simplicianus at once conducted him
to it. Victorinus passed through the various stages of a
catechumen, " *mirante Roma, gaudente ecclesia*," St Augustine
says. When the day came on which, as was customary,
he was to make his public profession of faith, the Roman
clergy offered to read it to him behind closed doors so as to
spare his *amour propre*. Victorinus refused. He mounted
on the platform. His name passed from mouth to mouth,
then a great silence fell and " he pronounced the formula
of truth with such a fine confidence that all would have liked
to seize him and give him a place in the deepest recesses of
their hearts " (. . . *volebant eum omnes rapere intro in cor
suum*).

Up till then he had given himself up to learned works and
metaphysics. It is not easy to discern in the *Ars Grammatica*
what portion properly belonged to him and what should be
attributed to a grammarian, by name Aphtonius, whose
work seems to have been compiled with his own. His
commentary on Cicero's *Inventione* is not important otherwise
than in informing us of the method of instruction followed
by the rhetoricians in the IVth century. A *De Definitionibus*
which had strayed in among the writings of Boethius should
be restored to him. But it was in philosophy that Victorinus
interested himself far more than in philology or grammar
(" qui philosophorum tam multa legerat et dijudicaverat,"
St Augustine remarks). As a confirmed neo-Platonist he

had translated Porphyry's *Isagogé*[1] and apparently various works of Plotinus.[2] It was he who initiated St Augustine into neo-Platonism at a critical period in his views, and it was from his example that he received a decisive impulse. *Exarsi ad imitandum,* he confesses. Victorinus also translated Aristotle's *Categories* and the Περὶ ἑρμηνείας, thereby exercising a leading influence on the logicians of the Middle Ages through the intermediary of Boethius.

A dialectician before everything else, he applied his aptitude and taste to the defence of the Christian faith once he had embraced it. The Arian dispute attracted him especially on account of its metaphysical rather than its historical character. He brought to it his customary charm[3] sounding a different note amid those hard-hitting polemics, and his firm belief in the sovereign competence of the reason even where it bases its support on Scripture.[4] St Jerome appraised the works of Victorinus somewhat harshly. He finds them very obscure and accessible only to the learned (". . . valde obscuros, qui nisi ab eruditis non intelliguntur ").[5] In another place[6] he reproaches him with his ignorance of Holy Scripture (certain portions of which he had commented upon). " It is no use being eloquent," Jerome remarks ; " it is not possible to discuss competently a subject one knows nothing of." As a matter of fact, there is no doubt that Victorinus had read the Bible closely ; but as he had become a Christian very late, and was wholly penetrated with neo-Platonism, he did not see his way, like so many others, to renounce the philosophy which had been dear to him ; he endeavoured rather to draw attention to the help which even orthodoxy might derive from it in the arduous comprehension of the relationship of the Son to the Father (which he

---

[1] A restored version by P. Monceaux of this Latin *Isagogé* by Porphyry appears in *Mélanges Havet,* Paris, 1909, pp. 296–310 (following one of the commentaries of Boethius).

[2] On this point see Alfaric, *L'Evol. intell. de St Augustin,* 1918, p. 375.

[3] In his discussion with Candidus, the Arian, of which a little work entitled *Liber de generatione divina* (P.L., VIII, 1013–1020) has been preserved, and which is connected with the refutation of the Arians, he calls his adversary *O generose Candide, O mi dulcissime Candide,* etc. . . . There is also a letter from Candidus to Marius Victorinus (P.L., *ibid.,* 1035).

[4] He felt the danger of this prepossession and says : ". . . Ne quis blasphemiter intellegens meum dogma dixerit, omnia enim a sancta Scriptura et dicuntur et sunt " (*Adv. Arium,* I, xlvi ; P.L., VIII, 1076-C.).

[5] *De Vir. Ill.,* ci.

[6] *Comm. in Gal.,* Praef.

represents as analogous to that of the One and the νοῦς of the metaphysics of Plotinus),[1] of the theory of creation,[2] and the explanation of original sin.[3] Deep down in the mind of Victorinus, the system of Plotinus holds a place of first importance. From this proceeded certain statements and certain rather disquieting reserves,[4] sincerely Christian as he had become. He would never have accepted the Christian doctrine if he had not had the happy astonishment of finding so many occasions of " utilising " his favourite concepts, to which he strains in more than one place to refer it.

His style has force, movement and even a kind of pious melody (as for example in his three hymns to the Trinity). Victorinus formed for the Latin of the West a new language of philosophy which was to be of great help to the logicians and metaphysicians of the Middle Ages. He tried, as far as he could, to transpose Greek expressions into Latin and apologises when he cannot find the equivalents.[5] To sum him up, Victorinus, without having a great mind himself, has influenced great minds. In the history of ideas he has his place, more by what he has transmitted than by what he created himself.

[1] See details and references in Tixeront, *Hist. des Dogmes*, II, 266 ; 268.
[2] *Ibid.*, p. 273.
[3] p. 278.
[4] He admits that man is under the influence of the stars so long as he is not a Christian and has not acquired *in suis actibus libertatem* (*ad Gal.*, II, 3 ; P.L., VIII, 1175–6). The same idea comes out also in Hippolytus of Rome and Clement of Alexandria. The manner in which he expresses himself on the resurrection of the body has an idealism which might lend itself to equivocal interpretation (*ad Eph.*, ii, 9 ; P.L., VIII, 1274 A). He seems to attribute to matter a maleficent power by which original sin might be explained (*Adv. Arium*, I, xxvi ; P.L., VIII, 1060 A), etc.
[5] V.g. *Adv. Arium*, II, ix (P.L., VIII, 1095 A) ; *ibid.*, II, xi (1097 A).

CHAPTER II

ST AMBROSE, BISHOP AND DIPLOMAT

BIBLIOGRAPHY

THE first edition of the works of Ambrose appeared in Venice in 1485. No decided progress in establishing the text was realised before the edition brought out by the Benedictines Du Frische and Le Nourry, published in two sets in Paris between 1686 and 1690. The Benedictine edition was reproduced by Migne, P.L., vol. XIV-XVII. A very faulty re-impression of Migne, with fresh pagination, was brought out in 1879. It also served as the basis of P. A. Ballerini's edition, published in Milan between the years 1875 and 1883. Ballerini was satisfied with collating certain Milanese manuscripts. His work, handsomely produced, has been severely criticised. A large portion of Ambrose's exegetic treatises have found a place in the *Corpus Script. Eccl. lat.*, through the labours of Schenkl. See Table V.

Consult: Tillemont, vol. X (1705), p. 78, a conscientious and indispensable guide; A. Baunard, *Histoire de St Ambroise*, 2nd ed., Paris, 1872, very ably combined, but more literary than scientific; Th. Foerster, *Ambrosius, Bischof von Mailand, eine Darstellung seines Lebens und Wirkenes*, Halle, 1884, an excellent monograph; Duc de Broglie, *Saint Ambroise*, Paris, 1899, important for the political activity of Ambrose.—A large number of pieces have been translated by P. de Labriolle, and combined with analyses, in his *St Ambroise*, Paris, 1908 (P.C.).—Ihm has set out the chronology of Ambrose's works in the *Jahrbucher fur Klassische Philologie, Supplementband*, XVII (1890), p. 1 et s., following the results already obtained by the Benedictines Du Frische and Le Nourry. Many fertile discussions are included also in Rauschen's work, *Jahrbucher der christlichen Kirche unter dem Theodosius dem Grossen*, Freiburg-im-Breisgau, 1897.

The language of Ambrose has not yet been thoroughly studied. Useful indications will be found in Steier's *Jahrbucher fur Klassische Philologie, Supplementband*, XXVIII (1903), pp. 553-562; Francesco Lora, *Saggio sintatico comparativo su Girolamo, Agostino, Ambrogio*, Padova, 1900; Engelbrecht, *Philologisches aus Augustinus und Ambrosius* (*Zeitsch f. die oesterr. Gymnasien*, LVII, 7), C.W. (Carl Weyman), Rh.M., 1909, p. 328; P. Canata, *De Synt. Ambrosiana in libris qui inscrib. de Officiis*, Catanna, 1911.—We may mention also in connection with the iconography of Ambrose an article by Wieland in the *Römische Quartalschrift*, 1909, p. 132 et s.

SUMMARY

I. A Bishop in the IVth century. The rôle of St Ambrose.—II. His life until becoming a Bishop.—III. His intellectual formation.—IV. His political action. The Altar to Victory. The affair of Callinicum. The Penance of Theodosius.—V. His literary work. The *De Officiis*.—VI. Treatises on the ascetic life.—VII. Exegetic Treatises.—VIII. Dogmatic Treatises and the Ambrosian Hymns.—IX. The Prestige of St Ambrose.

I

On a page of his Etudes Historiques,[1] Chateaubriand has
given in forcible language the *rôle* of a Bishop in the IVth
century : " There is nothing more complete or well filled
than the life of the prelates of the IVth and Vth centuries.
A Bishop baptised, acted as confessor, preached, prescribed
private and public penances, issued anathemas and lifted
excommunications, visited the sick, ministered to the dying,
buried the dead, ransomed captives, gave relief to the poor,
the widows and orphans, founded hospitals and lazar-houses,
administered the goods of his clergy, adjudicated as a Justice
of the Peace in private suits and arbitrated on the quarrels
between different cities. At the same time he published
treatises on moral, discipline, and theology, wrote against
heresiarchs and philosophers, interested himself in science
and history, dictated letters to people who consulted him
on one or other religion, corresponded with Churches and
Bishops, monks and hermits, sat in Councils and Synods,
was called in by Emperors to advise them, was charged with
the arrangement of affairs, and despatched to usurpers and
barbarian princes to disarm or restrain them : three powers—
religious, political, and philosophical—were concentrated in
the Bishop."

The features of this picture drawn by Chateaubriand were
provided for the most part by the life of St Ambrose ; and
we are not surprised a few lines further on to encounter the
name of the Bishop of Milan.

In St Cyprian and St Hilary we have already admired
finished examples of those magnificent churchmen who were
the light and support of so many souls. But how different
was their lot to that of Ambrose ! Proscribed and hunted
down by the Roman authority, Cyprian could only develop
his initiatives in a setting that was relatively narrow. For
reasons of another kind, Hilary felt in an equal degree the
weight of the animosities engendered by power. Ambrose,
during nearly twenty years, from 378–397, was the adviser
of Gratian, Valentinian II and Theodosius, and the dispenser
of imperial favours, and on more than one occasion gave them

---

[1] *Etude, Œuvres complètes*, ed. Pourrat, Paris, 1836, vol. V, p. 268.

the assistance of his diplomacy [1] when their authority was in need of it. This favour, however justified it was, suffered its eclipses, we need hardly say ; it could not fail to exasperate those at the imperial court who wished to monopolise it to the exclusion of Ambrose. The Bishop rode victoriously over the most dangerous crises. He had made himself too formidable owing to the close solidarity uniting him with his people, and too necessary on account of the wisdom of his counsels, that he could easily be put down and dispensed with. Responsible for the future prosperity of the Empire, how could Gratian, Valentinian II, and Theodosius have misunderstood the absolute devotion with which the fervour of his Roman patriotism inspired the Bishop ? The interests which he defended were as dear to him as to themselves ; with them he suffered the first assaults upon the majesty of Rome inflicted by the barbarians ; his reverence for the *res publica* was part and parcel of his faith itself.

Little by little there formed in this lofty mind the magnificent idea of a Christian Empire whereof the Catholic faith should be the cement : " O sacred nail," he cried in his funeral oration on Theodosius (alluding to the Nail of the Cross which Helena had sent to Constantine to set in his diadem), nail which holds the whole world together, and which serves as ornament to the brow of sovereigns in order that those who have long persecuted the faith may become its heralds : *ut sint praedicatores, qui persecutores esse consueverunt !* " [2] Dying before the taking of Rome by Alaric, Ambrose did not live to see the overthrow of this grandiose dream under the shock of invasions. That he should have been able to conceive it is a sign of the times, and marks the fresh stages that Christianity had passed through on its painful and then triumphal road.

II

WE do not know the exact date of the birth of Ambrose. [3]

---

[1] See P. de Labriolle, *op. cit.*, p. 95 et s., on his painful missions to Maximus.

[2] P.L., XVI, 1465.

[3] We have three principal sources for learning the character and life of Ambrose : (1) Ambrose in his works, especially his correspondence (91 letters) ; and a passage in *Ep.* xlviii, 7, enables us to conjecture that he took pains himself to form a kind of collection of his letters. (2) The biography of Ambrose, written by the deacon Paulinus about twenty-five years after the death of the Bishop. This *Vita*

It should be placed between the years 330 and 340.[1] His family had been Christian for a fairly long time ; among its members it counted a martyr, Sotheris a virgin, who had been put to death during the persecution of Diocletian. Ambrose's father exercised the high function of Pretorian Prefect among the Gauls, at Trèves. When he died, his widow brought her three children, Ambrose, Satyrus and Marcellina, to Rome. We have hardly any details of the early life of Ambrose ; but he undoubtedly received the education of the young of his class. He passed through the school of grammar and rhetoric, and received the imprint of this intellectual discipline like so many others.

The example of his father could not but incite him to enter upon the same *cursus honorum*. He attached himself to the person of Sextus Petronius Probus, Pretorian Prefect of Italy from 368–376, and his powerful protector conceived so much esteem for him that it was not long before he entrusted him, after a short period under his own immediate direction, with the government of the Provinces of Liguria and Aemilia, with the title of Consul.

Ambrose thus settled at Milan, the Episcopal See of which was then filled by Auxentius who belonged to the Arian party. When Auxentius died a year after the arrival of Ambrose, the choice of his successor occasioned lively debate among the Christians of Milan, of whom some were partisans of Arius, while others held firmly to the orthodox faith. The opposing factions met in the basilica to discuss the matter. Ambrose, fearing trouble, felt he ought to be there in person. Paulinus, his biographer, tells us (§ vi), " He was haranguing the crowd when the voice of a child suddenly cried, ' Ambrose Bishop ! ' All the people repeated this cry, and thereupon the disputing between Arians and Catholics gave place to a marvellous and incredible unanimity." Ambrose was little expecting such an honour. His first motion was to

---

Anbrosii was translated into Greek. Papadopoulos-Kerameus published in 1891 at St Petersburg a Greek text which should go back to the VIIIth or IXth century. Paulinus throughout aims at edification. (3) Indications and testimony of ecclesiastical contemporaries ; these *testimonia* are to be found in Ballerini's edition, I, p. xvi et s. There is in existence a *Commentary* on the blessing of Jacob (cf. Genesis, xlix) which is ascribed to Paulinus of Milan. It is printed in P.L., XX, 715–732. Dom A. Wilmart has recently drawn attention to a manuscript of Troyes, no. 804, IXth century which gives the real author as Adrevald, doubtless the monk of Fleury-sur-Loire who died in 878 or 879. See *R. Bén.*, 1920, pp. 57–63.

[1] Cf. *Ep.* lix, 4.

fly from it. But unexpected though it was, the choice appeared so excellent to all that he had to resign himself to submit. The Italian Bishops and then the Emperor Valentinian gave it their approval. Ambrose received baptism (it had been deferred until then according to the custom of those times), and eight days after, the priesthood, on the 7th December, 374.

III

AMBROSE, suddenly made a Bishop under the impulse of popular enthusiasm, found himself in a very paradoxical position. Without any preliminary theological training or any special education for it, he had, right from the outset, to exercise Episcopal authority, " to instruct before having even learnt," [1] as he confesses with his customary simplicity. If we may attribute to him with certainty a rather free translation of the *Wars of the Jews* by the historian Josephus, which several manuscripts ascribe to him (while others give a certain Hegesippus as the author),[2] we must conclude that even before his episcopate he had interested himself in religious history. But taking everything into account, the attribution of the authorship to him rests extremely doubtful.

The very high conception which he formed of his duties made him feel keenly what was wanting in him on the speculative side proper. His first care then was to read assiduously Holy Scripture in order to make of it his life's blood and his food. There are few ecclesiastical writers as fruitful as he in quotations from the Bible. I would not dare to say that the modern reader would always find them perfectly opportune or could bear them without some impatience. But Ambrose would not have understood that anyone could

---

[1] *De Off.*, I, l. 4 : ". . . Factum est ut prius docere inciperem quam discere." Cf. *de Paenit.*, II, viii, 72.

[2] Text in P.L., XV, 1961–2224 ; special edition by C. Fr. Weber and J. Caesar, Marburg, 1864. Bibliog. in O. Scholz, *die Heges. Ambrosius Frage*, Breslau, 1913.—The translator alludes in his preamble to a Latin transposition in the form of a historical account of the four books of Kings which he had already made. This indication led Dom Morin (*R. Bén.*, 1914, pp. 83–91) to suppose that the true author was Dexter, the son of Pacian of Barcelona, to whom St Jerome dedicated his *De Vir. Illustr.* The work on the Kings was preserved in a Latin account of the death of the Machabees which may be read in twenty manuscripts.

wish to divert him from exploring as widely as possible the source of all truth and all philosophy.

Again, he had to make himself familiar with the workings of Christian thought, whether to fit himself to be able to interpret the Scriptures, or for theological controversy. The curious thing is, that in spite of his practical and realistic mind which should have brought him in touch with the West, he almost entirely neglected their writings. He was unacquainted apparently with Tertullian and St Cyprian. There is hardly anyone except Hippolytus of Rome who drew his attention. It was to Eastern writers that his sympathies and curiosity went out. He felt their superiority from the speculative point of view, and that in them he would find ready to his hand the weapons he needed in his struggle against the heterodoxy of the times. It was a short step for him to find himself at once on their side. Philo and Origen became his masters in exegesis. For moral and dogmatic instruction he had recourse to the most well-known Greek ecclesiastics of his day, Athanasius, Basil, Cyril of Jerusalem, Didymus, Epiphanius and Gregory of Nazianzen, making himself master of their writings with avidity, even of those which had only just appeared. We see him making use of the theological discourses given by Gregory of Nazianzen at Constantinople in 380, for his own *De Spiritu Sancto* which was written during the first half of 381.

In this way, by constant study of the sacred Books and the best Greek and Hellenistic exegetists and theologians, he was successful in acquiring the foundations of ecclesiastical learning in which he was wanting; these were rather jumbled and lacking in order, but failing any striking originality it revealed in him a remarkable power of assimilation.

The constant practice of public speaking obliged him to filter and clarify this adventitious theology for the benefit of those he was instructing, and he made it his own, thanks to his labour in adaptation. His catechetical instructions at the same time provided him with the matter for nearly all his works. After he had spoken he wrote it down either from his own notes or memory, or from a report taken down in shorthand; it sufficed him to arrange the subject matter and any connecting links, and the book was ready at the cost of a slight revision. This was clearly a risky method as far as artistic presentment was concerned. How could Ambrose prevent a few of the gaps permissible in a spoken discourse, and even some of the ready witticisms in which a public audience delight, from creeping into his explanatory renderings ? He remained faithful to this method, however, to the end of his career ; it economised valuable time, and once he saw that it did not compromise edification which was his sole thought, it mattered little to him that a few fastidious minds were so narrow as to find fault with it.

IV

MOREOVER, the domain of literature properly speaking was not that in which Ambrose showed his full capacity, and in which his labour was most fruitful. Direction of souls, and the utilisation of different characters and circumstances for the benefit of the Church formed the real field in which he triumphed. We must therefore first study his practical activity—not in all its consequences, but selecting a few significant features.

One of the most famous episodes of his public life, the matter of the Altar to Victory, brought him up against the followers of the pagan religion. From the year 380 his ascendancy over Gratian was firmly established. Gratian was pleased to regard him as a father and guide, and possibly it was at his (Ambrose's) instigation that in 382 he decided to renew the struggle against paganism which had been suspended for the past eighteen years by the policy of toleration pursued by Valentinian I. By an edict he deprived the colleges of their priests and the vestals of their revenues. The allocations allotted to the exercise of their religion were suppressed for the benefit of the public treasury, and the same thing happened to the foundations bequeathed to these colleges by legacy. Finally, as the crowning point of these vexations, Gratian ordered the removal from the Chamber of the Curia of the famous statue to Victory which from the time of Augustus had stood upon an altar, as the symbol to the Senators in their Assembly of the glorious Roman past.

The Senators who were pagan resolved to send a deputa-

tion to Gratian praying him to annul so wounding a measure.
But their Christian colleagues, who already formed a majority
in the Curia, formally refused to associate themselves with
them and, through the intermediary of Ambrose and Pope
Damasus, made known to the Emperor their decision.
Gratian did not receive the deputation.

In the following year, on the 25th August 383, Gratian
fell at Lyons beneath the blows of the usurper Maximus.
Valentinian II, still very young—he was about twelve years
old—assumed the responsibilities of power.   The pagan party
thought this a good opportunity to return to the charge.
At that time, in 384, Symmachus, one of the most distinguished representatives of that party, occupied the position
of Prefect of Rome.   The Pretorian Prefect of Italy, Vettius
Agorius Praetextatus, was also a confirmed follower of the
ancient religion.   The occasion seemed to be propitious.
Towards the middle or the end of the summer, Symmachus
drew up his famous Report which a delegation of Senators
placed in the hands of the young Emperor.[1]

Modern critics have found this petition cold and half-
hearted.   It is deserving of a more favourable appreciation.
Written in a style of sober elegance, its mission was to defend
" ancestral institutions, and the rights and destinies of the
fatherland " :

> " What !   Is the Roman religion outside the rights of
> Romans ? " exclaims Symmachus.   " Freedmen share
> the legacies which have been bequeathed to them :
> we do not refuse to slaves the legal advantages which
> testamentary dispositions concede to them : and shall
> noble virgins, ministers of a sacred cult, be excluded
> from the possessions which come to them by succession ?
> What profit to them to devote their chastity to the public
> safety, to assure protection from on high for the Empire
> so long as it shall last, to bring to your arms, to your
> eagles, the agency of friendly powers, to offer up for
> you their efficacious vows, if they have not the enjoy-
> ment of common law ? " (§ 13).

And, calling up the mighty image of Rome in a kind of
prosopopoeia, he puts into its mouth words instinct with

[1] Ed. Seeck, M.G.H., VI, 1, p. 280.

majestic sorrow in order to deplore the assaults of which such venerable traditions had just been the victim.

When read at the Emperor's Council this document produced a powerful effect. Christians and pagans seemed for one moment to be agreed to give it a favourable reply. Ambrose understood that he would have to act at once. In a letter to Valentinian (*Ep.* xvii) he took steps to show him how groundless were the grievances of which Symmachus had made himself the interpreter :

> " They come and make complaint of their losses—those who were so little sparing of our blood and who have laid our Churches in ruins ! . . . They claim their privileges from you when, but yesterday, the laws of Julian refused to us the right devolving upon all to speak and instruct. . . ." (§ iv).

By what right did the pagans claim to impose on their Christian colleagues, in the same Curia even, the statue of a religion condemned by them ? Ambrose implored Valentinian in the name of his dead brother and on the conscience of a Christian Emperor, to reject the petition :

> " The present question is one concerning religion, and I intervene therefore in my capacity as a Bishop. . . . If a decision contrary to us be taken, we Bishops cannot accommodate ourselves to it with a light heart, nor dissimulate our opinion. You may lawfully come to Church, but you will not find there any priest, or he will only be there for the purpose of protesting " (§ xiii).

This warning had its full effect. Valentinian decided, against the advice of his council, to make no change in the measure proposed two years before by Gratian. The rebuff to the pagan party was complete. To make it still more damaging, Ambrose drew up a detailed reply to the petition of Symmachus in the form of a letter to Valentinian (*Ep.* xviii). Taking the arguments of Symmachus one by one, he set himself to destroy any close connection between the glory of Rome and the sacred rites of the official religion. He let fall the heavy weight of his irony on the desolation of the vestals and the priests deprived of their revenues, and to these well-paid offices of devotion opposed the magnificent disinterestedness of the Church :

> " The Church possesses nothing, except it be the faith : therein are her revenues, therein her benefits. The maintenance of the poor is her patrimony. Let our adversaries tell us how many captives their temples have ransomed, how many poor they have supported, and to how many exiles they have provided the means to live ! "

Then sharply rebuking the reactionary complaints of Symmachus and his superstitious cult of the past, he does not hesitate to affirm the inevitable character of the evolution through which humanity, freeing itself from religious forms henceforth passed away, was advancing towards a truth becoming more and more luminous and complete.

His cause was heard. In spite of many attempts ventured upon before Theodosius, Valentinian II and Eugenius, the pagan element never succeeded in regaining entirely what it had lost. And it is an undoubted fact that the Bishop of Milan was the principal instrument in this humiliating defeat.

The affair of Callinicum, quite a local incident, only deserves to be mentioned here because we see in it very fully the inflexible and high-handed firmness of the Bishop once the *prestige* of the Church appeared to him to be threatened.

During the year 388, Theodosius was informed by a report from the *Comes Orientis*, the commander of the Roman troops in the East, that very serious disorders had broken out in the town of Callinicum, one of the chief cities of the province of Osroene (Mesopotamia). Some monks who had been roughly handled by the partisans of a Gnostic sect had set fire in reprisal to one of their sanctuaries. A still more vexatious proceeding, and one to which the Emperor gave special attention, was the burning of a Jewish synagogue at the instigation of the Bishop of the town.

Anxious for the preservation of public order, Theodosius judged that strong measures should be taken. He ordered the synagogue to be rebuilt at the cost of the Bishop, whom he considered to have been responsible.

On receiving news of this, Ambrose, who was at Aquileia,

returned in all haste to Milan, with the intention of formally opposing the step taken by the Emperor. Seeing that he was by no means inclined to grant him an audience, he addressed a letter to him (*Ep.* xl), in an attempt to induce him to withdraw his decision. He reproached him for not having even called for a report from the Bishop, and for having condemned him unheard. He recalled to his recollection similar proceedings on the part of the Jews, when they had often taken the gravest responsibilities upon themselves without much notice having been taken of them. He protested, above all, against the injury done to the Catholics, who had been humiliated before the Jews and obliged to rebuild with Christian money a synagogue, a den of impiousness. " If my personal credit is too weak," he concluded, " deign to call together any Bishops you please. Let them examine what can be done without bringing harm to the faith. In questions pertaining to money, you consult your Comites : is it not still more just to consult, in matters of religion, the ministers of the Lord ? " (§ 27).

This urgent presentation of the case did not produce at first the effect which Ambrose had hoped. The Emperor made no reply to it. Ambrose then resolved on a bold stroke. He has himself related in a letter to his sister (*Ep.* xli) the setting of the scene he made use of. In a full Church he reminded the Emperor in a series of allusions from his Bishop's throne of the responsibility of his duties, and of the debt of gratitude to heaven he had incurred, and invited him to " protect the body of Christ " in order that Christ Himself might protect his Empire. At the conclusion of his sermon he stepped down :

> " ' Is it of me that you have been speaking ? ' the Emperor asked : ' I said what I thought to be my duty in order to help you.' ' Yes,' he replied ; ' the order I gave to have the synagogue restored by the Bishop was too harsh, but I have softened it down. The monks are much too forward ! ' I remained standing some little time, and then said to the Emperor, ' Act so that I can offer the Holy Sacrifice for you in full assurance. Lift the weight off my soul.' The Emperor, who was seated, made a gesture of agreement but without any

formal promise. I stayed planted in front of him. He told me he would amend his rescript. I asked him to issue at once his commands on the matter. . . . He promised me that this should be done. ' I have your word ? ' ' I give it.' Then only did I go up to the altar which I should not have approached if he had not made me a positive promise " (§ 27–28).

Such was the firmness with which Ambrose dared to speak to so powerful a man as Theodosius once it seemed to him that the Emperor was trespassing beyond his right.

Still more famous is the penance which he imposed upon him after the massacre of Thessalonica. The seat of the Governor of Macedonia, Thessalonica in 390 was the theatre of a rising springing from trivial causes in which a certain number of functionaries perished. Theodosius was profoundly annoyed at this. Ill advised by his counsellors, he sent a savage order which he did his best to revoke soon afterwards, but when too late. A large part of the people of Thessalonica, who were assembled in the circus under the pretext of a display, were massacred by soldiers let loose upon them.

When the news of this dire event became known in Milan, many Bishops happened to be assembled at a Synod there. The general view was that a public expiation should be demanded from the Emperor. Ambrose, whose close relations with Theodosius were well known, felt that it was incumbent upon him to obtain his submission and to make him understand that he was excluded from the Church on account of his crime and that he could only obtain re-admission at the price of sincere repentance. He did not wait for Theodosius, then absent from Milan, to return ; though in great ill-health himself, he left the city and addressed confidentially letter li to the Emperor from a distance. After some discreet remonstrances that Theodosius had purposely kept himself away while he was devising these abominable reprisals, he made known to the Emperor categorically the duty incumbent upon him—the duty to repent and do penance, the example of which had been given to him by David and other personages in the Bible. Together with phrases testifying to his affection he introduced a note of menace : it would be impossible for him as a Bishop to offer the Holy Sacrifice before a sinner who had done nothing to restore the communion of the Church.

What was the attitude of Theodosius in face of this respectful summons ?   That he brought himself to repent is certain ; but over the details of this historic penance modern criticism raises serious difficulties.[1]   According to the Greek historian Theodoret,[2] when the Emperor wished to enter the Church Ambrose stepped in front of him and forbade him to set foot within the sacred precincts.   Even to this day, in Milan, an ancient column marks the spot where tradition states the Bishop and Emperor met.   Unfortunately Theodoret has mingled many blunders with his account, which renders it suspect.   Neither Rufinus, St Augustine, nor Ambrose himself, speak of any such impressive exclusion. There is here then a very obscure historic problem.[3]   Moreover, the renown of Ambrose does not rest in any degree on one or other of the solutions presented to us ; if the episode related by Theodoret were nothing but pure fiction, we still have the fact that the confidential letter of Ambrose to Theodosius was sufficient to decide the Emperor to undergo the humiliation of a public penance, which is attested unanimously by contemporary evidence.

Taken as a whole, we can say that the religious policy of Ambrose had a triple object in view : first, the protection of the Church against all violence or indiscretion on the part of the State : " In questions affecting the faith, it is the Bishops who are the judges of Christian Emperors, and not the Emperors who are the judges of the Bishops." [4]   Next, to make the civil power respect the moral law, even in acts deprived of any religious character, under pain of the censure of the Church.   And lastly, to seal a close union between Church and State of such a kind that, far from placing the different religions on the same level, the State should unfailingly show its special and single favour to the Catholic religion, and discourage all others.

We are not called upon to approve *en bloc* all the steps taken by Ambrose in the politico-religious affairs in which he was mixed up.   Was his success over the incident of

---

[1] Cf. my *Saint Ambroise*, p. 136–147.
[2] *Hist. eccl.*, V, xvii (P.G., LXXXII, 1232).
[3] It deserves fresh examination.
[4] *Ep.* xxi, 4.

Callinicum of such a kind that we can give whole-hearted praise to it ? Certainly Theodosius might have proceeded with less heat and more caution than he first showed, by waiting for an explanation from the Bishop, and making the town pay the expense, and not the Bishop in his own person. But in all justice, total immunity would have been to show excessive leniency likely to encourage the promoters of disorder.

With this reservation once made it is impossible not to see in Ambrose a habitual and very noble regard for equity. Thus he did not hesitate to brand in most vigorous terms the inhumanity of the Bishops who wrung from the imperial power the punishment of death for Priscillian and his partisans under the pretext of magic and immorality, but in reality for heresy.[1] He was far from thinking that the State should be indifferent in matters of doctrine, and freely suffer them to dispute for the possession of souls ; but he did nothing to counteract that genuine liberalism towards persons which the State observed. Never were high pagan officials discharged from their posts once they were serving well,[2] and St Ambrose was the first to render service to them when he could.[3]

It was a benefit that, outside any desire for political domination, there should rise in face of the all-powerful Emperor another power strong enough, although unarmed, to impose a moral check upon him, and oblige him to confess his faults when the occasion arose. It was through Ambrose that the people learnt what clement mediation, what sheltering guardianship the Church was henceforth to offer to the caprice and violence of their princes—a lesson it was not likely to forget through succeeding ages.

V

It is time we came to the literary work of St Ambrose. I have already hinted that it provides some disappointments. Ambrose had neither the depth and gift of verbal creation of

---

[1] *Ep.* xxvi.
[2] The poet Prudentius noted this : *Contra Symmachum*, I, 616 et s.
[3] See the letters of Symmachus to Ambrose, M.G.H., VI, 1, 80 and 82, with introduction, p. cxxviii.

a St Augustine, nor the ardent imagination, the impassioned fire, and scientific aptitude of a St Jerome. The most interesting portion is his Correspondence. In it the man of action is depicted, with his energy, practical wisdom, and real goodness, the attractiveness of which was felt so keenly by those who knew him. In some places, occasionally, we are a little disappointed to see him wasting time over the little elegances of style, and the imitations and mannerisms of a past age which the taste of the period represented as literary excellence. Ambrose's composition is seldom irreproachable, and his form of expression itself lacks originality. Burdened with more urgent tasks, he never had the time to improve on the form or to aim at perfection.

Nevertheless his books, into which he was far from putting his principal energy and the best of himself, do not fail to offer considerable interest from the point of view of a record of his ideas. They are of value as documents on the moral doctrines of Christianity in the second half of the IVth century.

We know with what subtle and penetrating considerations St Ambrose's *De Officiis Ministrorum* has inspired a critic like R. Thamin.[1] The work is one of those which enable us to *mark the point* forming a landmark on the road followed by succeeding generations. Certainly Christianity has been incessantly concerned with moral problems, both theoretical and practical, but with the exception of the *Institutiones* of Lactantius, a very miscellaneous work by an honest, conscientious mind of limited scope, there was not yet in the IVth century any synthesis comparable to those which the Greeks, and after them, the Romans, had sometimes attempted.

In his *De Officiis* Ambrose nowhere assumes the tone of a thinker who is proposing to give a *Summa* of the moral principles with which he had identified his faith and life. Far from proclaiming any such ambition he seeks the most modest *formulæ ;* it is a simple conversation on moral questions which he wished to have with his clergy, by means of which he took occasion to rectify many philosophic ideas current among the pagans. He even declares that he is little concerned to present any methodical explanation and that it is

---

[1] *Saint Ambroise et la morale chrétienne au IVᵉ siècle. Etude comparée des traités De Officiis de Cicéron et de Saint Ambroise,* 1895.

sufficient for him to paraphrase the beautiful examples of which the Scriptures offer such a rich harvest.[1]

In fact, there is much freedom of choice and disconnectedness in the work. There, as elsewhere, Ambrose observes a very free style, to which his habit of preaching had accustomed him. Again, whom was he addressing ? Were they the clergy only, or the Christian body ? Was it a strictly clerical system of moral doctrine that he outlined, or one that was simply Christian ? His hesitation is sometimes excusable ; hence a certain lack of clearness and unity.

It remains to say that Ambrose followed Cicero very closely both in his general scheme (in spite of certain digressions which were necessary to his particular point of view) and in the setting forth of his ideas, and sometimes even in his expressions. I have already indicated in what spirit he made this kind of transposition,[2] and the fresh support he supplied to many precepts of tradition. In each one of his exhortations we find, on analysis, an amalgam of Stoicism and Christianity, but it is the latter which forms the preponderating and decisive element. Nowhere do we obtain a clearer idea at what particular point the basic doctrines of Christianity— the belief in a Providence, the firm trust in the immortality of the soul and of a reward beyond the grave, and especially faith in Jesus Christ—have ousted numerous moral problems.[3]

VI

THE treatises on the ascetic life present a special side of the moral teaching of Ambrose, and make us understand one of the favourite forms of his propaganda among the faithful.

From all parts of Italy, and even from Africa, young girls were coming to Milan to take the veil. These *opuscula* are derived, at least partly, from the sermons delivered by Ambrose in honour of virginity. The *De Virginibus*, the first in point of date, goes back probably to 377. In it Ambrose states that when he wrote it he was *nondum triennalis sacerdos*. It was addressed to Marcellina, his sister, who

---

[1] Cf. I, xviii, 72.
[2] Introd., p. 31.
[3] In this connection see Brochard's reflections, *Etudes de Philos. anc. et de Philos. moderne*, p. 493.

had herself made her profession of virginity, and who, associating herself in all the works of her brother, had become the spiritual directress of some young girls who had resolved to live in the same state. Shortly afterwards, the *De Virginitate* appeared (in which Ambrose refutes objections raised by the *De Virginibus*), and the *De Viduis* in which the Bishop addressed himself exclusively to widows. In 391, thirteen or fourteen years afterwards, he wrote the *De Institutione Virginis*, on the occasion of the taking of the veil by Ambrosia, a young girl who had been intrusted to his ministrations. Lastly, the *Exhortatio Virginitatis*, published in 393, is nothing else than a sermon preached by Ambrose at Florence on the occasion of the commemoration of the martyrs Vitalis and Agricola.

Ambrose did not nourish any systematic hostility against marriage. With his customary good sense and his care for strict fairness, he also abstains from certain brutal misogynisms of which ecclesiastical writers have not always been sufficiently sparing. He guards himself against wishing to discountenance or discredit marriage. He regarded it as a permanent union which divine law forbids to be broken, and one in which the husband should predominate and be the *gubernator*. On the question of re-marriage, he is much more severe. From an early date Christian tradition had looked suspiciously at a second marriage. Ambrose too saw in it a mark of weakness, a want of self-control. Notwithstanding this, he refuses to consider it in the light of a sin: *Neque enim prohibemus secundas nuptias, sed non suademus.*[1] And if he discountenances it, this is entirely from ascetic reasons and considerations of a practical order which he does not omit to develop in full detail. As regards the state of virginity, it is in his eyes that virtue which is pre-eminently Christian. It existed of course among the pagans, but in their case it was inspired by purely temporal motives. In the Christian religion alone was virginity practised from supernatural motives and it enhanced itself by an incomparable moral purity. He had no hesitation, therefore, in order the more cogently to urge souls to renunciation, in marking the worries which usually accompany the state of marriage, and in praising in the most enthusiastic terms the incom-

---

[1] *De Viduis*, xi, 68.

parable sacrifice consummated by the virgin.   He endeavoured
also to unravel the difficulties in the moral and even economic
order which were raised in Milanese society against the
maxims he was advocating.   Furthermore, all these criticisms,
although he refuted them one by one, must break in pieces
against an argument which, in the opinion of Ambrose, would
dispense with the necessity of giving any others.   And this
was that virginity, as a vocation freely chosen, is of divine
institution which the Virgin Mary protects with her example
and patronage.

Such in broad lines is the doctrine of Ambrose on marriage,
re-marriage, and virginity.   He has certainly contributed
in large part to attach to the ideal he thus traced the high
value it has retained in the bosom of Catholicism.

VII

As I have already said, nearly all the works of Ambrose were
spoken before being written out ; and if they were put into
writing it was because he wished that what he preached
should be heard beyond the circle of his Milanese audience
which was too narrow for his taste.   It was to his pastoral
eloquence that he owed his most efficacious influence over
souls.   On this point, we have the direct testimony of St
Augustine, a constant hearer of Ambrose even before his own
conversion : " I was very zealous," he relates in his *Confessions* (V, xiii), " in hearing him deliver his dissertations
in the midst of the people, and his words held my irresolute
attention.   In truth, I was not curious, I was even disdainful,
over the deeper matters, *but the sweetness of his discourse
enthralled me.*"

We know that one of the favourite themes on which
Ambrose loved to expatiate was the immorality of the contrast existing between the extreme poverty of some and the
unbridled luxury of others.   Particularly significant from
this point of view is his sermon on Naboth which most likely
dates from one of his last years.   With a vigour which recalls
the invective of the Roman satirists and moralists, he brands
the greed of the rich and the oppression they make weigh
heavily on the poor.   He even does not shrink from reminding

them of the altogether conventional and arbitrary character of human property. The " political economy " of Ambrose, if it is not too ambitious a term, is penetrated through and through with charity and love.

To gain an idea of his catechizing, we must read his *De Mysteriis*. In it St Ambrose addresses the catechumens who had already received Baptism and the Eucharist, and explains to them the profound signification of the ritual which had been carried out before them or upon them. In order to anticipate objections or doubts which might arise in their minds, he takes pains to demonstrate to them that nothing is indifferent in what they had seen, that everything carried a mysterious meaning and a moral efficacy, and was the instrument of regeneration prefigured in so many writings of Scripture.

Constant recourse to Scripture was the usual method of St Ambrose in his sermons. " Holy Scripture," he wrote to Bishop Constantius,[1] " is a sea which has in itself deep meanings and all the mystery of prophetic riddles." To the deciphering of these riddles he devoted his exegetic treatises which form the bulk of his work.

At the outset we are astonished that St Ambrose found leisure to draw out such copious paraphrases from the Scriptures in the midst of a life taken up by so many diverse cares. But when we come to analyse them the matter is fairly intelligible. It was out of his daily task of preaching that he produced the greater part of these lesser works.[2] Thus the *Exameron* (to take this as an example) is made up of nine sermons which were preached on six days running during Lent. Six homilies are included in the first, third, and fifth books—two in each book. The other books, the second, fourth and sixth, are composed of only one homily each. And here and there we are able to mark traces of their origin, which Ambrose had not troubled to remove : the finishing words or resumption of a sermon ;[3] an allusion to the day which is declining ;[4] and to the fatigue of his listeners.[5]

It is beyond dispute that in his time Ambrose had real renown as an exegetist. From all parts people consulted

---

[1] *Ep.* ii, 3.

[2] Sauvage and Tougard re-edited (Paris, 1895) a sermon by Victricius of Rotomagus (Rouen), *De Laude Sanctorum :* cf. P.L., XX, 443. See E. Vacandard's *Saint Victrice, Evêque de Rouen* (iv–v cent.), 1903 (Coll. *Les Saints*).

[3] *Exam.*, I, vi, 24 ; V, xxiv, 92.   [4] V, xxiv, 84.   [5] VI, 1, 1.

him on difficulties presented by the Old and New Testament. Nevertheless, from the historical point of view, his method of interpretation offers nothing really fresh. In no way aiming at writing scientific treatises on sacred hermeneutics, but solely desirous of offering his sheep the truths pertaining to salvation in a form most fitted to move them, Ambrose from preference employed what is called the allegorical method of exegesis. From the first days of Christianity St Paul had employed it ; it had, besides, for long been held in honour among the Jews, who themselves owed the idea to Greek philosophy. Thus quite a tradition authorised its use ; but it was especially in the East, in the hands of Clement of Alexandria and Origen, that the use of allegory had been raised to a system with deliberate intention. According to Origen, allegory should serve to exclude from Scripture any contradictions, improbabilities, and those " stumbling blocks," " pitfalls," and " mysteries " which it had pleased the Spirit of God to sow " in the faith and the records," and conse-quently it should distinguish the real intentions of the inspired authors from appearances, and render clear the sub-stance of their teaching.

It would not be accurate to say (as sometimes has been wrongly said), that St Ambrose was the first to introduce allegorical exegesis in the West. In order to render this assertion null and void, it is sufficient to mention the names of Tertullian, the author of the *De Cibis Judaicis*, and St Hilary of Poitiers. But Ambrose gave to it special import-ance because it enabled him to multiply *ad infinitum* edifying considerations in connection with texts, and to combat effectively the heretics with whom he happened to be dealing. Was it not by this means that he made a conquest of the intelligence of Augustine who was still imbued with very many Manichaean prejudices ? [1] His special authorities were Philo the Alexandrine Jew, and Origen. He mentioned them but rarely by name ; he even came to combat their views. But in point of fact he used them as his favourite guides to get beyond the literal meaning to what he calls the *sensus altior* or the *subtilior interpretatio*.[2]

Allegorical exegesis is no longer to modern taste. We know the Bible far less well than the Christians of the first

[1] *Confessions*, vi, 4.
[2] A very accurate analysis of his different methods will be found in Kellner's *Aubrosius als Erklarer des alten Testaments*, Regensburg, 1891.

centuries who made it their favourite and almost sole sustenance.

Let us learn however to recognise in it the principle of an art which, at least in the order of architecture, was to produce marvels, and of a profoundly idealistic conception of the universe. It is the allegorical interpretation of the Bible which has habituated Christian thought to seek symbols for everything, to go in search of pure spirit behind outward appearances, and to see in each form the mark or covering of an idea. This mystical conviction, so different from the proceeding usual in science, was to impose upon generations of writers, liturgists, and artists, the search to decipher the handiwork of God, wherein everything consisted of prefiguration, instruction, and mystic concordance suitable to engendering piety. The genius of the Middle Ages already was breathing in the exegetic work of St Ambrose.[1]

It is in this class of writing too, especially in the *Exameron*, that Ambrose most developed literary quality properly so called, rhetorical effect and distinction. The *Exameron* became the model and the principal source of those *Mirrors* from nature in which the theologians of the Middle Ages represented the picture of the universe even in the order of the creation. At Chartres, Laon, Auxerre, Lyons, Bourges, and many other towns, the six days' work has been sculptured in synthetic representations on the sides of our Cathedrals.[2]

VIII

WE do not possess all the dogmatic treatises of St Ambrose. Three works at least have been lost, the *De Sacramento Regenerationis sive de Philosophia*, to which St Augustine often alludes ; the *Ad Pansophium Puerum*, attested by Paulinus, his biographer (§ 28) ; and the *Expositio Fidei*, from which Theodoret, Bishop of Cyr, quotes a fragment.[3] Among those which have come down to us we must mention first the *De Fide*. The two first books, written in 378 at the express desire of Gratian, bear the impress of the haste in

---

[1] See H. Hauvette, *Dante*, 1911, p. 281 et s.

[2] The Greek and Latin *Examerons* have been studied by F. Egleston, in *The Hexaemeral Literature*, Chicago, 1912 ; cf. K. Gronau's *Posidonios und die judisch-christliche Genesisexegese*, L. and B., 1914. A special study of St Ambrose's *Exameron*, its sources and its philosophy, would be a useful contribution to the history of Christian thought.

[3] *Eranistes*, ii.

which Ambrose had composed them. The general outlines
of the subject are sketched out rather than deeply fathomed,
as even the author acknowledges.[1]　In 380, two years later,
Ambrose revised his treatment of it and gave it all the fulness
which he thought it deserved. At this period of controversies and heresies it was important to fortify the young
Emperor with precise ideas upon the *depositum fidei*. Ambrose
wrote this treatise at the very time when Gratian, informed
of the disasters which the imprudence of Valens was preparing
for the Empire, was making ready to start for the East. This
is how at the end of the second book (II, xvi, 136), Ambrose
breaks off for a moment in his exposition of doctrine to express
to the Emperor in a " chant de guerre à la fois pieux et
patriotique," [2] his good wishes for his victory, and to affirm
the solidarity henceforth established between the religion of
Christ and the destinies of Rome. The three books of the
De Spiritu Sancto, likewise dedicated to Gratian, were put
together in 381. In order to deal with this difficult question
Ambrose availed himself of the principal resources of contemporary Greek theology. We recognise in the *De Spiritu
Sancto* ideas from Athanasius, Cyril of Jerusalem, Basil,
Didymus of Alexandria, Gregory of Nazianzen, and Epiphanius of Salamis. St Jerome, who always was very
sparing in his praise of Ambrose, could not refrain from discharging an epigram at his indiscretion shown in these
borrowings.[3]　Even before Ambrose had completed the work,
the challenge of two Arian chamberlains at the court of
Gratian [4] led him to deliver a public statement on the mystery
of the Incarnation; from this instruction issued the *De
Incarnationis Dominicae Sacramento* which appears to have
been published between the *De Fide* and the *De Spiritu
Sancto*. The *De Paenitentia* was written between the years
380 and 390, and was directed against the partisans of
Novatian who had remained faithful to that heresiarch's
ideas after the lapse of a hundred and thirty years. In the
first book Ambrose claims the absolute right of the Church
to bind and loose sins, and refutes the arguments which

[1] III, l, 1.
[2] De Broglie, *Saint Ambroise*, p. 28.
[3] P.L., XXIII, 103 (Preface to the translation of the *De Spir. Sancto* by Didymus
of Alex.).
[4] Cf. the *Life* of Ambrose, by Paulinus, § 18.

those rigorists deduced from certain texts from Scripture. The object of the second book is to inculcate the necessity of penance for expiation and pardon. In fact, it does not enter into the mind of Ambrose to mitigate in the slightest degree those just satisfactions which are required for the wiping out of sins ; but his natural moderation made him feel acutely the imprudence of the attitude of the Novatians, and the danger arising from the apparently heroic demands which that sect did not shrink from proclaiming.

Doctrinal considerations are not absent from the *De Excessu Satyri* either. The first book is nothing more than the setting down in writing of the touching funeral oration which Ambrose delivered in the Cathedral at Milan on the day of his brother Satyrus' funeral. In the second book is incorporated the sermon given seven days later before the tomb. It contains further outpourings of memories and regrets, but also quite philosophic developments on the universal and beneficent law of death, the rigour of which was wonderfully softened by the promise of the resurrection. The same concern is evident in the hymns which Ambrose wrote in iambic dimeters to serve as a useful vehicle for the propagation of orthodox ideas against the Arians, as St Hilary had done before him. Of the hymns, which are called Ambrosian, four are certainly authentic,[1] the *Æterne Rerum Conditor*, the *Deus Creator Omnium*, the *Jam surgit Hora Tertia*, and the *Veni, Redemptor Gentium*. Eight others are doubtful, and critics differ in their opinion as to the correctness of attributing them to Ambrose. In 386 Ambrose had preferred to undergo a regular siege, shutting himself up in the Porcian basilica with a multitude of the faithful, rather than hand it over to the Arians as the Court had ordered him to do at the instigation of the Empress Justina. In order to keep up the spirits of this crowd of people who had nothing to do, it occurred to him to introduce into the office the alternating chant of psalms and hymns. This custom seems to have had its rise at Antioch, and from there it had passed into use among the Christian communities of the East. Thanks to Ambrose, it soon spread throughout the West.[2]

[1] See Ermoni's " Ambroise (saint) Hymnographe ", in the *Dict. d'Arch. chr. et de Lit.*, I, 1347 et s. ; Walpole, Notes on the text of the Hymns of S. Ambrose, in J.T.S., 1908, p. 428–436.

[2] Paulinus, *Vita S. Ambrosii*, § 13, Saint Augustine, *Conf.*, ix, 7.

IX

IT is sufficient to run through the list of *testimonia* collected in modern editions to realise that Ambrose was soon considered by his contemporaries, in the East as well, as a " pillar of the Church," " the pearl glistening on the finger of God," and " the flower of Latin writers." From his see at Milan he exercised a kind of moral primacy over the Churches in Illyria. This was well seen at the Council of Aquileia (3rd September, 381); it was manifestly he who laid down the summary procedure through which, in spite of their subterfuges, the Arian Bishops Palladius of Ratiara and Secundianus of Singidunum found themselves punished by being deposed.[1] He laboured from a distance at the conversion of a German tribe, the Marcomanni. His biographer relates (§ 36) that in the last years of the IVth century, Frigitil, their queen, asked him to instruct her in the Christian religion by correspondence. Ambrose acceded to her wishes and, animated always with his desire to serve Rome, begged her to work upon the mind of her husband to remain at peace with the Empire. A few years later, Ambrose, together with Jerome, Gregory and Augustine, was to be numbered among the Doctors of the Church, who at first were four in number, as we know—" like the four rivers of Paradise," remarks a monk of the Middle Ages.[2]

[1] J. Zeiller, *Le Christianisme dans les Provinces Danubiennes,* p. 328 et s.

[2] *Ioannis monachi liber de miraculis* (viii–ix cent.), ed. Hoferer, Wurzburg, 1884, p. 47.

CHAPTER III

THEOLOGIANS OF THE SECOND ORDER

BIBLIOGRAPHY

I. AMBROSIASTER (c. 366-384), P.L., XVII, 45-508.—Consult: Cumont, R.H.L.R., 1903, p. 417; Wittig, *der Amb. Hilarius (Sdraleks Kirchengesch. Abh. 4,* Breslau, 1906); Souter, in *Expositor*, 1914, pp. 224-232.

II. DONATISM.—Consult: Monceaux, vols. IV and V.

III. ST OPTATUS.—P.L., XI, 883-1082; Ziwsa, in C.V., vol. XXVI (1893). One of the *tractatus* published by Dom Morin in 1917 *" Sermo in Natale infantium qui pro Domino occisi sunt"* (p. 170) is attributed to Optatus in the *Cod. Aureliensis,* 154, s. vii/viii.—French Translation by Pierre Viel, 1664.—Consult: L. Duchesne, *Le dossier du Donatisme,* in the *Mél. d'Arch. et d'Hist. publiés par l'Ecole franc. de Rome,* X (1890), p. 589-650; Monceaux, V, 241-306.

IV. TYCONIUS.—P.L., XVIII, 15-66; F. C. Burkitt in T.S., 3, 1 (1894). The *Commentary on the Apocalypse* was still in existence at St Gall in the IXth century. Some fragments of it have been published in the *Spicilegium Casinense,* III, 1 (1897), p. 261 et s. An attempt at its reconstruction by J. Haussleiter in *Zeitsch. f. Kirchl. Wiss. u. Kirchl. Leben,* VII (1886), pp. 239-257. Cf. H. L. Ramsay in R.H.L.R., 1902, pp. 433-444.—Consult: Hahn, *Tyconius-Studien,* L., 1900 *(St. zur Gesch. der Theol. u. der Kirche,* 6, 2); Monceaux, V, 165-219.

V. PACIAN.—P.L., XIII, 1051-1090; Peyrot, Zwolle, 1896 (mediocre). Dom Morin, from reasons of similarity of style which are hardly conclusive, attributes to Pacian the *Liber ad Justinum* often imputed to Victorinus *(R. Bén.,* 30 [1913], p. 286-293).

VI. FILASTER OF BRESCIA.—P.L., XII, 1111-1302; Marx, in C.V., vol. XXXVIII (1898).

VII. GAUDENTIUS.—P.L., XX, 827-1006.

VIII. ZENO OF VERONA. — P.L., XI, 253-528. A critical edition by Giuliari, Verona, 1883; 2nd ed., 1900, unchanged.—Consult: Monceaux, III, p. 365-371.

IX. HILARIANUS.—P.L., XIII, 1097-1114. These works are dated the 24th and 25th March 397. Re-edited by C. Frick, in the *Chronica Minora,* I, Leipzig, 1892 (B.T.), p. 153-174. See also Mommsen, M.G.H., XIII, 415.

X. NICETA OF REMESIANA.—P.L., LII; A. E. Burn, *N. of R.,* Cambridge, 1905: The *Sermones de Vigiliis* (Burn, pp. 55-67) are in P.L., LXVIII, 365-376; the *Sermones de Psalmodiae Bono* (Burn, pp. 67-82), in P.L., XXX, 232; the *De Ratione Paschae* (Burn, pp. 93-111), in P.L., LXXII, 49-52 and P.G., XXVIII, 1605-1610; the *Ad Lapsam Virginem Libellus* (Burn, pp. 112-131), in P.L., XVI, 367-384. Burn's edition has all the importance of a leading basic work. Consult: W. A. Patin, *N., Bischof von R.,* Munchen, 1909.—Numerous observations on the language of Niceta in A.L.L., 1906, p. 481 et s. See also Patin, chap. v.

XI. PRISCILLIAN.—Schepss, in C.V., vol. XVIII (1889).—Consult: E. Ch. Babut, *Pr. et le Priscillianisme (Bibl. de l'Ecole des Hautes-Et.,* sc. histor. and philol.), fasc. 169. A. Puech, in the *Journal des Savants*, 1911, and B.A.L.A.C., 1912, p. 81 ; 161.

SUMMARY

I. Ambrosiaster. — II. Donatism.   Optatus of Milevis.   Tyconius. — III. Pacian of Barcelona.—IV. Filaster of Brescia.   Gaudentius.   V. Zeno of Verona.—VI. Hilarianus.—VII. Niceta of Remesiana.—VIII. The Affair of Priscillian.

I

SINCE the XVIth century, under the name of Ambrosiaster (pseudo-Ambrose), people have designated the anonymous author of a commentary on the Epistles of St Paul (excluding the Epistle to the Hebrews), which was incorrectly ascribed to St Ambrose in the Middle Ages and possibly even in the time of Cassiodorus.[1] This paraphrase is really remarkable and is one of the most interesting bequeathed to us by Christian antiquity.   Of an original mind, well versed in the methods of the Law, and possessing very positive views combined with pointed satirical humour in regard to prominent men in the Church, the author carefully avoids losing himself in the mists of allegory.   This disregard of the allegorical method is almost a unique case at that period. Before everything else he aims at a clear comprehension of his text, and sets himself to draw practical lessons therefrom for the use of Catholics.   Let me add, he had his eyes open as to the times in which he was living.   His commentary is a precious source for understanding the pagan mysteries—those of Anubis, Mithra and especially Cybele— whose vitality remained still so powerful in the second half of the IVth century, and we can gather from it the persistence of the belief in astrology by the Christians themselves.[2]

The problem of the identity of Ambrosiaster is particularly irritating.   We even know that he wrote in Rome soon after Julian the Apostate,[3] in the time of Pope Damasus [4] (366–384).   Now this period is fairly well known to us, and it is strange that so vigorous a personality as this " Ambrosiaster," should not be able to be clearly established   All the more

[1] *Instit. Div.*, viii (P.L., LXX, 1120).   Ambrose had promised some homilies on St Paul in one of his letters (*Ep.* xxxvii, 1–2).
[2] Cf. Cumont, R.H.L.R., VIII (1903), p. 417 et s.
[3] *In II Thess.*, ii, 7 (P.L., XVII, 457).
[4] *In I Tim.*, iii, 14 (XVII, 471).

so because another work, the *Quaestiones Veteris et Novi
Testamenti*,[1] (wrongly printed among the writings of St
Augustine), presenting a series of discussions on doctrine,
Scripture, and polemics which are nearly always interesting,
must be restored to him.[2]

Conjectures are not wanting. Dom Morin has shown
a special fecundity in this respect. He first thought of the
Jew Isaac,[3] and the combination offered sufficient attraction for certain critics still to adhere to it, even after he
had relinquished it. This Jew Isaac, after having been
converted to Catholicism, took an active part in the com-
petition of Ursinus with Damasus for the Episcopal See
of Rome; he even brought a serious accusation in law
against Damasus, the matter of which we are ignorant; his
suit went against him and caused him to be exiled to Spain
by Gratian. Isaac ended by returning to the synagogue.[4]
A Paris manuscript (VIIIth–IXth centuries) has preserved
a *Liber Fidei de Sancta Trinitate et de Incarnatione Domini*
by him.[5] Dom Morin thought he noted certain analogies of
language between it and the *Quaestiones* and *Commentary*
on St Paul. Also the caustic turn of mind of Ambrosiaster,
and the special importance he appears to attach to a host of
particulars more or less connected with Judaism were
features which seemed to him remarkably applicable to the
accuser of Damasus. The identification, however, entails

---

[1] *Quaestio* in ecclesiastical language means an examination of passages of
Scripture which are hard to understand. Several of St Augustine's works contain
this word in their title: *De diversis quaestionibus ad Simplicianum*, etc. Cf.
Souter, in T.S., VII, 4, p. 8. Ed. in P.L., XXXV, 2213–2416, and C.V., vol. L
(1908), by Souter. There have been three renderings of the *Quaestiones*: one
contains 151 questions, the second, amended and abridged, 127 questions, and the
third (which was made between the VIIIth and IXth centuries) 115 questions.

[2] The demonstration given by Al. Souter, *A Study of Ambrosiaster*, in T.S.,
VII, 4 (1905), p. 23–160, is quite conclusive.

[3] R.H.L.R., IV (1899), p. 97.

[4] Cf. Mansi, *Conc.*, III, 626, and *Coll. Avellana*, no. 13. Isaac is probably
alluded to by St Jerome, *in Tit.*, iii, 9 (P.L., XXVI, 595).

[5] P.G., XXXIII, 1541–1546 (published shortly after 374).—Certain recent
critics (Wittig, Scholz, etc.) have ascribed to Isaac various works of unknown
origin; for example, the *Gesta inter Liberium et Felicem episcopum* (C.V., XXXV, 1),
the *Fragmenta contra Arianos* (S.B.W., 146 [1903], p. 11), the *de Bello Judaico* of
Hegesippus (P.L., XV, 1962), the *de Concordia Matthaei* (P.L., XVII, 1011), a tract
on St Matthew (Mai, *Nova Patr. Bibl.* I, 1, 477), the famous *Mosaicarum et
Romanarum legum Collatio* (Hyamson, Oxford, 1913; Mommsen, *Coll. libr. juris
ante-justiniani*, B. 1890) wherein several provisions in Roman Law are represented
as being already in existence in the Bible, the fragment of a Comm. on St Matthew
(Mercati, *Studi e Testi*, Rome, 1903; Turner, J.T.S., 1904, 218), and an *Expositio
Fidei Catholicae* (K.A., p. 304).

serious difficulties.[1]   Four years later,[2] Dom Morin brought forward another person, Decimus Hilarianus Hilarius,[3] a man connected with the State, concerning whom, moreover, there is no evidence enabling us to say that he made any practice of writing, even occasionally.   Finally, in 1914, after comparing the biography written by Evagrius with the personal information escaping from the writings of Ambrosiaster, and the Latin of the translation of the *Life of St Antony*, by Evagrius, with the Latin of Ambrosiaster, he decided to identify the latter with Evagrius of Antioch.[4]   It may be that this fresh conjecture in spite of its being presented as " undeniable and certain," may not enjoy a longer fortune than its predecessors.[5]   The worst thing that minds curious about Christian literature will have to fear is to read the works of Ambrosiaster, resigning themselves to remaining ignorant of the real name of this penetrating and caustic exegetist.

II

WE need not relate in detail here the history of Donatism which absorbed almost all the vitality of the Church in Africa in the IVth century.   Taking birth shortly after the persecution under Diocletian, under the pretext that certain Bishops who had handed over the Sacred Books (*traditores*) were unworthy any longer to remain as directors of their flock, this movement quickly developed, and neither the

---

[1] (1) The author says himself (*Quaestio* cxiii ; Souter, p. 310, 22) : " Cum in errore degeremus in quo nunc manent Pagani . . .", which seems to imply that he had been previously a pagan, not a Jew.   Other texts to the same effect, but not so pronounced, are quoted by Brewer, Z.K.T., 1913, p. 214–216.—(2) The beginning of *Quaestio* cxx resembles completely the opening of a homily by a priest ; now it does not appear that Isaac belonged to the clergy.

[2] R.B., XX (1903), p. 113.

[3] Pro-Consul of Africa in 377 ; Prefect of the City in 383 and 408 ; Pretorian Prefect of Italy in 396.   Cf. C.I.L., VIII, 1219 (an inscription at Vaga, in Africa). Ambrosiaster is quoted by St Augustine under the name of " Sanctus Hilarius " (*Contra duas Epist. Pelag.* IV, iv, 7 ; cf. *Ambros.* v, 12 [P.L., XVII, 92]).

[4] R.B., XXXI (1914), p. 1–34.

[5] The expressions *ac per hoc*, and *hinc est unde*, real peculiarities of style with the author of the *Commentary* on the Epistles of St Paul, and of the *Quaestiones*, are not found in the *Life* of St Antony.   Ambrosiaster shows a certain antagonism to the Greek ecclesiastical writers.   Now Evagrius was from the East and did not come to Italy before 363–4, when he was already married.   Lastly the silence of St Jerome in his *De Vir. Illustr.* on such important works is difficult to understand.   His notice of Evagrius (§ cxxv) only makes very vague allusion to *diversarum ὑποθεσέων tractatus* not yet published.   Dom Morin points out these objections himself, but does not succeed in lessening their importance.

intervention of the imperial power nor the conferences arranged between Catholics and Dissidents succeeded in checking it. Very many elements foreign to the initial causes of this crisis violently stirred up the passions of both sides :—old disputes in connection with the necessity of re-baptising, on the duty of keeping the Church immaculate, and on the obligation to seek martyrdom. Local patriotism and personal matters ended by embittering the conflict in which " circumcelliones," [1] robbers and incendiaries, mingled their lawless violence.

Like all great movements based on ideas, Donatism brought forth a fairly considerable amount of literature, of which we are in a position to form an approximate estimate thanks to the detailed refutations of orthodox polemists,[2] which remained for long without any serious reply from the Catholic side. It will be noticed that Donatism, unlike Arianism, had its seat in the West. There do not appear to have been any Greek Donatists, and there was no Greek Donatist literature.

Ought we to make a distinction between Donatus the Great, Bishop of Carthage, and Donatus, Bishop of *Casae Nigrae ?* [3] It is at least doubtful, and it is possible that this duplication of names may have been invented afterwards by the Donatists. However this may be, the head of the sect composed a large number of writings, also a *liber de Spiritu Sancto*, which bordered on Arianism according to St Jerome.[4] All of this is lost.

Parmenianus is known to us through St Augustine's *Contra Epistulam Parmeniani* and the treatise of Optatus of Milevis. Although a Spaniard or a Gaul, he became the head of the schismatic church in Africa, and Bishop of Carthage after the death of Donatus. He only took posses-

---

[1] The original form of the word seems to have been *circelliones* (from *circellus* meaning *fibula :* cf. schol. *ad* Juvenal., vi, 379), that is, the " continent ". The sobriquet *circumcelliones*, grafted in derision on to the first, has another signification, that of *circum cellas vagantes*. Donatus restored the original sense by the term *agonistici* (Optat. III, iv) : *agonisticus* meaning *miles Christi :* cf. St Augustine, *Enarr. in Ps.* 132. See Reitzenstein, in the *Nachrichten Gott.*, 1914, 1, p. 90.

[2] Monceaux (V, 35 et s.) has devoted a special study to the *passiones* of the Donatist martyrs.

[3] Cf. Dom Chapman, in R.B., 1909, p. 13 et s. ; Monceaux, IV, p. 20, note 1 ; V, 99 et s.

[4] *De Vir. Ill.*, xciii.

sion of his Episcopal See just after the abrogation by Julian the Apostate of the Edict of Constantius, which from the year 347 had kept the Donatist leaders in exile.   He had the heavy task of reorganising the sect in the midst of the trouble which Julian (perhaps purposely) had let loose, and he was remarkably successful.   He was a man of high intellect and a certain moderation ;   his Catholic opponents spoke of him with deference.   In a long treatise of five books written possibly about the year 362–3 immediately after his return to Africa, he attempted an apology of the Donatist Church [1] to the detriment of Catholicism.   In his *Letter to Tyconius* he hit back vigorously against his criticisms in regard to his co-religionists.   His collection of *Psalms* was intended as an incentive to the piety of the Donatists.[2]

In 411, Gaudentius of Thamugadi (Timgad) was one of the seven advocates of Donatism at the Conference of Carthage presided over by Marcellinus, who helped to win the cause for the Catholics, and was a delegate from the Emperor Honorius.   In 420, when the Tribune Dulcitius promulgated his edicts against the Donatists, Gaudentius declared that rather than hand over his basilica he would prefer to be burnt in it together with his following.   It was then that at the request of the embarrassed Tribune St Augustine wrote his *contra Gaudentium* which brought him a pamphlet in the form of a letter from his opponent which he answered in a second book.   We do not know the issue of this affair,[3] which should be placed about the year 420–1.

We must further mention Vitellius to whom Gennadius [4] ascribes a *De eo quod sint mundo Dei servi*, and *Adversus Gentes*, and divers works relating to the *regula ecclesiastica ;* Cresconius the grammarian, also refuted by Augustine in 406 ;   the priest Macrobius [5] who later on was to become the secret head of the Donatist community at Rome and had written, when still a Catholic, a *Liber moralis ad Confessores et Virgines*.   The *dossier* of Petilianus, the Donatist Bishop of

---

[1] There is a reconstruction of the plan of this treatise by Monceaux in the *Journal des Savants*, 1909, p. 158 et s., i.e. the *Hist. litt. de l'Afr. chr.*, v, 227 et s.

[2] Cf. St Augustine, *Ep.* LV, xviii, 34.

[3] Monceaux has described it in detail in the *Rev. de Philol.*, XXXI (1907), p. 111–133.

[4] *De Vir. Ill.*, iv.   Gennadius places him in the time of Constantius (337–350).

[5] *Ibid.*, v.   The *de Singularitate clericorum* has been attributed to Macrobius : see above, and Monceaux, V, 151 et s.

Cirta, has become far more important,[1] thanks to the research of M. Monceaux ; it comprises an *Epistola ad presbyteros et diaconos Donatistas adversus Catholicam,* two letters to St Augustine, a *Liber de Schismate Maximianistarum,* an *Epistula de ordine partis Donati,* a *de Unico Baptismo,* and different discourses given at the Conference of Carthage in 411. These titles and a few meagre fragments can be established by the writings of St Augustine.

The most interesting personality among the Donatists is this same Tyconius over whom Augustine was so much exercised. " He was a Donatist, but of a very special kind, a layman who mixed himself up in theology and was able to enlighten the Bishops thereon, a man of study who observed with interest the disputes between the Churches, and who in the independence of his views claimed to preserve his freedom of speech, a philosopher who knew the Bible better than anyone else but interpreted it in his own way without fearing to clash with opinions already established . . . , lastly, a polemist solicitous for the truth, ready to allow that his opponents were not always in the wrong and to tell his friends that they were not always in the right." [2] There is nothing so detestable to parties as those censorious minds who refuse to submit their judgment to sectarian catchwords. In two works which have been lost, the *de Bello Intestino,* written about the year 370, and the *Expositiones Diversarum Causarum,* in 375,[3] but of whose contents we have some approximate knowledge thanks to allusions thereto by St Augustine, Tyconius did not hesitate to controvert the Donatists on a certain number of points without making any breach with the Donatist Church. Parmenianus, the head of this schismatic Church, refuted him in that *Letter to Tyconius* which, some years later, St Augustine in his turn was to turn against him.[4] Tyconius was finally condemned in 380 by a Donatist Council.

He also wrote a *Commentary on the Apocalypse* of which

---

[1] *Rev. de Philol.,* XXX (1906), p. 218 et s. ; XXXI (1907), 28 et s. *Hist. litt. de l'Afr. chr.,* V, 309–328.

[2] Monceaux, *Journal des Savants,* 1909, p. 162 : cf. *Hist. litt. de l'Afr. chr.,* V, 165 et s.

[3] Titles mentioned by Gennadius, *de Vir. Ill.,* xviii.

[4] The *Letter to Tyconius* is analysed by Monceaux, *ibid.,* p. 164 et s. *Hist. litt.,* V, 231 et s.

various later commentaries on the same book enable us to form some idea. But the work which is most admired was his *Liber Regularum*, written about 382, which may be considered as the first manual of Biblical hermeneutics to appear in the West. The object of Tyconius was to establish rules of interpretation enabling edification to be drawn from the Bible from every portion as it were, even from passages the most unpromising in appearance. From the first beginnings of Christianity texts from the Bible had largely been used by exegetists, polemists, compilers of *tractatus*, etc.; repertories had even been formed in which every one might seek according to his requirements. But there remained a considerable residue, a *prophetiae immensa silva*, in the words of Tyconius, the moral and religious significance of which did not appear at first. Tyconius flattered himself that he had discovered a method by means of which these sterile and neglected texts might be assimilated with the efficacious ones : " Si ratio regularum sine invidia, ut communicamus, accepta fuerit, *clausa quaeque patefient et obscura dilucidabuntur*. . . ." These *regulae* seem to us to be passably ingenious ; what is certain is that his contemporaries were enraptured with them. While recommending that Tyconius should only be read with due care,[1] St Augustine embodied his seven rules of exegesis in his *De Doctrina Christiana*,[2] thus perpetuating the influence of this vigorous, original, and in more than one case, disconcerting mind.

III

THE first Catholic champion against Donatism, and the most remarkable before St Augustine to do full justice to it, was Optatus, Bishop of Milevis, in Numidia. In 366 or 367 he undertook to reply to Parmenianus, whose subtile dialectics troubled many of the faithful. The Donatists avoided debates in public ;[3] it was in order to reach them in spite of their evasiveness that he wrote his *Libri contra Parmenianum Donatistam*.

The work originally comprised six books. In the 1st

---

[1] *De Doctr. Chr.*, III, xxx.
[2] *Ibid.*, xxx–xxxvii. These rules are explained in Monceaux, V, 182 et s.
[3] *Contra Parm.*, I, iv.

Book Optatus traces the history of Donatism. To do this, he collected ten salient points which he placed in an appendix, and refers his reader to them on different occasions. The authenticity of these documents thus inserted has been contested. Optatus has even been suspected of having been only a forger. Mgr. Duchesne has conclusively proved, as against Seeck, the hollowness of these accusations. The following are the conclusions at which he arrives : " There is no possible reason to doubt the sincerity of St Optatus of Milevis, but we must recognise that he did not handle his documents with the same skill as St Augustine. Neither the accounts given by St Optatus, nor the arguments brought forward by him, should be struck out from the list of historic sources as regards the origins of Donatism. We only need the assistance of other information at our disposal for purposes of classifying and interpreting them." On the other hand, his most recent historian, M. Monceaux, notes in him " two fundamental qualities—loyalty and a taste for precision." The polemics of Optatus present valuable information to theologians ; for instance, when he opposes the great Catholic Church, whose centre and connecting point [1] is Rome, to the little Donatist Church ; when he defines the " marks " of the Church ; when he lays down the rôle of the minister in the administration of the Sacraments (V, iv : *sacramenta per se esse sancta, non per homines*). Let us note too that in Book III, vi–vii, he outlines some kind of justification for the action of the secular power against heresy. His style slightly errs in over-emphasis, but it is clear, accurate, and not without humour.

Twenty years after the publication of his treatise, Optatus took it up again, as it seems, and retouched it in places ; then he added a seventh book of a gentler tone addressed to the Donatists in general (Parmenianus died in 391), in order to answer the contradictions which his criticisms had provoked. This seventh book was not finished, and it is possible that other hands may have inserted certain rather maladroit interpolations. St Jerome was not yet aware of it in 392 when he wrote his notice of Optatus in § cx of his *De Viris Illustribus*.[2]

[1] II, ii.
[2] Cf. Dom Wilmart, in R.S.R., 1922, p. 271-302, on a sermon by St Optat. for the Feast of Christmas.

Pacian need not detain us long. Before everything else he was a somewhat reactionary theologian who thrived on the legacy of ideas bequeathed by Tertullian and St Cyprian, but he knew how to combat with tact and humanity certain rigorist prejudices which went so far as to exclude in perpetuity the sinner from the Church under the pretext of preserving her entire " virginity."

When Bishop of Barcelona, a recrudescence of Novatianism brought him up against a certain Sympronianus, who approved of the severity affected by that sect. Three letters of Pacian remain to us out of the correspondence exchanged between them. In the first, the Bishop claims for the orthodox Christian the right to call himself Catholic in view of the multiplicity of sects. In it this oft-quoted phrase appears : " Christianus mihi nomen est, Catholicus vero cognomen " (1, 4). Sympronianus having again written to him sending at the same time a tract on Novatianism, Pacian gives expression to his views on Novatian himself in a second letter. Then, after having read over again at his leisure the objections of his adversary, he refutes them radically in a third letter in which he quotes numerous extracts. The main idea of Sympronianus is summed up at the beginning of the letter in these words : " . . . quod post baptisum paenitere non liceat ; quod mortale peccatum Ecclesia donare non possit, immo quod ipsa pereat recipiendo peccantes." It is the same spirit as Tertullian's in his *de Pudicitia* when he had become a Montanist, and, whose side the Novatianists of the IVth century still took.

Pacian wrote with taste ; his irony is not lacking in point. He was a lettered man who had read and retained his Cicero, Virgil, and Horace. We have further a *Sermo de Baptismo* in which he points out the renovating effects of baptism on the soul (" . . . aperiam quid fuerit ante gentilitas, quid fides praestet, quid baptismus indulgeat ") ; a *Paraenesis, sive Exhortatorius Libellus ad Poenitentiam,* in which he defines the different kinds of sins, and upbraids those of the faithful who from false pride conceal their faults or who after confessing them evade the necessary expiation, and ends by setting forth the rewards promised to those who loyally carry it out.

He also wrote a *Cervulus* directed against the amusements

of an altogether pagan license which marked the new year. There are numerous allusions in Christian literature to this kind of Carnival which was accompanied by many disorders.[1] Pacian gives such a *piquant* description of them that he was accused (he himself mentions ironically this insinuation at the beginning of the *Paraenesis*) of encouraging the very people he was endeavouring to dissuade from them. Unfortunately the work has not been preserved.[2]

According to St Jerome he died in the reign of Theodosius in extreme old age, before the year 392, the date on which Jerome wrote a short notice of him in his *De Viris Illustribus* (§ cvi).

IV

THE immense heterodox literature of the first Christian centuries has almost entirely perished, such of it, at least, as remains in its original tenor. We are able to form some idea of it from Catholic refutations and the works of heresiographers. The list which in a certain number of manuscripts is joined to Tertullian's *De Praescriptione*,[3] is one of the first specimens of this kind of investigation, a fresh attempt at which we find in the mediocre compilation of Filaster.

" You express a keen desire that I should write something short on all the heresies contrary to the doctrine of our Lord which have swarmed since His coming. . . . Filaster, the Bishop of Brixia (Brescia), whom I have seen with St Ambrose of Milan, wrote a book on the above ; he even made mention of the heresies which showed themselves among the Jewish people before the coming of the Lord, and he counted twenty-eight ; as regards the heresies which have arisen since the establishment of Christianity he counted one hundred and twenty-eight. Epiphanius, Bishop of Cyprus . . . collecting the heresies during the time preceding and following our Lord, only found eighty. Both were endeavouring to

---

[1] Cf. *The Mediaeval Stage*, Oxford, 1903, vol. II. App. N. ; see also the thesis of Boethius mentioned further on, on St Caesarius of Arles.

[2] Dom Morin, basing his view on similarities in language, further ascribes to Pacian : 1. the *De Similitudine carnis peccati*, included in the Paris MS. 13344, IXth cent. (R. Bén., 1912, p. 1 et s.) ; 2. the *Liber ad Justinum Manichaeum* (P.L., viii, 999–1010), usually imputed to C. Marius Victorinus (R. Bén., 1913, 286 et s.).

[3] See above, p. 222.

L

do what you are asking of me, and you see how the number of sects differs ; this would not have happened if what had seemed a heresy to the one had also seemed a heresy to the other. We must not believe that Epiphanius was unaware of the heresies which Filaster knew of, for I find Epiphanius far more learned than Filaster. . . . But it cannot be doubted that over such a matter the two authors were not in agreement as to what was and what was not heretical ; and as a matter of fact, it is difficult to decide this fully. . . . Consider then whether perhaps I had not better send you St Epiphanius' book ; I think he has spoken on this matter with more light than Filaster. . . ."

This appreciation of St Augustine in a letter to Quod-vultdeus [1] should be borne in mind, but we cannot avoid still further accentuating our unfavourable opinion of Filaster from it.

We know very little of even the personality of Filaster. A sermon by Gaudentius, his successor, suggests the idea of a restless and travelled controversialist [2] who throughout the Roman world disputed with pagans, Jews, heretics (especially with Auxentius, the Arian Bishop of Milan), and entered into private and public oratorical contests, even in Rome itself. Whatever Marx, the last editor of the *Liber de Haeresibus* may say, Filaster was most likely of Latin origin ; the characteristics of his language are in favour of this hypothesis. [3]

As to his low intellectual level, it is as low as you like to place it. He had a clumsy mind and though professing to be a heresiologist was incapable of defining with any precision the very concept of heresy, [4] and sought in a puerile manner to

---

[1] *Ep.* ccxxii.

[2] See the *Sermo de vita et obitu Filastri* (P.L., XX, 998) : ". . . Circumiens universum paene ambitum Romani orbis, dominicum praedicavit verbum. . . ."

[3] A good demonstration of this is to be found in P. C. Juret's *Etude gramm. sur le Latin de Saint Filastrius*, a thesis at Fribourg-en-S, 1904 (Roman. Forsch., xix [1906], p. 130 et s.), p. 4–5.

[4] We should say in exculpation that this concept was only made clear fairly late. *Heresy* and *schism* were for long rather confused : see Buonaiuti in *Athenaeum*, IV (1916), p. 168–180 ; Monceaux, IV, 161–2 ; Bayard, *Le Latin de Saint Cyprien*, 1902, p. 183. But how can we admit statements like this (§ cii) : " Alia est haeresis quae terrae motum non Dei jussione et indignatione fieri, sed de natura ipsa elementorum opinatur " ?

establish an artificial symmetry in his notices.[1] There is a paragraph in the *Liber de Haeresibus* which defies the most careful endeavours to interpretate. With all the assurance of mediocrity, Filaster rejects *en bloc* human science, the *inanes sententiae philosophorum*, and the *deliramenta poetarum*, the *mendacia historiographorum ;* every quotation he makes from profane works seem to have been drawn, not from the original texts, but from the ecclesiastical sources he utilises. It is difficult to verify these sources for he mixes up his own extracts with others and with his own personal discoveries.[2] It hardly seems open to doubt, although this has been contested, that he had before him the *Panarion* of St Epiphanius. The *Panarion* must have been finished towards the end of 376, or in the course of the year 377. A thorough examination of the ideas given in the *Liber de Haeresibus* leads us to place its compilation between 385 and 391. Now at this time important works passed very quickly from the East to the West.

We know from Gaudentius, the panegyrist of Filaster, that he was in the East when news came to him of his election as Bishop of Brixia. He hesitated to assume the responsibility of this charge, but St Ambrose and other Bishops wrote to him such pressing letters that he decided to accept it. A highly considered personage, he took part in the embassy sent to the imperial court at Constantinople by Honorius and Pope Innocent I, when St John Chrysostom was condemned to exile. His sermons were held in high esteem. A chance circumstance decided him to put in writing a few of them. A certain Benevolus, *magister memoriae* to Valentinian II, and a pious official who was so attached to the faith of Nicea that he gave up his position rather than collaborate in the law of the 23rd January 386 drawn in favour of the Arians, had been unable through illness to hear the ten sermons delivered by Gaudentius during Easter week. At his request, the Bishop consented to write them out.[3] He added five *tractatus*, four of which were on the Gospel and one on Machabees. Six other writings may be

---

[1] Augustine gives the division selected by Filaster (28 + 128). Filaster divides these 128 heresies which arose during the Christian era into two series of 64 + 64, the first of which is classed κατὰ διαδοχήν, and the second κατὰ δόξαν.

[2] For a full discussion see my *Sources de l'Hist. du Montanisme*, 1913, p. **xxxvi** et s.

[3] Gaudentius gives these reasons himself (P.L., XX, 827 ; 830).

ascribed to him for serious reasons, namely, the *De Ordinatione sui*, the *De Dedicatione Basilicae*, the *Ad Paulum Diaconum*, the *De Petro et Paulo*, and the *De Vita et obitu b. Filastrii* (groundlessly suspected by Marx). His style is simple and correct and shows a classic formation.

V

It is not open to doubt that there was a Zeno, Bishop of Verona, during the second half of the IVth century. In a letter addressed to Syagrius, Bishop of that city, about 386, St Ambrose expresses himself as follows regarding a nun unjustly suspected : " Before giving the matter any consideration you have formed a preconceived opinion against a girl *to whom Zeno, of holy memory, had given his esteem and whom he had sanctified with his blessing.*" [1] We also possess a sermon of Petronius of Bologna delivered at Verona for the anniversary of Zeno, who was the patron of that city.[2] It is singular that neither St Jerome nor Gennadius mention him in their lists of *illustres*. St Jerome seems to have been unaware that his contemporary Zeno possessed any qualifications as a writer. Nevertheless a dozen manuscripts have preserved to us sixteen well-developed sermons and seventy-seven much shorter under his name.[3] Certain indications make us think that Zeno must have been of African origin. One of these *tractatus* is devoted to Arcadius of Cæsarea, an obscure martyr of Mauretania. The author closely imitates Tertullian, St Cyprian, Lactantius, and even Apuleius ; he has gone so far as to find some of his similies in the most *risqué* scenes from the voluptuous sophist of Madaurus.[4] Several of these writings are directed against the Arians,

---

[1] *Ep.* v, 1.

[2] The most recent edition is that given by Dom Morin in the *R. Bén.*, XIV (1897), p. 3 et s. Dom Morin has published *ibid.* for the first time following the *Monac.* 14386, Xth cent., another sermon of Petronius " *in die ordinationis vel natale episcopi.*" The contents of these sermons prove that Petronius was not the Bishop of Verona, contrary to the superscription on the manuscript. The notice by Gennadius (*De Vir. Ill.*, xlii) styles him as Bishop of Bologna.

[3] The manuscripts in reality give 104 sermons, but 11 of them are not by Zeno. A difference in the writing of the oldest manuscript, the codem *Remensis*, has enabled this discrimination to be made.

[4] Compare Zeno, iv, 3 (p. 38, Giuliari) : " Venerem . . . connexis manibus se tegere conantem, immo animi sui vitium et corporis demonstrantem " ; and Apuleius, *Metam.*, II, xvii : " In speciem Veneris . . . reformata . . . feminal rosea palmula potius obumbrans de industria quam tegens verecundia."

pagans and Jews. Others are dissertations on doctrine or moral exhortations. In connection with the history of dogma in the IVth century, as also with that of the Christian religion, the liturgy, and Christian archæology, much may be gleaned from his pages, with their studied and even flowery arguments.

VI

JULIUS QUINTUS HILARIANUS was a Bishop in the Pro-Consulate of Africa. In his *De Mundi Duratione*, he endeavoured to define the duration of the universe by the light of the *Lex Dei*, disregarding the " verbiage " of profane science.[1] As reckoned by Hilarianus, there still remained to humanity 101 years of life at the end of the IVth century.[2] Towards the end, Antichrist would prevail ; then after the revolution of the 6000 years allotted to the world, there would come the resurrection of the dead, the reign of 1000 years (the millennium), the universal judgment, the total destruction of the heavens and earth, and finally, the descent of the City described in the Apocalypse, wherein the just would be happy for ever. In order to understand the importance attached during the first centuries to this kind of calculation, we must remember the long continued anxiety of the Christians regarding the date of Christ's second coming. Practically the Christians were resigned to dispose themselves and arrange their daily life as though the *parousia* were only an uncertain quantity. Nevertheless belief in an end of the world that was fairly imminent remained alert and active : it was one of the mainsprings of their individual morality. The benefits to be anticipated from a Christian chronology were to enlighten them as to whether this gloomy disquietude as to the future might be laid to rest in each one's mind, or whether, on the contrary, it should make them more anxious on account of the proximity of the final catastrophe. At that time they would have deemed rather strange the discouragement felt by modern exegetists when confronted with the difficult task of reconciling the chronological ideas of the Old Testament either with each other, or with those of profane history. Hence the zeal of the old interpreters. However irksome to us their calculations may be, we should under-

[1] Cf. the opening. [2] § xvii.

stand the value they had for their contemporaries.   Where we see only a skeleton framework of somewhat fantastic additions, they read the secret of their own personal destiny and that of the universe, and believed that they had pierced the riddle of the mysterious and dreadful to-morrow.

In the *De Die Paschae et Mensis*, Hilarianus develops and claims to unravel three problems relating to the fixing of the festival of Easter from the course of the moon.   He sums up his conclusions in § xiv, and establishes the difference between the Jewish and Christian calculation.   " Aliud est pascha nostrum, aliud Judaeorum."   In all this chronology, there is more numerical fantasy than solid and real science.   According to the *De Duratione*, § 1, the two *opuscula* form a division into two of a previous work in which they were at first united.

VII

NICETA of Remesiana was the apostle of Catholicism among the Danubian races.   His Episcopal city of Remesiana (Palanka), not far from Nisch, was in Lower Dacia on the road from Naissus to Sardica.   But the evangelising activity of Niceta certainly extended beyond the limits of his ecclesiastical boundary.

Christian antiquity has not overlooked his name.   Paulinus of Nola, who received two visits from him, expresses in his poem XXVII his joy at the thought of seeing him soon,[1] on the occasion of the approaching anniversary of St Felix. Poem XVII is a " Proempticon "[2] in 85 strophes addressed to Niceta on his return to his own country.   In it Paulinus alludes to the happy propaganda carried out by Niceta amidst the barbarian tribes as far as the Riphaean mountains (in the north of Scythia) :[3]

> " Quaque Riphaeis Boreas in oris
> Adligat densis fluvios pruinis,
> Hic gelu mentes rigidas superno
> Igne resolvis."

Again in another place he speaks of the " venerabili

[1] Verses 148 et s.
[2] Cf. F. Iager, *das antike Propemptikon u. das 17 Gedicht des Paulinus v. N.*, Munich, 1913.
[3] Lines 201 et s.   Cf. v. 249.

episcopo atque doctissimo Nicetae, qui ex Dacia Romanis
merito admirandus advenerat. . . ." [1] The second visit of
Niceta to Paulinus of Nola should be placed in 400. He
also figures as one of those to whom the letter of Germanius
to his colleagues in Illyria was addressed in 366 or 367.[2]
Letters XXI and XXII of Pope Innocent I imply that he
was still living in 409–414.[3] The above are the only data
left to us concerning his life.

We should do wrong to regard as certainties the hypotheses tending to ascribe to Niceta various anonymous
writings. Paulinus of Nola informs us that Niceta encouraged
around him a taste for Church hymns.[4] Two treatises, the
de Vigiliis Servorum Dei, and the de Psalmodiae Bono, are
attributed to him in several manuscripts : the first enumerates
the advantages of meditatio nocturna during which the soul
retreats better into itself than in the midst of the bustle of
the day ; [5] the second combats the view of those who did not
see the use of Church music,[6] and explains to them their
error both from the point of view of tradition as also of the
evident benefit their piety draws from it.[7] People have been
led on this account to think that Niceta might very well
have been the author of the Te Deum which was already
known everywhere by the IVth century.[8] Various manuscripts of this rhythmic prose give the name of Niceta or
Nicetius : " Thus," Mgr. Duchesne remarks, " this celebrated hymn, which all Christendom sings in its moments of
deep emotion, may have first resounded from a hidden
corner of ancient Moesia." [9] It would be an interesting fact.
Nevertheless, specialists in Latin euchology are far from
considering this as definitely established. Similarly the
reasons given for placing to the account of Niceta the de

[1] Ep. xxix, 14.
[2] Quoted in Burn, p. 138.
[3] Cf. Burn, p. liv.
[4] Carmen xvii, 90 ; 109 ; 262 ; xxvii, 315 ; 500.
[5] Cf. § viii (Burn, p. 65).
[6] § ii : " Scio nonnullos, non solum in nostris, sed etiam in orientalibus esse
partibus, qui superfluam nec minus congruentem divinae religioni aestiment
psalmorum et hymnorum decantationem."
[7] It will be noted that Niceta ascribes the Magnificat to St Elizabeth (§ ix ;
Burn, p. 76, l. 21 ; § xi, Burn, p. 79, l. 4). Origen had already been aware of this
attribution (Hom. vii in Luc ; P.G., XIII, 1897 c.). Cf. Burn, p. clv in the edition
mentioned.
[8] From the testimony of Cyprian of Toulon in the year 530 (M.G.H., Epist. III,
436). Cf. Dom Morin, R. Bén., XI (1894), p. 48–77, who favoured the conjecture.
[9] Hist. anc. de l'Egl., III, 181.

Ratione Paschae and the *Epistula ad Virginem Lapsam* present nothing to carry our assent.

The notice by Gennadius (*de Vir. Ill.*, xxii) has enabled the *Libelli Instructionis*, written for candidates for baptism, to be reconstructed through the accident of a series of learned discoveries. Niceta is here seen, in his polemics against Arianism or Macedonianism, in the light, not of a theologian of complicated speculations, but as a catechist skilful in simplifying difficult questions. He shows the gift of lucid explanation for which Cassiodorus later on was to praise him:[1] "Si quis vero de Patre et Filio et Spiritu Sancto aliquid *summatim* praeoptat attingere, *nec se mavult longa lectione fatigari*, legat Niceti (sic) episcopi librum quem de fide conscripsit. . . ." Gennadius had said of him, *Simplici et nitido sermone*. It is in a style suited to pastoral instructions in which only the essential points of doctrine require to be touched on and defined. Elsewhere Niceta could be vehement and almost pathetic when he wished to appeal to the deeper sensibilities of his hearers.

On the whole, it is fortunate that the efforts of philologists have been successful in restoring some kind of vitality to this apostolic figure who from the time of Baronius had been confused with Nicetas of Aquileia or with Nicetius of Treves. " In studying the sum total of his work we are led to conceive that at various periods in Illyricum, first in connection with Victorinus of Pettau and afterwards with Niceta at the end of the IVth century, a centre of theological activity hitherto little known, to which the situation of this country lying between the two worlds which met there, give it a place apart."[2] In any case, a history of Christian evangelisation should keep a place for the name of the Bishop of Remesiana, the civiliser of the barbarians, whom he made Roman in making Catholic.

> "Orbis in muta regione per te
> Barbari discunt resonare Christum
> Corde Romano placidamque casti
> Vivere pacem."[3]

[1] *Inst. Div litt.*, § xvi.
[2] J. Zeiller, *Les orig. chrét. dans les Provinces Danubiennes*, p. 556.
[3] Paulinus of Nola, *Carmen* xvii, 257 et s.

VIII

THE question of Priscillian has always aroused particular interest among Church historians, whether orthodox or not. Has not Priscillian been considered as the first victim of the " secular arm," of the power of the State put at the disposal of the Church ? The facts are well known, and it will be enough to recall them very briefly.

Born in Spain in the middle of the IVth century, of noble birth, wealthy, and a man of high culture, Priscillian began to spread abroad his theories of doctrine about 370–375, especially, as it appears, in the district of Merida Cordova. He found numerous adherents among educated people and women. Two Bishops, Instantius and Salvianus, joined him. But his propaganda was violently opposed by two other Bishops, Hydatius of Merida and Itacius of Ossonaba, who displayed extraordinary zeal to compass his ruin and were capable of every sort of violence and deceit. In October 380, a Council at Saragossa had to pronounce on the Priscillianist " heresy," and condemned, if not Priscillian by name, at least the ideas which were attributed to him.[1] Hydacius and Itacius thereupon turned to the imperial power and obtained from Gratian a decree of banishment against the " Manichaeans," a term sufficiently vague which comprehended in the current usage the Priscillianists themselves. Priscillian, who had just been consecrated Bishop of Avila, was obliged to go to Aquitania. There too he made proselytes ; Euchrotia, the wife of Delphidius the rhetorician, and her daughter Procula, attached themselves to him and followed him to Italy, where his personal pleading before Pope Damasus and St Ambrose did not obtain for him any advantage. However, thanks to the good offices of Macedonius, *magister officiorum*, and of Volventius, Pro-Consul of Africa, he secured the annulment of the edict issued by Gratian and was able to return to his own country. Meanwhile Maximus had been proclaimed Emperor by the legions in Britain, and, desirous of securing the support of the Catholic clergy, he relegated the matter to a synod assembled

---

[1] On this vexed question, cf. Cirot, in *Bull. Critique*, 1897, no. 18 ; Babut, *Priscillien et le Priscillianisme*, p. 40 ; Puech, in the *Journal des Savants*, 1891, p. 343, and in B.A.L.A.C., 1912, p. 173.

at Bordeaux (384).   Instantius was deprived of his Episcopal
See.   Priscillian refused to recognise the competence of
the Council of Bordeaux, and committed the imprudence
of appealing to Maximus himself.   After being taken to Trèves
he was condemned to death on the report of the prefect
Evodius, together with four of his partisans, including
Euchrotia, and was executed.   Sulpicius Severus [1] has
acquainted us with the motives of this condemnation :
" . . . convictumque *maleficii* nec diffitentem obscenis se
studuisse doctrinis, nocturnos etiam turpium feminarum
egisse conventus nudumque orare solitum . . ." : immorality
and magic were the charges brought, to the exclusion of the
crime of heresy.[2]

Hydatius and Itacius had worked underground in order to
obtain this bloody outcome.   Violent protests were raised
among the Catholics themselves against their abominable
proceedings.   The former was obliged to resign from his see ;
the latter was deposed.   St Martin of Tours and St Ambrose
gave expression to their reprobation in forcible terms.   The
scandal also was great on the part of the pagans.   In his
panegyric on Theodosius, written in 389, the Gallic rhetorician,
Latinus Pacatus Drepanius, a friend of Ausonius, speaks with
horror of these Bishops turned executioners " who assisted
in person at their torture and went to feast their eyes and ears
on the sufferings and groans of the accused." [3]

The curiosity of learned people was therefore keenly excited
when eleven treatises ascribed to Priscillian appeared in
1889 in the *Corpus Script. eccles. latinorum*, vol. XVIII,
thanks to the labours of Schepss.   These treatises, with no
name of the author, figure in a manuscript of the Vth or VIth
century belonging to the library of the University of Wurzburg.   They had drawn the attention of Ruland, the librarian,
who made a copy of them.   This copy passed into the hands
of Dollinger, the historian, who did not edit it himself but
suggested that Priscillian must be the author.   Dollinger's
conclusion was accepted by Schepss.

[1] *Chron.*, II, L, 8.
[2] As regards the *nudum orare solitum*, we must remember that nudity, partial or
complete, was one of the conditions exacted in magic practices.   See references in
Lejay, R.H.L.R., 1903, p. 317.
[3] *Paneg. lat.* (Baehrens, p. 217).

The hopes aroused by this discovery have been sadly deceived. In the first place, the style of the collection is very different from what one had a right to expect from an author whom Sulpicius Severus represents as *facundus . . . , disserendi ac disputandi promptissimus*, etc. Clumsy, obscure, and involved lucubrations, scarcely relieved here and there by specimens of a rather fervid form of dialectics, constitute the sole profit gained by the disappointed scholars. Secondly, the enigma of Priscillian's doctrine was made little clearer by the publication from which so much had been expected. The most qualified historians of dogma had sadly to acknowledge this on the morrow of the appearance of Schepss' work. From his languid and dreary sentences one can certainly pick out statements that might be held suspect on the right of freely interpreting the Scriptures in the name of the gift of prophecy whose prerogatives God had not limited,[1] and on the use of apocryphal writings which the author would have liked to incorporate in an enlarged canon of Scripture.[2] But these indications do not go far.

The results of this disappointment have been twofold. If it is so difficult to discern " heresy " in any definite form in the writings of Priscillian, might this not be because his orthodoxy was not deserving of the disqualifications to which it was subjected ? M. Babut undertook with vigour and skill the paradoxical task of the rehabilitation of Priscillian in history. After examining the *dossier* of Priscillianism, he distinguishes two groups of documents. First, what he calls the " dossier primitif," wherein he includes among other writings the treatises of Schepss. If we are reduced to this series, " the condemnation of Priscillian would appear to have been not only unjustifiable, but also inexplicable." [3] Secondly, the accusing documents which appeared, especially after the year 400, imputing to Priscillianism an extraordinary multiplicity of errors. According to Babut's conception of him, Priscillian was above all things " a man of opposition and an innovator " [4] who " sincerely attempted a compromise between the free tendencies of his own personal religion and the demands of orthodoxy " [5] and finally became the

---

[1] Schepss, p. 32.   [2] *Ibid.*, p. 44, 10; 52, 11; 53.
[3] Babut, p. 15.   [4] P. 167.   [5] P. 128.

victim of the " machinations of worldly Bishops who feared the rigour of his precepts and the purity of his ideal."

An ingenious thesis, which raises more difficulties than it solves. If Priscillian's ideal was irreproachable, why did the Council of Saragossa condemn him ? Why did Ambrose and Damasus show the door to the Bishop of Avila ? Why did Bishop Delphinus, who was present at the Council of Saragossa, forbid him to enter Bordeaux ? Why has Sulpicius Severus, who esteemed the condemnation of Priscillian iniquitous, such harsh words for his errors ? How likewise explain the severity of St Jerome ?[1] Lastly, if Priscillian had not been a heretic, through what misunderstanding did his immediate followers undoubtedly so become ?

In spite of the generous efforts of Babut, a revision of the question of Priscillian is not incumbent upon history.

An examination of the Wurzburg treatises led Dom Morin[2] to a conclusion of another kind from which it is far more difficult to escape. Out of these eleven treatises, there are eight which are hardly more than homilies devoid of historic value. The three first, namely the *Liber apologeticus*, the *Liber ad Damasum episcopum*, and the *De Fide et Apocryphis* have an entirely different bearing. Critics are agreed in considering the *Liber Apologeticus* as a plea delivered before the Council of Bordeaux in 384. On this count, remarks Dom Morin, it is impossible to admit that Priscillian can have been the author. As a matter of fact, Priscillian denied the competence of his ecclesiastical judges ; he refused to be heard by them and preferred to appeal to the Emperor.[3] Under these circumstances it was another who pleaded the cause of the Priscillianists, and Sulpicius Severus mentions him by name : *Instantius prior jussus causam dicere. . . .*[4]

The Wurzburg treatises therefore cannot have been written by Priscillian ; they should be restored to Instantius. Another indication strengthens this conjecture. We read in the *Liber ad Damasum* (p. 46, l. ii) the following passage : *nos tamen non omittentes in causa fidei sanctorum judicium malle quam saeculi.* These words are suitable in the mouth

---

[1] *Ep.* lxxv, 3 ; *Comm. in Is.* xvii, 64 (P.L., XXIV, 622) ; *Ep.* cxxxiii, 3.
[2] R. Bén., 1913, p. 158 et s.
[3] Cf. Sulpicius Severus, *Chron.*, II, xlix.
[4] " Jussus causam dicere " was what Sulpicius Severus wrote. " Quod jubetis " he said at the beginning of the work (Schepss, p. 4, I. 2).

of Instantius who undertook to defend his ideas before the Bishops assembled at Bordeaux. How can we attribute them to Priscillian since he rejected the authority of the ecclesiastical tribunal in order to entrust his case to a secular court ?

Dom Morin's hypothesis seems to be very judicious. It explains the literary mediocrity of the Wurzburg treatises, and the mild note of heretical " pravity " which we are astonished to notice therein. If it definitely stands the proof of time and the acuteness of the critics, there will hardly remain anything else to the credit of Priscillian except the *Canones in Pauli Apostoli epistulas*.[1] These are a kind of theological digest of St Paul composed of quotations and references which for a long time were held to have been written by St Jerome, and after the mistake had been discovered, were retouched by a Bishop of the name of Peregrinus to insure their perfect orthodoxy. Attempts have been made (on no serious grounds) to identify Peregrinus with the Spanish monk Bachiarius, to whom we are also indebted for a *Liber de Fide* and a *Liber ad Januarium de Reparatione Lapsi*.[2]

Priscillianism kept up a disquieting vitality up to the Vth century. The sect approached nearer and nearer to Manichaean ideas. A fairly abundant literature was born from these polemics ; on the Priscillianist side we may mention the names of Tiberianus,[3] Asarbus,[4] Latronianus (a very distinguished poet, if we may credit St Jerome),[5] and Dictinius,[6] and on the Catholic side those of Itacius,[7] Olym-

---

[1] This compilation, likewise published by Schepss, p. 107 et s., was fairly well known in Spain and France during several centuries. Schepss was aware of 17 manuscripts dating from the IXth to the XVth centuries. It is possible that in the mind of Priscillian it was originally meant for a controversial work for the purpose of showing the conformity of his theology with that of St Paul.

[2] P.L., XX, 1019–1062. Th. Stangl (B. ph. W. 1917, p. 868–888) considers this identification doubtful. Dom de Bruyne (R.B., XXXI [1914–19], p. 384) rejects it expressly. I have analysed Stangl's interesting notice of Bachiarius in the *Revue de Philologie* (*Revue des Revues*, 1918). Dom Morin has published in B.A.L.A.C., 1914, p. 117 et s., divers hitherto unpublished fragments of which Bachiarius might be the author. The whole work of this personality seems to merit a study ; his writings are not at all insignificant.

[3] St Jerome, *De Vir. Ill.*, cxxiii.

[4] Priscillian, *Liber Apol.*, I (Schepss, p. 3).

[5] *De Vir. Ill.*, cxxii.

[6] Cf. *Ep.* xv, 16, of Pope Leo Ist. We can reconstruct the main gist of his work entitled *Libra*, from St Augustine's *Contra Mendacium*.

[7] Isidore of Seville, *De Vir. Ill.*, xv.

pius,[1] Pastor,[2] Syagrius,[3] and Turibius of Astorga.[4] St Augustine himself attacks the Priscillianists more than once in his letters, in his *Contra Mendacium*, and his *Ad Orosium contra Priscillianistas et Origenistas*.

[1] Gennadius, *De Vir. Ill.*, **xxiii**.
[2] *Ibid.*, lxxvii.
[3] *Ibid.*, lxvi.
[4] Cf. Migne, LIV, 693.   On these different personages, see Kunstle, *Anti-priscilliana*, Fr. i. B., 1905, and Dufourcq, *Etude sur les Gesta Martyrum romains*, vol. IV (*Le Néo-Manichéisme et la légende chrétienne*).

CHAPTER IV

CHRISTIAN POETRY IN THE IVᴛʜ CENTURY

BIBLIOGRAPHY

I. The Small Poems. See Table VI.—There is a general *resumé* in Manitius, *Gesch. d. christlich-lat. Poesie*, Stuttgart, 1891 (mediocre, but useful analyses); G. Boissier, *La Fin du Paganisme*, vol. II, book IV.

II. Juvencus.—P.L., XIX, 53-346; Marold, in B.T. (1886); C.V., XXIV (1891, Huemer); some translations in F. Clément's *Les Poètes chrétiens*, 1857, p. 1-11.

III. Paulinus of Nola.—His works are in Migne, vol. LXI, and in C.V. (Hartel, 1894), vols. XXIX and XXX. Hartel has included in an appendix four poems whose authenticity is contested, the *Carmen ad conjugem*, the *C. de nomine Jesu*, the *C. ad Deum post conversionem et bapt. suum*, and the *C. de domesticis suis calamitatibus*.—A French anonymous translation of his letters in prose, Paris, 1703; 1724. Some pieces in verse and prose are translated in Anot. de Maizières' *Nouveaux choix de Pères latins*, 1853, vol. IV and V; the notice of Pacatus written by his pupil Uranius (Migne, LIII, 866), is included in the above, vol. II, p. 144. See also the *Chefs-d'oeuvre des Pères de l'Eglise*, vol. XIV; Félix Clément, *op. cit.*, pp. 88-161. P. de Labriolle's *la Corresp. d'Ausone et de Paulin de Nole*, 1910.—The chronology of Paulinus' works is often a difficult matter; cf. E. Ch. Babut, in the *Annales du Midi*, XX (1908), pp. 18-44, and Rauschen's *Jahrbucher der christl. Kirche*, 1897.—On his works as a whole, consult: Lagrange, *Hist. de saint Paulin de Nole*, 2 vols., 1882; A. Baudrillart, *Saint Paulin, évêque de Nole* (coll. *les Saints*), 1905.—There are many useful observations in P. Reinelt's *Studien uber die Briefe des hl. P. v. N.*, Breslau, 1904, and Philipp's *Zum Sprachgebrauch des P. v. N.*, Erlangen, 1904 and L. Kraus' *die poetische Sprache des Paulinus Nolanus*, Augsburg, 1918.

SUMMARY

I. General view of Latin Christian Poetry.—II. Paraphrases of the Bible. Juvencus. Cyprian's *Heptateuchos*.—III. Didactic Poems.—IV. The *Centos*.—V. Paulinus of Nola. The Conversion of Paulinus. Paulinus and Ausonius.—VI. The Letters of Paulinus.—VII. His Poems.

I

In his History of the Church (III, xvi), the Greek historian Socrates relates that following the edict of the Emperor Julian which forbade the Christians to explain the pagan classics, the two Apollinares, father and son, the former

311

a professor of grammar at Laodicea in Syria, and the latter Bishop of Laodicea, made an attempt to reconstitute *en bloc* for the benefit of educated Christians the profane works on which they were forbidden to comment in public. The father drew up a grammar " consonant with the Christian faith," which doubtless means that his examples were taken from Christian authors or counterfeited in conformity with the faith ; he translated the books of Moses into heroic verse, paraphrased the historical books of the Old Testament, and drew from them epopees and tragedies. He purposely made use of the greatest possible number of the traditional metrical forms of Hellenic literature in order to popularise them among the Christians. His son transposed " the Gospels and the doctrine of the Apostles " in the form of Platonic dialogues.

Julian died soon after ; the law he had introduced became inoperative, and all this counterfeiting of profane literature, in the words of Socrates, " retained no more importance than if it had never existed." [1]

It is well to know something of the attempt by the Apollinares in order to understand the spirit inspiring the majority of the Christian poets in the Latin tongue whom we are going to review. What slightly diminishes the interest of their works is that we are too much aware of a desire to assimilate them to profane literature ; we can discern a concerted purpose, an artificial effort, rather than the freedom of spontaneous inspiration which relieves itself in its utterance. Their intention is to oppose the *certa fides* to the *mendacia* of the classics (these are the terms used by Juvencus), and by the same forms as those employed in the classics. In order to reach a public very different from the cultivated circles at which they usually aim, they only very exceptionally shake themselves free from these forms consecrated by long usage.[2] Christian poetry in Latin was only able to rise to real and true originality in the Church hymn. Nevertheless the IVth century offers us one name at least which

---

[1] Sozomenes, who also gives details of this improvisation (H.E., V, xviii), judges it differently : " If mortals did not attach value solely to what is old, if they could shake themselves free from inveterate routine, the writings of the Apollinares would have been read with no less pleasure than the works which they were intended to supersede."

[2] This was the case with St Augustine in his *Alphabetical Psalm*.

should be remembered—that of Paulinus of Nola,—and a talent exceeding the mediocrity of the common level.

II

THERE is a whole group of poems which are nothing else than paraphrases of episodes, more or less developed, taken from the Old Testament, and, less often, from the New. The magnificent poetry of the Bible, the Mosaic cosmogony in particular, offered rich material which was largely exploited. In order to realise the secret of the Christian versifiers, we must understand the ideas which they obeyed. It was a question with them, in the first place, of being helpful to young minds by instilling into them sacred teaching transposed in an attractive form, expurgated of those difficult details with which certain episodes in the Bible might oppress their youthful imaginations.[1] Then, imbued with another thought which as we know obsessed the cultivated Christians, they hoped to conquer the intellectual and learned *élite* by the charm of their poetry, and bring them back to God by those flowery paths which were not forbidden by Him. " It matters little," Sedulius was to say in the dedicatory Epistle of his *Carmen Paschale*, " it matters little by what path each one arrives at the Faith, provided that once he has entered upon the road to liberty he does not fall again into the pitfalls of servitude which lately held him captive." Lastly, a commentary of the Bible in verse enabled them to develop certain dogmatic and moral interpretations, to refute adverse doctrines on the origin and formation of the earth, and to unveil the mystic signification hidden beneath the dry covering of the texts. Apologetics also thus found their place in it. One would not like to say that poetry always comes into its own. In any case this series of poems, without being absolutely barren of happy features, does not reveal any original talent,—no Milton, Tasso, not even a du Bartas or a Maurice Scève. Description abounds formidably, the kind of description defined by Guizot,[2] " which is less anxious

---

[1] We shall notice that with the exception of Dracontius, who allows himself some rather profane details, the creation of woman in Eden does not provoke any perilous descriptions. The *Metrum in Genesin* (v. 123) drily gives in a hemistich : *Mulier de costa viri fit :* that is all.

[2] *Hist. de la Civilis. en France*, vol. II, ch. xviii, p. 60.

to make people see objects than to make them understand them, which observes and goes through them, taking pains to enumerate and display every part ; in such a way that such and such a person, such and such a fact, if it had been simply mentioned or indicated by one sole characteristic, would have been real and visible to the imagination, but now only appears discomposed, cut in pieces, dissected, and destroyed." Again, these professorial amplifications are supported entirely on quotations. The author of the *Metrum in Genesin* [1] becomes moved over Adam and his posterity in terms recalling the melancholy of Virgil when deploring the sad destiny of the young Marcellus : " O happy man, formed by the same hand of God which hurleth the thunderbolt (*summi cui dextra tonantis est pater*) ; O too happy, thou who takest from heaven (*Olympo*) both thy origin and thy shape ! If thou dost not become the prey of the deadly vices of the earth, if thou dost not allow thyself to be seduced by error, thou shalt be a god (*numen eris*) and, mounting to heaven, shalt marvel at the kingdom which by His own mouth the Father hath promised to virtuous men ! " I have underlined certain expressions of " classicism " rather foreign in a Christian subject. Tartarus, the vale of Tempe, the Styx, Avernus, the Elysian Fields, and material from mythology of every kind find a place in these verses aiming at being epic, amid a quantity of shreds torn from Ovid and Virgil. It is something like Claudian with less colour, brilliancy, and richness of imagination. At any rate, this rather servile respect for past masters, shared alike by Christians and pagans, preserved the art of poetry from a ruin still more complete by substituting imitations which are not always without skill, in place of their feeble inspiration.

If Commodian must be put on one side as certain critics (wrongly without doubt) wish to do as far as the IVth or even the Vth centuries are concerned, the Spanish priest Gaius Vettius Aquilinus Juvencus should be reckoned the first Christian poet in the Latin tongue.

We must, however, mention a little poem anterior by a few years, the *Laudes Domini*, in which the anonymous author who knew his Virgil very well, in connection with a miracle which had taken place " in the country of the Eduens "

[1] Lines 125-30 (P.L., L, 1287 ; C.V. III, 283, and XXVII, 231).

(a Gallic tribe whose capital was Bibracte, Autun) sings the praises of Christ Who, together with the Father, created the world and came to ransom it.   In any case, Juvencus was the first to try and utilise Christian ideas in any large measure by methods borrowed from traditional classic technique.

> " Versibus ut nostris divinæ gloria legis.[1]
> Ornamenta libens caperet terrestria linguæ . . ."

St Jerome informs us that he wrote his *Evangeliorum Libri* in the reign of Constantine, about the year 329.[2]   The idea of drawing from the sacred Books matter for a Christian epopee must have come naturally to lettered Christian writers.   The literary Roman criterion (the most perfect expression of which we find in Horace) was firmly bound up in a hierarchy of subject matter, and gave the palm to the epic poem.[3]   What honour to the Faith to prove that it could become the principle or leaven in a revival of this kind of literature which was so highly esteemed !

" I would sing," Juvencus declares, " the noble deeds of Christ on earth."   In his conception, therefore, it was highly appropriate to reproduce the Gospel in a kind of epopee, and his invocation to the Holy Spirit takes the place of the Prologue, the traditional invocation to the Muses.   As his basis he takes St Matthew's text which he read from one, or several, pre-Hieronymic Latin versions, and availed himself on occasion of St Luke, St John, and, more rarely, of St Mark.   The 3190 lines of the poem are divided into four books which otherwise do not coincide with the contents of each of the four Gospels.

The great difficulty encountered by Juvencus—many other Christian poets after him were to bruise themselves against this stumbling-block—was his very respect for the Word of God, and his fear of offending God by misrepresenting the fabric of the sacred Books.   By applying in all its rigour such a principle or scruple all poetic endeavour would have become impossible.   Juvencus was obliged here and there to prune, transpose, and even elaborate—especially in his descriptions of nature, where his ready and *facile* talent found

---

[1] iv, 805.
[2] *De Vir. Ill.*, lxxxiv ; *Chron. ad annum* 2345 ; cf. Juvencus, iv, 806 et s.
[3] Cf. Horace, *Sat.*, I, iv, 43.

itself more justified in breaking ground. But he is not at his ease, and this is somewhat too apparent. Equally timorous both as a classic and as a Christian, he has no other concern than to plant his footsteps as closely as possible in the tracks of Virgil—his favourite model—or in those of Lucretius, Statius, and a few others.[1] Evangelical simplicity does not emerge without damage from these laborious adaptations. The *Transeat a me Calix Iste* is watered down as follows :

> " Si fas est, genitor, calicis me transeat hujus
> Incumbens valido nobis violentia tractu,
> Sed tua jam veniat potius quam nostra voluntas
> Quæ tibi decreta est tantis sententia rebus."

The *Jam foetet* becomes :

> " Crediderim corpus motu fugiente caloris
> Fetorem miserum liquefactis reddere membris."

Modern critics are very sensitive to these errors of taste. A certain phrase of St Jerome seems to imply that he had already felt their maladroitness (*Ep.* lxx, 5). Nevertheless, Juvencus founded a tradition, and his initiative sufficed to assure him the respect of his Christian successors who often essayed to imitate this imitator.[2] His renown was widespread throughout the Middle Ages,[3] but it hardly lasted beyond it.

The *Heptateuchos* of the poet Cyprian has only been known to us in its present form for a few years. In 1560, G. Morel, following a manuscript in the library of the Abbey of St Victor, Paris—to-day this manuscript is in the Bibliothèque Nationale, and is numbered 14758—published a short poem of 165 lines entitled *Genesis*. In 1735, the Benedictines Dom Martène and Dom Durand added to this fragment 1276 lines after a MS. in the Abbey of Saint Germain-des-Prés (Bibl. Nat. no. 13047). In 1852, Cardinal Pitra completed this *Genesis* by the addition of 57 lines (*Spicil. Solesm.*, vol. I). The three manuscripts which he had examined, namely two at Laon (IXth century), and one at Trinity College, Cambridge (Xth century), enabled him in 1888 to include

---

[1] The peculiarities of his versification are mentioned in edition C.V., p. 163. He frequently makes use of rhyme. He ventured on some verbal creations : *auricolor* (1, 356) ; *flammivomus* (*Prol.*, 23) ; *flammicomans* (iv, 201) ; *flammipes* (ii, 546) ; *altithronus* (*Prol.*, 24 et *passim*) ; etc.

[2] Cf. Huemer's edition (C.V.), p. viii.

[3] *Ibid.*, p. xiv.

in his *Analecta novissima Tusculana,* six other poems on the books following *Genesis,* viz. Exodus, Leviticus, Numbers, Deuteronomy, Josue and Judges. The " Heptateuch " was complete. The name of Cyprian was found in an old catalogue of the Xth century of the manuscripts of St Nazaire de Lorsch, and in one of the manuscripts at Laon. Who was this Cyprian ? Was he the author of the *Caena Cypriani* which had been inserted among the apocryphal writings of St Cyprian, or the priest Cyprian to whom Letter CXL of St Jerome is addressed ? This we cannot venture to decide. In any case, he was a lettered man, familiar with Virgil, Ovid, Persius, Juvenal, and Lucan, and also with several Christian poets, and one who was not without a certain technical skill : thus, for different portions of a more lyrical turn, he substitutes the phalecian hendecasyllable in place of the hexameter (v.g. *Exodus,* 507–542 ; *Numbers,* 557–567 ; *Deuteronomy,* 152–278). His prosody is otherwise somewhat fanciful, and he makes an unpleasing abuse of the old Roman practice of alliteration.

It is probable that the poetic efforts accomplished by Cyprian were more numerous than we can judge at the present time, for isolated verses have been discovered relating to the four books of Kings, the two Paralipomena and Job. We find also in old catalogues traces of a translation in verse of Judith and Esther. Perhaps Cyprian had attempted to put into verse the whole of the Old Testament, leaving himself free to omit from his scheme (as we see he had done in different places) those portions which did not lend themselves to transposition.

III

ANOTHER series of writings is connected with the didactic order which enjoyed a long popularity in Rome. " We may say . . . that by recalling Lucretius, Virgil, and even Manilius, it aimed at the highest elements in the Roman soul, and that it responded to its most noble and most treasured aspirations." [1] Since the IIIrd century this vigorous tradition had lost its flavour in mediocre works such as the *Cynegetica* of Nemesianus, the *de Re Rustica* of Palladius

[1] A. Puech, *Prudentius,* p. 161.

and several others. The Christian writers had the merit of understanding the advantages of a method of exposition or of polemics, offered by a class of literature which had such deep roots in the Roman past.

The *de Cruce*[1] (called also the *de Pascha*, and the *de Ligno Vitae*) deserves special mention. The " tree of life " was the cross raised on Golgotha, wood " cut from a barren tree " which notwithstanding " extended its branches on both sides," and " covered the whole world in order that the nations of the earth might ever find in it their nourishment and their life, and might learn that death also could die." And its fruits savouring of salvation produce a marvellous renewing in those who before having recourse to it " have obliterated the shameful defilements of their past life, and have washed their bodies in the sacred stream." All this symbolism is presented with simplicity and feeling. The *de Ternarii Numeri Excellentia*,[2] attributed to St Ambrose, celebrates in 14 hexameters the surpassing virtue of the number three. Subtilty delighting in refinements, and making play in allegory and symbol, had for long been exercised on the mystery attaching to numbers and to their secret correspondence with certain beliefs. Did not St Augustine himself take pleasure in it ?[3] The *de Naturis Rerum*, which an Oxford manuscript likewise attributes to St Ambrose (it is not known whether rightly or wrongly), celebrates the almightiness of God in nature under a title very similar to that chosen by Lucretius the Epicurean.[4] The *Ad quemdam Senatorem*[5] is an urgent, but courteous warning to a Senator and former Consul (v. 27), who, after having embraced Christianity for several years (v. 43–44), had abandoned it for the religion of the *Magna Mater*. The author (he is given as St Cyprian in the manuscripts !) is astounded that a man of his distinction should return to those absurd and bloody rites, and expresses the hope that when he grows old the backslider will abjure them. " As I am not unmindful that you are a lover of poetry," he remarks, " I have tried to turn poet

[1] TABLE VI, no. 3.   See Brandt in B. ph. W., 1920, 424–432 (a study of the text : Hartel cannot have followed the best MSS.).
[2] *Ibid.*, no. 22.
[3] Cf. Knappitsch, *Augustins Zahlensymbolik*, Progr. Graz, 1905.
[4] TABLE VI, no. 16.
[5] No. 21.

in order to make answer to you, and I hasten to write these verses to make you ashamed." The piece is very clear in language and of a very lively turn. The *Invectiva contra Nicomachum* was written during or immediately after the pagan reaction attempted by the Emperor Eugenius, in 392–394. Virius Nicomachus Flavianus, several times Praetorian Prefect, Consul in 394, and an historian of a certain talent, had shown himself one of those most attached to the ancient religion [1] among the members of the Roman aristocracy ; he died before the Emperor Eugenius. The *Invectiva* celebrates the fall of this influential adversary of Christianity and draws therefrom a pretext to turn into somewhat heavy ridicule the superstitions of the pagans, and the cult of Isis and of the *Magna Mater*. This poem, whose style is clumsy and versification rather incorrect, has been preserved to us in one single manuscript, the *Cod. Paris. 8084*, of the VIth century, which also includes the poems of Prudentius. The *Carmen adversus Marcionem*,[2] in five books and 1302 lines, was published in 1564 by George Fabricius from a manuscript now lost, but which doubtless came from the monastery of Lorsch where the poem was ascribed to Tertullian. Comparison with the authentic treatise of Tertullian against Marcion proves that the poem was incorrectly attributed to him. The names of Marius Victorinus, Victorinus of Pettau, and Commodian, have been suggested. The date of the writing of the *Carmen*, as also the place where it was written, cannot be defined with certainty.[3] In addition to Tertullian, the author exploits a few other Christian writers, Theophilus, St Cyprian, etc. His narrative is dull and confused in spite of a certain correctness of diction, and is strangely flat after Tertullian's ardent, caustic, and passionate prose. Fabricius made the mistake of retouching the text arbitrarily with the view of giving it a more classic colour. Certain restorations of the original text are possible, thanks to a poem

---

[1] He translated into Latin, with hostile intent, the *Life of Apollonius of Tyana*, by Philostratus.

[2] No. 14.

[3] A recent study by Karl Holl, S.B.B., 1918, p. 514–559, comes to the conclusion that this poem must have been written in the south of Gaul during the last quarter of the Vth century. His argument relies on two passages, the list of the Popes (iii, 275 et s.), and the legend that Adam was buried at Golgotha (ii, 160 et s.). See my analysis in the *Revue de Philologie, Rev. des Rev.*, 1919, p. 53 ; also T.U., XLII, 4 (1919), p. 161–2

entitled *Versus Victorini de Lege Domini*,[1] made up of lines taken from the *Carmen adversus Marcionem*.

Two manuscripts, the *Codex Veronensis* 163 (IXth century) and the *Vossianus* Q 33 (Xth century), St Gregory of Tours,[2] and an anonymous grammarian of the early Middle Ages,[3] attribute the *Carmen de Ave Phoenice*[4] to Lactantius. This poem relates in 85 distiches the legend of the Phœnix, its life in a sacred wood in the remote East (v. 1–58) as the bird-priest of the Sun, its voluntary death every thousand years on a palm-tree in Phœnicia in which it builds a nest for this purpose (v. 59–98), and finally its resurrection and the transfer of its remains to the Temple of the Sun in Egypt (99–170). The legend of the Phœnix was popular in antiquity. Herodotus[5] had learnt it from Egyptian priests without attaching too much credence to it. More than one Roman writer had re-echoed it, among whom was the sober-minded Tacitus, in his *Annales*.[6] Tacitus relates it in full detail in connection with the alleged reappearance of the Phœnix in Egypt during the Consulate of Fabius and Vitellius (34 A.D.). Always distrustful and divided as regards the " marvellous," he adds, " all this is uncertain and exaggerated by fables. Moreover, it is incontestable that this bird sometimes appears in Egypt." Pliny the Elder[7] too had his doubts : *haud scio an fabulose*. The legend, developed and added to in a greater or less degree, was to preserve its vitality down to the last days of Latin literature, and Claudian was to sing it in one of his idylls. Quite early the Jews had appropriated it as a symbol of the resurrection. The Christians followed their example. Towards the end of the Ist century, Clement of Rome considered the story of the Phœnix in his letter to the Corinthians,[8] and concluded in these words, " Can we then find it strange and astonishing that the Creator of the Universe should make those creatures live again who served Him in a holy manner and with the confidence of a perfect faith, since He makes us behold in a bird the magnificence of His promise ? " A large number of Christian authors treated

---

[1] Cf. Brandes, in *Wiener Studien*, XII (1890), p. 310. This poem is included in the *Vaticanus Regin.* 582, of the IXth or Xth century.
[2] *De Cursu Stell.*, § 12 (M.G.H., *Scr. rer. Merov.*, I, 2, p. 861).
[3] G.L., v.g. 477, 14 et s.   [4] TABLE VI, no. 1.
[5] II, lxxiii.   [6] VI, xxviii.
[7] *H. Nat.*, X, ii.   [8] xxv–xxvi.

it in the same spirit. At the beginning of the VIth century, the poet Dracontius again brings it forward among examples of resurrection offered by nature.[1] This form of zoology applied to Christian doctrine was altogether to the taste of the first centuries.

The author of the *Carmen de Ave Phoenice* only makes extremely discreet use of the fable in the service of Christianity, so much so that we might feel some doubt whether he had any other object in view than to develop incidents which provided him with a sufficiently brilliant poetic theme. Nevertheless, certain features, without being very clearly marked, reveal the Christian, and under the rather ordinary guise of description there is hidden a mysticism which knew how to extract from traditional common-places congruities suited to the faith.[2] It can neither be proved, nor is it unlikely, that it was Lactantius who adapted the story in this manner.

The idyll *de Mortibus Boum*,[3] in 33 asclepiad strophes, is a work by a friend of Paulinus of Nola,[4] the rhetorician Severus Sanctus Endelechius, a man of Gallic origin, who taught in Rome at the end of the IVth century. Aegon is struck by the sadness of Buculus. The latter informs him that in two days the terrible epidemic which, starting in Pannonia had spread through Illyria and Belgium, had carried off his whole flock. Tityrus, another drover, had preserved his own intact. Tityrus explains how a cross laid on the foreheads of his cattle had protected them efficaciously. Buculus and Aegon at once decide to have themselves initiated in the safe-guarding faith. Without equalling the great descriptions of the classics, that given by Buculus of this scourge is rather expressive and strong.

IV

THE universal admiration in which Virgil was held had early provoked certain minds gifted with ingenuity to compose whole poems out of verses taken from the *Bucolics*, *Georgics* and the *Æneid*, and twisted more or less skilfully into meanings

---

[1] *Carmen de Deo*, I, 650–660.
[2] For example, v. 93 : " Animam commendat " (cf. St Luke, xxiii, 46) ; v. 64 : " hunc orbem, mors ubi regna tenet " ; v. 25 : " fons in medio est, quem vivum nomine dicunt " ; v. 163–170 : in praise of chastity.
[3] TABLE VI, no. 15.
[4] Paulinus, *Ep.* xxviii, 6.

quite unforeseen by the bard of Mantua : " We see to-day," Tertullian had already noted,[1] " issuing from Virgil some entirely different fable in which the subject is adapted to verse and the verse to the subject. Hosidius Geta ' pumped up ' entire (*plenissime exsuxit*) his tragedy *Medea* from Virgil. One of my relations, among other literary pastimes has explained the *Pinax Cebetis* by means of the same poet." This " labour of the rag-picker " (*more centonario*), as Tertullian calls it, had become the fashion : we possess fairly numerous specimens of " centos." [2] The poetess Proba, a Christian lady of the highest aristocracy, the granddaughter, daughter and mother of Consuls, conceived the idea of relating by the same method the principal episodes of the Old Testament as far as the Deluge,[3] and of the New Testament, to the Ascension.[4] She wished in this way to assist her children more easily to engrave the sacred history on their memory. It was a chimerical undertaking, the difficulties of which no device could surmount. Proba was compelled to substitute for the names of the personages in the Gospel vague designations such as *Deus, Dominus, Magister, Heros, mater, vates,* etc. Only the name of Moses, *Moseus,* due to its consonance with that of Virgil's *Musaeus,* succeeded in finding a place in her verses. And then how could she express in profane hemistiches the Conception of the Virgin, the flight into Egypt, the Crucifixion, etc., even by changing the circumstances of the events and persons as she sometimes permitted herself to do, or by allowing herself liberties in prosody which Virgil would not have tolerated ? We can understand the annoyance which these well-intentioned imitations (of which we have a few other specimens),[5] caused to St Jerome's good sense.[6] The decree ascribed to Gelasius places Proba's work among the " apocrypha " reserved for private reading.[7]

---

[1] *De Praescr. Haer.,* xxxix, 3.
[2] They are to be found collected in P.L.M., IV, p. 191–240.
[3] V. 29–332.
[4] V. 333–688.
[5] TABLE VI, nos. 2, 5, 23, 24.
[6] *Ep.* liii, 7 (C.V., LIV, 454, 1, i).
[7] P.L., LIX, 162. Cf. Isidore, *de Vir. Ill.,* xxii.

V

A PROFOUND sensation was created in high Gallo-Roman society when, in 393, it learnt that Meropius Pontius Paulinus, one of the foremost personages in the Empire, the owner of vast domains in Gaul and Italy, a Senator, and Procurator of Campania since his twenty-first year, was definitely renouncing the life of the world, and was thinking of becoming a monk. And this too, not in the decline of life when a man's powers become unsteady and disillusionment increases, but at the age of forty, in his full intellectual and physical maturity.[1]

For some years his friends had already seen that his soul was undergoing a change, and that he was gradually detaching himself from everything, and suspected that the influence of his wife, Therasia, a pious Spanish woman, strongly supported the secret working of his mind.[2] But could any-one have expected such a complete rupture, the alienation of his magnificent landed properties—the *regna Paulini*,[3]—which he was selling in order to distribute his wealth among the poor ? What was to become of the empire, menaced as it was by the barbarians, if its most valiant defenders thus made default ? Also was it right that at a time when the public offices of the State constituted so heavy a burden, the richest should dispense themselves from them, and leave all the weight on other men's shoulders ? The restless state of patriotism, the important interests affected, and lastly, the spirit of enjoyment humiliated by the spirit of sacrifice—all these sentiments of different value united to render the scandal more impressive. Paulinus was aware of the unpopularity of which he was the object. He suffered on account of it without doubt, but he was determined to effect the necessary cutting adrift. Besides, his wife, in complete harmony of soul, shared with him all his renunciations.

He had not reached this point all at once. Born of a Christian family, religious considerations were aroused in him fairly early. When quite a young man, he had been keenly struck by the miracles which he had seen taking place

---

[1] He was born at Bordeaux in 353 or 354.
[2] Cf. Ausonius, *Ep.* xxviii, 31 (Peiper, p. 284).
[3] *Id., Ep.* xxvii, 116.

at the basilica of St Felix, at Nola, which belonged to his family.[1] He had then entered upon his career of high position, and for some years lived happily the life of the world at Bordeaux. In a prayer to the Creator in 19 hexameters which he wrote at that time, he expressed no other desire than to take advantage of the lawful pleasures of life [2] in full security.

A somewhat mysterious occurrence, a grave peril from which he thought his escape had been wholly due to the protection of St Felix, seems to have contributed greatly to detach him from the life of the world: "Thy goodness, O my Father and guardian (he is addressing the Saint) hath never belied itself. Following after the death of my brother, I found myself in danger; out of the trial of my brother there arose against me a like accusation; the public assessor had already come to view my possessions in order to auction them. It was thou who wast able to remove my neck from under the sword, my patrimony from the state treasury, and thus save for the Lord Christ my goods and my person." [3] He had doubtless nearly fallen a victim to some juridical murder set on foot by the usurper Maximus with the sole object of confiscating his riches. What is certain is that from 390, his desire for "conversion" (we can see in what sense to understand this word) was more and more felt. He was baptised, which had been put off until then; he settled in Spain with Therasia, and remained there four years at least. There, about the year 393–4, husband and wife decided to live a life of continence and poverty.

We may truly say that no one was more painfully astonished at so disconcerting a report than Ausonius, the aged rhetorician. He had had Paulinus as his pupil at the University of Bordeaux. He had taken the greatest satisfaction in him, had placed his highest hopes on his future, and had continued his connection with him by the affectionate intercourse of letters, verses, and presents. He highly appreciated the poetic talent of Paulinus. An abridgment in verse, which he undertook, of three books of Suetonius on the Kings had delighted him especially.[4] He recognised therein the

---

[1] *Carm.* xxi, 367 et s. (Hartel, II, p. 170).
[2] *Carm.* iv.
[3] *Carm.* xxi, 414 et s. (Hartel, II, p. 171).
[4] Ausonius, *Ep.* xxiii (Peiper, p. 267).

happy fruits of the discipline he had inculcated; he saw
himself reflected in his disciple. And here was Paulinus,
so dear to him, renouncing the life of the world, leaving
Aquitaine to bury himself in Spain, and selling his worldly
possessions. . . . But what then? And his abstract of
Suetonius, his poetry, his Latin culture? Was he going to
deny himself all these things? Ausonius could not endure
such a perplexing condition of things, which was aggravated
by the long silence of Paulinus. He wrote to him four
letters in verse, one after the other, begging him to speak, to
give some explanation, and to come back; and in these
hexameters, full of the most cordial and sincere sentiments,
he multiplied choice legends of mythology, and the wide
common ground existing between themselves, as though the
better to recall to his old pupil the beautiful things he seemed
to be forgetting.

Paulinus at last replied, also in verse. A certain literary
coquetry was always to remain with him—the only vanity
in which he did not deny himself some pleasure. While
lavishing on his old master the most affectionate terms, he
gave him categorically to understand that the pastimes in
which he begged him to continue his interest seemed to him
from now onward to be too frivolous, and that another kind
of discipline, which monopolised his thought, his heart, and
his whole being, had taken the savour from that wherein
he had occupied his youth.[1]

In spite of all his protestations of respect and tenderness,
nothing could be more mortifying to Ausonius, nor make him
see better at a glance the chasm which had been opened between their two spirits, formerly so like-minded.

Looking around him, Ausonius began to perceive more
and more that to some minds elegant phrases were not a
sufficient incentive to life, and this discovery plunged him
into a kind of stupor. He saw Patrician men and women
undertaking long pilgrimages to the Holy Land. He saw an
illustrious advocate like Sulpicius Severus imitating the renunciation of Paulinus, and at the same time marvellous
fishers of souls like St Martin and Romanus of Blaye, bringing
about the most astounding conversions among the masses.
At the end of the IVth century a gust of asceticism was

[1] I have translated and commented on this *Correspondence*, Paris, (Bloud), 1910.

blowing over the whole of the West. Piety, confidence, and faith were stirring up Christian believers to the work of conquest and struggle. Even in the immediate surroundings of Ausonius, his grandson Paulinus (of Pella), although still quite a child, was giving indications of a desire to consecrate himself to the service of Christ, and just at first his parents were not opposed to this. The old man was able from his daily experience to observe the prodigious difference which separated his own quite external and formal Christianity from a Christianity that was truly felt and was deep.[1]

By contrast, the *prestige* of the sacrifices freely consummated by Paulinus and Therasia was extraordinary among the people. On Christmas Day 394, or 395, the population of Barcelona, in a tumultuous access of enthusiasm, practically compelled Paulinus to receive the priesthood at the hands of Bishop Lampius, although he was not at all in the prescribed canonical conditions.[2] Soon afterwards Paulinus decided to retire to Nola by the tomb of St Felix. He embarked with Therasia for Narbonne, and was welcomed most warmly by St Ambrose who wished to enrol him among his clergy,[3] at least nominally, and far more coldly by Pope Siricius, the reasons for which Paulinus does not define.[4] He passed the last thirty-five years of his life at Nola in the exercise of mortification and prayer. What remained to him of his patrimony he devoted to building a new basilica to St Felix, which was inaugurated in 403. In 409, on the death of Bishop Paulus, he received Episcopal dignity. If he had had a mind so commonplace as to wish to be revenged on those who had detracted from his life, he could have found a striking opportunity when in the year 410 he witnessed the arrival at Nola, miserable and frozen with terror, of the fugitives fleeing before the hordes of Alaric. The flood of the barbarians had passed over those rich domains, those white villas, and those good things which had rendered Gallo-Roman life so pleasant and so agreeable that to renounce them had seemed folly.

---

[1] On the Christianity of Ausonius, see *ibid.*, p. 53–63. Ausonius' works have been edited by Peiper (B.T., 1886) and Schenkl, M.G.H., 5, 2 (1883). French translation by Corpet in Panckoucke's and in Nisard's collection.

[2] Paulinus, *Ep.* l, 10 ; iii, 4.

[3] *Ep.* iii, 4.

[4] *Ep.* iv, 13–14. That he should have been suspected of Priscillianism (see Babut, R.H.L.R., 1910, p. 109 et s.), is a paradox which the most refined subtilty has not succeeded in rendering likely.

Latin civilisation, whose seductiveness and requirements they had lately opposed to his vow of asceticism had resolved itself into dust.

He died on the 22nd June 431, at the age of 76 or 77.   His body was buried in the basilica of St Felix ; later on, it was to be transferred to the Church of St Barthélemy in Rome.

VI

His work is divided in the *Corpus Scriptorum Ecclesiasticorum Latinorum* into one volume of prose and one of verse.

The prose writings are all in letters.   A panegyric on Theodosius, composed by Paulinus in 394–5 on the occasion of the victory of the Emperor over Maximus and Eugenius, has not come down to us.   Hartel gives 51 letters in his edition.[1]   *Ep.* xxxiv, which is a sermon on well-doing, must be set apart.   We possess only a fragment of *Ep.* xlviii. The authenticity of *Ep.* xlvi and xlvii, addressed to Rufinus, without being improbable, is uncertain.[2]   These letters are scattered between the years 394 and 413 ; one only, the 51st, must be placed between 423 and 426.   Their chronology is rather difficult, for they are not disposed in the manuscripts according to their order in point of time.

It is not open to doubt that Paulinus was esteemed by his contemporaries as one of the most remarkable of letter writers. St Augustine,[3] and St Jerome [4] speak of his letters with an enthusiasm which appears to be sincere ; St Jerome goes so far as to compare him to Cicero : " *In epistolari studio prope Tullium representas,*" he wrote to him.   We find less pleasure in them than these eminent correspondents, and for these reasons.

In the first place, there is an excessive abundance of quotations from the Bible which is rather overwhelming. " More than any other Catholic writer of the time," Babut very well remarks,[5] " he multiplies extracts from the Bible. Sometimes there are passages or entire verses, more often

---

[1] There are at least 14 or 15 which have been lost, according to the allusions given in them : cf. Reinelt, p. 54 et s.
[2] There are arguments in a contrary sense in Reinelt, p. 45, Philipp, p. 67.
[3] *Ep.* xxvii, 2 ; clxxxvi, 40.
[4] *Ep.* lviii, 11, and lxxxv, 1.
[5] R.H.L.R., 1910, p. 129.   Cf. Philipp, p. 77.

scraps of two or three words or simple allusions. . . . The quotations, or quasi-quotations, are only on rare occasions distinguished from the text by a word which qualifies them, such as *scriptum est* or *dicente apostolo*. As a rule, they are incorporated in the sentences. Paulinus tangles up his own words and what he quotes. He incessantly expresses his own thoughts by means of expressions taken from Scripture, or rather his own thoughts seem made up of a continuous flow of Biblical *souvenirs*. We have here a special kind of literature written for a scholarly few, the full savour of which escapes us. . . ." Let me add that Paulinus, beneath his camel's hair shirt, which was a present from his friend Sulpicius Severus, was a man of letters according to the taste of his age and of his old professor Ausonius. He takes care to excuse himself here and there when any reminiscences of profane literature come into his mind,[1] but these repentances are fugitive. As a matter of fact, his prose is adorned with all the flowers of rhetoric, and nowhere exhibits any repugnance to diffuse developments carefully and even meticulously prepared.[2] He is regardless only of the fact that there should be some limit even to what is pleasing, and that discretion is a virtue in a writer. Lastly, his letters in prose all refer to the time when the form of his thought and life was definitely settled. He gives us no confidences in connection with the stages through which he passed as an opulent patrician before arriving at this point of humility and detachment. Hence our curiosity is somewhat disappointed.

Notwithstanding, this part of his work offers some interest. Many illustrious names of the period are mentioned. His correspondence with Sulpicius Severus is particularly attractive. Linked with Sulpicius in close friendship, Paulinus had preceded him in the path of asceticism, and Sulpicius wished to regard him as his spiritual guide, although the modesty of Paulinus refused to allow this. They had been victims of the same adverse comments, and the same outcry, on account of their breach with the world. They felt themselves so fully united in heart that Paulinus liked to consider that their affection had been predestined.[3] It is in their

---

[1] See Philipp, p. 58 et s.
[2] E.g. : *Ep.* xxiii, 10 et s. (Hartel, I, p. 167).
[3] *Ep.* xxiii, 15.

letters especially that the quality of the religious sentiment residing in the choice souls of those times can be seen. The letter to Jovius [1] fairly well indicates the position taken by Paulinus in the debated question of the lawfulness of utilising the old learning, which was always arising again. A cultured Christian, Jovius took pleasure in Plato, Xenophon, Demosthenes, Cato, Varro and Cicero, and allowed himself to be imbued with certain ideas on chance and fortune somewhat incompatible with Catholic sentiment. While giving large praise to his intellectual qualities, his *facundia* and his *doctrina*, Paulinus begs him not to allow himself to be captivated by the " pernicious charm " of pagan literature. Let him take from it the qualities it is able to impart, *linguae copiam et oris ornatum*, but as a man who arms himself with hostile weapons in order to make a better use of them, and let him turn them to the service of true wisdom. It is practically the theory of Jerome ; from this time onward there was agreement on this question among minds of any scope of vision. Disputes on matters of doctrine are not absent even from these letters. But Paulinus was not of a bellicose temperament ; he was a gentle and modest man of profound humility and charity who did not at all think that he need espouse the heated quarrels of the great champions of orthodoxy, although on fundamental points he sided with them.

VII

THERE is general agreement in according a marked preference to his work in verse. Paulinus was thoroughly acquainted with the *technique* of poetry ; he had been educated in a good school. Like Ausonius he uses great diversity of metres. In the same piece he passes on from the hexameter to the iambic trimeter, then to the elegiac, to go back finally to the form used at the commencement.[2] Like Ausonius again, he had at his service the whole lexicon of the revered poets Virgil, Horace, Ovid and Statius ; from Ausonius himself he made flattering extracts.[3] His memory was so loaded with reminiscences that he, so scrupulous about everything bearing on the

[1] *Ep.* xvi (Hartel, I, 120).
[2] *Carm.* xxi : cf. x, xi, xxxiii.
[3] See Philipp, p. 19–57.

M

faith, came to apply to his own beliefs turns of expression coming in a straight line of descent from the poets of paganism. He calls St John the Baptist " *semideumque* virum " ; [1] he depicts Christ enthroned on high in heaven in these words : " *Inridebat eos caelesti Christus ab arce.*" [2] He said of the child Celsus, who died at the age of eight and whose intelligence appeared to be full of promise, that his parents feared the revenge of some kind of jealous Nemesis : " *Gaudebant trepido praesagi corde parentes dum metuunt tanti* muneris invidiam.*" [3] This method, moreover, was customary with nearly all the Christian poets of the first centuries and only appears to have provoked very rare protests.

The classification of his poems does not present any difficulty. I have already drawn attention to his correspondence with Ausonius.[4] In it Paulinus does not seem to be so very different from Ausonius intellectually, but his Christianity awakened in him new refinements. When he describes the moral transformation which had taken place in him, his self-abandonment to the Divine will, his concern as to his state in the future life, it is *his* soul speaking to ours in spite of the trivial niceties of style over which he still lingers.[5] The group of poems in honour of St Felix include no fewer than 14 pieces of varying length.[6] Every year Paulinus wrote one for January 14th, the anniversary of the death of the saint and of his " birth " into life eternal.[7] The subject ran the risk of seeming monotonous. Without completely avoiding this difficulty Paulinus very skilfully diversified his matter, relating either the chief episodes in the life of the Saint, or the miracles that had been accomplished through his intercession. These poems provide a host of original features in connection with the history of popular devotions.[8] His description of the new Basilica of St Felix is deserving of the attention of those interested in Christian art.[9] We can also

---

[1] *Carm.* vi, 252. [2] *Carm.* xvi, 122. [3] *Carm.* xxxi, 29.

[4] *Carm.* x ; xi. On the course taken by this correspondence, see P. de Labriolle, *op. cit.*, p. 51.

[5] Cf. x, 19 et s.

[6] *Carm.* xii–xvi ; xviii–xxi ; xxiii ; xxvi–xxix. *Carmen* xii has 29 lines, *Carmen* xxi, 858. These poems were written between the years 395 and 407.

[7] *Carm.* xiv, 2 : " Qua corpore terris occidit et Christo superis est natus in astris ". Hence its title *Natalicia* (cf. *Ep.* xxviii, 6).

[8] G. Boissier has skilfully brought some of these out (*Fin du Pagan.*, II, 94 et s.).

[9] *Carm.* xxvii–xxviii.

gather precious sidelights on the interior evolution of Paulinus [1] who is less discreet here than in his prose, and on the religious struggles of the period which he visualises more than once without however falling into the tone of the polemist.[2]

He found another source of inspiration in the Bible whose inexhaustible fruitfulness for a poet in search of a style worthy of the pen of a Christian he pointed out to Jovius.[3] Paulinus was the first of the numerous line of poets to imitate the Psalms.[4] Renewing the attempt of Juvencus, he also paraphrased the Gospel in 330 hexameters in order to celebrate St John the Baptist.[5] He has been reproached with emasculating the Hebrew poetry to excess; desirous of edification before everything else, his tender and restrained soul chose instinctively the points likely to touch, while doing his best to tone down what might give offence to unbelievers.

He did not go so far as certain kinds of literature much favoured among the pagans, which he only appropriated in order to infuse a new spirit into them. Of this kind is the *Epithalamium* which he composed for the marriage of Julian (the future Julian of Eclana, the opponent of St Augustine) and Titia; [6] his Christian spirituality eliminates from it all appeal to voluptuousness to the taste of writers like Catullus and Claudian; the *Propemticon* addressed to Niceta, the apostle of the Dacians, and Bishop of Remesiana; [7] the *Consolatio* in which, in connection with the mourning of Pneumatius and Fidelis who had lost their son Celsus, he tenderly recalls the memory of his only son who had died not long since in Spain shortly after his birth.[8] Other pieces resemble the familiar swing of one of Horace's epistles,[9] or assume the gravity of inscriptions intended to explain to the people the mural paintings in their Churches.[10]

[1] *Carm.* xxi.
[2] *Carm.* xxvii. R. Pichon has shown that Paulinus, without naming him, refutes some of the arguments of Vigilantius, the heresiarch (R.E.A., XI [1909], p. 237–242).
[3] *Carm.* xxii, 149 et s.
[4] *Carm.* vii, viii-ix (Ps. 1, 2, 136).
[5] *Carm.* vi.
[6] *Carm.* xxv.
[7] *Carm.* xvii. Lucilius, Corn. Gallus, Propertius, Tibullus, Horace, and Statius had largely exploited the same class of writing. See above, p. 302.
[8] *Carm.* xxxi.
[9] *Carm.* xxii; xxxii.
[10] Compare the *Dittochaeon* by Prudentius. If the *de Obitu Baebiani* (*Carm.* xxxiii) is by Paulinus that would prove that he composed *epigrammata* of the same order for private and domestic use.

We see how varied was his *facile*, smooth and limpid talent, and how much his efforts must have contributed to the Christianising of Latin poetry. Paulinus had no genius, but he possessed the gift of restraint, a delicacy that is sometimes charming, and a happy turn of mind for intimate and personal poetry. "We see springing forth in him some drops from that stream which overflowed so abundant and clear from St Gregory of Nazianzen, and so tumultuous from St Augustine." [1] It was largely due to him that Nola became "one of the holy cities of the West." [2] Paulinus himself was admired less for the quality of his poetry than for that of his soul, and for the magnificent example which he had given of the renunciation of his worldly possessions. *Praestantissimum praesentium temporum exemplum* Sulpicius Severus called him. [3]

[1] A. Puech, *Le poète Prudence,* p. 157.
[2] H. Delehaye, *Les Orig. du Culte des Martyrs,* Brus., 1912, p. 347.
[3] *Vita Martini,* xxv.

CHAPTER V

ST JEROME AND HIS TIMES

BIBLIOGRAPHY

I. St Jerome.—See Table No. VII. The fundamental work on St Jerome is no longer Grutzmacher's *Hieronymus*, 3 vols. L. and B. 1901-1908, but Cavallera's still unfinished *St Jérôme, Sa Vie et ses Oeuvres*, 2 vols. (Paris and Louvain, 1922). On St Jerome's language, cf. H. Goelzer's *Etude lexic. et gramm. de la latinité de S. Jérôme*, 1884 ; A. Ottolini's *La rettorica nelle Epist. de Girolamo da Stridone*, Cremona, 1905 ; C. Kunst's *de S. Hier. studiis Ciceronianis* (Diss. *philol. Vindob.*, vol. XII, p. 2 [1918]) ; Reiter in *B. ph. W.*, 1919, pp. 642, 666, 690 ; L. Laurand, in R.S.R. 1919, pp. 371-2.

II. Rufinus.—The work of Rufinus is very scattered and has not yet been collected into a *Corpus*.—A. Translations. St Basil's *Instituta monachorum* were published by Holstenius, *Codex regularum monasticarum et canonicarum*, Augsburg (1759), I, 67-108 ; the nine discourses of St Gregory of Nazianzen appear in C.V., XLVI (1910): Migne, P.G., XXXVI, 735, only gives the prologue. Origen's *de Principiis* is to be found in P.G., XI, 111-414, and in C.B. (1913, by Koetschau) ; *the History of the Church* by Eusebius of Cæsarea, in P.G., XX, 45-906, and C.B. (1903-1909, by Schwartz and Mommsen): the two last books, which deal with the years 324-395, are by Rufinus himself, and are also to be found in P.L., XXI, 461-540 ; O. F. Fritzsche issued at Zurich in 1873 the *Epistula Clementis ad Jacobum;* the *Sententiae* of Sextus are in Gildemeister, Bonn 1873, and A. Elter's *Gnomica*, L. 1892 ; the *de recta in Deum fide*, in C.B. (1901, by Van de Sande Bakhuyzen). The other translations are included in vols. I, XII, XIII, XIV, XVII, XXXI, XXXII, of *Patr. Grecque;* the *Historia Monachorum* is in P.L., XXI, 623-688.—B. Personal works. P.L., XXI, 295-688.—C. Works unauthenticated. *Ibid.* The *Commentarius in prophetas minores tres Osee, Joel et Amos* should be by Julian of Eclana, according to Dom Morin, *R. Bén.*, XXX (1913), 1-24. Dom Wilmart, *R. Bén.*, XXXI (1914), 258-276, restores to Lithbert, Abbot of St Rufinus Abbey (XIIth century) the *Commentarius in LXXV Davidis psalmos.*

III. The Pilgrimages to the Holy Land.—*Itiner. Burdigalense* (in the year 333), P.L., VIII, 783-796 ; Geyer, in C.V., XXXIX, 1-33 ; *Peregrinatio Aetheriae* (about 395), C.V., *ibid.*, 35-101 ; W. Heraeus, Heidelburg 1908 (*Samml. vulgarlat. Texte*, I) ; *Eucherii quae fertur de situ Hieros. urbis* (Vth century), C.V., pp. 123-134 ; *Breviarius de Hieros.* (Vth to VIth century), C.V., pp. 151-155. See Geyer for accounts of a later date.—Consult: F. Cabrol, *Étude sur la Peregrinatio Silviae, les Eglises de Jérusalem, la discipline et la liturgie au IVᵉ Siècle*, Paris and Poitiers 1895 ; J. Anglade, *de latinitate libelli qui inscriptus est Peregrinatio ad loca sancta*, 1905 ; E. Lofstedt, *Philol. Kommentar zur Per Aetheriae*, Upsala 1911. English translation of the *Peregr. Aetheriae*, by J. H. Bernard, London 1891.

IV. Sulpicius Severus.—P.L., XX, 95-248 ; Halm, in C.V., vol. I (1866) ; text and French translation of the *Chronica* by Lavertujon, 2 vols. 1896-1899 ;

the edition of the *Vita Martini*, by Dubner-Lejay, 1890.—Consult: H.
Goelzer, *Gramm. in Sulpitium Severum observationes*, 1883.—French transla-
tion of the works of Sulpicius Severus by Herbert and Riton in the *Biblioth.
Panckoucke*, 1848-9, 2 vols.

SUMMARY

I. St Jerome's Destiny.—II. His early years.—III. The Biographies of the
Monks.—IV. The *Chronica.*—V. The translations of Origen.—VI. St
Jerome in Rome. The Council of Patrician Women. The Satirist.
—VII. The *Discussion between a Luciferian and an Orthodox.* The *Adv
Helvidium.*—VIII. St Jerome the Translator of the Sacred Books.
The First Phase.—IX. His Departure for the East. The Second
Phase.—X. St Jerome and the *Hebraica Veritas.* St Augustine's Reser-
vations.—XI. The Commentaries on the Bible—XII. The *de Viris
Illustribus.* The *Adv. Jovinianum.* The *Contra Vigilantium.* The
Dialogues against the Pelagians.—XIII. The Origenist Dispute.
Rufinus of Aquileia.—XIV. The Personality of St Jerome.—XV. The
Pilgrimages to the Holy Land. The *Peregrinatio Aetheriae.*—XVI.
Sulpicius Severus.

I

Among the leading representatives of Christian thought in
the IVth century St Jerome had a special career.

At a time when high ecclesiastical positions already
possessed influence and *prestige*, he was neither a Bishop as
were St Hilary, St Augustine, or St Ambrose, nor an Arch-
bishop, as was St Basil, nor a Patriarch, as was St John
Chrysostom. It is true he might have been Pope but for the
animosities he aroused. He himself tells us that from the date
of his sojourn in Rome, from 382 to 385, the close intimacy
which united him with Pope Damasus had marked him
out in the eyes of almost every one as his eventual successor.
" . . . *Totius in me Urbis studia consonabant. Omnium
paene judicio dignus summo sacerdotio decernebar.*" [1] A cabal
drove him from the Pontificate, and we can believe that he
consoled himself for this without difficulty since he was able
to retain his precious liberty. He accepted the priesthood
on one express condition namely that of remaining a monk
and free from any link with the life of the world.[2] We can
see in him a very clear purpose to eliminate from his life anything that could intrude upon his complete independence
and impair its fruitfulness.

Neither had he, like the great pastors whose names I have
recalled, vast congregations to feel the power of his words.

---

[1] *Ep.* xlv, 3.   [2] *Contra Ioh. Ierosolym.*, c. xli.

We have some homilies of St Jerome; nearly a hundred have been discovered during the last few years.[1] But these are altogether familiar allocutions, " whispered in a corner of the monastery," [2] as he himself says, and delivered to his monks at Bethlehem. Properly speaking, they did not reach the Christian public.

And so this man who for nearly forty years was one of the lights of Christianity and fashioned so many souls after his own ideal, owed all his influence to his qualities as a scholar and still more to his initiatives as a man of action. Cut off from external aids his own personality accomplished everything. Let me endeavour to describe him in his process of formation and in the work of his maturity.

II

THE exact date of the birth of Jerome (*Eusebius Hieronymus*) is unknown. Plausible calculations place it between the years 340 and 350.[3] In his *de Viris Illustribus* [4] he informs us that he was born at Stridon, and that this town before its destruction by the Goths was situated on the confines of Dalmatia and Pannonia. An inscription, published in 1882,[5] enables us to localise Stridon in the neighbourhood of the modern town of Grahovo Stridon belonged to the Roman province of Dalmatia.

His parents were Christian. " From the cradle I was brought up on the milk of the Catholic faith," [6] he wrote. He was, however, not to receive baptism until much later, in accordance with the custom at that time very general, which theologians such as Gregory of Nazianzen, Gregory of

---

[1] Dom Morin in 1897 brought to light 59 homilies by Jerome on the Psalms, 10 on the Gospel of St Mark, and 10 more on different texts from the Bible (A.M., III, 2, p. 373). For an account of his discovery see R.H.L.R., I (1896), p. 393–434, *Revue d'Hist. eccl.*, I (1900), p. 75 and 78, and R.B., XIX (1902), p. 113–144. In 1903 Dom Morin further published 14 homilies on the Psalms, and 2 homilies on Isaias, known already, but whose authenticity was disputed (A.M., III, 3).

[2] *Ep.* cxii, 22 : " Mihi sufficit cum auditore vel lectore pauperculo in angulo monasterii susurrare."

[3] Cf. Grutzmacher, vol. I, p. 45 et s.

[4] § 135.

[5] *Corpus Insc. lat.*, III, 4, 9860. This inscription was found graven on a stone marking the boundaries of Stridon and Salviae. Mgr. Bulic has shown that the doubts cast on its authenticity have no serious foundations (*Festschrift fur Otto Benndorf*, Vienna, 1898, p. 276–280).

[6] *Ep.* lxxxii, 2.

Nyssa, and St John Chrysostom were already combating. His family was in easy circumstances; they held landed property, and there still remained a few more or less dilapidated *villulae* [1] even after the passage of the barbarians. As a young man Jerome went to Rome to finish his education which had begun in his native town. He there had for his professor in grammar, the famous Donatus, the commentator on Terence and Virgil, and the author of the manuals *Ars Major* and *Ars Minor*, on which from the end of the IVth century to beyond the IXth the interpretation of .grammarians was to base itself. With the exception of St Augustine perhaps no other Christian author was more strongly nurtured on the pith of the classics than Jerome.

His life as a student was not irreproachable. As often happens in the case of those who resolve to live a stricter life after a period of dissipation, Jerome was to retain in his heart both the sting and the remorse for his past as a young man. He carried away from it the conviction that the dangers offered by life are such that inevitably frail souls (that is to say almost all) must succumb to them unless they place between themselves and temptation a barrier that is almost impassable. This was the leading motive for his asceticism and the reason why, without making of the religious life an absolute obligation, he constantly praised it as the best, and as the one offering the greatest moral security.

It was in Rome, however, that he was ultimately baptised. At the conclusion of his studies he travelled in Gaul with his friend Bonosus. He touched at Trèves, and there seems to have resolved to embrace a life of mortification.[2] We find him shortly afterwards at Aquileia in Illyria. He formed one of an association given up to the practice of asceticism, of which Chromatius, the future Bishop of Aquileia, was the leading spirit.[3] Then, coming to an abrupt decision, he left for the East after bidding farewell to his relatives at Stridon.

A group of pilgrims set forth with him on the road to Jerusalem. But he saw his companions dropping off on the

---

[1] *Ep.* lxvi, 14. Jerome was obliged to sell these in 397 in order to maintain his institution at Bethlehem.

[2] *Ep.* iii, 5 ; *Comm. in Gal.*, Preface of I, II.

[3] Some Commentaries (P.L., XX) by Chromatius, Bishop of Aquileia, still exist (P.L., XX). Cf. P. de Puniet in the *Rev. d'Hist. Eccl.*, VI, 1905, p. 15–32 ; and Paschini in *R. Bén.*, 1909, 469–475.

journey; Innocent and Hylas the slave died, and Niceas, a sub-deacon, returned to his own country. Jerome himself fell ill at Antioch. After recovering, he delayed some time in that city to attend the lessons of Apollinaris of Laodicea. His vocation as a great "intellectual" had already been indicated. He would not separate from his books which he had bought not so long back in Rome, and which he was shortly to carry with him into solitude. He had also just applied himself to the study of the Greek language which was an indispensable instrument for his future task.

Nevertheless, he felt his desire for the monastic life to be swerving. The news that his friends Bonosus and Rufinus had already made the sacrifice, and had settled, one on the coast of Dalmatia, and the other in Nitria, made him blush at such vacillations. He buried himself in the desert of Chalcis on the frontier of Syria, fifty miles from Antioch. He was to remain there three years, from 375 to 377.

He courageously accepted the hard life practised by the monks of the desert. He gives a picture of himself, his body covered with a hideous sack, black with sweat and dust, lying on the bare ground, drinking water and sustaining life on uncooked food. This physical wretchedness did not guarantee him from the worst temptations :

> " I, even I, who from fear of Gehenna had condemned myself to such a prison tenanted only by scorpions and wild beasts, often felt myself transported into the midst of girls dancing. I was pale from fasting, and my imagination was boiling over with desire in a frozen body wherein the fire of my passions wrought frenzy." [1]

After days and entire nights passed in groanings and anguish, fearing his cell as though the accomplice of his thoughts,[2] he would take flight anywhere to still more rugged spots, and sometimes a kind of ecstasy came to flood him with sweetness in the midst of his prayers and tears.

Happily intellectual work brought him its aid which was sometimes painful, but always efficacious. It was in the desert of Chalcis that he learned the Hebrew tongue under the

---

[1] *Ep.* xxii, 7.
[2] "Ipsam quoque cellulam meam, quasi cogitationum mearum consciam, pertimescebam." (*Ibid.*)

direction of a lettered Jew who rendered him the most scholarly service.[1] His initiation was a severe penance :

> " Relinquishing there," he relates,[2] " the skilled turns of Quintilian, the flood of eloquence overflowing from Cicero, the gravity of Frontonius, and the charm of Pliny, I set myself to learn the Hebrew alphabet and to study a language of guttural and heavy-breathing words.[3] Much effort as I had expended and many the difficulties I had suffered, how many times in desperation did I not break off from a study which the stubborn desire for knowledge made me resume again afterwards, I alone can testify, I who have toiled so hardly, and with me those who then shared my life. And I render thanks to God for any delicious fruit I now gather from so bitter a sowing."

Moreover, except during those periods when his vexed soul sought isolation, he was not too far from the civilised world so as not to be able to keep up a connection with his friends through the interchange of letters. He had books [4] sent to him through them, and he offered them in exchange Bibles copied under his own supervision by *alumni* trained for the purpose. He even had the happiness of receiving a visit from his friend Evagrius.[5] An essay (lost) commenting on the prophet Abdias dates from this period, also the *Life of Paul of Thebes* of which I shall speak further on.

The desert would have held a real attraction for him if he had been allowed to live there in peace. But the interests and concerns which Jerome had thought to flee soon came to start him off again. Antioch, the metropolis of Syria, had for many years been a prey to disputes on matters of doctrine which kept on increasing in intensity, and its echoes reached the desert of Chalcis. Three parties, those of Miletius, Paulinus, and Vitalis, were affirming with equal asperity their orthodoxy as regards the Trinity ; all three could boast of sympathies that were worthy of respect and alleged themselves to be in full agreement with the *cathedra Petri*.[6] The *formulæ* on which they were disputing were not very familiar

---

[1] *Ep.* xviii, A, 10. [2] *Ep.* cxxv, 12. [3] *Stridentia anhelantiaque verba.*
[4] See *Ep.* v, 2. [5] *Ep.* vii, 1.
[6] *Ep.* xvi, 2, *ad Domasum :* " Meletius, Vitalis atque Paulinus tibi haerere se dicunt."

to the western mind of Jerome, who suspected some snare.[1]
Moreover, almost every day fanatics from the different parties
came to extort from him his profession of faith, and treated
him as a heretic when it did not square with their own.[2] In
his uncertainty Jerome thought to solicit the advice of Pope
Damasus. He wrote to Damasus a first letter in which he
celebrated the unique *prestige* of the See of Rome and declared
himself ready to side with the opinion of Damasus whatever
it might be.[3] This letter received no reply. He wrote
a second,[4] to which Damasus does not appear to have replied
either. Jerome was feeling weary of these continuous
summonses to which he was being subjected by the monks,
his brethren in the desert.[5] Their pretensions to regulate
consciences became unbearable to him. " I am ashamed to
say this ; " he wrote, " we condemn the universe from the
depth of our cells ; huddled under sackcloth and ashes we
pass judgment on our Bishops. What is this pride, more
suited to kings, doing under the habit of the penitent ?
Chains, squalor, and long hair are outward signs of a remorse
which groans, and not emblems of domination ! " [6] Many
solitaries, vexed by this indiscreetness, abandoned the desert
where they had previously shut themselves off, " preferring,"
as they said, " to live in the midst of wild beasts rather
than with Christians of that kind." [7] As soon as the season
permitted Jerome bent his footsteps towards Antioch.

Rome had just recognised Paulinus as an orthodox
Bishop.[8] He conferred, or rather imposed, the priesthood
on Jerome.[9] It was understood that he was to remain
free from any pastoral or liturgical obligation. Notwithstanding his troublesome experiences in the desert of Chalcis,
he remained profoundly attached to his monastic ideal, and
to his twofold profession of scholarship and asceticism, upon
which he had already begun to regulate his life.

He knew Gregory of Nazianzen at Constantinople whither
he went shortly, and learned to profit by his instructions in
exegesis[10] while at the same time he conceived from his studies
an admiration for Origen, for which he was later on to repent

---

[1] *Ep.* xv, 3-4.   [2] *Ep.* xvii, 2-3.   [3] *Ep.* xv.
[4] *Ep.* xvi.   [5] *Ep.* xvi, 2.   [6] *Ep.* xvii, 3.
[7] *Ibid.*   [8] St Ambrose, *Ep.* xii.
[9] *Contra Joh. Hierosolym.*, xli.
[10] *Comm. in Is.*, vi, 1 (Migne, xxiv, 93) ; *Ep.* i, I ; lii, 8, etc. He willingly
called Gregory *praeceptor meus.*

for having given too strong expression. He was still living there when the second Oecumenical Council began in May 381. But another Council was about to open in Rome. He decided to accompany thither Paulinus of Antioch and Epiphanius of Salamis.[1] Possibly Pope Damasus, to whom his talents were known, had given him a personal invitation to come and meet him there.

III

HE settled there in the year 382.

His reputation as a writer had preceded him. Let us cast an eye over his labours prior to his sojourn in Rome (382–385).

He had already inaugurated with his *Life of Paul* that series of biographies of monks which he was to continue a little later with his *Life of Malchus* and his *Life of Hilarion* (published between the years 386–391).[2] Already stories about these holy people were popular, at least in the countries where they had lived. Jerome was content to gather them together, giving to them of set purpose the charm of a very simple style, and to reconstitute the atmosphere of the marvellous with which the imagination of the crowd surrounded the anchorites. In this way he made up real little historical romances which were amusing as fairy tales, but which were profitable to the conscience in quite another way on account of the moral lessons emerging from them. Just like one of Perrault's Fairy Tales he began " Once upon a time there was an old man called Malchus. . . ." And then were seen the extraordinary adventures of young men who, disgusted with the world, or driven away by persecution, had taken refuge in the desert. Jerome outlined certain features of the usual scene with a few touches which were always the same— a grotto serving as the cell of the hermit, a spring at which he quenched his thirst, and a palm-tree whose leaves woven together supplied a ready-made garment. He depicts the solitaries giving themselves up to the most rigid fasting in

---

[1] *Ep.* cviii, 6 ; cxxvii, 7.

[2] He had formed the project of writing a kind of history of the Church in a series of monographs of the same kind (cf. *Vita Malchi*, I). He did not follow up this idea, neither that of a history of the reigns of Gratian and Theodosius which he was considering in 381 (*Chronicle*, ed. Helm, p. 7).

order to mortify their flesh and to free their souls from evil suggestions. Thus Hilarion, the founder of monachism, from the age of 21 to 27 years, during the first three years consumed only 17 gallons of lentils soaked in cold water, and for the three following years dry bread and water and salt ; from the age of 27 to 30, he supported himself on wild herbs without oil. But illness compelled him nevertheless to add a little oil to his frugal *régime,* which he kept up to his 63rd year. Then, feeling his strength growing weaker, he thought that an old man had fewer needs than a young one. He therefore cut down his bread from the age of 64 to 80. His daily food and drink then weighed barely five ounces. He passed the rest of his life in this manner. This practice of abstinence won for him great renown and also a special power over created beings. By killing in himself all material desires he made himself master over matter and made it subject to his law. Not only did he exorcise those possessed, and heal the sick, but even the animals and the elements became subject to him. At his bidding the devil came forth from the body of a camel which had been all foaming and maddened by it. He compelled a boa to climb upon a heap of logs and allow itself to be burnt. And with three signs of the Cross he caused the sea, which a cataclysm had projected beyond its limits, to retire to its bed.

The History of Paul and Antony contains the same mixture of facts which are probably accurate (they are rather difficult to disentangle) and of more or less fantastic poetic rendering. There is no reason to add that in Jerome's mind these stories were solely meant to amuse. They are consistent with his apostolate, although possessing somewhat more liberty of fancy. Jerome was not unaware that in all great matters some element of imagination and fantasy finds entrance. Why should not the very strangeness of these far-off stories be the prelude to some generous vocation by stirring up the imagination ? In any case, the edifying intention in them is strongly marked here and there. Thus the Life of Paul introduces a parallel between the deceits of the joys of the world and the happiness, fruitful in quite another way, of the eremitic or monastic life. The monks themselves gathered useful lessons from the life of Malchus who had retired from the world, and then experienced a nostalgia, and had tried to get back to it, and thereby exposed himself to tragic misadventures the vicissitudes of which Jerome gives in detail.

We may say that through these lives of solitaries, the success of which was considerable, Jerome gave a fresh character to hagiographic literature. For long the acts of the martyrs, and the heroism of " witnesses " to the faith, had constituted its basis. But the era of bloodshed was finished. The struggle now, no less bitter, was that of man against himself, the example of which must be set forth for the piety of the faithful. Henceforward, the lives of saints, their works, and their *traits* were to become the food of religious souls—the genuine romance of which they would be justified in reading with pleasure because at the same time they would purify themselves.

IV

In the year 379–380, doubtless during his sojourn at Constantinople, Jerome wrote the *Chronicle* dedicated to a certain Gallianus, and to Vincentius, to whom was also to be dedicated another of his works, namely his translation of Origen's *Homilies*.

The χρονιχόι κανόνες of Eusebius of Cæsarea served as his model. We no longer possess the original work of Eusebius, but we are able partly to reconstruct it, thanks to an Armenian version published for the first time in 1818,[1] and to a large number of *excerpta* transcribed by other chronographers. In a first part (χρονογραφία), Eusebius set forth the chronological systems of the Chaldeans (according to Alexander Polyhistor, Abydenos,[2] and Josephus) ; of the Assyrians (according to Abydenos, Castor, Diodorus and Cephalion) ; of the Hebrews (according to the Old Testament, Josephus, and Clement of Alexandria) ; of the Egyptians (according to Diodorus, Manetho, and Porphyry) ; of the Greeks (according to Castor, Porphyry, and Diodorus) ; and of the Romans (according to Dionysius of Halicarnassus,

---

[1] In Armenian, by J. B. Aucher, at Venice ; in Latin, by J. Zohrab and A. Mai, at Milan. A German translation of the Armenian *Chronicle* has been given by J. Karst, 1911, in C.B., *Eusebius*, vol. V.

[2] The author of a history of Chaldea, written in the time of Antoninus (*Fragm. hist. gr.*, iv, 279–285).

Diodorus and Castor). The second part, by far the most important, was made up of a series of synchronous tables (χρονικόι κανόνες), in which figured the principal facts of universal history, especially those of sacred history, together with references to different computations (the years of Abraham, the Olympiads, the years of Rome, and the dates of Dynasties). The object set himself by Eusebius was to show the great antiquity of Moses ; [1] in addition, he desired to provide for the period posterior to the coming of Christ a chronological equipment for the *History of the Church* he was meditating. For his point of departure he took the year of Abraham's birth (2016–5 B.C.) and defined five divisions : (*a*) from Abraham to the taking of Troy ; (*b*) from the taking of Troy to the first Olympiad ; (*c*) from the first Olympiad to the second year of the reign of Darius ; (*d*) from the second year of the reign of Darius to the death of Christ ; (*e*) from the death of Christ to the twentieth year of the reign of Constantine.

Such is the work which Jerome undertook to introduce into the West in a Latin translation. He contented himself with making a translation pure and simple of the first part. In the sections following, inasmuch as his work was destined for the West, he felt he ought to insert a large number of facts dealing with general history, and especially with Roman history and even Roman literature. Lastly, this time without any guide, he continued the *Chronicle* of Eusebius from the twentieth year of Constantine down to the year 378, the date of the death of Valens.

This *opus tumultuarium*, as Jerome himself calls it, who confesses to have dictated it *velocissime*,[2] thus offers to us a threefold aspect in the form of a translation, a revision, and an original work. He had, however, felt its technical difficulties ; he indicates them in his preface [3] while apologising beforehand for any negligences of his scribes.[4] He conscientiously prepared his ground. His own personal sources have been carefully marked down ; [5] they are numerous

---

[1] Schoene, II, p. 5 (cf. Helm, p. 9, I, 5 et s.) : " Nam Moyses . . . omnibus . . . quos Graeci antiquissimos putant senior deprehenditur, Homero scilicet et Hesiodo Trojanoque bello ", etc. . . .
[2] Helm, p. 2, I, 12.   [3] *Ibid.*, p. 4–5.   [4] *Ibid.*, p. 6, l. 4.
[5] Mommsen, *Gesamm. Schriften*, VII, p. 606 ; Bauer, S.B.W., vol. CLXII (1909), 3 Abt., p. 42, 1.

—Eutropius, Suetonius, Rufius Festus, Ammianus Marcellinus, Aurelius Victor, etc. But we suspect that the *taedium operis* dulled his brain in more than one place. There are mistakes in translation and an often arbitrary and strange choice of events in what he writes down as memorable. Thus in the year 356 A.D., the murder of a monk by the Saracens; referring to the year 374, the following note occurs: " *Aquileienses clerici quasi chorus beatorum habentur* "; he does not seem able to get away from himself nor from anything that interested him personally. The same thing applies to his likes and dislikes: for this same year he had noted down the departure of Melania, the elder for Jerusalem, and in this connection recalls that she had deserved the name of Thecla [1] on account of her virtues, especially her humility; he crossed out this flattering mention when he fell out with her over Origenism. [2]

Notwithstanding, the work has rendered great service. To judge of this it is only necessary to examine a modern history of the Church, or even a history of Roman literature. The history of empires was represented to the Middle Ages, " just as the history of the Popes was contained in the notices in the *Liber Pontificalis*." [3] The *Chronicle* has been one of the fundamental books upon which all researches on the past of mankind have been based. [4]

V

WE know Origen's singular fate. This eminent mind, this powerful intellect, and the glory of Christianity in the IIIrd century, was to become a hot-bed of disputes and a firebrand of discord for a long series of generations. Familiar with all the systems of Greek philosophy and the speculations of the Gnostics, but at the same time deeply attached to the

---

[1] Helm, p. 247.

[2] Rufinus, *Contra Hier.*, II, xxv. But it is incorrect to accuse him of having substituted the name of Florentius for that of Rufinus: cf. Cavallera, in B.L.E., 1918, p. 318.

[3] Duchesne, *Liber Pontif.*, Preface to vol. I.

[4] To understand the different lists in the *Chronicle* requires a certain preliminary initiation. One will do well to consult the *Paléographie Latine* by Steffens-Coulon, Paris, 1910, p. 17. Useful concordance tables of the different reckonings are given by Schürer, *Gesch. der judischen Volkes*, 3rd ed., I, p. 773, and by Ginzel, *Handbuch der mathem. Chronologie*, at the end of vol. II.

rule of faith, Origen had conceived the idea of a vast synthesis in which to incorporate the fundamental principles of the Christian doctrine about God, Man, the Universe, and Scripture which was the source of all truth. This " summa " of theology, the book of *the Principles* (Περὶ Ἀρχῶν), Origen wrote at Alexandria shortly after the year 220, no doubt making use of the conferences which for twenty years he had been giving at the Catechetical School, to which educated Christians and half-converted pagans, or at least people curious about matters pertaining to Christianity, came in crowds. In spite of the respect which Origen's admirable clearness and genius had won for him, his methods did not escape arousing uneasiness. These misgivings only grew more pronounced in certain circles later on. Origen's orthodoxy was furiously attacked and passionately defended. These quarrels lasted for centuries, always being rekindled after long periods of quiet. The " errors " of Origen were to be explicitly condemned at Constantinople by the Councils of 543 and 553.

That Jerome was at first an admirer of Origen, and his faithful disciple, was evidence which one day his adversaries were to exploit against him, and which he himself was not able to cover up. The immense erudition of the Alexandrine Doctor had literally subjugated him and he found no words too strong to express his enthusiasm for such a model. We shall speak of the disagreeable consequences he was thus preparing for himself.

During the years 379 to 381, St Jerome rendered in Latin fourteen homilies of Origen on Jeremias, a like number on Ezechiel, and nine on Isaias.[1] He was to continue these translations during subsequent years. He had a clear conception of the character of his task as translator and explains himself in more than one passage.[2] His view was that the interpreter should translate *latine* (that is, *in good Latin*) and not merely *in latinam linguam*. A word-for-word servility seemed to him an absurd subjection ; he claimed for himself the examples of Terence, Plautus, Caecilius, and Cicero himself the translator of Plato, Xenophon, Æschines and Demosthenes. But he also indicated that a translation of the Scriptures demanded a much more scrupulous literalness

[1] For the manuscript translation, see B.A.L.A.C., 1914, 309.
[2] See his Preface to Origen's *Homilies* on Jeremias and Ezechiel ; *Ep.* lvii to Pammachius ; *Ep.* cvi, 3.

than that required for a non-canonical text, even the order of the words having a symbolic value in the Bible. Here, where we are able to compare his Latin with the Greek of Origen, we see how alert in him was that taste for humanism and fitting language which is one of the surest marks of his talent.[1]

VI

JEROME's memory is indissolubly bound up with that of the Roman Patrician ladies whose counsellor and friend he was. In Albina, Marcella, Asella, Fabiola, Principia, and still more, perhaps, Paula, her daughters and her grand-daughter (for Jerome knew the two generations of which Paula was the grandmother),[2] we hear the echo of the names which Jerome's correspondence brings down to us, in whose souls he could contemplate the most faithful reflection of the ideal he carried in his own heart.

Before Jerome came to Rome a certain number of Roman ladies belonging to the highest nobility had been accustomed to meet at the house of one of them, Marcella, who had established a kind of conventicle in her palace on Mount Aventine. She wished to create in the midst of the town which was still half pagan, and in which the Christians themselves did not always set an example, a little Thebaid where they could freely discourse upon holy things, read the Scriptures, and sing Psalms. This *coterie* of women was persuaded of the super-eminent virtues of the religious life, whose austerities they endeavoured to imitate in the midst of the bustle of the world.

When Jerome arrived in Rome in 382, his activity as a letter-writer had already made him known as a Hebrew scholar of the first order.[3] It was soon learnt that he was much appreciated by Pope Damasus, and that on questions of

---

[1] Cf. Klostermann, in T.U., N.F. I (1897), p. 2 and 33.

[2]

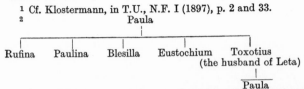

[3] Eighteen letters in our collection are anterior to 382. Cf. the list drawn up by Grutzmacher, *op. cit.*, I, p. 99.

philology he readily consulted him. Lastly his letters revealed his proselytising interest in the eremitic life which
he had himself lived in the desert of Chalcis, and which he
was in a position to advocate from his own knowledge. One
of his letters in particular, addressed to his friend Heliodorus,[1]
who had at first thought of following Jerome into the desert
and had then reconsidered it, had vividly struck the minds of
people on account of its eloquence (very artificial in our
opinion), but altogether to the taste of the time.[2]

Jerome was greeted with enthusiasm by the circle whose
aspirations I have described. During the three years which he
passed in Rome he became the centre and oracle of the
gatherings on the Aventine. There existed a kind of harmony,
already established between the souls which he was called
upon to direct, and his own tastes. These women of quite
superior education were passionately interested in Biblical
studies. Many of them, Marcella, Paula, Blesilla and
Eustochium, already knew Hebrew, or learnt it in order to
study the Scriptures and sing the Psalms in the same language
in which they had been written. To Jerome they were not
only his pupils, but his fellow-workers. Marcella especially,
according to the testimony of Jerome, put such intelligent
questions as to be instructive in themselves,[3] and Jerome
published a volume of letters written in reply to the difficulties which she submitted to him. We can see from them
that scholarship retained all its severity in this intellectual
intercourse. Jerome had no need to vulgarise nor render it
insipid. We may say that the influence of this feminine
curiosity, which here took so noble a form, reappears in all
the works of Jerome. How many times did he not decide to
put himself to the task of translating some commentary of
Origen, or to clear up some portion of Scripture, only because
Marcella, Paula, or Eustochium had asked him to do so![4]
In dedicating to them a certain number of his driest works,[5]

---

[1] *Ep.* xiv.

[2] Jerome himself recognised later on that this declamatory letter, at least in its
form, was a *jeu d'esprit* of his earliest youth. Cf. *Ep.* lxx, 2.

[3] *Ep.* lix, 11 : *Magis nos provocas quaestionibus, et torpens otio ingenium, dum
interrogas, doces.* Cf. *Ep.* cxxvii, 7.

[4] For the *Homilies* of Origen, cf. P.L., XXIV, 219 ; for the commentary on
Ezechiel and Isaias, P.L., XXV, 76 ; XXIV, 17 ; for the commentary on *Ecclesiastes*, P.L., XXIII, 1061 ; for the *Epistles of St Paul*, P.L., XXVI, 440.

[5] The commentaries on *Sophonia* (P.L., XXV, 1337), on *Isaias* (XXIV, 17),
and on *Ezechiel* (XXV, 15) are addressed to Paula and Eustochium.

Jerome might draw upon himself the ridicule of foolish men : [1] in reality he was only acquitting himself of a debt of gratitude towards those women who had inspired them.

But St Jerome's intercourse with these remarkable women was not limited to questions of scholarship and exegesis. He was really their director ; that is to say, by tracing out for them a certain type of life accounted the most perfect, he assisted them to get nearer to it in the midst of the miseries and weaknesses of everyday life. In this capacity he was the first of the line of such men as St Francis of Sales, Bossuet, and Fénelon. " Like them, he had the privilege of being the confidant of the most aristocratic souls of his time and of working upon moral material of a high quality." [2] But he counselled them to make sacrifices and renunciations far sterner than Fénelon ever required of the Comtesse de Montberon, or Bossuet of Madame de Luynes. Real religious life as conceived by Jerome consisted in the giving up of all joys, in fastings, mortifications, and tears ; above all, in celibacy, to the preservation of which all the other ascetic exercises co-operated. There are moments when we might say that Tertullian's spirit, violently hostile to nature and rejoicing in the deprivations which he imposed upon it, lived again in Jerome, so much vigorous conciseness, such plain-spoken directness does he use in inculcating the virtues which he loved.

Moreover, those to whom he addressed these rigorous counsels were not likely to find them too inexorable. They had already given up all those vanities whose nothingness he was seeking to show them. He confirmed them in a disposition they had already acquired, rather than imposed any change of life. But on numerous occasions, when going outside this circle thus won in advance, his efforts to expand the ascetic life encountered, even in Rome, the most violent opposition, and not only among laymen.

He was not spared either equivocal insinuations or direct attacks. " Why does he occupy himself always with women, and never with men ? " " If the men would question me about the Scriptures, I should not talk to the women," he

---

[1] Cf. *Praef. in Sophon. ;* Rufinus, *Apol.,* ii, 7 (P.L., XXI, 589) : *Puellis quoque et mulierculis scribens.* . . .

[2] Thamin, *Saint Ambroise et la morale chrétienne au IVᵉ siècle,* Paris, 1895, p. 386.

replied. What provoked the greatest exasperation were the *piquant* phrases he discharged at society in Rome. In Jerome there was the stuff of a Juvenal ; he readily compared himself to Lucilius. His letters are full of satirical portraits of extraordinary *verve*. One day he was denouncing worldly women, " the women who daub with vermilion and I don't know what other paints, their cheeks and eyelids ; whose plastered faces, disfigured with too much whitening, make one think of idols ; who cannot drop an involuntary tear without it hollowing out a streak ; . . . who make-up their heads with the hair of others, and furbish up for themselves a tardy youth over their senile wrinkles." [1] Another time it was false devotees who suffered : " A robe of dirty brown, a coarse belt, unclean hands and feet . . . but the belly which is not seen gorged with meats." [2] Even the clergy were not spared. For certain smart ecclesiastics, with curled hair, perfumed, skittish, and of the butterfly kind, prototypes of the gallant abbés of the XVIIIth century, Jerome reserved his most biting ridicule. A frame of mind whose sharpness his friends endeavoured to temper with a half-laugh,[3] was bound in the nature of things to create a coalition against him of all those whom he had belaboured. When Blesilla, the daughter of Paula, died, they accused Jerome of having killed her with fasts. The people tried to knock him down and all the monks with him, on one occasion.[4] We can guess too whether their tongues did not shoot forth their most viperish gibes against the school of asceticism (*castitatis chorus*) of which Jerome was the spiritual master. Not one of those noble women on the Aventine was spared.[5] As long as Pope Damasus lived, Jerome held up against the storm. But after the death of his protector all support was withdrawn from him and he had no other resource but to leave that " Babylon " [6] where it was not permitted to be a saint with impunity.

VII

DURING these three years of Roman life, during which he contracted strong friendships and tenacious enmities which

[1] *Ep.* xxxviii, 3.   [2] *Ep.* xxii, 27.   [3] *Ep.* xxvii, 2.
[4] *Ep.* xxxix, 5.   [5] *Ep.* xlv, 4.   [6] *Ibid.*, 6.

were to accompany him right to the end, Jerome did not
write any very important work. Twenty-six letters (*Ep.*
xix to xliv) belong to this period.   It is not certain that the
Discussion between a Luciferian and an Orthodox was not written
a little earlier, in the year 379 or 380 : in a tone of moderation
which he was not to practise very much longer, Jerome sets
forth the reasonable requirements of the Church as regards
the Arians who desired to re-enter her bosom, and he makes a
fictitious adversary, the disciple of Lucifer of Calaris, recognise
the enormity of the punishments which the latter demanded
against these repentant men.   The debate centred in a very
lively engagement between the two disputants, while stenographers took down their arguments.

The *Adversus Helvidium* strikes a *piquant* note in another
way.   Jerome's ascetic propaganda in Rome, in addition to
so many other forms of opposition, had brought forth a polemical pamphlet wherein a layman named Helvidius thought
there was no better way to ruin Jerome's contention as to the
superiority of celibacy than to attack the doctrine of the
perpetual virginity of Mary.   We do not know exactly who
Helvidius was.   Gennadius puts him down as a pupil of
Auxentius, the Arian Bishop of Milan.[1]   According to Jerome,
he was a man of mediocre talent.[2]   However, he thought it
advisable to reply in a short work of twenty-two chapters.

Helvidius directed his principal attack upon the belief
in the immaculate virginity of Mary *post partum*.   He made
much of certain texts in the Gospel, such as Matth. i, 18–20 ;
i, 25 ; Luke ii, 7, and viii, 20.   He also invoked the authority
of Tertullian (*de Mon.*, viii ;   *de Virg. Vel.*, vi ;   *de Carne
Christi*, vii) and that of Victorinus of Pettau.   Jerome
rejected the authority of Tertullian :   " De Tertulliano quidem
nihil amplius dico, *quam Ecclesiae hominem non fuisse.*"   He
affirms that Helvidius interpreted badly the views of
Victorinus.[3]   But he takes particular exception to the passages
from the Gospel on which Helvidius had set store.   He discusses them with power and precision, and most of the solutions which he favours, for instance the question of the

---

[1] *De Vir. Ill.*, xxxii (P.L., LVIII, 1077).
[2] 1: " . . . Hominem rusticum et vix primis quoque imbutum litteris ; . . .
ut discat aliquando reticere, qui numquam didicit loqui." § xvi : " Praetermitto
vitia sermonis, quibus omnis liber tuus scatet.   Taceo ridiculum exordium :
O tempora ! O mores ! etc. . . ."
[3] § xvii (P.L., XXIII, 201).

" brethren " of Jesus, have become traditional in the bosom of the Catholic Church. The *Adversus Helvidium* is the first treatise by a Latin specially devoted to Mariology, and this realm of ecclesiastical knowledge is largely due to Jerome.[1]

The two last chapters oppose the moral and religious advantages of celibacy to the worries entailed by marriage. After discussing many trivial details Jerome gladly gives rein to his rhetorical eloquence. He confesses that *rhetoricati sumus, et in morem declamatorum paululum lusimus.* Helvidius emerges from this bout riddled with shafts : [2]

> " O thou most ignorant of men," Jerome exclaims, " without taking the trouble of consulting the Scriptures thou hast soiled with thy slime the Virgin. Legend speaketh of a fool who, in order to be talked about, found nothing better to do than to set fire to the temple of Diana. . . . Following the example of this monstrosity, thou also hast fouled the sanctuary of the Holy Spirit by presuming to make issue therefrom a whole cartload of brothers and sisters. . . . Behold thee arrived at thy goal ; thy crime hath rendered thee famous ! "

VIII

It was when in Rome that St Jerome entered upon the task which was to fill twenty years of his life, namely the revision and translation of the Sacred Books.

At the end of the IVth century many far-seeing minds felt the need of a general recasting of the Latin translations of the Bible. Pope Damasus had the good sense to see that he had ready to his hand the kind of man required to carry out successfully such a task. He knew Jerome for a technician familiar with the Greek language and one who was capable of clearing up delicate questions of *textual* criticism. He therefore begged him to take in hand, not a fresh translation of the New Testament,—an initiative which at the outset would have seemed too daring,—but a simple revision of the Latin translations.

[1] Cf. J. Niessen, *die Mariologie des hl. Hieronymus*, Munster i W., 1913 (and B.A.L.A.C., 1914, p. 304).

[2] § xvi (Turmel's translation, p. 174).

" You wish me to draw forth from an old work a new
one," Jerome wrote to him. " I shall have to become
the judge of copies of Scripture scattered over the whole
world, and after having seen their discrepancies to
decide on the text which is conformable with the Greek
original. A pious labour without doubt, but what
peril in this presumption to judge others, to be judged
by opinion in my turn, to change the language of old
men, and to bring the world already growing grey to
the first beginnings of infancy ! " [1]

In spite of his misgivings which were not fantastic Jerome
set himself to the work. His method was the following :
He took a certain number of Latin versions and the oldest
Greek manuscripts which he could procure ; [2] where the Greek
disclosed evident misinterpretations in the Latin he corrected them ; when the versions offered meanings which
were sufficiently divergent, he chose the one which seemed
to him to approach most nearly to the Greek.

His retouches were not equally thorough in the different
portions of the Gospels. He was deeply concerned to upset
as little as possible anything that western Christianity was
accustomed to, and proceeded with greater or less discretion
according to his mood.[3] Did he likewise revise the remainder
of the New Testament ? The matter is not certain, and since
the time of Erasmus and Lefèvre of Etaples it has often been
disputed ; it seems at least to be very likely.[4]

In any case, the revision of the *Psalter* from which came

---

[1] *Praef. in quattuor Evang.* (P.L., XXIX, 525).

[2] He seems to have examined the versions of the Italo-Roman type to the
exclusion of those of the African type. One of these manuscripts in our possession, the *Codex Brixianus,* provides a text fairly close to that used by Jerome.
Cf. Harnack, *Beitr. zur Einl. in das Neue Test.* VII (1916), p. 6. His Greek manuscripts resembled those represented to us by the *Sinaiticus* and the *Vaticanus.*
Taking all in all, Harnack is of opinion that the critics have not up till now attached
sufficient value to Jerome's revision, and that not one of our Greek manuscripts
is as near to the original text as Jerome's Latin translation (S.B.B., 1915, no
xxxvi–xxxvii, p. 569).

[3] His adjustment to the *graeca veritas* is seen especially in the beginning of
Matth. and in the second portion of John ; it appears less in Mark, and very little
in Luke.

[4] See Durand in R.S.R., 1916, p. 531 et s. ; Harnack, *Beitr. zur Einleitung in
das Neue Test.,* VII (1916), p. 11. The texts which make one lean towards the
affirmative are *Ep.* lxxi, 5 (Hilberg, in C.V., LV, p. 6, I. 10) ; *Ep.* cxii, 20 (*ibid.,*
p. 391, I. 3) and *de Vir. Ill.,* cxxxv. Cf. however Lagrange, in R.B., 1917, pp. 445–
447, and 1918, pp. 254–257 : Fr. Lagrange does not think that Jerome revised the
Epistles of St Paul.

the *Psalterium* called *Romanum*, dates from this same period.[1]
Jerome amended the text according to the Greek of the
Septuagint.

On the whole, the labours of Jerome marked a progress
of which competent people were sensible. St Augustine,
whose express reservations on certain of Jerome's later
undertakings we shall mention, gave his approval to this one.
Nevertheless, criticism was not wanting already. In his
Letter XXVII to Marcella, Jerome takes exception to
certain *homunculi* whom he calls two-legged asses, who, in
the name of tradition and of the inspired nature of the Gospels,
were protesting against his corrections. This was only the
prelude of storms to come. The first phase was to a great
extent accomplished without too many obstacles. Besides,
the protection of Damasus was extended over Jerome.

IX

FROM the day when he no longer possessed it, he understood
that he must leave. He departed for the East. His special
friends Paula, and Eustochium, her daughter, soon decided to
follow him. Jerome has recounted their journey (*Ep.* cviii).
In spite of the entreaties of their family they embarked,
taking with them a few young girls destined, as they hoped,
to form the nucleus of a convent. They made a prolonged
stay in Palestine and Egypt, and contemplated the spots
with which Scripture had familiarised them beforehand.
In 386, they finally settled in Bethlehem. Paula employed
what she had kept of her fortune to build several convents—
one for men over which Jerome took the direction, and three
others for women which she administered herself.[2] Hostels
for the use of pilgrims were also built. Then began the
happiest period in the life of Jerome and of his companions.
Shortly after their arrival the latter wrote to Marcella a letter
full of mysticism and tenderness in which they depicted their
joy.[3] While watching over strict economy in the convent

[1] Jerome states this formally (P.L., XXIX, 117).
[2] Up to the time of her death in 404. Eustochium succeeded her.
[3] *Ep.* xlvi. They begged Marcella to come and join them. She did not
come. There was much more independence and self-possession in her than in her
friends. The latter only lived upon feeling: Marcella was an " intellectual "
before everything else.

they delighted in humbling themselves to the most lowly duties, attending to the lamps, sweeping the rooms, and lighting the fires.[1] Jerome often saw his friends; he commented on the Scriptures for them, and charged them with many duties which helped him in his work. It was at Bethlehem, in his cell which he called his paradise, that he wrote the greater part of his works. In addition, he opened a school for young boys whom he instructed in grammar, and commented upon the classic authors.[2] But the best part of his time was absorbed by the monastery; he showed his monks how to copy manuscripts, thus giving the model to those laborious communities who in the Middle Ages saved so much of the *débris* of the old civilisation.

He had already learnt Hebrew in the desert of Chalcis. He took it up again with renewed ardour under the direction of a Jew named Bar Anina who gave him lessons for money— by night in order to avoid the animosity of his co-religionists.[3] Gaston Paris has remarked, not without astonishment, that " not one of the Fathers of the Latin Church up to the time of St Jerome appears to have known Hebrew nor to have been concerned to learn it." [4] The Septuagint had sufficed to establish the authority of the Old Testament in a world in which the Greek language predominated. But Jerome possessed the critical capability which drove him to go back to the sources, for he knew how many deformations a text must inevitably undergo when it is transposed into another language.

Origen's *Hexaples* which he went through in the library at Cæsarea,[5] strengthened this conviction in him. The object of Origen in this vast work had been not so much to give a correct edition of the Greek Bible as to establish, with the view of composing so many disputes between Jews and Christians who were each reciprocally dealing with forgeries, the status of the Jewish and Christian Bible respectively. Arranged in six columns, the *Hexaples* (the original manuscript of which was in fifty large rolls) presented

---

[1] *Ep.* lxvi, 13.
[2] Cf. Rufinus, *Apol.*, ii, 8 (P.L., XXI, 592).
[3] *Ep.* lxxxiv, 3 (Hilberg, in C.V., LV, p. 123, l. 8).
[4] *Journal des Savants*, 1883, p. 387. Cf. the article *Hebrew Learning among the Fathers*, by the Rev. C. J. Elliot, in D.C.B., II, 851–872.
[5] " Ἑξαπλοῦς Origenis in Cæsariensi bibliotheca relegens semel tantum scriptum repperi." (*Commentarioli in Ps.*, ed. Morin, p. 5.) See Cavallera, II, p. 88.

synoptically the Hebrew text of the Old Testament in Hebrew characters, the Hebrew text in Greek characters, the Greek translation of Aquila, the Jew, contemporary with Hadrian, the Greek translation of Symmachus, the Jew, in the time of Septimus Severus, the Greek translation of the Septuagint, and lastly that of the Jew Theodotion (about 180 A.D.). For certain books there were three more supplementary columns in which anonymous Greek versions were inserted.[1] In addition, the text of the *Septuagint* was marked with certain signs (which had become traditional since the time of Alexandrine criticism)[2] intended to show the bearing of this text upon the Hebrew text. The *obelus*[3] signified words or passages added in the Greek ; the asterisk disclosed the *lacunae* appearing in the Greek ; the termination of the additions or omissions was shown by two dots.

This methodical arrangement decided Jerome in the autumn of 386 to enter upon new undertakings. He revised the *Psalter* for the second time, following the system of the *Hexaples* by using the critical signs employed by Origen.[4] From this revision emerged the *Psalterium* called *Gallicanum* from its having been the first to be in general use in Gaul. He also translated the book of Job[5] from the Greek of the *Hexaples*, using the same system of signs, the *Proverbs*,[6] *Ecclesiastes*,[7] the *Canticle of Canticles*,[8] and the *Paralipomena*.[9] It is possible that he may have proceeded further in this work, of which a theft almost completely defrauded him.[10] We only have in their entirety the Psalter, and the book of Job.[11]

[1] There is a description of the *Hexaples* by Jerome in the *Comm. in Titum*, iii, 9 (P.L., XXVI, 595).

[2] The origin of these goes back to Aristophanes of Byzantium about 257–180 B.C. or even to Zenodotus (IIIrd century). See J. E. Sandys, *A History of classical Scholarship*, Cambridge, 1906, p. 127.

[3] From the Greek ὀβελός, a brooch. The form was this ÷ or –. On these critical signs, cf. St Epiphanius, *de Mens. et Ponder.*, viii and xvii (P.G., XLIII, 243–244 and 265) : Isidore of Seville, *Orig.*, I, xx. Serruys has shown that Anastasius the Sinaite has given a clearer and more satisfactory interpretation of them than that by Epiphanius, which is derived from his, but has mistakes in it (*Mél. de l'Ecole de Rome*, XXII [1902], p. 189 et s.).

[4] Cf. P.L., XXIX, 117.

[5] St Augustine, *Ep.* civ, 3, in Hilberg, C.V., LV, p. 239, l. 21.

[6] *Praef. in libr. Salomonis*, P.L., XXIX, 403.

[7] *Ibid.*

[8] *Ibid.*

[9] XXIX, 401.

[10] *Ep.* cxxxiv, 2 (P.L., XXII, 1162).

[11] We must add to these extracts from the three books of Solomon in the St Gall manuscript no. 11 (cf. C. P. Caspari, *das Buch Job*, 1893, pp. 5–7) ; S. Berger, *Quelques textes latins inédits de l'Ancien Testament* (notices and extracts from the

X

BUT more and more one thing became obvious to his mind. Any critical investigation of the Old Testament should be based neither on the Latin texts which were often faulty, nor on the Greek of the Septuagint, which was not sufficiently close, but on the original text wherein God Himself had spoken, the *Hebraica veritas*. The only rational solution therefore was to neglect the intermediaries and translate direct from the Hebrew. This was a considerable undertaking but one from which St Jerome did not recoil once his conscience as a scholar had decided, sustained as he was by the thought that he was at last to dispossess the Jews of the privilege upon which they plumed themselves, of being the only people to read the Divine Word in its authentic tenor. This he accomplished between the years 390 and 404. As he finished a book or group of books he dedicated it to one of his followers, together with a foreword which provides us with more than one valuable piece of information. He only left on one side the books which he considered as non-canonical or doubtful, *Wisdom, Ecclesiasticus, Baruch* with the *Letter of Jeremias*, the first and second Book of *Machabees*, the third and fourth Book of *Esdras*, and the additions to the Book of *Esther*. Considerations foreign to canonicity, properly so called, decided him to translate also the additions to the Book of *Daniel* (but marking them with the *obelus*), and the Books of *Tobias* and *Judith*. For the portions written in Chaldaic he obtained the assistance (at least at the commencement) of a Jewish interpreter who translated to him aloud the Chaldaic into Hebrew, and Jerome transposed it accordingly into Latin.[1]

How was this enterprise, so honourable to Catholic scholarship, received by St Jerome's contemporaries? With great distrust and even hostility outside the group of his faithful

MSS., vol. XXXIV, 2); quotations from the *Proverbs* in a Pelagian writing of the year 430, and in Cassian (cf. P. Vaccari, *Un testo dommatico e una versione biblica*, in *Civilta Cattolica*, vol. IV [1913], p. 196). Dom de Bruyne drew attention in the R. Bén., July 1914, pp. 229–236, to fragments of the preface to the book of *Esther*, which, contrary to the opinion of Martianay, he wished to connect with Jerome's version from the *Hexaples*. The result of this would be, therefore, that Jerome must have also revised the book of *Esther*.

[1] *Prol. in Tob.* (P.L., XXIX, 23 et s.).

friends. He was doing nothing less than relegating to a second place the translation of the Septuagint : this was the delicate point. " People must consider the attachment of the first Christians to the letter of the Scriptures, and to the authority of the Septuagint which had been universally used by the Fathers in their commentaries, was accepted and read in the churches, and held as inspired by the unanimous opinion of the Doctors. It was not a question of completing them in Hebrew, but of a total recasting. Thousands of phrases were to disappear, others were to be added, the order of several books was to be changed, and at every step a different sense was to be encountered. It was a matter of reducing to silence the Messianic prophecies, of abandoning the text used by the Apostles which they had consecrated by their infallible authority ;—in other words, as the conservatives said, Jerome intended to lower the Catholic Church before the pretended scholarship of the Jews." [1] There was a wild outcry against this *falsarius et sacrilegus* [2] who dared to lay hands upon the venerated text of the Septuagint which was authenticated by every tradition. Despite his natural moderation, St Augustine himself was moved. The first revision from the Greek accomplished by Jerome had met with his full approval. But the idea of a new translation from the Hebrew was invincibly repugnant to him. He could not restrain himself from letting Jerome hear his views. " And in the first place," he asked him, " can you seriously hope to do better than the former translators of the Hebrew text ? "

" It is a matter of astonishment to me that there is still in the Hebrew something which has escaped so many interpreters, past-masters in their knowledge of this language. I am not speaking now of the Septuagint ; I do not wish to formulate any precise opinion on their conformity in design or inspiration which is more noticeable in them than if they had been by one and the same author, still more, because such a privilege should, in my opinion, indisputably extend to them a

[1] Lagrange, in B.L.E., 1899, p. 41.
[2] *Prol. in Evang.*, P.L., XXIX, 558 ; *Apol.*, II, xxiv (P.L., XXIII, 468) ; *in Ezech.* (P.L., XXV, 327). And again P.L., XXVIII, 179, 505, 1137, 1141, 1308, etc. . . .

pre-eminent authority. But what strikes me especially is that those who after them laboured to translate the Scriptures and who are accounted to have been most careful to render accurately the genius of the Hebrew expressions and turns, not only are not agreed among themselves, but further have passed over so many difficulties which must now be exhumed and placed in their proper light. For, to come to the point, those passages are clear or obscure. If they are obscure, we may permit ourselves to believe that it is possible for you to be mistaken about them just as much as they were. If they are clear, how can we suppose that they were mistaken ? " [1]

St Jerome's retort to this dilemma is an argument *ad hominem* and betrays a little nervousness :

" I will borrow from you," he wrote to Augustine, " your own argument. What the former writers who have preceded us in the Lord have explained in their commentaries on Holy Scripture is either obscure or clear. If it is obscure, how have you dared to discuss after them matters which they did not know how to elucidate ? If it is clear, it were a vain undertaking to search out explanations which could not have escaped them." [2]

But Augustine had further objections, and other scruples, and after having read the translation from the Hebrew of Job he laid them before Jerome with his customary gentle firmness, as a Bishop desirous for the good of souls before all else. If the West were to adopt the new version and read it in public, would there not then be disagreement between the Latin Churches and the Greek, who were firmly attached to the Septuagint ? [3] If a controversy arise on any passage in Scripture, recourse to the Greek is easy, but could they imagine having recourse to the Hebrew with which no one was acquainted ? [4] And then, too, was Jerome's translation so reliable as he believed it to be ?

[1] *Ep.* lvi, 2, *Ap.* St Jerome (Hilberg, C.V., LIV, p. 497, l. 1).
[2] *Ep.* cxii, 20 (Hilberg, C.V., vol. LV, p. 389, l. 25).
[3] *Ep.* civ, 4 (in Jerome ; Hilberg, C.V., LV, p. 240, l. 15).
[4] *Ibid.*, p. 240, l. 19.

" We have come to this that a brother Bishop, having ordered your translation to be read in the church to which he was accredited, people were disturbed because you had rendered a passage from the prophet Jonas in a very different manner from that which had grown old in all their memories and which so many generations had repeated. All the people were in an uproar; the Greeks, especially, passionately accused you of having falsified the text; so much so that the Bishop (the scene took place at Oea) was obliged to consult the Jews. Whether from ignorance or malice the latter affirmed that the tenor of the Hebrew was conformable to that given in the Greek and Latin copies. Our Bishop found himself obliged to rectify the passage as being erroneous in order to retain his people who were on the point of abandoning him. It seems to me therefore that you, even you, may have misunderstood certain passages, and you can guess to what consequences that might lead in the case of a text which it is impossible to correct from the point of view of the original, the language of which is not in use." [1]

The fact was that Augustine saw no serious reason to upset so many interests and venerable traditions, and energetically counselled Jerome to confine himself to giving a good translation of the Septuagint which was known everywhere and which the Apostles themselves had used.[2]

We can guess how much Jerome suffered at seeing the advantages of his initiative thus misunderstood. " If my work gives offence," he observed sadly, " no one is bound to read it. I leave people to find delight in drinking the old and in despising my new wine." [3] To reasons in the practical order he opposed reasons in the scientific, namely, the value of a translation made from the original, *ut scirent nostri quid Hebraea veritas contineret;* [4] his own care for accuracy despite stories like that of the Bishop of Oea, the foundation for which he formally disputed; [5] the mistake of thinking

---

[1] *Ibid.*, 5 (p. 241).
[2] *Ibid.*, 4 and 6.
[3] *Ep.* cxii, 20 (Hilberg, in C.V., LV, p. 390, l. 24).
[4] *Ibid.*, 20.
[5] *Ibid.*, 21. See also P.L., XXVIII, 604, 1185, 1394; 1473; XXIX, 426.

that the Greek Bible presented any unity, or had undergone
no alterations,[1] and the occasional independence of Christ
and the Apostles as regards the Septuagint in their quotations
from the Old Testament.[2]

He felt himself sustained by his profound conviction
that the future would decide the dispute in his favour. In
this he did not deceive himself. Jerome's version was gradually introduced into the practical use of the Churches. St
Augustine himself had recourse to it in certain cases.[3] It is
not our task to describe here the history of the Vulgate in
the Middle Ages,[4] nor the vicissitudes which resulted in the
declaration of the Council of Trent ordering " *ut haec ipsa
vetus et vulgata editio, quae longo tot saeculorum usu in ipsa
ecclesia probata est . . . pro authentica habeatur.*" [5]

XI

St Jerome did not rest satisfied with translating Holy
Scripture ; he endeavoured also to facilitate its understanding
by following it up with commentaries. He completed these
exegetic works at Bethlehem. I have already described
with what ardour the admirable women who lived under
his eyes demanded fresh lights without ceasing.

In these, as elsewhere, Jerome's method in working was
not irreproachable. His natural impulsiveness made the
meticulous slowness required in critical work painful to him ;
he yielded to a haste which he acknowledged with humility

---

[1] *Ep.* cxii, 19 ; and P.L., XXVIII, 1389 et s.
[2] *Apol.* II, xxxiv (P.L., XXIII, 477), etc.
[3] Cf. *de Doct. Christ.*, IV, vii.
[4] See Samuel Berger's fundamental work, *Hist. de la Vulgate pendant les
premiers siècles du moyen-âge.* It will be noticed that St Jerome employs the word
vulgata to describe the translation of the *Septuagint* (*In Is.*, lxv, 20 ; *in Oseam,*
vii, 13) : it is a translation of the Greek word κοινή. In the Middle Ages the term
vulgata editio was still sometimes used to designate the *Septuagint*. It was only
after the Council of Trent that it was ordinarily applied to St Jerome's translation.
In its present condition, the *Vulgate* comprises (1) the old Latin translation not
revised by Jerome (as regards certain non-canonical books of the Old Testament) ;
(2) the old Latin translation revised from the Greek (in the case of the Gospels ;
possibly for the rest of the New Testament ; and for the Psalter [Gallican]) ; (3)
the translation made by Jerome from the Hebrew (for the Old Testament, with
the exception of certain apocrypha). For present-day schemes for the revision of the
Vulgate, cf. Jaquier, *Le N.T. dans l'Eglise Chrétienne*, Paris, 1913, II, 195 ; J.
Denk, *der neue Sabatier*, L. 1914.
[5] Denzinger-Bannwart, *Enchir. Symbol. et Definitionum*, 1908, no. 785. The
principal modern edition of the *Vulgate* is that of Wordsworth & White, Oxford,
1889 et s.

in order to be excused, but without always succeeding in being pardoned. The *Commentary* on Abdias was dictated in two nights ; that on St Matthew in two weeks ; he cleared off the Epistle of St Paul to the Ephesians at the rate of a thousand lines a day.[1] From this arose a prolixity which nearly approaches to chatter, also an annoying tendency to pile up opinions which had been given at an earlier date on any particular Scriptural difficulty, instead of making his own selection and putting it forward. His lexicographical and topographical writings on the Bible come from Origen especially, and also from Philo (through the intermediary of Origen), but Jerome has also included in them the results of his original researches. Richard Simon irreverently declared as regards the *Liber de nominibus Hebraicis* that " if any one were to think of presenting to the public a work like that he would be hissed by everybody." [2] Far better equipped with implements, modern minds have been quick to look down upon the toil of the first clearing of the ground. Let us at least recognise St Jerome's great merit and his truly scholarly concern to make comprehensible the texts he was endeavouring to explain, by surrounding them with all positive information capable of elucidating them. With rare exceptions this was not at all the form of exegesis in favour in his time. They much preferred allegorical exegesis, which, starting from the principle that the sacred text hid a mysterious meaning which the letter veiled far more than it explained, endeavoured to extract it even by means of the most fantastic interpretations. The fashion was so strong that Jerome himself could not get away from it. His ideal would also have been, so far as we can see, to mingle the two forms of interpretation, historical and allegorical,[3] or to overlay one with the other.[4] In any case, he strove to associate with this somewhat puerile bent, wherein vanity found play,[5] investigations less flattering to the imagination, but fruitful in other ways for a full understanding of the past.[6]

[1] I have mentioned other facts in B.A.L.A.C., 1914, p. 238.
[2] *Lettres choisies*, I, 310.
[3] *Comm. in Nahum*, § 2 (P.L., XXV, 1243).
[4] *In Isaiam, Pref.* (P.L., XXIV, 20).
[5] *Ibid., Pref.* 1. V (P.L., XXIV, 158).
[6] He remarks in the *Prologue* to Isaias how little prepared was Roman taste, permeated with rhetoric as it was, to understand the importance of these researches.

XII

WE must cast an eye over those works of his mature age which do not enter into the ample framework of his Scriptural writings, especially the *De Viris Illustribus* and the *Adversus Jovinianum*.

The *De Viris Illustribus* was written at Bethlehem in the year 392 at the request of Dexter, the son of Pacian (Bishop of Barcelona then dead) and a Pretorian Prefect. This work was dedicated to Dexter.

The idea of Jerome was to draw up a list of Christian writers, but in a much briefer form, on the lines of the *De Viris Illustribus* of Suetonius, which was a series of notices written in the year 113 in which the most distinguished representatives in Roman literature found a place. " Suetonius enumerated the poets from the time of Livius Andronicus, the orators from Cicero, the historians from Sallust, the philosophers, and lastly, the grammarians who formed only one book. In each of these books he doubtless gave the names in chronological order, as in the last." [1] It was a common practice among the pagans to jeer at the intellectual mediocrity of the Catholics. What better means could be found to show them their error or bad faith than to enumerate the writers by whom Christian literature was honoured ?

> " Let them learn then—men like Celsus, Porphyry and Julian, those mad dogs raving against Christ—let their partisans learn, men who imagine that the Church has neither philosophers, orators or doctors, the breadth and the talent of the men who founded, developed and embellished her ; let them cease accusing our faith of having nothing else to show than rustic simplicity, and let them rather recognise their own ignorance."

Jerome therefore took in hand to supply a few brief notices of all those who " from the time of the Passion of Christ up to the fourteenth year of Theodosius *de scripturis sanctis memoriae aliquid tradiderunt.*"

The list comprised 135 sections, the first of which is

[1] Macé, *Essai sur Suétone*, Paris, 1900, p. 244.

devoted to Simon Peter, and the last to St Jerome himself, who kept back to the end his own notice among this succession of " illustrious men." The first 78 are closely dependent upon the *Ecclesiastical History* and the *Chronical* by Eusebius of Cæsarea. Jerome is content to include the particulars found therein save in a few rare cases (*e.g.* 12 ; 53 ; 58 ; 66 ; 67 ; 68 ; 72 ; 74 ; 75). It thus happens that he reproduces the mistakes of Eusebius, and even makes others himself, which we can rectify by reading his model.[1] In reality, he was rather poorly acquainted with the early Christian literature of the IInd century, or rather, being contented to transcribe Eusebius, he did not take the trouble to revive what he knew. From § 79, Jerome continues by himself. As regards a certain number of writers, such as Tertullian, Minucius Felix, Cyprian, Novatian, Victorinus of Pettau, etc., he is our one and precious source.

We must bear in mind the particular object he proposed to himself if we would understand certain of his methods. Thus, in his desire to enhance the importance of the writers he speaks about, he is prodigal to excess of laudatory epithets —*elegans, utilis, pulcherrimus, valde utilis*, which he adds to the information copied from Eusebius. Further, desirous of swelling his list at all costs, he does not hesitate to enter the names of heretics, such as Tatian (§ 29), Bardesanus (§ 33), Asterius (§ 94), Photinus (§ 107), and even under various pretexts, profane writers such as Philo the Jew (§ 11), Flavius Josephus (§ 13), and Justus Tiberiensis (§ 14). St Augustine expressed his regret to him that he had not taken the trouble to insist more strongly on the errors of the heresiarchs whom he thus incorporated in the ranks of the Christian phalanxes.[2] The fact is that they played somewhat the *rôle* of " substitutes " destined to make up the number, and Jerome had not been at pains to blacken them too much.

Even in these simple notices the personality of the author betrays itself in a curious manner. More than once Jerome makes the length of his chapters accord with his sympathies or antipathies. When dealing with a Didymus (§ 109),

---

[1] E.g. § **xxxix**, he includes under one person Quadratus the author of an apology presented to Hadrian in 124, and Quadratus Bishop of Athens who lived in the time of Marcus Aurelius (161–180). See also P. de Labriolle, *Les sources de l'Histoire du Montanisme*, Paris, 1913, p. xx et s.

[2] *Ep.* xl, 6 (P.L., XXXIII, 157).

or a Gregory of Nazianzen (§ 117), he makes generous allow-
ance. To make up for this, St John Chrysostom (§ 129),
then but a simple priest at Antioch it is true, only has three
lines. As for St Ambrose (§ 124), Jerome metes out to him the
following statement :

> " Ambrose, the Bishop of Milan, is still writing to-day ;
> as he is living, I shall avoid giving my judgment in order
> not to expose myself to the contradictory reproach of
> too much flattery or too much frankness (*ne in alterutram
> partem aut adulatio in me reprehendatur aut veritas*)."

The serenity proper to the historian and critic was not his
strong point. But after all the work has left landmarks
for posterity whose loss would be irreparable. He kindled
the zeal of various writers to continue his work, such as
Gennadius in the Vth century ; Isidore of Seville in the
VIIth, and Honorius of Autun in the XIIth. An unknown
hand translated it into Greek between the VIIth and IXth
centuries. This translation has been preserved in MS. C. 11,
XIVth century, in the Library at Zurich.

The *Adversus Jovinianum* was written in 392–3 at the
request of Pammachius, the son-in-law of Paula. According
to St Jerome Jovinian had at first led a very severe life, then
little by little he was seen to be giving up this first rigour,
and to be taking to a much freer manner of living. Perhaps
he had made an endeavour to react against the excesses of
the asceticism of the East such as were becoming naturalised
more and more among a portion of Roman society, and which
Jerome did not cease to recommend. Was he influenced by
personal motives which were more or less unmentionable ?
We can only suppose so if we listen to Jerome alone. Nevertheless, neither St Ambrose, nor Pope Siricius, nor St Augustine
insinuate anything of the kind against him, and our sense of
justice demands a due reserve. Already in 390 a Council
held in Rome had condemned him, together with eight of his
partisans. He took refuge in Milan, but St Ambrose was
swift to renew this condemnation by a Synod held in 391.
Meanwhile, Jerome received in Rome the *Commentarioli*
composed by the heresiarch, and notwithstanding the poor
style of Jovinian (I, i), he determined to write a refutation.

Jerome reviews Jovinian's doctrine in four theses.

In the first place, Jovinian had proclaimed the equal merit after baptism of virgins, widows, and married women, provided that their " good works " were of equal merit. He was concerned to vindicate the state of marriage against its detractors, including among them those who, without formally discrediting it, showed a greater esteem for celibacy. He based his contention upon Genesis ii, 24 ; and Matthew xix, 5 ; he appealed to the example of persons in the Old and New Testaments who were married ; he also invoked the authority of the Apostle Paul in his Ist Epistle to Timothy. And from all these examples he made the deduction that marriage, even when repeated, was not in itself inferior to any other manner of life. St Jerome's reply is a discussion of the texts before everything else. He exerted himself to prove that those relied upon by his opponent were misleading or were annulled, or at any rate were limited, by other texts in an opposite sense. In addition, he did not deny himself any extravagance in his views or any violence in his expressions. It is a kind of semi-paradoxical contest from which the *prestige* attaching to marriage emerges somewhat impaired.

We must realise that this question of marriage, its advantages and its disadvantages, had much concerned the moralists of old. The theme " εἰ γαμητέον " (ought one to marry ?) was dear to popular philosophy. We see it treated of by Hierocles, the Stoic, in the Ist or IInd century of our era, and in the *excerpta* which Stobaeus, the compiler, has preserved of him. Hierocles recommended marriage from the political and civic point of view. For him it represented, as Cicero has said in his *De Officiis* (I, xvii, 54), *principium urbis et quasi seminarium reipublicae.* He also extols it as the entire union of two beings, a union of the body, and a union of the soul, ". . . μεχρὶ τῶν σωμάτων, μᾶλλον δὲ κὰι αὐτῶν τῶν ψυχῶν." He mentions the benefit of the presence of an industrious woman in the house, the useful help which the children, when they have grown up, give to their parents, and the care which the latter receive from them in their old age. In his eyes, marriage from its nature was a light burden. What weighed it down to the point of rendering it unbearable to many was the lack of reason, the ἀφροσύνη of so many men, who allow themselves to be drawn into it by the sole consideration of beauty or fortune.

These discussions περὶ γάμου, in which Chrysippus had already perhaps had a hand, recur in the writings of many other Stoic moralists, or of those with Stoic tendencies, such as Dion Chrysostom, Seneca (*Ep.* 94), Eudorus, etc., and even the rhetoricians had taken it up. We also hear therein the arguments of the detractors of marriage. He who marries, they contended, exposes himself to the humiliation of being deceived by his wife, to the grief of losing his children, to the prolonged weariness of living side by side with a woman who is a *coquette*, extravagant, cross-grained, etc. . . . Tertullian certainly had made use of this satirical tradition in his work (now lost) *de Nuptiarum Angustiis.* Jerome in turn appropriated it in his *Adversus Jovinianum,* happy in the thought that the worldly women of Rome would rear up under the pricks of the expressions which he was letting loose against their sex.[1]

His refutation of the second proposition of the heresiarch was appreciably shorter.[2] In addition, it was far more abstract in character, and more specifically theological, and in this domain of speculation Jerome is rather less at his ease. Jovinian claimed that whosoever received baptism in full faith could not, after this rebirth, be led into sin by the devil. Perhaps there was in his mind a secret co-relation between this second thesis and the first. From the moment that it was enough to receive baptism in the requisite conditions in order to become the permanent habitation of God, it mattered little what was the particular state adopted by anyone after baptism. It became then only a secondary element, the importance of which there was no need to accentuate. To this line of argument Jerome replied with facts not with reasoned statements; it was a fact that the best may fall, as had Moses, Aaron, David, Solomon, and Peter the Apostle. How then could they believe in the indefectibility of those who had been baptised ?[3]

The third thesis of Jovinian[4] went to maintain that there

---

[1] I, x: "Licet enim in me saevituras sciam plurimas matronarum . . . tamen dicam quod sentio." On all these matters, see Bickel's *In Senecae philosophiae fragmenta,* vol. I. *Fragm. de Matrimonio,* L. 1915, p. 191 et s., 356; Fr. Buggenhagen, Περὶ γάμου . . . Bale, Zurich, 1919.

[2] II, i–iv.

[3] II, iv : "(Baptisma) sicut priora peccata dimittit, sic in futurum servare non potest, nisi baptizati omni custodia servaverint cor suum."

[4] II, v et s.

was no difference between abstaining from food and partaking of it with thanksgiving. He thus aimed at diminishing the merit of fasting. Here Tertullian's *de Jejunio* provided Jerome with the greater part of his arguments (he also borrows some from the philosopher Porphyry), and prompts him as to the tactics to pursue. It consisted in treating his opponent as a glutton who erects an array of imposing principles in order to mask the hankerings of his voracity. Nevertheless in this apology of the practice of fasting he is careful at times not to go too far, and shows that he does not share in any degree the error of certain heretics who condemned the work of the Creator.[1]

In his fourth and last proposition, Jovinian asserted the identity of the rewards which all who had preserved their baptismal faith and purity would obtain in heaven. Therefore we were to conclude from this that the hierarchy which people wished to establish between the different *states* was chimerical. One just man was worth as much as another just man, by whatever means he had preserved himself in his state of justice. Jerome met him with reasons from Scripture (*e.g.* I *Cor.* xv, 22 ; 39 et s. ; II *Cor.* v, 10) and also from good sense ; how could God be so unjust as to reward with identical remuneration merits which were so obviously of unequal value ? There were shades and degrees of good as well as of evil.

In his peroration,[2] he resumes his abusive and truculent tone :

" And now for a last word to our Epicurus sweating out passion (*subantem*) in the midst of his gardens among young men and young women. Thou hast for thy followers the plump, the well-fed, the well-washed. All the pretty boys, all the youth with curled hair that I see, and their well kept locks and cheeks painted with vermilion, form thy flock, or rather all that trash grunts among thy pigs. . . ."

The work finishes with an enthusiastically-worded reproach against the city of Rome where the doctrine of Peter is seated unshakable upon the rock of Christ.

This work, full of vigour, if not of good taste, did not

---

[1] II, xiv.   [2] II, xxxvi.

meet with the success which Jerome had promised himself.
His friend Pammachius had bought a good number of copies
of it in Rome : he made speed to withdraw from circulation
those upon which he could lay hands, in face of the impression
that was produced.[1] From another quarter Domnio communicated to Jerome quite a long list of passages begging
him to correct or to explain them.[2] Jerome had to defend
himself in an apologetic letter addressed to Pammachius.[3]
In it he repeated that he had not at all intended to condemn
marriage, nor to glide into a kind of Manichaeism on account
of his misgivings about flesh-meat and wine ; he also invoked
the liberty permitted to a polemical work.[4] These were
grumbling excuses, in which were mingled sharp attacks
against certain people who, he affirmed, only gave themselves airs of indignation in order to defame him.

Thirteen or fourteen years after, in 406, he had again to
break a lance against Vigilantius, a priest from Gaul, who was
reviving certain theses which had already been combated by
Jerome, and in addition attacked the veneration with which
the tombs of the martyrs were surrounded, the vigils which
it was customary to pass in their Churches, and various
liturgical practices. Jerome had personal reasons for little
liking Vigilantius whom he had welcomed with goodwill at
Bethlehem on the recommendation of Paulinus of Nola,[5]
and who had repaid him by retailing unfriendly stories about
him.[6] As soon as his works came into his hands he retorted
with a short and furious diatribe in which reasoning holds
only a feeble place, as though such a sorry adversary was not
worth the trouble of refuting in detail, and in which he hustles,
abuses, cleaves him in two, and even reproaches him with his
name, on which he does not disdain to make puns.[7]

This wordy vigour seems to have already been somewhat
appeased by the year 415, in which Jerome wrote his *Dialogues*
against the Pelagians. It was St Augustine who, through the

[1] *Ep.* xlviii, 2 (Hilberg, in C.V., LIV, 347).
[2] *Ep.* L. 3 (*ibid.*, p. 391, l. 16).
[3] *Ep.* xlix (xlviii, in Vallarsi).
[4] For a curious theory as to the duplicity that was permissible in works of this
kind, see *ibid.*, 13 (Hilberg, p. 368).
[5] *Ep.* lviii, 11.
[6] *Ep.* lxi.
[7] He calls Vigilantius *Dormitantius* (as an enemy to pious vigils). I note
that Cicero expressly approved of this play of words on proper names : *de Orat.*,
II, lxiii, 257.

intermediary of his disciple Orosius, had engaged him in a struggle which he held so much at heart. St Augustine praised the accurate expression of Catholic doctrine [1] contained in his *Dialogues*. Of the two disputants, the one, Atticus, represents the orthodox point of view, the other, Critobulus, the opposite opinion; the theses are presented in the presence of each other, turn by turn, and this alternation obliged Jerome to observe the form of a certain amount of impartiality.

XIII

THE evening of his life was saddened by quarrels over Origenism in the course of which he had to struggle against the most mortifying personal attacks. There is no reason to relate here all the phases of this unhappy strife; [2] we must at least give an outline of the character of some of the protagonists who were mixed up in it, and point out where they parted company.

In the last years of the IVth century the renown of Origen was still shining with a bright light in spite of the efforts of certain men to cloud it over. The entry of a redoubtable adversary into the lists was to change all that. At the beginning of the year 374, Epiphanius, the Bishop of Salamis, assigned to himself the task of ruining Origen and Origenism in Catholic opinion. To anyone who may still doubt that the most extensive erudition can be joined in the same mind to a real mediocrity of intelligence and the most obstinate prejudices, Epiphanius may be presented as a fairly successful specimen of this displeasing amalgam. Personally he was a man of edifying piety and of a life worthy of respect; but burning over with a somewhat mischievous zeal he had constituted himself a hunter of heresies, and scented in Origenism a magnificent prey.

We have mentioned all that Origen represented to the laborious youth of Jerome, the respect and admiration which he had devoted to that illustrious exegetist, and his promptness in taxing with ignorance anyone who refused to

---

[1] *Ep.* clxxx, 5.

[2] It is traced in a very vivid manner in J. Brochet's work, *Saint Jérôme et ses ennemis*, 1905. But Brochet is not always correct in the chronology of his facts : see the important studies of Holl and Julicher in S.B.B., 1916, p. 226 et s. (and my analysis in the *Rev. de Philol.*, *Rev. des Revues*, 1917).

recognise in him the Instructor of the Churches from the time of the Apostles (*post apostolos Ecclesiarum magistrum nemo nisi imperitus negabit*).[1] What then were the influences under which this unexpected revival took shape in his mind about the year 400 ?

We must here introduce upon the scene a new personage who was to play an important *rôle* in this crisis, the enigmatic Tyrannius Rufinus.

Rufinus was born at Concordia, near Aquileia. He had made the acquaintance of Jerome in Rome where they were both studying, and their friendship was strengthened into affection in the ascetic little circle at Aquileia. When this group was scattered, Rufinus, who had become a monk, attached himself to the person of Melania, a rich patrician lady ;[2] he became in some degree her director of conscience and her indispensable counsellor. In November 372, they both left for the East. They first stopped in Egypt ; Rufinus prolonged his stay there while Melania went on to Jerusalem and there founded a monastery where Rufinus rejoined her in 378. The influence of Origen was at that time altogether predominant in the East, especially in Egypt with the monks. Rufinus submitted to it all the more readily because he had not any very vigorous originality of mind. If we cast an eye over his works (almost all of them written after the year 397), we see that, apart from his polemical writings and one or two exegetic treatises, they are made up of translations. Rufinus had observed that in the West people knew Greek less and less, while thinkers of the breadth of mind of Origen were entirely ignorant of it, even in high ecclesiastical spheres. He told himself that it would be a useful task to translate the leading works of Greek theology, even at the cost of a few free renderings and amendments, into as correct and elegant Latin as possible.[3]

When Jerome and Paula arrived in Palestine (386),

---

[1] *De Nomin. Hebr. Praef.*

[2] She was Melania, the elder, the daughter of Marcellinus who was Consul in 341. Her grand-daughter, Melania, the younger, the wife of Pinianus, settled at Bethlehem in 414 with her mother Albina, and Pinianus, her husband.

[3] Let me mention here the anonymous Latin translation of the *Acta Archelai* (C.B., Beeson), which must have been made at the end of the IVth century. These two dialogues between Bishop Archelaus and Manes constitute one of the most important sources of the History of Manichaeism. The " palatine " translation of the *Pastor of Hermas* (ed. Gebhardt and Harnack, in *Patrum apost. op.*, fasc. 3, L. 1877) is of the same date.

Melania and Rufinus held a leading position in Jerusalem. Inasmuch as pious pilgrims were settling in Jerusalem, little jealousies and occasions of variance were successfully avoided for several years. But in 392, a certain Aterbius (possibly sent by Epiphanius) came to ask Jerome and Rufinus to condemn Origenism, the progress of which was then evident in Palestine. Jerome could not fail to experience some perplexity. Up till then he had before everything else regarded Origen as the interpreter of the Scriptures rather than as a bold constructor of ideas ; the sanctity of Epiphanius, his wide erudition, and zeal for orthodoxy, must have intimidated his judgment and have awakened in him a fear of deviating from the right path if he obstinately clung to defending an entire theological system which he had hardly investigated up till that moment. Briefly, he associated himself in the reprobation of the errors of the great Alexandrine which Aterbius pointed out to him. Rufinus entirely refused to receive Aterbius. This different attitude created at the outset a certain constraint between the two friends.

Meanwhile Epiphanius, who was almost an octogenarian, thought good to come in person to Jerusalem (doubtless about Easter of the year 392) in order to combat directly the epidemic of Origenism with which John, the Bishop, was infected. An oratorical duel, wherein, under an external aspect of palpitating courtesy, opposing passions were boiling, set them one against the other in the chapel of the Holy Sepulchre. John refused all disavowal of Origenism. Epiphanius then left the city in the dead of night and took refuge in the monastery at Bethlehem. He formally invited the monks to break off from Jerusalem, and in order that they might not advance the necessity of their liturgical requirements he ordained almost by force Paulinianus, Jerome's own brother. Some months later he launched against John of Jerusalem a decisive ultimatum wherein he summoned him to pronounce his views as regards Origenism. Jerome translated this letter in order to place *au courant* his friend Eusebius of Cremona who did not know Greek. His translation fell into the hands of Rufinus. John and Rufinus might well believe that Jerome associated himself personally with the campaign opened by Epiphanius.

Then began a war of subterranean manœuvres, intrigues

and traps, with intervals of rest, and verbal reconciliations, to begin again with still more intensity and treachery. In 397, Rufinus, who had returned to Italy, made the Origenist quarrels fashionable there, and enlisted in his rancour Jerome's old enemies. With a cleverness which was very like perfidy he affected to place under the patronage of Jerome his own efforts in favour of Origen, and recalled the numerous evidences he had given in former days of his admiration for the author of the treatise *de Principiis*. Jerome protested : " I praised," he stated, " the exegesis of Origen and not his doctrine, his genius, not his faith, the scholar and not the propagandist." [1] Driven by these polemics far beyond his first hesitations, he opposed to the toned-down translation of the *de Principiis* which Rufinus had just given, another translation in which the systematic omissions of Rufinus were repaired, in order that the perilous temerities of Origen might appear in their full light.[2] But shortly after, Rufinus by a singular *volte-face* disavowed Origen in order to concentrate all the ardour and all the spleen of his polemics upon Jerome. To the *Apologies* of Rufinus Jerome felt bound to reply with his three books *Contra Rufinum*, in which he laid bare the crookedness of his old friend, his quibbles, and his " traps for foxes," and congratulated himself that he was at last able to tear off the mask from him : *levius est inimicum cavere quam hostem latentem sub amici nomine sustinere* (ii, 35).

This time his vigorousness got the better of the elusive suppleness of his adversary. Rufinus took the course of silence. He shut himself away at Aquileia and buried himself in his labours as a skilful translator up to the day when fleeing from the barbarians he was obliged to take flight to the East with Melania, accompanied by her daughter Albina, Melania the younger and Pinianus the husband of the latter. But death overtook him in Sicily (410).

Jerome himself died on the 30th September, 420, in his cell at Bethlehem. He had experienced the sorrow of seeing the passing away before him of his pious and learned friends who had remained tenderly faithful to him through all his troubles.

[1] *Ep.* lxxxiv.
[2] Of these translations see the large edition of the *de Principiis* by Koetschau (C.B., 1913) and my review of them in B.A.L.A.C., 1914, pp. 287–290.

XIV

I HAVE endeavoured to give a succinct idea of the *rôle* and personality of St Jerome. I have thinned down as little as possible the magnificent *relief*, while quite realising that certain features of it may have seemed singular to minds who conceive of sanctity under the somewhat conventional aspect of benevolent gentleness. At this valuation Jerome would be a saint out of his frame. His ardent imagination, his fiery though disciplined passions, and his violent and eruptive nature, connect him with all sides of humanity as it is. He is profoundly human. But what is most remarkable about him is it not just this, that with his altogether impulsive temperament he consistently subordinated the multifarious activities of his life to a sharply defined end ? The goal to which his every effort converged was the good of the Church. He rendered immense services to her. By his revision of the Bible he unified and fixed the text in which Christians read the Word of God. By his fervour for the ascetic ideal he indirectly raised the moral level of the faithful and the clergy, for the sight of renunciations is assuredly the best propaganda, even for those who are not willing or who dare not raise themselves to such a height. And at the same time, he spread appreciation of a celibacy devoted to good works, a fruitful celibacy, thereby preparing the way for the marvellous monastic expansion of the Middle Ages. Lastly, as a writer, he has enriched the entire domain of classic literature— exegesis, literary history, biography, polemics, and even the funeral oration, for certain letters of his on his friends who had died are nothing else. He was thus assured of the greatest influence upon the literature of the Middle Ages in the West. And by an exceptional fate his gifts as a man of letters and as a scholar, and the brilliancy of his style closely resembling the classics which he imitated even in their methods, preserved for him a like admiration among the men of the Renaissance. There were perhaps among the Fathers of the Church characters more delicate, more nicely shaded, more subtile—that of an Ambrose or an Augustine, for instance. But there was not one more vigorous, nor one whose life, expression, and fire, we can better grasp through the dead letter after the lapse of so many centuries.

XV

IN a letter addressed to Marcella, Jerome's friends; Paula and Eustochium described with pious and *naïve* ardour their happiness in the privileged East : [1]

" We are able to see here the foremost personages in the world. . . . All the most brilliant people in Gaul hasten to come here. From the recesses of his land, which the ocean separates from our own world, the Briton, as soon as he has made any progress in religion, leaves behind his Western sun and seeks a city he only knows by reputation, and because he has read of it in Holy Scripture. How describe the Armenians, Persians, the people from India, Ethiopia, and Egypt neighbour to Palestine and so fruitful in solitaries, from Pontus, Cappadocia, Coele-Syria, Mesopotamia, and the entire East ?

" Here the only rivalry is in humility. The least of all takes rank with the first. We have no difference in our garb, nothing which seeks to be admired. We dispose ourselves as we will without risk of censure or praise. We do not rend each other here with gnashing teeth as people do elsewhere. No luxury, no voluptuousness : but so many spots for prayer that one day would not suffice to visit them. . . . Oh ! when will come that day when a breathless courser will bring us the news that our Marcella hath set foot in Palestine, when the choirs of monks and the multitude of virgins will everywhere spread abroad the news ; . . . that day when it will be vouchsafed to us to enter with thee the grotto of the Saviour, to weep with His sister at the sepulchre of Christ, to mourn there with His Mother, to kiss the wood of the Cross, and to ascend in mind and soul with the Lord the Mount of Olives ; to see Lazarus rise again swathed in bands, and to contemplate the waters of the Jordan purified by the baptism of Jesus. . . . We will go to Nazareth, and will see the ' flower ' of Galilee, for Nazareth meaneth ' flower.' Not

[1] *Ep.* xlvi, 10 et s.

far from there we will visit Cana, where the water was changed into wine. We will climb up to Itabyrium, etc. . . ."

One of the notable facts of the IVth century was just this ardent piety which from this period carried so many Christian men and women to the Holy Land there " to adore " as St Jerome says (*Ep.* xlvii, 2), " the track of the footsteps of the Saviour, and to see there in all their freshness the traces of the Nativity, the Cross and Passion."

The influx of pilgrims into Jerusalem was not however without its disadvantages. Less optimistic at certain times than these patrician mystics, St Jerome does not hesitate to dissuade Paulinus of Nola from going there : [1]

" Do not imagine that your faith will suffer some loss from not coming to Jerusalem, and do not think that we are better because we live here. . . . If the spots which have witnessed the accomplishment of the mystery of the Cross and of the Resurrection were not in a city which is over populated, wherein we find a Curia, a garrison, prostitutes, actors, and buffoons, just like in other cities ; if they (the Holy Places) were only frequented by solitaries, all the solitaries assuredly should wish to fix their habitation here. But what folly to give up the world, to leave one's country, to leave the cities behind and to follow the calling of monk in order to live far from one's own house amid a population far denser than in one's own fatherland ! People flock to Jerusalem from all the corners of the universe. This city is full of all sorts of people, and we see here such a throng of men and women that one is obliged to put up with many a sight here which one may succeed in some measure in avoiding elsewhere."

He had however not so long back said that pilgrimages to the Holy Places were " a part of the Faith " (pars fidei),[2] and a passing fit of ill-humour did not alter this conviction in him. We see this well from the way in which he relates in his *Epitaphium Paulae* the journey of Paula to Galilee.

---

[1] *Ep.* lviii, 4 et s. (C.V., LIV, 532). Compare St Gregory of Nyssa, *Ep.* ii.
[2] *Ep.* xlii, 2.

This letter of consolation (*Ep.* cviii), addressed to Eustochium
—one of the most moving which came from his pen—is
further interesting from its detailing the whole series of stages
by which the descendant of the Gracchi and the Scipios
travelled, up to the point of her settling in her cell at Bethlehem : the island of Pontia, Methone (south of Messenia),
Cyprus, Seleucia, Antioch, Coele-Syria and Phœnicia, various
spots in the Holy Land, Jerusalem, and lastly, Bethlehem,
which was to be the point of departure for another tour which
she made through Palestine and Egypt.

We possess other accounts of travels in the Holy Land,
written by the pilgrims themselves. There are two which
belong to the IVth century, the *Itinerary from Bordeaux to
Jerusalem* which refers to the year 333, and the *Peregrinatio*
called *Aetheriae*, which the opinion of the most competent
critics assigns to the last quarter of the IVth century.

The *Itinerarium a Burdigala Hierusalem usque et ab
Heraclea per Aulonam* (Aulona in Illyria, on the coast of the
Ionian Sea) *et per urbem Romam Mediolanum usque*, with no
name of the author, is hardly more than a list of names of
places written by a pilgrim who leaving Bordeaux for Jerusalem returned to his native town by way of Constantinople,
Rome, and Milan, after a sojourn of some months in the
Holy Land. His wellnigh only concern is to take note of the
distances between the stages of the posting houses (*mutatio*)
at which he stopped, the cities which he passed through,
and the rest-houses (*mansio*) where he stayed the night.
The portion devoted to the Holy Land assumes a slightly
less arid turn, but still closely resembles a simple catalogue,
with the addition of references to the Bible. The whole work
is of the most forbidding dryness.

The *Peregrinatio Aetheriae* has a different character. It
was discovered by Gamurrini in the same manuscript at
Arezzo which also provided him with the *De Mysteriis* and
fragments of hymns attributed to St Hilary. This manuscript of the XIth century had previously belonged to Monte
Cassino. Dom de Bruyne [1] has discovered since then some

---

[1] R. Bén., XXVI (1909), p. 481 et s. The work by Petrus Diaconus, *de locis
Sanctis* (XIth century), in which the *Peregrinatio* is utilised, also enables us to fill
in certain *lacunae* (cf. Geyer, in C.V., vol. XXXIX, p. xiv).—History of the
manuscript of Arezzo in the Revue du Monde catholique, 1888, I, p. 21 et s.

fragments of the *Peregrinatio* in a manuscript at Madrid ⟨IXth century⟩.

It is the account of a pilgrimage to the Holy places made by a woman. She addresses her " sisters " (*dominae venerabiles sorores, dominae animae meae, dominae sorores, dominae, lumen meum*) in an affectionate and sprightly tone, and it is on their account that she puts down in writing her impressions and recollections. The account is incomplete. The portion which has been preserved shows us the traveller at the foot of Mount Sinai. From there she goes to Jerusalem which is her connecting point. Some time after she proceeds to Mount Nebo in Arabia (x, i), comes back to Jerusalem, starts again for the *Ausitis regio* on the confines of Idumaea and Arabia in order to see the tomb (*memoria*) of Job there (xiii, i), and, after another stay in the Holy City, considers returning to her own country. But before doing so she is anxious to go further, into Mesopotamia, in order to visit the solitaries living there, whose wonderful lives she had heard people speak of, and also the tomb of St Thomas, at Edessa (xvii, i). She sets out therefore from Antioch to Mesopotamia and, after her curiosity has been satisfied (*ut sum satis curiosa*, she confesses, xvi, 3), she makes her way to Constantinople by way of Antioch, Cilicia, Cappadocia, Galatia, Bithynia, and the sea (xxii–xxiii). It is at Constantinople too that she writes the account of her travels (xxiii, 10). Thinking that her " sisters " will be interested in it she adds a kind of appendix on the liturgy followed by the Church in Jerusalem (xxiv, i). This supplement by itself is almost as long as the portion of the narrative proper still remaining ; further, the end is missing.

The tone of the work is perfectly simple and relieved from all rhetorical phraseology. The interest proceeding from it is real, but we must describe its nature. Amateurs of the picturesque would be disappointed. The pilgrim is not insensible to the beauties of nature ; the powerful and " terrible " volume of the Euphrates reminds her of the course of the Rhône,[1] but on a larger scale ; she finds pleasure in describing the wide views she obtained from the top of Mount Nebo.[2] But she does not drive to death the epithet " rare " ; *vallem infinitam, valde pulchram, vallem pulchram satis et*

---

[1] xviii, 2 (Geyer, p. 61).   [2] xii, 3, p. 53.

amoenam, vallem amoenis˛imam, hortos pulcherrimos, hortus gratissimus, are the sober adjectives which suffice for her.[1] What she is eager for (and it is almost the on₁y thing), is to contemplate the spots whose names she knows from the Scriptures or from pious legends, and to realise at first-hand the moving stories with which her nun's imagination is full. Guided by the monks whom she collects around her with a *naïve* confidence very sure of itself, she makes them show her, as she says, " singula loca, quae semper ego juxta scripturas requirebam." [2] A prayer, and a repetition from the Psalms carry to God on each occasion the testimony of her gratitude for the happiness she has just tasted.

If we exclude the specifically literary point of view, the *Peregrinatio* is a precious document. We find in it a host of topographical information, sufficiently succinct for scholarship to draw material from it. Philology can gather therein specimens of late Latin in general use. But it is especially in the history of the liturgy that we are appreciably enriched : " The woman who wrote these pages gives us in their most minute detail a description of the liturgical ceremonies and the offices of each day. She tells us of the principal Feasts in the ecclesiastical year at a time when other writers remained mute upon this subject, or only furnished a few vague and incomplete particulars." [3]

Who was the author of the *Peregrinatio ?* It is a much-discussed question which seems to have received a solution, not indeed certain, but one that is reasonable and plausible. The pilgrim must have occupied a certain rank, if one may judge from the regard with which she was received both by the clergy and the official authorities who placed at her disposition soldiers for her protection. Gamurrini proposes that she should be recognised as the sister-in-law (he was wrong : the sister) of the Consul Rufinus who, on the testimony of Palladius (*Hist. Lausiaca,* LV, i), made the journey from Jerusalem to Egypt at the end of the IVth century. She was called Σιλβανία, and Gamurrini renders this name in Latin by Silvia. A work by Dom Férotin, which appeared in the *Revue des Questions Historiques* [4] in 1903, reopened the debate. Dom Férotin draws attention to a letter included in a manu-

---

[1] I, i ; xiii, 2 ; xvi, 2 ; ix, 4 ; iv, 7.   [2] vii, 2, p. 47.
[3] Dom Cabrol, *op. cit.,* p. 5.   [4] Vol. LXXIV, p. 367 et s.

script in the Escurial, wherein Valerius, a Spanish monk,
who lived in Galicia in the second half of the VIIth century,
writing to the monks of Vierzo (*fratres Bergidenses*) in order to
kindle their zeal puts before them the admirable example
of the journey to the East accomplished by the virgin Aetheria
through every kind of difficulty.[1] From the way in which
he describes the meritorious trials of Aetheria we can see to all
appearances that he has in his mind the alleged Silvia.[2]

Was Aetheria a native of Galicia, or did she come
from one of the convents of Marseilles or Arles ? The researches of philologists have not cleared up this debated point.
It is still very difficult in the present state of our knowledge,
and it may always remain so, to distinguish precisely the
specific characteristics of different forms of national Latinity,
and to be able to state for certain what is a " Gallicism,"
a " Hispanism," or an " Africanism." Neither does the comparison between the Rhône and the Euphrates, which I
mentioned above, authorise a very solid conclusion : the
traveller may have seen the Rhône and noticed its impetuous
course without having lived on its banks.

There is no decisive reason to bring down the date of the
Peregrinatio[3] to the middle of the VIth century. Attention
has been drawn to the relatively few sanctuaries of the martyrs
which attracted her notice : in the VIth century these would
have been looked for in more places. The *terminus post
quem* is provided in § xx, 12 : to a request by the pilgrim
who was desirous of visiting the country where Thare lived
(cf. *Genesis* xi, 28), the Bishop to whom she wrote informed
her that the cities of Nisibis and Hur were not accessible to
the Romans, this region being under Persian domination.
Now the Persian rule was extended over the country from the

---

[1] This letter had been printed already in Migne's *Patr. Lat.* (LXXXVII, 421).
There is a critical edition by Z. Garcia, in A.B., XXIX (1910), p. 393 et s. The
manuscripts of the letter of Valerius (several have been discovered) give the following forms : Etheria, Echeria, Eiheria, Aeiheria, Egeria. The form Aetheria
is to be preferred on account of a passage in which the author appears to suggest
a play upon the words : " . . . ut . . . *aetherea* hereditaret regna " (Garcia,
p. 398).

[2] M. Paul Lejay is rather sceptical (R.C., 1909, i, 165) : " The combination
which has provided the name Etheria is ingenious ; but a fresh discovery would
suffice to overturn this house of cards. An agreement in literals between two
texts of this kind proves nothing : there were already Baedekers or Vasari, copied
without shame by the Stendhals of the period."

[3] This is Meister's theory (Rh.M., LXIV [1909], 327–392), refuted by Deconinck
\R.B., 1910, pp. 432–445), Baumstark (*Oriens Christ.*, I [1911], pp. 32–86), Weigand
Byz. Zeitsch., 1911, pp. 1–26), Delehaye (A.B., XXXI [1912], p. 346).

year 363 : after the death of the Emperor Julian (26th June, 363) Jovian was forced to cede to Sapor the five provinces on the other side of the Tigris in return for a thirty years' peace.[1] The *terminus ante quem* is doubtful : Aetheria wrote (xix, 2) : " Pervenimus Edessam. Ubi cum pervenissemus, statim perreximus ad ecclesiam *et* ad martyrium sancti Thomae." At first sight we should be tempted to say that she made a distinction between the Church and the tomb of the Apostle. Now we know that the relics of St Thomas were transferred in 394 to the Church itself. But it is not certain that the " et " is disjunctive.[2] However this may be, a certain number of indications, especially in the liturgical order, strongly urge us to place the *Peregrinatio* at the end of the IVth century.

It would be a departure from our plan to examine in this place the other accounts of pilgrimages which succeeding centuries from the Vth to the VIIIth have bequeathed to us. But we may at least draw attention to the importance of these narratives of travel, and, speaking generally, of the journeys to the Holy Land, from the point of view of the history of civilisation. They had the effect of widening in the West the knowledge of geography and history which was tending to become restricted on account of the breaking up of the great Roman unity. They prepared the way from a distance for the great crusading movement. The veneration of relics and the liturgy received the impression of Oriental usages, especially of those of the Church in Jerusalem. Many a legend (like that of the Grail) had the same origin, and there is nothing in the monumental, iconographic, and decorative art of the Middle Ages which does not reveal the influence of Syria and Palestine.

XVI

SULPICIUS SEVERUS also powerfully collaborated in developing in the West the taste for asceticism. He was a native of Aquitaine.[3] Born in the year 360 of Christian parents, a student at Bordeaux, and an advocate of renown, a rich marriage

---

[1] Ammianus Marcellinus, XXV, ix.
[2] See p. 65 and p. 70, two passages which provide significant parallels.
[3] Gennadius, *de Vir. Ill.*, xix ; *Dial.*, I, xxvii, 2.

which had united him with a family of consular rank seemed to bring him every chance of happiness, when his young wife died. From that moment Sulpicius Severus resolved to turn to a life of piety and renunciation. The example of his special friend Paulinus—the future Paulinus of Nola—offered him encouragement during this turning-point in his conscience, and his wish was likewise favoured by Bassula, his mother-in-law, by whom he was loved affectionately. For some years he lived in the neighbourhood of Elusa (Eauze) in Aquitaine, and also at Toulouse and Elusio (Font d'Alzonne) in Narbonne. The reputation of St Martin gave him a keen desire to know the illustrious Bishop. He went to Tours in 396, having in his mind, as he later confessed, to write his biography one day.[1] From that time, as he states, he did not fail to visit him at regular intervals, as often as twice in the same year. Martin's influence put an end to the trouble that was working in his soul. From another quarter the letters of Paulinus exhorted him from a distance to complete his sacrifice. Sulpicius had sold already a portion of his goods, but poverty made him afraid.[2] It was only in 399 that he realised his project of breaking with the world, thereby stirring up a scandal almost as lively as that recently aroused by Paulinus. Paulinus dissuaded him from replying to the abuse of his detractors.[3]

Sulpicius settled at Primuliacum [4] with his mother-in-law and a group of pious friends, giving himself up entirely to his literary labours from which he hoped for some glory for the Church and for himself. According to the notice of him given by Gennadius, he received the priesthood : what is certain is that the " lay " note is appreciable in his writings. Gennadius states that after having had some leanings towards Pelagianism he soon recognised his error, and punished himself by inflicting on himself an absolute silence up to the day of his death. We have no means of checking this information.[5]

---

[1] *Vita M.*, xxv.
[2] Paulinus of Nola, *Ep.* xi, 12–13.
[3] *Ep.* 1, 2.
[4] There is some controversy in localising *Primuliacum*. See Abbé L. Ricaud, *Sulpice-Sévère et sa Villa de Primuliac à Saint-Sever-de-Rustan*, Tarbes, 1914, who reviews these discussions, p. 179 et s.
[5] It should be taken with caution. See T. R. Glover, *Classical Review*, 1899, p. 211.

The *Chronica* is only a " popular " work. Sulpicius wished to present a short history of Christianity written in an attractive manner, and capable, in spite of its pre-determined brevity, of interesting the educated public.[1] This sort of abridgment was then much in favour ; we may call to mind the *Breviarium* of Eutropius, and that of Festus, etc. Sulpicius begins his narrative with events at the Creation, and takes it down as far as the Consulate of Stilicho (400). Giving special attention to the chronology, he analyses the books of the Old Testament which he read from the Greek of the Septuagint ; as regards the New Testament, he abstains out of respect from mentioning the historical events related therein.[2] He found a useful guide in Eusebius of Cæsarea whose *Chronicle* he makes use of without mentioning the name of the author, nor those of any of his profane authorities, contenting himself with informing his reader[3] once for all that he was going to avail himself of *historicis mundialibus*.[4] As regards certain episodes about which he was especially informed his account is more fully developed, as for example the Priscillianist affair at the end of the second book. M. Babut thought he had detected certain affinities in Sulpicius with that sect. Certainly Sulpicius felt keen animosity against some of those who had most warmly combated the doctrines of that heresiarch ; he did not forgive the partisans of Itacius the accusations which they had dared to bring against St Martin himself, and the indignation which he felt on this account may have had its counterpart in diminishing his personal objections to the theories of Priscillian. But if each of the expressions which he employed in his *Chronicle* to qualify Priscillianism be weighed, it will be seen whether gentleness is their leading characteristic.[5] This little work is written in a quick, nervous style, showing much distinction. Sulpicius, from the moment of his conversion, had made an undertaking with himself not to read profane[6] authors any more, but he continued to profit by the solid grounding he

---

[1] See the beginning, I, i.
[2] *Chron.*, II, xxvii, 3 (Halm, p. 82).
[3] I. i.
[4] Bernays (*Ueber die Chronik des S.S.*, in *Ges. Abhandl.*, II, 167 et s.) remarks that he ransacked the works of Greek historians unknown to us for the account of the Diadochi.
[5] II, xlvi, 1 ; 4 ; 5 ; 6 ; 7 ; xlvii, 3, 4 ; xlviii, 2, 3 ; xlix, 9 ; li, 5.
[6] Cf. Paulinus of Nola, *Ep.* xxii, 3 ; cf. v, 6 and xxx, i.

owed to them. Very little read in the Middle Ages—we only have one single manuscript of it, a *Palatinus*, now *Vaticanus* 824, of the XIth century—the *Chronicle* regained the high favour of scholars after the Renaissance.

His immense literary popularity Sulpicius Severus owes to his works on St Martin : his *Life*, written during the last months of 396 and appearing in 397, after the death of Martin ; the three complementary letters recording his last moments ; and the two *Dialogues* [1] only published in 403–4. These last are made up of a conversation lasting two days between Sulpicius Severus, Gallus, a former monk from Marmoutier and a pupil of St Martin, and one Postumianus returned from the East, during which they compare some of the wonders wrought by St Martin with those of the Eastern Christian ascetics.

If there is one saint with whom the most " independent " of historians have dealt sympathetically, or even with some sort of piety, it is assuredly St Martin. Gaston Boissier hails him as " the ideal French saint." [2] " Excluding Christ," Camille Jullian [3] wrote, " no character in Christianity has exercised, whether living or above all dead, such a lasting influence. . . . In all the history of Christianity he is the phenomenon most like the initial phenomenon, the name, the life and the memory of Christ." E. Ch. Babut [4] reproaches these learned men for continuing a hagiographic tradition the authority for which he thinks is more than suspect, without taking this into account. He is concerned to diminish the value of the testimony of Sulpicius Severus concerning St Martin. Babut states that in order to put together the portrait of his hero, Sulpicius Severus borrowed more than one *trait* from the *Life of Antony* by St Athanasius, and from St Jerome, and St Hilary, and utilised a quantity of material taken from books which he boldly incorporated in his biography, presenting them as authentic facts concerning St Martin. " The Life of St Martin," Babut wrote, " is a veritable anthology of marvellous events taken from different sources which Sulpicius arbitrarily placed to the credit of his

---

[1] Editions anterior to those of Halm give three; but the best manuscripts show no division in the middle of the first dialogue (cf. Halm, p. vii).
[2] *Fin du Pagan.*, II, 59.
[3] R.E.A., vol. XII (1910), p. 260.
[4] *Saint Martin de Tours*, Paris, p. 146.

hero." The literary habits of the time authorised, it is true, a large amount of fiction in narratives of this kind, but Sulpicius would have somewhat abused the right of *mendacium* which was then allowed to " aretologists " or recorders of miracles. Babut's conclusion is that we know almost nothing of the real character or of the authentic *rôle* of St Martin ; that he must have been a poor man whose reputation was much contested during the second part of his life ; and that the historians, too partial to the writings of Sulpicius Severus, have *naïvely* indulged in the " sophisme du document " which " consists in presuming, when dealing with times about which few texts have been preserved, that men and facts have had in real history the same importance as written history had assigned to them."

In order to appraise with justice Babut's contention the work of Sulpicius Severus should be read through again. A somewhat puzzling impression is left. The literary ability of Sulpicius is outside the question. Possibly too Babut was wrong in disputing, as he has done, the facts narrated, since he allows that Sulpicius may have stayed " some months " at least in close contact with Martin (p. 60). What is more disturbing are his asseverations as to his veracity which, amid so many strange and sometimes burlesque and even " scatological " [1] episodes, he awards to himself. If his conscience had been easy, would he have felt the need of making oath at every incident that he was speaking the truth ? In fact Babut has shown in an excellent chapter (p. 73 et s.) how Sulpicius more than once enriched his narrative by covertly copying from antecedent *Lives*, or by exploiting traditional themes. This does not denote the scrupulous accuracy which he would have us believe was so alert in him. Since the famous *Life of Antony* by Athanasius, it was an understood thing that all Christian biography had to be a kind of " epopee of miracles." [2] Hence the necessity for the biographer to make search on all sides for the means to swell the number of these *virtutes*. More than once we ask ourselves which of these two dispositions we must suspect in Sulpicius— a boundless credulity, or the secret wish to amuse himself at the expense of his readers. Babut is not the first critic to

---

[1] For instance, *Vita M.*, xvii, 7.
[2] The expression of Cam. Jullian in R.E.A., 1911, p. 328.

raise doubts as to his perfect ingenuousness, but he adduced new reasons to mistrust him, and we must agree after reading it that to write a historically true life of St Martin is a difficult matter in the present state of our sources of information.

We must not conclude from this, as Babut has done, that St Martin was only a personage of limited consequence in real history. If he had left behind in Gaul no profound memory, no luminous track, would the work of Sulpicius Severus, however enthusiastic and skilful, have been sufficient to elevate him to such a destiny ? Such a consideration is not without its difficulties.

Babut attaches great importance to the fact that, apart from Sulpicius Severus and Paulinus of Nola, and excepting also the epitaph by Foedula in Vienne (which must have been engraved between the years 410 and 440), Martin's name was not mentioned in the literature of Gaul of the first half of the Vth century. From this he concludes that the Bishop did not occupy in the counsels of his time the place assigned to him by Sulpicius, and that the effects of the apotheosis stage-managed by him were only realised after the generation which had known the real Martin had disappeared. These deductions are rather hazardous. In the history of the literature of the first centuries of Christianity there are many of these disconcerting silences. Could it be believed that Tertullian nowhere makes mention of Hippolytus of Rome nor of Clement of Alexandria, or that neither Hippolytus nor Clement of Alexandria quote Tertullian ? St Ambrose does not speak of St Jerome, nor does Athanasius mention the name of St Hilary. We could find other puzzling instances of the same kind. To be in a position to impute them to ill-will, or a voluntary indifference, we should have to possess in its integrity the literature of the period. And again, pure chance sometimes plays singular tricks.

Such as it is, the portrait of St Martin, more hagiographic in the *Life*, and more familiar in the *Dialogues*, gave keen delight to the first readers to whom it became known. In Rome people disputed for copies of it.[1] It became the model for lives of the Saints. Paulinus of Nola, Hilary of Arles

---

[1] See especially *Dial.*, I, xxiii (Halm, p. 176) : " Deinde cum tota certatim urbe raperetur, exultantes librarios vidi, quod nihil ab his quaestuosius haberetur, siquidem nihil illo promptius, nihil carius venderetur."

in his *Life of St Honoratus*,[1] Uranius in his *Death of Paulinus of Nola*,[2] Possidius in his *Life of Augustine*, Paulinus of Petricordia (Périgueux) in the six books of his *Vita Martini*,[3] Gregory of Rome in his *Dialogues*, Gregory of Tours, and Fortunatus, all took their inspiration from it. Hundreds of manuscripts of the work of Sulpicius exist,[4] the fame of which has come down to modern times.

The character of the author himself is one of the most complex of the end of the IVth century. There is some enigma about Sulpicius Severus : how far did this finished man of letters, *ecclesiasticorum purissimus scriptor*, as Scaliger called him, personally credit the stories he related so well ? We can suspect a good deal of malice in him if we are to judge from the caustic terms in which he censures certain monks, and the Bishops of his time, above all.[5] He remains an interesting and original figure, even if we refuse to attribute to him all the *arrière-pensées* with which people have been pleased to complicate his personality.

[1] Migne, L, 1249–1272.

[2] *Ibid.*, LIII, 859–866.

[3] *Ibid.*, LXI, 1009–1076. C.V., XVI (1888, Petschenig). It is a panegyric in verse, written about the year 470, the three first books of which are based on the *Vita S. Martini* of Sulpicius, the two following on the *Dialogues*, and the sixth on information furnished by Perpetuus, Bishop of Tours. French translation by Corpet, 1852 (Coll. Panckoucke). Some pieces are translated in F. Clément's, *Les Poètes chrétiens*, 1857, pp. 267–281.

[4] Halm distinguishes two groups, the *Italica* (a basic manuscript, a *Veronensis* of the VIIth century) ; the *Gallica* and the *Germanica* (a basic manuscript, a Quedlinburgensis [Quedlinburg in Saxony] of the IXth century).

[5] *Vita M.*, II, xx, i ; xi ; xxvii ; *Dial.*, I, ii, 3–4 ; I, xxiv, 3 ; I, xxvi, 3, etc. ; *Chron.*, II, li, 19. Halm has not sufficiently studied the written tradition concerning Sulp. Sev. See Delehaye, art. quoted, p. 8 et s.

BOOK IV
THE BREAK UP OF THE EMPIRE

CHAPTER I

SAINT AUGUSTINE AND AUGUSTINIANISM

BIBLIOGRAPHY

THE Benedictine edition of St Augustine has quite a history (cf. Kukula, in S.B.W., 1890, 1893, 1898; and Ingold, *Hist. de l'éd. Bénéd. de S. Augustin*, Paris, 1903). Begun, at the suggestion of the great Arnauld, by the labours of Dom Delfau and Dom Robert Guérard, the work appeared to be imperilled on a first occasion in 1670, these two religious having been relegated to a distant abbey possibly on account of certain outspoken views on the abuses to which the *commendam* of the abbey had been put. Dom Blampin took their place and prosecuted their task with zeal. The printing was put in hand on the 5th October 1677, and the first volume appeared in the beginning of 1679. A staff of diligent workers, among whom were Dom Pierre Coustant, Dom Claude Guénié, Dom Nicolas Goyzot, and Dom Martène, pushed the work on with their best endeavours. A few slight skirmishes had already revealed that unfriendly eyes were watching the undertaking from afar. The real battle opened in 1678 with an anonymous pamphlet which purported to have been written by "one of the most important ecclesiastics in Germany," in which the Congregation of St Maur were accused of favouring the errors of Jansenius. Suspicion naturally fell upon the Jesuits, and, as a matter of fact, the letter seems to have been written by one of them, Père Langlois.

Certain members of the Episcopate already were showing some feeling in the matter. But Bossuet energetically took up the defence of the Benedictines before the king. Other anonymous libels were published. The Benedictines had decided at first to make no reply. They were soon obliged to abandon these tactics which might have turned to their prejudice. Replies and counter-replies were abundant. The most skilful plea put forth in favour of the Congregation of St Maur was that by Bernard de Montfaucon (under the signature of D. B. de Rivière). This strife, the many episodes of which it is impossible to relate here, was terminated on the 7th June 1700 in the complete victory of the Benedictines: a decree of the Holy Office condemned three of the pamphlets which had been directed against them, in particular the famous letter of the "German" ecclesiastic which had kindled the fire. Some weeks later, the General of the Congregation presented to the king the last volume of "this edition of St Augustine which had caused them so much trouble." On different occasions, 1707, 1712 and 1730, their adversaries endeavoured to revive the quarrel, but without success.

For the different editions, see TABLE VIII.

A good French biography of St Augustine is still wanting. Very attractive from its charm of style as is Louis Bertrand's *Saint Augustin* (Paris, undated), with its sequel *Les plus belles pages de Saint Augustin*, published in 1912, it is far from reproducing the complex character of the original.

The Bibliography of St Augustine is given in the *Dictionnaire de Théol.*

Cathol., vol. I (1909), 2284-2286, 2457, art. *Augustin*, by E. Portalié. The recent study by Père Batiffol, *Le Catholicisme de Saint Augustin*, 1920, is of first importance for understanding the mind of Augustine. There are many interesting views in Père Alfaric's *L'Evolution intellectuelle de Saint Augustin*, published in 1918.

Detailed studies will be mentioned in the foot-notes.

SUMMARY

I. The taking of Rome by Alaric.—II. The Soul of Augustine.—III. His Life. The Stages of his Conversion.—IV. Augustine after his Conversion.—V. Polemics : Manichaeans ; Donatists ; Pelagians ; Arians. Exegetic Treatises.—VI. *The City of God.*—VII. The *de Catechizandis Rudibus.*—VIII. The *de Doctrina Christiana.*—IX. Correspondence.— X. Sermons.—XI. Conclusions on St Augustine.—XII. The Disputes for and against Augustinianism. Cassian. St Vincent of Lerins. Faustus of Riez. Arnobius the Younger. Marius Mercator. St Prosper of Aquitaine.—XIII. Evagrius.

I

ON the 24th August 410, Rome was taken by Alaric, defaced, and profaned,—Rome, the Mother of all civilisation, the creator of Law, the mistress of the races of the earth. It was an appalling event and produced a feeling of stupefaction. " My voice left me," wrote St Jerome, " and sobs choked my speech. The city which had conquered the whole world is herself captive. What can I say ? She perished from hunger ere perishing by the sword.[1] That famous city, head of the Roman Empire, is laid waste by fire. There is no spot which is not receiving fugitives from Rome.[2] I was desirous of setting to work to-day studying Ezechiel, but at the very moment when I began to dictate, I felt such anguish in thinking of the catastrophe in the West, that the words ceased to come to me. For long I remained silent, bethinking me well that this was a time for weeping. . . ."[3] The idea of the eternity of Rome was deeply rooted in all minds. Without denying themselves occasional mention of the blemishes which had soiled the history of the city, the Christian apologists themselves willingly accepted this idea since the close union between Church and State had been realised.

All these illusions found themselves weakened, and, while the faith of some was shaken, paganism, harassed by the laws in force against it, but always alive and sullen in many hearts, reiterated the old grievances which attributed

[1] *Ep.*, cxxvii, 12.　　[2] *Ibid.*, cxxviii, 4.　　[3] *Ep.*, cxxvi, 2.

all the misfortunes of the empire to the anger of the gods who had been outraged and disowned.[1] " Ah ! if sacrifices were still offered ! If they immolated on the altars of the gods as in former times, the ills under which we now suffer would not have come, or they would have been over by now ! " [2] " The body of St Peter is in Rome," people murmured, " the body of St Paul is in Rome, the body of St Laurence rests in Rome, the bodies of so many other holy martyrs find their resting-place in Rome, and Rome is destitute. . . . Where then are the *memoriae apostolorum ?* " [3] Such were the comments heard in Africa.

Under these mournful aspects the Vth century opened. And they knew not the succession of misfortunes to which Western civilisation had been handed over. Never had mankind greater need of a consoler and guide capable of raising their souls above their material and moral misery, and of bringing the virile encouragement of *Sursum corda.*

II

" From his distant Africa," wrote Mgr. Duchesne, " Augustine shed his light over the whole of Christendom. To the men of his own time he uttered profitable words. He knew how to explain their own souls to them, to console them for the calamities of the world, and to guide their understanding through mysteries. He was amiable to all. Fanatics were calmed down by him, the ignorant were enlightened, and thoughtful minds were sustained in the traditions. He was the instructor of the entire Middle Ages. Even now, after the inevitable attrition of so many centuries, he is still the great authority in theology. It is through him in a special manner that we have

[1] See the *Carmen de Providentia* (P.L., LI, 617–638), written about the year 415 in South Gaul. Translation in Poizat's *Les poètes chrétiens,* Lyons, p. 291 (reproduced in Dom Leclercq's *les Martyrs,* III [1904], p. 313).

[2] " Non enim desunt quorundam voces titillantes aures ecclesiae dicentium : O si sacrificaretur ! O si diis immolarentur solita ! Quoniam aut non venissent, aut iam finirentur ista quae patimur mala." These lines are taken from a sermon *de Tempore barbarico,* which Dom Morin, the editor of St Augustine's *Tractatus* (1917), attributes to Quodvultdeus.

[3] St Augustine, *Serm.*, ccxcvi, 6 ; cf. cxi ; cxxxvi, i ; cv, 12.

intercourse with Christian antiquity. In certain aspects he is for every age. His soul—and what a soul! passed into his writings ; in them he still lives ; on some pages he will always cause tears to fall. . . ." [1]

Theologian, philosopher, moralist, and tireless champion, it is really through his exquisite sensibility that St Augustine has remained the contemporary of successive generations. Who does not call to mind the meditations of the mother and son in the discreet household at Ostia, and the intimate tenderness of these loving hearts who for long had been separated by the " tumults of the flesh " and were reunited on the eve of the day on which Monica was to die, in order that they might dream together rapturously of eternal things without forming any other wish than to taste in heaven a joy similar to what they were then feeling (*ut talis sit sempiterna vita quale fuit hoc momentum intellegentiae cui suspiravimus*) ? [2] No convert knew how to pray like Augustine, with such humility, compunction, remorse for his *prisca flagitia*, and such astonishment that God had not damned him for his long ingratitude. He would love God alone, but he reminds himself that he had loved " the perishable beauty of the body, the brightness of the light, the soft melody of *cantilenae*, the delicious scent of the flowers, and limbs made for embracing by the flesh," [3] and out of all these sweet things purified, transfigured, and idealised, he made the mystic perfume of his love for the " Father of mercies."

Let no one be deceived however ! In that soul of burning charity, expert in discovering words of flame wherewith to address his love to God,[4] there dwelt also the formidable rigour of the dialectician. Into how many anxious hearts has not his doctrine on grace struck dismay, and the terrifying fate reserved for the greater part of the mass of lost ones (*massa perditionis*) of which humanity consisted in his eyes ! Did he not go so far as to consign to hell little children who had died before being baptised, depriving them even of that

[1] *Hist. anc. de l'Eglise*, III, p. viii.
[2] *Conf.*, IX, x, 25.
[3] *Ibid.*, X, vi, 8.
[4] " Unum et multa, pulchritudo, dulcedo, Deus pulcherrimus, Deus dulcissimus, odor suavitatis, interior melodia, motus cordis, affectus, passio, suspirare, accendi, flagrare, ascendere, rapi, intrare, deseri, sponsus, sponsa, amplexus, frui Deo mihi adhaerere Deo bonum est," etc. It was Augustine who created a large number of the expressions of Catholic piety.

medietas, that intermediate state which the Pelagians claimed for them ? [1]

Let me add that his interest in scholarship was moderate. From this point of view he differed profoundly from St Jerome, whom he little understood, and whose efforts in the domain of Scripture he appeared to discourage.   Exegetists who wish for a broader interpretation of the Bible are disappointed not to find any support in Augustine.   The perfect accuracy of the Biblical chronology,[2] the reality—historic and not symbolical—of all the events recorded, the greater weight of the account in the Bible over profane history, and a refusal of any checking by means of the latter—such were the principles of Augustine, and time was only to further strengthen them in him.

How came these inflexible theories to be firmly set in a mind formerly accustomed to so many metamorphoses ? And how could this theological rigorism be united with a foundation most richly endowed with humanity, moderation, and kindness ?   It would require a very delicate psychology to unravel this.   Nevertheless the history of his previous life is significant : it is in his personal experiences that we shall find the starting-point of several of the conceptions with which his name is connected.

III

WE possess three sources for the history of the life and works of St Augustine.   First his biography by Possidius,[3] Bishop of Calama in Numidia, who had been his pupil and remained his friend.   Written shortly after 430, this panegyric contains interesting details on the inner life of Augustine and on his last moments.   Then we have the *Retractations*.[4] The Latin word *retractationes* does not convey quite the same sense as the corresponding word in French (or English). It was like a synonym for *curae secundae*, and indicated the

---

[1] *De peccat. meritis et remiss.*, I, xxviii, 55.   He makes however one concession to pity : the *damnatio* to which these little ones are vowed will be *omnium mitissima* (*ibid.*, I, xvi, 21).   Public sentiment around him protested against the rigorousness of his interpretations : *Sermo*, ccxiv, 1 et s.

[2] See, on the other hand, St Jerome's perplexities, *Ep.*, lxxii, 5, *ad Vitalem*.

[3] P.L., XXXII, 33–66.   French translation in the *Œuvres de Saint Augustin* by Péronne, Ecale, Vincent, etc., Paris, 1870, vol. I, p. 1 et s.

[4] There is an important study by Harnack, S.B.B., 1905, II, 1096–1131.

work of the author in going over his writings at a distance of time in order to bring them into line. Possidius calls this work *de Recensione librorum ;* the title is significant. He could not otherwise make headway against the traditional title attested by St Augustine himself. From the year 412, Augustine was thinking of looking over his writings and calling attention in a special work to passages which seemed to him to be capable of improvement.[1] He did not find the leisure to do this until much later, in 427, when he was 72 years old ; he was still only able to revise his treatises, to the exclusion of letters and sermons. The *Retractations* are divided into two books. The first is devoted to the treatises which Augustine had written as layman and as priest : in it he examines 167 passages. The second deals with his treatises written when he was a Bishop ; the progress of his thought rendered it necessary for him to retouch 52 passages. It will be noted that in his last thirty works he raises only 13 sentences for discussion. The reason is that his orthodoxy had become more and more scrupulous and circumspect. This tendency shows itself on almost every page of the *Retractations*. With absolute frankness Augustine blames and disavows his former complaisance in regard to profane philosophy, that of Plato especially, and of other Christian authors of insufficient orthodoxy, such as Origen. He corrects some of his Scriptural interpretations, and softens down some of his statements on doctrine, for example on the question of the soul's origin, in regard to which he hesitates in choosing between " traducianism " and " creationism." Henceforth he was determined to seek his rule of thought in the Bible only, and not elsewhere. The *Retractations*, taken as a whole, amount to a theological *erratum*, and form a very valuable descriptive list. Lastly, there are the *Confessions*, so highly valued since their first appearance,[2] and which stand out as the most moving book of antiquity on the interior history of a soul.[3] St Augustine did not utter these confidences to justify himself in the eyes of posterity, as did Jean Jacques Rousseau, nor to compel it to agree that no one was a better man than he. Penetrated

---

[1] *Ep.*, cxliii, 2.

[2] *De dono persever.*, xx ; *Retract.*, II, vi.

[3] On the " form " *Confessions*, cf. Misch, *Gesch. der Autobiographie*, I, Berlin, 1907, and the study of this work by Paul Lejay, R.C., 1908, II, p. 313.

through and through with remorse for his sins, if he made up his mind to recall them it was because he wished the marvellous effects of divine grace to be seen in his own case. In considering from what an abyss Augustine had been rescued every sinner was to feel heartened to deserve his own redemption through his own efforts. Augustine " confesses " therefore his own falls at the same time as the glory of God. The absolute veracity of this document has been often suspected. In comparing with it his writings very nearly contemporary with the final crisis related in it, we have to ask if Augustine did not unconsciously project over his past certain dispositions of his soul which in point of time came after the phase to which they relate. Such self-deception would only be very natural. We shall see, however, if the difference in *tone* between the *Confessions* and the writings of Augustine as a catechumen are not explicable by very simple reasons, and if there is any just cause to substitute far less authorised conjectures for the testimony he brings himself concerning his moral and religious evolution.

Aurelius Augustinus was born on the 13th November 354, at Thagaste, a small town in Numidia.

In his *Confessions* he begins the history of his life at the cradle, anxious to note down the awakening of evil inclinations, even in his heart as an *infans*.[1] He attended the school at Thagaste to learn the first rudiments. His mother, Monica, a very fervent Christian—his father, Patricius, was a pagan— did her best to develop the sentiment of religion in him. Later on he was to say, " *Religionis verissima semina mihi a pueritia salubriter insita.*"[2] Nevertheless, in accordance with the custom prevailing in the IVth century, she did not have him baptised, foreseeing the temptations he would one day have to encounter and the wisdom of an amnesty thus deferred.[3] Having been sent to Madaurus, the next village, to follow his studies, he there learnt Greek; it is not correct to allege that he forgot [4] it afterwards, but he was only in

---

[1] See I, vii, 11.

[2] *De duabus anim.*, i.

[3] I, xi, 18.

[4] He acknowledges in two places that he was not much of a scholar as regards Greek (*Contra litt. Petil.*, II, xxxviii, 91 ; *de Trin.*, III, i, i). Nevertheless the texts collected by H. Becker, *Augustin, Studien zu seiner geistigen Ertwicklung,* L. 1908, pp. 122–131, prove that he had picked up more than a superficial acquaintance with it.

moderate sympathy with that language from that time, as a brutal master had disgusted him with it. Mathematics likewise interested him very little. To make up for this he read with delight the *Æneid*, and his compositions in style won him many little successes.

Notwithstanding his limited means Patricius had conceived high ambitions for his son. He had in mind to send him to Carthage to finish his education. While he was getting together the necessary money, Augustine came back to Thagaste, in the summer of 369. He was then sixteen years old. These months of idleness did his morals no good. He turned into an open *mauvais sujet*. He tells us that among other exploits he and some comrades one day robbed the pears from a pear-tree—not a very serious peccadillo—for which, however, he preserved a keen remorse because he had felt for the first time his inclination to do evil for evil's sake, and to taste what was forbidden simply because it *was* forbidden.[1] Thanks to the munificence of Romanianus, a rich inhabitant of Thagaste, he was able at last to set out for Carthage, a seat of learning, but also a city of pleasure.[2] There he threw himself into pleasure with all the ardour of a passionate soul eager for a risky life, dreading nothing more than a " pathway without snares." [3] " *Nondum amabam et amare amabam. . . .*" From the day when he was loved and loved in return, there were jealous suspicions, quarrels, and all the ardour and all the misery pertaining to sensual *liaisons*. As with the emotions of the heart and the flesh, those aroused by the theatre also awoke in him a profound echo, especially when they caused him to shed tears, stirring him to the bottom.[4] Nevertheless he attended assiduously the school of rhetoric, and took no part in the turbulent proceedings of some of his comrades who had formed themselves into bands of *eversores* (smashers) who were much dreaded by quiet folk. He preserved a substratum of seriousness even in his life of dissipation, the irregularity of which moreover we must not exaggerate, since he informs us himself that he was faithful to his concubine as *to a wife*.

When he was 19 (373) he read Cicero's *Hortensius*. In this dialogue, of which we only possess fragments, Cicero

[1] II, iv, 9.
[3] " *Viam sine muscipulis* " (*Conf.*, III, i. i).
[2] Cf. *Contra Acad.*, II, ii, 3.
[4] III, ii.

replied to the criticisms of Hortensius against philosophy
with a magnificent eulogy of this form of intellectual activity,
more capable than any other of setting a man in the way of
real happiness, which consisted, not in deceptive material
enjoyments, but in the life of the mind. From reading this
Augustine himself dates the awakening of his desire for
" wisdom," and a kind of renewal of his sensibility : " *Ille
vero liber mutavit affectum meum. . . .*" [1] " *Surgere coeperam,
ut ad te redirem. . . .*" The call of the infinite sounded
low in his predestined heart. Here we see him started on
the road ; and through many a stage, often painful, he was
not to pause right to the end.

He set himself to study the Scriptures, for owing to the
evident influence of his early education he could not rest
satisfied with any wisdom which was absolutely stranger
to the name of Christ. But the unskilful form of the Latin
translations of the Bible soon repelled him.[2] Disappointed,
he threw them aside as incomprehensible and barbarous.

He turned to the Manichaeans, who were very numerous
in Africa.[3] The sect promised him " truth," and that promise
alone was sufficient to draw him in his then eager state of
mind.[4] It kept its hold over him for some time afterwards
by many ties which he well defined. (*a*) The Manichaeans
claimed to impose no truth on any one before that truth had
become evident to the one who was to accept it. Now,
just then, his own understanding, sharpened by his school
exercises, was very strong in Augustine, and rendered the
method of authority used among the Catholics painful to
him.[5] (*b*) The criticisms directed by the Manichaeans
against the Old Testament, and the ironical questions they
put regarding certain licences granted by God to the Patriarchs, disconcerted Augustine. Having as yet only a very
imperfect idea of the working of Revelation, he was not far
from considering their objections unanswerable.[6] (*c*) He also
acknowledges that he had some difficulty in conceiving
God as a purely spiritual Being. It seemed to him that all
that is must be corporal, in whatever rarefied and quintessen-
tial manner the word be understood. Now the Manichaeans

---

[1] III, iv, 7. Cf. *de Vita beata*, I, iv.
[3] III, iv, 8 ; cf. III, vi, 10.
[5] *Conf.*, III, vii.

[2] III, v.
[4] *De Util. Credendi*, i.
[6] VII, vii, i.

precisely admitted nothing but matter more or less subtilised.[1] (d) The doctrine of the Manichaeans of two co-eternal Principles—the one the principle of good, and the other of evil—having both placed their imprint on every creature, made clear in his eyes the problem of the origin of evil, and exonerated him from his sins before his own conscience.[2] (e) Lastly the name of Jesus Christ, which the sect mingled with their metaphysical conceptions, effectually reassured him and made him in sympathy.

During nine years, from the age of 19 to 28, he was to continue this sympathy, in spite of the grief of the pious Monica, whom these aberrations greatly distressed.

About his twentieth year (c. 374), he had become a professor in his native town, Thagaste.[3] He continued his *liaison* with the same woman who had presented him with a son, Adeodatus. In spite of his adhesion to Manichaeism his soul was unsatisfied, and he sought his path in books. Curious to understand everything, astrology attracted him for a time, but a certain Vindicianus, a man of Pro-Consular rank, and better instructed than he in the nothingness of that pseudo-science, half succeeded in undeceiving him.[4] Then the death of a dear friend reduced him to such an extremity of sorrow [5] that he determined to leave Thagaste for Carthage where a post as rhetorician had been offered him.[6]

He remained there about eight years. It is here that he wrote his first work, which we no longer possess, the *de Pulchro et Apto*. He was not long in casting away his illusions regarding Manichaeism. The fantastic conceptions of Manes on certain questions of accurate knowledge where it was possible to verify them personally, had always seemed strange to him, and it astonished him that Manes represented them as being inspired. The Manichaeans whom he continually interrogated evaded his questions. Now there arrived at Carthage a Manichaean Bishop named Faustus, who was reputed by all to be eloquent and learned. Augustine hastened to place before him his doubts. But he only could reply with elegant phrases and ended with the simple con-

---

[1] V, x, 18.
[2] III, xi, 20 ; IV, i, i.
[3] *Conf.*, IV, iv, 7. Cf. Possidius, *Vita*, i–ii.
[4] IV, iii, 5.
[5] See his fine pages on friendship : *Conf.* IV, v, 10, to IV, viii, 13.
[6] IV, vii, 12 ; cf. *C. Acad.*, II, ii, 3.

fession that he did not understand much about those kind
of things. Thereupon Augustine felt his keen ardour of
hitherto sensibly cooled down.[1]

In the autumn of 383 (it seems) he left Carthage for Rome,[2]
where higher appointments and more disciplined classes of
students were held out to him. Although disabused of the
sect, he had kept up some acquaintance with the Manichaeans; he first lodged with an " auditor " and fell seriously
ill. What proves that the idea of becoming a Christian
still held only a very moderate influence over him, is that
he had no wish to be baptised at this critical moment.[3] He
had reached a certain scepticism which caused him to find
some semblance of good sense in the doubts of the academician
philosophers, in whose view man could not attain to the full
understanding of any truth.[4]

He had already opened his classes in Rome and collected
a certain number of students. These proved themselves to
be less boisterous than those at Carthage. But Augustine
discovered that it was no unusual thing for these young
people, notwithstanding the engagement they had entered
upon, to leave one school *en masse* and betake themselves
to another. Such want of good faith displeased him, and
he gladly seized the opportunity given to him, thanks to the
recommendation of Symmachus, Prefect of Rome, to go to
Milan in the capacity of master of rhetoric (384).

He was going to meet there the chief instrument in his
definite conversion. St Ambrose was such an important
personage at Milan that Augustine could not refuse to go and
present himself to him. He was touched with the fatherly
kindness with which the Bishop received him : " *Eum amare
coepi,*" he said.[5] He was drawn to attending the sermons
of the Bishop. The outer form of these allocutions attracted
him from the beginning. He flattered himself that he was
attentive only to the quality of his language. But the teaching of St Ambrose little by little penetrated into his mind,
and forced him to reflect. Up till then he had considered
certain Catholic doctrines to be untenable, and to his surprise
he was beginning to find out that they were nothing of the
kind. Explanations of the Sacred Books such as St Ambrose

---

[1] V, iii, 6 ; V, v, 8 ; V, iii, 2.   [2] V, viii.   [5] V, xiii, 23.
[3] V, ix, 16.   [4] V, x, 19.

was giving appeared to him to be fully satisfactory. His
intellectual appreciation, freshly conceived, decided him to
break definitely with Manichaeism. Monica, who had rejoined him, learnt of this breach with joy, and could not refrain
from telling him that she was convinced that she would see
him a faithful Catholic before she died.[1] She began to follow
assiduously with her son Ambrose's pastoral instructions.
Augustine would have liked well to confide himself more
completely to Ambrose, but the Bishop's life was so wholly
taken up that he found neither opportunity nor courage to
have a thorough explanation with him.[2]

He thus remained in a state of suspense and perplexity,
half won over, but fearing to deceive himself once more,
and dreaming somewhat *naïvely* of obtaining " in the order of
things not seen " the same certainty which made him affirm
that seven and three make ten.[3] He felt however that it
was a greater test of loyalty to require a belief in what was
not susceptible of demonstration, as did Catholicism, than to
undertake to prove everything, and then to extricate themselves by means of ridiculous fables according to the tactics
of the Manichaeans. He had lost his prejudices against the
Bible. In considering the problem of liberty the riddle of
which pursued him, a profound instinct warned him that
responsibility was not a vain word : " *Cum aliquid vellem aut
nollem, non aliud quam me velle ac nolle certissimus eram et
ibi esse causam peccati mei jam jamque animadvertebam.*" [4]
But with these accurate intuitions there were still mingled
many divagations. Also he felt himself unable to shake off
the bonds to which his senses had accustomed him. Without
pleasure, life did not seem to him to deserve the name,
and became a kind of punishment, *non vita, sed poena.*[5]
His mother thought of arranging a marriage for him. The
woman with whom he was living was removed : he lost no
time in taking another. He was then nearly thirty years old.
Eleven years had already passed since he had felt himself
inflamed with a fine ardour for wisdom. He experienced
profound bitterness at finding himself still so far from the
ideal which in his youthful enthusiasm he had formerly set
before himself.

[1] VI, i.
[2] VI, iii, 3.
[3] VI, iv, 6.   [4] VII, iii, 5.   [5] VI, xii, 22.

Meanwhile, certain Platonist books which had been translated into Latin by Victorinus the rhetorician came into his hands.[1] Augustine does not mention the titles. It is commonly thought that they referred to works by Plotinus and Porphyry.[2] He was keenly struck by the points of resemblance between the teaching he found therein and certain articles of Catholic doctrine, on the Word for instance ; he was also struck by what was wanting in them : " *Non habent illae paginae vultum pietatis hujus, lacrymas confessionis, sacrificium tuum, spiritum contribulatum, cor contritum et humiliatum. . . .*"[3] His reading of these books was the point of departure of new reflections on God, on himself, and on the true nature of the evil which is in the world, and correspondingly many metaphysical difficulties with which he had hitherto been confronted, vanished. He felt in himself a great impulse towards God, but this uplifting was still hampered by many a fall back, in which his will to become better gave way.[4] For beneath the intellectual drama whose vicissitudes were being enacted within he perceived the insidious murmur of his passions, his " old friends " which " drawing him by their garb of the flesh," [5] cunningly counted over the sacrifices to which he would have to consent if he wished to be logical with himself. Certain examples of recent conversions, that of Victorinus in particular,[6] made him ashamed of his weakness and indefinite temporising : " *Ita rodebar intus et confundebar pudore horribili vehementer. . . .*"

The decisive moment in the crisis came in July 386.[7] The scene is well known : a day of poignant struggles between the " two wills," *illa carnalis, illa spiritalis ;* an immense desire to weep ; Alypius, his special friend, present and awaiting the issue of a battle which was nearing its end before his eyes ; the solitude he had sought at the foot of a tree in a garden ; the cry of a child coming from a neighbouring

---

[1] VII, ix.
[2] Cf. *Contra Acad.*, III, xviii ; *Ep.* cxviii ; *de Vita Beata,* iv (the text from *Plotinus* is the only one to remember) ; *Cité de Dieu,* VIII, vii and xii ; Grandgeorge, *S. Augustin et le Neoplatonisme,* published 1896, p. 36 et s. ; Ch. Elsee, *Neo-platonism in relation to Christianity,* Cambridge Univ. Pres. ; P. Alfaric, *L'Evol. intell. de Saint Augustin,* 375 et s. ; 400 et s. See also Boyer, *op. cit.*
[3] VII, xxi, 27.
[4] VII, xvii, 23 : *pondus hoc, consuetudo carnalis.* . . .
[5] VIII, xi, 26.
[6] See above p. 259.   [7] VIII, xii.

house : [1] " *Tolle, lege ; tolle, lege :* take it and read " ; the Bible opened at hazard, and Augustine's eyes falling on the verse from the Epistle to the Romans wherein St Paul calls upon the faithful to renounce voluptuous pleasures and to " put on Jesus Christ " ; all the shadows dissipated and the sense of security coming to inundate his soul with sweetness. . . .

Augustine did not receive baptism until eight months later, on the 24th April 387. In the interval he retired to a property situated at Cassiciacum, not far from Milan, which his friend Verecundus the grammarian had placed at his disposal, and he stayed there till the beginning of Lent 387. He had need of mental quiet ; in addition, he was suffering from his chest. He shared this studious retreat with Monica, his mother, his brother Navigius, his son Adeodatus, and some friends among whom were Alypius and Romanianus. The *contra Academicos,* the *de Vita Beata,* and the *De Ordine* resulted from the philosophic discussions which constituted the favourite recreation of the learned and pious company with which Augustine had surrounded himself. A stenographer took them down, and the transcriptions, revised and retouched by Augustine who adapted them to a Ciceronian style, formed the matter of these " dialogues," which cannot be said to be fictitious since they more or less reproduce faithfully authentic conversations.

Critics have been astonished to find in them no traces of the moral torment which is unburdened in the last chapters of the *Confessions.* The peaceful calm of these metaphysical discourses scandalises them. Just as if on the morrow of this dearly-bought victory some kind of relaxation must not have made itself felt in the soul of Augustine, and as if in these same works whose tranquil tone amazes them one is not able here and there to mark the track left by his inner life, his devotion, and tears in secret to which his companions were in no way privy ! [2]

[1] *De vicina domo.* Knoll has had the maladroitness to accept the text *de divina domo,* on the authority of only one manuscript, the *Sessorianus,* of the VIIth–VIIIth century.

[2] See especially *De Ordine,* I, iii, 6 ; I, viii, 22 ; I, x, 29. He was hoping that philosophy would assist him to *understand* what he already *believed* (*C. Acad.,* III, xx, 43). In a letter to Nebridius (*Ep.* iv, 2), which should belong to this period, he expresses his surprise at his craving to reason things out at those very moments when he *felt* his faith most vividly.

A few months after his baptism, his thoughts turned to going back to Africa with his relatives. But his mother died at Ostia on the journey, in the autumn of 387. In the immense sorrow which he felt Augustine could tell himself that she had at least enjoyed in her last days the full realisation of the dream of her whole life.

IV

AT this point the narrative portion, properly speaking, of his *Confessions* comes to a halt. Augustine could have continued further the history of his life from 388 to 398, the approximate date of his writing the work. But he only wished to relate the thirteen years of vagueness and uncertainty during which he was seeking for the *truth* which he had found and cherished ever after. Certainly the development of his views was not at an end ; it was to remain ceaselessly active and vibrating, with a strong tendency to eliminate all those elements not specifically Christian which he had at first fostered : from the year 386 their standpoint was fixed, and only that mattered in the eyes of Augustine. Moreover, the three last books of the *Confessions* consist of little more than mysticism and philosophy.

After a short stay in Carthage, he retired to Thagaste and remained there three years (388–391) in laborious meditation in which he associated his friends. He was considering a kind of encyclopædia of the " liberal arts "—grammar, logic, rhetoric, music, geometry, arithmetic, and philosophy (to take the place of astronomy) ; he only realised a small portion of this. He also began his polemics against the Manichaeans ; still quite close in point of time to the errors in which he had remained so long, it was from them that he wished especially to preserve men's minds. In order the better to mark his renunciation of his previous ambitions he sold his little inheritance and distributed the proceeds among the poor. In his own words, he had bid good-bye to all the hopes of the world.[1] He would have liked to establish a monastery and live there in piety, work, and friendship. His elevation to the priesthood in 391 was quite unexpected. He had gone to *Hippo Regius* in the hope of winning a soul there which seemed

---

[1] *Sermo,* ccclv, 2 (P.L., XXXIX, 969).

ready to offer itself to God ; he discovered that Valerius, the old Bishop, who felt a keen desire to be supported in his public preaching by an assistant priest, was opening his mind to his people at that very moment. The acclamation of all at once designated Augustine. He received the priesthood with anxious humility, requested of Valerius a leave of some months in order to make a profound study of the Scriptures which he would be obliged to teach, and then came back to set himself to his task. The Bishop made over to him a garden near the church, and half realising his own personal design, Augustine founded there a kind of community where his friends formed a group from which, on the testimony of Possidius,[1] ten Bishops were later to come. Towards the end of 395, Valerius made known his intention of conferring Episcopal ordination himself upon Augustine. The practical unanimity of the African Bishops approved his initiative, in spite of the canonical difficulty created by the 8th Canon of Nicea, which forbade duality of Bishops in the same city. Valerius died shortly afterwards. Augustine remained Bishop of Hippo until his death. He died at the age of 76 on the 28th August, 430, at the beginning of the siege of the city by Genseric, king of the Vandals.

V

DURING nearly thirty-five years he guided with pre-eminent authority the religious thought of his age, and even drew fresh ardour from the opposition he encountered. He was a polemist of prodigious resources who in the height of his debates had always present the law of charity in his heart, and was the great sower of ideas over which theology was to dispute indefinitely.

It would be a disproportionate task to examine here every one of the treatises composing his immense output of work. We must content ourselves with a rapid classification which will be followed by a more detailed examination of some of his writings of preponderating historical importance.

---

[1] Possidius does not give their names. We know at any rate Alypius who became Bishop of Thagaste in 394 ; Evodius, Bishop of Uzalum (the *de Fide contra Manichaeos* [P.L., XLII, 1139–1154] is very probably by Evodius) : see also Dom Morin, *R. Bén.*, XIII [1896], pp. 481–486, and XVIII [1901], pp. 241–256) ; Severus, Bishop of Milevis ; Profuturus, Bishop of Cirta ; Possidius himself, Bishop of Calama.

Manichaeans, Donatists, Pelagians, and Arians were the principal adversaries with whom Augustine had to measure himself.[1]

Manichaeism had spread through every part of the Roman[2] world in the IVth century. Its partisans were recruited both from the old Gnostic sects (the Marcionists in particular), and from among those who were seeking to reconcile as far as they could some sort of link between Christianity and their taste for rationalism and freedom of criticism. Of the fantastic theories of Manichaean mythology the West scarcely knew any but that of dualism : the others were carefully wrapped in mist so as not to startle people. It was this reasonable attitude which had formerly attracted Augustine's youth. The principal promoter of Manichaeism in Africa since 383 was Faustus of Milevis, a Bishop of the sect, one of the most skilful sophists but a man of very superficial learning, whom Augustine had consulted. Various Manichaean works were current in the country—the " Letter on the Foundations of Mani," a work by Adimantus, and another by Faustus himself.[3] At Hippo, Fortunatus a Manichaean priest had made many partisans. Augustine entered on the contest, as I have said, in 388 directly after his baptism. He only had to follow it up actively until about 405. His method consisted not only in written refutations, but in public addresses. A disputation begun on the 28th August 392 ended in the overthrow of Fortunatus. Another conference held on the 7th December 404, against the Manichaean priest Felix, turned out likewise a complete success for Augustine ; Felix agreed to anathematise Mani and his doctrine. Naturally anxious to probe the matter to its depths Augustine was not content to refute the theories of the sect. From these debates he drew positive conclusions in the philosophic and theological order on the relationship between knowledge and faith, on the origin and nature of evil, on free will, and on the economy of Revelation whether shown in the Old or the New Testament.[4]

[1] For the history of heresies in general, see TABLE VIII, no. 114.
[2] Cf. Em. de Stoop, *Essai sur la diffusion du Manichéisme dans l'Empire romain* (derived from the labours of the Univ. of Ghent, Fac. de Phil. et Lettres, 38 fasc. (1909)) ; Dufourcq, *Et. sur les Gesta Martyrum romains*, vol. IV, published 1910 (and my account in the *Rev. Crit.* of the 16th June, 1910, pp. 463–470) ; Prosper Alfaric, *Les Ecritures manichéennes, leur constitution, leur histoire*, 1918 ; *id., L'Evolution intell. de S. Augustin*, p. 65 et s. ; 279 et s. (important).
[3] *Conf.*, V, iii ; cf. A. Bruckner, *Faustus v. Mileve*, Bâle, 1901.
[4] TABLE VIII, nos. 14, 15, 16, 18, 20, 21, 22, 30, 35, 42, 54, 55, 56, 81, 103.

In the same way, his polemics against the Donatists drew him on to define with wonderful penetration the essence of the Church, without ever losing sight of the sentiment of her vitality in this subtle investigation. The Donatists, puritanical and mischief-makers, kept up an epidemic state of discord in Africa which was tormented by this perpetual anarchy. Much more, they awakened terrible scruples in the hearts of numerous Catholics by continuing to repeat that the efficaciousness of the Sacrament depended upon the state of holiness of the minister, and that their Catholic ministers were under the grave suspicion of administering only invalid sacraments. Augustine had a formidable combination to deal with : men like Petilianus, Gaudentius, and Parmenianus were by no means opponents of a negligible quantity. Apart from his numerous polemical treatises,[1] in order to discomfit them by reaching the masses he wrote an *Alphabetical Psalm* in 287 lines, each strophe of 12 lines being followed by this refrain : "*Omnes qui gaudetis de pace, modo verum judicate.*" M. Monceaux[2] has remarked how wrong the learned writers who make a study of the origins of our versification have been to neglect this piece. A fixed number of syllables, the *caesura* always in the same place, rhythm or assonance, balanced hemistiches with two fixed accentuations — these " fundamental elements of Roman verse " discover themselves in the *Alphabetical Psalm*, from which Augustine of set purpose had excluded entirely all the prosody of tradition.[3] It was in the course of these struggles with Donatism that Augustine, who had at first favoured as wide a toleration as was possible,[4] was led to express a wish for the direct coercion of the State in certain cases, and to acknowledge that some " wholesome fear "[5] might be of advantage since in actual fact it brought back to the fold the hesitating and timorous, or prevented them from leaving it—a principle which he himself would never have applied except with his customary moderation,[6] but one in the course of centuries that was to produce formid-

---

[1] TABLE VIII, nos. 25, 47, 48, 51, 57, 64, 65, 66, 90, 91, 102. Cf. Batiffol, *op. cit.*, I, 125 et s.

[2] III, 495 et s. See also Monceaux, VII, 81 et s.

[3] *Retract.*, I, xx.

[4] *Ep.* xxiii, 7.

[5] *Ep.* xciii, 10 (P.L., XXXIII, 326) ; *Contra litt. Petil.*, II, lxxxiii.

[6] Cf. *Ep.* c and cxxxiv. See Batiffol, *op. cit.*, II, 228 and 335. See also Monceaux, VII, 215 et s.

able results which Augustine for certain would not have advocated.

In his works written against Pelagianism,[1]—the first in date, the *De Peccatorum Meritis*, is of the year 412,—St Augustine has perhaps given the best expression of his inner nature as fashioned by the experiences of his life. In the course of those long years of uncertainty and painful interior struggles he had tasted in very truth all the joys of a passionate existence. Rhetoric, philosophy, dialectics, music, mathematics, poetry—none of the walks of knowledge known in his time were strangers to him. He had felt the keen delights of friendships and of love. The satisfaction springing from a career in life had likewise not been denied to him. But these pleasant things had been more than half spoiled by the weaknesses of a will which had been too easily overcome by the " bird-lime " of pleasure. He retained from those years a fear of his senses, of the *inquietus ardor libidinis*, and a sure knowledge of the infirmity of the human will. He conceived life as a long succession of temptations (*ista vita, quae tota temptatio nominatur*),[2] and as " a forest full of ambushes and perils." [3] To cut off the various forms of concupiscence, both of the flesh and of the mind,[4] was the task to which he had consecrated his efforts. We can guess what he must have thought of the ideas of Pelagius, the British monk,[5] and of his disciple Caelestius, on the radical soundness of nature and the absolute power of free will.[6] They repre-

---

[1] TABLE VIII, nos. 70, 71, 77, 78, 85, 89, 98, 99, 100, 104, 108, 109, 116, 117, 118. The doctrine of Augustine on grace did not take clear shape until the year 397 (*de div. quaest. ad Simplic.*). In his *de libero Arbitrio*, he had not given to grace its full share, and from this fact the Pelagians later on were careful to make objections to it.

[2] *Conf.*, X, xxxii, 48.

[3] X, xxxv, 56 ; cf. 60.

[4] Cf. X, xxx et s.

[5] Pelagius was more probably a Briton than an Irishman (cf. Roger, *L'enseign des Lettres class. d'Ausone à Alcuin*, 1905, p. 214). Gennadius devotes a short notice to him, *de Vir. Ill.*, § xliii. Of his numerous writings we have an *Epistola ad Demetriadem* (412 or 413) : (P.L., XXX, 15–45 and XXXIII, 1099–1120), a *Libellus fidei* addressed to Pope Innocent 417 (P.L., XLV, 1716–1718 and XLVIII, 488–491). A. Souter has restored the original text of his *Commentarii in epistulas S. Pauli*, London, 1907. Dom Morin attributes to him a work, *De Induratione Cordis Pharaonis* (*R. Bén.*, XXVI, 163). On Pelagius consult Batiffol, *op. cit.*, vol. II, p. 349 et s. ; Bruckner, *Quellen zur Gesch. d. Pelag. Streites*, S.Q. ii, 7 (1900). All we know of Caelestius are the names of certain of his works. There is a notice of him in Gennadius, § xlv.

[6] In 1890 Caspari published at Christiania some writings of Pelagian origin which Dom Morin attributes to the British Bishop Fastidius (*R. Bén.*, XV, 1898, 491–493). Gennadius (*De Vir. Ill.*, LVI) mentions a *De Vita Christiana* by this

sented to him a formidable psychological misinterpretation. His opposition to these enormities was so keen that it disconcerted a large number of theologians and of the faithful. We shall follow the current of ideas arising from his opposition to these theories.

His anti-Arian writings are far fewer than the preceding.[1]

It was not until 418 that Augustine was led to concern himself with Arianism in connection with an anonymous Arian sermon which had been submitted for his examination. Two years before his death he again provoked a debate in public with Maximinus, an Arian Bishop, who took up a very disloyal attitude in it.

We will only say a word here on his exegetic treatises which are, in contradistinction, very numerous.[2] It was from the Bible, the *veracissima Scriptura*, wearied as he was with the speculations over which he had delayed too long, that he asked for the solution of the riddle of man and the universe. Time caused his evolution to take the form of a fidelity becoming increasingly more strict to the letter of the sacred Books, and to a certainty of their indefectibility becoming more and more strengthened. We shall find again in his *de Doctrina Christiana* an indication of some of the principles from which he formed the substructure of his commentaries on the Old and New Testament.

Let us now fix our attention at rather greater length on some of his leading works.

VI

It would be difficult to meet with one more ample, more rich in ideas, than the *City of God*. This book which originally had only been begun to meet a " particular case," or for a polemical purpose between the years 412 and 426, was developed into a masterly synthesis of doctrine, wherein place was found for an entire history of mankind, the whole system of Christian beliefs, and all the imposing drama exhibiting

---

Fastidius, which is perhaps the same as that appearing in P.L., XL, 1031, and L. 383. We have a *De Damnatione Pelagii atque Caelestii Hereticorum*, by Aurelius of Carthage, written in the year 419 (P.L., XX, 1009).

[1] TABLE VIII, nos. 92, 112, 113.

[2] TABLE VIII, nos. 15, 24, 26, 28, 29, 37, 38, 39, 43, 53, 82, 83, 84, 95, 96.

before our eyes the old struggle between the " Divine City "
and the " Terrestrial City," right up to the final apotheosis
of the one and the swallowing up in the abyss of Gehenna of
the other.

After the fall of Rome, as we know, many went about
repeating the old accusation against Christianity that it had
been a leaven of decadence for the City. Uneasiness was
general in all classes of society. Augustine understood
that this could only be dispelled by a real renewing of public
mentality.[1] This was the reason of his writing the *City
of God*. He worked at it for thirteen or fourteen years ;
but from the beginning he had conceived its vast proportions,[2]
and it was owing to his responsibilities which were too heavy [3]
for him that he delayed its completion for so long.

Whoever has read the *City of God* from beginning to end
will recall having felt here and there some misgivings the
causes of which, on analysing them, have been fairly apparent
to him. In the first place, the composition of the book is
much too lax for modern tastes. Augustine had a plan :
he summarised it in his *Retractations*, II, xliii, and we see
him taking trouble to mark the different divisions in the *City
of God* (cf. II, i ; III, i ; IV, i and ii ; VI, i ; IX, i ; XI, i ;
XVIII, i ; XIX, i). But he is nowhere in a hurry to come
to a head and, anxious before anything else to bring peace
to men's minds, he approaches as he goes along all the questions with which he knows they were preoccupied at the
time. These digressions have their interest : in the long run
they become somewhat fatiguing.

What is much more disconcerting still is the apparent lack
of preciseness in his notion of the " city " which is floating
between heaven and earth without our being able to understand in places if we are to attribute to it a value which is
purely metaphysical, or if we ought to understand it in
a realistic sense.

Augustine uses the words " City of God," and " terrestrial
city " right from the beginning of the work. He does not
think it necessary to excuse the novelty of the expression
which he would not have failed to do if he had run any risk

---

[1] His first attempt to combat this spirit is in *Ep.* cxxxviii.
[2] See the first pages of the *De Civit.*, and I, xxxv.
[3] *Retract.*, II, xliii.

of mystifying his public. We must therefore look for ante-
cedents for this conception of the word " city." We find
very striking ones in Plato (in *Leg.*, p. 713 A), and among the
Stoics (according to Clement of Alex., *Strom.*, IV, xxvi), less
pronounced in Philo, Seneca, and Plotinus. In reality it was
the Bible which had familiarised Christian readers with the
notion of the divine " city." At the beginning of Book XI
Augustine refers expressly to Scripture ; he quotes *Psalm*
LXXXVI, 3 : " Gloriosa dicta sunt de te, civitas Dei,"
and also *Psalms* XLVII, 2, 3, 9 ; XLV, 5 et s. The writer
of the *Epistle* to the *Hebrews* alludes to the πόλις promised
by God to men who believe (xi, 10, 16 ; xii, 22 ; xiii, 14).
Likewise the *Apocalypse*, iii, 12 ; xxi, 2. The concept was
therefore traditional. Moreover, Tyconius the Donatist,
whose exegetic skill was held in high appreciation by Augustine, had appropriated it and had brought it out in strong
relief in his *Commentary* on the Apocalypse written shortly
before 380. He marks the opposition between the *civitas Dei*
and the *civitas diaboli* in the following terms : " Hae duae
civitates, una mundo et una desiderat servire Christo : una
in hoc mundo regnum cupit tenere, et una ab hoc mundo
fugere. . . . Hae utraeque ita laborant in unum, una ut
habeat unde damnetur, altera ut habeat unde salvetur."
Augustine was struck by this parallel and registered it in his
memory. He makes use of it in his *De Catech. Rudibus*,
§§ 31 and 37, in the *De Vera Religione*, § 50, in the *Enarr. in Ps.*
LXI and LXIV, and in the *in Ps.* CXXXVI ; he also amply
developed it in the *De Civitate Dei*, as we know.

What then was this " city " as conceived by Augustine ?
Primarily the grouping, which is ever being renewed, of men
who regulate their lives in accordance with the Divine Will,
or upon purely worldly and almost always corrupt principles.
" Quod (genus hominum) in duo genera distribuimus, unum
eorum, qui secundum hominem, alterum eorum, qui secundum
Deum vivunt ; *quas etiam* MYSTICE *appellamus civitates
duas. . . .*" (XV, i). These two cities, considered thus in
their mystical and symbolic aspect, are intermingled and confused together down here, " perplexae in hoc saeculo invicem-
que permixtae " (I, xxxv), until their sorting out at the Last
Judgment. Further, in composing his picture of each of these
cities Augustine borrows numerous traits from the historical

realities of the past and present. His terrestrial city was really the *societas improborum*, but it was also the State, pagan in so far as it was wanting in justice, which should be its principal mainspring, owing to the failures of its rulers. In the same way the divine city was the collectivity into which enter the souls liberated from sin by grace, the *communio electorum*, but it was also the Church Militant struggling against her enemies while awaiting the triumph reserved for her. Augustine invariably places in juxtaposition the realistic and the symbolic point of view : hence arises some confusion to anyone not alive to this.

" What an occasion and what a theme ! Rome taken, paganism imputing to the new faith this last downfall, this irreparable overthrow of all the grandeur of the past ; in its turn, Christianity throwing back these misfortunes upon the entire ancient civilisation, and to that frail city which had been vaunted as eternal opposing another city which was really eternal and could only accomplish her destiny in the bosom of God, but which was beginning already in the souls of those who believe and pray." [1] Augustine has been accused of ungraciousness in regard to Rome in the hour when this noble victim succumbed. However, he was not insensible to the magnificence of her past *rôle*. He praises her worship of honour and her love of glory—very mixed virtues doubtless, but yet worthy of drawing a divine blessing—which had made her historical greatness.[2] But all the same one feels a sense of solidarity unfolding itself in the *De Civitate Dei*. Christianity had realised, in the light of facts, that it bore within itself the principle of its own development and the guarantee of its destinies, and that— whatever useful support the power of Rome had been able to bring to it—it was henceforth strong enough to prosper without that support, or to create others. Though the City of man might topple in ruins there would still remain the fervent and luminous City of God, to which all upright wills and all pure hearts had access.

Generations of men were to nourish their thoughts and their hopes on all these similitudes.[3] I would not dare to

---

[1] Paul Janet in the *Rev. des Deux Mondes*, March 15th, 1856, p. 388.
[2] V, xv and xxi.
[3] See B. Gaffrey, *die augustinische Geschichtsanschauung im liber ad amicum des Bischofs Bonitho v. Sutri*, Langelsalza, 1918 ; E. Bernheim, *Mittelalterliche Zeitanschauungen . . . ,* Tubingen, 1918.

affirm that a study of this grandiose work to-day would make it appear equally convincing in all its parts.[1] But the idea of co-ordinating the evolution of humanity with the great battle between believers and unbelievers is a general view which has as much value and more, without doubt, than many other generalisations of the same kind. It requires a certain amount of prejudice to declare that one must not speak of the philosophy of history in connection with the *City* because divine foreknowledge " renders nugatory the evolution of history," and that the conception of " progress " would have been lost upon Augustine.[2]

We must also emphasise (since this is sometimes misunderstood) the features which Augustine gave to his definitions of the pagan State, at first sight so severe and crushing. Its formidable antagonism to the *civitas caelestis*, as represented by him, would make one think that he wished it to come to a miserable end. He does manage however to allow it a certain *justitia civilis ;* he praises the State in its capacity of guardian of public order, the safeguard against anarchy, and the power that produces the incontestable benefit of peace. In addition, faithful to the precepts of St Paul, he commends to Christians a patient submission to established authority, whatever it be : " pessimam etiam, si ita necesse est, flagitiosissimamque rempublicam . . . tolerare . . . jubentur." [3] His personal ideal is a Christian State in which true faith reigns, a pledge for the welfare of all, wherein the Church is recognised as the dispenser of all higher moral life, and can count upon the secular arm in its struggles against heresy, and where the king has no other care but to use his authority in the service of God : " suam potestatem ad Dei cultum maxime dilatandum majestati ejus famulam facit." [4] From this point of view the policy of the Christian emperors already gave him wide satisfaction, and he does not hesitate to characterise

---

[1] It would be an interesting thing to draw up a table on this matter. The question of the sources used by Augustine have hardly been studied, except for the first ten books, by S. Angus, in " The Sources of the first ten Books of A. *De Civit. D.*," Princeton, 1906. The *City of God* provides considerable material in the matter of history, political science, and theology. Cf. Schilling, *die Staatsund Soziallehre* des hl. Augustinus, Freib. i. B., 1910, a systematised repertory of the writings of Augustine on politics and sociology.

[2] H. Scholz, *Glaube u. Unglaube in der Weltgeschichte*, L. 1911, p. 150 et s.

[3] II, xix.

[4] V, xxiv.

his age as truly Christian.[1] But it was in the Middle Ages especially that the principles of Augustine were to exercise their most efficacious influence. Gregory VII was often to avail himself of them in his struggles with the civil powers. St Thomas of Aquinas incorporated a large number in his theory of the State. And was Charlemagne, a great reader of the *City of God,* dreaming of anything else than a Christian conqueror such as Augustine had already defined as one who " places his authority at the service of Divine Majesty in order to spread the worship of Him as widely as possible " ?

VII

THE *De Catechizandis Rudibus,* written in 400, is addressed to Deogratias, a deacon of Carthage. " On the Art of Catechising, for the use of those who are ignorant of Christian Doctrine," is the sense of this title. Deogratias had admitted to Augustine the embarrassment and discouragement he had more than once experienced in his duties as catechist, and had asked him for his advice and a system. Augustine begins with kind consolation, showing him that there is nothing exceptional in his case. That thought is always in advance of its expression was a fact well known to all who speak or write, and it required to be somewhat simple to be disturbed over translating badly into speech what one felt strongly :

> " I myself am almost always dissatisfied with what I have said. I would like to say something better ; I play with this something in my mind before trying to express it in speech. And when I perceive the inferiority of this expression I suffer because my tongue renders so imperfectly the sentiments of my heart." [2]

The essential thing was to love what one was doing ; and very usually the pleasure which one derived from the task of teacher passed on to the listeners and became the measure of the attention they would give. There was nothing that communicated itself so easily as tediousness if there be no alacrity proceeding from a cheerful teacher.

[1] *De Vera Rel.,* III, iii ; *De Cons. Evang.,* I, xxvi, 40 ; *Sermo,* cv, 6, 8 ; *Ep.* cxi, 2 ; *De Gratia Christi et de pecc. or.,* ii, 17–18, etc.
[2] § ii.

For the teaching of Holy Scripture, of the Old Testament especially, experience suggested certain principles with which it was good to inspire oneself. In the first place, not to put oneself to the pains of either relating or even summarising all the facts included therein, but to choose a few of the most wonderful and most moving, and then extract all the juice, and be satisfied with brief allusions for the rest. To inculcate in their minds the essential idea that everything in Scripture up to the coming of Christ was a figure of what had been realised in Christ and His Church. Once this truth was grasped it mattered little if the details were omitted. Also, to make the catechumens understand that the Redemption was essentially a work of love, and that human love ought to respond to divine love by passionate obedience to the divine law. To question each one as to the personal motives which were urging him to the faith in order to make him feel God better in the changes through which his own experiences were passing. Lastly not to be afraid of insisting on the promises of the Resurrection which were so much laughed at by pagans and sceptics, and upon the punishments beyond the grave, not forgetting to forewarn the simple of the scandal which the feebleness of some of those already in the Church might offer to them.

Such is the general system recommended by Augustine. But he takes pains also to foresee and study certain special cases.

First, the case of the merely educated man (*liberalibus doctrinis* excultus) [1] who reaches Christianity. It was probable that a postulant of this quality had already occupied himself for some time with matters concerning the faith. There was no need therefore to weary him with making him go over the rudiments. But it would be a good thing to enquire what books he had read and how and when his aspiration towards the faith took shape. If by chance these have been heretical works, he should enlighten him upon them by basing himself on the authority of the universal Church. Certain authors, Catholics who were dead, favoured heresy, however, in some pages of their writings : he must equally know in what points their views were incompatible with true orthodoxy.

[1] § viii.

More delicate was the case of a catechumen who was an " intellectual," a former pupil of grammarians and rhetoricians, and already initiated into all the curiosities of the mind.[1] The first step to attempt was to give him a taste for Christian humility, and to show him that it was a more serious thing to sin against good morals than against grammar. If he was successful in piercing the envelope containing his classical prejudices, in making him understand the seriousness of human life, and the greater importance of what one does than of the refinements of the intellect, a considerable step would have been made. As regards Holy Scripture, the taste for this could not be given to people of this kind except by representing it to them as a book of mystery, fruitful in deep meanings upon which the intellect must exercise itself in a broad manner. This is a significant passage which helps one to penetrate the state of mind of the lettered pagans, and explains the fondness of the Christian interpreters for allegorical exegesis.

> " One must make them see how great is the profit from these matters which are hidden beneath a veil, and for that very reason are called mysteries, and how much these obscure riddles sharpen a love for truth and dissipate the weariness and distaste inspired by any notion too easy to discover."

Lastly Augustine enlarges upon the disposition of mind in which the catechist should endeavour to place himself in order to react against moments of dryness and carelessness. He shows him how to arouse the attention of a class which has become a little sleepy and how to keep up their spirits. As a conclusion to the treatise, he gives a specimen " instruction " for the use of uneducated postulants, which is simple, direct, practical, and wonderfully adapted to the minds of common people.

VIII

WE have already marked the importance of the *De Doctrina Christiana* from the point of view of the destinies of the old learning during the preceding centuries of Christianity.[2]

---

[1] § x.   [2] Cf. p. 27.

There are certain notions developed in this work which are worth while drawing attention to again, all the more that Augustine, having completed his work three years before his death, must have given them in their final form.[1]

Augustine's object was to provide a method of interpreting the Scriptures both for the understanding of the text itself and also for giving an account of the results attained (*modus inveniendi quae intellegenda sunt et modus proferendi quae intellecta sunt*).

Of the first three books, which are of an altogether technical character, only a few features need be specified here. In chapter x of book II, Augustine recommends the Christian exegetist to learn Greek and Hebrew for cases where the Latin translations appeared obscure or doubtful. He was ignorant of Hebrew himself ;[2] we remember that he had not supported St Jerome when the latter made his vigorous attempt at *Hebraica veritas*.[3] Some change had thus come over his sincere mind ; he no longer limited the investigations of the exegetist to the Latin translations, nor even to the *Septuagint* —which, nevertheless, still remained in his eyes the privileged version.[4]

In chapter xv of book II we find the famous passage on the *Itala*, which has been the cause of so much vexatious confusion. St Augustine mentions the multiplicity of Latin versions of the Bible, some very servile, others rather more free, which latter he prefers. There was one to which he assigns the palm, the *Itala*, in which clearness was united to a scrupulous fidelity : " Among the translations we must place the *Itala* above all others for it comes closest to the words, and the idea stands out clear in it : *In ipsis autem interpretationibus Itala ceteris praeferatur ; nam est verborum tenacior cum perspicuitate sententiae.*"

---

[1] The original text, which was abandoned by Augustine in 397, went as far as chapter iii, xxxvii, of the complete work finished in 427. " Cum imperfectos (libros) comperissem," Augustine explains (*Retr.*, II, iv, i), " perficere malui quam eis relictis ad alia retractanda transire. Complevi ergo tertium. . . . Addidi etiam novissimum librum et quatuor libris opus illud implevi." To attempt to restore the first edition, as Dom de Bruyne has done, who supposes that Augustine remodelled the work from cover to cover in 427 (*R. Bén.*, 1913, p. 301 et s.), is an undertaking which seems to be rather chimerical (cf. Cavallera, B.L.E., 1915–6, p. 420 et s.).

[2] *De doct. chr.*, II, xvi, 23 ; cf. *Conf.*, XI, iii, 5.

[3] See above, p. 357.

[4] *Ep.* lxxi ; lxxxii ; *Enarr. in ps.* 87, 10 ; *de Civit. Dei*, XVIII, xlii–xliv.

What exactly was this Itala ? Many different answers have been given. To Ronsch, the *Itala* was . . . the *Afra*, a version of African origin ! Other modern critics, F. C. Burkitt, for instance (*The Old Latin and the Itala*, in *Texts and Studies*, IV, 3), and, more recently still, Dom de Bruyne (*Rev. Bénéd.*, XXX [1913], pp. 294–314), have wished to identify the *Itala* with St Jerome's version. In the VIIth century this was already the interpretation of Isidore of Seville (*Etym.*, VI, iv). This gives rise to such great difficulties that it must be rejected deliberately.[1]

The *Itala*, as its name indicates, could be no other than a version accustomed to be used in the " diocese " of Italy, which at the time of Augustine included Verona, Aquileia, Brescia, Ravenna and Milan.[2] From the moment that Augustine put it forward against the other translations which were current in large numbers (" *Latinorum interpretum infinita varietas*," he wrote in the *De Doctr. Chr.*, II, xvi), it is altogether unreasonable to attribute this name to the Latin translations anterior to St Jerome taken in bulk, and it is an erroneous assignment which must at last be given up.[3]

In interpreting the Scriptures, all the resources of profane knowledge, with the exception of those confined to superstition, would not be superfluous. Nevertheless Augustine is careful to mark that the Bible to a certain degree surpassed all other books : " Nam quidquid homo extra didicerit, si noxium est, ibi damnatur ; si utile est, ibi invenitur." [4]

In book III he indicates with much minuteness the different ways of solving the difficulties which result from the letter of the Scriptures, or from the apparent sense of certain passages which are disconcerting as regards morality. Allegorical exegesis should render good service [5] in the last case.

---

[1] See Cavallera, in B.L.E., 1915–6, p. 416 et s., and W. Ruting, *Unters. uber Augustins Quaestiones u. Locutiones in Heptateuchum*, Paderborn, 1916, pp. 360–366.

[2] The adjective *Italus* is a poetic use. But the prose writers of the imperial age employed it fairly frequently instead of *Italicus* (e.g. Pliny, *Hist. Nat.*, III, liv ; Arnob. *Adv. Nat.*, II, lxxiii ; St Augustine, *City of God*, III, xxvi, etc.). Cf. Sittl, in A.L.L., XI (1900), p. 124 ; Wölfflin, in S.B.M., 1893, I, p. 256.

[3] The Commission of the *Thesaurus Linguae Latinae* of Berlin has incorporated it in its system of reference. Wölfflin nevertheless in 1893 drew attention to the inconveniences it presented (S.B.M., 1893, I, p. 273). The two books *De Vocatione Omnium Gentium* (P.L., XVII, 1073, and LI, 647) have likewise wrongly been attributed to Prosper. The author is unknown.

[4] II, xlii.

[5] III, xxii.

No interpretation which set forth the *caritas Dei et proximi* could be altogether erroneous.[1] He counsels the use of the seven rules of Tyconius the Donatist which were excellent notwithstanding the partial heterodoxy of their author.[2]

Book IV is very important from the point of view of the literary ideas of St Augustine.[3] He recommends the Christian professor to study rhetoric. When any technique of eloquent phraseology was encountered it should be assimilated, lest a bad service be done to the interests of truth by excluding it with less skill than that shown in the passage it was intended to combat. To instruct, to please, to touch, were, in the opinion of Augustine as of Cicero, the ends of eloquence. But it was only in St Paul and the prophets that he sought for his examples. According to him, Scripture offers specimens of every variety of style. It was lawful to follow the models presented in it, or those put forward by the best Christian writers, such as St Cyprian or St Ambrose. But the rule governing all presentation of the truths of faith was clearness ; the susceptibilities of good language must not prevail against that fundamental law. If one spoke, it was in order to be understood.[4]

IX

OF the 276 letters of St Augustine [5] which we possess 53 have reference to his correspondents. This series is spread over forty years (from 386–7 to 429) : it therefore only reflects in a very incomplete manner Augustine's immense activity as a letter writer.

His letters do not possess the literary and brilliant turn of those of St Jerome. There are no animated scenes, and no

---

[1] I, xl.

[2] III, xxx et s.

[3] There are some views in Zurek, *Diss. philol. Vindobonenses*, VIII (1905), pp. 69–109. Hendrickson's article in the *Amer. Journ. of philol.*, 1905, p. 276 et s., treats of little more than the differences of style in Augustine.

[4] *De Doctr. Chr.*, IV, x, 24.

[5] 270 were collected and classified by the Benedictines ; 2 letters and a fragment have been discovered since the Benedictine edition, and figure in Migne (XXXIII, 751 ; 789–792 ; 929–938) ; 2 letters published by Goldbacher (C.V., XXXIV, 2, p. 444 and XLIII, p. 648), following manuscript 3479 in Cambridge University ; 1 letter published by Dom Morin in R. Bén., XVIII (1901), pp. 241–256, from the *Monacensis* Clm 8107, IXth century. Goldbacher also gives in vol. LVII of the C.V., p. 44, an unpublished fragment of four lines of a letter to Bonifatius, from the *Codex Augiensis* XCV, Xth century. The letters of Augustine are in P.L., XXXIII, and in C.V., vol. XXIV, XXXIV and LVII.

biting satires. He only very rarely betrays himself or becomes expansive.[1] Sometimes we meet with a slight trace of malice, but he very soon recovers himself, being entirely taken up with his purpose and bent solely on the demonstration he wishes to give.

They are of varying length. Some are compressed into short notes. Others take the form of veritable treatises which can only be classed as letters from the fact of the names which appear at the beginning and end : for instance *Ep.* clxxxv to Count Boniface, which St Augustine in his *Retractations* himself entitles " *liber de correctione Donatistarum.*" [2] Letter ccxiii is still further removed ; it is a stenographic report of a meeting held in the Church of Peace at Hippo on the 26th September 426, at which Augustine obtained the assent of his flock to the priest Heraclius being his successor in the Episcopal chair of that city.

From the point of view of the history of religion, and even that of civilisation, this collection is of first importance. Year by year we feel the *prestige* of Augustine growing. He is the revered *Pope* to whom the eyes of Western Christendom were turned, and to whom the Emperors themselves judged it indispensable to address a copy of the official letters which they sent to the Primate of Carthage. He was consulted on every side, and these enquiries, even on the most delicate [3] and sometimes preposterous matters,[4] brought forth replies full of forbearance. He gives comfort and advice with eagerness and inexhaustible kindness, and is as ready to provide a community of religious women with a detailed rule of life,[5] as to treat of the great questions of grace, free will, or the lawfulness of a career as a soldier.

X

St Augustine was not accustomed to write out beforehand the sermons he was to deliver, except on rare occasions.[6]

---

[1] *e.g.* at the beginning of *Ep.* cclxi.

[2] Likewise the letters mentioned in Table VIII.

[3] Cf. *Ep.* cclxii : the wisdom of his directions in the case of a private quarrel between husband and wife will be noted.

[4] Cf. *Ep.* ccv, in which we see Consentius enquiring of him " utrum nunc corpus Domini ossa et sanguinem habeat, aut reliqua carnis lineamenta."

[5] *Ep.* ccxi.

[6] Cf. *de Trin.*, XV, xxvii, 48 ; *Retract.*, II, xxxii, 2.

He would not have had the time to do that. He contented himself with a preliminary meditation bearing principally on the texts from Scripture which he intended were to form their structure. If we are to believe his biographer Possidius he sometimes even abruptly changed his subject under the pressure of some unexpected circumstance. Stenographers,[1] sometimes the faithful themselves, took down his words.[2] This is how a certain number of them have survived. Victor of Vita informs us that this ran away with much of his time.[3] Among the sermons to which Possidius, Cassiodorus and others, allude, there are some which do not figure in our very incomplete collection. To make up for this, many were fraudulently written under Augustine's name. The task of modern editors has been to separate the genuine from the false. Unfortunately the valuable revision represented by the *Retractations* is wanting in his sermons and letters.[4]

The interest offered by these sermons is very unequal. Many are made up merely of paraphrases of verses from the Bible over which the attention of the most zealous reader wavers a little. The interest revives upon seeing Augustine unfolding not only the strength of his deep faith, but also the candour of his humility, in order to reach the inner feelings of his hearers which was the source of his invigorating power. Far from placing himself above the heads of those he was instructing in doctrine, he acknowledges himself to be as weak as they, and includes himself in the rebukes he delivers to them. The language in which he speaks to them is curiously composite. The methods of rhetoric betray themselves on more than one page; there are alliterations, metaphors, plays upon

---

[1] *In Ps.* li, 1 (P.L., XXXVI, 600).

[2] Possidius, § vii.

[3] *Hist. Persec.*, I, iii, ii.

[4] The Benedictines have distinguished 363 authentic sermons, 31 doubtful, and 317 apocryphal. They divide the sermons into four classes—*sermones de Scripturis* (1–183); *s. de tempore* (*i.e.* Feasts of the Liturgical year, 184–272); *s. de sanctis* (273–340); *s. de diversis* (341–363). The oldest sermon we possess is no. 214, of the year 391; the latest, sermon 345, after the year 428 (cf. P.L., vol. XXXVIII–XXXIX). Since the Benedictine edition, other sermons have been published by Michel Denis (P.L., XLVI, 813–940); Fontani (XLVII, 1113–1140); Frangipane (XLVI, 939–10004). Dom Morin has discovered in a manuscript of the IXth century, now at Wolfenbüttel (no. 4096), a collection of homilies, forty-one of which are not yet published. He attributes thirty-three of these to St Augustine (*S. Aurelii Augustini tractatus sive sermones . . . edidit G. Morin*, Campoduni and Monaci, 1917). This collection must have been made in the time of Cæsarius of Arles. Dom Morin had published previously two other authentic sermons (R. Bén., VII, 260; 592; VIII, 417; cf. IX, 173).

words,[1]etc.; but he approaches closely turns of phrase which are in distinctly popular language wherein we see certain marks similar to those in use in languages of Latin origin : *Nunquam fecit tale frigus* (never before was it so cold) ; *metuo ne ibi vos habeam fatigatos ; multa habemus dicere vobis*,[2] etc. He wrote in his *de Doctrina Christiana* (IV, x) : " More often than not, to speak in popular language (*loquendi consuetudo vulgaris*) is more useful for expressing things than the correctness of language of lettered men." There should be much material in the sermons for reconstructing life in Africa at the beginning of the Vth century, the survivals of paganism, the relations between the pagans and Christians, as well as the frenzy for public shows and the sensual ardour of those races upon whom Augustine essayed unweariedly to impose the law of Christianity, with its refinements and austerities.

XI

Noverim me, noverim te (*Solil.*, II, i) : to know God, and to know the human soul formed the twofold object towards which the mind of Augustine was drawn with an ever fresh impetus. He was the most philosophic of the Fathers of the Primitive Church. We will say more : among the Latin Fathers he is the only one who really possessed speculative genius and the gifts of a close thinker. He embodied some of the purest sources of the old philosophy, especially those of Platonism ; but he searched into them with a gaze that was too *clairvoyant* not to enrich with his own personal contribution their lofty lessons which he made his own.

Moreover, his philosophy did not pride itself on any independence. He made his submission resolutely to the faith and to the Church. Augustine accepted whole-heartedly the authority of Catholicism, and all his dialectic efforts were used only to justify it in a rational manner, and to make it understood by those who had not yet felt its benefits. The Bible and the Church were for him the very foundations of truth, and every construction not based upon them seemed in his eyes destined to ruin. Notwithstanding, he appreciated

---

[1] " Distulit *securim*, dedit *securitatem* (72, 2). *Perpetua et Felicitas*, coronis martyrii decoratae, *perpetua felicitate* floruerunt," etc.
[2] S. 25, 3 ; 37, 17 ; 215, 9.

learning, and was less distrustful of it than a St Hilary or a St Ambrose ; he would not subject his faith to it, but his mentality in deciphering its riddles, and his life.

Minds inclined to be critical find more satisfaction in the works of St Jerome than in his. His very humility sometimes rendered him credulous, and Manichaeism had made the minutiæ of exegesis excessively distasteful to him. The vigorous mind of Jerome had more defensive power than Augustine's and greater resistance to what was unacceptable. But what detachment from self was in Augustine, what true modesty in face of the admiration which his contemporaries were not sparing in showing him, what passionate flights, what ardent meditations ! He was all charity and all love.

In a letter to St Bernard, Peter the Venerable calls him *maximus post apostolos ecclesiarum instructor*. Not that certain of his teachings did not provoke, as we shall see, bitter opposition. But his thoughts have become as it were the substance of Christian literature ; they have been present in the thick of all the battles of the spirit during the centuries past.

XII

THE thesis of Augustine on human free will and predestination—that harsh doctrine which consigned to Hell the greater part of the human race, the real " leaven of iniquity," with the exception of a privileged few to whom God had vouchsafed the wholly gratuitous gift of His grace—aroused keen opposition in several quarters of the Christian world. Eighteen Bishops in Italy and Sicily preferred to resign their Episcopal sees rather than subscribe to the condemnation of Pelagius and Caelestius formulated in the *Tractoria* of Pope Zosimus. The most irreconcilable of them was Julian of Eclana, a polemist formidable from the force of his logic and the clearness of his language.[1] Deposed and in exile, Julian waged strife with Augustine who during twelve years found himself obliged

---

[1] Cf. A. Bruckner, *Julian von Eclanum*, in T.U., XV, 3 (1897) *id., die vier Bucher Julians von Ecl. an Turbantius*, B. 1910 ; Batiffol, *op. cit.*, II, 490 ; Dom Morin, R. Bén., 1913, pp. 1–24, wished to restore to Julian the commentary by the Pseudo-Rufinus on the Prophets Osee, Joel, and Amos (P.L., XXI, 959–1104), and that this commentary be re-edited from the *Parisinus* 12148. Alb. Vaccari attributes to him a commentary on Job, published in 1897 in the *Spic. Casinense* under the name of the priest Philippus (*Un commento a Giobbe di Giuliano di Eclana*, Rome, 1915). There is a notice of Julian in Gennadius, *de Vir. Ill.*, xlvi.

to sustain his attacks and reply to them. It is only from numerous and long quotations copied out by Augustine that we are able to form any idea of the *Four Books to Turbantius* and the *Eight Books to Florus*, in which Julian combated his views. The ideas of Pelagius had also found some favour in Britain. Many Bishops were advocating them there, and their moral integrity brought much support to the doctrine they defended. In order to refute them Pope Celestine was obliged to send Bishop Germanus of Auxerre, who crossed over the English Channel accompanied by St Lupus, Bishop of Troyes.[1] In spite of the thoroughness of the efforts of Germanus, who soon became a legendary figure among the Britons, the concepts of Pelagius lasted on for a long time still in the land of his birth.

But it was especially in southern Gaul that opposition to him was organised and vigorous.[2] At Marseilles, John Cassian (c. 360–435) openly took part against Augustine. His influence was great. Born in Scythia,[3] if we may give credence to Gennadius, and brought up in a monastery at Bethlehem, he had lived for ten years with the monks of the Egyptian Delta and Desert of Nitria. Ordained deacon at Constantinople in 404 by St John Chrysostom, next a priest in Rome, Cassian founded about the year 415 two monasteries at Marseilles, one for men and the other for women. His twelve books *de Institutis coenobiorum et de octo principalium vitiorum remedio*,[4] finished in the year 426, give in detail, with numerous examples, the stern rules of the monasteries in Palestine and Egypt, and the moral tribulations to which the monks were specially subjected (among these eight *vitia*,

[1] A letter from Lupus to Talasius of Angers appears in P.L., LVIII, 66.

[2] In addition to the names we are about to mention, we must bear in mind those of various Gaulish ecclesiastical writers, such as Petrus Chrysologus, Bishop of Ravenna, 433–450 (his sermons, many of which are not authentic, are in P.L., LII, 183 and 665) ; Valerianus, Abbot of Lérins, and Bishop of Cemele (homilies and a letter are in P.L., LII, 691–758) ; Bishop Maximus (a letter to Theophilus of Alexandria ; cf. Dom Morin, R. Bén., XI [1894], p. 274) ; Leontius of Arles (a letter to Pope Hilary, written in 462, in P.L., LVIII, 22–23) ; Ruricius of Limoges (82 letters in two books : P.L., LVIII, 67–124, C.V., XXI, p. 348 et s. [1891, Engelbrecht], and M.G.H., VIII [1887, Krusch]).

[3] *De Vir. Ill.*, lxii. According to Merkle, this should refer to the Dobroudja, cf. T.Q., 1900, pp. 419–441. See the discussion by Petschenig in C.V., vol. XVII, p. iiii, who thinks that he was a native of Provence. There is no doubt that Gennadius intended a Latin town in Scythia, which presents nothing extraordinary.

[4] Migne (who reproduces the edition of Gazet, Douai, 1616), XLIX, 53–476 ; C.V., vol. XVII (1888, Petschenig). French translation by Saligny, published 1663, Lyons, 1685. Study by Paucker on the Latinity of Cassian in the *Romanische Forschungen*, II (1886), pp. 391–448.

he mentions " sadness ") together with the means of healing
them. His twenty-four *Collationes* (c. 429),[1] in three parts
(i–x ; xi–xvii ; xviii–xxiv) and each preceded by a preface,[2]
initiate the Christian public into the spiritual life of the monks.
These two works formed a kind of code of monachism.[3]
They were translated into Greek,[4] a privilege the exceptional
character of which I have already mentioned. Lastly the
de Incarnatione Domini contra Nestorium in seven books
written in 430 by request of the future Pope Leo, give evidence
of the zeal of Cassian for orthodoxy.[5] Now this stern writer,
holding profane [6] learning in little favour, steeped in asceticism
and austere studies, and a man whose influence was great
with the most pious minds in Gaul, distinctly attributed
the initiative to good to the human will in his thirteenth
Collatio (§ viii, ix, xi), divine grace coming afterwards to add an
incrementum.

The solitaries of the Isle of Lérins (to-day St Honorat)
on the south-east coast of France were hardly more favourable
to Augustine's views. Founded by St Honoratus, afterwards
Metropolitan of Arles (426), in the first years of the Vth century, the Monastery of Lérins had become one of the centres
of Catholic theology in Gaul, and a nursery of Bishops for
that country.[7] In his *de Laude Eremi* [8] St Eucherius, the

---

[1] The *collatio* was an exercise much in vogue amongst the monks. They
made known their personal difficulties, and those in the intellectual and moral
order, to their Abbot, who suggested a solution for them. This custom was already
enjoined in the rule of St Pachomius for the East, and in the XIIth century it
was still in existence in the West.

[2] P.L., XLIX, 477–1328 ; C.V., vol. XIII (1886, Petschenig). French translation by Saligny, P. 1667, Lyons, 1687 (excluding the thirteenth *Collatio*).

[3] Herwegen, *Beitr. zur Gesch. d. alten Mönchtums*, Munster i. W. 1912 (an
analysis of Cassian's rules).

[4] On the testimony of Photius, *Bibl.* 197. A *résumé* in Greek of the *de Instit.
Coen.* may be found in the *Patr. grecque*, XXVIII, 849 et s. under the wrong title
of *Epist. ad Castorem.* K. J. Dyovouniotis published in 1913 from *Cod.* 593 in
a Meteorite monastery, *Collationes*, i, ii, vii, viii, in Greek. Cf. *R. Bén.*, 1913,
477, on the Greek translations of certain of Cassian's works.

[5] P.L., L, 9–272 ; C.V., vol. XVII.

[6] Cf. *Coll.*, XIV, xii et s.

[7] Cf. Cooper-Marsdin, *The History of the Islands of the Lérins*, Cambridge
Univ. Press, 1914.

[8] § xlii. St Eucherius wrote various works destined to spread the taste for
monastic life and to facilitate the understanding of the Bible : cf. P.L., L. vol.
XXXI of the *Corpus* of Vienna (1894, Wotke) includes the *Formulae spiritalis
intellegentiae*, the *Instructionum libri duo*, the *Passio Agaunensium martyrum*,
the *Epistula de Laude heremi ;* also different letters addressed to Eucherius by
Salvianus, Hilary and Rusticus. French translation by Gregory and Collombet
(together with Vincent of Lérins), published 1834. Salonius and Veranius, the
two sons of Eucherius, were Bishops like their father ; we owe to the former a few
writings of mystical exegesis (P.L., LIII, 967–1012).

future Bishop of Lyons, who had joined the community in
410, extolled the charm of the setting chosen by Honoratus :
" Watered by health-giving springs, rich in verdure, spangled
with flowers, full of the charm of fragrance and sweet sights,
my dear Lérins presents to those who enjoy her an image
of that paradise which they should possess."

From Lérins came the famous *Commonitorium*,[1] written
in 434 [2] by that enigma " Vincent of Lérins." [3] Few works of
Christian antiquity have had such striking attention as the
Commonitorium, I mean in modern times.[4] Not that Vincent
gives evidence of much individual originality as regards the
fundamentals of his doctrine.[5] We can discern in the
Commonitorium many echoes of Tertullian's *de Praescriptione*,
and it is equally certain that Vincent derived much profit
from his reading of St Augustine's writings, in spite of certain
hostile *arrière-pensées*. But he has the merit of having
meditated on the ideas of his predecessors and of having enclosed them in clear, striking, and decisive formulæ, which
seem to have imposed themselves in some cases upon posterity.
We know his famous criterion, so often invoked, so seldom
applicable, and which the Church has never made her own
except under reserve : [6]

> " In the Catholic Church we must carefully adhere
> to what has been believed everywhere, always, and by
> all (*quod ubique, quod semper, quod ab omnibus creditum
> est*). For that is what is truly and properly ' Catholic,'
> as is shown by the meaning and etymology of the word
> itself, which comprehends the universality of things." [7]

To make up for this, his theory of progressive doctrine [8]—
operating through organic growth and not by the addition of
elements which were originally foreign to it, and consisting

---

[1] *Commonitorium* properly means "notes consigned to writing to aid the
memory " (Baluze). Cf. F. Brunetière and P. de Labriolle, *St Vincent of Lérins*,
Paris, 1906 (French translation with detailed introduction), and Koch, in T.U.,
XXXI, 2 (1907). P.L., L, 637–686 (which reproduces Baluze). Special editions
by Jülicher, in S.Q., 1895, and Rauschen, in F.P., 1906.

[2] We gather the date from § xxix, 7.

[3] We owe the little we know of him to Gennadius, *de Vir. Ill.*, § lxv.

[4] More than 150 editions and translations can be counted since the XVIth
century.

[5] Cf. Brunetière and P. de Labriolle, p. lxiv et s.

[6] *Ibid.*, p. lxxxv et s.

[7] *Common.*, ii, 6.

[8] xxiii.

P

in disengaging and placing in their own proper light the truths
implicit in the *depositum fidei* and not yet perceived—has
become the *quasi*-official doctrine of the Church.[1] Vossius [2]
was the first to suspect that this work of St Vincent of Lérins
might well have formed a portion of the semi-Pelagian
dossier. What Vincent says in chapter xxvi, 8, of this
sect which held out to its adherents " a special and strictly
personal grace " which people received " without labour,
without effort, without giving oneself any trouble, and without
even asking, or seeking, or knocking at the door for it," [3]
is very congruous, according to Tillemont himself,[4] " to
the unfavourable meaning which the semi-Pelagians gave
to the doctrine of grace, in order to discredit it in the minds of
people." Other indications suggest the same conclusion.
Without doubt it would be an altogether exaggerated view
to uphold (as some have done) that the *Commonitorium* as
a whole is fundamentally only a polemical treatise against St
Augustine. Vincent of Lérins had an intention which was
much more general : he wished to place in the hands of the
Church a weapon which might serve for all time against
heretics. But it is also strongly probable that he had in his
mind the illustrious Doctor of Hippo on more than one
page, and that Augustine's personal point of view remained,
in short, *privata opiniuncula* (xxviii, 8), and was not capable
of prevailing against the old unanimous view of the Church.

In the year 433, Faustus, the future Bishop of Reji (Riez,
in Provence), was appointed Abbot of the Monastery of Lérins.
In his *de Gratia libri duo*, written against the priest Lucidus,
a partisan of predestination, Faustus adhered to the views of
Cassian in his essentials. Moreover the decree of the pseudo-
Gelasius included this work, together with all the writings
of Cassian himself, among the *apocrypha*. A prolific writer,
Faustus in the words of Gennadius had the reputation of
" an eminent Doctor," [5] and we possess a fairly large number

---

[1] Whatever may have been said, Newman did not have a very different conception of the development of doctrine : cf. *Critical and Historical Essays*, London,
1871, vol. I, p. 287.
[2] *Hist. de controversiis quas Pelagius ejusque reliquiae moverunt*, Leyden, 1618,
1. I, § 9.
[3] " Etiamsi nec petant, nec quaerant, nec pulsent." Cf. St Augustine, *de
Dono Persev.*, xxiii, 64 : " Adtentant ergo quomodo falluntur, qui putant esse
a nobis, non dari nobis, ut petamus, quaeramus, pulsemus."
[4] *Mém.* . . . , XV, 860–1.
[5] " Viva voce egregius doctor et creditur et probatur." (*De Vir. Ill.*, lxxxvi.)

of his writings. The assignment of certain of them to him is open to discussion.[1]

Arnobius the Younger, who was thus named in order to distinguish him from Arnobius the rhetorician, the master of Lactantius, has attracted the attention of critics during recent years. It is impossible to gather any explicit account of him from the writings of antiquity. He appears to have given himself out as a monk.[2] There is no decisive reason to suppose he was a Gaul.[3] In any case, he lived in Rome, or was in very close relations with people in Rome about the year 450. We have some *Commentarii in Psalmos* [4] of his, in which he too combats the views of St Augustine upon grace. Possibly he is the author of the *Expositiunculae in Evangelium*,[5] short notes of no great significance, and of the *Conflictus Arnobii Catholici cum Serapione Aegyptio*,[6] directed against Monophysitism. Dom Morin attributes to him in addition a curious *Libellus ad Gregoriam* which Isidore of Seville ascribed to St John Chrysostom : [7] the work is addressed to Gregoria, a Roman lady, who lived in the imperial palace on the Palatine, and found herself in disagreement with her husband ; the author points out to her the virtuous diplomacy which will again insure happiness in her household.[8]

Dom Morin likewise restores to Arnobius the Younger the treatise in three books known by the name of *Praedestinatus*,[9] which was discovered by J. Sirmond the Jesuit in a manuscript of Rheims Cathedral, and published by him in 1643.

---

[1] Texts in P.L., LVIII. The *Corpus scrip. eccl. lat.*, vol. XXI (1891, Engelbrecht) includes the *de Gratia*, the *de Sp. Sancto*, twelve *Epistulae*, of which two are addressed to Faustus, and thirty-one *sermones*. Others yet to appear are the sermons edited by Gagny, 1547 ; the *Tractatus* edited by Pierre Pithou, 1586 ; the *Tractatus de Symbolo*, edited by Caspari (*Alte u. neue Quellen zur Gesch. d. Taufsymbols*, Christiania, 1879, p. 250). The authenticity of certain sermons has been discussed (cf. Dom Morin, R. Bén., IX, 49 ; X, 62), and of a letter (*ibid.*, VIII, 97), and the identification of the *Adversus Arianos et Macedonianos* mentioned by Gennadius (cf. Dom Cabrol, R.Q.H., XLVII, 232). The letters of Faustus appear also in M.G.H., VIII. French translation of the letter to Lucidus, in *l'Histoire de Boëce*, by Gervaise, 1715.

[2] Comm. in Ps., P.L., LIII, 486 and 552.

[3] Cf. Dom Morin, *Etudes, Textes, Découvertes*, I, p. 341.

[4] Migne, LIII, 327–570.

[5] LIII, 569–580, published completely for the first time by Dom Morin, *Anecd. Mareds.*, III, 129–151 (cf. R. Bén., XX [1903], pp. 64–76).

[6] LIII, 239–322.

[7] *De Vir. Ill.*, xix.

[8] Critical text published for the first time by Dom Morin, *Etudes, Textes, Découv.*, I, pp. 383–439.

[9] P.L., LIII, 587–672.

The purpose of the *Praedestinatus* was to attack the doctrine of predestination in a roundabout and circumspect form and with every kind of effusive respect for St Augustine.   In the first book the author, careful to vouch for his own personal orthodoxy, ushers in his exposure of the " heresy " of pre-destination by drawing up a list of heresies teeming with involuntary carelessness, wilful misrepresentation, facts very like the latter, and falsehoods.[1]   The second book offers a defence of the said heresy, which is refuted in the third. Dom Morin, basing himself on parallelisms of expression and thought, supposes [2] that the preface, the first, and the third book, are the work of one and the same author, and that this author is no other than Arnobius the Younger.

Whatever value we should attach to the resemblances indicated by Dom Morin, a grave difficulty makes us hesitate to ascribe to Arnobius the responsibility for the whole of these writings, which Dom Morin is disposed to swell still further. How could the convinced semi-Pelagian who betrays himself in the *Commentarii* and in the *Praedestinatus*, finally subscribe in the *Conflictus* to the Augustinian thesis ?   Dom Morin supposes that Arnobius had thrown off the ideas of Pelagius " as the increasingly clear action of the authority of Rome, which did not take a light view of questions such as these, made him see his opportunity."   If such an evolution was really produced in the mind of Arnobius, the case of this monk toning down from motives of prudence and discipline the *odium theologicum* which he had at first shed forth so bitterly, would be an interesting one.[3]

Some of the most convinced admirers of St Augustine hesitated to follow him on the question of grace.   Such, on the testimony of St Prosper, was the state of mind of Hilary,[4] the Bishop of Arles, " a man of great authority and much addicted to spiritual studies," who expressly

---

[1] See my *Sources de l'Hist. du Montanisme*, pp. cxiv–cxxvii.

[2] *Etudes*, etc., p. 315 et s.

[3] The most complete work upon Arnobius is Dom Morin's, *Etudes, Textes*, etc., pp. 309–382.   See also H. Kayser's, *die Schriften des Arnobius Junior, dog-mengesch. u. litt. unters.*, Gutersloh, 1912 ; J. Scharnagl, *Zur Textesgestaltung des Arnobianischen Conflictus*, in *Wiener* Studien, 1916, 2, pp. 382–384.

[4] *Ep.* ccxxv, 9, ad Augustinum.   Cf. the notice of Gennadius on Hilary of Arles, § lxix.   He wrote the *Life of Honoratus*, his predecessor (P.L., L, 1249–1272). A few other pieces are doubtfully assigned to him, e.g. the *Metrum in Genesin*, and the *Versus in natali Machabaeorum*.

reserved himself upon this point. But none the less Augustine did not lack warm partisans quite ready to enter the lists on his side, such as the Gaulish monk Leporius,[1] whom he had succeeded in turning from Pelagianism in 418, and who wrote a book in order to give an account of his error and of his recovery therefrom, and Aurelius, Bishop of Carthage.[2] Among his most active supporters, two laymen, Marius Mercator and Prosper of Aquitaine, take the first place.

Marius Mercator was probably a native of Africa. In the year 418 he sent to Augustine from Rome two works (apparently now lost) against the partisans of Pelagius and Caelestius.[3] A few years later, in 429, he is to be found at Constantinople, ever active against Pelagianism, and also against Nestorianism. His knowledge of Greek enabled him to make known in the West various works by heresiarchs such as Theodore of Mopsuesta, Nestorius, and Proclus, which would not have come down to us without him. He also translated into Latin the polemical writings of Nestorius against Pelagianism, and of St Cyril against Nestorianism. He thus undertook a task very similar to that which Rufinus had so usefully fulfilled.[4] Mercator died probably after the year 451.

The personality of Prosper, although not commanding, and of a too abject docility, deserves a more careful study.

Born in the South of Gaul in the year 390, Prosper of Aquitaine (*Tiro Prosper* was his name, according to the manuscripts of his *Chronicle*) learned to understand Pelagianism about the year 428 from St Augustine's *de Correctione et Gratia*. The purpose of his life and the field for his activity were revealed to him by reading this work; although only a layman, he determined to follow up Pelagianism under all its forms and to defend the illustrious Bishop of Hippo

---

[1] *Libellus emendationis sive satisfactionis ad episcopos Galliae* : P.L., XXXI, 1221–1230.

[2] *De damnatione Pelagii atque Caelestii haereticorum* (419) ; P.L., XX, 1009–1014.—Capreolus (430–437), the successor of Aurelius, reserved his efforts to combat Nestorianism : P.L., LIII, 843–858.

[3] Cf. letter cxciii of Augustine to Marius Mercator. It has sometimes been wished to identify one of the two works to which St Augustine alludes with the *Hypomnesticon contra Pelagianos et Caelestianos* (P.L., XLV, 1611–1664).

[4] The fragments of his translations are in P.L., vol. XLVIII. Likewise his own works : the *Commonitorium super nomine Caelestii* (published first in Greek [429], then in Latin [431]) ; the *Commonitorium adv. haer. Pelagii et Caelestii vel etiam scripta Juliani* (431–2) ; the *Comparatio dogmatum Pauli Samosateni et Nestorii* (431), and the *Nestorii blasphemiarum capitula* (431).

against his detractors. He did hardly anything else, both in prose and verse, during the space of thirty years.

In 428 or 429 he warned St Augustine [1] of the opposition aroused by his writings on grace among certain circles in Marseilles, who judged his theory of gratuitous predestination to be contrary to the traditional feeling of the Church, and even dangerous from the point of view of edification. He begged him to throw light on these difficult questions by further explanations. We know that St Augustine, urged on likewise by Hilary,[2] another layman, wrote for both of them the *de Praedestinatione Sanctorum* and the *de Dono Perseverantiae*.

Prosper then undertook to explain to Rufinus, one of his friends, the nature of the problem of grace (*Ep. ad Rufinum de gratia et libero arbitrio*),[3] next he fell upon St Augustine's opponents (he died in 430) with ever fresh ardour, without allowing himself to be intimidated either by the talent of men like Vincent of Lérins (*Pro Augustino responsiones ad capitula objectionum Vincentianarum*), or the prestige of Cassian the model of the ascetics (*De gratia Dei et libero arbitrio liber contra Collatorem*).[4] His most curious work is the Περὶ ἀχαρίστων, *hoc est, de ingratis*, in 1002 hexameters. He plays upon the double meaning of the word *ingratus*, " unprofitable " and " despiser of grace." This poem, which Guizot hails as " one of the happiest essays in philosophical poetry which have been attempted within the bosom of Christianity," [5] is entirely made up of theological disquisitions against semi-Pelagianism, the heir to Pelagianism. In the first part are found the well-known verses (quoted in honour by Bossuet in his *Sermon sur l'Unité de l'Eglise*) upon Rome who " held captive by the authority of religion what she no longer held by the force of arms," [6] as well as a fine eulogium of St Augustine.[7]

Although Prosper in his prose recognises the virtues of his opponents (in his letter to St Augustine), he treats them with no benevolence in his verse. The disquisition in the *de*

---

[1] *Ep.* ccxxv (among the letters of Augustine).
[2] *Ep.* ccxxvi.
[3] Translated into French in the *Œuvres de Saint Augustin*, by Péronne, Ecalle, Vincent, vol. XXXII.
[4] Translated *ibid*.
[5] *Hist. de la civil. en France*, IVth.
[6] Line 39 et s.
[7] Line 99 et s.

Ingratis is at least clear and bright, however difficult the subject may be ; sometimes even it warms into elegance born of the ardour of his belief in St Augustine, which accepts with enthusiasm the rigorousness and even the obscurity of his master's doctrine.

> " If you ask why from among the innumerable multitude of men upon earth, God chooses some to be re-born in Jesus Christ and leaves others to perish, although the same condemnation surrounds all men, and nothing but grace distinguishes creatures who are equal in merit, *we are not so rash as to seek further* in order to penetrate into channels hidden from us or to plant our footsteps in inaccessible paths."

To the *de Ingratis* we may add a series of short poems, for example, two epigrams in verse against an *obtrectator Augustini*, the sarcastic epitaph on the Nestorian and Pelagian heresies, and 106 epigrams in which are transposed into verse various views from the *Liber Sententiarum* which Prosper had himself compiled from the writings of Augustine.

The only work in which Prosper partially gets away from the sole idea which absorbed his intellect and devotion, is his *Chronicle*. In it he develops St Jerome's *Chronicle* by calling to his aid the annals of the Consuls (*consularia Italica*), and brings it down at first to the year 445,[1] and then in a second revision, to the year 455.[2] The work has no real historical importance until after the year 425, on which date the information given by Prosper becomes independent.

He died in 463. It is not correct to make him Bishop of Riez. He remained a layman to the last, but owing to the favour in which he was held by Pope Celestine, and Pope Leo I, whose secretary he became in 440, and to his solid theological foundation and the consistent character of his ardent con-

---

[1] This is the *Chronicon* called *vulgatum*.

[2] This is the *Chronicon* called *intergrum*. Among the Chronicles more or less directly related to the Chronicle of St Jerome, we might also mention that of Hydatius († in 468) which goes from 370 to 468 (Migne, LXXIV) ; that of Count Marcellinus († after 534), from 379 to 534, interesting on account of the Empire of the East (Migne, LI) ; that of Marius of Avenches († 593), from 455 to 581 (Migne, LXXII) ; that of Victor of Tunnuna († 569), from 444 to 567, in the portion which has been preserved (Migne, LXVIII) ; and that of Jean de Biclaro who continued after Victor the years 567 to 590 (Migne, LXXII). All these Chronicles were collected by Mommsen in the *Chron. Minora*, vol. II (M.G.H., XI [1894]).

victions, he exercised considerable influence on ecclesiastical thought in the middle of the Vth century.[1]

Without entering into the views of semi-Pelagianism the Roman Church displayed much reserve on the theories of Augustine. The ardent controversies of that period were to revive many centuries later with a virulence which is well known.

XIII

In the year 440 Evagrius the Gaulish priest endeavoured in his *Altercatio legis inter Simonem Judaeum et Theophilum Christianum*,[2] to go back to the tradition of the literary dialogue in use in Christian apologetics in the middle of the second century. His rendering is of an almost *naïve* simplicity. " Fuit igitur altercatio legis inter quemdam Simonem Judaeum et Theophilum Christianum. Judaeus igitur sic ait. . . ." This forms all the prelude. Once the discussion is entered upon Theophilus takes a larger and larger share in it and lavishes on his opponent significant texts from the Old Testament. Soon the Jew begins to waver; for conscience' sake he still brings forward a few objections, which are quickly refuted ; finally he acknowledges himself beaten, asks to be baptised and utters a prayer to God to give him grace, which closes the colloquy : The forfeit had been fixed from the beginning : " Quod si tu me hodie viceris, facito Christianum : aut ego cum te superavero, faciam Nazaraeum Iudaeum." We are far from the zest and *finesse* of the *Octavius*, or even from the supple dialectics of one of St Augustine's similar dialogues.

[1] The history of the editions of St Prosper is summarised by L. Couture, in B.L.E., 1900, pp. 270–282, which shows the use of his works made by Jansenism in the XVIIth century. There are interesting modern quotations in J. J. Ampère's *Hist. litt. de la France avant le XIIth century*, II, p. 50 et s. Migne (vol. LI) reproduced the edition of Luc Urbain Mangeant (Paris, 1711). The *Chronicle* is also printed in M.G.H., IX, 1, p. 341 (1892, Mommsen). We cannot assign to Prosper with any certainty the *De promissionibus et praedictionibus Dei* (P.L., LI, 733) ; the *Poema conjugis ad uxorem* (P.L., LI, 611 ; C.V., XXX, 344) ; the *De Providentia Divina* (P.L., LI, 617) ; the *Confessio Prosperi* (P.L., LI, 607) ; the *Praeteritorum sedis apostolicae episcoporum auctoritates de gratia Dei* (P.L., LI, 205 ; L, 531). The matter is discussed in Valentin's *S. Prosper d'Aquitaine*, Paris, 1900, who likewise makes a study of the language and style of Prosper. French translation of the *de Ingratis*, by Lemaistre de Sacy, 1646 and 1650 ; of the complete works of Prosper, by Lequeux, 1762 ; various of his writings have been inserted in the translation of St Augustine, vol. XXXII.

[2] P.L., XX, 1165–1182 ; Harnack, T.U., I, 3 (1883) ; Bratke, in C.V., vol. XLV (1904). Critical notes by Stangl, in B. ph. W., 1915, nos. 23 to 26. Harnack's thesis, according to which the *Altercatio* was a translation or a resetting of the *Debate between Jason and Papiscus*, by Ariston of Pella (about the year 140) has not been favourably received.

CHAPTER II

THE CHURCH AND THE BARBARIANS—OROSIUS—
SALVIANUS—LEO THE GREAT—VICTOR OF VITA

BIBLIOGRAPHY

I. OROSIUS. The *Commonitorium de errore Priscillianistarum* appears in P.L., XXXI, 1211-1216 (and XLII, 665-670), also in C.V., vol. XVIII, pp. 149-157 (Schepss): the *Liber Apologeticus* is printed in P.L., XXXI, 1173-1212, and C.V., vol. V, 600-664 (C. Zangemeister); the seven books *Historiarum adv. Paganos*, are in P.L., XXXI, 663-1172; C.V., vol. V, 1-564; B.T. (Zangemeister, 1889). A letter to St Augustine *de Haeresibus* is mentioned in S.B.W., vol. LXXXIV (1877), p. 533; it is in the British Museum, Add. MSS. 24902, fol. 37 v.—Consult; G. Boissier, *Fin du Pagan*, vol. II, p. 398 et s.

II. SALVIANUS.—Text in P.L., LIII; M.G.H., I, 1 (Halm, 1877); C.V., VIII (Pauly, 1883). French translation by Grégoire and Collombet, 2 vols., Paris, 1833. A reliable study of the language of Salvianus, which is very interesting, is needed. J. H. Schmalz has drawn attention to certain grammatical peculiarities in B. ph. W., 1915, No. 32/33, cols. 1041-1046. —Consult: Boissier's *Fin du Pagan*, vol. II, p. 410 et s.; Waltzing's *Tertullien et Salvien*, *Mélanges de Borman*, 1919, pp. 13-17.

III. LEO THE GREAT.—P.L., LIV-LVI (116 Sermons, of which 96 are authentic; 173 letters, of which 143 are by Leo himself). Amelli published in 1882 two letters written to Leo, one from Flavianus of Constantinople, and the other from Eusebius of Dorylaeum: these documents were re-edited by Mommsen in 1886, in the *Archiv. d. Ges. f. aelt. Geschichteskunde*, XI, 361-8.—Consult: Turner in the *Miscellanea Ceriani*, Milan, 1910; Ad. Régnier, *S. Léon le Grand*, 1910 (coll. *les Saints*). French translation of ten sermons and nine letters in the *Chefs-d'oeuvre des Pères de l'Eglise*, vol. XIV (1838), pp. 129-310; translation of all the sermons by the Abbot of Belle-garde, 1701.—The *Sacramentarium Leonianum* has been edited by Feltoe (c. 1897); cf. Migne, LV, 21-156.

IV. VICTOR OF VITA.—P.L., LVIII, 180-216; Halm, in M.G.H. (1879), III, 1; Petschenig, in C.V., VII (1881). French translation in Dom Leclercq's *Les Martyrs*, III (1904), pp. 348-407.

SUMMARY

I. Orosius and Augustine. — II. The Seven Books *against the Pagans.*— III. The *de Gubernatione Dei*, by Salvianus. — IV. Pope Leo the Great.—V. *The History of the Persecution by the Vandals*, by Victor of Vita.—VI. Vigilius of Thapsus.

I

THE name of Orosius is naturally connected with that of St Augustine. Like Alypius, Quodvultdeus,[1] and many others, Orosius was his disciple and friend, and had scarcely any other ambition than to live upon his doctrines, and to develop them subject to his master's corrections.

Paulus Orosius was a native of Spain, perhaps of Tarragona.[2] Born about the year 390, he entered orders and was attached apparently to the clergy at Bracara, in Gallecia. His admiration for Augustine brought him in 414 to Hippo. Augustine welcomed him kindly, and quickly recognised his real moral and intellectual[3] qualities, and after keeping him a short time with him sent him to St Jerome in Palestine in order both to help him to finish his education in doctrine, and to transmit to Jerome by a trusty messenger certain questions on the origin of the soul,[4] over which he was preoccupied at that time.

In the meantime, Orosius, who had been able to observe at close quarters in his own country the Priscillianist doctrine, inscribed to Augustine a *Commonitorium de Priscillianistis et de Origenis errore.* Augustine replied to it without delay with a treatise *contra Priscillianistas et Origenistas ad Orosium.*

Having arrived at Bethlehem, Orosius soon became St Jerome's auxiliary in his polemics which at that time were being directed against the Pelagians. In this way he felt sure of giving pleasure to St Augustine and no thought could have acted as a keener spur to him. In the last months of 415 he wrote a *Liber Apologeticus*, a veritable indictment of Pelagian-

---

[1] Various works have been recently restored to Quodvultdeus with more or less probability: sermons (*S. Aur. Augustini tractatus sive sermones inediti*, published by Dom Morin in 1917, pp. 181, 191, 196, 200); a *Liber de promissionibus et praedictionibus Dei*, reproduced by Migne in the appendix to the works of St Prosper of Aquitaine, P.L., LI, 734–838 (see Schepens, R.S.R., 1919, pp. 230–243).

[2] He wrote *Tarraconem nostrum* (*Adv. Pag.*, VII, xxii, 8).

[3] *Ep.* clxvi, 2.

[4] *Ep.* clxvi. It appears probable that Orosius also took with him *Ep.* clxvii and certain other writings for the purpose of placing Jerome *au courant* with Augustine's ideas on grace. Cf. Brochet, *Saint Jér. et ses ennemis*, 1906, p. 451 et s. In December 415, during his stay in Jerusalem, the relics of St Stephen discovered by the priest Lucianus of Kaphar Gamala, who wrote out in Greek an account of this *inventio*, which was soon translated into Latin by Avitus of Bracara, a Spanish priest, who happened to be there (P.L., XLI, 805–818). Orosius later on brought some of these relics to Minorca, where many Jews were converted on this account: related by Severus, Bishop of Minorca, in P.L., XLI, 821–832, and XX, 731–746.

ism, for the use of the Fathers assembled at the Council of
Diospolis (on the coast of Palestine) in December of that
same year.[1] But this "lamentable" Council, as Jerome
called it, in no way resulted in the confounding of Pelagius,
and Orosius returned disappointed to Augustine at the beginning of 416.

Acting on his advice he set himself to his great work,
the *Adversum Paganos Libri VII*, and laboured at it with so
much ardour that by 417 he had almost finished it.[2]

II

THIS history is directly connected with the *City of God*,
particularly with Book III wherein Augustine set down the
reckoning of the evils suffered in former days by Rome which
the gods had been powerless to avert. Augustine considered
that his outline might be gone over and amplified with
advantage in order to do away with the grievance of the pagans
over what they supposed were exceptional misfortunes at
the beginning of the Vth century. Orosius clearly explains
this design in his preface. What he wished to do was to collect
from the record of different nations the most significant
examples of the ills of humanity—wars, pestilences, famines,
earthquakes, floods, the ravages caused by thunderbolts and
hail, cases of parricide and turpitude—and to classify these
calamities in the form of a kind of history of the world.[3]

In the nature of things Orosius could not examine a very
large number of documents in only two years. He would
very much like us to believe that he made use of very many
sources of information. As a matter of fact, he extracted
what he knew from a small number of Latin authors (not
counting the Old and New Testament). The *Chronicle*
of Eusebius, remodelled and continued by St Jerome, provided him with the outlines of his plan. He supplied himself
with his facts from an *Epitome* of Titus Livius, from Cæsar's
Commentaries (which he attributed to Suetonius),[4] from
Tacitus, Justin, Florus, Eutropius, Rufinus, and St Augustine

---

[1] Cf. Frankfurth, *Augustinus u. die Synode zu Diospolis*, B. 1904.
[2] He gives the number of years since the creation of the world to the time
at which he was writing as 5618 (VII, xliii, 19 ; Zangemeister, p. 564).
[3] See the Prologue ix–x ; cf. I, xxi, 21.
[4] VI, vii, 2.

himself.[1] His account has special interest after the year 378, for his written sources of information for that period have not been preserved.

This abundant subject matter, with which he confesses he is somewhat overwhelmed,[2] is divided into seven books : I. A short description of the terrestrial globe. A history of the world down to the founding of Rome, which he places in the year 752 (B.C.). II. A history of Rome down to the conquest of the city by the Gauls, together with a synchronous account of the history of the Persians from the time of Cyrus, and of the Greeks down to the battle of Cunaxa. III. Events in Roman, Greco-Macedonian, and Hellenistic history down to the year 290 before the Christian era. IV. The Pyrrhic wars down to the destruction of Carthage. V. Rome, from the destruction of Corinth to the first civil war. VI. The wars against Mithridates down to Augustus and the birth of Christ. VII. The period of the Emperors down to 417 A.D.

In order to understand the methods employed in the *Adversum Paganos*, we must remember that considerations of a mystical order, rather than technical requirements, suggested them to Orosius in more than one place. If he divided his work into seven books, it was because St Augustine had given prominence in his *City of God* (XI, xxxi) to the special virtues of the number 7—the total made by the first uneven number (3) and the total of the first two even numbers (4)[3]—the number of the day on which God rested after the Creation, etc. . . . In the same manner, if he admitted four great Empires—the Macedonian in the North, the Assyrio-Babylonian in the East, the Carthaginian in the South, and the Roman in the West—it was because the Prophet Daniel's interpretation (VII, 3–27) of his dream favoured that classification. He thought he saw mysterious chronological coincidences between the refounding of Babylon by Semiramis and the conquest of that city by the Medes, and he notices that the same lapse of time separated the founding of Rome and her conquest by Alaric. These enigmatic coincidences appearing among the multiplicity of events in history disclosed in his eyes the constant

---

[1] The verification is easy thanks to the notes in Zangemeister's edition, and to the index, pp. 684–700.

[2] *Pref.* to Book III.

[3] Augustine makes 4 the first even number (*totus par*).

action of Providence which had ordained them and which regulates the onward march of humanity down to its minutest detail.

But the considerations which had determined him to undertake his work inclined him also to emphasise especially events of the past of a particular kind. What mattered to him was to demonstrate that in spite of their childish bewailings, his contemporaries were not appreciably to be more pitied than those of any other period in the world's history. He remarks on that illusion of the imagination or of the sensibility which readily makes us believe that no misfortune can be worse than what we are suffering at the present moment, like some man who, after having been devoured by fleas all night, is of opinion that his loss of sleep was more trying than when a raging fever had recently held him in its grip.[1] It is therefore upon the sufferings of generations of men, on the harsh dealings of nature, and on the ferociousness of mankind, that Orosius dwells more readily in order to arrange an instructive picture, a kind of chamber of horrors of history, looking at which his contemporaries shall blush for their grumblings. Besides, was the present as appalling as they pretended ? For his part, Orosius doubted it, and resolutely held out an optimistic view. Thus, after tracing the war between Sparta and Athens, he makes this observation : [2]

" We esteem lightly those afflictions which weighed down Greece during so many long years. What we cannot put up with now is that the course of our pleasures should be interfered with, and that our passions experience some weariness. There is, however, this difference between those times and our own, that they put up with those intolerable ills with a steadfast heart because they were born to them, because they lived among them and knew no other better state, while our people, accustomed from long date to the serenity of their undisturbed condition and of their pleasures, are moved by the slightest shadow of worry and anxiety. Please God they may pray to Him who can dissipate this alarm however

---

[1] Preface to Book IV (Z., p. 204).
[2] I, xxi, 18 (Z., p. 78).

trifling it be, and to Whom they owe a continuity of peace unknown to other periods ! "

In another place,[1] in connection with a terrible invasion of locusts which had alighted upon Africa during the Consulship of M. Plautius Hypsaeus and M. Fulvius Flaccus (in the year 125 B.C.), he remarks that no such formidable scourge had ever been reproduced since the era of Christianity. There were still many incursions of these insects, *sed tolerabiliter laedunt.*

Even towards the barbarians only recently so hateful in the eyes of an Ambrose, or a Prudentius, Orosius feels within himself much indulgence. Of course he loves *Romania,*[2] and appreciates the benefits springing from Roman civilisation, and appears to believe still in the solidity of its foundations. But he considers the barbarians to be capable of improving. They perpetrated horrors, it was true : at least they were not incapable of repenting[3] of them. In short, without his views on the future of Latin Hegemony being very clearly pronounced, Orosius was half resigned already to vicissitudes which the preceding generation could not accept without revolt.

Written with a certain warmth of eloquence in language wherein an imitation of the classics, particularly of Virgil, has left many traces, the Histories of Orosius enjoyed a wide influence in the Middle Ages. We possess more than two hundred manuscripts, one of which is a *Laurentianus* of the VIth century. Their compiler became in his turn a source of information for Count Marcellinus, Jordanis, Bede, Isidore and Gregory of Tours. At periods of an inferior state of learning this kind of work was preferred to all others. Moreover, its leading idea was interesting : Orosius contributed in a remarkable degree to make the history of Christianity a field for apologetics by using it to describe the action of Providence in the vicissitudes of mankind.

---

[1] V, xi, 6 (p. 302). We may also compare III, ii, 14 (p. 145).

[2] He is one of the first to employ this term as a literary expression (III, **xx**, ii ; VII, xliii). We also meet with it in the *Vita Augustini*, by Possidius, VI. It is of older use in Greek. See Gaston Paris, *Mél. linguist.*, I, p. 18.

[3] VIII, xl, 10.

III

MORE than twenty years passed between the appearance
of the work of Orosius, written in 417–418, and that of the
de Gubernatione Dei by Salvianus, composed between the years
439 and 451. The advance of the barbarians had become too
evident, their strength had been too brutally asserted for any
observer capable of perspicacity to retain the least doubt
as to the final overthrow of the Roman power. Already
they held the greater part of Gaul, Spain and Africa ; every
year the independent territories were becoming more shrunk.
In the face of all these calamities the Christians themselves
were murmuring vehemently against Providence which was
allowing the arms of the orthodox to be defeated by Arian
or pagan invaders, and seemed to be heedless of the fate of
the Christian Empire.

It was Salvianus who set himself to reassure the despondency of public opinion on this point.

Gennadius informs us in his de Viris Illustribus, § lxvii,
that Salvianus was a priest of the Church at Marseilles. We
have a few letters of his, nine, to be exact ; we see from the
fourth that he had married, when quite a young man, Palladia
the daughter of a pagan, and that he had a daughter, Aus-
piciola ; that he and his wife a few years later both resolved
to embrace the ascetic life, and that the parents of the young
woman were so vexed over it that they quarrelled with them.
From certain indications in his writings, Salvianus must
have been a native of Trèves.[1] Part of his life was passed at
Lérins, and then at Marseilles ; he also made a sojourn in
Africa.[2] He died at a fairly advanced age.[3] This is about
all we know of him.

Gennadius mentions different works by Salvianus which
have been lost. Besides the above-mentioned letters, and the
de Gubernatione Dei, we have nothing else but a work in 4 books
called by Gennadius Adversus Avaritiam, but Ad Ecclesiam
in the manuscripts, and by Salvianus himself,[4] and anterior
to the de Gubernatione, because it is mentioned in it.[5] Under

---

[1] De Gub., VI, xiii, 72 (text doubtful) ; VI, xv, 84 ; VII, vi, 25 ; Ep. i, 5.
[2] V, xvi, 70.
[3] " Vivit usque hodie in senectute bona," Gennadius wrote, about the year 470.
[4] Ep. ix.
[5] IV, i.

the pseudonym of Timothy, Salvianus addresses those who on their death-bed neglect to leave of their possessions to the Church, and who end by placing the seal on their lifelong cupidity by this last exercise of avarice. According to him, this oblation of their earthly riches for the benefit of the Church, provided that it was accompanied by tears and compunction, was the best way to blot out the sins of the past.[1] He imposed this obligation upon all states of life, lay as well as religious, and claimed to justify it by a series of texts from Scripture with which he confronted good common-sense motives, especially the perplexity of parents who may be disturbed at the thought of leaving their children deprived of all resources.

Such an uncompromising injunction leads us to distrust somewhat his good judgment and critical sense. Possibly the *de Gubernatione Dei* may go some little way to remove this ambiguous impression.

This work comprises eight books, the last of which was uncompleted.[2] Salvianus begins by reproving those whom the despondency caused by those melancholy times had induced to have doubts of Providence. Afterwards in book III he enters upon the essence of his thesis.

If Christians complained, it was doubtless because in worshipping the true God they thought they were entitled to have the benefit of a protecting guardian. But in what does this faith consist from which they claim exceptional treatment as their proper due ? Does it not consist essentially in observing the commandments of God ? Salvianus had now reached his point. He then goes on to endeavour to demonstrate that not only did the ills under which Christians were suffering in no way reflect upon Providence, but that if Providence did not chastise so many outrages daily committed against His law, only in that case might they doubt the reality of His action. The crimes, shameful actions and wickedness of the *plebs Romana* were the direct cause of so many calamities. " (Deus) ideo nos perferre haec mala patitur, quia meremur ut ista patismur." [3]

He then contrasts in a long catalogue abounding in

---

[1] *Ad Eccl.*, I, x.
[2] An argument begun in VII, i, 2, does not appear in it either.
[3] IV, liv.

picturesque features, the vices of the Roman civilisation
with the qualities of the victorious races, which were mingled
with faults, without doubt, but were unquestionable. This
arresting comparison is continued right to the end of the work.

To the Romans he attributes every kind of moral enormity
—drunkenness, lying, pride and perjury. *Proprium est
Romanorum paene omnium malum.*[1] He considers the Africans
still worse : they might be called the sink into which the
turpitude of the whole world had come to empty itself.

> " From the point of view of our lives and our acts,
> we are worse than the barbarians, heretics, and pagans.
> No exception can be made to this, except for the religious
> (*omnes religiosos*), and a few lay people who are like
> religious (*deinde nonnullos etiam saeculares religiosis
> pares, aut, si id nimis grande est, aliqua tamen religiosis
> honestorum actuum probitate consimiles*). As for the rest,
> all, or nearly all, are more culpable than the barbarians."[2]

To possess the Catholic law was, without doubt, an
immense advantage, but all the more must they render themselves worthy of it. " Quod lex bona est, nostrum non est ;
quod autem male vivimus, nostrum est."[3] Equal in vice,
their knowledge of this divine law only aggravated the
responsibility of the Romans as compared with the responsibility of the barbarians.

Salvianus admired many virtues in the invaders. They
loved one another : " *Mutuo amant*, omnes paene Romani
se mutuo persequuntur."[4] They also saw poor people,
widows and orphans preferring to go and live among the Goths
and Bagaudi, and that they were not at all disappointed
with their choice. They were chaste, especially the Goths
and the Saxons.[5] They were unacquainted with the impure
exhibitions of the circus and theatre.[6] With them, fornica-
tion was a crime, while the Romans gloried in it.[7] By
certain energetic measures they had put an end, especially in
Africa, to horrors at which the Romans did not blush.[8]
" An incredible and unheard of thing, they had succeeded in
obliging them to observe modesty."[9] It must not be denied

[1] VII, lxii.   [2] IV, lxi.   [3] *Ibid.*
[4] V, xv.   [5] VII, lxiv.   [6] VI, xxxv.
[7] VII, xxiv.   [8] VII, xciv.   [9] VII, cvii.

that they were heretics ; but that again was the fault of the Romans. " Etiam ipsae quondam haereses barbarorum de Romano magisterio fluxerunt, ac perinde etiam hoc nostrum crimen est, quod populi barbarorum haeretici esse coeperunt." [1]

How could they be surprised that God had given them Aquitaine and almost the whole of the Empire, inasmuch as they were accomplishing therein a wholesome work ? [2] In short, theirs was a purifying *rôle :* " Barbari ad emendandam nostrarum turpidinum labem extiterunt." [3]

This comparison between *Romania* and Barbary all to the honour of the latter marks a new development in the evolution sketched by Orosius. Salvianus already was half resigned to the fall of Rome. Certain historians, like Hauréau,[4] have angrily reproached him for this kind of treason. Even among the Gallo-Roman aristocracy such instances of turning round were by no means rare in the Vth century.[5] Moreover, we must guard ourselves against unreserved agreement with the fervid paradoxes of Salvianus. One or two generations after him St Cæsarius gives us a lively picture of the bestiality of these barbarians who were so dear to the heart of Salvianus, and of their propensity to drunkenness, homicide and sensuality. But it would not be surprising if, with his fiery eloquence, his highly-coloured fervour and thundering rhetoric formed in the school of the Fathers more than in that of the classics, Salvianus contributed to incline men's minds to accept the new state of things which was in process of formation amid so many tribulations and trials.

IV

HOWEVER, the cult of Rome the eternal had not been crushed out of all hearts. Pope Leo the Great celebrated in magnificent terms in the middle of the Vth century the wonderful fortunes of that City which had placed under her hegemony so many different races in order to diffuse the Gospel more efficaciously and had now become still more majestic in her spiritual power than ever she had been in former days in

[1] V, xiv.
[2] VII, xxiv.
[3] VII, xciv.
[4] *Mém. de l'Acad. des Inscr. et belles-lettres,* vol. XXVI (1867), p. 142.
[5] Cf. Roger, *L'Enseign. des lettres class. d'Ausone à Alcuin,* p. 62.

all her grandeur of the flesh.[1] The short sermons of Leo are full of doctrinal vigour which was not impaired by any excessive seeking after verbal effects. His language is strong and simple, altogether worthy of that admirable Pontiff, who knew how to protect Rome from the threat of Attila,[2] who ransomed her from the cruelty of Genseric [3] and more than any other of his predecessors strengthened the sovereign power of the Papacy.[4] But it was not only by his practical skill and firm suppleness that St Leo acquired œcumenical authority ; it was also by his wide knowledge as a Doctor [5] of the Church. In the course of the disputes relating to Eutychianism, in his famous letter to Flavianus [6] he provided the Council of Chalcedon with the elements essential to the dogmatic decisions which were there arrived at. At the same time in the West he followed up the active remnant of Manichaeism and Priscillianism, exacted a formal retractation from those Pelagians who were anxious to re-enter the Church, and imposed on all the feeling that in the universal anarchy of the time there was no other form of method and unity than in the Catholic Church.

V

THE *Historia persecutionis Africanae provinciae temporibus Geiserici et Hunirici regum Vandalorum* which we owe to

---

[1] *Sermo 82, In natali apost. Petri et Pauli*, § 1 (P.L., LIV, 422).
[2] Cf. St Prosper's *Chron. ad a.* 452.
[3] *Ibid., ad a.* 451.
[4] Cf. *Ep.* xvi ; xlvi, 2. It was he who, in face of the encroachments of Bishop Hilary of Arles, obtained from the Emperor Valentinian III in 445 an edict " ne quid praeter auctoritatem sedis istius inlicitum praesumptio attentare nitatur " (v. *Ep.* x–xi). We must mention here a few of the Popes who had preceded him. The letters and decretals of Pope Siricius (384–399) are in Migne, XIII, 1115–1196 ; those of Anastasius I (399–402), *ibid.*, XX, 51–80 (a letter to Venerius, discovered in 1871 in a manuscript in Brussels, has been re-edited by J. Van den Gheyn in R.H.L.R., IV [1899], pp. 1–12) ; those of Innocent I, XX, 463 et s. ; those of Zosimus (417–418), XX, 639 et s. ; those of Boniface I (418–422), XX, 749 et s. ; those of Celestine (422–432), L, 417 et s. ; those of Sixtus III (432–440), L, 581 et s. Cf. K. Silva-Taronca, *Ueberlieferungsgesch. der Papstbriefe des 4, 5 u. 6 Jahrhund.*, in Z.K.T., 1919. The famous decretal *de recipiendis et non recipiendis libris*, attributed, without doubt inaccurately, to Pope Gelasius, and which might pass as the prototype of the *Index librorum prohibitorum*, has been much studied in recent times : Dobschutz, in T.U., 38, 4 (1912), de Bruyne, R. Bén., 1913, 187–207 and 315–333. The authentic writings of Gelasius are in P.L., LIX : there is a study of his language in A.L.L., XII, 1 et s.
[5] The title of Doctor of the Church was decreed to him by Benedict XIV in 1754.
[6] *Ep.* xxviii (of the 13th June, 449).

Bishop Victor, of Vita in Byzacene (south of Tunisia), comprises three books—and not five according to the incorrect division of the old editions.[1] The work relates the persecutions which the Vandals made the Christians undergo from the time of their invasion of Northern Africa (429) down to the death of Huneric (484). Victor wrote it in the year 486 when in exile on the confines of Tripoly. He made a special point of describing the abominations committed by the Arian barbarians, and the appalling sufferings inflicted on Bishops, priests, consecrated virgins, and simple believers. The history of Victor of Vita gives the impression of a long and painful *Passio martyrum*. In more than one case the author is at pains to note that he was a witness of the facts he is reporting, or that he saw the victims. He is careful to insert official documents in his narrative, for instance, Huneric's edict authorising all liberty of preaching to be given to the Arian Bishops ; the mandate preparing the conference of Carthage in 484 ; the *libellus fidei* of Eugenius, Bishop of Carthage (1. II) ; and a second edict of Huneric against the Catholics, the prelude to fresh atrocities (1. III). The accounts given by Victor have the attraction of the horrible : he lingers over descriptions of the worst tortures, counting up the blows and making you see the palpitating flesh. He seeks after oratorical effects and willingly borrows turns and words from the language of poetry ; but this striving after effect is joined to a remarkable lack of concern for, or ignorance of, the traditional morphology and syntax.

VI

VIGILIUS of Thapsus (Thapsus in Byzacene) was present at the Conference held in Carthage (1st February 484) between Catholic and Arian Bishops,[2] described by Victor of Vita in his *History of the Vandal Persecution*. Of the treatises claimed for him by Chifflet, a Jesuit, in his edition of 1664 (reproduced by Migne),[3] there are only two which are certainly authentic—

---

[1] Cf. F. Ferrère, in the *Rev. de Philol.*, 1901, pp. 110–123, 320–336.

[2] Among the works which kept alive the persecution of Arianism, and polemical writings, we should mention a letter by Eugenius of Carthage (P.L., LVIII, 769), an *opusculum* by Cerealis of Castellum in Mauretamia (*ibid.*, 757), and a letter of condolence by Autoninus Honoratus of Cirta (L. 567).

[3] T. LXII.

the dialogue *contra Arianos, Sabellianos et Photinianos,* and the five books *contra Eutychetem.*[1] In the first of these two works Vigilius mentions a book written against the Arian Bishop Marivadus (II, xlv), and another work against the Arian Bishop Palladius (II, L). These appear to have been lost ; the works printed by Chifflet under the same headings are not by Vigilius.[2] There are no serious reasons for claiming for him the other treatises collected by Chifflet.

[1] For the different literary and theological problems connected with the works of Vigilius, cf. Ficker's *Studien zu Vigilius von Thapsus,* Leipzig, 1897.

[2] The first probably belongs to Itacius of Ossonuba ; the second to Phebadius of Agen, as regards book II at least (*de Fide orthodoxa contra Arianos*), for book I simply reproduces the acts of the Synod of Aquitaine (381).

CHAPTER III

CHRISTIAN LATIN POETRY IN THE Vth CENTURY

BIBLIOGRAPHY

I. PRUDENTIUS.—Bergman, a learned Swede (S.B.W., CLVII [1908], Abh. V), has enumerated 320 manuscripts of the poetry of Prudentius. Of these manuscripts 27 only contain all the works of the poet; the greater number belong to the Xth century; they are divided into two classifications which enable us to distinguish the order of succession of the poems, and in the second, the relationship of the last two hymns of the *Cathemerinon* to the *Peristephanon*. The most important manuscript is the Puteanus *sive* Parisiensis 8084, of the VIth century (*Bibl. Nat.*). Bergman has promised a critical edition of Prudentius. The last in date is that of Dressel, Leipsic, 1860. Migne (vols. LIX and LX) reproduced the edition of Arevalo, Rome, 1788. Special edition of the *Psychomachia* by Bergman, Upsala, 1897 (with commentary). A good selection by Lietzmann, K.T., No. 47/49 (1910). The most important work on Prudentius is undoubtedly A. Puech's thesis, *Prudence, Etude sur la Poésie latine chrétienne au IVᵉ siècle*, Paris, 1888. To this must be added the series of articles by Paul Allard in R.Q.H., vol. XXXV to XXXVII, and P. Chavanne's work on the *Patriotisme de Prudence* in R.H.L.R., IV (1899), p. 385. A study on the language of Prudentius will be indispensable after Bergman's edition has appeared. The *Apotheosis* has been partially translated in Felix Clément's *Les Poètes chrétiens* . . . , 1857, pp. 139-161. The *Cathemerinon* is also translated in Bayle, 1868, and in Anot de Maizières, *Nouveau Choix de Pères latins*, 1853, vol. V, pp. 126-199 ; specimens of the *Contra Symmachum*, in Clément, *op. cit.*, pp. 88-138. Poizat has translated a few of the hymns of Prudentius into French in *Les Poètes chrétiens*, Lyons-Paris, 1902, p. 243.

II. ORIENTIUS.—Text in P.L., vol. LXI, 977-1000 (reproducing Martène), and in C.V., XVI, 171 (1888, R. Ellis). French translation of the *Commonitorium* and of the prayers in Louis Bellanger's *Etude sur le poème d'Orientius*, Paris, 1902, pp. 293-339.

III. ALETHIA.—P.L., LXI, 937-970 (Migne was so mistaken as to reproduce the fantastic edition of Gagny (Lyons, 1536) instead of that of G. Morel (1560)) ; C.V., vol. XVI, p. 335 (1888, Schenkl).

IV. PAULINUS of PELLA.—The *Eucharisticos* is not included in Migne ; the best edition is that of Brandes, in C.V., XVI, pp. 263-334. French translation by Corpet, in *Les Oeuvres d'Ausone* (Panckoucke's collection), I, 348 et s.—For the language of Paulinus, cf. Devogel's *Etude sur la Latinité et le style de Paulin de Pella*, Brussels, 1898.

V. CLAUDIANUS MAMERTUS.—Text in P.L., LIII, 697-790 (reproducing Gallandi) ; and in C.V., vol. XI (1885, Engelbrecht), which only gives the *de Statu animae* and the *Letters*.

VI. DRACONTIUS.—Text in P.L., LX (the *Hexaemeron* [i.e., *Laudes Dei*, I. 118-754] also figures as a separate piece in vol. LXXXVII) ; in M.G.H., XIV (1905, Vollmer) ; and in P.L.M., vol. V (1914, Vollmer, amended).—

The *Orestis Tragoedia* and the *Carmina minora* (an anthology of Verona gives to them the title of *Romulea*, probably a synonym for *Latina* [*carmina*]) is in M.G.H., pp. 197 and 132, and in P.L.M., V.—For their language, see M.G.H., p. 431 et s.

VII. Sedulius.—There are numerous manuscripts of the poems of Sedulius, of which two are *Bobienses* of the VIIth century giving the *Carmen Paschale*, whose *prestige* was considerable in the Middle Ages (see Manitius, *Gesch. d. lat. Litt. d. Mittelalt.*, under *s. u. Sedulius* in the Index).—Text in P.L., XIX, 533-754 (reproducing Arevalo, Rome, 1794); C.V., vol. X (1885, Huemer).

VIII. Sidonius Apollinaris.—Text in P.L., LVIII (reproducing Sirmond, Paris, 1614); and in M.G.H., VIII (1887, Lutjohann). A small edition by P. Mohr, 1895 (B.T.).—French translation by Grégoire and Collombet, 1836, 3 vols., and by Eug. Baret, 1887 (Nisard's collection).—Consult: Paul Allard's *Saint Sidoine Apollinaire* (*les Saints* collection), 1910. There are some valuable remarks on the grammar in Eug. Baret's *Oeuvres de Sidoine Apollinaire*, 1879, pp. 106-123. Cf. especially Lutjohann's *Index*, p. 449 et s.

SUMMARY

I. Prudentius. His Life.—II. The *Cathemerinon.*—III. The *Peristephanon.* —IV. Didactic Poems. The Patriotism of Prudentius. The *Psychomachia.* The *Dittochaeon.*—V. The Poetry of Prudentius.—VI. The Poem of Orientius. The *Alethia.*—VII. Paulinus of Pella.—VIII. Claudianus Mamertus.—IX. Dracontius.—X. Sedulius.—XI. Sidonius Apollinaris.

I

" I HAVE lived, if I mistake not, for fifty years, to which seven more must be added. . . . Their limit is not far off, and I see coming the days which are near to old age. What have I done of any use in so long a time? My childhood shed tears beneath the resounding strokes of the ferule. Then, already disabused, I put on the toga, and learned to utter culpable lies. Then came vice unabashed, and outbursts of sensuality, and every foul and perverse naughtiness soiled my youth—what remorse and what disgust! Wordy battles next armed my restless spirit; an unreasonable obstinacy to come off best threw me into painful predicaments. Twice I have governed noble cities under the authority of the laws, rendering justice to the good, and bringing fear to the guilty. At last the good pleasure of the Prince honoured me with a high post in the army and placed me near his person in the highest rank. And all this time life was in flight, my hair was growing white, and I forgot that I was born when old Salia was Consul (348). . . . Well, well! May my sinful soul cast off its follies, and if it cannot render homage to God through its merits, may it do so at least by its voice ! ''

These biographical details and the secret of his call to poetry are given to us by Prudentius in the Preface to his Poems, published by himself in the year 405. An advocate, a high official, perhaps even a *comes primi ordinis*, he felt the need of making amends for the sins of his life, and for his tardy poetical efforts he predicated the merit of repentance and expiation.

In this same preface (v. 37 et s.) he enumerates the series of poems which he is presenting to his readers :

> '' May these hymns string together day to day, and may no night pass without singing praises to the Lord (the *Cathemerinon*), may my voice combat heresies (the *Apotheosis*), defend the Catholic faith (the *Hamartigenia*), tread the pagans under foot (the *Psychomachia*), prepare, O Rome, the way for the fall of thine idols (the *Contra Symmachum*), and dedicate its verses to the martyrs, and laud the Apostles (the *Peristephanon*).''

Apart from the poems thus designated by Prudentius in paraphrases (the vagueness of the term *Psychomachia* will be noted), Gennadius ascribes to him a *Tropaeum*—doubtless it should read *Dittochaeon*—and a *Hexaemeron* of which we have no other source of information.

The traditional division of the works of Prudentius is into lyrical and didactic poems, and it is best to keep to it.

II

THE *Cathemerinon* is a collection of twelve hymns, the first six of which are intended to celebrate the different '' mystical moments '' of the Christian's day. A hymn for cock-crow (i) ; the morning hymn (ii) ; a hymn for before and after meals (iii–iv) ; a hymn for the hour when the lamps are lighted (v) ; a hymn before going to sleep (vi). The round of daily acts is now closed. Hymns vii and viii praise the virtues of fasting, the latter being specially written for the ninth hour which marks the end of the day. Hymn ix (*Hymnus omni horae*) is a canticle of thanksgiving to Christ,

whose chief miracles are recalled. Hymn x is addressed to
the dead, and holds out to them the resurrection. Hymns
xi and xii celebrate the Feasts of Christmas and Epiphany.

Only a small portion of this lyrical work has passed into
use in the liturgy of the Church.[1] The reason for this is because Prudentius of set purpose departed from that extreme
simplicity which St Ambrose and St Hilary had made the
rule by their Church hymns. Side by side with the popular
acatalectic (i, ii, xi, xii) iambic dimeter, and catalectic (vi),
he made use of metres and strophes of a far more ambitious
character—the iambic in six feet (vii) ; the catalectic trochaic
tetrameter (ix) ; the hypercatalectic dactylic trimeter (iii) ;
the catalectic anapæstic dimeter (x) ; the phalecian hendecasyllable (iv) ; the short asclepiad (v) ; and the sapphic
strophe (viii). He wished to write a literary work, that of
a *scholarly* poet as they would have called it in the days of
Catullus and Horace. The same claim is betrayed in the composition of his pieces. Prudentius endeavoured to amplify
and illustrate his subject by inserting extracts and descriptions
from the Bible. He cultivated a literary development with
the conscious and avowed desire of embodying some little
of the distinction still shed by the classic poets. " A sentiment which was not Christian, that of human renown, a love
which was not Christian, that of art esteemed and aimed
at for its own sake, are seen to be at the bottom of this new
form of inspiration, and the genius of other days on its way to
disappear, but immortal in spite of all, creeps in and mingles
with that of the age which was springing to birth." [2] This
great attempt was not without its fruit. Prudentius hits
upon some happy developments, and verses of bright and
delicate colouring, such as the following on the Holy Innocents,
in the hymn of the Epiphany (v. 125 et s.) :

" Hail, ye blossoms of martyrdom, whom, on the very
threshold of life, Christ's persecutor hath mown down,
like budding roses in a sudden gust of wind—First
victims of Christ, tender flock of sacrifice, innocently ye
sport with palm and crown at the very foot of the
altar. . . ."

[1] For example, some of the strophes in hymns i, ii and xii.
[2] A. Puech, *Prudence*, p. 97.

We have to recognise that such touching and original accents are very seldom repeated in these hymns. For so grandiose an attempt Prudentius had need of greater inspiration; he required also a more accurate appreciation of proportion which would have warned him against writing at such length,[1] and would have obliged him to subordinate the different parts of the same piece to the general purport, instead of making each development bring out everything he thought possible to extract from it.

III

THE same failings of taste sometimes obtrude themselves in a still more glaring manner in the *Peristephanon* (i.e. a poem " on the crowns " [of the martyrs]), the leading idea of which is nevertheless so interesting.

The eminent dignity of the martyr in the eyes of the primitive Church is well known. The sentence of Pascal : " Je crois volontiers les histoires dont les témoins se font égorger," [2] sums up the impression of every age. In the eyes of the first Christian generations the martyr represented the perfect Christian in faith and love ; on the part of his brethren he was esteemed worthy of eternal veneration as the highly-privileged depositary of the power of the Holy Spirit. In order to do honour to the dead martyrs Christianity appropriated the traditional funeral customs of the pagans, leaving itself free to modify them in accordance with its own ideals. The bodies of the martyrs were laid in the midst of the tombs of simple believers, outside the town ; and it was there that the people gathered for the usual commemorations. When once security had been definitely achieved in the IVth century, these ceremonies were surrounded with more imposing circumstance, and assumed the character of real popular festivals. In every spot of Roman territory basilicas were rising up from the ground. The celebration of the feasts of a great number of martyrs tended by degrees to break through the restricted limits in which they were at first confined. An anniversary, which originally had been a kind of family affair, and special to a particular community, became almost general.

---

[1] The shortest piece, the viiith, is in 80 verses ; the xiith has 208.
[2] Brunschvigg's edition, § ix, pensée 593, p. 595.

The custom was established of invoking the martyrs and of begging their intercession. From their relics power was held to emanate which appeared to be capable of being communicated, and the efficaciousness of which made itself felt both in healing and exorcism. Many of the faithful sought the privilege of being buried in the vicinity of their tombs, and the names of martyrs were readily given to children in order to assure them protection and safeguard.[1]

Prudentius who shared in these sentiments of veneration for the *witnesses* to the faith with a full union of heart and enthusiasm, conceived the bold project of making their martyrdom the subject of a series of lyrical poems.

We can mention hardly any former attempt other than that made by Damasus, Bishop of Rome (366–384), the first Pope (as appears likely) to have endeavoured to accomplish any literary work in Latin.[2] But the attempt by Damasus had a very different character. A great builder and restorer of edifices intended for worship, his design, in the words of Rossi, was " to include not only certain chosen monuments of the Roman Church, but indeed all, and especially those connected with the martyrs, in the ample circumference of the suburban cemeteries, and to adorn them with historic *tituli*, for present and future instruction." Majestically engraved by Furius Dionysius Filocalus, an engraver of much taste, the inscriptions of Damasus were eagerly read and copied out by pilgrims visiting the *mirabilia* of Rome. Many of these marbles were broken by the Goths in the VIth century ; fortunately collections of them in manuscript had been early made. The interpretation made by Rossi has largely contributed to determine the tests of authenticity of these inscriptions composed by Damasus.[3] From the literary

---

[1] See the excellent book dealing with all these matters by Delehaye, *Les Origines du Culte des Martyrs*, Brussels, 1912.

[2] See above, p. 52, for Victor I ; for Sixtus II, and the treatise by the pseudo-Cyprian *ad Novatianum*, p. 163, note 1. Two letters in Latin of Pope Cornelius (251–253) figure in the series of letters of St Cyprian (*Ep.* xlix, L) ; five others have been lost, which we can take note of, thanks to allusions by St Cyprian (*Ep.* xlv, i ; xlviii, i ; L ; lix, 1–2). There is a special edition of the two letters which have been preserved, by G. Mergati, *D'Alcuni nuovi sussidi per la critica del testo di S Cipriano*, Rome, 1899, pp. 72–86. A decision of Pope Stephen relative to the baptism of heretics is quoted by St Cyprian (*Ep.* lxxiv, 1). The letters of Pope Liberius (352–366) are in P.L., vol. VIII : of these there are four (*Studens paci, Pro Deifico, Quia scio,* and *Non doceo : ibid.,* 1365–1372) which have occasioned much discussion as to the orthodoxy of Liberius : See Zeiller, in B.A.L.A.C., 1913, pp. 20–51.

[3] These tests are three in number : the testimony of Damasus himself, the style, and the form of the characters. Cf. Ihm, in Rh. M., vol. L (1895), p. 491 et s.

point of view it must be confessed that they hold little but disappointment : " No worse verses," Mgr. Duchesne somewhat irreverently declares, " have ever been transcribed in such profusion. If only they had been merely bad ! But they are void of all history, obscure, and contain scarcely anything but banalities." [1]

There does not seem to be any doubt that Prudentius knew these vague and colourless Virgilian inscriptions, with their metrical inaccuracies. *Peristephanon XI* is, in one portion at least, only an amplification of one of the inscriptions of Damasus. Notwithstanding, Prudentius has nowhere made mention of Damasus by name. Such attempts must have appeared paltry to him by the side of the series of poems he had in view.

It was especially Spanish and Roman legends which he undertook to adorn with his art and poetry in the fourteen hymns of the *Peristephanon.*

" Hispanos Deus adspicit benignus ! " [2]

His local patriotism reserved to the Spanish martyrs poems i, iii, iv, v, vi, and viii, in which he celebrates in succession two Spanish soldiers, the brothers Hemeterius and Celedonius, who had been put to death for having refused to sacrifice to pagan altars ; Saint Eulalia of Merida ; eighteen martyrs of Cæsaraugusta (Saragossa) ; the deacon Vincentius, also of Saragossa ; Bishop Fructuosus of Tarraco (Tarragona), and his two deacons ; and the martyrs of Calagurris (Calahorra). To this series we may add poems vii and x, the former relating to the Pannonian martyr Quirinus, Bishop of Siscia (Sissek in Croatia), and the latter to St Romanus, a deacon of Cæsarea, veneration for whom had been spread in Spain, also poem xiii consecrated to the life and death of St Cyprian, a martyr reverenced by the whole Church. The other poems were inspired in Prudentius by a journey he made to Rome in the year 402 or 403. A moved and fervent pilgrim, he went through the Holy City, its sanctuaries, and

---

[1] *Hist. anc. de l'Egl.*, II, 482. Cf. *Anal. Bolland.*, XVI, 239. Migne reproduced in P.L., vol. XIII Merenda's edition (Rome, 1754). The best edition is Ihm's *Damasi epigrammata* (*Anthol. lat. supplementa.* I, Leipzic, 1895), French translation by Dom Leclercq in the *Dict. d'Arch. chr. et de Lit.*, art. *Damase.*

[2] Hymn vi, 4. Paul Allard has given in R.Q.H., 1885, p. 353 et s., a very successful specimen of criticism on the sources of Prudentius. The enquiry might be further developed.

its catacombs, studied the tablets in the churches and deciphered the inscriptions, and in this way he was able to mingle many descriptions with the accounts of the martyrdom of such Roman martyrs as St Laurence (II), St Cassian (IX), St Hippolytus (XI), St Peter and St Paul (XII) and St Agnes (XIV), wherein modern archæologists find valuable aid for their own personal investigations. The words in which he gives his impression of the catacomb in the Tiburtine Way, though less " romantic " than the famous account of St Jerome in his *Commentary on Ezechiel* (XL, 5), is not lacking either in accuracy or picturesqueness :

> " Not far from the walls of Rome and the cultivated zone which surrounds them a concealed crypt opens its deep entrenchments. The steep slope of a path returning on itself leads through the windings of this retreat, from which light is absent. For daylight hardly reaches the first opening of the entrance and only then lights up the threshold of the vestibule. In proportion as one advances into the labyrinths of the cavern darkness becomes denser, although from time to time openings made in the vault of the roof permit a brilliant ray of sunlight to penetrate. In the midst of the obscure turnings formed by narrow chambers and dark galleries crossing each other, a little daylight thus falls from above into the entrails of the hill. In the bottom of the subterranean crypt it is still possible to see the gleam and to follow the light of the absent sun." [1]

Rome the beautiful, *pulcherrima Roma* [2] from the magnificence of her buildings, if not from the purity of her morals, had inspired in Prudentius an admiration of which the *Peristephanon* [3]—as also other works of this poet—bears the mark. He commiserates his compatriots living so far from her. But it was Christian Rome, with her basilicas, baptisteries, marbles, paintings and mosaics, which had especially attracted the gaze of the wonderstruck provincial ; and Prudentius was capable of being a close observer and a trusty

[1] *Perist.*, xi, 155–168. I am using Paul Allard's translation, R.Q.H., XXXVI (1884), 48.
[2] *Perist.*, xi, 231. Cf. Virgil, *Georg.*, ii, 534.
[3] *Perist.*, ii, 529.

witness of the manifold outward signs by which victorious Christianity then gave evidence of its vitality.

As regards the real character of these poems and their artistic construction, more than one reservation must be made. Prudentius nourished his inspiration from various sources—*fama*, that is popular traditions, the liturgy of the Church, figured representations, inscriptions, especially the literature of the later *Acta*, so different from the admirable and touching accounts written in the first centuries (such as the *Martyrdom* of St Polycarp, the *Letter* relating to the martyrs of Lyons, the *Passio* of Perpetua and Felicitas, etc. . . .). He accepts and reproduces the current stories, conventions, and declamatory rhetoric of their vexatious form of hagiography. Let us not condemn the scenes of torture which he is pleased to describe : " the rare cruelty " (as d'Aubigny was to say in his *Tragiques*)[1] of these " exquisite deaths " have their place in the oratorical jousts between judge and accused. What is most painful is the grandiloquent verbosity which he puts into the mouths of his martyrs : by turns ironical and losing all self-control (did not the gentle Eulalia, brought up under her mother's wing, spit in the face of the Praetor ?), his heroes and heroines weary the patience of the magistrates and that of the reader by interminable harangues in which the commonplaces of traditional apologetics are mingled with still more tiresome notions. St Romanus develops at great length the strange idea that torture is not so exceptionally dreadful inasmuch as ordinary illnesses, such as pleurisy, fever, gout, rheumatism and surgical operations, inflict almost parallel sufferings on the patients.[2] St Laurence draws an almost ludicrous parallel between physical ills and the ills of the soul, and ends his list with a pun at the expense of the judge to whom he declares that he (the judge) is suffering from *morbus regius* (i.e. jaundice).[3] One, " under examination," utters no fewer than six tirades—the two last of 32 and 93 lines—after his tongue had been cut out ![4] Prudentius does not know how to keep himself within limits ; he has a tendency to prolixity and declamation owing to the natural bent of his Spanish temperament nourished on Roman

---

[1] Lalanne's, ed. 1857. *Les Feux*, p. 178.
[2] *Perist.*, iii, 127.
[3] *Ibid.*, ii, 264.
[4] *Perist.*, x, 133 et s. ; 426 et s. ; 587 et s. ; 801 et s. ; 928 et s. ; 1007 et s.

rhetoric but little understanding the models of lofty reason offered by the classics which he was endeavouring to out-rival.

This lack of literary tact is all the more regrettable because brilliant pieces, well-finished developments, and skil-fully arranged strophes are not rare in the *Peristephanon*. The attempt realised by Prudentius is worthy of respect. And what variety of metre, what technical virtuosity ! [1] But all the archæological and historic interest of this work, and certain happy successes, cannot hide its weakness of con-struction and the mistakes of a somewhat uncertain good taste.

IV

ANOTHER series of poems is of the didactic kind, so well suited to the Roman temperament, and to the best and most glorious Latin tradition, and it was natural that Christianity, eager to instruct souls in order to conquer them, should appropriate it in its turn. These are the *Apotheosis*, the *Hamartigenia*, the two books *Contra Symmachum*, the *Psychomachia* and the *Dittochaeon*.

Preceded by a double prelude, one in 12 hexameters, the other in 56 iambic lines grouped together in twos and threes, the *Apotheosis* refutes in 1084 hexameters a certain number of errors concerning the Trinity, and the Divinity of Christ. Prudentius first takes to task the " Patripassionist " heresy of Praxeas (1–177), and then Sabellianism (178–320). His polemics are then turned against the Jews (321–551), a " blind and deaf " nation who obstinately shut their ears to the Divine voice whereas almost the whole world had learned to listen to its accents :

" It hath known the coming of the Lord, this people
whom the sun of Iberia sees when it sets, and whom
the East lightens with its first rays. The penetrating

---

[1] Here is a table of the metres he employs : i (120 lines) ; in catalectic trochaic tetrameters ; ii (584 lines) : acatalectic iambic dimeters ; iii (215 lines) : hyper-catalectic dactylic trimeters ; iv (200 lines) : sapphic strophes ; v (575 lines) : acatalectic iambic dimeters ; vi (162 lines) : phalecian hendecasyllables ; vii (90 lines) : glyconics ; viii (18 lines) : elegiacs ; ix (106 lines) : dactylic hexa-meters and iambic trimeters grouped together in verses ; x (1130 lines) : iambic trimeters ; xi (246 lines) : elegiacs ; xii (66 lines) : archilochian ; xiii (106 lines) : archilochian ; xiv (133 lines) : hendecasyllable Alcaics.

force of the word of the Gospel hath pierced the frosts of
Scythia, and its warmth hath dissipated the misty cold
of Hyrcania ; delivered from its icy bonds, the Hebrus,
coming to birth in the Caucasus, rolls to the foot of
Rhodope its cool waters. The Getae are made gentle ;
the Gelonian, ferocious barbarian, fills with pure milk
his cup emptied of blood ; the blood of Christ will
furnish him with a holy potion. Already the countries
of Atlas inhabited by the perfidious Moor have learned to
consecrate on the altars of God their bearded kings. . . .
And among the sons of Aeneas, the purple prostrates
itself suppliant before the altars of Christ, and the
lord of the world adores the standard of the Cross ! " [1]

Like the Jews, the Ebionites denied the divinity of
Jesus. Prudentius opposes to them the prodigies which
surrounded His birth, and especially the succession of His
miracles (552–781). He declares that those who deny
Christ will be the prey of everlasting night, and this gives him
occasion to study the nature of the soul, its origin, and the
punishments beyond the grave (782–951). Christ alone
escaped death. Prudentius launches a final assault against
the Manichaean docetism, and concludes his poem with a
vigorous affirmation of his belief in the Resurrection.

The *Hamartigenia*, in 966 hexameters preceded by a preface
of 63 iambic trimeters, treats of only one question, the origin
of evil as connected with Marcion's Gnostic dualism, which is
interpellated right from the beginning. Prudentius arraigns
dualism : he who admits two gods can just as well admit
thousands. The father of evil was Satan, the corrupter of
mankind and of nature. In this connection the poet gives
some specimens of the vices of his times, and with special
vigorousness takes exception to the artifices of the *toilette*
in blameworthy use among women—Why has God permitted
evil ? (637 et s.) :

"Si non vult Deus esse malum, cur non vetat? inquis."

Because that was the sole means of leaving to human
action man's free choice between the lord of life and the lord of
death. This choice will be confirmed by posthumous rewards.

[1] *Apoth.*, 424 et s.

The description given by Prudentius of the torments of Hell
(824 et s.) and the joys of Paradise is one of the most circumstantial left to us by Christian literature of the first centuries :

> " Carpunt tormenta foventque
> Materiem sine fine datam : mors deserit ipsa
> Aeternos gemitus, et flentes vivere cogit."

In conclusion, he expresses the hope of meriting a not too
vigorous punishment, if the " immense light " be denied him.

These two poems are not at all negligible. Certainly the
doctrine contained in them is hardly original. Although he
was treating of questions in which his age took a lively
interest, Prudentius avoided throwing himself into the quarrels
of the time. Some people have thought to discover allusions
to Priscillianism in them.[1] They must be very vague ; and
why should Prudentius have avoided mentioning Priscillian
by name ? As a matter of fact, he preferred to inveigh
against errors which had been classified and refuted long
before. Nearly all the substance of his theology comes
from Tertullian, whose *Adversus Marcionem, Adversus Praxean*,
the *De Carne Christi*, and perhaps the *De Patientia*, he had
read. Where Prudentius is seen to advantage is in explanation
and detail. He had an appreciation of ideas, and the gift
of explaining clearly and of illustrating them with significant examples. He had that passion which animates
and gives colour to everything, and a sincere attachment
to the beliefs he was burning to propagate, like some Christian
Lucretius. A great number of his developments are interesting in connection with the history of manners, and there is
something in his poetical mythology, and in his race of demons,
the enemies of mankind whose ambushes he describes,
which has made certain possibly too indulgent critics, think
of the pictures of a Dante or a Milton which are powerful in
another way.

Written between the spring of the year 402 and the summer
of 403, the two books *Contra Symmachum* came twenty years
after the famous incidents the vicissitudes of which we have
related.[2] M. A. Puech [3] is inclined to think that there may

---

[1] Kunstle, *Antipriscilliana*, Freib.-i.-B., 1905, p. 170 et s. Cf. Bergman's
ed. of the *Psychomachia*, p. xxviii ; he is much less positive than Kunstle.

[2] P. 270 et s.

[3] *Op. cit.*, p. 195.

Q

have been, shortly before 402, a fresh attempt on the part of Symmachus, or of his party, to extort from the son of Theodosius the favourable decision which had been obstinately refused by his predecessor. At the beginning of book II Prudentius seems to say that the *orator catus* had come back to the charge. The allusion is however very far from being explicit. Doubtless Prudentius simply saw in this episode an interesting historical subject the rich matter of which he tried to exploit.

The work comprises two books. The first opens with a preface in 89 asclepiads in which Prudentius recalls the shipwreck of St Paul on the coast of the island of Malta, and how he rendered the bite of the viper innocuous : in this account in the Acts (xxviii) the poet saw in miniature a symbol of the destiny of Christianity itself. There follow 658 hexameters in which the triumph of the faith is celebrated, notwithstanding the vitality which, thanks to certain influences, paganism still preserved. Theodosius pronounces a long discourse summoning Rome to detach herself from her gods and to adore the Cross. Further, it was to Christianity that all the promises of the future were to come :

> " Turn your looks towards the people : how many are there who do not shun with disgust the altar of Jupiter, tainted with impure blood ? All those people who dwell in high garrets and run about the muddy streets of the city, and who eat the bread which is served out to them from the high steps, hasten to visit on Mount Aventine the tomb wherein repose the ashes of Peter, our beloved Father ; or else they go in crowds to the palace on the Lateran whence they return with the holy Chrism and the sacred character of the Christian. What then ! Can we still doubt, O Christ, that Rome is consecrated to thee and hath passed under thy laws ? . . ." [1]

The first book closes with a fine eulogium on Symmachus, *Romani decus eloquii*, in regard to whom the poet observes in this polemical work the most exact rules of courtesy.

In the preface to the second book, in 66 eloquent glyconics

---

[1] I, 545 et s. ; 579 et s.

Prudentius invokes the presence of Christ. Then he unfolds in 1131 hexameters a refutation of the *Relatio* of Symmachus, making use of almost the same answer which St Ambrose had given.

The work is interesting for more than one reason. We find vigorous traits in it worthy of the strong realism of Juvenal; for example, when Prudentius jeers at the tardy marriages of the Vestals (II, 1080 et s.):

> "Vesta on her return is weary at last of all this virginity; her period of service over, her sacred work accomplished, the aged Vestal is in haste to marry; she leaves the hearth she has guarded all her youth; she carries to the nuptial couch her well-won wrinkles and, newly married in a frozen bed, learns to know transports that are but lukewarm." [1]

But the most curious aspect of this work is the ardent patriotism breathing through it, which the poet associates with his beliefs without any difficulty. Prudentius had a respect and a love for Rome, and accepted the doctrine of her immortality in the same spirit that Horace or Virgil would have felt. He venerates all the outward marks by which the might of Rome was expressed, whenever they were not opposed to the faith. The *prestige* of the Senate remains unimpaired in his eyes; he calls the Senators *pulcherrima mundi lumina*. He uses words of respect and devotion in speaking of the emperors. Even to Julian the Apostate he had previously rendered impartial justice in the *Apotheosis :*

> "He flourished in the days of my childhood, and I remember him. A very courageous general, a wise lawgiver, famed for his eloquence and his valour, he preferred the religion of his fathers to the true religion, and was the zealous upholder of three hundred thousand gods. I have seen that prince, faithless to God, but not to Rome (*Perfidus ille Deo, quamvis non perfidus Urbi*), bowing his august head before the feet of a Minerva made of clay, etc." [2]

The reverence of Prudentius for Rome, and his confidence in her eternal destinies, are closely bound up with his religious

---

[1] II, 1078 et s.   [2] *Apoth.*, 450 et s.

convictions. Looking down the vista of past centuries Rome seemed to him to have fulfilled a kind of mission set by Providence. By grouping together under her hegemony all the peoples of the world she had been a powerful instrument for the propagation of Christianity :

> " Would you know, O Romans, the true cause of your accomplishments, the real reason of that glory which hath placed the world under your yoke ? These races speak different languages, their kingdoms have diverse religions : God willed to make of them a society, to submit their customs to the unity of the same empire, and to make all accept the same yoke, in order that religion might draw together the hearts of men ; for there could not be a union worthy of Christ unless one spirit only held all nations joined together. . . . In every part of the world men live this day as fellow-citizens of the same city, and their children by the same hearth. The administration of justice, the forum, commerce, the arts, and marriages, draw together the inhabitants of the most distant shores. These are the fruits of the victories and triumphs of the Roman Empire : in this way was the path prepared for the coming of Christ, and the road constructed by a long peace under Roman government. . . . The world, O Christ, now possesseth Thee, the world brought into unity by the *Pax Romana*." [1]

In the *Peristephanon*, II, 433, he placed this prayer in the mouth of the martyr Laurence :

> " O Christ, grant unto thy Romans that their city may be Christian, that city through whom Thou hast given the same faith to all the cities of the world (*per quam dedisti ut ceteris mens una sacrorum foret*). May all their scattered members be united under one sign ! May the universe turn in submission, may their city, mistress of all, turn ! . . . May Romulus become a believer, and Numa himself believe in thee ! "

---

[1] II, 582 et s. Compare Claudian's lines, *de Consul. Stilich.*, III, 138 :
" Haec est in gremium victos quae sola recepit,
Humanumque genus communi nomine fovit."

The Roman patriotism of Prudentius is so sensitive on this point that he surpassed that of Symmachus. The poet does not mean to admit that the gods had nothing to do with the working out of the grandeur of Rome, for their action might be enlarged on by only recalling the exploits of a Corvinus or the Fabii (II, 555 et s.). He protests against the pessimism into which Symmachus was tempted to fall when he gave importance to certain indications of the wrath of heaven against Rome for being heedless of her traditions. No, never had the Empire been so happy, so flourishing ; as for those who were threatening her, as for the Barbarians, there was more difference between them and the Romans than " between the quadruped and the biped, between the dumb and one able to speak, between the Christian and the pagan " (II, 814 et s.).

A curious state of mind which facts, the rulers of the world, were not long in modifying at the centre of Christendom. We have already followed this transformation in the case of St Augustine, Orosius, and Salvianus. During all these first years of the Vth century before the inrush of the barbarians, it became still more general, and the vehemence with which Prudentius knew how to give expression to it should suffice to lend an exceptionally historic bearing to the *Contra Symmachum.*

The battles of the soul, and the struggle between Christianity and paganism, form the subject of the *Psychomachia,* a kind of epopee with an apologetic intention, which takes the shape of a long allegory. The preface, in 68 iambic trimeters, relates an episode in the history of Abraham ; then the poem, in 915 hexameters, opens with a Virgilian ring :

"Christe, graves hominum semper miserate labores[1] . . ."

First the Faith is advancing :

". . . agresti turbida cultu,
Nuda humeros, intonsa comas, exserta lacertos."

The first enemy who dares to come to the attack is the *veterum Cultura Deorum* (l. 29). But the faith lays it low, and the *legio victrix* composed of a thousand martyrs shouts

---

[1] Cf. *Æneid*, VI, 56 : " Phoebe, graves Trojae semper miserate labores."

with joy. Other battles take place between *Pudicitia* and
Sodomita Libido (l. 40–108), Patience and Anger (109–177),
Superbia and the army led by Humility and Hope (178–309).
Superbia falls into a pit digged by *Fraus*, and Humility
cuts off her head. But here a more formidable enemy comes
forward, *Luxuria*, with her perfumed hair, wandering eyes,
and languid voice. . . .

> " Delibuta comas, oculis vaga, languida voce.
> Perdita deliciis, vitae cui cause voluptas " (l. 310).

She hurls at the army composed of the virtues, not
javelins, but violets and rose leaves whose corrupting scent
(*male dulcis odor*) insinuates itself languorously among them.
Fortunately *Sobrietas* finds the words necessary to reanimate
their failing courage, and *Luxuria* falls under their blows.
Her army, made up of *Jocus, Petulantia, Amor, Pompa,* and
Voluptas, scatters, leaving behind an ample booty of which
Avarice and her daughters, true Eumenides, wish to take
possession. Pity (i.e. *Operatio*) [1] saves the situation. The
army of the Virtues is then victorious. Concord (l. 644)
gives the signal to go back to the camp to which the triumphant troops take their way singing like the Israelites after
the passage of the Red Sea. But she is wounded by a
treacherous blow from Discord (l. 665) who, summoned to
give her name, confesses that she is called *Haeresis* (l. 710).
Discord develops her views on Christ (Prudentius is hitting
at Arianism and Gnosticism—perhaps also at Priscillianism,
but that is open to doubt) ; Faith ends by piercing her tongue
with a dart, and invites the holy assembly to raise in honour of
Christ a temple spangled with gems, sapphires, amethysts,
and topazes. A prayer of thanksgiving to Jesus concludes
the poem (888–915).

Thus the method consistently employed in the *Psychomachia* is allegory, in the sense of personifying purely abstract
notions. This method was no stranger to Greek literature, [2]
and Roman taste had accepted it from a long date. We
have only to call to mind the abstractions so often deified
in the old religion of the Romans [3]—the dialogue between

---

[1] L. 573.

[2] An example in Egger's *Essai sur l'hist. de la Critique chez les Grecs*, Paris,
2nd ed., 1886, p. 41.

[3] Cagnat-Chapot's *Manuel d'archéol. Rom.*, I (1917), pp. 460–466.

Luxury and Poverty in the prologue to the *Trinummus* of Plautus, the *mala gaudia mentis* of the Hades of Virgil (*Aen.*, VI, 273 et s.), Claudian's description of the gardens of Venus in the *de Nuptiis Honorii et Mariae*, peopled by *Pallor, Irae, Licentia, Perjuria, Voluptas* and *Lacrimae ;* and again in Christian literature itself, we have the portrait of Patience as drawn by Tertullian : " If we would like to picture her countenance and apparel, her face is tranquil and peaceful, her forehead smooth with no wrinkles from anger or grief . . ." (*de Pat.*, xv) ; and there is the procession of adultery in the *de Pudicitia*, v, led by idolatry which goes before, and by homicide which follows after, both of whom protest their complete solidarity with her. " It is very natural," observes M. Puech, " that a Christian who sees in temptation the work of the Devil, should be led, more than another, to translate into exterior images the struggles of within, and to give a visible reality to the adversaries whom he supposes present to him." This was very much the view of Prudentius : he intended, under a poetical form, to translate the " inner sedition " of the soul, the tumult of which was only appeased by faith :

" Et omnes
Virtutum gemmas componat sede piata " (l. 910).

Taken as a whole the poem leaves an impression of pedantic heaviness clinging to an almost continuous imitation of the epic style of Virgil. All these abstractions abuse one another, embrace, and put each other in the wrong, repeating the words and gestures of the heroes in the *Æneid.* And what eloquence is expended in these fictitious encounters from which flows blood too pale to cause emotion ! Discourses on Chastity, Anger, Patience, Pride, Hope, Sobriety, *Operatio*, Discord, Concord, Faith—there is scarcely one of these vices or virtues which the poet does not dower with his inexhaustible verboseness, interrupting his narrative, and again resuming it with a *Dixerat* or a *Haec ubi dicta dedit* after the manner of Virgil. Furthermore we should be ignorant of the spirit of the Middle Ages to be astonished that this was recognised in the *Psychomachia*, and that this poem became one of their favourite books. Their theologians, miniaturists, and sculptors (the Roman more than the

Gothic) on many an occasion found in it matter for their dialectics or the motives of their inspiration.[1]

There remains the *Dittochaeon*. The title of this work is rather enigmatic : without doubt we must derive it from the two Greek words διττὸς ὀχή meaning " twofold nourishment," in allusion to the Old and the New Testaments. It is a collection of 49 quatrains in hexameters intended for the explanation of pictures : twenty-four refer to the Old Testament, and twenty-five to the New. Paintings and mosaics were largely employed in the religious edifices from the IVth century,[2] and inscriptions were often placed before them in order to interpret them to the faithful, " ut littera monstret quod manus explicuit," as Paulinus of Nola expressed it.[3] The following are the subjects of some of the works of art briefly commented on in the *Dittochaeon*—in what Church we do not know : *Adam and Eve ; The Oak of Mambre ; Sara's Tomb ; Joseph recognised by his brethren ; Moses receiving the Law ;* the *House of Rahab the Harlot ;* the *Captivity of Israel ; Mary and the Angel Gabriel ;* the *Angels announcing the Glad Tidings to the Shepherds ;* the *Massacre of the Innocents ;* the *Resurrection of Lazarus ;* the *Passion of the Saviour ; St Peter's Vision,* etc. . . . The descriptions of these historic scenes are of great interest in the study of Christian iconography.

V

CONSIDERING the work of Prudentius as a whole we cannot refuse to admire a poetical effort which transformed the liturgical hymn into a Christian ode, which drew from the ample literature of the *Acts of the Martyrs* rich epic and lyrical material, which placed didactic poetry at the service of the new faith, and largely exploited the allegorical method. The poetry of Prudentius is absolutely Christian in its inspiration. Certain private opinions have been noticed in him, for instance,

---

[1] See Mâle's *L'Art relig. au XIII s. en France*, 3rd ed., 1910, p. 124 et s., 150 ; L. Bréhier's *L'Art Chrétien*, 1918, p. 203 et s.

[2] Cf. St Paulinus of Nola, *Natale*, IX, 515–635 ; X, 15–27 ; 167–179 ; *Ep.* xxxii, 17 ; Biraghi, *Disticha ad picturas sanctas in Basilica Ambrosiana*, in continuation of the *Inni sinceri di sant. Ambrogio*, Milan, 1862.

[3] *Natale*, IX, 584–585.

concerning the rest accorded to the damned on the night of the Resurrection : [1] there are hardly any authentic Fathers of the Church in whom analogous views may not be noted. Prudentius does not pride himself in playing at being an original thinker, and his sole wish is to infuse into the souls of his readers the enthusiasm for the faith held in common by the faithful with which he himself is animated. But this singer of Catholic doctrines is at the same time a Roman of the good old stock, formed in the school of Lucretius, Virgil, Horace and Juvenal, familiar, too, so it appears, with the Greek language. He accepts all the firm Roman traditions on condition that he may purify them. Although impassioned, there is nothing of the fanatic or iconoclast about him. He respects the manifestations of Roman genius both in art and literature, and in their civil and political life :

" O Senators," he exclaims, " wash ye your marbles stained with the blood of victims : may the statues, works of great artists, rear themselves white and pure. In them we have the fairest ornaments of our fatherland ; but may no unworthy use from henceforth soil these monuments of an art which has for too long been turned aside from its proper end." [2]

Bentley calls him " *Christianorum Maro et Flaccus.*" Virgil and Horace were in truth his favourite models. A rather bold innovator as regards matter and verbal creations, his style is closely imitated from the phraseology of Virgil, and he tried to reproduce in his metres, so varied in form, the technical suppleness and dexterity of Horace. He had no need, in speaking of himself, to exclaim : " *Audi poetam rusticum,*" [3] or to declare that " a love for the precious names of the martyrs interferes little with the rules of versification, for when one speaks of the Saints one never speaks amiss or incorrectly." [4] Such commonplaces are somewhat insincere. In fact he emancipated himself from the popular forms preferred by Christian poets anterior to him, and almost the only one with whom he may be compared as regards diversity of metre, is Ausonius.

[1] *Cathem.*, L, 125.
[3] *Perist.*, II, 574.
[2] *Contra Symm.*, I, 501–5.
[4] *Ibid.*, L, 165.

This combination of Christian thought and classic forms often produces curious incongruities in Prudentius. Like the great Venetians of the XVIth century, he intermingles heterogeneous elements in his composition. He describes Sodom as being destroyed with its *tabularia, forum, balneae, templa* and *madidae propinae*.[1] At the marriage of Cana, Christ changes the water into Falernian wine, "*fit falernum nobile*."[2] Biblical and Roman forms are constantly mixed up in his verses, together with anachronisms whose simplicity is not without its savour.

Taken as a whole, he is not far short of deserving to be called a great poet. With a little more moral substance, or originality in psychological observation, and with a finer sense of proportion, he would almost have realised that fusion of the two "learnings" which the most lettered Christians of the first centuries had always dreamed of, without daring to acknowledge it.

VI

"IN the towns, estates, country-side, cross-roads, villages, and all along the roads wherever you looked, nothing was seen but death, woe, destruction, disaster, fire, and mourning ; in short, entire Gaul was nothing but a smoking funeral pyre." These lines from the *Commonitorium*[3] of Orientius make us think that this poet must have witnessed the vast desolation of Gaul ravaged by invasions since the first years of the Vth century. At the beginning of his *Life of St Martin*,[4] Fortunatus mentions Orientius after Juvencus and Sedulius, and before Prudentius, Paulinus of Périgueux and Avitus. Scrupulous critics have decided to identify him with St Orens, the Bishop of Auch,[5] who in 439, in the name of Theodoric king of the Visigoths at Toulouse, presented himself before the Roman generals Aetius and Littorius, in order to solicit peace from them.[6]

Orientius, whose birthplace the three *Lives* drawn up by the Bollandists give as in Spain, must have been living in

---

[1] *Hamart.*, 758 et s.
[2] *Cathem.*, IX, 28.
[3] *Common.*, II, 181 et s.
[4] I, 140.
[5] L. Duchesne, *Fastes Episc. de l'Anc. Gaule*, II, 96.
[6] *Acta Sanctorum*, 1st May, p. 62.

Gaul in the first half of the Vth century. His *Commonitorium* is an exhortation in elegiacs written for the purpose of instructing his readers as to " what are the means which open Heaven to us and put death to flight." Without concealing that he himself had escaped with great difficulty from the " slough of sensuality " he wishes the experiences of his life to be serviceable for their good. In the first book, after having besought Christ in a prayer, which takes the place of the old invocation to the Muses, for " the gift of good speech and thought," he enumerates the blessings of God, recommends the law of charity to one's neighbour, and details the promises of the Resurrection and immortality ; he then goes on to precepts in the practical order—to beware of women, " the first cause of evil on earth," whose deceptive beauty turns into hideousness with advancing years : " When therefore thou dost behold a young girl of fair countenance and charming manner, turn aside thine eyes, or lower thy head " ; to preserve oneself also from envy and cupidity, and to love peace. The second book enjoins mistrust of praise, draws a rather spirited portrait of the drunkard losing his dignity and his equilibrium, and lays bare how vain do honours appear at the approach of inevitable death, the prelude to the tremendous divine judgments.

This poem, or rather sermon in verse (for the tone is consistently oratorical) on the vanities and miseries of the world, reads easily. What is especially wanting is originality of expression. There is some truth in Fauriel's [1] judgment when he is astonished at the " inability of ecclesiastical literature to rise to simple and severe forms—forms in harmony with the basic nature of its subject." If we take away from this poem of Orientius (as we might from many other productions of this period) what the poet owes to Virgil, Ovid, Horace and even Martial, Catullus, and Juvenal, without counting the Christian poets, little else remains but the merit of having pieced together this *marqueterie*, and the honour due to his outspoken convictions.

The *Commonitorium* has come down to us in only two manuscripts, an *Aquicinctensis* (i.e. a MS. of Anchin, near Douai), now lost, which only contains the first book and formed the basis for the edition of Martin Antoine Delrio

[1] *Hist. de la Gaule mérid.*, I, 430.

(Antwerp, 1600), and a *Turonensis* of the Xth century, which contains the two books and was used by Dom Edmond Martène in his edition of 1700. Stolen from Tours by the famous Libri, this manuscript was sold to Lord Ashburnham; thanks to Leopold Delisle, the French Bibliothèque Nationale regained possession of it in the year 1888. It announces " twenty-four prayers of Orientius " to follow the *Commonitorium*,[1] but only gives two, in iambics of 6 feet; the strophes are of three lines with a refrain of two lines. It is probable that these pieces were written for liturgical use.

The *Alethia*—the Latin for the Greek word Ἀληθεία, Truth—follows the story in Genesis from the creation of the world to the destruction of Sodom. The first book (547 hexam.) corresponds to the three first chapters of Genesis; the second (558 hexam.) to the four following; the third (789 hexam.) embraces chapter viii, verse 20, to chapter xix, verse 29. In spite of certain slight difficulties, we can identify this poem with that attributed by Gennadius (*de Vir. Ill.*, lxi) to one Victorinus or Victorius, a rhetorician of Marseilles: the only manuscript of the *Alethia*[2] gives as the author " Claudius Marius Victor, *orator Massiliensis*." Victor was a lettered man, familiar with Lucretius, Virgil and Ovid. His object, as he shows in the *Precatio* at the beginning, is to instruct the youth, *teneros formare animos* :[3] he also carefully leaves out indecent incidents, such as that relating to the daughters of Lot, and dissembles the wickedness of Sodom. It is with the same intention to instruct that he outlines certain philosophic doctrines, such as atomism and the eternity of matter,[4] and certain practices such as astrology.[5] While paying homage to his " truly Christian and pious sense," Gennadius declares that Victor " only expressed ideas of a very slight value because no one had instructed him how to understand the Scriptures." It is not impossible that Gennadius, with his known tendencies, was rather annoyed

---

[1] We must note that this title is not provided by the manuscripts, which only give *S Orientii versus* and *Versus libri S Orientii.* It goes back to Sigebert de Gembloux, a writer of the XIth century, and was preferred by Delrio and Martène.

[2] *Parisin.* 7558, IXth century (which comes from Tours).

[3] V, 1, 104–5.

[4] I, 22–32.

[5] III, 139–148.

that a layman and a man of letters like Victor should dare to appropriate the Bible and effect a number of transpositions of the facts in the sacred narrative, even though he offered his excuses [1] while doing so.

Following the *Alethia,* a *S. Paulini Epigramma* in 110 hexameters figures in the manuscript : it is a satirical dialogue upon Gallo-Roman morals—masculine and feminine—at the beginning of the Vth century. The unknown author (he has been sometimes identified, at a guess, with Paulinus, Bishop of Béziers [c. 400–419]), gives his opinion that the hardest trials have not reformed the vices of his compatriots.[2]

VII

WE see clearly in the *Eucharisticos* (616 hexameters) which Paulinus of Pella wrote in 459 when he was over 80 years old among what vicissitudes certain lives were passed in those troublous times.

"Conditio instabilis semper generaliter aeví." [3]

He was born at Pella in Macedonia. His father there fulfilled the office of Prefect, and then was given the high position of Pro-Consul of Africa, and the child was taken to Carthage. Eighteen months later he was brought to Rome, and then to Bordeaux, the home of his ancestors : *Tandem majorum in patriam. . . . Burdigalam veni.* There he first came to know his grandfather, who was then Consul.

It has been deduced from these indications that Paulinus must have been the grandson of Ausonius, who was Consul in the year 379. Two different theories have been put forward by the critics : some identify the father of Paulinus with Hesperius, the son of Ausonius, who was Pro-Consul of Africa in 376 ; [4] others with Thalassius, the son-in-law of Ausonius, who was Pro-Consul of Africa in 378, whose son

[1] *Prec.*, 119.
[2] V. 91 et s. Text in Migne, LXI, 969–972, and in C.V., xvi, 499 ; French translation in Clément, *op. cit.*, pp. 247–252. This passage should be noted : " If St Paul and Solomon be left on one side, if a Dido recite Virgil, a Corinna Ovid, if they (women) applaud the lyre of Flaccus or the Muse of Terence, it is we (men) who are responsible."
[3] *Euchar.*, v. 540.
[4] Tillemont, *Hist. des Empereurs*, V, 710–11 : Kruger in R.E., article *Paulinus v. P. ;* Schenkl, in his edition of Ausonius.

was Paulinus by a first marriage.[1] In any case, we do not
know of any other Consul than Ausonius connected with
Bordeaux during those years. The relationship of Ausonius
to Paulinus is therefore hardly open to doubt, although
the former has nowhere made any allusion to his grandson
Paulinus.

> " The enlightened solicitude of my irreproachable
> parents fashioned my mind from childhood so as never to
> expose my reputation to the attacks of scandal. And
> although this reputation, surely acquired, obtained its
> measure of esteem, I would nevertheless have preferred
> the kind of praise which would have been reserved for
> me if, in agreement as were the wishes of my parents
> at first with my own, these had persisted in the design
> of consecrating me from my childhood to Thy service,
> O Christ. More wisely inspired for my welfare, their
> pious solicitude would have freed me from the passing
> pleasures of the flesh in order to enable me to gather the
> eternal fruits of the future life." [2]

There seems to emerge from this enigmatic passage that the
parents of Paulinus, after favouring a precocious religious
vocation, afterwards withstood it. They somewhat spoilt
the child who was of rather delicate health, and he obtained
from their indulgence the gratification of all his whims—
horses, dogs, hawks, toys, rich clothes, etc. . . . Paulinus
gives us the information that during his adolescence he
restrained himself from yielding to the seductions of women of
independent position in life, who were much disposed not to
show themselves too timid, and that he contented himself
meritoriously with availing himself of the charms of the
domestics who were in the service of his parents (*contentus
domus illecebris famulantibus uti*) ! At the age of twenty he

---

[1] Peiper, in his edition of Ausonius, pp. ci and cxv ; Brandes, in his edition
of Paulinus of Pella ; Seeck, M.G.H., VI, i, p. lxxvii. Seeck remarks that instructions xv, 7, 3 (10th March, 376), and 1, 32, 2 (8th July, 376) of the *Theodosian
Code*, are addressed to Hesperius, Pro-Consul, while instructions 1, 15, 8 (21st
January, 377), and viii, 5, 34 (25th February, 377) are addressed to Hesperius,
Praetorian Prefect. Hesperius was therefore Prefect of the Gauls from the beginning of the year 377. Now Paulinus informs us that his father was at Pella when
he was born and that afterwards he was for eighteen months in Africa as Pro-
Consul, that is to say, up to the end of 377. This raises a difficulty.—I remark
that this would form a more serious difficulty if we were not aware of the lack of
preciseness customary with the ancient poets on questions of chronology.

[2] Cf. Brandes, C.V., vol. XVI, p. 295.

was married off; he became a man settled in life, active, but fond of a comfortable existence, the security of which was not long in being endangered by subsequent events :

> " I desired a commodious house with large apartments arranged for all kinds of weather according to the different seasons of the year, a table neat and well garnished, slaves young and numerous, furniture in plenty and suited to different uses, silver plate more valuable from its design than from its weight, artists of every kind skilful in promptly carrying out my commissions, stables full of well-fed horses, and strong and elegant carriages for taking drives."

He was thirty when the barbarians penetrated into the " very entrails of the Roman Empire." At first he had only praise for the Goths, who bestowed upon him important positions of dignity. But, by a grievous change of fortune, he soon saw himself despoiled of his possessions, driven from his home which was left in ashes, and besieged in Bazas by the Goths and Alani whom he skilfully found means to set against each other. He would have liked to flee to the East where he still retained a few possessions. He was unable to succeed in doing this, and moreover his wife had no desire to take this step. All these trials ripened his conversion, which he did not complete until fairly late, when he was about 46 years old. In addition, he lost successively his mother-in-law, his mother, his wife, and one of his sons who was already a priest. He lived poverty stricken on the meagre remnant of his patrimony, first at Marseilles and then at Bordeaux. A Goth had the honesty to remit to him the money for a small property which had formerly belonged to him, thus saving him from a too lamentable old age.

The account of this progressive downfall, interspersed with words of thanksgiving after the manner of St Augustine in his *Confessions*, is very attractive, and reflects the uncertainty and misery of that period of dissolution.

VIII

BROTHER of the Bishop of Vienne in Dauphiny, Claudianus Mamertus was a priest in that same town, where he died in

474. " In this master," Sidonius Apollinaris declares in the epitaph which he wrote on him, " a three-fold literature (*triplex bybliotheca*) shone forth—Roman, Attic and Christian. . . . Orator, dialectician, poet, author of sermons, geometrician and musician, he excelled in unravelling the knots of problems and in striking with the sword of his speech the sectaries who harass the Catholic faith. . . ." The generous terms employed by Sidonius in praising his friends are well known. Moreover Claudianus Mamertus is not at all wanting in merit. Gennadius [1] rightly calls him " *Vir ad loquendum artifex et ad disputandum subtilis.*" In his *De Statu Animae* in three books written in 469 and dedicated to Sidonius, he defends the theory of the incorporeity of the soul—substance without doubt, but not quantitative nor subject to the category of space—against the contrary speculations of Faustus of Riez and Gennadius. We have, further, two letters in his name addressed, one to Sidonius Apollinaris, and the other to the rhetorician Sapaudus of Vienne, in which he deplores in significant terms [2] the lack of intellectual curiosity of his contemporaries ; also a few poems which we cannot attribute to him with certainty, or which we should even formally deny having been written by him. A mention added to the notice in Gennadius, missing in most of the manuscripts of the *De Viris Illustribus*, attributes to him the *Pange Lingua Gloriosi*. But it appears certain that Venantius Fortunatus was the author of this famous hymn. Sidonius makes two allusions to hymns written by his friend [3] which may account for this erroneous attribution.

IX

The principal work written by Dracontius, the *De Laudibus Dei*, was not published in its entirety until 1791 by the Jesuit Arevalo, from two manuscripts in the Vatican which ascribe it inaccurately to St Augustine. Up till then only the portion relating to the history of the Creation, the *Hexaemeron*, was known, which had been detached at an early date from

---

[1] *De Viris Ill.*, lxxxiv.
[2] P.L., LIII, 783 ; C.V., XI, p. 203.
[3] *Ep.* IV, iii, and in the *Epitaph* to Cl. Mamertus.

the poem, and had been touched up in the VIIth century
and 59 lines added by Eugenius II, Bishop of Toledo.

The *Laudes Dei* was written by Dracontius under rather
tragic circumstances. An advocate of repute at Carthage,
vir clarissimus, a poet skilled in the art of exploiting the traditional themes of rhetoric and mythology (we possess
a certain number of detailed narratives of his, and even a
tragedy, the *Orestes*, in 974 hexameters),[1] he had the misfortune to displease Gonthamond (484–496) king of the Vandals,
for having lauded in one of his poems an enemy of his. Gonthamond confiscated his goods and cast him into prison.

Under the title of *Satisfactio ad Guthamundum*, Dracontius
endeavoured to excite the pity of his persecutor by a humble
avowal of his fault, the exposure of his misery in prison, and
a promise to celebrate the exploits of the king. This elegy in
153 verses did not succeed in altering the mind of Gonthamond.
It was then that Dracontius set himself to his great didactic
poem in three books. He still makes a few allusions in it to
his sad state : *Quanto cecidi de culmine lapsus* (III, 653),
Me . . . catenarum ferrato pondere pressum (III, 721). But
he rises above these personal considerations to celebrate the
action of Divine grace in the world wherein everything hangs
upon the *irae* and the *pia vota* of God (I, 10). Descriptions
and didactic pieces—for example, in the second Canto on
Arianism,[2] and on the origin of evil,[3] and in the third Canto,
his criticism of paganism [4]—alternate with passages of a more
lyric character, with prayers in the form of hymns,[5] and
with regrets for his own past.[6] The part wherein he relates
the Six Days' Work is one of his most successful. Striking
analogies have been noticed between Canto VIII of Milton's
Paradise Lost and the happy developments wherein Dracontius
describes the wonder of Adam at the spectacle presented by
the earthly Paradise, and then the desire he feels for some other
created being with whom to share his happiness.[7] There are
real beauties of detail in this poem, which was greatly appre-

---

[1] It is really a narrative in epic form.
[2] II, 60 et s.
[3] II, 245 et s.
[4] III, 257 et s.
[5] I, 683 et s. ; II and IV, at the beginning ; II, 154 et s.
[6] III, 566 et s.
[7] I, 348–358.

ciated in the Middle Ages and reveals the familiarity of Dracontius with Christian as well as with classic poets.

X

WE know next to nothing about the life of Sedulius. In a dedication in prose addressed to the priest Macedonius, he informs us that while he was spending his time to no purpose in *saecularia studia*, the Divine pity touched him and decided him to write some work which might strengthen his readers in the right way after he had first attracted them by the " honey " of his poetry for which they were so eager. According to an indication which appears in trustworthy manuscripts,[1] he learnt " philosophy " in Italy when still a layman, and wrote his works in Greece in the time of Theodosius II and Valentinian III, that is to say, in the middle of the Vth century.[2] A flattering mention of Sedulius in the decree *de libris recipiendis*, issued by the pseudo Gelasius, and the fact that his *Paschale Carmen*, discovered among his papers, was collected and put in order by Turcius Rufus Asterius, who was Consul in 494,[3] are indications which hardly allow of any doubt as to the period in which he lived.

> " While pagan poets delight to celebrate fictitious events in pompous and emphatic terms, under the mask of tragedy, or in the language of the comedy of Geta, or in any other form of poetry ; while they cause to live again the poison of impious events, and laud heinous crimes, and, from no other necessity but custom, trace on papyrus from the Nile thousands of falsehoods, why should I, who am used to chant the Psalms of David to the sound of the ten-stringed instrument, keep silent on the resplendent miracles of Jesus Christ, our Saviour ? "[4]

[1] C.V., X, p. 5.

[2] The anonymous author of this short notice gives it as having been taken from the appendix added to St Jerome's *de Viris Ill.*, by his disciple Paterius (?). If it was Gennadius (the text is evidently mutilated), we shall have to admit that the paragraph relating to Sedulius must have been lost for it does not appear in the *de Vir. Ill.* of that author.

[3] We derive this information from a mention which appears in the oldest manuscripts of Sedulius. This Asterius is the same man who made a revision of Virgil (cf. the celebrated *subscriptio* to the *Codex Mediceus*, 39, i, Vth century, now at Florence).

[4] *Carmen Pasch.*, I, v. 17–26.

St Paul wrote in his 1st Epistle to the Corinthians (v, 7) : "Etenim Pascha nostrum immolatus est Christus." It was this verse which suggested to Sedulius the title of his poem, *Paschale Carmen*. His object was to celebrate the wondrous facts of the life of Christ, His miracles especially, not simply for the pleasure of describing them in verse, but also to draw from them the doctrinal and moral teaching to which they lent themselves. Of the five books, written in hexameters, the first, a kind of introduction, after an appeal to the pagans who found themselves being impelled to give up their sterile errors,[1] treats of some of the wonderful events in the Old Testament, without regard to abrupt transitions ; the three following give an account of the wonders of Christ from His birth to His triumphant entry into Jerusalem ; the fifth comments on the episodes of the Passion, making use of rhetorical description and allegory. Sedulius bases himself throughout on St Matthew and St Luke ; from the beginning of book V, he *alters* the information given by the four evangelists. He avails himself, on occasion, of authorised commentaries, such as those of St Ambrose and St Augustine. He does not bind himself to a strictly literal rendering of the sacred text, and allows himself free paraphrases whenever he sees it is advantageous for the edification of the reader.

Later on he took the trouble to transpose his poem into prose. He entitled this reconstituted work *Opus Paschale*, to distinguish it from the *Paschale Carmen*. His friend Macedonius got him to undertake this work in order that he might repair (as he explains in the preface), the omissions which the *angustia metricae necessitatis* [2] had imposed upon him.

Gaston Boissier, who some time back had the curiosity to compare the *Opus Paschale* with the *Paschale Carmen*,[3] found the verse of Sedulius much more simple and easy to understand than his prose. This inferiority in the *Opus Paschale* does not proceed simply from the difficulty of finding fresh expressions in which to repeat the same things ; it consists in the abuse (of which Sedulius was also guilty) of the employment of terms of forcible signification to express

---

[1] V, 38 et s.

[2] The most accurate analysis of the poem is that made by Th. Mayr, in his *Studien zu dem Paschale Carmen*, a thesis written at Munich, 1916, pp. 5–33.

[3] *Revue de Philol.*, VI (1882), p. 28 et s.

the simplest things,[1] and especially in his mania for para-
phrasing, which was held in check by the rules of versification
but which freely found vent in prose, often for the childish
pleasure of giving a more suitable termination to a sentence.[2]
Briefly, in his poetry, the imitation of the classic poets—of
Virgil, who was the model consistently studied—maintained to
a certain point the old language, and even the old prosody.[3]
Less fettered by tradition, his prose was susceptible in a greater
degree of being infused by the bad taste of the period.

Sedulius further wrote two hymns in honour of Christ,
one of 55 distiches which affected the form of *versus echoici*
or *serpentini*, in which the first words of each hexameter
were repeated in the second part of the pentameter ;[4] the
other, which is alphabetical, is in iambic dimeters grouped in
verses of four lines. The Catholic liturgy has taken a few
of the verses óf the second poem into use—the *A solis ortus
cardine* for the Feast of Christmas, and the *Hostis Herodes
impie* for the Epiphany.

XI

SIDONIUS APOLLINARIS (*C. Sollius Modestus Apollinaris
Sidonius*) was born at Lyons on the 5th November 431 or
432 at the time when the city was still entirely Roman,
and died in 487, the subject of a Visigoth king. Brought up
on the strong traditions of Rome, whose majesty he keenly
appreciated, and whom he calls *domicilium legum, gymnasium
litterarum, curiam dignitatum, verticem mundi, patriam liber-
tatis, unicam totius mundi civitatem,*[5] he thought it right to

---

[1] *Adorare consulatum,* for " sing the praises of a consulate " ; *sublimare con-
vivium,* for " to honour a festivity with his presence " ; etc.

[2] The man born blind begs his sight of Jesus. Sedulius expressed this in his
verse by *lumen petere,* in prose by *oculatae copiam claritatis postulare* (IV, 212).
In connection with the massacre of the Innocents, he writes in the *Paschale Carmen,*
" *Haec laceros crines nudato vertice rupit, illa genas secuit* " ; and in the *Opus
Paschale,* IV, 123 : " Haec effusam vultibus comam miseranda dilacerans crinalis
damni foeditate nudum cervicem sauciabat ; illa madidas lacrimosis imbribus
genas unguium protervitate sulcabat." The terminations of Sedulius have been
studied by J. Candel, Latin thesis, Toulouse, 1904.

[3] We notice besides in Sedulius some irregularities in his prosody—syllables
of short accent made long when he wishes to be emphatic, and long syllables
shortened when he wishes to express hesitation, etc. . . . See Huemer's edition,
p. 394.

[4] Ex : *Primus ad ima ruit* magna de luce superbus : Sic homo, cum tumuit
primus ad ima ruit.

[5] *Ep.* I, vi.

repay with his verses the forbearance of the invaders " having their heads perfumed with rancid butter." The life of this great personage, somewhat puerile as regards his literary performances, but of great honesty and good intentions, embodies the best elements of Gallo-Roman nobility in the Vth century, faithful to Rome, sacrificed by her, and finally reduced to relying only on themselves.[1]

His grandfather, Pretorian Prefect of Gaul, was converted in 408 in the reign of Theodosius.[2] His father held the *insignia* of the same high post under Valentinian III. In 452, Sidonius, when still very young, married Papianilla, a young girl who belonged to an illustrious family of Auvergne. On the 1st January 456 he was called upon to deliver before the Roman Senate the panegyric upon his father-in-law, Flavius Eparchius Avitus, who had been chosen emperor the previous year by the deputies from the Gaulish nobility assembled at Beaucaire (*Ugernum*). The success of this poetic feat won for him a bronze statue in the Forum of Trajan.[3] Shortly afterwards Avitus, owing to the threats of certain disaffected members of the Roman aristocracy, found no other means of saving his life than to accept the Episcopal see of Plaisance. Another panegyric,[4] this time addressed to the Emperor Majorian, preserved Sidonius from the animosity of the new prince, and even advanced him in his estimation.

From 461 to 465 Sidonius led the comfortable life of a great landed proprietor on his estate at Avitacum, with his wife and three children. A fresh literary exploit—the panegyric on Anthemius, who in his turn had become Emperor of the West [5] —obtained for him in 468 the dignity of Prefect of Rome, and, at the expiration of his term of office, the title of Patrician.

He looked forward to enjoying in peace his remaining years, when, in circumstances of which we are ignorant, he was elected in 471 or 472, to the Episcopal see of Arverna (Clermont-Ferrand). His social *prestige*, his talent as a writer, his administrative experience, and also his great piety (which often finds expression in his *Letters*) marked him out for this high office with the lively approbation of the Gallo-Roman

---

[1] Sources of his biography : a notice in the *de Viris Ill.*, of Gennadius, § xcii ; the works of Sidonius and especially the poem included in *Ep.* IX, xvi.
[2] *Carmen* xii, 7.   [3] *Carmen* vii.
[4] *Carmen* iv.   [5] *Carmen* ii.

Episcopate. He had not sought this unexpected promotion, but he did not flinch from any of his new duties which political events rendered heavy and formidable. He organised the resistance against Euric the Arian and his Visigoths who, in 474, had attempted the invasion of Auvergne. But that province was soon after handed over to them by a duly authorised treaty signed by Nepos, the Emperor. *Facta est servitus nostra pretium securitatis alienae*, as Sidonius,[1] who had raised courageous protests, mournfully stated. As a punishment, Euric had him taken to the fortress of Livia not far from Carcassonne,[2] but decided afterwards to give him back his liberty. Sidonius, whose material interests were rendered very precarious, once more made use of his familiar methods with a view to soften the disposition of his new master ; the poem included in *Letter* viii could not but be pleasing to the vanity of Euric. Sidonius was bound to acknowledge that throughout his career, at the price of certain necessary concessions, his writings had served him well.

Twenty-four poems and one hundred and forty-seven letters in nine books make up the works of Sidonius, who was much admired by his contemporaries in the Middle Ages, and whose high favour only paled in the time of the first humanists.[3] In his poems, the show pieces and the *nugae* (detailed descriptions, letters in verse, epithalamia, etc.), should be distinguished ; his favourite metres are the hexameter, elegiacs, and the hendecasyllable. His prosody is correct, and he only allows himself licences on very rare occasions. As regards his letters, they were collected and published by himself at the request of his friends in successive portions, the Ist book in 469, the IInd about 472, books V to VII about 474–475, book VIII a little later, and book IX about 479. When once he had become a Bishop he deemed it suitable to give up the " frivolous exercises " in which he had delighted until then. " I fear," he declares, " that a reputation as a poet may in some degree sully the strictness necessary in a priest." [4] Notwithstanding, on more than one occasion he falls into introducing some passages in verse into his letters.

The fundamental interest of the writings of Sidonius lies

---

[1] *Ep.* VII, vii.
[2] *Ep.* VIII, iii ; IX, iii ; Vaissette, *Hist. du Languedoc*, I, 501.
[3] As evidenced by Baret, *op. cit.*, pp. 102–106.
[4] *Ep.* IX, xii, and IX, xvi, line 45 et s.

in their being historical documents. Even from his most artificial productions from the point of view of composition, historians and lovers of the picturesque are able to glean valuable details : for example, the portrait of the Huns in his *Panegyric* on Anthemius, and of the Franks in his *Panegyric* on Majorian ; and there are many other revealing sketches which Chateaubriand in the course of his immense reading as a young man was careful to note. Without the letters and poems of Sidonius the political and social history of Gaul at this period would be almost empty of facts for us. When by chance Sidonius resigns himself to be simple and to describe without adding any embroidery any incident which he has witnessed, he is a *piquant* and amusing story-teller.[1] He also knew how to render himself an eloquent interpreter of Gallo-Roman patriotism on more than one occasion : letter VII, vii, written when Auvergne was about to be detached from *Romania*, is a noble page which deserves not to perish. Devoted to his province and to his flock, faithful to his friends and profoundly " sociable," the character of Sidonius commands our sympathy.

He has also made known to us the literary life of Gaul in the Vth century. Personally, he was a very learned man.[2] Upon his numerous correspondents [3]—poets, orators, philosophers, lawyers and simple men of letters,—he lavished such laudatory epithets that if we took them seriously we should have an impression of an immense intellectual activity flourishing within the Gallo-Roman society. The following is a specimen of his amiable hyperbole :

> " When your book," he writes to Claudianus Mamertus who had sent him his *De Statu Animae*, " unfolds its scholarship against what it is opposing, it proves itself equal to authors in both languages in point of morals and learned attainments. It thinks like Pythagoras, it distinguishes like Socrates, it explains like Plato, it shrouds its meaning like Aristotle, it flatters

[1] See *Ep.* V, xvii ; I, xi ; III, xii (with P. Allard's interpretation of certain details which are often little understood, *Saint Sidoine Apoll.*, p. 75).

[2] The echo of Tibullus and Silius Italicus, almost forgotten for at least two centuries, comes back with him. The history of Roman literature owes some interesting scraps of information to him, for example, on the wife of Lucan, who married again ; and on Seneca the tragedian, whom he formally distinguishes from the philosopher Seneca (*Carm.* ix, 232), etc.

[3] They will be found mentioned in Teuffel, III, no. 466, p. 435.

like Aeschines, it is impassioned like Demosthenes, it is flowery like Hortensius, it inflames like Cethegus, it urges on like Curio, it temporises like Fabius, it feigns like Crassus, it dissimulates like Cæsar, it counsels like Cato, it dissuades like Appius, it persuades like Tullius ; and, to come to a comparison with the holy Fathers, it instructs like Jerome, it is destructive like Lactantius, it establishes like Augustine, etc. . . ." [1]

Then follow in succession : Hilary, John (Chrysostom), Basil, Gregory, Orosius, Rufinus, Eusebius, Eucherius, Paulinus and Ambrose. . . . A quotation like that is sufficient to gauge the watermark of any mind. It warns us also to check the grandiloquent admiration of Sidonius. We can then see that these vaunted correspondents, however slightly acquainted, or however saturated, with literary ability they might be, did not surpass the level of Sidonius himself ; they have the same touching fervour for things of the intellect, the same insufficiency in power of criticism, and in profound learning.[2] In his moments of *clairvoyance* Sidonius has well glimpsed certain aspects of this decadence,[3] but he did not succeed in correcting all its effects on his own account.

Where this is most apparent is when he strives to imitate the methods, the routine, and the pseudo-literary commonplaces of which Juvenal had declared himself to be already weary three and a half centuries before.[4] We see him furbishing up in his verse and prose the forms of address, the enumerations, the amplifications, the scholarly echoes, and the mythological banalities with which his memory, loaded up with so much reading,[5] unremittingly supplied him. And all this is set in tortuous phraseology, painful, and often obscure owing to its far-fetched and affected character, wherein worldly elegance finds itself side by side with obsolete phrases of a Latin which was already breaking up,[6] and

---

[1] *Ep.* IV, iii.

[2] See Roger's *L'Enseign. des lettres class. d'Ausone à Alcuin,* 1905, pp. 67–75.

[3] *Ep.* V, x, 4 ; II, x, i (he was complaining that the rush of barbarism was eating into the Latin tongue) ; IV, xvii, 2.

[4] *Sat.,* i.

[5] An attempt to reconstruct his library appears in Allard, *op. cit.,* p. 133. A notice of the " sources of information " in M.G.H., VIII, p. 384 et s.

[6] The comparative in two words (*Plus celsos* . . .) ; inflections replaced by prepositions (*nebula de pulvere*) ; an infinitive replaced by *quod* or *quia,* with the indicative or subjunctive, etc.

with unexpected verbal creations.[1] It requires an effort to read Sidonius Apollinaris, and one dare not say that it invariably finds its reward.

This was not the opinion of the learned men of his time. Sidonius largely contributed to the formation of the poetic style then in vogue, and this imitator was almost as often copied as some of the authorised classics.

---

[1] Cervicositas, saeculiloquus, familiarescere, phthisiscere, crepusculasceus, etc. ...

BOOK V

ON THE THRESHOLD OF THE MIDDLE AGES

CHAPTER I

WORKS IN VERSE

BIBLIOGRAPHY

I. AVITUS.—Text in P.L., LIX, reproducing Sirmond (Paris, 1643); in Ul. Chevalier, *Oeuvres complètes de Saint Avite évéque de Vienne*, Lyons, 1890; in M.G.H., VI, part 2 (1883, Peiper [excellent]).—Various pieces translated in F. Clément, *op. cit.*, pp. 323-353.—Consult: H. Goelzer, *Le Latin de Saint Avit* (*Biblioth. de la Faculté des Lettres de Paris*, fasc. XXVI [1909]).

II. ENNODIUS.—The manuscripts give the works of Ennodius in a very confused order. Sirmond (Paris, 1611), reproduced by Migne, LXIII, 13,364, and followed likewise by Hartel, C.V., vol. VI (1882), attempted to introduce a logical classification. Vogel, M.G.H., VII (1885), preferred to keep to the order, or rather disorder, of the manuscripts.—French translation of the *Letters* by the Abbé Léglise, Paris, 1906.—Consult: A. Dubois, *La Latinité d'Ennodius* (Clermont-Ferrand), 1903.

III. VENANTIUS FORTUNATUS. — Text in P.L., vol. LXXXVIII, reproducing the edition of the Benedictine A. Lucchi (Rome, 1786-7). For an account of the history of the editions of Fortunatus, see Ch. Nisard, in the *Rev. de l'Enseign. second.*, 1885, II, p. 276 et s. (cf. id., *le Poète Fortunat*, 1890, chap. i). The *Parisinus*, No. 13,048, VIIIth/IXth century represents a special tradition, and provides 31 pieces not contained in the manuscripts of the other tradition. These poems were published by Guérard in 1835. They do not appear in Migne, except the first three, which had already been published before. The most complete edition is the *Mon. Germaniae histor.*, vol. IV (1881-1885: Leo, for the poetry; Krusch, for the works in prose): the criticism is very conservative, perhaps excessively so (see Rey in the *Rev. de Philol.*, XXXI, 190).—French translation of the poetry of Fortunatus by Ch. Nisard and E. Rittier, Paris, 1887 (Nisard's Collection); translation of the *Life of St Radegonde*, by R. Aigrain, 1910. Study of the grammar of Fortunatus by A. Meneghetti in the *Didaskaleion*, 1916, pp. 195-298; 1917, pp. 1-166 (*La Latinita di Venanzio Fortunato*, Turin, 1917).

N.B.—The writings placed under the name of Amoenus in P.L., LXI, 1075-1082, belong to Prudentius and Fortunatus. This Amoenus was doubtless a mere compiler of extracts.

SUMMARY

I. The Decline of Latin Learning. — II. Avitus. — III. Ennodius.—VI. Venantius Fortunatus.

I

WE know to what degree the mournful presentiments which
strained at the hearts of men at the time of the first inrush
of the Vandals, Alani, and Suevi at the beginning of the Vth
century were justified and even surpassed by events. During
all that century torrential invasions broke like surf over Gaul,
Italy, Spain and even Africa. The wealth, works of art,
and all the refined outer garb of the privileged classes were
scattered and broken up by ignorant and brutal hands,
and, what was still more disastrous,—for it was not only the
upper classes who were to suffer from it—the established
institutions were included in the catastrophe, or at least
seriously shaken. The public schools in particular found
themselves almost wholly disorganised in more than one part
of the Empire. They were able to maintain at first in the
principal cities a small handful of active and lettered men.
Then they became rarer, and the greater number disappeared.
Teaching was only given, when it could be provided at all,
by private tutors to whom the members of the aristocracy
entrusted their children. There were still educated individuals
who sometimes associated together in groups when circumstances permitted, but the general level of education—
that culture which can only be handed on by uninterrupted
effort—declined progressively, and presented a fragile and
precarious appearance when once the framework, indispensable to its continuity, had been rent asunder.

Those who endeavoured to become writers in the midst
of the prevailing ignorance deserved some merit. The infinite
value of the privileged ages during which good taste had
acquired all its delicacy and preserved all its balance cannot
be better understood than by reading them. There were,
however, cultivated intelligences who retained the taste for
good style and a genuine respect for that literary tradition
which they flattered themselves they were perpetuating.
They sought to preserve themselves from the incorrectness of
language spoken all around them—two specimens quoted by
H. Goelzer in his fine work on St Avitus (p. 2) give a sufficient
idea of this increasing corruption. But they seem to have
grown unaccustomed to attach importance to the root base of

things, to thought itself; they are only careful of their language, and its expression, which they embroider in order to please. They endeavour to overdo each of their phrases. Nothing can be more insipid than their niceties. Also they make few innovations in matter of style. H. Goelzer and Max Bonnet have taught us to recognise in the system they followed the methods used in rhetoric during the first centuries of the Empire; they did nothing more than press them to their utmost limits, sometimes even to absurdity. The already distant influence of an Apuleius developed all its harmful effects in them.

II

BORN at Vienne in Dauphiny about the year 450 of a family from Auvergne who had settled in Burgundy, the son and grandson of Senators, Avitus was raised to the Episcopal chair of his native town in 490 and died in 518. His *rôle* as a Bishop was extremely important. He presided as Metropolitan of the Gauls at the Council of Epaonia in 517.[1] From Arianism he brought back to Catholic orthodoxy, Sigismond, the son and successor of Gondebaud, king of Burgundy. He had the reputation of being a formidable extirpator of heresy.[2] We still possess his *Contra Eutychianam Haeresim Libri Duo*, which dates from 512–513, and his *Dialogi cum Gundobado Rege vel Librorum contra Arianos reliquiae*.[3] His works in prose consist of 98 letters, 2 homilies on the Rogations, and 72 short fragments of sermons. Among his contemporaries he was considered one of the most brilliant writers of his time. It was to his poetry especially that he owed this reputation. The *De Laude Virginitatis* in 666 hexameters, addressed to his sister Fuscina, develops the ecclesiastical theories on the inconveniences of marriage and the advantages of virginity.[4] The work in which Avitus shows his full scope is the *Libelli de Spiritalis Historiae Gestis* (he thus names it in one of his letters),[5] which may be

---

[1] Hefele Leclercq, *Hist. des Conc.*, II, 2, 1031 et s.
[2] Gregory of Tours, *History of the Franks*, II, xxxiv.
[3] The *Collatio Episcoporum contra Arianos coram Gundobaldo Rege* (P.L., LIX, 387) is a mistake of Vignier's. Cf. Julien Havet, *Questions Méroving*, 1885, vol. II.
[4] Note especially this development (line 164 et s.) : ". . . Dominum passura cubilis Servit in obsceno tolerans conubia lecto."
[5] *Ep.* xliii.

considered the most remarkable poem inspired by the Book of Genesis in the Vth century. The first book (325 lines) treats of the origin of the world ; the second (423 lines), of original sin ; the third (425 lines), of the Judgment of God. Guizot remarked that these three cantos form a whole, the strong texture of which is a forerunner of the *Paradise Lost.*[1] A fourth book follows on the Deluge (658 lines) and a fifth on the Passage of the Red Sea (721 lines). Avitus published the work himself in 507, without having had, as he tells us, leisure to correct it. He confesses that he had thought of making up a collection of his poems to form a volume of a fair size, but the sack of Vienne in 500 caused the loss of nearly all of them.[2]

Once we admit the principle of his poetry which treats subjects specifically Christian by means of the methods inherited from the classics, and in order to build Noah's Ark takes toll of Pelion, Pindarus, Ossa and Atlas,[3] we must acknowledge that brilliant and happily-conceived pieces are not wanting. In the scene of the Temptation, the gradual rising of evil curiosity in the soul of the woman and the trembling concessions which lead her on to the full accomplishment of her fault—all these *nuances* are described with a psychological *finesse* which is too rare in these essays of schoolmen grown old. The preacher of chastity reveals himself in the complaints which he puts into the mouth of Adam :

> " Alas ! It was then for my destruction that this woman was joined to my life ! She whom Thy command hath given me for companion is the woman who, herself overcome, hath undone me by her baleful counsels, and hath driven me to taste the fruit which she knew already. . . . I have been deceived, but it was Thou who hadst made me trusting by giving marriage unto me and by tying these knots full of delight. *Happy man had I spent my life alone without ever knowing hymeneal bonds !* "[4]

While freely exploiting the Genesis of old, Avitus does not

---

[1] *Hist. de la Civil. en France*, II (1840), 71.
[2] See the *Prologue* in prose to his brother Apollinaris, Bishop of Valence.
[3] Cf. *de . . . Gestis*, IV, 299 et s.
[4] III, 98–107.

forget the times in which he was living, and compares the sorrows of Adam and Eve with those endured by their sad posterity—devastated cities, social upheavals, and the calamities of invasion. " There is no evil which this world, full of iniquity and woe, doth not commit and endure : its downfall is imminent, the measure of crime is full up. . . ." [1]

Avitus was a lettered man, a *scolasticus*, as they said in those days. He had received lessons from the rhetorician Sapaudus whom Sidonius and Mamertus held in high esteem. He knew grammar very well,[2] and included in an almost equal admiration Virgil and . . . Sidonius Apollinaris. Consistently concerned with good diction, he only made rare concessions to popular language. His style, refined and artificial, precious and dainty, also furnishes an excellent choice of examples whereby to illustrate the history of literary decadence. All the methods dear to Latin writers from an early date (fulness of expression, paronomasia, antithesis, alliteration) are used by him without discretion. H. Goelzer [3] considers, nevertheless, after an " exhaustive " examination, that, though completely bound to the same school as the other Gallo-Roman writers, Avitus is less inflated and less obscure than most of them.

III

ENNODIUS was a native of southern Gaul. He was born probably at Arles, in the year 473 or 474, of a family of consular rank, but his education and ecclesiastical career were passed in northern Italy. Like Sidonius Apollinaris he realised the type of rhetorician-Bishop, but with more sonorous humanism and unprofitable virtuosity than even the former possessed.

Becoming Bishop of Ticinum (Pavia) about the year 513, he was charged with important missions. Pope Hormisdas sent him on two occasions, in 515 and 517, as Legate to the court of the Emperor Anastasius at Constantinople, in order to bring about unity between the churches of the East and the West. He also mingled in politics. He believed in the benevolent intentions of Theodoric, accepted his advances,

---

[1] III, 359–361.
[2] See *Ep.* lvii (p. 85, Peiper).
[3] *Op. cit.*, p. 713 et s.

R

and in 507, a few years before his Episcopate, delivered a grandiloquent panegyric in honour of the king.

He was considered a fine scholar. But his writings consisted of little else than uttering mere trifles in harmonious and well-balanced phrases, or in verse formed on Virgilian *recipes*. His 297 letters are of an elegant turn, and incredibly void of ideas, although some of his correspondents bore the names of Symmachus, Boethius, Hormisdas, etc. Ennodius lingers over academic exercises on the model of the *controversiae* of old : " Against a man who placed a statue of Minerva in a wrong place " ; " Against a father who had been unwilling to ransom his son who had fallen into the power of pirates and who later begs him to come to his assistance." He pushes his admiration for the classics as far as to imitate the licence of a Martial in several of his epigrams. The Christian does however appear in a certain number of pieces, for example, in a *Life of Epiphanius*, Bishop of Pavia (conspicuous for its harangues like those put into the mouths of their characters by the old historians) ; in a *Life of Antony* a monk of Lérins, a *Eucharisticum de Vita sua*, a *Libellus* supporting the Synod of Rome in 502, a *Paraenesis Didascalica*, addressed to two young people, etc. The last-mentioned exhortation mixes up in a strange way the most contradictory points of view : Ennodius recommends to his young friends the Christian virtues, *verecundia, fides, castitas*, but also the assiduous practice of the liberal arts, especially rhetoric, which at its good pleasure can make an innocent man appear guilty, and a guilty man innocent !

" Qui nostris servit studiis, mox imperat orbi."

Most of his productions which have come down to us seem to have been written before his Episcopate. That is perhaps an excuse. In any case they betray the superficial and entirely academic character of the culture with which he was enamoured, and which in some amusing commonplace he sometimes made a pretence of repudiating : " Cessent anilium commenta poetarum, fabulosa repudietur antiquitas ! " [1] A study of his language reveals a real effort at correctness of grammar. He tried his best to keep to the rules. But he could not succeed in the impossible attempt to perpetuate the

[1] *Ep.* I, ix (Léglise's translation, p. 96).

old rules of Latin literary style in an age when Latin was becoming more and more corrupt; some colloquial expressions mingle strangely with the traditional rhetorical language.

What one would like to find among so many faded elegancies, and phrases made up from the *recipes* of the schools, would be some energetic language based on a vigorous thought, some idea springing from a fresh sensation. But his exaggerated literary mould comes between himself and reality.[1]

IV

THE life of a troubadour wandering through the countries of the West, impelled by curiosity and a liking for scenes on a large scale, and especially by devotion; repaying in complimentary verses the good offices of those who gave him shelter; and then his vagrant career finding its *métier* once for all in the most fervent, the most respectful, the most enthusiastic friendship for a most charming and pious woman —these traits sum up the career of Venantius Honorius Clementianus Fortunatus, whom we may regard as the last representative of Latin poetry on the threshold of the Middle Ages.

Born about the year 530 at Duplavilis near Treviso, Fortunatus was educated at Ravenna, and received there some smattering of grammar, rhetoric, and law. His fortunate recovery from an affection of the eyes led him to set out for the tomb of St Martin to whom he attributed his cure.[2] He took by no means the shortest route to reach Tours. He travelled by way of the Julian Alps, Noricum and Rhetia, crossed the upper Danube and the Rhine, and stopped for some time at the court of Sigebert, king of Austrasia, whose marriage with Brunehaut in 566 he celebrated in an *epithalamium* in which he entrusted to Venus and Cupid their

---

[1] We may connect the name of Ennodius with that of Rusticus Helpidius, the author of a *De Christi Jesu Beneficiis*, in 149 hexameters (P.L., LXII, 545–548), and of certain inscriptions written for the purpose of explaining representations from the Bible (*ibid.*, 543–546). The *De . . . Beneficiis* was re-edited by W. Brandes, Brunswick, 1890. A protégé of Ennodius, Arator, subdeacon of the Church in Rome, published in 544 a paraphrase in verse of the Acts of the Apostles (P.L., LXVIII, 63–246) dedicated to Pope Vigilius. New edition by Hubner, Neissen, 1850.

[2] Cf. his *Vita Martini*, IV, 689 et s. ; Gregory of Tours, *De Virt. Mart.*, I, xv.

glory and happiness.　On arriving at the end of his journey after two years of adventurous travels, " sometimes asleep, fatigued by my tramping when not made heavy with wine," [1] his pilgrimage accomplished he pushed on again to the Pyrenees, came back to Poitiers and there came to know Radegonde.[2]

The wife of the murderer of her parents and the oppressor of Thuringia her fatherland, Queen Radegonde had finally obtained the permission of her husband Clotaire to consecrate herself to the monastic life.　She had founded at Poitiers the monastery of Notre Dame (soon afterwards called the monastery of Sainte-Croix), the direction of which she entrusted to her spiritual daughter Agnes.　Both highly cultivated, the two nuns had no difficulty in winning the devotion of the itinerant poet who was doubtless little accustomed to such delicate attentions as theirs, and who received from them mystical intercommunion of soul, and flattering praise, and even a certain amount of innocent spoiling in the way they skilfully humoured a slight greediness which was his favourite shortcoming.[3]　Fortunatus did not forget Italy, but yielded to the powerful attraction which kept him at Poitiers (567) ; besides, his country was at that time invaded by the Lombards.　He became Radegonde's secretary, perhaps her responsible agent (*agens in rebus*), at least occasionally.　He was ordained priest, and in 597 succeeded Bishop Plato in the Episcopal see of Poitiers. Radegonde had already been dead some ten years (13th August, 587).　Fortunatus constituted himself the first biographer of that incomparable woman, *gemma Galliae pretiosissima*, as he described her in his litanies.

His works consist of Lives of saints, hymns and circumstantial poems.[4]

Besides his biography of St Radegonde, he wrote in prose a life of St Albinus, Bishop of Angers († 550 c.), and of St

---

[1] *Carm., Praef.*, § iv.

[2] See R. Aigrain's *Sainte Radegonde* (coll. les Saints), 1918.　An excellent critical account.

[3] The scandal which certain critics, like J. J. Ampère, have experienced over these little mouthfuls which are in fact somewhat frugal, does honour to their own sobriety.　See *Carm.* xi, xvi et s.

[4] There is no serious reason to ascribe to St Radegonde the poem on the devastation of Thuringia and the letter to Artachis (M.G.H., IV, 271 and 278) as proposed by Ch. Nisard (*Rev. Histor.*, 1888, *Le Poète Fortunat*, 1890, chap. iii). Cf. E. Rey, *Rev. de Philol.*, XXX (1906), p. 124 et s.

Hilary of Poitiers († 367), as well as a *Liber de Virtutibus S Hilarii ;* a life of St Germanus of Paris [1] († 575 c.), of St Paternus of Avranches († 565 c.), of St Marcellus of Paris, and of St Severinus of Bordeaux († 482), which last has not been preserved. Historians can find in them much interesting information about the times in which his heroes lived.

The *Life of St Martin,* dedicated to Gregory of Tours, with whom Fortunatus had been in relations since 573, comprises no less than 2243 hexameters, in four books. The poet does little more than embellish the outline drawn by Sulpicius Severus and Paulinus of Périgueux ; [2] moreover he was able to complete his poem in two months.

Partially incorporated in the liturgy of the Catholic Church, his hymns represent the best claim to his moderate reputation, which the mediocrity of his other writings would have only indifferently assured. Fortunatus is the author of the *Agnoscat Omne Caelum* and the *Vexilla Regis Prodeunt,* in acatalectic iambic dimeters and verses of four lines in almost regularly recurring rhyme, and of the *Pange Lingua Gloriosi* in catalectic trochaic tetrameters and verses of three lines. Possibly from among the seven hymns considered as doubtful by modern critics, two or three should also be ascribed to him. [3]

It is in relation to the eleven books of *Carmina,* [4] or *Miscellanea,* together with certain prose writings, that we can best judge his literary ability. Letters, elegies, consolatory addresses, epithalamia, panegyrics of kings, Bishops, important personages, churches, country houses, etc., " toasts," funeral inscriptions (intended to be read rather than engraved), nearly always in elegiacs—the foregoing form

---

[1] See Batiffol's *Etudes de Liturgie et d'Archéologie Chrétienne,* 1919, p. 245 et s. on an *Expositio Liturgiae Gallicanae* attributed to St Germanus of Paris (P.L., LXXII, 83–98).

[2] Book I is the *Vita Martini* to xviii, 3 ; II, the same, to the end of the work ; III, forms the *Dialogues* ii, 1 to 13 ; IV, the *Dial.* iii, 1 to 17.

[3] Dreves (in V.M., 3, 3 [1908]) attributes to him hymns i, vii, viii in the *Appendix spuriorum* of M.G.H.

[4] Note the preface addressed to Gregory. He expresses a modest astonishment that his friend attaches so much importance to these *nugae,* and mentions that he wrote them haphazard in the course of his wanderings in the West (. . . *paene aut equitando aut dormitando conscripserim*). Books I–VIII comprise the poems written up to the year 576 ; Book IX, those of the years 577–584 ; Book X (note at the beginning his explanation of the *Pater*), those of the year 585 ; Book XI and appendix nos. x–xxxi which opens with an *Expositio Symboli* in prose taken from Rufinus, embody the pieces addressed to Radegonde and Agnes. Possibly these two last books may not have been published by Fortunatus himself.

practically the entire subject matter of the collection which
the poet exerted himself to put together at the request of
Gregory of Tours.[1] His social position—very different from
that of Sidonius, Ennodius, and Avitus—and the long-con-
tinued precariousness of his means of existence, had forced
him to flatter abundantly, and of this he made a speciality.
In cases where we can check what he metes out to his protectors we can see the quality of this court homage. He
lauds Chilperic's taste for letters ; now Gregory of Tours
relates that when the king meddled in versification he mixed
up short syllables with long, and did not conform to any
known system of metre.[2] J. J. Ampère[3] speaks in fairly
appreciative terms, though somewhat ill-naturedly, of the
" literary career of Fortunatus, the last of its kind, humble,
traversed, subservient, ever bowing before the conquerors,
but possessed of a kind of childish vanity and pitiful satisfaction." We see, he adds, " his decrepit and mincing muse,
smirking in superannuated coquetry as the barbarian chiefs
passed before him, and paying them his humble reverence
and little pretentious compliments. . . ."

The talent of Fortunatus lay especially in his facility :
he triumphed in poetic improvisation. But his insufficient
education (although he knew Horace, Virgil and some of the
Christian poets) was a poor safeguard against grammatical
irregularities and faults in quantity.[4] He was well aware of
this, in which connection he has made very humble confessions
whose sincerity might be believed more easily if their form
had been less affected.[5] His own shortcomings in no way
discouraged his output, which brought him honour and profit,
and, however mediocre, caused once more a last reflection of
Latin culture to gleam forth among the barbarians whom he
portrays with " their goblet of maple wood in their hands,
drinking health after health, and uttering a thousand follies
calculated to arouse their God Bacchus " (*Carm., Praef.*, § v).

---

[1] *Carm.* IX, i, 99 et s.
[2] *Hist. Franc.*, V, xlv, and VI, xlvi.
[3] *Hist. litt. de la France avant le douzième siècle*, vol. II (1839), p. 350.
[4] See the *Indices* in M.G.H., IV, 389 et s.
[5] *De Vita Mart.*, I, xxvi, 30 et s. ; *Carm.* X, iii, i ; II, ix, 5 et s.

CHAPTER II

WORKS IN PROSE

THE HANDING ON OF THE LEGACY OF ANTIQUITY

BIBLIOGRAPHY

I. FULGENTIUS of RUSPA.—P.L., vol. LXV, reproducing L. Mangeant, Paris, 1684. See notes further on.

II. ST CAESARIUS of ARLES.—P.L., vol. LXVII. Besides the sermons collected in Migne under the name of Caesarius, several appear in vol. XXXIX of the *Patrologie Latine* in the appendix to St Augustine's sermons (the list is drawn up by Paul Lejay in R.H.L.R., 1905, p. 184), and Dom Morin has published six hitherto unpublished sermons in the *R. Bén.*, XIII (1896), p. 97 ; fifteen others, *ibid.*, XVI (1899), pp. 241, 289 and 337.— A portion of the homilies of Caesarius were translated into French in the XVIIIth century by Dujat de Villeneuve, Paris, 1760, 2 vols. A reliable study on the language of Caesarius is wanted ; see Dom Morin's observations in *Mélanges Cabrières*. Later on the writings attributed to Caesarius will be mentioned.

III. BOETHIUS.—The works of Boethius are in P.L., LXIII-LXIV. The *De Consolatione Philosophiae* (523-4) has been edited by Peiper, Leipsic, 1871.—French translation by Oct. Cottreau, Paris, 1889. The *Commentaria in Porphyrium* (506-7) are in C.V., vol. XLVIII (1906, Schepss and Brandt). Special editions of the *De Arithmetica L. Duo* and the five books *De Musica*, by G. Friedlein, in B.T. (1887) ; of the two books *In Librum Aristotelis de Interpretatione*, by C. Meiser, in B.T. (1897-1900) ; of the *Liber de Diffinitione*, by Th. Stangl (*Tulliana et Mario-Victoriniana*, Munich, 1888) : as a matter of fact, this last work is by Marius Victorinus.

IV. CASSIODORUS.—Texts in P.L., vol. LXIX-LXX, reproducing, with certain additions, the Benedictine Garet (Rouen, 1679). The chapter in *Inst. Div.*, relating to grammar figures in Keil's *Gramm. Latini*, VII, 210-216 ; the chapter on rhetoric is in R.L.M., p. 495 et s. Mommsen has given the *Chronicle* in M.G.H., XI (1894), pp. 109-161 ; the *Variae, ibid.*, xii. (1894), in collaboration with Traube.—A *Compendium* of the *Inst. Div.*, going back to the Middle Ages, has been published by Lehmann in the *Philologus*, 1914/1916, pp. 253-273, following the *Vat. Lat.* no. 4955, XIth century.—Translation of the treatise *On the Soul* by Stephane de Rouville, 1874 ; and of the *Historia Tripartita*, by Loys Pianeus, 1568.

V. ST GREGORY of TOURS.—Texts in P.L., LXXI, 161-1118, and in M.G.H., *Scriptores Rerum Meroving.*, vol. I (Arndt. Krusch and Bonnet). The *Liber de Miraculis b. Thomae* was published by Max Bonnet, *Supplem. Codicis Apocryphi*, I (L. 1883), pp. 96-132. — French translation of the *Historia Francorum* by H. Bordier, Paris, 1859-1862 ; by the same, the *Book of the Miracles and the other works of Gregory of Tours*, 4 vols., Paris, 1857-1865 (Société de l'Histoire de France).

VI. ISIDORE of SEVILLE.—The works of Isidore of Seville figure in vols. LXXXI-LXXXIV of Migne, reproducing Arevalo (Rome, 1797-1803). Vol. LXXXI includes interesting data on the life and writings of Isidore.— Special editions of the *De Natura Rerum* by G. Becker, Berlin, 1857 ; of the *Chronica* and the *Historica Gothorum*, by Mommsen, M.G.H., vol. XI (1894) ; of the *Etymologiae* or *Origines*, by W. M. Lindsay, Oxford, 1911 (with useful *Indices*).—Dzialowski, *Isidor u. Ildefons als Literarhistoriker*, Munster i. W., 1898, has amended the text of the *De Vir. Illustribus*, from Arevalo.—The Arevalo-Migne edition is of great value on account of the commentaries which are included.

SUMMARY

I. Fulgentius of Ruspa.—II. St Caesarius of Arles.—III. Boethius, "The First of the Scholastics." — IV. Cassiodorus. — V. St Gregory of Tours. His Hagiographic Works. The *History of the Franks*. Gregory's Learning.—VI. St Isidore of Seville.—VII. Conclusion.

I

THE contention which identifies Claudius Gordianus Fulgentius, Bishop of Ruspa in Byzacene, with the mythologist Fabius Planciades Fulgentius is based on specious reasons, to say the least, drawn either from certain coincidences in their lives, or from certain analogies in their style.[1]

We possess various works by this mythologist,[2] the best known of which is the *Virgiliana Continentia*, wherein the mystical sense attaching to the *Æneid*—taken as a figure representing human life—is elucidated by the methods of allegorical exegesis. The episodes related in the poem are represented as so many veiled lessons suitable to make people love virtue. As regards the Bishop, we know that he was born in 468 at Telepta, in Byzacene, of a Senatorial Carthage family, and that he died in 532. According to his *Life*, written by one of his pupils in 533-534,[3] he knew Greek and also spoke it (§ iv-v). He was exiled to Sardinia by king Thrasamund, together with more than sixty Bishops, and was recalled first in 515, and definitely in 523. A faithful disciple of St Augustine, whose trend of thought he diligently assimilated, he combated Arianism and Semi-Pelagianism in a series of works of which the literary capacity is not always equal to the vigour of his religious views (*Contra*

[1] Cf. O. Friebel, *Fulgentius, der Mytholog und der Bischof* (in the *Studien zur Gesch. u. Kultur des Altertums*, V, 1-2 [1911]), which gives a bibliography of the historical facts connected with the question.

[2] R. Helm's edition, L. 1898. He has made clear the identity of the two Fulgentii with the best arguments (Rh. M., LIV [1899], pp. 111-134).

[3] P.L., LXV, 117-150. Mentioned by Isidore of Seville, *De Vir. Ill.*, xiv.

Arianos ; De Trinitate ad Felicem Notarium ; De Veritate Praedestinationis et Gratiae Dei ad Joannem et Venerium, etc.). Bossuet calls him " the greatest theologian of his time," which does not mean that Fulgentius was an original thinker, but that he had formed a most lucid and sure conception of doctrine from Augustine's writings.

II

CAESARIUS was born in 470 in the district of Chalon-sur-Saône. He joined the clergy at Chalon in 484, was instructed at Arles by the priest-rhetorician Julianus Pomerius,[1] and succeeded Eonius, Bishop of Arles, in 503. On two occasions, in 505 and 513, he incurred the disfavour of Alaric II, and Theodoric, for political reasons. The restoration of the seat of the Primacy of the Gauls to Arles, which he secured from Pope Symmachus (514), still further increased the *prestige* which his personal gifts had won for him. He died on the 27th August 543.[2]

It is not possible to determine the order in which his works were written nor to assign to them any precise dates. We possess a *Regula ad Monachos*[3] of his, and a *Regula ad Virgines*[4] (he founded in his diocese a convent of nuns over which he placed his own sister as Superior) ; four *Epistulae,* and a Testamentum.[5] Various other works are attributed to him.[6] But the best part of his pastoral activity Caesarius

---

[1] Pomerius wrote various works (cf. Gennadius, § xcviii) : his *De Vita Contemplativa* is in Migne, LIX, 415–520.

[2] Noticed in Gennadius, § xcvii. *Vita Caesarii* by his pupil Cyprian of Toulon (P.L., LXVII, 1001–1121, and M.G.H., *Script. rer. Meroving.*, III [1896], 433–501). We have a letter of Cyprian's addressed to Maximus of Geneva (M.G.H., Epist. iii [1892], pp. 434–436).

[3] P.L., LXVII, 1099–1104.

[4] *Ibid.*, 1105–1121. Cf. Dom Leclercq on these *Regulae*, *Dict. d'Archéol. chr. et de Lit.*, art. *Cénobitisme*, col. 3199 et s., and Malnory especially, *Saint Césaire d'Arles*, Paris, 1894. One will notice that one of the articles of the *Rule* of St Caesarius enjoined on the nuns the transcribing of manuscripts.

[5] P.L., LXVII, 1135–1138. The *Testamentum* has been re-edited by Dom Morin, *R. Bén.*, XVI, 1899, p. 100 et s.

[6] (1) A Treatise on the Trinity for the fragments of which we must go to Mai's *Nova Patrum Bibliotheca*, I (Rome, 1852), p. 407 ; Reifferscheid's *Bibl. Patrum Italica*, I, 174, note 5 ; Dom Morin's *Mélanges Cabrières*, I (Paris, 1899), p. 109.— (2) A work against the Semi-Pelagians, published by Dom Morin, R. Bén., XIII (1896), p. 433 et s.—(3) *Capitula Sanctorum Patrum, ibid.*, XXI (1904), 225–239.— On the other hand, Dom Morin disputes the authorship by Caesarius of the *Statuta Ecclesiae Antiqua* (cf. R. Bén., XXX [1913], pp. 334–342), which L. Duchesne and P. Lejay attribute to him.

gave to his sermons.[1] The author of the *Vita Caesarii* informs us that he despatched some copies of them throughout Gaul, Italy and Spain. Critics have succeeded in restoring to him a good number which had been confused under other names, or had remained anonymous, and which certain favourite tricks of style have enabled them to identify.

The form of eloquence shown by Caesarius is familiar and animated, entirely bent upon being practical, even when it touches on what is speculative. He largely utilised his predecessors, the homilists. He copied out sentences or even whole pages from Origen, St Augustine, Fulgentius, and Faustus of Riez, but with adaptations and abridgments, in which he reveals his concern not to disconcert his hearers who for the greater part were uneducated [2] and whose moral sustenance consisted in his sermons, and to only use forms of expression which might be understood by all.

" If I wished to explain the Scriptures in the order and in the language used by the holy Fathers, the food of doctrine could only reach a few learned men, and the rest of the people, the multitude, would remain famished. That is why I humbly beg that the ears of the learned will consent to tolerate unpolished expressions in order that the Lord's flock may receive the celestial food in simple and plain language ; and since the ignorant may not rise to the height of the learned, may the learned deign to descend to the ignorance of their brethren. . . ."

This popular way of speaking revivified the society of that period with all its brutality, vice, and secret and stubborn attachment to pagan practices.[3] The historian would be very wrong to neglect the *Homilies* of Caesarius. As regards

---

[1] Other writers of sermons or letters in his time were Eleutherus, Bishop of Tournai (cf. P.L., LXV, 83–102) ; Remigius, Bishop of Rheims (*ibid.*, LXV, 963–975, and M.G H., *Epist.* iii [1892], pp. 112–116) ; Aurelianus, Bishop of Arles (P.L., LXVIII, 385–408, and M.G.H., *Epist.* iii, 121–126).

[2] Cf. P.L., XXXIX, 2325.

[3] Cf. A. Malnory's *Saint Césaire, Evêque d'Arles*, 1894 ; P. Lejay's *Le Rôle Théologique de Césaire d'Arles*, in R.H.L.R., 1905, pp. 444–487 ; R. Boese's *Superstitiones Aretalenses e Caesario collectae*, Marburg, 1909 (an interesting study which embraces sermons, canons of the Councils, books on penance, etc.). Very significant too, from the point of view of the survival of pagan practices, is the *De Correctione Rusticorum* by Martin of Bracara (Caspari's edition, Christiania, 1883), who was writing in the north of Spain between the years 560 and 580. Martin's writings (P.L., LXXII) are full of reminiscences from Seneca.

his claim to be called a theologian, he will notice the fidelity with which he followed the views of St Augustine on grace. He had however visited Lérins, the old stronghold of Semi-Pelagianism. But it was to the tradition of Prosper and Hilary that he adhered and not to that of Cassian and Faustus of Riez. Moreover, even in Rome Popes Gelasius I (492–496) and Anastasius II (496–498) resolutely favoured Augustine's views and pushed them further on certain points than Augustine himself would have liked to do. The Semi-Pelagian reaction had been greatly checked by the end of the Vth century even in Gaul where not long since it had seemed to be winning the day.

A man of action, preacher, moralist and instructor of the barbarians, Caesarius at the beginning of the Merovingian age was " one of the leaders of the Church in Gaul, one of the founders of her discipline and of any learning she was to retain through two centuries of twilight." [1]

III

The " first of the Scholastics," Anicius Manlius Severinus Boethius belonged to the illustrious *gens* of the *Anicii*, who, in the course of the IVth and Vth centuries had given to the Empire a long series of high officials.[2] They had become Christians in the middle of the IVth century : [3] we shall see that we have no reason to doubt that Boethius was one himself like all his race. Born in the year 480, Boethius entered the service of the Arian king Theodoric. His father had been Consul in 487 ; he himself became Consul in 510, and had the pride of seeing his son promoted to the same dignity in 522.[4] Theodoric readily entrusted him with the most delicate missions. Deep disgrace brutally cut short this brilliant career. For having undertaken the defence of the Senator Albinus who was accused of maintaining secret correspondence with Justin I, the Emperor of the East, Boethius found himself thrown into chains (doubtless at

---

[1] Paul Lejay, in R.H.L R., 1905, p. 137.
[2] P.W., I, 2198 et s. Genealogical table, *ibid.*, p. 2201.
[3] Prudentius, *Contra Symm.*, I, 548 et s. ; Zosimus, VI, vii, 4 ; C.I.L., XIV, 1875.
[4] Cf. the *Variae* of Cassiodorus, II, 40 ; II, 41 ; I, 45.

Pavia). Accused of high treason, and also of magic, he died under torture in 524.

The motives for his condemnation were solely political. Nevertheless he had served the Catholic cause in face of the hostility of his irascible master, and died with admirable resignation. He was included among the martyrs [1] at an early date and honoured as such at Pavia and Brescia.

In spite of the heavy administrative functions whose charge he had assumed, Boethius only lived for things of the mind : " Cum in omnibus philosophiae disciplinis ediscendis atque tractandis summum vitae solamen existimem . . ." : it is with these words that the *De Syllogismo Hypothetico*, one of his treatises, opens, and they sum up wonderfully the rule of his life. After learning Greek at Athens a knowledge of which had become very rare in the West, he assigned himself the task of translating into Latin the whole of Aristotle, and the whole of Plato, of commenting on them, and of showing their fundamental agreement in the majority of the problems of philosophy.[2] In this way he resumed the *rôle* (to the profit of Catholic theology) of interpreter played by Rufinus and St Jerome more than a century before.

He was only able to carry out a small portion of his plan. Those of his works which remain deal with Aristotle as an eminent theorist in logic, and with his commentators and imitators, such as Cicero and Porphyry. Thanks to Boethius the Middle Ages learned how to discourse on the five " universals " and on the " categories," and to construct syllogisms in accordance with the rules laid down by Aristotle ; it was not until much later, at the beginning of the XIIIth century, and through the intermediary of translations from the Arabic, that they came to know the moral and metaphysical works of this philosopher.

Boethius likewise provided the schools with precious manuals in his *Institutio Arithmetica*, wherein he paraphrased the *Introduction to Arithmetic* by Nicomachus of Jerassa, the Pythagorean ; in his *Institutio Musica*, proceeding from the same source, and in his *Geometria*, derived from Euclid.

But his greatest renown rests upon his *Consolations of*

---

[1] Martyrology of Adonius (P.L., CXXIII, 107).
[2] In *Libr. Aristot. de Interpret.*, II, ii, 3 (a leading passage) ; cf. *In Categ.* (P.L., LXIV, 201).

Philosophy, which, as the Abbé Gervaise wrote at the beginning of the XVIIIth century, " has been the delight of all thoughtful minds for twelve centuries, and has been translated into as many different languages as there are races in Europe." With prose and poetry[1] intermingled the work is divided into five books of which the following is the gist.

It opens with a few mournful verses which Boethius wrote in prison " at the dictation of the stricken Muses." Suddenly he seemed to see by his side " a woman of imposing countenance, with eyes full of brilliancy and possessed of wonderful penetration, of bright complexion, and imbued with youthful vigour although she was so full of years that she had all the appearance of belonging to another age." With a few angry words the apparition put to flight the group of the Muses, and then bending over Boethius she dried his eyes dim with tears. Boethius then recognised the companion of his youth and mistress of his life, Philosophy.

She had come to console him. She reminded him of the injustices of which thinkers like Socrates, Anaxagoras, Zeno, Seneca and others, had been the victims, and invited him to lay bare his wounds that she might dress them. Boethius related to her the intrigues under which he had fallen. What they had aimed at was his integrity as an administrator whose uprightness wearied their wicked envy, and as the defender of the Senate which had so ill repaid him its debt of gratitude. In his own personal misfortunes Boethius perceived (and it was this that disconcerted him most) the triumph of injustice, and a serious check inflicted upon the eternal rules of right morality.

To this cry of distress Philosophy replies with calm firmness. She undertakes to reveal to him the fundamental truths wherein his ulcerated soul may find healing.

" It is because thou dost not know what is the last end of things that thou believest in the power and the happiness of wicked men and criminals. It is because thou hast forgotten by what laws the world is governed

---

[1] The same arrangement is found in the Encyclopædia of Martianus Capella, in the Vth century, in Alexander's Greek story revised by Julius Valerius at the beginning of the IVth century, and in the *Satiricon* of Petronius in the Ist century. It has its remote origin in the *Satire* of Menippus.

that thou dost imagine that all these vicissitudes of destiny float about without any direction." [1]

She begins by pouring out for him a first soothing draught (1, II). He grieves over the caprices of Fortune : but was it not the practice of that witch to abandon in an inexplicable manner those on whom she had been lavishing her favours ? Did it count for nothing that he had been loaded with good things by her ? And in his trials did not Boethius still retain a few of them ? [2] Moreover were these benefits, if estimated at their true value, worth the attachment which the generality of men gave to them ? Fortune did better service to mortals when she is contrary to them than when favourable, because she then reveals herself in her true self and frees them from the superstition with which they honour her unduly.

Boethius confesses that he is already somewhat softened and relieved (Book III). But Philosophy holds in reserve a still more efficacious moral therapeutic. She goes back to the quality of the good things pursued after by mankind. Riches, honours, power, glory and pleasure have after all no other value than that which unstable opinion attaches to them. " Not only are they unable of themselves to procure happiness, but they cannot even be considered as the road leading to it." In reality, it is God who is the sole, the sovereign good. It is through Him alone that man can be happy. In him are reconstituted the scattered elements of happiness, on which man lays a greedy hand almost blindly, without knowing that their only value lies in their being brought together in the Divine Unity.

Boethius, although half won over by this persuasive reasoning, still retains a grievous objection (Book IV). How " under the rule of the beneficent Master who governs the world, doth evil pass unpunished or how can it exist ? " Philosophy disposes herself to initiate him into still more lofty problems in order to resolve this difficulty :

---

[1] P.L., LXIII, 654.
[2] " Sed hoc est quod recolentem vehementius coquit. Nam in omni adversitate fortunae infelicissimum genus est infortunii, fuisse felicem," Boethius replies. Dante, who was familiar with the *Consolatio* recollected this passage in the well-known lines, " Nessun maggior dolore, che ricordarsi del tempo felice nella miseria." *Inferno,* V, 119 et s.

" I will fasten wings to thy soul which shall enable it to mount up to higher regions in order that henceforth delivered from all anxiety thou mayst regain safe and sound thine own country under my guidance, by following my paths, and suffering thyself to be borne on by me." [1]

She then enters upon the mysterious question of the nature of good and evil. The good is the opposite of evil : if it be proved that the former possesses power, it is therefore because the latter has none ; and reciprocally, if the powerlessness of evil be demonstrated, the force of good must be recognised. This is the conclusion to which Philosophy leads Boethius by a succession of subtle remarks. Evil is synonymous with *nothing*. In the absolute meaning of the word, wicked men *are not*, since they depart from those very laws which make man what he is by nature destined for.—But, retorts Boethius, they do not persecute the good any less for all that !—Their misfortune is all the greater, and if they rejoice in impunity, it is an added calamity since it perpetuates their iniquity. Philosophy declares that she is not willing to invoke another kind of argument taken from the rewards beyond the grave. She prefers to reply to a fresh question put by Boethius who cannot see how, in the obscure apportionment of good things and misfortunes, God is different from blind chance. She discloses to him the real nature of Providence to whom fate itself is subordinate, being only " the variable and succeeding chain of all those events the working out of which God hath prepared." If happiness and misfortune seem to be distributed without discernment, it is because we are ignorant of the designs by means of which God apportions to each one of us the trials from which we are able to draw our own purification.

What is Chance (Book V) ? Philosophy hesitates over this secondary question. Finally she decides to give a definition of Chance, but in order to pass at once to the essential problem of free will. Liberty was an undoubted truth. Nevertheless it had its degrees :

" The human soul is necessarily more free so far as it is permitted to remain in the contemplation of the Divine

[1] P.L., LXIII, 788.

Intelligence ; it is already less so when it turns its migration in the direction of the body, and still less when it finds itself imprisoned in its wholly material members. But its slavery is extreme when, given up to vice, it forfeits the possession of Reason which is proper to it." [1]

How was liberty to be reconciled with the Divine foreknowledge ? Philosophy scouts certain current solutions of this difficult problem to bring forward another. The knowledge possessed by the Divine Being in no way resembled our own. It soars above the succession of time, and sees, in the simplicity of its cognition, all things as though they were present.

The *Consolatio* has no conclusion. Evidently Boethius had not time to put the last touches to it.

This work seems beforehand to give the lie to Rochefoucauld's ironical maxim : [2] " Philosophy triumphs easily over past and future ills ; but ills that are present triumph over her." Even in the agony of a harsh captivity Boethius was able to free himself from the dejection caused by his own misery in order to raise his eyes to the great problems of the destiny of man. Who cannot admire the strength shown in such an emancipation ? Even to-day the *Consolatio* is read with interest in spite of its certain lack of balance—more evident in the last three books especially—the forerunner of the quibbles dear to the Middle Ages. A compelling and soothing movement carries the discussion to higher and higher altitudes. Boethius gathers together all the lessons of the noble wisdom of antiquity to create from them the substance of his Προτρεπτικός εἰς Θεόν, of his exhortation to turn towards God which is the end and aim of all creatures. Turn by turn we hear echoes of Aristotle, Plato, Seneca, Cicero, also Tibullus and Virgil. Many other reminiscences mingle in the *Consolatio* with no displeasing incongruity because Boethius blends them with skill into a whole which is his special gift.

This idealistic discussion is nowhere based on the Scriptures, and the name of Christ does not appear in it. It was from considerations of the reason alone that Boethius

---

[1] *Ibid.*, 836.
[2] Gilbert's edition, I, p. 39, and especially p. 22.

drew the material for his argument. People have wondered
at this so far as to allege that he was not a Christian.[1] There
is one difficulty nevertheless in accepting this interpretation :
several treatises on Catholic theology under the name of
Boethius have come down to us. Must we then deny his
authorship ? Some critics do not recoil from this excision.
But this hypothesis is shown to be without foundation since
Alfred Holder [2] discovered at the end of a manuscript of the
Xth century coming from Reichenau and belonging to the
library at Karlsruhe, an extract in which Cassiodorus attri-
butes to his kinsman and friend Boethius by name the *De
Sancta Trinitate, Capita Dogmatica*, and the *Liber contra
Nestorium*. The debate is thus closed : Boethius was a
Christian. Let us not compare him, as has Gaston Boissier,[3]
with the Tertullian of the *De Anima*, nor with Minucius
Felix, nor with Ausonius : analogies could be but superficial.
Let us rather compare him, in company with Boissier, this
time more happily inspired, with the St Augustine of the
treatises written at Cassiciacum. However profoundly convinced of the truths of the faith, Boethius recognised the
right which Augustine had claimed not long before, of advancing solutions of the problems dominating life and giving
to it its meaning and proper end, which were purely philosophical but fully compatible with the faith. The Middle
Ages were nowhere shocked at this method. The *Consolatio
Philosophiae* was one of the books on which it was brought
up.[4] We possess some 400 manuscripts [5] of it, and we know
of more than 20 commentaries. These figures are significant,
and from them we are able to estimate the action of this
masterpiece on Western thought.[6]

[1] On this question cf. A. Hilderbrand's *B. und seine Stellung zum Christentum*,
Regensb. 1885 ; G. Boissier, *Journal des Sav.*, 1889, 449.
[2] Cf. Usener's *Anecdoten Holderi, ein Beitrag zur Gesch. Roms in ostgotischer
Zeit*, published in *Festschrift der 32 Philolgenvers, zu Wiesbaden*.
[3] *Journal des Sav.*, 1889, 456.
[4] As regards religious art in particular, see E. Mâle's *l'Art Religieux au XIII*e
siècle, 3rd ed., Paris, 1910, p. 114 et s. ; Bréhier's *l'Art Chrétien*, 1918, p. 284.
[5] There are some views on the manuscripts of Boethius in S.B.W., vol. 144,
pp. 1–8 : Engelbrecht claims that a distinctly conservative criticism should be
reserved for the *Consolatio*. Observations on his style, *ibid.*, pp. 15–26, his syntax
(pp. 16–36), his choice of words (pp. 36–51), his metre (pp. 53–58). F. di Capua
has shown in the *Didaskaleion*, III (1914), pp. 269–303, that Boethius observed the
rules concerning the ending off of sentences with infinite natural good taste.
[6] The question of the sources used in the *Consolatio* deserve to be studied.
According to Usener (Rh. M., XXVIII, 398), Boethius borrowed from Aristotle's
Protrepticos, either directly, or through a translation, the greater portion of books

IV

THE family to which Flavius Magnus Aurelius Cassiodorus belonged was one of those which deemed it wise and politic to place themselves in the service of the barbarian kings as the Roman power declined. His father was Pretorian Prefect at the court of Theodoric. Born at Scylacium (Squillace),[1] on the south-east coast of Italy, Cassiodorus was himself Quaestor (507–511), Consul (514), Governor of Lucania, *Magister Officiorum* and Pretorian Prefect (from 533–536). His *cursus honorum* thus followed its course uninterruptedly during forty years, and under four successive kings, to whom his administrative aptitude and scholarly gifts ˙rendered him indispensable. In 540, he renounced his worldly honours and retired to the monastery of Vivarium.[2] Beyond his desire to render his salvation more sure another preoccupation had decided him upon this retreat. He was concerned at the lack of serious interpreters of Holy Scripture.[3] Already some years previously, in agreement with Pope Agapetus he had thought of founding in Rome a school of Biblical studies [4] similar to that which had been the glory of Alexandria in the days of Clement and Origen, or to the one which was still flourishing at Nisibis in Mesopotamia. The death of Agapetus after only one year of his Pontificate, and unfavourable political circumstances had brought this project to nothing, and he now resumed it in a more modest form at Vivarium. Here he wrote his theological works and died shortly after the year 575 at the age of nearly one hundred.

Even during his life in the world, Cassiodorus had written

II and III, and the beginning of book IV. The two-thirds of the remainder of the work was made up of reminiscences from Aristotle and neo-Platonism. The observations made by E. Kennard Rand (*Harvard Studies in Classical Philology*, XV [1904], pp. 1–28) tend to recognise much more independence in Boethius than Usener supposes. G. A. Muller, *die Trotschrift des Boethius*, Berlin, 1912, insists on the connection between Boethius, and Plato, Aristotle, and Cicero's *Hortensius* (see pp. 40 and 51 for certain significant resemblances to this last work).

[1] There is a fascinating description of Scylacium in the *Variae*, XII, xv.

[2] The *Monasterium Vivariense* took its name from the fish ponds constructed by Cassiodorus, who was then Pretorian Prefect, near his native town (cf. *Variae*, XII, xv, 14). Another habitation, more secluded, was arranged by the monks who desired solitude, on Mount *Castellum* (*Inst.*, I, xxix).

[3] *Inst.*, I, *Praef.*

[4] *Ibid.*

historical works—a Chronicle of the Universe (*Chronica*) from Adam down to the year 519, drawn up at the request of Eutharic, Consul that same year, from the records of Titus Livius, Aufidius Bassus, the Chronicle of Ravenna and that of St Jerome ;[1] a History of the Goths (*de Origine Actibusque Getorum*) written between the years 526 and 533 at the command of Theodoric (the original has been lost and we only get an idea of it from the *Getica of Jordanis*, who made extensive use of it) ;[2] twelve books of *Variae*, or 468 pieces of an official character, worded in a grandiloquent, florid, and unmeaning style, which became the model of the chancelleries of the Middle Ages ; the last in date is of the year 527 ; and a *De Anima* reflecting the ideas of St Augustine and Claudianus Mamertus.

With the assistance of a collaborator, Epiphanus the *scolasticus*, he wrote in his retreat at Vivarium the *Historia Tripartita*, compiled rather carelessly from Socrates, Sozomenes and Theodoret ; and a translation of the *Antiquities of the Jews* by Josephus whom he qualifies with some exaggeration as *paene secundus Livius*. To these we must add the *Complexiones in Psalmos*, a wordy commentary on the Psalms.

The work on which his best reputation rests is the *Institutiones Divinarum et Saecularium Litterarum* in two books.[3] The first treats of spiritual reading, that is to say, the study of the Bible. The purpose of Cassiodorus, to which he desired to incline his monks, was a full understanding of the sacred Books. He taught them that the mere reading of the canonical texts was not sufficient to grasp all their meaning and that profane sciences—geography, grammar, rhetoric, dialectics, and astronomy—powerfully co-operated to this end.[4] He also exhorted them to copy manuscripts of the Scriptures with a care worthy of such a task, renewing

---

[1] On the subsequent fate of this *Chronicle* in the Middle Ages, cf. Paul Lehmann, *Cassiodorstudien*, in *Philologus*, LXXI (1912), pp. 278–281.

[2] The works of Jordanis are in M.G.H., V, 1 (1882, Mommsen). French translation by A. Savagnier, in the Panckoucke collection, vol. LXXI (1842), and in the Nisard collection.

[3] This is the most authentic title according to V. Mortet, R. ph. XXIV (1900), pp. 103–110. The work must have been written about the middle of the VIth century, in 543–4 according to Franz, Ebert and Mortet ; in the years 543–555, according to Mommsen. Lehmann, *Philologus*, 1912, p. 290, does not think that the *Div. Inst.* could have been finished before 551–562.

[4] I, xxv et s. (P.L., LXX, 1139).

the advice which St Martin had previously given to the
cenobites of the monastery at Tours [1] a hundred and fifty
years before, and laid down the prudent limits within which
their fondness for making corrections in the text should be
restrained through respect for the divine Word, even though
the grammar or style should suffer from this forbearance.
A library of books, purchased at great expense and kept
in nine *armaria*, provided them with all the necessary requirements.[2] To those of them who did not feel an aptitude for
literary work he recommended agriculture and gardening,
bringing to their notice the help they would find in the works
of certain specialists of former days, Gargilius Martialis,
Columella, and Aemilianus Macer. The second book of the
Institutiones comprises seven chapters concerned with the
" liberal " arts, whose method and precepts, as represented
by the theorists of antiquity and by certain Christian authors
like St Augustine and Boethius, Cassiodorus reviews.

The *De Orthographia*, written at the age of 93, completes
the *Institutiones* by giving rules for the art of writing and
punctuating correctly.

We have already mentioned, when treating of the preservation of the old learning,[3] how fruitful in initiative
Cassiodorus was. He communicated to his monks a taste
for intellectual work ; he provided them with books and
taught them how to profit by them ; and while co-ordinating
in the exegesis of the Bible the methodical researches to
which he impelled them—the somewhat narrow view previously held by the Fathers of the IVth century—he guarded
against all condemnation of the pagan writers and made many
extracts from them. In this way he founded a tradition of
work and criticism which was to be renewed after him, and
which assures for him the eternal gratitude of Western
civilisation.

In addition, some of his friends under his persuasion
devoted themselves to render in Latin a selection of Greek
works. One of them, Mutianus, translated the *Homilies*
of St John Chrysostom on the Epistle to the Hebrews.[4]

---

[1] Sulp. Severus, *Vita S. Martini*, vii.
[2] For the probable contents of this library, see Olleris, *Cassiodore Conservateur
des livres de l'Antiquité Latine*, 1841, pp. 54–68 ; A. Franz, *M. Aurelius Cassiodorus
Senator*, Breslau, 1872, pp. 80–92.
[3] P. 28.
[4] P.G., LXIII, 237.

Denys the Less attacked a series of Greek writings with special reference to the domain of Canon Law ; [1] Bellator translated Origen's *Homilies ;* [2] Epiphanus the Scholastic took as his share Socrates, Sozomenes, Theodoret, and a compilation of what he thought he recognised (but erroneously) as a Commentary by Didymus on the Catholic Epistles.[3] The translation of the *Hypotyposes* of Clement of Alexandria probably came from this same group of writers [4] of whom Cassiodorus was the soul, and whom he inspired with his own love of work. This is the last time that Greek learning, soon to be consigned to oblivion in the West, excited the zeal of an intellectual *élite*.

V

THE " Father of our History," as Claude Fauchet called him in the XVIth century, was born on the 30th November, probably of the year 538, at Arverna (Clermont-Ferrand). He came from a family of Senatorial rank on the side of his father Florentius and of his mother Armentaria, and was " allied both by birth and piety [5] with all that was most illustrious." He was called Georgius Florentius, but took the name of Gregory in memory of his maternal great-grandfather St Gregory, Bishop of Langres from 506–7 to 539–540. After a pious and studious youth under the direction of his mother, his paternal uncle Gallus, Bishop of Clermont, and Avitus who succeeded Gallus in the same Episcopal See, he went to Tours in 563 in the hope of recovering his health at the tomb of St Martin, and he was not disappointed. He had then just been ordained deacon. Ten years later, in 573, at the age of 35, he was chosen to be Bishop of Tours, the religious centre of Gaul. He devoted himself to his charge with complete abnegation amid innumerable difficulties during the twenty years of his episcopate. " In him we possess an admirable type of the Bishop of the VIth century," wrote Gabriel Monod. " The *rôle* that he played

---

[1] P.L., LXVII.
[2] Cf. Cassiod., *Inst.*, I, vi.
[3] P.G., XXXIX, 1749.
[4] Cf. Cassiod., *Inst.*, I, viii.
[5] Cf. genealogical table drawn up by G. Monod in his *Ét. crit. sur les sources de l'Hist. mérov.*, in the *Recueil de Travaux Originaux ou Traduits Relatifs aux Sciences Historiques,* fasc. 2 (1872), p. 27.

in the events of his time, together with the respect of all his contemporaries by which he was surrounded, and his remarkable intellectual activity joined to his ceaseless practical zeal, disclose in him an intelligence superior to the times in which he lived however much, in his humility, he pretended the contrary. But it is his character which commands our respect. . . . A Bishop devoted to the interests of his diocese and those of the whole Catholic Church, he drew from his faith an intrepid courage to withstand the acts of violence and injustice committed by the barbarians, and a moral nobility and a spirit of charity and disinterestedness which rightly won for him the title of Saint. He was a perfect representative of the Church which alone in the world at that time represented intellect and morality." [1]

Gregory died on the 17th November 593 or 594.

His work as a hagiographer [2] is full of curious features. From nowhere else can lovers of folk-lore draw more abundant material. The miraculous, of course, has the first place, because Gregory aimed at edification before all things, and because in the eyes of his somewhat rough public these strong methods appeared much more compelling than theological arguments. He himself thought likewise. He built up rather a strange conception of the power of miracles (*virtus*), an emanation of the Infinite *Virtus* and liked to describe their beneficent or terrifying effects. One quotation will suffice :

> " The tomb (of St Peter) placed beneath the altar (of the church in the Vatican) is a most rare piece of work. He who would offer prayers at it opens the *grille* surrounding it, approaches the sepulchre, and passing his head through a small window in it, asks what he has need of ; his prayers are granted immediately provided only that they be lawful. Should he wish to take back some relic from the tomb, he casts upon it a piece of cloth which he has first weighed, then with vigils and fasting he prays fervently that the

---

[1] *Ibid.*, p. 142.

[2] The *Septem Libri Miraculorum* comprise the *In Gloria Martyrum* (written in 590), the *De Virtutibus S. Juliani* (between 581 and 587), the four books *De Virtutibus Martini* (I and II, written between 574 and 581 ; III in 587 ; IV between 591 and 593). The first six books were touched up afterwards by Gregory.

power of the Apostle will deign to grant his wish. If the faith of one acting thus be sufficient, the cloth, when he has taken it from the tomb, is so filled with divine power that it weighs much heavier than before." [1]

" This page," remarks H. Delehaye, the Bollandist, " has a very legendary colouring, and it is difficult to persuade oneself that the strange experience of weighing was ever put to the proof. But what can be said of the state of mind of a man who does not hesitate to recount anecdotes like these ? " [2] Gregory was living in the VIth century, and we must not expect from him a critical mistrust which did not exist in his times. The flowers of pious expression sometimes found in his *Lives* of the Saints have at least original freshness and charm.

Gregory, from his character and inner disposition, was the most loyal of historians. It is this very candour which gives so much value to his *History of the Franks*, especially in regard to events which he personally records.[3] The first four books which go down to the death of Sigebert (575), form one complete whole and end in a chronological summary. In the first book he gives a history of the world from Adam down to the death of St Martin (397), based on the Bible, St Jerome, Orosius, the Martyrologies, etc. Beginning with the second book, he unfolds the history of the Frankish kings, luxurious, brutal, and good from caprice or under the influence of Heaven. From the fifth book, his work assumes the character of personal memoirs, which are those of a well-informed observer. Gregory nourished a vigorous hatred against the enemies of the Church, but as he quotes his facts conscientiously, the impartiality of his account enables us to rectify the partiality of some of his judgments. As for the " phlegm " with which he has been sometimes reproached,[4] is it not preferable that he should

---

[1] *De Gloria M.*, I, xxviii.

[2] *Les Origines du Culte des Martyrs*, Brussels, 1912, p. 142. Other texts are noticed by Hébert, R.E.A., XVIII (1916), pp. 123–141. See also A. Marignan's *Etudes sur la Civilisation Française*, vol. I, *La Société Mérovingienne ;* vol. II, *Le Culte des Saints sous les Mérovingiens*, 1899.

[3] Cf. a list of these events in Monod, *op. cit.*, p. 105. For Gregory's sources, *ibid.*, p. 73 et s. Books I–IV of the *Historia Francorum* were written in 575 ; V–VI, in 580–585 ; VII–X, § 30 in 585–591, and § 31 of book X, in 594.

[4] Ampère, *Hist. Litt.*, II, 300–301.

have maintained it amid all the horrors which he relates, rather than weary the reader with repeated outbursts of indignation ?

The *De Cursibus Ecclesiasticis*, written between the years 575 and 582, enumerates in succession the seven wonders of the world (the foremost, according to Gregory, was Noah's Ark), and then the seven marvels wrought by God (the tides, the germination of plants and fruits, the phœnix, Mount Etna, the fountain at Grenoble, the sun and the moon). Gregory is thus led to give some indications on the movement of the stars. He gives his purpose in the following words :

> " I do not instruct in science, and I do not aim at sounding the future, but I will show how the course of the day should be filled logically with the praises of God, *that is to say, at what hours he who desires to pursue with diligence the service of God should rise during the night to pray.*"

Modern opinions differ somewhat on the question of Gregory's " learning." Let us hear him defining his abilities with his customary ingenuousness : [1]

> " The cities of Gaul allowed the cultivation of literature to decline, or rather to perish. . . . Not one man could be found who, as a grammarian versed in dialectics, was able to depict (the events of the time) either in the language of prose or that of verse. The greater portion often bewailed this and said : ' Woe upon our times, for the study of letters hath perished from among us, and no one in the whole world can be found to tell us by his writings what is happening in our days ! ' Pondering over these laments . . . , I could not keep silent, in my uncouth style, either upon the strife of the wicked or the lives of the good, attracted especially by that saying which hath often struck me among our people when I heard it, that ' very few understand a rhetorician when he offers a dissertation, but many, an ignorant man when he speaks (*philosophantem rhetorem intelligunt pauci, loquentem rusticum multi*).' "

[1] *Hist. Franc., Prœmium.*

And again :

"Although these books be written in an unpolished style (*stilo rusticiori*), I conjure nevertheless all the priests of the Lord who shall rule over the Church at Tours after me, who am unworthy, never to cause them to be destroyed. . . ." [1]

"I fear," he confesses elsewhere,[2] "that if I undertake to write, people will say to me ; 'Dost thou think, ignorant man that thou art, who hast not the calling thereof (*O rustice et idiota*), to place thy name among those of the writers ; or dost thou hope to gain acceptance by the competent of this work of thine, void of grace and of art, and lacking all knowledge of style ? Thou, who hast no practice in letters, who knowest not how to distinguish the nouns, who often takest the masculine for feminine, the feminine for neuter, and in place of the neuter dost use the masculine ; who canst not even employ the prepositions [3] as is suitable, the proper use of which hath been regulated by the most illustrious authors, since thou dost place them on occasions which require the accusative before words in the ablative, and inversely ; dost thou think that people will not see that it is a case of a slow heavy ox trying to play in the *palaestrum*, or of a sluggish ass endeavouring to flit across the court of players at ball ?' Nevertheless, I will make reply, 'It is for you that I labour, and thanks to my rusticity (*per meam rusticitatem*), you will be enabled to exercise your knowledge.' . . ."

Critics like Ozanam,[4] and even Fustel de Coulanges,[5] agree in seeing in these apologies only a half sincere affectation of modesty, or only an echo of that long tradition which liked every ecclesiastical writer to oppose his *rusticitas*, solely desirous of the truth, to the inflated, cadenced and

---

[1] H.F., X, xxxi. See the whole of the end of the chapter.
[2] *De Gloria Conf., Prooemium.* See also the *Preface* to the *Vita Martini*, and *passim* (M.G.H., p. 33, 12 ; 668, 27, etc.).
[3] According to a computation by Max Bonnet in his *Le Latin de Grégoire de Tours*, 1890, p. 522, Gregory makes about 20 per cent. of mistakes in his use of his prepositions.
[4] *La Civil. Chrét. chez les Francs*, 1872, p. 479.
[5] *La Monarchie Franque*, 1888, pp. 2–3.

frivolous language of the rhetoricians.   Ozanam found Gregory
" *tout pénétré d'antiquité.*"   This was coming to too quick
a conclusion.   Gregory knew Virgil [1] rather well ; he quotes
two passages from Sallust ; [2] he speaks of Pliny, Aulus Gellius, [3]
Cicero [4] and the Theodosian Code, [5] but there is nothing to
show that he had read them.   This is all that his alleged
impregnation with profane learning comes to.   Besides,
does he not himself say that he had been drawn exclusively
towards sacred literature ? [6]   As regards his language, the
ample work of Max Bonnet provides us with all the elements
of a practical appreciation.   " The extremely rich vocabulary
of Gregory," the eminent philologist writes, [7] " owes its
abundance, after preserving an immense majority of the old
words, not only to his use of expressions borrowed from all
the different varieties of Latin, Greek, and sometimes the
languages of the barbarians, but especially to his adoption of
new preferences which are very diverse and often very
unexpected.   Briefly, the inflections were preserved.   However, some breaches were made in them, both by alterations
in sound which naturally extend to all, and by false analogies
which only show themselves very capriciously.   One word will
follow ten times the old inflection, and at the eleventh he
will confuse it in a new rendering, led away by some kind
of resemblance.   His syntax and vocabulary are furthest
removed from classic Latin.   *There is hardly one line that one
could pass as having been written at the good period.*   His
tendencies and methods of style are those of a self-taught
man anxious to do like the professional writers, but who feels
his powerlessness to imitate them.   Time after time he
strives after this, and then gives it up.   From this results
a strange contrast between worn-out forms of eloquence
and a fresh and rugged originality ! "

Taken as a whole, we have reason to believe that the
declarations of Gregory were sincere.   He had a profound and
sorrowful feeling of his literary insufficiency, and it was well
founded.   It was a scrupulosity which did him honour,

---

[1] Numerous instances are noticed by Karl Sittl, A.L.L., VI, 560.
[2] H.F., IV, xiii ; VII, i.
[3] *Vitae Patr., Proœm.*
[4] *Gloria Conf., Proœm.*
[5] H.F., IV, xlvii.
[6] *Vitae Patr.,* ii.
[7] *Op. cit.,* p. 751.

as it proves that having had a glimpse of some few classics or imitators of the classics, Gregory understood his shortcomings, and regretted that his early bringing up had not enabled him to repair them. It remains to be said that modern readers find a charm in this *naïveté* which did not exclude the language of rhetoric, but was incapable of sustaining the effort for long, and which preserved him throughout from those *finesses* of the *littérateur* in an age when imitation of the old writers was so rapidly degenerating into a perverted taste. What could he not have given us if he had known how to " develop " (*dilatare, extendere*) and " embellish " his writings (*ornare paginam*),[1] instead of having left this perilous task to more skilful hands, as he regretted ?

VI

A WRITER who undertook to-day to treat single-handed of theology, heresiology, polemics, chronology, history, biography, symbolism, law, the liturgy, grammar, etymology, cosmography, natural history, mineralogy, ethnology, agriculture, and the arts of building, clothes and cooking, would have hard work to make himself taken seriously. The Middle Ages, which did not always distinguish very clearly between real knowledge and compilation, nevertheless celebrated Isidore of Seville as the embodiment of the *doctor egregius*. If they mistrusted the quality of Isidore's vast range of knowledge at least they had good reason to feel very grateful to the laborious excerptor who did not spare any pains in collecting and handing on to future generations the positive information he had culled in the course of his immense reading. Far less original than Boethius whom on more than one occasion he has utilised, Isidore fulfilled an analogous *rôle* in a much more varied domain. He provided for later centuries a useful *summa* of the science of antiquity the results of which he condensed in his manuals. Not that he was particularly favourable to Greco-Latin learning. He counselled his monks against the reading of " gentile "[2] books. But, without ignoring the danger of profane literature, he loved it for its own sake, and flattered himself with

---

[1] *Vita M.*, II, Pref.

[2] *Regula Monach.*, viii, 3 (P.L., LXXXIII, 877): " Gentilium libros vel haereticorum volumina monachus legere caveat."

having drawn therefrom valuable material for the elucidation of the sacred Books.

Isidore was born in the year 570 of a family belonging originally to Carthage, who had migrated to Seville, doubtless after the destruction of Carthage in 552. He was brought up by his brother Leander, one or two of whose works we have,[1] and who became Bishop of Seville, the chief city of Betica, in 576. Isidore succeeded him twenty-five years later and died on the 4th April 636. His biographers highly praise his character and piety. He also held a certain place in the religious history of his time. It was he who presided at the fourth national Council at Toledo held in December 633. He read continuously, pen in hand, extending his investigations far beyond the circle of Christian authors to profane writers and scholiasts, and copied out everything that seemed to him worthy of interest, without troubling himself to indicate the sources upon which he had drawn.[2]

His master work was the *Etymologiae* or *Origines*, a veritable encyclopædia of human knowledge, which his friend Braulio, the Bishop of Saragossa,[3] received from his hands unfinished, and divided it into twenty books, after having made perhaps a few corrections : I. Grammar ; II. Rhetoric and Dialectic ; III. The four mathematical disciplines (Arithmetic, Geometry, Music, Astronomy) ; IV. Medicine ; V. The Laws and the Times ; VI. The Ecclesiastical Books and Offices ; VII. God, the Angels, the Faithful ; VIII. The Church and the Sects ; IX. Tongues, Nations, Kingdoms, the Army, the Citizens, and Parents ; X. Etymological Lists ; XI. Men and Monsters ; XII. The Animals ; XIII. The Universe and its Divisions ; XIV. The Earth and its Parts ; XV. Buildings and the Fields ; XVI. Stones and Metals ; XVII. Rural Matters ; XVIII. War and Games ; XIX. Ships, Buildings and Clothes ; XX. Food and Domestic and Agricultural Utensils. Isidore himself confesses that

---

[1] A *De Institutione Virginum et Contemptu Mundi* and a *Homilia de Triumpho Ecclesiae ob Conversionem Gothorum* : P.L., LXXII, 873–898.

[2] There have been numerous works in recent years on the sources used by Isidore : Manitius, G.L.L.M., p. 62 et s. ; H. Philipp, *die histor. u. geogr. Quellen n den Etymologiae des Is. v. Sev.*, Berlin, 1913 ; O. Probst, *Isidors Schrift de medicina,* taken from the *Archiv. fur Geschichte der Medizin*, VIII, i (1916) ; P. Lehmann, *Kassiodorstudien* (*Philologus*, vol. 71 [1912] and 72 [1913]) ; P. Wessner, *Isidor und Sueton* (*Hermes*, 1917, pp. 201–300).

[3] Some writings of Braulio are included in Migne, vol. LXXX.

he has hardly done more than put together notes which he had culled from the " Ancients " : " En tibi, sicut pollicitus sum, misi opus de origine quarundam rerum *ex veteris lectionis recordatione collectum* atque ita in quibusdam adnotatum *sicut extat conscriptum stilo majorum*." [1] But a twofold purpose dominates this collection of extracts which are sometimes lengthened to prolixity, but more often are condensed to the extent of dryness. The leading idea is that in order to study deeply any science, the etymology of the words used must be understood accurately : " Etymology," he declares, " is the knowledge of the origin of words when we explain by the reason the value of a verb or a noun. Aristotle called this σύμβολον, Cicero *annotatio*. Thus the word *flumen* takes its form from *fluendo*, because the *fluvius* increases by flowing. The very name of this science makes us realise its utility and necessity. For when we see whence a noun has issued, we can more quickly understand its value." [2] The greater part of the etymology advanced by Isidore is arbitrary,[3] but not more so than that furnished by Plato in the *Cratyle* or the learned Varro in his works on grammar. The other purpose animating Isidore was to turn into edification details which at first sight seem the least capable of lending themselves to it. He even speculates on the letters of the alphabet and gives them a mystic sense. In this, too, he was only continuing a far more ancient tradition.

In addition to the *Etymologiae*, we must mention the *De Natura Rerum* dedicated to King Sisefuth. It is a kind of cosmography in which theology has its place. Thus at the end of § xxvii Isidore asks himself what will happen to the stars at the Resurrection if they really have souls. Already in his dialectical arguments there is that imperturbable confidence which was to encourage the Middle Ages to discuss minutely the most inaccessible questions. The *Chronicle*, in two parts, goes from the beginning of the world to the year

---

[1] *Ep.* vi ad Braulionem.
[2] *Etym.* I, xxviii.
[3] *Segnis*, without spirit, without fire, according to him should come from *sine igne ; amicus*, from *hamus* a clamp, a friend being one on to whom one clamps oneself ; *pectus* is the part covered with hairs (*pexus*) between the two breasts ; *avis* from *avia*, because the bird flies hither and thither where there is no road, etc. Isidore fairly often uses Greek words. Certain blunders make one think that he could not have been very familiar with that language (*e.g.* III, xxi, 6).

615 ; following the example of St Augustine, he divides the history of the universe into six periods, corresponding to the six days of the Creation. The *De Viris Illustribus*, in which probably he was not the only one to have a hand, provides a useful supplement to similar works by St Jerome and Gennadius. His *Historiae* open with a eulogy of Spain which is celebrated.

This great worker of no critical ability or method exercised an immense influence. To form some idea of the prodigious and widespread diffusion of the *Etymologiae* in the Middle Ages, one must read the *Isidor Studien* by Ch. H. Beeson,[1] in which he has grouped together all the *non-Spanish* manuscripts up to the IXth century which he could trace, and gives a list of them by their countries. This simple list is instructive by itself and gives evidence of Isidore's brilliant reputation. It was in France that his knowledge was first received with special acclamation ; but a great number of manuscripts of his works also came from Ireland, and we know the important *rôle* played by Ireland in the development of education in the Middle Ages.

VII

AFTER Boethius, Cassiodorus and Isidore of Seville, the framework of the intellectual life of the Middle Ages was established for a long time. A natural line of demarcation at this point closes the history of Latin Christian Literature.

I believe I have not over-estimated its merits. I have not concealed the fact that really finished literary authors are rare. With his vibrating sensibility and warm imagination St Augustine possessed that quality : a life of practical action held him at an early stage, and it is only occasionally that we find in his polemical or exegetic writings pages to equal certain wonderful chapters in his *Confessions*. St Jerome too could have been a master of style had he so wished, as is sufficiently shown by his letters; but he subjected and

---

[1] In the *Quellen und Unters. zur lat. Philologie des Mittelalters*, IV, 2 (1913). At the end of his work, basing them on some fifteen manuscripts Beeson published several *tituli* in verse which he is inclined to attribute to Isidore on the formal testimony of the written tradition, in spite of the contrary opinion of Ebert and the doubts of Manitius. These short pieces have otherwise very slight interest.

sacrificed himself to his labours on the Scriptures. We must not forget Tertullian when stirred by passion, although he is half spoilt by his own subtilty. In the case of all of them, rhetorical phraseology did their works much harm in the sense that their efforts to write cleverly were satisfied by the traditional methods it enjoined on them, and, owing to religious scruples, or to errors of taste, it too rarely sought after a choicer originality. The Christian poetry cannot bear comparison with the pagan. It produced no epic poet of any great breadth of vision, no dramatic poet, not even a fabulist ; a few passably happy lyrical poems and a few beautiful church hymns form the only productions which will really live.

But let us guard ourselves against a certain rather rigid type of " humanism " which would only judge the Christian writings from the point of view of the classic ideal. When we recognise in the profane writers a more marked diversity of tone and subject, and a more sustained perfection, ought this concession in any way to militate against the admiration with which the Christian writers inspire us ? [1]

Whatever be its defects, this vivid Latin Christian Literature deserves to be more carefully studied than appears to be generally the case, and whoever is interested in the history of ideas will not regret having made the effort. There are numerous historical and literary problems which can only be grasped fully after we have seen their factors coming to light during the period we have just traversed. And again, how many strong personalities are revealed, how many magnificent minds and pathetic souls anxious for the destiny of mankind, each one preserving, in spite of the community of their faith and the identity of its theoretic solutions, their original action upon this eternal enigma ! On the day when our Higher Course of Studies shall have taken a more generous interest in some of their masterpieces, scholarly research will again turn in the direction of patristic study, and we shall then be on the road to win back our former hegemony in this domain of which a prolonged lack of interest has dispossessed us.

---

[1] Remy de Gourmont, who does not shrink from giving a paradoxical form to ideas that are otherwise correct, writes : " The Latin Church is, we think, rather more attractive than that of Horace, and the soul of the ascetics more rich in ideals than that of the *egotistical and sly* (*sic*) *old victim to gout.*" (*Le Latin Mystique*, 1913, p. 5.)

TABLES REPRESENTING
LATIN CHRISTIAN LITERATURE

N.B.—Table I will enable the reader to obtain a synoptic view of Latin Christian Literature and to appraise (1) the contribution of each province in the Roman West; and (2) side by side, the contribution of contemporary Greek Christian Literature, and Latin and Greek Profane Literature. In the tables following, the classification of the works varies with the authors. In cases where the chronological order is sufficiently established and has special value (as for instance as regards St Augustine) this order has been adhered to. In other cases, I have preferred to classify by the matter, or even alphabetically.

TABLE I

General View of Latin Christian Literature

ROMAN EMPERORS	LATIN CHRISTIAN LITERATURE					PRINCIPAL CONTEMPORARY GREEK CHRISTIAN WRITERS	CONTEMPORARY PROFANE LITERATURE	
	ITALY	AFRICA	SPAIN	GAUL	ILLYRIA		GREEK	LATIN
100 Trajan (98-117) .						Ignatius of Antioch, Polycarp of Smyrna	Plutarch (c. 46-125)	Pliny the Younger, Tacitus (c. 55-120) Juvenal (c. 60-130) Suetonius (c. 75-160)
117. Hadrian						Papias of Hierapolis	Arrianus	Justin Gaius (110-180 ?)
138. Antoninus Pius						Aristides, Hegesippus, Aristo of Pella, St Justin		Frontonius (c. 90-168)
161. Marcus Aurelius 161-9. Lucius Verus . .		First Latin versions of the Bible (?)						Apuleius (c. 125 ?)
180. Commodus .		Acta of the condemnation of the martyrs of Scillium				Tatian, Athenagoras, the letter concerning the martyrs of Lyons (177), Theophilus of Antioch, St Irenaeus	Lucian (c. 125-190)	
193. Pertinax .						Epistle to Diognetes (?) Pantaenus, Clement of Alexandria (c. 160-215)		
193. Julianus . 193. Septimus Severus . .		First writings of Tertullian : the Apologeticum (197)						
200	Fragment of Muratori					Homilies of Clément		

Chronological table (rotated on page). Columns of authors/events aligned against the list of emperors and dates.

Emperors / Dates	Latin Christian writers	Juvencus	Gaul / Itineraries	Victorinus	Greek Christian writers	Greek writers	Latin historians
211. Caracalla					Origen (185-254), Inscription of Abercius, Julius the African	Philostratus, Dion Cassius	
217. Macrinus 218. Heliogabalus 222. Alexander Severus 238. Maximin Military Anarchy	Death of Tertullian (?) Minucius Felix						
250 Decius (249-251)	Novatian St Cyprian, Firmilian of Cesarea, Commodian (?)				St Gregory Thaumaturgus		
251. Gallus 253. Æmilianus					Denys of Alexandria		
253. Valerian and Gallienus					Oracula Sibyllina	Plotinus (204-270)	
268. Claudius II.					Theognostis		
270. Aurelian 275. Tacitus 276. Florianus 276. Probus 282. Carus						Longinus (c. 220-273) Porphyry (233-c. 301/5)	Spartianus, Capitolinus, Vulcatius Gallicanus Trebellius Pollio
283. Carinus and Numerianus 284. Diocletian (286) Maximian	Arnobius			Victorinus de Pettau	Pierius	Heliodorus	Vopiscus, Lampadius
305. Constantius 306. Constantine	Lactantius		Reticius of Autun, Itinerarium Burdigalense		S. Pamphilius, S. Méthodius of Olympia		
313. (Edict of Milan)	Donatus the Great						
Constantine (306)-337		Juvencus			Eusebius of Cesarea	Philostratus	Compilation of the History of Augustus

S*

TABLE I—*contd.*
General View of Latin Christian Literature

Roman Emperors	Latin Christian Literature					Principal Contemporary Greek Christian Writers	Contemporary Profane Literature	
	Italy	Africa	Spain	Gaul	Illyria		Greek	Latin
337. Constans, Constantius II	Firmicus Maternus (Sicily)	Marius Victorinus	Hosius of Cordova	St Hilary of Poitiers		Saint Athanasius		
361. Julian	Proba, Lucifer of Calaris (Sardinia) Eusebius of Vercelli		Pacian of Barcelona Gregory of Elvira	Phebadius of Agen		Saint Gregory of Nazianzen (c. 330-c. 390)	Libanius	Aurelius Victor, Eutropius
363. Jovian		Zéno Bishop of Verona				Apollinaris of Laodicea	Themistius Himerius	
423. John 425. Valentinian III				Orientius, Hilary of Arles, Evagrius, Prosper of Aquitaine		S. Cyril of Alexandria (c. 380-444) Socrates Sozomenes		
455. Petronius	Sedulius, Leo the Great, Arnobius the Younger			Faustus of Riez, Vincent of Lerins, Salvianus		Theodoret (386-c. 458) Basil of Seleucia	Proclus	Nicomachus Flavianus
455. Avitus 457. Majorianus 461. Libius Severus 467. Anthemius				Gennadius of Marseilles, Claudianus Mamertus, Sidonius Apollinaris				Nicomachus Dexter
472. Olybrius								

Date								
473. Glycerius								
474. Julius Nepos								
475. Romulus Augustulus								
Goth Kings								
476. Odoacer		Dracontius Victor of Vita		Avitus of Vienne		Gelasius of Cyzicus	Stobaeus	Asterius
493. Theodoric							Procopius of Gaza	
500	Boethius, Cassiodorus St Benedict	Eugippius Fulgentius of Ruspa		The poet Cyprian, Ennodius, St Cesarius of Arles	Denys the Little			Priscian
526. Athalaric						Justinian, Denys the Areopagite	Closing of the schools of Athens (529)	Vettius Agorius Mavortius
534. Theodahad	Victor of Capua Arator	Facundus of Hermianum						
536. Vitiges								
541. Totila								
550.	Collectio Avellana, Venantius Fortunatus				Jordanis	Cyril of Scythopolis		
560.						John Malalas		Maximianus
570.				S. Gregory of Tours				
580.								
590.	St Gregory the Great		St Isidore of Seville			Evagrius the Scholiast		
600								

TABLE II

TERTULLIAN	DATES [1]	EDITIONS			FRENCH TRANSLATIONS
		MIGNE	CORPUS SCR. ECCL. LAT.	VARIOUS	
1. de Anima	208/211	2, 687-798	20, 298	EHLER, L., 1851/4 / 2, 553	DE GENOUDE, Paris, 1852 / 2, 1
2. Apologeticum	end of 197	1, 305-604	"	1, 111; RAUSCHEN, in F.P. (1916); MAYOR, Camb. 1917	—, 251 / WALTZING, Liége, 1919
3. de Baptismo	200/206	1, 1305-1334	20, 201	1, 619; RAUSCHEN, in F.P. (1912); LUPTON, in C P. T. (1908)	3, 239
4. de Corona	211	2, 93-122	"	1, 415	2, 130
5. de Carne Christi	208/211	2, 797-838	"	2, 423	1, 389
6. de Cultu feminarum lib. II	200/206	1, 1417-1448	"	1, 701	3, 305
7. de Exhortatione Castitatis	208/211	2, 963-978	"	1, 737	—, 357
8. de Fuga	213	2, 123-142	47, 126	1, 461	2, 423
9. adversus Hermogenem	200/206	2, 219-264	20, 30	2, 337	3, 51
10. de Idololatria	211/212	1, 737-774		1, 67	2, 217
11. de Jejunio	after 213	2, 1003-1030	—, 274	1, 851	3, 377
12. adversus Judaeos	200/206	2, 633-682	"	2, 699	—, 1
13. adversus Marcionem l. V	207/8 [3]	2, 263-556	"	2, 45	1, 1
14. ad Martyras	Jan.-Feb. 197	1, 691-702	"	1, 3	2, 449
15. de Monogamia	after 213	2, 979-1004	"	1, 761	3, 409
16. ad Nationes l. II	after Feb. 197	1, 629-680	20, 59	1, 306	2, 465
17. de Oratione	200/206	1, 1243-1304	—, 180	1, 553	3, 263
18. de Pallio	209	2, 1083-1106	"	1, 913	2, 153
19. de Poenitentia	200/206	1, 1333-1360	"	1, 643	2, 197; P. de Labriolle, in H.L. (1906)

	Date				
20. de Patientia	do.	1, 1359-1386	47, 1	1, 587	2, 173
21. de Praescriptione	about 200	2, 9-92	,,	2, 1	2, 343 ; P. de Labriolle in H.L. (1907)
22. adversus Praxean	after 213	2, 175-220	—, 227	2, 651	3, 177
23. de Pudicitia	217/222	2, 1029-1084	20, 219	1, 791	3, 443 ; P. de Labriolle, in H.L. (1906)
24. de Resurrectione carnis . .	208/211	2, 837-934	47, 25	2, 465	1, 435
25. ad Scapulam	212	1, 773-784	,,	1, 539	2, 457
26. Scorpiace	221/2	2, 143-176	20, 144	1, 495	3, 137
27. de Spectaculis	about 200	1, 701-738	—, 1	1, 17	2, 391
28. de Testimonio animae . .	197/200	1, 681-692	—, 134	1, 399	—, 117
29. ad Uxorem	200/206	1, 1385-1418	47, ,,	1, 669	3, 333
30. adversus Valentinianos . .	208/211	1, 559-632	47, 177	1, 381	—, 103
31. de Virginibus velandis (4) .	208/211	2, 935-962	,,	1, 883	—, 277

(1) The dates given above are taken from Monceaux's *Rev. de Philologie*, XXII (1893), p. 77-92 (cf. *Hist. Litt. de l'Afrique chrét.*, I, 256-296). We may compare those suggested in Harnack's *Chronol.*, II (1904), 256-296, and by K. Adam in *Der Katholik*, XXXVII (1908), 341-370, 416-434. There are no important divergences except in the case of No. 10 (Harnack giving 198-202/3) ; No. 11 (Harnack, shortly after 217/18 ; Adam, after 217) ; No. 15 (Harnack, 217-221 ; Adam, about 220) ; No. 27 (Adam, shortly before 197).

(2) Many portions are translated in Turmel's *Tertullian* (1905).

(3) This work has appeared in several editions. See page 86.

(4) Treatises lost : adv. Apelleiacos (cf. de Carne Christi, 8) ; de Aaron Vestibus (cf. saint Jerome, *Ep.*, 64, 23) ; de Aaron Submissione (mentioned in the index to the *Agobardinus*) ; de Carne et Anima (*ibid.*) ; de Censu animae adv. Hermogenem (cf. de Anima, I ; 11 ; 21) ; de Ecstasi (in Greek) ; de Fato (cf. de Anima, 20) ; Liber ad Amicum philosophum (cf. Saint Jerome, *Ep.* 22 ,22 ; adv. Jovinianum 1, 13) ; de Paradiso (cf. adv. Marcionem V, 12 ; de Anima, 55) ; de Spe fidelium (cf. adv. Marc. III, 24 ; Saint Jerome in Ezech. 36 [P.L., 25, 339]) ; de Superstitione Saeculi (mentioned in the index to the *Agobardinus*).

TABLE III

SAINT CYPRIAN	DATES	EDITIONS			FRENCH TRANSLATIONS
		MIGNE	CORPUS SCR. ECCL. LAT.	VARIOUS	
1. Epistulae	248/9-258	**4**, 191-438	**3**, 2, p. 465	"	DE GENOUDE (1) 5bis, p. 30-334
2. ad Donatum	246	—, 192-223	—, 1, p. 3	LÉONARD (2) ; KRABINGER (3)	— 19
3. de Habitu Virginum . .	249	—, 440-464	—, 187	KRABINGER (4)	— 337
4. de Lapsis	251	—, 465-494	—, 237	ID. (ibid.)	— 353
5. de catholicae Ecclesiae unitate .	2nd half 251	—, 495-520	—, 209	"	— 378
6. de dominica Oratione . .	251/2	—, 519-544	—, 267	"	— 397
7. ad Demetrianum . . .	251/2	—, 544-564	—, 351	LÉONARD (2)	— 422
8. de Mortalitate . . .	252/6	—, 583-602	—, 297	ID. ; KRABINGER (5)	— 447
9. de Opere et Eleemosynis .	252/6	—, 601-622	—, 373	KRABINGER (3)	— 463
10. de Bono patientiae . .	begun 256	—, 622-638	—, 397	ID.	— 483
11. de Zelo et livore . .	256/7	—, 638-652	—, 419	ID. ; GASSNER (6)	— 501
12. ad Fortunatum . . .	257	—, 651-676	—, 317	"	— 513
13. ad Quirinum (Testimoniorum libri III)	before 249	—, 675-780	—, 35	"	— 538
14. Quod idola dii non sint . .	date uncertain	—, 564-582	—, 19	"	— 440
APOCRYPHA					
1. de laude Martyrii . .	252/3 (7) 249/250 (8)	—, 787-804	—, 3, p. 26	"	— 685
2. adversus Judaeos . . .	III Cent.	—, 919-926	—, 133	"	"
3. de Montibus Sina et Sion . .	210/240 (9) end of II Cent. (10)	—, 909-918	—, 104	"	"
4. ad Vigilium Episcopum de Judaica Incredulitate	235/260 (11)	**6**, 49-58	—, 119	"	"

5. de Spectaculis	III Cent.	**4**, 779-788	**3**, 3	A.L.L., 8 (1892)1-22 (WOLFFLIN)	— 660
6. de Bono pudicitiae	id.	", 819-828	", 13		THIBAUT, 1868, **2**, 86
7. ad Novatianum	middle III Cent. [12]	**3**, 1205-1218	", 52		"
8. adversus Aleatores	260/300 [12]	**4**, 827-836	", 92	T.U.V. I, p. II (HARNACK); MIODONSKI [14]; HILGENFELD [15]	"
9. Liber de rebaptismate	middle III Cent. [13]	**3**, 1185-1204	", 69	F.P. fasc. XI (1916, RAUSCHEN)	"
10. de Pascha computus	243 before Easter	", 939-972	", 248	"	"
11. de Singularitate clericorum	2nd half IV Cent.	**4**, 835-870	", 173	MIODONSKI (Cracow, 1893)	"
12. Exhortatio de paenitentia	middle III Cent. [16]	"	"	"	"
13. de duodecim Abusivis saeculi	VII Cent. [17]	", 869-882	", 152	T.U., XXXIV, 1 (1909, HELLMANN)	"
14. de duplici martyrio ad Fortunatum [20]	1530	", 881-906	", 220		GUILLON, 1837, **1**, 272
15. Oratio I	V Cent. [18]	", 905-906	", 144	"	"
16. Oratio II	id. [18]	", 905-910	", 146	"	"
17. Epistulae I	date uncertain	"	", 272	"	"
18. — II	id.	"	", 272	"	"
19. — III	IV Cent. [19]	"	", 273	"	"
20. — IV	date uncertain	"	", 274	"	"
21. Caena Cypriani	V Cent. [18]	", 925-932	"	HAGEN in Z.f. wiss. Theol., 27 (1884), 164; HARNACK in T.U. N.F. IV, 3b (1899)	"

[1] Les Pères de l'Eglise, Paris, 1842.
[2] Namur, 1887.
[3] Tubingen, 1859.
[4] Ibid. 1853.
[5] Ibid. 1859.
[6] Salzburg, 1882.
[7] Monceaux, II, 104.
[8] A.C.L., II, 2, 406.
[9] Ibid. 384.
[10] Corssen, Z.N.W. 1911, p. 1-36.
[11] A.C.L., II, 2, 393.

[12] A.C.L., III, 2, 380.
[13] A.K.L., II, 500.
[14] Erlangen et Leipzig, 1889.
[15] Fribourg-i-B., 1889.
[16] Monceaux, II, 87. The work was edited in 1751 by Trombelli.
[17] Hellmann, op. cit.
[18] T.U. xix, 3b (1899, Harnack).
[19] Mercati, in Rendiconti del R. Instituto Lombardo, di sc. e. l. Ser, II, XXXII (1899), p. 986 et s.
[20] The work of Erasmus.

TABLE IV

SAINT HILARY OF POITIERS	DATES	EDITIONS			FRENCH TRANSLATIONS
		MIGNE	CORPUS SCR. ECCL. LAT.	VARIOUS	
1. Commentarii in Matthaeum . . .	about 355	**9**, 917-1078		,,	GUILLON, 1837, **1**, 272
2. Liber I ad Constantium . . .	356	**10**, 557-564	**65**, 180	,,	
3. de Trinitate	356/359	—, 25-472	,,	,,	Chefs-d'œuvre " des Peres de l'Eglise, 1838; Vol. V, p. 33.
4. de Synodis	begun 359	—, 479-546	—, 196	,,	,,
5. Liber II ad Constantium . .	Jan. 360	—, 563-572	,,	,,	,,
6. contra Constantium Imperat .	361	—, 577-603	,,	,,	,,
7. Tractatus super Psalmos . .	360/367	**9**, 231-908	**12**	,,	
8. contra Auxentium . . .	364/5	**10**, 609-618	**65**, 3	,,	Ibid. V, p. 5-19.
9. Tractatus Mysteriorum . .	364/6	,,	—, 208	J.-F. GAMURRINI, Rome, 1887.	,,
10. Hymni (1)	,,	—, 551	—, 245	K. T. No. 47/49 (1910).	CLÉMENT, Les Poetes chretiens, 1857.
11. id. (2)	,,			BLUME et DREVES, Anal. Hymn., L. 1908; Z. K. T. 13 (1889) 737	
12. Tractatus in Job (3) . . .	,,	—, 723-4	—, 229	,,	LARGENT, Saint Hilary, 1902, p. 55.
13. Epistula ad Abram filiam (4) .	,,	—, 549-552	—, 236	,,	,,
14. Fragmenta historica . . .	359 et s.	—, 627	—, 98	,,	,,
Fragmentum I . . .	,,				
— II . . .	,,	—, 632	—, 103	,,	,,

III	. . . . .	"	„ 658	„ 49	"
IV	. . . . .	"	„ 678	„ 155	"
A	. . . . .	"	„ 681	„ 89	"
VI	. . . . .	"	„ 686	„ 164	"
VII	. . . . .	"	„ 695	„ 93	"
VIII	. . . . .	"	„ 699	„ 78	"
IX	. . . . .	"	„ 703	„ 87	"
X	. . . . .	"	„ 705	„ 174	"
XI	. . . . .	"	„ 710	„ 43	"
XII	. . . . .	"	„ 714	„ 156	"
XIII	. . . . .	"	„ 717	„ 47	"
XIV	. . . . .	"	„ 718	„ 159	"
XV	. . . . .	"	„ 719	„ 160	"

(1) Contained in the Arezzo manuscript.
(2) Ascribed to Hilary.
(3) Two fragments.
(4) Of doubtful authenticity.

TABLE V

SAINT AMBROSE	DATES	EDITIONS			FRENCH TRANSLATIONS
		MIGNE	CORPUS SCR. ECCL. LAT.	VARIOUS	
1. de Officiis ministrorum libri tres	386	16, 25-184	„	KRABINGER, Tüb. 1857	ABBÉ DE BELLEGARDE, 1689. DURANTI DE BONRECUEIL, 1729.
2. de Virginibus libri tres	v. 377	—, 187-232	„	„	„
3. de Viduis l. unus	do.	—, 233-262	„	„	do.
4. de Virginitate l. unus	shortly after 377	—, 265-302	„	„	do.
5. de Institutione Virginis l. unus	392	—, 305-334	„	„	do.
6. de Mysteriis liber	387	—, 389-410	„	RAUSCHEN, F. P., fasc. VII, 1909	P. DE LABRIOLLE, Saint Ambroise, 1908, p. 273.
7. Exhortatio virginitatis	393	—, 335-364	„	„	„
8. de Sacramentis libri sex (1)	date uncertain	—, 417-462	„	„	„
9. de Paenitentia l. duo	about 384	—, 465-524	„	„	„
10. de Fide l. quinque	379/381	—, 527-698	„	„	„
11. de S. Spiritu libri tres	381	—, 703-816	„	„	„
12. de Incarnationis dominicae sacramento l. unus	379/383	—, 817-846	„	„	„
13. Fragmentum Ambrosianum ex Theodoreto desumptum	„	—, 847-850	„	„	„
14. de lapsu virginis consecratae (2)	date uncertain	—, 367-384	„	„	„
15. de Excessu fratris sui Satyri l. duo	Sept. 375	—, 1289-1354	„	A. E. BURN, Nicela of Remesiana, Camb. 1905, p. 112	„
16. Hymni nonnulli	„	—, 1409-1412	„	SCHENKL, in Ambrosiana, Milan, 1897, ch. V BLUME et DREVES, Anal. hymnica medii aevi, L. 1907	„
17. de Obitu Valentiniani consolatio	July 392	—, 1357-1384	„	„	anon. 1876.
18. de Obitu Theodosii oratio	26 Feb. 395	—, 1385-1406	„	„	„
19. Sermo contra Auxentium de basilicis tradendis	386	—, 1007-1018	„	„	„

	379/396	—, 875-1286	"	"	P. DE LABRIOLLE, *Saint Ambroise*, 1908.
20. Epistulae . . .	379/396	—, 875-1286	"	"	"
21. Hexaemeron l. VI	after 388	**14,** 123-274	**32,** 1, 3	"	"
22. de Paradiso l. I	375/378	—, 275-314	—, 265	"	"
23. de Cain et Abel l. II	id.	—, 315-360	—, 339	"	"
24. de Noe l. I	378	—, 361-416	—, 413	"	"
25. de Abraham l. II	after 388	—, 419-500	—, 501	"	"
26. de Isaac et Anima l. I	id.	—, 501-534	—, 641	"	"
27. de bono mortis l. I	after 391	—, 539-568	—, 703	"	"
28. de Fuga saeculi l. I	after 388	—, 569-596	—, II, 163	"	"
29. de Jacob et vita beata l. II	do.	—, 597-638	—, 2	"	"
30. de Joseph patriarcha l. I		—, 641-672	—, 73	"	"
31. de benedictionibus patriarcharum l. II	do.	—, 675-694	—, 125	"	"
32. de Helia et Jeiunio l. I	after 386	—, 697-728	—, 411	"	"
33. de Nabutha . II	date uncertain	—, 751-756	—, 469	"	"
34. de Tobia l. I	do.	—, 759-794	—, 519	"	"
35. de Interpellatione Job et David l. IV	about 383	—, 797-850	—, 211	"	"
36. Apologia prophetae David	383/386-7	—, 851-884	—, 299	"	"
37. — altera prophetae David (4)	do.	—, 887-916	—, 359	"	"
38. Enarrationes in XII Psalmos Davidicos	384-5/397	—, 921-1180		"	"
39. Expositio in Ps. CXVIII	after 387	**15,** 1197-1526	**62,** 1 "	"	"
40. Expositio Evangelii secundum Lucam	386/388	—, 1527-1850	**32,** IV, 1	"	"
41. de Excidio urbis Hierosolymitanae l. V (5)	date uncertain	—, 1961-2205	"	C. F. WAEBER et J. CAESAR, Marburg, 1864	"
42. Commentarius in Cantica Canticorum (6)	XII Cent.	—, 1851-1962	"	"	"

(1) Authenticity disputed.
(2) Authenticity doubtful.
(3) Numerous letters translated in P. de Labriolle, *op. cit.* p. 37-161.
(4) Unauthenticated.
(5) Authenticity doubtful.

(6) Drawn up in the XII Cent. from various passages in the writings of St Ambrose.

N.B.—Various *apocrypha* are included in Vol. XVII of the *Patr. Lat.* col. 9 to 1160. It is quite possible that the *Explanatio Symboli ad Initiandos* (17, 1155-1190) may have been by St Ambrose.

TABLE VI

THE SHORT POEMS OF THE IV CENT.	DATES	EDITIONS			FRENCH TRANSLATIONS
		MIGNE	CORPUS SCR. ECCL. LAT.	VARIOUS	
1. de Ave Phoenice	2nd half IV Cent.	7, 277-284	27, 2, 1,135	A. L., No. 731; P. L. M., III, 247	
2. Cento (the poetess Proba)	"	19, 803-818	16, 1,568	"	Gamber (1), ", p. 119.
3. de Cruce	"	2, 1113-1114	3, 305	"	"
4. de Evangelio	"	"	23, 270	S.S., I, 166	"
5. de Ecclesia	"	"	16, 1,621	A.L., I, 1, No. 16; P.L.M., IV, 214	"
6. de Fratribus septem Macchabaeis	"	50, 1275-1286	23, 240 et 255		"
7. in Genesin fragmentum (2)	end of IV Cent.	2, 1097-1102	3, 283 et		"
8. Geneseos liber	"	19, 345-380	23, 1	J. E. B. Mayor, Lon. 1889	"
9. de Judicio Domini	date uncertain	"	3, 308-325	Œhler, Op. Tertulliani, II, 776 Ibid., p. 769.	"
10. de Jona	"	"	23, 221	Rivinus, Sanctae reliquiae duum Victorinorum, Gothæ 1652.	"
11. de Jesu Christo Deo et Homine	"	"	"		"
12. Laudes Domini	316/323	19, 379-386	"	Brandes, progr. Braunschweig, 1887.	"
13. de Ligno Vitae (3)	"	51, 1091-1094	"		"
14. Marcionem (adversus)	see p. 319	2, 1051-1090	"	Œhler, op. cit. II, 781	"

	Date				
15. de Mortibus boum	end of IV Cent.	**19**, 797-800	,,	A.L., I, 2, No. 893.	CLÉMENT, *op. cit.* p. 82.
16. de Naturis rerum	,,	,,	,,	A.S.C., I, 121	DOBBELSTEIN, diss. Louvain, 1879, p. 49.
17. Nicomachum (contra Flavianum) [4]	394/5	,,		P. L. M., III, 286; A.L. No. 4; HERMES, IV (1870) 354.	,,
18. de Pascha (or de Resurrectione) [5]	,,	**2**, 1101-1106	**3**, 289 et **23**, 212	ŒHLER, *op. cit.* II, 769.	,,
19. de Sodoma	,,	—, 1105-1108	**3**, 302 et **23**, 227	,,	,,
20. Senatorem (ad quemdam)	,,				,,
21. de Ternarii numeri excellentia	,,	**125**, 821-2	,,	MERCATI, *Studi e Testi*, 12 (1904) p. 23	,,
22. Tityrus [6]	,,	**19**, 773-780	**16**, 1,609 —1,615 et **10**, 310	A.L., I, 2, No. 719a	,,
23. de Verbi incarnatione [6]	,;				,,
24. Versus ad gratiam Domini [7]	,,	,,	,,		,,

(1) *Le livre de la Genèse dans la Poésie Latine du Ve S.* 1899.
(2) Forms the beginning of the *Geneseos Liber*.
(3) See *de Cruce*.
(4) See Ch. Morel's commentary, *Revue Archéol.*, XVIII (1868), p. 51-55.
(5) See *de Cruce* (No. 3).
(6) Centos.
(7) See *Tityrus* (No. 22).

TABLE VII

SAINT JEROME	DATES	EDITIONS			FRENCH TRANSLATIONS
		MIGNE	CORPUS SCR. ECCL. LAT.	VARIOUS	BAREILLE, P, 1878-1885 (3)
Treatises, Opuscula, various, Sermons					
1. Vita Pauli.	374/9	**23**, 17-28	"	TAMIETTI, Turin, 1903.	**2**, 408; P. DE LABRIOLLE, 1907
2. Altercatio Luciferiani et Orthodoxi.	382/5	—, 155-182	"	"	—, 450
3. adversus Helvidium.	382/4	—, 183-206	"	"	—, 477
4. Liber hebraicarum quaestionum in Genesin.	386/391	—, 935-1010	"	"	**3**, 507
5. Liber de situ et nominibus locorum hebraicorum	id.	—, 859-928	"	"	—, 501
6. Liber de nominibus hebraicis	id.	—, 771-858	"	"	—, 438
7. Vita Hilarionis	id.	—, 29-54	"	id.	**2**, 417; id.
8. Vita Malchi	id.	—, 53-60	"	id.	—, 441
9. de Viris illustribus	392	—, 601-720	"	S. Q. fasc. XI (1895)	**3**, 270
10. contra Jovinianum (2)	392/3	—, 211-338	"	"	**3**, 500
11. contra Johannem Jerosolymitanum	395/6 (1)	—, 355-396	"	"	**3**, 15
12. contra Rufinum l. II	402	—, 397-456	"	"	**3**, 60
13. contra Rufinum liber III	c. 403	—, 457-492	"	"	**3**, 60
14. contra Vigilantium	406	—, 339-352	"	"	**3**, 1
15. Tractatus in Psalmos	392/401	"	"	A.M. III, 2 (1897) 1	"
16. — in Marci Evangelium	id.	"	"	— 319	"
17. — varii	id.	"	"	— 373	"
18. Tractatuum in Psalmos series altera	id.	"	"	III, 3 (1903) 1	"
19. Dialogus adv. Pelagianos	415	**23**, 495-590	"	"	**3**, 163

Commentaries

20. On the Epistle to Philemon	386/7	"	**26**, 599-618	**11**, 50; P. DE LABRIOLLE
21. —— the Galatians	id.	"	—, 307-438	**10**, 221
22. —— the Ephesians	id.	"	—, 439-554	—, 374
23. —— Titus	386/7	"	**26**, 555-600	**11**, 1
24. —— Ecclesiastes	389/390	"	**23**, 1009-1116	**4**, 1
25. —— Nahum	c. 392	"	**25**, 1231-1272	**9**, 92
26. —— Micheas	id.	"	—, 1151-1230	—, 1
27. —— Sophonias	id.	"	—, 1337-1388	—, 214
28. —— Aggeus	id.	"	—, 1387-1416	—, 272
29. —— Habacuc	id.	"	—, 1273-1338	—, 139
30. —— Jonas	395/6	"	—, 1117-1152	**8**, 509
31. —— Abdias	id.	"	—, 1097-1118	**8**, 487
32. —— Isaias (13-23)	before 398	"	**24**, 901-942	**5**, 4
33. —— Saint Matthew	398	"	**26**, 15-218	**9**, 524
34. —— The Psalms	392/402	A. M. III. I (1895)	—, "	"
35. —— Osee	406	"	**25**, 815-946	**8**, 166
36. —— Joel	id.	"	—, 947-988	—, 317
37. —— Amos	id.	"	—, 989-1096	—, 365
38. —— Daniel	406/8	"	—, 491-584	**7**, 390
39. —— Isaias	408/410	"	**24**, 17-678	**5**, 1 et **6**, 1
40. —— Zacharias	406	"	**25**, 1415-1542	**9**, 305
41. —— Malachias	406	"	—, 1541-1578	—, 451
42. —— Ezechiel	410/5	"	—, 15-490	**6**, 422 et **7**, 1
43. —— Jeremias	415/20	**59**, REITER (1913)	**24**, 679-900	**6**, 161

Revision of the Bible

44. Revision of the Latin Versions of the Gospels	384	"	**29**, 541-726	"
45. Revision of the Epistles of St Paul	before 385	"	—, 727-822	"

(1) According to Holl, S.B.B., 1916, No. viii/ix.

(2) Bickel's *Diatribe in Senecae phil. fragmenta*, I (L. 1915), p. 382 et s. edits critically § I, 41-46; II, 5-14; 28.

(3) Fairly numerous pieces translated in Turmel's *Saint Jerome*, 6, 1906 (P. C.).

N.B.—For the Commentary on the *Apocalypse*, see Victorinus of Pettau, p. 221.

TABLE VII—contd.

SAINT JEROME	DATES	Editions			FRENCH TRANSLATIONS
		MIGNE	CORPUS SCR. ECCL. LAT.	VARIOUS	
46. Revision of the rest of the New Testament	before 398	—, 823-872	,,	,,	P. DE LABRIOLLE
47. 1st Revision of the Psalms (*Psalt. Romanum*)	384	**29**, 120-398	,,	,,	,,
48. 2nd Revision of the Psalms (from the **Greek**) (*Psalt. Gallicanum*)	386/391	—, 119-397	,,	,,	,,
49. Revision (from the **Greek**) of the Book of Job	386/391	—, 61-114	,,	,,	,,
50. Revision (from the **Hebrew**): Pentateuch	398/404	**28**, 163-462	,,	,,	,,
51. —— Josue	404/5	—, 461-504	,,	,,	,,
52. —— Judges	id.	—, 503-542	,,	,,	,,
53. —— Ruth	id.	—, 543-548	,,	,,	,,
54. —— Samuel	before 392	—, 547-664	,,	,,	,,
55. —— Kings	before 392	—, 663-672	,,	,,	,,
56. —— Malachias	id.	—, 673-772	,,	,,	,,
57. —— Isaias	id.	—, 771-848	,,	,,	,,
58. —— Jeremias	id.	—, 847-938	,,	,,	,,
59. —— Ezechiel	id.	—, 937-1014	,,	,,	,,
60. —— 12 Prophets	id.	—, 1013-1075	,,	,,	,,
61. —— Job	393	—, 1083-1122	,,	,,	,,
62. —— Psalms	before 392	—, 1123-1240	,,	,,	,,
63. —— Esdras	before 395	—, 1404-1434	,,	,,	,,
64. —— Books of Solomon	398	—, 1241-1292	,,	,,	,,
65. —— Paralipomena	396	—, 1323-1402	,,	,,	,,

66. (from the Chaldee) Esther . . .	before 404 (?)	—, 1433-1450	"	"	"	"
67. — Judith . . .	date uncertain	29, 37-60	"	"	"	"
68. — Tobias . . .	id.	—, 23-38	"	"	"	"
Various Translations						
69. Chronicle of Eusebius .	379/381	27, 33-702	"	"	"	7, 543 et 8, 1
70. Origen's Homilies on Jeremias .	id.	25, 583-692	"	"	"	8, 48
71. — Ezechiel	id.	—, 691-786	"	"	"	4, 554
72. — Isaias . .	id.	24, 901-936	"	"	"	
73. — the Canticle of Canticles . . .	382/4	23, 1117-1144	"	"	"	—, 105
74. de Spiritu Sancto, by Didymus	386/391	—, 101-154	"	"	"	
75. Origen's Homilies on St Luke .	388/391	26, 219-306	"	"	"	10, 114
76. Monastic Rule of Pachomius, Theodore, and Orsenius . . .	end of 404	23, 65-100	"	"	"	
77. **Letters** . . .	370 to 419	22	54, (*Ep.* I. à LXX) ; 55, (*Ep.* LXXI to CXX), 56 (*Ep.* CXXI à CLIV) (1)	"	"	1 et 2

(1) The *Indices* of this edition, given by Hilberg, are still wanting.

TABLE VIII

SAINT AUGUSTINE (1)	DATES	EDITIONS			FRENCH TRANSLATIONS
		Migne	Corpus Scr. Eccl. Lat.	Various	Peronne, Ecalle, Vincent, etc. Paris (Vivès) 1869 et s.
1. de Pulchro et Apto (2)	about 380	"	"	"	"
2. Panegyric on Bauton et Valentinian (3)	385	"	"	"	"
3. contra Academicos l. III	386	32, 905-958	"	"	2, 400
4. de Vita beata	id.	", 959-976	"	"	", 476
5. de Ordine l. II	id.	", 977-1020	"	"	", 502
6. Soliloquiorum l. II	386/7	", 869-904	"	"	", 565
7. de Immortalitate animae	id.	", 1021-1034	"	"	3, 1
8. de Grammatica (4)	id.	", 1385-1408	"	Keil, G. L. 5,496	4, 1
9. de Musica l. VI (5)	387/391	", 1081-1194	"	R. L. M., 137	3, 93
10. Principia rhetorices	id.	", 1439-1448	"	"	4, 104
11. Principia dialecticae (6)	id.	", 1409-1420	"	W. Crecelius, Elherfeld, 1857	", 52
12. Categoriae X ex Aristotele decerptae (7)	id.	", 1419-1440	"	"	", 71
13. de Quantitate Animae	387/8	", 1035-1080	"	"	3, 24
14. de Moribus eccl. cathol. et de moribus Manichaeorum	388/9	", 1309-1378	"	"	", 493
15. de Genesi c. Manichaeos l. II	388/390	34, 173-220	"	"	", 423
16. de libero Arbitrio l. III	388/395	32, 1221-1310	"	"	", 292
17. de Magistro	389	", 1193-1220	"	"	", 253
18. de Vera religione	389/390	34, 121-172	"	"	", 596
19. de diversis quaestionibus LXXXIII liber unus	389/396	40, 11-100	"	"	21, 1

20. de Utilitate credendi ad Honoratum	391/2	**42**, 65-92	**25**, I, p. 3	„	**25**, 271
21. de duabus Animabus contra Manichaeos	id.	—, 93-112	—, I, 51	„	—, 315
22. contra Fortunatum disputatio	392	—, 111-130	—, I, 83	„	—, 343
23. de Fide et symbolo	Oct. 393	**40**, 181-196	**41**, 1	„	**21**, 223
24. de Genesi ad litteram liber imperfectus	393/4	**34**, 219-246	**28**, 1	„	**3**, 490
25. Psalmus abecedarius c. partem Donati	393/4	**43**, 23-32	**51**, 3	„	**28**, 24
26. Epist. ad Galatas Expositio	id.	**35**, 2105-2148	„	„	**11**, 60
27. Ep. XXVIII ad Hieronymum (de nova Vet. Test. versione)	id.	**33**, 111-114	**34**, 103	„	**4**, 320
28. de Sermone Dei in monte l. II	about 393	**35**, 1229-1308	„	„	**9**, 19
29. Expositio quarundam propositionum ex. Epist. ad Romanos	about 394	—, 2063-2088		„	**11**, 1
30. contra Adimantum	394/5	**42**, 129-172	**35**, 1, 115	„	**25**, 365
31. de Mendacio	id.	**40**, 487-518	**41**, 411	„	**22**, 1
32. de Continentia	id.	—, 348-372	—, 139	„	**21**, 444
33. de diversis quaestionibus ad Simplicianum l. II	id.	—, 101-148		„	—, 117
34. de Agone christiano	396/7	—, 289-310	—,„ 99	„	—, 364
35. contra epistulam quam vocant Fundamenti l. I	id.	**42**, 173-206	**25**, l. 193	„	**25**, 431
36. Confessionum l. XIII	id.	**32**, 659-866	**33**, 1	Gibb and Montgomery, C.1908	**2**, 103
37. de Doctrina Christiana	397/8 [8]	**34**, 15-122	„	„	**6**, 439
38. Quaestionum Evangeliorum l. II	397/427 [9]	**35**, 1321-1364	„	„	**9**, 135
39. Annotationes in Job	397/400	**34**, 825-886	**28**, III, 509	„	**8**, 110
40. de Trinitate l. XV	398/416	**42**, 819-1098	„	„	**29**, 595

[1] For lost or unauthenticated works, cf. Teuffel, *Röm. Litter*, III (1913), p. 364 et s.

[2] Lost. See *Conf.* IV, xiii.

[3] Lost. See *ibid.* VI, vi et *Contra Litter. Petil*, III, xxv, 30.

[4] A fragment in Mai, N. P.B., I, 2, 165; re-edit. by C. W. Weber, Marburg, 1861. It is not in Migne.

[5] A fragment in Mai, C. V. S., 3, 116.

[6] Authenticity disputed. See Zurek, *De S. Aug. princ. rhetoricis* Diss. Vindob. 1905, p. 73.

[7] Authenticity doubtful.

[8] According to Monceaux, *C. R. de l'Acad. des Inscr.*, 1908, p. 53.

[9] See p. 416, N. 1.

TABLE VIII—contd.

SAINT AUGUSTINE	DATES	EDITIONS			FRENCH TRANSLATIONS
		MIGNE	CORPUS SCR. ECCL. LAT.	VARIOUS	
41. de Catechizandis Rudibus	400	40, 309-348	"	FAUSSET, Lon. 1896 / KRUGER, S. Q., Heft IV (1909)	21, 393
42. contra Faustum Manichaeum l. XXXIII	id.	42, 207-518	25, 1, 251	"	25, 480
43. de Consensu evangelistarum l. IV	id.	34, 1041-1230	43, 1	"	8, 422
44. ad inquisitiones Januari l. II (Ep. LIV-LV)	id.	33, 199-223	", "	"	4, 449
45. de Opere monachorum	id.	40, 547-582	41, 529	"	22, 84
46. de Fide rerum quae non videntur	id.	—, 171-180		"	21, 209
47. contra Epistulam Parmeniani l. III	id.	43, 33-108	51, 19	"	28, 40
48. de Baptismo c. Donatistas	id.	40, 107-244	—, 145	"	—, 142
49. de Bono coniugali	400-401	40, 373-396	41, 185	"	21, 476
50. de Sancta Virginitate	400-401	—, 397-428	—, 233	"	—, 511
51. contra litteras Petiliani l. III	401/403	43, 245-388	52, 3	"	28, 350
52. ad catholicos epistula de secta Donatistarum (de Unitate Ecclesiae)	end of 401	—, 391-446	28, I, 3	"	29, 4
53. de Genesi ad litteram l. XII	401/415	34, 245-486		"	7, 39
54. de actis cum Felice Manichaeo l. II	404 (¹)	42, 519-552	25, 1, 801	"	26, 331
55. de Natura boni	405	—, 551-572	—, 1, 855	"	—, 379
56. contra Secundinum Manichaeum l. I	405/6	—, 577-602	—, 1, 905	"	—, 411
57. contra Cresconium grammaticum partis Donati l. IV	406/7	43, 445-594	52, 325	"	29, 81
58. de Divinatione daemonum l. I	406/411	40, 581-592	41, 597	"	22, 130
59. Ep. XCIII ad Vincentium (de haereticis vi coercendis)	408	33, 321-347	34, 445	"	4, 628

	Monceaux date				
60. Ep. LII ad Deogratiam (Sex Quaestiones c. Paganos)	408/9	—, 370-386	—, 544	,,	—, 702
61. Ep. CVIII ad Macrobium (de non iterando baptismo)	409	33, 405-417	34, 612	,,	5, 2
62. Ep. CXVIII ad Dioscorum (de philosophiae erroribus)	410	—, 439-449	—, 665	,,	—, 40
63. Ep. CXX ad Consentium (de Trinitate)	id.	43, 452-462	—, 704	,,	—, 70
64. de Unico baptismo c. Petilianum	id.	43, 595-614	53, 3	,,	29, 286
65. Breviculus conlationis cum Donatistis	411	—, 613-650	—, 29	,,	—, 309
66. contra partem Donati post gesta	412	—, 651-690	—, 97	,,	—, 362
67. Ep. CXXXVII ad Volusianum (de Incarnatione)	id.	33, 515-525	44, 96	,,	5, 160
68. Ep. CXXXVIII ad Marcellinum (id.)	id.	—, 524-535	—, 126	,,	—, 174
69. Ep. CXL ad Honoratum (de gratia)	id.	—, 538-577	—, 155	,,	—, 191
70. de peccatorum Meritis et Remissione et de baptismo parvulorum l. III	id.	44, 109-200	60, 3	,,	30, 3
71. de Spiritu et littera ad Marcellinum	end of 412	—, 201-246	—, 155-229	,,	—, 126
72. de Fide et operibus	413	40, 197-230	41, 3	,,	21, 242
73. Ep. CXLVII ad Paulinam (de videndo Deo)	id.	33, 596-622	44, 274	,,	5, 273
74. de Civitate Dei	413-426	41, 11-804	40, I et II	DOMBART, dans B. T., t. I (1909), t. II (1905)	23, 442
75. Ep. ad Julianam (de bono viduitatis)	414	40, 429-450	41, 303	,,	21, 587
76. Ep. CLVII ad Hilarium Siculum (de Pelagianismo)	id.	33, 674-693	44, 449	,,	5, 315
77. de Natura et gratia liber I	415	44, 247-290	60, 233	,,	30, 193
78. ad episcopos Eutropium et Paulum de perfectione Justitiae hominis	id.	—, 291-318	42, 3	,,	30, 253
79. Ep. CLXVI ad Hieronymum (de origine animae)	id.	33, 720-733	44, 545	,,	5, 450
80. Ep. CLXVII ad Hier. (de sententia Jacobi)	id.	33, 733-741	44, 586	,,	5, 469

(1) December 398, according to Monceaux, *C. R. de l'Acad. des Inscr.*, 1908, p. 58.

(2) Authenticity disputed. See Batiffol, *Le Cathol. de S. Aug.*, 1920, t. I, p. 132.

TABLE VIII—*contd.*

SAINT AUGUSTINE	DATES	EDITIONS			FRENCH TRANSLATIONS
		MIGNE	CORPUS SCR. ECCL. LAT.	VARIOUS	
81. ad Orosium presbyterum contra Priscillianistas et Origenistas .	id.	**42**, 669-678	,,	,,	**26**, 555
82. Enarrationes in Psalmos .	415	**36**, 66-1906	,,	,,	**11**, 15
83. in Joannis Evangelium tr. cxxiv .	416/7	**35**, 1379-1976	,,	,,	**9**, 10
84. in Epist. Joannis ad Parthos .	416	—, 1977-2062	,,	,,	**10**, 450
85. de gestis Pelagii ad Aurelium episcopum l. I	beginning of 417	**44**, 319-360	**42**, 51	,,	**30**, 292
86. Ep. CLXXXV ad Bonifacium (de correctione Donatistarum)	417	**33**, 792-815	**57**, 1	,,	**5**, 547
87. Ep. CLXXXVI ad Paulinum Nol. (de Pelagianismo)	id.	—, 815-831	—, 45	,,	—, 579
88. Ep. CLXXXVII ad Dardanum (de praesentia Dei)	id.	—, 832-848	—, 81	,,	—, 603
89. de Gratia Dei et de peccato originali l. II	418	**44**, 359-410	**42**, 125	,,	**30**, 343
90. Sermo ad Caesareensis ecclesiae plebem	Sept. 418	**43**, 689-698	**53**, 167	,,	**29**, 414
91. Gesta cum Emerito Caesareensi Donatistarum episcopo	id.	—, 697-706	—, 181	,,	—, 426
92. contra sermonem Arianorum l. I. .	418	**42**, 677-708	,,	,,	**26**, 566
93. de Patientia .	about 418	**40**, 611-626	,,	,,	**22**, 170
94. de adulterinis Coniugiis l. II .	419	**40**, 451-486	**41**, 345	,,	**21**, 588
95. Locutionum in Heptateuchum l. VII	id.	**34**, 485-546	**28**, I, 507	,,	**7**, 383
96. Quaestionum in Heptateuchum l. VII	id.	—, 547-824	—, III, 3	,,	—, 469
97. Ep. CXCIX ad Hesychium (de fine saeculi)	id.	**33**, 904-925	**57**, 243	,,	**6**, 68

98. de Nuptiis et concupiscentia l. II	419/420	**44**, 413-474	**42**, 211	,,	**30**, 421
99. de Natura et origine animae l. IV	end of 419	—, 475-548	**60**, 303	,,	**20**, 508
100. contra duas epistulas Pelagian. ad Bonifacium	420	**44**, 549-638	—, 423	,,	**31**, 4
101. contra mendacium liber ad Consentium	id.	**40**, 517-548	**41**, 467	,,	**22**, 40
102. contra Gaudentium Donatistarum episc. l. II	id.	**43**, 707-752	**53**, 201	,,	**29**, 440
103. contra adversarium Legis et Prophetarum l. II	id.	**42**, 604-666	,,	,,	**26**, 458
104. contra Julianum haeresis pelagianae defens., l. VI	421	**44**, 641-874	,,	Krabinger, Tübingen, 1861, S. Q, 2, 4	**31**, 123
105. Enchiridium ad Laurentium	id.	**40**, 231-290	,,		**21**, 287
106. de Cura pro mortuis gerenda	421	**40**, 591-610	**41**, 619	,,	**22**, 143
107. de octo Dulcitii quaestionibus liber	422 (or 425)	—, 147-170	,,	,,	**21**, 179
108. de Gratia et libero arbitrio l. I	426/427	**44**, 881-912	,,	,,	**31**, 465
109. de correptione et gratia	id.	—, 915-946	,,	,,	—, 515
110. Retractationum l. II	id.	**32**, 583-656	**36**, 1	,,	**2**, 1
111. Speculum de Scriptura (1)	427	**34**, 887-1040	**12**, 3	,,	**8**, 203
112. Collatio cum Maximiano Arianorum episc.	428	**42**, 709-742	,,	,,	**27**, 3
113. contra Maximinum	id.	—, 743-814	,,	,,	—, 47
114. de Haeresibus ad Quodvultdeum l. I.	id.	—, 21-50	,,	Welchmann, Oxford, 1871; Oehler, Corpus Haereseologicum I, 187 (B. 1856)	**25**, 211
115. Tractatus adv. Judaeos	id.	—, 51-64	,,	,,	—, 248
116. de Praedestinatione Sanctorum liber ad Prosperum et Hilarium	428/429	**44**, 959-992	,,	,,	**31**, 578
117. de dono perseverantiae liber	id.	**45**, 993-1034	,,	,,	—, 627
118. Opus imperfectum contra Julianum (2)	429/430	—, 1049-1608	,,	,,	—, 704

(1) The two Speculum Peccatoris (P.L., 40, 967, and 983) are unauthenticated. The Speculum audi Israel is not in Migne, but only in C. V. 12, 287. Leop. Delisle defended its authenticity, 1884.

(2) For the letters see p. 418 ; for the sermons and the fresh *tractatus* published by Dom Morin, *ibid.* p. 420.

INDEX

A

Adeodatus, 398, 402
Alphabetical Psalm, 183, 406
Abra, 239
Academe (New), 15, 113, 399
Acrostics, 176
Acta Pauli, 59, 167
Acta Pilati, 167
Acts of the Martyrs, 454 ; Apollonius, 53 ; Martyrs of Scillium, 55 ; SS. Perpetua and Felicitas, 102 ; St. Cyprian, 136 ; Donatist martyrs, 291 ; Passio Agaunensium martyrum, 424 ; Victor of Vita's History of the Vandal Persecution, 443
Adimantus (the Manichaean), 405
Adonis, cult of, 234
Adversus Omnes Haereses, 222
Aemilianus Macer, 508
Aetheriae Peregrinatio, 376 et s
Africa, Christian, 5, 55
Agapetus, Pope, 506
Agnes, 492
Agnoscat omne Caelum, 493
Agricola, martyr, 279
Alaric, 18, 390
Alès, A. d', 130, 163, 165
Alethia, 446, 468
Alfaric, 261, 390
Allard, Paul, 452, 453
Allegory, in Greek Literature, 462 ; in Latin profane literature, 462 ; in Christian tradition, 282, 462
,, Theory of, 415, 418
,, Author's views on, 283
,, History of, 167, 173, 243, 345, 400, 461, 475, 496
Altercatio Heracliani laici, 227, 257
Alypius, 401 et s. ; 404
Ambrose, St., 31, 230, 255, 263 et s. ; 299, 318, 364, 399, 418, 459, 475
Ambrosiaster, 286 et s.
Ammianus Marcellinus, 230
Amoenus, 485
Anachronisms in Prudentius, 466
Anastasius I, Pope, 443, 499
Ancyra, the 12 Anathemas of, 241
Anger of God, 191, 211
Anti-Christ, 180
Anthemius, Emperor, 477
Antioch, Synod of (A.D. 341), 241
Antony, Life of, 384

Anubis, Mysteries of, 288
Apelles, the Gnostic, 59
Aphtonius, 260
Apis, Cult of, 97
Apocalypse of Peter, 54
Apocrypha, St. Cyprian, 163 et s.
Apollinaris of Laodicea, 311, 337
,, of Valence, 488
Apollonius, Apologist, 53
,, of Tyana, 319
Apollyon, 179
Apologetics, Christian, 71, 109, 189, 203, 318, 408, 435, 439, 457
Apuleius, 9, 101, 110, 218, 300, 487
Aquila, the Jew, 355
Aquileia, Council of, 255
Arator, 491
Arcadius of Caesarea, 300
Arcani, Disciplina, 122
Archelai, Acta, 370
Arevalo, 472
Arezzo, Manuscript of, 243, 248, 376
Arianism, 238, 241, 244, 247, 248, 408, 473
Contra Sermonem Arianorum, 254 et s.
Arian Commentary on Job, 254
,, *Fragmenta* from Bobbio, 254, 289
Fragmenta contra Arianos, 289
Aristeus, Letter of, 174
Aristides, Apologist, 212
Ariston of Pella, 432
Aristotle, 18, 70, 202, 500, 504
Arnobius, 19, 109, 188, 200, 237
,, the Younger, 427 et s.
Art, Christian, 210, 231, 283, 330, 332, 453, 464
Asarbus, Priscillianist, 309
Ascension of Isaias, 254
Asceticism, Christian, 14, 63, 81, 94, 187, 209, 278, 336 et s. ; 348
A Solis Ortus Cardine, 476
Asterius, 363
Asterius, Turcius Rufus, 474
Astrology, 232, 262
Athanasius, St., 244, 251, 253, 268, 385 ; Pseudo A, 253
Atys, Cult of, 234
Audentius, 186
Aufidius Bassus, 507
Augustine, St., 10, 14, 23, 26, 27, 64, 162, 229, 259, 280, 293 et s. ; 298, 310, 327, 357, 368, 471, 475, 498, 505, 507 et s. ; 518

Aurelianus of Arles, 498
Ausonius, 324 et s. ; 329, 469
Altar of Victory, 269
Auxentius of Durostorum, 254
„ Milan, 266, 298, 350
Avellana, Collectio, 227, 252
Avitus, St., 485, 487
„ Emperor, 477
„ of Bracara, 434

B

Babut, E. Ch., 12 ; 307 et s. ; 327, 382
Bachiarius, 309
Baehrens, 117, 120, 123
Ballerini, 252, 261
Baluze, 188
Baptism,' second, 140, 163, 252 ; deferred B., 267, 335
Barbarians, feeling in regard to the, 439
Bardesanus, 363
Barnabas, Epistle of, 174
Bartas, du, 313
Basil, St., 25, 268
Basilides, Bishop, 143
Batiffol, 144, 188, 203, 229, 258 et s.
Bede, 438
Bellator, 509
Benedictines, their method (MSS.), 34
Benedictine Edition of St. Augustine, 389
Bérenger, 238
Bernardine of St. Pierre, 202
Bible, in the life of the Christians, 44, 46, 313 ; in Christian prose, 327 ; in Christian poetry, 313 et s. ; 331 et s. ; 448 et s. ; 487 et s. ; in Tertullian, 61 ; in Minucius Felix, 121 ; in Arnobius, 190 ; in Lactantius, 204 ; in St. Ambrose, 268, 278 ; in Priscillian, 307 ; in Tyconius, 294 ; in St. Augustine, 393, 408, 417
Bible, First Latin Translations of, 16, 39–49, 131, 157, 256, 397 : Revision of, by St. Jerome, 351 et s. ; Influence of the, on the French language, 46 ; Exegesis of the, 10, 58, 220, 239, 281, 360 et s. See also Allegory
„ Classes, 345, 506
Biography, Christian, 135, 239, 265, 340, 383, 385, 393, 466, 490, 492, 496, 509 ; Auto-, 60, 239, 324, 394, 429, 447, 469, 477
Blesilla, 346, 349
Bobbio, 30, 254, 289
Boethius, 260, 499 et s. ; 508
Boissier, Gaston, 116 et s. ; 120, 199, 236, 475, 505
Boniface I, Pope, 443
Bonnet, Max, 487, 514

Bonosus, 337
Bossuet, 204, 348, 389, 430, 497
Braulio of Saragossa, 516
Brewer, 184, 290
Bruyne, Dom de, 309, 356, 376, 417
Bulic, Mgr., 335
Burn, 287, 303
Burkitt, 39, 45, 417

C

Cabira, Cult of, 234
Cabrol, Dom, 33
Caecilius Natalis, 111
Caelestius, the Pelagian, 407
Cagnat, René, 61
Callewaert, 51, 68
Callinicum, 272 et s.
Callixtus, Pope, 98, 149
Candidus, the Arian, 261
Canon of Scripture, 4, 54, 58, 356
Capreolus, 429
Carmen de Providentia, 391
Carnival, 297
Carneades, 208
Carthage, 56, 60, 77, 398
Cassian, 423 et s. ; 430
Cassiodorus, 28, 495, 505, 506 et s.
Catullus, 467
Cavallera, 416, 417
Cave, G., 222
Caecilius, Comic Poet, 345
Celestine, Pope, 592
Celsus, polemist, 22, 23, 194
Centos, 321
Caesarius of Arles, St., 496, 497 et s.
Cæsar, 435
Chapman, Dom J., 54, 139, 144, 146
Charismata, 120
Charlemagne, 30, 413
Chateaubriand, 14, 71, 264, 479
Chilperic, 494
Christianity and Pagan Society, 13, 19, 76, 81, 203, 209
Chromatius of Aquileia, 386
Chronicle of Ravenna, 507
Chronology, Christian, 166, 301, 342, 393, 431, 436, 507
Chrysippus, 72
Church, Conception of in St. Cyprian, 139 et s. ; in St. Augustine, 421 ; in St. Leo, 443
Cicero, 27, 31, 127, 181, 197, 199 et s. ; 277, 296, 345, 396, 418, 500, 506, 517 ; his view of art of translation, 46 ; and new words, 49
Circumcelliones, 291
City of God, Origin of the idea, 409 et s.
Claudius, Emperor, 41
Claudian, 314, 320
Claudius Herminianus, 74

Clausules (terminations) in Tertullian, 101 ; in St. Cyprian, 134 ; in Arnobius, 198 ; in Lactantius, 218 ; in St. Hilary, 250 ; in St. Jerome, 333, 373 ; in Sedulius, 475 ; in Sidonius, 480

Clement of Alex., 17, 24, 60, 197
,, Rome, St., 42, 320
Cluny, Monastery of, 50
Collatio, 424
Columban, St., 29, 254
Columella, 508
Commerce and Christianity, 209
Commodian, 176 et s. ; 212, 314
Commonitorium, 425
Concordia Matthaei, 289
Confessions of St. Augustine, character of, 394
Conscience, liberty of. See Tolerance
Consolatio of St. Paulinus of Nola, 331 ; of Boethius, 500
Constantius, Emperor, 229, 238, 241, 251
Constantine, Emperor, 228
Cooper-Marsden, 424
Cornelius, Pope, 170, 451
Cornelius Labeo, 197
Cornutus, Stoic, 42
Corpus Script. Ecclest. Lat., 3, 35
Corssen, 48, 167
Corybantes, Cult of the, 234
Coustant, Dom P., 245
Cresconius, Donatist, 292
Crimes against nature, 78
Croiset, Maurice, 4
Cruce, de, 318
Cuq, E., 84
Cybele, Cult of, 97, 233, 288
Cyprian of Antioch, 162
Cyprian, poet, 316
Cyprian of Carthage, St., 9, 65, 132 et s. ; 187, 204, 237, 264, 268, 300, 319, 418
Cyprian of Toulon, 303, 497
Cyril of Jerusalem, 268
Cyrus, 179

D

Damasus, Pope, 201, 289, 339, 346, 351, 451
Dante, 457, 502
Decius, Emperor, 147, 332
Delehaye, Père H., 162, 332, 511
Delisle, Leopold, 468
Demetrianus, the Pagan, 208
,, the Christian, 201
Denk, J., 39
Denys of Milan, 239
Denys the Less, 509
Deogratias, 413
Dexter, 267, 362
Dialogue, in Apologetics, 127, 257, 350, 368, 383, 402, 432, 469

Diatribe, 82
Dictinius, Priscillianist, 309
Didactics, 317, 455, 473
Didymus, St., 268
Diospolis, Council of, 435
Dissertatio Maximini contra Ambrosium, 255
Doctors of the Church, 238, 286
Dollinger, 306
Dombart, 169, 183
Dominici, Fra Giovanni, 13
Domnio, 368
Donatus and St. Cyprian, 154
,, the Grammarian, 336
,, of Casae Nigrae, 291
,, the Great, 291
Donatism, 131, 287 et s. ; 290, 406
Dracontius, 313, 321, 446, 472
Dräseke, J., 184
Duchesne, Mgr., 228, 295, 303, 344, 452
Dufourcq, A., 310
Duruy, 216

E

Easter, the Christian, 166
Ebionites, 456
Education, Roman, 6
Ehrhard, 144
Eleutherus of Tournai, 498
Elienus, 42
Elliot, C. J., 354
Empedocles, 15
Ennodius, 486, 489 et s.
Ephesus, Council of, 162
Epictetus, 8
Epicurus, 15, 202
Epigramma S. Paulini, 469
Epiphanius of Salamis, St., 268, 340, 494 et s.
Epiphanius, the Scholastic, 507, 509
Episcopate, the, St. Cyprian's view, 141 ; in the Vth cent., 264
Epithalamium, 331
Epopee, Christian, 315, 468, 488
Erasmus, 352
Eschatology, 178, 207
Etymology, Science of, 516
Eucherius of Lyons, St., 424
Euchrotia, 305
Euclid, 500
Eugenius of Carthage, 444
Eugenius II, of Toledo, 473
Euric, 478
Eusebius of Cæsarea, 217, 342, 363, 382 et s.
,, Vercelli, 227, 239, 256
Eustochium, 346, 353
Evagrius, priest of Gaul, 432
,, of Antioch, 290
Evhemerism, 156, 196, 234
Evodius of Uzalum, 404
Examerons, see Hexamerons
Ecstasy, 91

F

Faith (in Arnobius), 194
Fasts, 96, 367
Fauriel, 467
Faustinus, 227, 252
Faustus, the Manichaean, 398, 405
  ,, of Riez, 426, 472, 498
Favorinus, 41
Faye, E. de, 15, 145
Feder, Père, 245 et s.
Felicissimus, 138, 146, 186
Felix, St., 324 et s.
  ,, the Manichaean, 405
Fénelon, 202, 348
Flight, during Persecution, 63, 77, 93, 137
Filaster of Brescia, 173, 287, 297
Firmicus Maternus, 228, 232 et s.
Firmilian of Caesarea, 141
Flaccilla, Empress, 253
Florus, 110
Foebadius of Agen, 228, 256, 445
Fortunatus of Thuccabori, 157
Fortunatus (Venantius), 239, 386, 472, 485, 491 et s.
Foucart, Paul, 147, 234
Fragmenta contra Arianos, 289
Francis of Sales, St., 348
Frick, 287
Frigitil, Queen, 286
Frische, Dom du, 262
Frontonius, 8, 110, 124, 338
Fuldensis, 51, 61
Fulgentius of Ruspa, 495 et s.
Funk, 144
Furius Dionysius Filocalus, 451
Fustel de Coulanges, 513

G

Galerius, 201
Gall, St., 30
Gallus, Emperor, 138
Gambling, 164
Gamurrini, 243, 376, 378
Gargilius Martialis, 508
Gaudentius of Brescia, 298 et s.
  ,, Thamugadi, 287, 292
Gelasius I, Pope, 198, 322, 443, 499
Gennadius of Marseilles, 175, 186, 292, 304, 364, 426, 439, 448, 468, 472
Germanus of Auxerre, 423
Germinius of Sirmium, 257
Gesta inter Liberium et Felicem, 289
Gnosticism, 15, 59, 116, 168, 192, 203, 247, 344, 405
Goelzer, H., 333, 486, 489
Gonthamond, 473
Goths, 179, 185. See Invasions
Grace, Doctrine of, 117 et s. ; 407, 422. See Pelagianism and Semi-P.
Gratian, Emperor, 354 et s.

Greek (in the West), 4, 40 et s.; 57, 134, 249, 370, 395, 416, 429, 500, 508, 517
Gregory of Elvira, 228, 252, 257
  ,, Nazianzen, St., 18, 24, 259, 268, 339
  ,, Rome, St., 386
  ,, Tours, St., 386, 438, 493, 495, 509
Grievances, Pagan against Christianity, 155, 190, 260, 391, 409
Guéranger, Dom, 33
Guignebert, 72

H

Hadrian, Emperor, 41
Hagiography. See Biography
Harnack, A. von, 27, 144, 164, 166, 222, 352, 432
Hartel, G. von, 35, 132
Hauréau, 442
Haussleiter, 220
Havet, Ernest, 135, 144
  ,, Julian, 487
  ,, Louis, 30
Hebraisms in the Bible, 48
Hebrew, the knowledge of, 249, 337, 347, 354, 416
Hegesippus, 267, 289
Heine, Gotthold, 258
Hell, description of, 457
Heliodorus, 7, 347
Hellenisms in the Bible, 47
Helvidius, 350
Heraclianus. See Altercatio
Heresy, Sense of the word, 299
Hermas, Pastor of, 42, 58 ; Latin translation of, 370
Hermes Trismegistus, 206
Hermogenes, Gnostic, 41, 59, 85
Herod Agrippa, 74
Hexamerons, 283
Hierocles, 203
Hilary, the Deacon, 252
  ,, of Arles, 385, 428, 443
  ,, of Poitiers, St., 227, 238 et s. ; 258, 264, 422
Hilarianus Hilarius Decimus, 290
  ,, Julius Quintus, 287, 301
Hippolytus of Rome, St., 43, 166, 223, 258
History, Christian conception of, 216, 340
Holder, A., 505
Holl, Karl, 319
Honoratus of Arles, 424
Honorius of Autun, 364
Horace, 181, 296, 329, 331, 465, 467
Hormisdas, Pope, 489
Hosius of Cordova, 227, 256
Hostis Herodes Impie, 476
Humanists and the Latin Church, 2
Hydatius, Chronicle of, 305 et s. ; 431
Hymns, Christian, 247, 262, 285, 303, 312, 448 et s.

I

Index Liborum Prohibitorum, 443
Instantius, 305 et s. ; 309
Innocent I, Pope, 443
Institutiones, Sense of the word, 204
Instrumentum, Sense of the word, 104
Invasions, Barbarian, 28, 390, 439, 466, 486
Invectiva c. Nicomachum, 319
Irenæus, St., 40, 59, 146, 223
Ireland, 29, 167, 518
Isaac, the Jew, 289 et s.
Isidore of Seville, St., 247, 364, 438, 495, 515 et s.
Isis, Cult of, 97, 233, 319
Itacius of Ossonaba, 305 et s. : 445
Itala, Meaning of the word, 416
Itineraries, 201, 302, 374 et s.
Itinerarium a Burdigala, 376

J

Jansenism, 432
John Chrysostom, St., 364, 508
John of Biclaro, 431
„ Jerusalem, 371 et s.
Jerome, St., 7, 8, 10, 26, 39, 42, 45, 52, 57, 60, 110, 136, 156, 165, 188, 198, 220 et s. ; 244, 250, 261, 284, 316, 327, 333 et s. ; 390, 434, 507, 511, 518 ; and new words, 49 ; the Dream of, 11 ; Art of translating according to, 345
Jesus, the brothers of, 350
Jordanis, 507
Josephus, 74, 267, 507
Jovinian, 364 et s.
Jovius, 329
Judaism and Christianity, 43, 67, 75, 86, 173, 177, 272 et s. ; 455
Julianus Pomerius, 497
Julicher, 40
Julian of Eclana, 331, 333, 422
Julian, Emperor, 23, 236, 250, 292, 311 et s. ; 459
Jullian, Camille, 32, 383
Juno Caelestis, Cult of, 233
Jupiter Sabazios, Cult of, 233
Justin, St., 19, 42, 59, 212
Justina, Empress, 285
Juvenal, 317, 459, 465, 467, 480
Juvencus, 311, 312, 314 et s.

K

Kauffmann, 255
Koch, Hugo, 142 et s.
Kroymann, 50

L

Labeo. See Cornelius
Lachmann, 34
Lactantius, 9, 75, 102, 109, 188, 199 et s. ; 251. 300
Lagrange, J. M., 352
Lapsi, 138, 147 et s. ; 170 et s.
Latin, Vulgar, 48, 164, 167, 181, 421, 480, 490, 494, 498, 512 et s.
Latronianus, 309
Laudes Domini, 314
Launoy, 220
Laurand, L., 145, 333
Leander of Seville, 516
Learning, Profane. And Christianity, 2, 6 et s. ; 11–36, 73, 82, 178, 193, 199, 328, 354, 373, 396 et s. ; 403, 414 et s. ; 421, 474, 504, 512 et s.
Leclercq, Dom, 147, 497
Le Fèvre, Nicholas, 244
Lefèvre of Etaples, 352
Lejay, Paul, 3, 34, 55, 184, 228, 231, 306, 379, 394
Lemaitre, Jules, 14
Leo I, Pope, 186, 309, 424, 431, 433, 442
Leontius of Arles, 423
Leporius, 429
Lerins, 424, 499
Letters, Symbolism of, 517
Libellatici, 148, 152
Libellus Precum, 227, 252
Liber, Cult of, 234
Liber de Fide, 259
„ *de Promissionibus*, 434
Liberius, Pope, 252, 451
Lindsay, 169
Litbert, 333
Literature, Greek Christian, 4 ; the destinies of Profane, 30, 230, 240 ; and of Heterodox L., 253 ; of Latin, Christian and Critical L., 1
Liturgy, 285, 378, 380, 448, 468, 476
Loofs, 144
Lupus óf Troyes, St., 423
Loyalty of Christians, 73, 125
Lucan, 317, 479
Lucianus of Kaphar Gamala, 434
Lucidus, 426
Lucifer of Calaris, 227, 239, 250 et s. ; 350
Lucilius, Satirist, 208
Lucretius, 5, 10, 49, 181, 193, 316, 318, 457, 465, 468
Lucula Noctis, 13
Luxueil, 30

M

Mabillon, 13
Machabees, *Passio* in Latin of the, 267
Macé, A., 40
Macedonius, 474, 475

Macrobius, Donatist, 292
Magna Mater, Cult of, 318
Magnificat, 303
Magnus (Orator Urbis), 18
Mai, Angelo, 220, 254
Majorian, Emperor, 477
Malebranche on Tertullian, 82
Mamertus, Claudianus, 446, 471 et s. ; 479, 507
Manichaeism, 371, 397 et s. ; 403, 405, 422, 443, 456
Mantique, Pagan, 92
Manuscripts, Unique, 109, 169, 188, 233, 383, 468
Marcella, 346 et s. ; 353
Marcellinus, Count, 431, 438
Marcellinus, 252
Marcellina, 266
Marcian of Arles, 143
Marcion, the Heresiarch, 15, 59, 78, 86, 456
Marcionem, Carmen Adv., 319
Marcus, Gnostic, 15
Marriage, Lawfulness of, 63, 95, 210, 279, 365, 487 et s. ; mixed, 78 ; re-marriage, 94, 279
• Mariology, 350
Marius of Avenches, 431
  ,,   Mercator, 429
  ,,   Victorinus, 228, 259 et s. ; 297, 319, 401
Marivadus, Arian Bishop, 445
Martial, Bishop, 143
  ,,   the Poet, 467, 490
Martin, J., 184
Martin of Tours, St., 306, 325, 381, 383, 491, 508, 511
Martyr, The, in the Primitive Church, 63, 113, 128, 140, 148 et s. ; 160, 342, 450
Martyrologies, 511
Martyrs of Lyons, 42, 454
Marvels of the World, 512
Massebieau, 128
Maurice, 217
Maximus, Emperor, 305, 324
  ,,   Bishop, 423
Maximinus, the Arian, 254, 408
Melania the Younger, 370
  ,,   the Elder, 344
Melitos of Sardis, 59
Mendicus Christi, 187
Metaphors, Military, 157
Middle Ages, Symbolism in, 174 ; philosophic language of, 262 ; the " Mirrors," 283 ; Allegory in, 463 ; and the " City of God," 411 ; and Boethius, 500, 505 ;—and Cassiodorus, 507 ;—and dialectics, 517
Migne, 33 et s.
Milan, Edict of, 228
Millenarism, 63, 178, 207, 210, 220, 301

Milton, 313, 457, 473
Minucius Felix, 5, 102, 109 et s. ; 156, 237, 258
Miracles, 119, 510
Mirandole, Pic de la, 199
Mithra, Mysteries of, 61, 233, 288
Moehler, 72
Mommsen, 40, 131, 495
Monachism, 337, 340, 424
Monceaux, Paul, 69, 127, 132, 136, 178, 182, 187, 188, 217, 261, 287, 291 et s. ; 295
Monica, St., 392 et s.
Montanism, 56, 59, 62, 89 et s. ; 99 et s.
Morel, G., 316
Morin, Dom G., 131 et s. ; 162, 267, 289 et s. ; 297, 300, 303, 308, 332, 335, 391, 420, 422, 427 et s.
Mortibus Boum, de, 321
Mosaicarum et Rom. legum Collatio, 289
Muratori, Fragm. of, 51, 53
Mutianus, 508
Mysteries, Pagan, 229, 234 et s.
Mythology, Christian criticism of, 114, 195, 205, 473, 498

N

Naturis Rerum, de, 318
Neologisms in the Latin Bible, 48
Neo-Platonism, 193, 260 et s. ; 401, 506. See Plotinus, Porphyry, etc.
Nero, Legend of, 179
Nestorius, 429
Newman, 426
Niceta of Remesiana, 287, 302 et s.
Nicetas of Aquileia, 304
Nicetius of Trèves, 304
Nicomachus of Jerasa, Neo-Platonist, 500
Nicomachus Flavianus (Virius), 319
Nichomachum, Invectiva Contra, 319
Nobilitas, 229
Numbers, Symbolism in, 222, 318, 436
Nourry, Dom le, 263
Novatian, 138, 153, 163, 169 et s. ; 171, 258, 284
Novatus, 138, 146
Nudity in magic practice, 306

O

Octavius, 109 et s.
Olympius, 309
Onochoetes, 67
Optatus of Milevis, St., 287, 294 et s.
Opus imperfectum in Matthaeum, 254
Oracles. See Sibylline
Orens, St, 466
Orientius, 446, 466 et s.

Origen, 57, 93, 194, 207, 213, 223, 242, 258, 268, 282, 344 et s. ; 354, 394, 498, 509
Orosius, 185, 369, 433 et s. ; 511
Osiris, Cult of, 233
Ovid, 182, 237, 314, 317, 329
Ozanam, F., 513

P

Pacatus Drepanius (Latinus), 306
Pacian of Barcelona, 286, 295 et s.
Paganism, Criticism of, 473. See Mythology, Survival of, 498
Palladius, Arian Bishop, 445
,, of Ratiara, 254, 255, 286
Pammachius, 364
Pange Lingua Gloriosa, 472, 493
Papacy, The, and St. Cyprian, 142 et s. ; and Prosper, 430 ; and Leo the Great, 443
Papias, 223
Paraclete, 63 et s.
Paris, Gaston, 43, 45, 47, 354
Parmenianus, Donatist, 291, 294, 295
Pastor, 310
Patricius, 395
Patrology, The Latin, 46 et s.
Paul, St., and profane writers, 20, 23 ; and marriage, 94
Paula, 346 et s. ; 353
Paulinus of Antioch, 338
,, Beziers, 469
,, Milan, 266
,, Nola, St., 302 et s. ; 310, 323 et s. ; 375, 385
,, Pella, 326, 446, 469 et s.
,, Petricordia, 386
,, Treves, 239
Pelagius, 407
Pelagianism, 393, 407, 422, 428, 443
Pilgrimages to the Holy Land, 325, 374 et s.
Penance, 97, 163, 209 et s. ; 274, 284
Peripatetics, 15
Perpetua and Felicitas, *Passio*, 41, 52, 102 et s. ; 454
Perpetuus of Tours, 386
Persius, 317
Persecutors, their punishment, 74, 214 et s.
Petronius of Bologna, 300
Petrus Chrysologus, 423
Phœnix, The legend of the, 320
Philo, 213, 268, 361, 363
Philosophy, the Old, and Christianity, 15, 18, 69 et s. ; 83, 112, 123, 158, 171, 193, 205, 212, 239, 249, 365, 394, 421
Philostratus, 319
Photinus, 363
Pichon, René, 1, 188, 199, 217, 218, 331
Piety, Catholic, 392

Pilate, 74
Pithou, Pierre, 244
Pitra, Cardinal, 33, 175, 316
Plato, 70, 192, 394, 500, 504
Plautus, 345
Pliny the Elder, 320
Plotinus, 237, 261, 401
Poitiers, 220, 239 et s.
Polemics, Theory of, 365 et s.
Political Economy (St. Ambrose), 280
Polycarp of Smyrna, 93
Pontius, the Deacon, 131, 135, 158, 161
Porphyry, Neo-Platonist, 23, 203, 237, 261, 401, 500
Possidius of Calama, 386, 393
Potamius of Olisopo, 253
Praedestinatus, The, 427
Praxeas, 455
Prescription, Theory of, 84
Prayer, Christian, 159
Priscillian, 276, 287, 305 et s. ; 443, 457
Proba (poetess), 322
Proclus, 429
Procula, Priscillianist, 305
Profuturus of Cirta, 404
Propempticon, 302, 331
Prose and verse, mingling of, 501
Prosper of Aquitaine, 428 et s.
Providence, Doctrine of, 74, 112, 114, 155, 201, 204, 214 et s. ; 436 et s. ; 440, 503
Prudentius, 162, 229, 230, 276, 331, 446 et s.
Psalterium Gallicanum, 355
,, *Romanum*, 353
Psalms, Alphabetical, 183, 406 ; Donatist, 292 ; paraphrased in verse, 331
Psychics, 64
Puech, A., 1, 3, 305, 332, 449, 457, 463
Pyrrhonism, 194
Pythagoreans, 15

Q

Quadratus, 363
Quaestio, Sense of, 289
Quirinus, 156
Quodvultdeus, 298, 391, 434

R

Radegonde, St., 492
Rancé, 13
Reitzenstein, 162, 167
Remigius of Rheims, 498
Renan, E., 41, 76, 109, 119, 120, 123
Reticius of Autun, 227, 237
Retractationes, The sense of, 393
Rhetoric in Roman education, 6 ; and Christian writers, 7, 15, 82, 155, 156, 166, 351, 558, 420, 515, 519
Romanus of Blaye, 325

Romania, 29, 438
Romanianus, 396, 402
Rome, Taking of by Alaric, 184, 390 ;
    Christian view of, 113, 126 (Minu-
    cius Felix) ; 179 (Commodian) ;
    206, 210 (Lactantius) ; 265, 284,
    286 (St. Ambrose) ; 334 (St.
    Jerome) ; 411 (St. Augustine) ;
    438 et s. (Salvianus) ; 442 (Leo the
    Great) ; 458 et s. (Prudentius) ;
    476 (Sidonius Apoll.)
Ronsch, 48, 417
Rossi, de, 42, 451
Rufinus of Aquileia, 26, 42, 333, 337, 370
Ruricius of Limoges, 423
Rusticus of Narbonne, 424
    „   Helpidius, 491

S

Sabatier, Dom, 39
Sabellianism, 455
Sacramentarium Leonianum, 433
Sacrificati, 148
Sallust, 181, 237, 514
Salonius, 424
Saltet, L., 55, 253
Salvianus, Priscillianist, 305
    „   433, 439 et s.
Sapaudus, 472, 489
Saturninus of Arles, 239
Satyrus, 266
Saumaise, Claude de, 82
Scapula, Pro-Consul, 56, 73 et s.
Scève, Maurice, 313
Schepss, 306 et s.
Schism, Sense of the word, 298
Scillium, Martyrs of, 55
Secundianus of Singidunum, 255, 286
Sedulius, 313, 447, 474 et s.
Seeck, 295, 470
Semi-Pelagianism, 422, 431, 499
Senate, Roman in IVth cent., 185
Senatorem, ad quemdam, 318
Seneca, the philosopher, 23, 31, 49, 119,
    120, 127, 174, 205, 479, 504
Seneca, the rhetorician, 8
Septimus Severus, Emperor, 42, 67
Serapis, Cult of, 234
Severus of Milevis, 404
    „   Minorca, 434
Sibylline Oracles, 206, 214
Sidonius Apoll., 447, 476 et s.
Silius Italicus, 479
Silviae Peregrinatio.   See Aetheriae
    Pereg.
Simplicianus, 259
Siricius, Pope, 364, 443
Sirmium, Formula of, 241
Sixtus II, Pope, 163
    „   III, Pope, 443

Slavery, 155, 470
Socrates, 76
    „   the historian, 18, 311, 509
Soden, H. von, 132
Sotheris, virgin martyr, 266
Souter, Al., 289
Sozomenes, 312, 509
Squillace, 28, 506
Spectacula, Condemnation of, 81, 87,
    163, 178, 421
Speusippus, 70
Stephen, Pope, 138, 141, 451
State, the Pagan and St. Augustine, 412
Statius, 316, 329
Stoicism and Christianity, 31, 57, 72,
    155, 159, 192, 278, 366
Style, Christianity and, 2, 15, 19, 81,
    249, 252, 268, 466, 518
Sulpicius Severus, 306 et s. ; 325, 328,
    333, 380 et s.
Syagrius, 310
Symbolism, 174.   See Allegory, Letters,
    and Numbers
Symbolum Quicumque, 257
Symmachus the Jew, 355
    „   Pagan writer, 229, 230, 399, 457
        et s.
    „   Pope, 490
Symposium, 201
Sympronianus, 296
Synesius of Cyrene, 18

T

Tacitus, 101, 127, 320, 435
Tasso, 313
Tatian, 363
Taurobola, 229
Te Deum, The, 303
Terence, 181, 237, 345
Ternarii Numeri Excellentia, 318
Tertullianists, 64
Tertullian, 5, 7, 9, 18, 50–105 ; and
    the versions of the Bible, 45 ;
    priority to Min. Felix, 128 ; in-
    fluence of, 110, 132, 156, 159, 192,
    197, 216, 218, 251, 256, 257, 258,
    268, 296, 300, 319, 322, 350, 366,
    425
Thamin, R., 204, 277
Theodore of Mopsuesta, 429
Theodoret, 275 et s. ; 509
Theodoric, 489, 499
Theodosius, 264 et s. ; the penance of,
    274 ; and Prudentius, 458
Theodotion, 355
Theophilus of Antioch, 19, 59, 194
Thessalonica, Massacre of, 274 et s.
Thomas Aquinas, St., 254, 413
Tiberianus, Priscillianist, 309
Tibullus, 181, 479, 504
Tillemont, 167